LETTER OF TRANSMITTAL

SMITHSONIAN INSTITUTION,
BUREAU OF AMERICAN ETHNOLOGY,
Washington, D. C., June 2, 1911.

SIR: Five years ago the Bureau published as Bulletin 33, under the title "Skeletal Remains Suggesting or Attributed to Early Man in North America," the results of Doctor Hrdlička's comprehensive researches on that subject. I now have the honor to submit for your consideration the manuscript of "Early Man in South America," the work of the same author in collaboration with Prof. W. H. Holmes, Mr. Bailey Willis, of the United States Geological Survey, and Messrs. Fred. Eugene Wright and Clarence E. Fenner, of the Geophysical Laboratory of the Carnegie Institution of Washington, and to suggest its publication, with your approval, as Bulletin 52 of the Bureau's series.

Yours, very respectfully,

F. W. HODGE,
Ethnologist in Charge.

DR. CHARLES D. WALCOTT,
Secretary of the Smithsonian Institution,
Washington, D. C.

III

PREFACE

Between the years 1899 and 1907 the writer carried on a series of investigations with regard to the various skeletal remains which suggested or were attributed to ancient man in North America. These studies resulted in a number of publications,[1] culminating in a general treatise comprehending the whole subject, which appeared as Bulletin 33 of the Bureau of American Ethnology. The results of the investigations seemed at first to lend support to the theory of considerable antiquity for some of the remains presented as evidence, as, for example, the two low skulls discovered at Trenton, New Jersey. Subsequent researches however, cleared up most of the uncertain points and the entire inquiry appeared to establish the fact that no specimen had come to light in the northern continent, which, from the standpoint of physical anthropology, represented other than a relatively modern man.

The possibility of discovering osseous remains of man of geologic antiquity in North America still exists, but, as was brought out in the studies referred to, any find to be accepted as establishing the existence of such man would have to be unequivocally authenticated by the anthropologist and the geologist working in cooperation. The various conclusions reached in these studies seem to have been quite generally accepted and no further discoveries of osseous remains pointing to the presence of early man in this part of the world have been made.

While occupied with the subject of man's antiquity in North America, the writer became more directly interested in the reports of related discoveries in South America, particularly in Argentina. It was soon found, however, that these reports, or at least those dealing with the finds of human remains up to 1907, were singularly incomplete and unsatisfactory. The records of the many cases were full of defects and uncertainties which, owing to the distance of the field and other difficulties, seemed insurmountable obstacles preventing the formation of a definite opinion as to the merit of any of the finds.

---

[1] The Crania of Trenton, N. J., and their Bearing upon the Antiquity of Man in that Region; in *Bulletin of the American Museum of Natural History*, XVI, pp. 23-62, New York, 1902.

The Lansing Skeleton; in *American Anthropologist*, N. S., V, 323-330, Lancaster, Pa., June, 1903.

A Report on the Trenton Femur (written in 1902), published with E. Volk's The Archæology of the Delaware Valley; *Papers of the Peabody Museum*, V, Cambridge, Mass., 1911.

Skeletal Remains Suggesting or Attributed to Early Man in North America; *Bulletin 33 of the Bureau of American Ethnology*, pp. 1-113, pls. I-XXI, figs. 1-16, Washington, 1907.

But before the close of the year which marked the conclusion of the writer's inquiries relating to ancient man in North America (1907), there appeared in Argentina an important résumé of the evidence relating to the man of the Pampean formations in that country, by Lehmann-Nitsche and a number of his associates, and this was soon followed by the reports on the apparently epoch-making discoveries of the *Tetraprothomo* (1907), *Diprothomo* (1909), and *Homo pampæus* (1909), by F. Ameghino, all of which stimulated to a high point the writer's interest in the question of early man in the southern continent. Then, with the earnest aid of Prof. W. H. Holmes, who has always had much at heart the impartial solution of the problem of man's antiquity in America, and through the good offices of the present Secretary of the Smithsonian Institution, it became possible for the writer to visit Argentina. In recognition of the importance of expert geologic evidence in studies of this kind, it was arranged that the writer should be accompanied by a competent geologist, acquainted with formations in other parts of the world allied to those of the pampas. The selection for this service fell on Mr. Bailey Willis, of the United States Geological Survey, who had done important work on the loess and related formations in North America and in China.

The chief objects of the expedition were the examination of the skeletal remains relating to early man that are preserved in Brazil and in Argentina; the study of at least the principal localities and of the deposits from which the finds were reported to proceed; and the discovery, if possible, and the collection of osseous, archeologic, or other specimens bearing on man's antiquity.

It was hoped that the work on the ground, carried to such extent as the circumstances might allow, would make it possible to form more definite conclusions concerning the individual finds than the literature on these warranted, and that possibly by means of new discoveries additional light might be shed on the whole subject of early man in South America, particularly in Argentina.

The journey was undertaken, it should be explicitly stated, with no prejudice or preconceived opinions, though in view of the defective reports skepticism concerning certain details or finds was unavoidable.

Argentina was reached early in May, 1910, and the stay of the writer in the country lasted two months and that of Mr. Willis somewhat longer; almost all of this time was given to the researches here recorded. The Argentine men of science, Srs. Ameghino, Ambrosetti, Lehmann-Nitsche, Moreno, Outes, Roth, and others, received Mr. Willis and the writer very cordially and facilitated their work with a liberality that has left a lasting impression and has placed them under many obligations. Señor Moreno and Professor Ameghino, with his brother Carlos, were particularly helpful; without their aid a large portion of the work could not have been accomplished. The specimens which it was important to examine, even those the descriptions of which had not yet been published, were placed freely at the disposal of the writer and his colleague; Professor Ameghino and his brother accompanied them, notwithstanding the inclement season, for nearly three weeks from point to point along the coast where vestiges of ancient man or his forerunners were believed to have been discovered; H. Santiago Roth visited Alvear with Mr. Willis; and de Carles, at the instance of Professor Ameghino, accompanied the party to the distant Ovejero. Finally, through the good offices of Señor Moreno, the writer received most valuable aid from the provincial authorities of Patagonia and from several prominent citizens of the city of Carmen. Sincere thanks are due to all of these gentlemen and to many others by whom assistance was rendered.

The first weeks of his stay were given by the writer to the study of the available skeletal material attributed to ancient man or his forerunners, in the Museo Nacional, the Facultad de Filosofía y Letras, and the Museo de La Plata; while Mr. Willis devoted his time to the examination at the same institutions of the many samples of baked earth, scoriæ, and other objects, believed to exhibit the activities of ancient man. Besides this, spare time was utilized by visits to places in Buenos Aires which show exposures of the local formation, and especially to the docks where the *Diprothomo* skull had been discovered, in search of first-hand information concerning this find.

On May 24 Mr. Willis and the writer set out for the coast, along which the more important specimens had been discovered, and a few days after, at Mar del Plata, were joined by Professor Ameghino and his brother Carlos. Examinations were made of the coast from north of Mar del Plata to the Barrancas de los Lobos (see maps, pls. 1, 21; figs. 1, 2), a section very important from the standpoint of archeology and geology; of the more inland Laguna de los Padres, the neighborhood of which was occupied up to late historic times by a small body of Indians; of the coast about and to the northeast of Miramar, a region interesting archeologically, geologically, and because of finds, slightly farther to the south, of two "fossil" human crania; of the Necochea and the Arroyo del Moro parts of the coast, highly interesting because of recent finds there of a number of "fossil" human skeletons; and finally of the Monte Hermoso barranca, which yielded the *Tetraprothomo*.

On the completion of the foregoing work, Professor Ameghino and his brother returned to Buenos Aires, the writer set out for the valley of the Rio Negro, whence came many years ago the "fossil" Patagonian crania, while Mr. Willis proceeded to visit certain of the inland hills for the purpose of supplementing his geologic observations on the coast, thence to the localities of Arroyo Siasgo and Alvear, the former the site of a recent find of "fossil" man, and the other a well-known place that has given many examples of baked earth and other apparent evidences of man's antiquity. Early in July Mr. Willis and the writer returned once more to Buenos Aires, completed as far as possible the work of research there, and then started with Sr. de Carles for Ovejero, a locality in the northwestern part of Argentina, which in the last few years has yielded a relatively large quantity of "fossil" human bones. Subsequently this trip was extended, for geologic as well as anthropologic purposes, to Tucuman, San Juan, and Mendoza. From the last-named place Mr. Willis returned to Buenos Aires, while the writer crossed the Andes on his way to Peru.

The writer left Argentina feeling that the time at his disposal there, though utilized to the utmost, was all too brief. The country abounds in anthropologic problems and material and large sections as yet have not been explored. But the opportunities suggested by these considerations belong to the future. The writer and his colleague were not able to visit some of the places where remains of presumably ancient man were found, because, the discoveries having been made many years ago by men no longer among the living, the exact localities are not known. There was no time to conduct more extensive excavations, and even the examinations of some of the specimens could have been made with advantage more detailed. The main objects of the journey had been accomplished, however, so that further particulars could not be expected to change or augment materially the essentials of the evidence. Whatever doubts remain are of such nature that only by justifiable inference and strictly scientific field work can it be hoped to effect their final solution.

Unfortunately the general results of the inquiry here outlined are not in harmony with the claims of the various authors who reported the several finds. As will be seen by the details, the evidence is, up to the present time, unfavorable to the hypothesis of man's great antiquity, and especially to the existence of man's predecessors in South America; and it does not sustain the theories of the evolution of man in general, or even of that of the American man alone, in the southern continent. The facts gathered attest everywhere merely the presence of the already differentiated and relatively modern American Indian.

A. H.

CONTENTS

CONTENTS   XI

ILLUSTRATIONS

EARLY MAN IN SOUTH AMERICA

By Aleš Hrdlička.

In collaboration with

W. H. Holmes, Bailey Willis, Fred. Eugene Wright, and Clarence N. Fenner.

I. GENERAL CONSIDERATIONS

By Aleš Hrdlička

In dealing on a large scale with a subject of so great importance as man's antiquity, it seems appropriate to consider briefly at least, before taking up the details of research, the essential conditions on which judgments regarding the various problems involved must depend. These conditions, or criteria, are of prime consequence, yet are often so simple as to be self-evident. But notwithstanding this, they are not infrequently lost sight of by the very students who need most to keep them clearly in view.

The antiquity of any human remains, skeletal or cultural, antedating the historic period, can be judged of only from the association of such remains with geologic deposits the age of which is well-determined, and with the remains of other organic forms, the place of which in time and in the evolutionary series is known. In the case of osseous specimens great weight attaches also to the morphologic characteristics and to the organic and inorganic alterations of the bones.

From the geologic standpoint, consideration of the antiquity of human remains involves not merely unquestionable stratigraphic identification, but, preeminently, the question, unnecessary in general in dealing with bones of animals, of possible introduction subsequent to the formation of the matrix which enclosed them.

On the morphologic side, in turn, we encounter the important and often very difficult task of distinguishing between characteristics normal to a definite stage of evolution and those due to reversion or other causes affecting only individuals. And in regard to the post-mortem alterations in the bones, great difficulties are encountered in the way of a precise physical and chemical determination of the changes that exist, and especially in the evaluation of their chronologic significance.

In general, to establish beyond doubt the geologic antiquity of human remains, it should be shown conclusively that the specimen or specimens were found in geologically ancient deposits, whose age is confirmed by the presence of paleontologic remains; and the bones should present evidence of organic as well as inorganic alterations, and show also morphologic characteristics referable to an earlier type. In addition, it is necessary to prove in every case by unexceptional evidence that the human remains were not introduced, either purposely or accidentally, in later times into the formation in which discovered.

It will be plain to every critical reader that the age of a find relating to early man in which the above-mentioned requirements have not been satisfied can not be regarded as definitely settled. To accept any specimen as representative of man of a definite geologic period on evidence less than the sum total of these criteria would be to build with radical defects in the foundation. It will be far more profitable to anthropology to wait for discoveries that will fulfill the conditions named than to accept cases, howsoever satisfactory they may seem to some, that leave in the mind of the unprejudiced and experienced observer serious doubt as to the true age of the remains.

Two of the above-named requisites, namely, the morphologic evidence of the bones and their post-burial alterations, call for further consideration.

On the basis of what is positively known to-day in regard to early man, and with the present scientific views regarding man's evolution, the anthropologist has a right to expect that human bones, particularly crania, exceeding a few thousand years in age, and more especially those of geologic antiquity, shall present marked morphologic differences, and that these differences shall point in the direction of more primitive forms.

Man can not have arisen except from some more theroid form zoologically, and hence also morphologically. No conclusion can be more firmly founded than that man is a product of an extraordinary progressive differentiation from some anthropogenic stock, which developed somewhere in the later Tertiary, among the primates. He began, then, as an organism that in brain and in body was less than man, that was anthropoid. From this stage he could not have become at once as he is to-day, though in some stages of his evolution he may have advanced by leaps, or at least more rapidly than in others. He must have developed successively morphologic modifications called for by his advance toward the present man, and have lost gradually those features that interfered with his advance or became useless—progress which is still unfinished. We know these to be the facts, (1) because all organic form is essentially unstable, plastic, reactive to changing influences, and to this law man's complex and relatively delicate organism can form no exception; (2) because the best-authenticated skeletal remains of early man show without exception a more or less close approximation to more primitive primate forms; (3) because these older human forms show, in general, more theroid features in proportion to their geologic antiquity; and (4) because morphologic differences have occurred in numerous historic groups of mankind within relatively recent times, are very apparent to-day in the various "races" of man, and are constantly arising in tribes, in lesser groups, in families, and in individuals.

Evolutionary changes have not progressed and do not progress regularly in mankind as a whole, nor even in any of its divisions. Such changes may be thought of as a slowly-augmenting complex of zigzags, with localized forward leaps, temporary haltings, retrogressions, and possibly with even occasional complete cessations. Thus it would not be reasonable to expect that at any given date in the past or present all the branches or members of the human or protohuman family would be of absolutely uniform type. At all periods some individuals, and even groups, were doubtless more advanced than others from the ancestral and nearer the present human type. Nevertheless, the morphologic status of man in each geologic period had, unquestionably, its boundaries, and there is no evidence or probability that two human beings, a geologic period or more apart, could be so closely related in form that their crania or skeletons would show strictly one and the same type.

The antiquity, therefore, of any human skeletal remains which do not present marked differences from those of modern man may be regarded, on morphologic grounds, as only insignificant geologically, not reaching in time, in all probability, beyond the modern, still unfinished, geologic formations. Should other claims be made in any case, the burden of definite proof would rest heavily on those advancing them.

Other considerations bearing on this point have been brought forth in the writer's report relating to ancient man in North America,[1] which should be read in connection with the present work. The essence of the subject is that the expectation of important form differences between all human skeletal remains of geologic antiquity and those of the present era is justified; that the differences presented by

---

[1] *Bulletin 33 of the Bureau of American Ethnology.*

the older remains should point in the direction of zoologic inferiority; and that where important structural differences pointing to an earlier evolutionary stage are not found in the human skeletal remains which are the subject of study, and especially where the given crania and bones show close analogies with those of a modern or even of the actual native race of the same region, the geologic antiquity of such remains may well be regarded as imperfectly supported, in fact, as improbable.

As to the evidence that anatomic changes in man or, more precisely, in his skeleton, have taken place during the present epoch, particularly during historic times, the following points deserve attention:

The earliest skeletal forms approximating closely to those of present man occur in Europe in the latter part of the paleolithic epoch, assigned to the Upper Quaternary. They belong to the so-called Aurignacean and Solutrean cultural periods. Yet even here, as shown especially by the very important Maška collection,[1] there are numerous and important characters distinguishing the skulls as well as other bones from those of the whites and even from those of the more primitive races of to-day. It is only when the Cro-Magnon and the latest Grimaldi skeletal remains are reached, both regarded as of the latest "diluvial" age and possibly more recent, that we find forms corresponding closely to historic man.

Numerous changes, however, have taken place in various groups of mankind ever since the time of the Man of Cro-Magnon or of Grimaldi. These have been more pronounced in some regions than in others but there are no examples of complete morphologic standstill. The inhabitants of Egypt have been repeatedly pointed to as an example of the stability of human characters. Their skeletal remains are now known for a period extending over 5,000 years. The Egyptians sprang apparently from a single physical type and while there were subsequent accessions to the population, they were in general of people of the same type. After reaching the valley of the Nile this group of humanity continued to live relatively isolated and under much the same environment. For thousands of years they had in general the same occupations, the same diet, the same habits and customs, and changed but slightly in the grade of their civilization. Here were almost ideal conditions for maintaining stability of physical type, and there is no doubt that a closer approximation to such stability has been realized than in other known regions of the world. Yet, as the writer, who made a journey to Egypt largely for the purpose of investigating this subject, has shown already in a preliminary

---

[1] Maška's collection from Předmost, Moravia, as yet unpublished but being studied, embraces more than a dozen skeletons of man, contemporaneous with the mammoth, in a relatively excellent state of preservation, from the Solutrean.

writing,[1] and as was shown lately by G. Elliot Smith and Derry also,[2] the susceptibility of the organism to modification, even under these exceptionally uniform environmental conditions, has not been overcome, and numerous changes in the Egyptian skeleton between the predynastic and middle dynastic, and again between that and the Coptic period, excluding from consideration the influence of negro infusion, are perceptible. In other countries such changes have been more pronounced. In Russia, Bohemia, Germany, France, England, cranial alterations have taken place within the last 2,000 years, all of which can hardly be explained by migration or admixture. In the American Indian many territorially localized morphologic modifications have become manifest within relatively recent times, for almost every tribe to-day possesses some distinguishing marks of body as well as of skeleton; and further modifications are certainly now taking place in the Indian with changing conditions.

All these facts bear evidence strongly against the persistence of the same type of man in any region from the Pleistocene or an even older period to the present. The fundamental causes of this incomplete stability are, on the one hand, the nature of the human organism, which like every other organism is in its ultimate analysis a chemical complex, living by chemical change and subject to physical and chemical influences, and on the other the variability of these influences. So long as the chemical status of the organism, especially that of the developing organism and of the perpetuating or generative elements of the species, is not in absolute and lasting harmony with the environment, so long, it is safe to say, will absolute fixedness of structure and form be impossible. This expresses the case in its extremes without considering its complexity, and applies to the ultimate components and coordinations of the organism, but the principle, which reduced to the simplest terms is that of action and reaction between the protoplasm and the environment, holds good for all variations in the human body. The bearing of these considerations in connection with the theme in hand will be more clearly apparent as the several special parts of this report are presented.

The second important subject which calls for brief discussion in this place is that of the alterations of bones after burial. Such alterations are partly organic, partly mechanical, and partly chemical, and may be classed as follows:

(1) General decay and disintegration; (2) loss of organic substance through bacterial or mineral agencies; (3) partial mechanical loss of organic and chemical elements, through erosion; (4) covering by

---

[1] Note sur la variation morphologique des Egyptiens depuis les temps préhistoriques ou prédynastics; in *Bull. et Mém. Soc. d'Anthr. Paris*, 5me sér., X, 1909, pp. 143–4.

[2] Smith, G. Elliot, and F. Wood Jones, The Archeological Survey of Nubia, 4°, 2 vol., Cairo, 1910. Also Smith, G. Elliot, and D. E. Derry, Bulletin 6 of the same Survey, Cairo, 1910, and G. Elliot Smith, The People of Egypt, in *The Cairo Sci. Jour.*, No. 30, III, Alexandria, 1909.

mineral substances that adhere; (5) simple mechanical or sedimental filling of the bone cavities by mineral substances; and (6) lithification, i. e., conversion, more or less complete, of the bone into stone or ore through both infiltration and the replacement by other elements or compounds of the original inorganic constituents of the osseous structure.

These classes of alterations are but rarely met with isolated or perfect, existing more frequently in various combinations and in various stages of incompleteness. Occasionally also one process may have superseded another, a condition especially apt to appear when the location of the specimen happens to be changed, or when the bone is acted on by water differing in mineral composition from that with which it came previously in contact.

The nature of the alterations depends altogether on the minerals, particularly those in solution, and perhaps also on the gases which come in contact with the skeletal remains,[1] the bones themselves, though differing to some extent chemically as well as physically, being on the whole fairly constant in composition. The conditions to which any particular bone is subject may be favorable or unfavorable to its alteration. The unfavorable conditions are those that bring about a rapid destruction of the bone, or a dearth or absence of such agencies as are capable of producing changes in the bone that make for durability; the favorable ones are the presence of modifying agencies, while destructive potencies are slow. Bones in dry sand or in a dry crypt, or in peat, where bacteria and fungi can not exist and where neither corrosive liquids nor gases occur, can undergo but little alteration; but if exposed for a time to air, sand blast, growing roots, or to water or gases of corrosive qualities, they will show scaling, erosion, or other forms of loss of substance; in acid soil or in a wet, warm, aerated mold they will disappear; in a limestone cave through which water percolates they will be covered with stalagmite, or cemented with earth, stones, shells, etc., and lose rapidly their organic matter; in a shell-heap or in calcareous ground, or where washed by mineral water or reached by underground water carrying minerals in solution, they will be partially infiltrated with lime and may be lined with and covered by a deposit, their inorganic constitution may be more or less changed and in some cases they will become thoroughly petrified. The rapidity of the various processes is proportionate to the nature, quantity, and facility of access to the bone of the various reagents.

It follows from what has been shown that alterations of any nature in a bone are first of all indications of the conditions under which the bone has existed or, briefly, of the environment of the specimen, and

---

[1] See data adduced by Gratacap, L. P., Fossils and Fossilization; in *The American Naturalist*, xxx, Phila., 1896, 902 et seq.; xxxi, Phila., 1897, 16 et seq.

only secondarily and in a very uncertain manner of the time required for the consummation of the changes.

Alterations produced in different bones are often seen to be alike, even though the specimens come from different localities and sometimes from apparently different investing conditions. This is explainable only on the assumption that the real conditions in the different places were similar. As the whole process of post-mortem change in bone is largely of the nature of chemical reactions, it will always lead, with the same elements, to much the same result. But such similarity of modification is no index of the quantity of the available reagents, of the facility of their action, or of the period during which they acted in the various cases and places, and hence alone is no measure of time. Two bones that show a like degree of "fossilization" are therefore not necessarily contemporaneous or even nearly so. This applies even to bones from the same locality, for some may have been subjected, through differences in depth or localized variation in soil or amount of moisture, to considerably different influences. For the same reason even the two extremities of the same bone may present differences in color, weight, and in other qualities.

Another important point is that each locality, each kind of soil, must necessarily have a limit to its possible effect on a bone, or at least there must be a point beyond which further alterations in the bone, unless new conditions set in, are extremely slow. Such limit reached, the bone may continue in the same place for ages as an inert, neutral object, and resemble closely other bones from the same cave, layer, or deposit, introduced at a much later time, but which likewise may have reached the limit or nearly the limit of their possible alterations under the local conditions.

The above facts demonstrate the futility of utilizing alterations in bones as a chronologic index. Yet it is this very unreliable factor of "fossilization" of human bones that is principally responsible for the "peopling" of North America, and especially of South America, with "fossil" ancient human forms.

The foregoing considerations make it clear that while geologically ancient bones may be confidently expected to show more or less decided alterations of both organic and inorganic nature,[1] such alterations alone can never become a criterion of antiquity.

In conclusion, it is necessary to refer to a certain class of other phenomena observed occasionally in connection with human and especially with animal bones, and sometimes brought forward as proofs of man's antiquity. This applies to the split or splintered bones and to those that show various scratches, striæ, cuts, or perforations, which appear to be due possibly to human agency.

[1] In very rare instances remains of some of the most recent but now extinct animals have been found apparently but little altered, but the date of death in these few cases has never been accurately determined.

It is seen in prehistoric European stations that in order to extract the marrow ancient man often broke the long bones of animals killed, but it does not follow that all similar fragments of bones have a like origin. The bones of dead animals, especially those of large size, often lie exposed for a considerable length of time on the surface of the ground. Animals die at pools where they become mired, or in localities where other animals pass, as can be seen in numberless cases on the prairies, deserts, pampas, and elsewhere. Their bones may be split longitudinally by the action of the elements, and are apt to be broken in every possible way by the feet of animals, by falling or rolling stones, or by pressure within the earth, and the fragments may differ in no way from those produced by man breaking long bones to extract the marrow. So far as the writer has been able to learn and so far as he can conceive, there is no safe means of distinguishing between the fracture effect of a blow by man on bone recent or ancient and that of a stroke on such bone by the hoof of an animal or by impact of falling stones or earth, fragmentation by the teeth of large carnivores, or, in the case of buried skeletal remains, crushing by the weight and movements of the earth. With all this in view, it is difficult to see how fragments of bones of any kind can of themselves ever materially assist in establishing the fact of man's agency, and especially of his presence at the time when the animal whose bones are found split or broken, lived and died.

Again, the fact is often overlooked that along with fragmentary long bones offered as evidence of man's agency are found fragments of other bones, without medulla and hence without the marrow for which bones are broken.

As to scratched, striated, incised, or perforated bones, it is sufficient to call attention to the fact that a sharp edge or point driven by force of any kind may produce simple effects similar to those due to an implement wielded by the human hand. Only in cases in which there is clear evidence of design may human agency be established. Mere possibilities or probabilities can not be accepted as positive evidence in dealing with the important problem of man's antiquity.

Many scratches found on bones are doubtless accidental, produced during the excavation, handling, or transportation of the specimens. As to the striæ and incised markings, in order to be accepted as due to human agency, it should be shown conclusively that they can not be attributed to other causes, as, for example, to the teeth of some rodent or carnivore, which sometimes cut as clearly and deeply as would a knife. It is often difficult and frequently impossible to distinguish cuts due to human agency from those due to animal agency. In some cases, however, we may detect the animal agency of the cuts by their lack of purpose (from the human point of view), by their parallel arrangement or similarity of direction (usually transverse to the axis of the shaft), by their presence on the ends or edges of the specimen, and by their close similarity in character.

As to perforations and grooves found in bones, it may be said that many of the most neatly made are due to insects or worms. Numerous examples of this kind due to worms were seen by the writer in the latter part of 1910, during excavations on the Isthmus of Panama. Roots also may produce perforations, especially by enlarging nutrient canals, which are liable to be mistaken for marks of artificial origin.

It is plain from the preceding remarks that, unless the opening in a bone presents evidence of design or other characteristic such as makes its human origin plainly manifest, it can not be accepted as artificial and is worthless as evidence of man's agency.

Moreover, even in cases in which perforation in or markings on bones are readily recognized as of human origin, it does not follow that man lived contemporaneously with the animals to which the bones belonged. To be of value as evidence on this point, it must be shown that man worked the bone during the life of the particular species and not later.

As to the bones of fossil animals which show the effects of fire, it needs only to be remarked that in order that such specimens should become available in any case as evidence of man's antiquity, it would be necessary to prove that the fire was due to the agency of man, and that the man was contemporaneous with those animals.

These various considerations, even though stated very briefly, indicate the complexity of the subject of evidence relating to the skeletal remains of man or those suggesting man. They show the necessity of taking into account every circumstantial detail regarding each distinct discovery of human skeletal parts and the necessity of scientific accuracy in weighing the observed conditions. It might seem that all the precautions above outlined should necessarily characterize any scientific procedure in this field, but it will be seen in the perusal of the following pages of this paper how readily some of these principles are slighted and even wholly neglected.

II. ENUMERATION OF THE SOUTH AMERICAN FINDS RELATING TO EARLY MAN

By Aleš Hrdlička

The discoveries, so far as published, of industrial and skeletal remains suggesting man's antiquity in South America, are restricted to Brazil and Argentina.

Brazil presents only one group of finds of this class, namely, those of the Lagoa Santa caves, in the Province of Minas Geraes. They consist of a relatively large series of skeletal remains of man and a single stone implement, which collectively have been considered as probably belonging to Quaternary times.

In Argentina, on the other hand, discoveries of relics attributed to ancient man and even to man's precursors, have been very numerous. These began with some débris of "fossil" human bones from the Rio Carcarañá, in the northern part of the Province of Buenos Aires, and with two "fossil" human crania reported from the valley of the Rio Negro, northern Patagonia. Subsequent finds, numbering in all several thousand specimens and including both human bones and what are assumed to be traces of human activity, with the exception of those from Patagonia and of the so-called Ovejero remains, have all been obtained from the Province of Buenos Aires.

The determinations of the geologic age of the numerous Argentine finds by the local authors who have reported on them are considerably at variance. There are in the main, however, two groups of opinions, one represented by Florentino Ameghino, the other by Santiago Roth and R. Lehmann-Nitsche. Below is given the classification of these finds by Ameghino, according to the geologic age assigned them by this author; the classifications of the other observers are more restricted in the number of finds regarded as ancient, and offer in general more moderate estimates of the ages of the specimens.

11

Skeletal remains of, and other indications pointing to, early man in South America, and their geologic age, according to F. Ameghino [1]

Period	Epochs and stages	Remains extant
Quaternary	Recent	
	Platean. Querandine transgression	
	Post-Lujanean hiatus	*Homo sapiens*
	Lujanean and corresponding marine transgression	Skulls of Arrecifes and Ovejero
	Post-Bonaerean hiatus	
Pliocene	Bonaerean {superior {inferior	Fontezuelas, Arroyo de Frias, Samborombón, Baradero, Chocori skulls and skeletons
		Homo caputinclinatus skeleton (Siasgo)
	Belgranean transgression	Industrial vestiges
		Homo sinemento (Moro)
	Post-Ensenadean hiatus	
	Cuspidal Ensenadean	*Homo pampæus*, or *Prothomo:* Miramar (La Tigra), Necochea skeletal remains
	Inter-Ensenadean transgression	Stone industry
	Basal Ensenadean	Industrial vestiges
	Pre-Ensenadean	*Diprothomo platensis* skull
Superior Miocene	Post-Puelchean hiatus	
	Puelchean and corresponding transgression	Industrial vestiges
	Post-Chapalmalean hiatus	
	Chapalmalean [2]	Industrial vestiges
	Post-Hermosean hiatus	
	Hermosean	*Tetraprothomo argentinus*, atlas and femur
Lower Miocene		Industrial vestiges (?)
Oligocene		Industrial vestiges
Upper Eocene	Patagonian	Industrial vestiges of man's precursors

[1] Based on the table published by that author in his Le *Diprothomo Platensis*, in *Anales del Museo Nacional de Buenos Aires*, XIX (ser. iii, t. XII), 1909, p. 124, and supplemented by more recently announced discoveries.

[2] Written also Chapadmalean.

The "industrial vestiges" can receive in this report, with two important exceptions, only general consideration. They consist of four main groups, namely: (1) Baked earth, or tierra cocida; (2) scoriæ; (3) used or worked stones; and (4) used or worked bones.

On the basis of these and the above-enumerated human specimens, coupled with the presence in South America of certain small fossil monkeys, Ameghino advanced the theory that mankind evolved on that continent, that it was represented there in the course of time by a number of genera of intermediary beings and by several species of man himself, and that he spread thence over the rest of the world. This elaborate theory can be given in this report only brief space; for the many details which it involves it will be necessary to consult Ameghino's original publications (see Bibliography). The following table, from Ameghino's Le *Diprothomo Platensis* (1909, p. 206), shows the views of that author as to the sequence of the evolution, though later his conceptions on that subject were probably even further developed.

AMEGHINO'S SCHEME OF MAN'S EVOLUTION

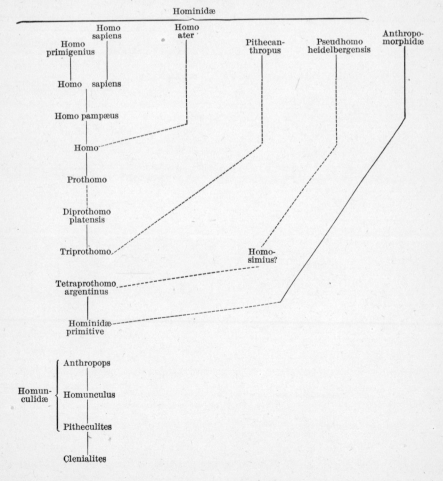

Having thus indicated in brief the status of the subject of remains relating to early man in South America at the time of the visit of the writer and Mr. Willis to Argentina, it is now appropriate to present the results of their observations. In general these lead, as already indicated, to conclusions different from those of the several Argentine authors, especially Ameghino, who have studied the anthropologic character, and have estimated the ages, of the various specimens.

III. GENERAL GEOLOGIC NOTES

By BAILEY WILLIS

INTRODUCTORY NOTE

The following geologic description is restricted to the writer's observations and to deductions from them. During four months, May to August, 1910, which he spent in Argentina, he visited the vicinity of Buenos Aires, the right bank of the Parana as far north as Rosario, the eastern part of the Province of Buenos Aires and the coast from Mar del Plata to Bahia Blanca, and the Sierra de la Ventana; all with reference to studies of the Pampean and post-Pampean terranes. Outside of this region his journeys extended to Tucuman on the north, to San Juan and Mendoza on the west, to Neuquen on the southwest, and to the Rio Colorado, including its delta, on the south. (See maps: Pls. 1 and 21; figs. 1 and 2.)

The writer is under great obligations to Dr. Florentino Ameghino and also to Prof. Santiago Roth, who not only gave valuable time to accompany his colleague, Doctor Hrdlička, and himself, but also most generously and frankly discussed the geologic phenomena. Their intimate knowledge and great experience entitle their views to the most serious consideration. The writer is happy to know that in many respects his inferences from observed facts agree with theirs, especially as to the Miocene and Pliocene age of much of the Pampean terrane.

He regrets that certain geologic relations, when interpreted in the light of his experience in other lands, lead him to conclusions that differ from theirs. There are some points on which they do not agree between themselves, notably as to the classification of the divisions of the Pampean. This problem is one that requires further investigation, both stratigraphically and paleontologically. The superficial formations of the pampas and of the coast are interpreted by the writer as of very recent origin. It is in them that human remains have been found. Were the remains as old as the deposits they would be geologically recent, but they are even younger, since the evidence of occurrence and character in every case that the writers could examine showed that the bodies had been buried in or had accidentally reached the positions in which they were found.

In warping, the old land of Buenos Aires on the whole was depressed during a long period. It has recently been raised again, though not to its former general altitude. There were, or are, two regions of greatest depression, one of which is the embayment of the Rio de la Plata, the other the bay of Bahia Blanca; each of these extends far

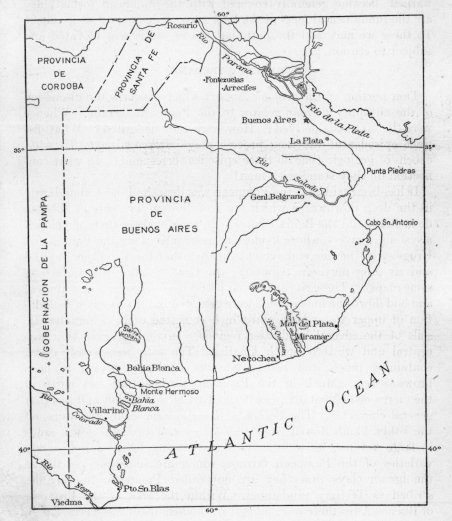

FIG. 1. Map of the Province of Buenos Aires.

inland. The intervening area did not sink so deep and within it lie the exceptional zones that were raised and became the Sierras of Córdoba, Tandil, and de la Ventana.

Over the sinking region superficial deposits of mud were spread, partly by rivers and partly by winds, and these constitute the

Pampean formation or terrane. They are no doubt thickest where the old rock floor lies deepest—in the downwarps of the Rio de la Plata and at Bahia Blanca.

These two facts—that there is a continental surface which was eroded on the ancient crystalline rocks, and that the surface, being warped, became generally covered with the Pampean formation—are the fundamental facts of the later geologic history of the pampas. To these we may add the note that the region is now elevated and subject to erosion.

PAMPEAN TERRANE

That portion of the geologic history which concerns the discussion of the antiquity of man relates to the Pampean terrane. Whence were the materials derived? How were they deposited? What distinct episodes of the long process may be recognized? To what epochs of geologic time do these episodes correspond? In what connection do they stand with man?

It has been said that the Pampean was deposited most abundantly in the deep downwarps which are now the embayments of the Rio de la Plata and the Bahia Blanca. In each of these there developed a system of rivers, whose modern representatives are the Parana and Uruguay in the one embayment, in the other the Rio Colorado and and its long northern tributary, the Gran Salado (Rio Curacó of some maps). These rivers, or their predecessors, brought, distributed, and laid down the muds which were gathered in the process of denudation of upper watersheds and which consisted of the characteristic soils of the several headwater regions. In the one case that was central and western South America. The soils were heavy clays, containing much iron and of various shades of brown to deep brownish-red. Much of the Pampean terrane that lies north of the Sierra de la Ventana, was derived from that region and has that general character. The Colorado River system, or its ancestors, on the other hand, flowed from the Andes and brought down sands in large volume, as well as clays, producing light-colored, sandy varieties of the Pampean terrane, which are sometimes so unlike the brown clays that they are not called Pampean, but are described as Tertiary sandstones. Within the area of the Province of Buenos Aires there rose, moreover, the heights of the Sierra Tandil and de la Ventana, which were eroded by rains and by winds, and which contributed more or less sand, together with clays, to the deposits laid down near the hills or in the valleys of streams which may have flowed from them.

Thus the sources of the Pampean earths were very unlike. The accumulation of so great a mass required a long time, during which conditions changed. Nevertheless, the Pampean terrane is on the whole a remarkably uniform and monotonous deposit, several agencies, among which wind has been the dominant one, having worked the material into a uniform condition.

Alluvial deposits, composed of unmodified river mud, such as rivers carry and deposit in regions of abundant rainfall and vegetation, consist of coarse as well as of fine clays and sands.—They contain also more or less carbonaceous matter derived from vegetation. But alluvium, which is spread and dries on flats that for any reason are not covered by vegetation, is sorted by winds, the fine clay being blown out and the coarse stuff being left behind. By being blown about or against one another the sand grains are worn down. There is also chemical disintegration. By many repetitions the process results in a fine flour of the most enduring universal substances, aluminous clay, silicious sand, and oxide of iron. Of such is the Pampean terrane.

Thus the Pampean, in the physical and chemical constitution of its materials, is a product of processes which require the interaction of rivers and winds. On the Arctic plains of northern Siberia, where the great rivers flood vast areas and retreating leave them bare, or in the immense delta of the Hwang River in eastern China, we may find modern illustrations of the Pampean conditions.

Climate is a factor of the first importance in modifying the effect of wind on alluvial deposits. Wind can not raise dust from surfaces that are frozen, moist, or sufficiently covered with vegetation, and it does not erode them. If alluvial deposits are dry and bare, wind does erode even plane surfaces, and when confined by the configuration of the surface to a hollow, or channel, it erodes rapidly. That the material of the Pampean has been blown about and sorted by wind is clearly proved by its uniform fineness, and hence we might conclude that the pampas have been arid and bare. But the Pampean is in large part a river deposit, such as the Hwang River has spread over the vast delta plain of China, and has been distributed by floods in a similar delta. The terrane contains abundant remains of large herbivorous animals, which lived on grass that must have grown rankly and in profusion. Thus there must have been rainfall sufficient to nourish vegetation. These evidences of aridity and humidity appear to be contradictory, but they are readily explained by geographic relations and by changes of climate.

The geographic relations of the Hwang River are to the point. The river rises in the mountains of central Asia, flows through desert basins, and descends to the head of its delta heavily laden with desert dust. The delta plain which is built of that dust is comparable in extent with the pampas of South America. The rivers that now flow from the Cordillera of Bolivia and Argentina southeastward also cross desert basins, which are arid because the mountains take the moisture from the air currents. They have been more or less arid ever since the uplift of the mountains occasioned the erosion which produced the Pampean sediment, and it is reasonable to infer that the fineness of the deposit is due to eolian sorting in the desert regions through which the rivers flow. This inference probably could not be extended to sediments derived from central Brazil, but it may be stated that the Pampean terrane which is so derived is less characteristically eolian than that which occurs farther west and south.

The parallel with the Hwang River may be extended to the action of the wind in the delta plain. During the winter months, in North China, when there is no rain or snow and no protecting vegetation dust is constantly in the air and dust storms are serious. Eolian drifts accumulate in eddies and lees. Similar conditions have existed during the formation of the Pampean, for it comprises both relatively modern and older deposits of a strictly eolian character occurring with others laid down by the river waters or in ponds.

It is possible that the geographic and seasonable conditions which have been described may be found sufficient to explain the various aspects of the Pampean terrane. But it is possible also that climatic cycles have been an important factor in determining the variation and succession of deposits in South America as they have been in the northern hemisphere. In order to present this question in the light of some of the known facts, we may digress at this point from the description of the Pampean terrane to a discussion of the climatic changes which characterize the Quaternary period in the Northern Hemisphere.

Here this period is distinguished from the Tertiary epochs which preceded it by the rigor of climate which occasioned the glaciation of northern Europe and northeastern North America. Ice fields of great extent spread from centers so conditioned by excessive snowfall and comparatively low temperature that they served as gathering grounds for the great névé which supplied the ice.

These centers were determined by meteorologic and also by topographic conditions. In North America two of them were situated in the great plains of northern Canada; another was in the northern Cordillera. In Europe the principal fields whence proceeded the dispersion of the ice were in northern Germany and in the Alps.

We were wont to speak of the Quaternary and of the glaciation which characterized it as though it were a single glacial period without intervals of milder climate. But this concept, which marked an early stage in the investigation of glacial deposits, has long since given way to the recognition of at least four epochs of glaciation and three epochs of general interglacial climate in those regions where the phenomena are most fully developed.

The several epochs of the Quaternary have received names which differ somewhat according to the center from which the ice spread.

Students of Alpine glaciation recognize the Gunz, Mindel, Riss, and Wurm stages, the Gunz being the earliest and the Wurm the latest glaciation, which spread from the Alps upon the plains of southern Germany. In the United States the deposits which were laid down by successive ice sheets that flowed from the great center in Labrador are known as the Wisconsin, Illinoian, Kansan, and Jerseyan. Those which spread from the other center in Keewatin, west of Hudson Bay, are similarly known as the Wisconsin, Illinoian (or Iowan), Kansan, and Nebraskan (or Pre-Kansan).

The deposits which have received these names have been traced over large areas in the respective regions in which they occur, and have been identified in each separate field as constituting in each case a sequence of formations due to recurrent glaciation, while between the deposits which indicate the former presence of ice there are found others whose character and included fossils demonstrate the existence of an intervening epoch of milder climate. Thus it is seen that the Quaternary period corresponds in duration with the development and retreat of at least four continental ice sheets, and that its time scale is marked off into eight epochs, namely, four which were characterized by glaciation and four which were marked by milder climate. We live in the latest of the milder epochs.

Having in mind the alternation of glacial and interglacial climatic epochs which have been distinguished in the Northern Hemisphere, it is reasonable to inquire whether the Pampean yields any evidence of similar climatic variations. Its general aspect is monotonous and readily suggests an initial inference that the general conditions of deposition were similarly uniform. But there are many local details which demonstrate the alternate action of wind and water, and hence in each such locality the alternation of climatic conditions favorable to one or the other agency. In so far as we may be justified in correlating the sequence of conditions in one locality with those in another, we may establish a presumption of general climatic epochs and of changes somewhat similar to those of the Northern Hemisphere. Let us hasten to say that this statement is not meant to imply that the Pampean formation contains a record of glacial and interglacial conditions. The writer has not observed the slightest evidence of glacial deposits in any part of the Pampean. Glacial deposits are entirely wanting in the delta deposits of the Hwang River, which the Pampean formation most closely resembles, and the origin of the Pampean material is to be sought rather in the region of the deserts, as has already been explained, than in one of the glacier-covered mountains. The fact that the loess deposits of the Mississippi Valley and of central Europe owe their origin to glaciers does not affect this statement, for the loess deposits of China, which are far more extensive, are independent of glacial origin. But the alternation of climate, of which there is evidence in the Pampean, is from humid to arid and back to humid, probably a number of times. It is theoretically probable that the epochs of humid climate were the more genial and those of arid climate the more rigorous as regards temperature, but of that we have as yet no satisfactory evidence.

With these suggestions we may consider some of the evidences of climatic variation in the Pampean.

Sections of the Pampean are to be seen at various points along the eastern coast of Argentina and have been observed by the writer north of Mar del Plata, in the Barrancas de los Lobos south of that city, and along the coast farther southeastward at Miramar, Necochea, and Monte Hermoso. The sections were carefully studied in each locality, but since we require here only an illustration of the kind of evidence of climatic change that may be adduced, it will suffice to describe a characteristic relation observed in the Barrancas del Norte, north of Mar del Plata.

The Barrancas del Norte are sea cliffs which vary but little from an average height of 10 meters. The constituent materials are earths which differ in color, texture, and arrangement, and which inclose secondary deposits of carbonate of lime forming more or less irregular bodies. The earths are characteristic loams of the Pampean terrane. They are very fine and uniform and usually very free from sands; pebbles, except those of the secondary limestone, are entirely wanting. In color, they present shades of brown which may be described as dark or reddish or fawn-colored. Gray tones also occur and certain strata are distinctly greenish. They are often compared to the Chinese deposits, to which Richthofen gave the name *loess*, and they share with the material the quality of uniform fineness. They are more compact, however, and exhibit many details of constitution and structure not found in loess, while at the same time they usually lack the columnar structure nearly always characterizing loess.

In the Barrancas del Norte the constituent formations might be variously classified as forming two, three, or four distinct horizons. From summit to base of the cliff one may recognize—

Plain: Meters.
    Black soil derived from the Pampean by the introduction of humus and
        possibly by accumulation of dust in the grass............................   1
    Fawn-colored to gray, or reddish, or yellow-brown Pampean earths, very
        irregularly distributed and varied in structure............................   4–8
    Greenish, stratified, sometimes sandy, but in general earthy, deposits not
        always present...   0–2
    Dark brown, very compact, dense earths, often sandy and constituting an
        earthy sandstone..   0–3
Beach..   10

The basal stratum of dark-brown, often sandy earth, marked by compactness and homogeneity and frequent stratification, is a continuous formation, which has the characters of eolian material redistributed by waters. The writer has seen very similar deposits in China in the banks of the Grand Canal south of Tientsin, where the material was loess redistributed in the vast delta of the Hwang River, but it was less compact. As the formation is homogeneous so far as traced in the Barrancas del Norte, and as it is very similar to the Pampean formations which extend from the Barrancas de los Lobos for many scores of miles southward, we can not ascribe it to strictly local conditions. On the contrary, it represents a general phase of erosion and deposition which corresponds apparently to the removal of fluvio-eolian formations from some one region and their redeposition where they are now found. The writer is inclined to regard this formation and similar deposits as due to river work on confluent flood plains and consequently as made during a relatively humid period.

The upper surface of the basal formation in the Barrancas del Norte is eroded and the hollows are filled by later deposits, sometimes of one character, sometimes of another. Characteristic examples are represented in the illustrations (pls. 2, 3). It will be seen that the formation was carved by an agent that undercut the sides and rounded the bottoms of the hollows, leaving masses with sharp points or edges in relief. Wind produces these effects in this material, whereas water cuts channels having nearly vertical walls. Thus it would appear that wind erosion, which is favored by, if not dependent on, aridity, succeeded an epoch of deposition that was conditioned by humidity. The eroded surface is not deeply carved but the extreme relief of about two meters which it exhibits is probably near the limit of height which the brown earth could maintain. It is impossible to say how much may have been removed above this surface, and we are thus left in doubt so far as this occurrence in the Barrancas del Norte is concerned whether the erosion was local and temporary or was occasioned by a general change. The phenomenon recurs, however, in other exposures of the formation at Miramar and at Necochea, and appears to be characteristic of the zone which is now laid open along the coast. Thus it is not improbable that the area of erosion was a broad one due to a somewhat general climatic and geographic change.

In the Barrancas del Norte the eroded surface of the Ensenadean comes into contact with several formations, which are unlike in color and constitution. The one which covers the longest stretches is a greenish stratified deposit formed of Pampean earth, which has been somewhat deoxidized. Similar greenish deposits occur here and there in the Pampean terrane up to the more recent formations, where they may be identified by their topographic relations on the present surface as having formed in ponds or lakes. The reduction of the iron oxide to which the green color is due is a natural effect of the presence of organic matter that gathers in ponds. Ameghino was the first to recognize their lacustrine origin. In the Barrancas del Norte they are sharply contrasted in color with the dark-brown Ensenadean, and the eroded surface is direct evidence of an interval between the episodes of deposition.

The eroded surface of the lower stratum worked out by wind and not by running water no doubt presented more or less extensive hollows in which pools or ponds would form and water-laid sediments would accumulate, provided there was sufficient rain. The deposits are water-laid and appear to constitute evidence of a return to conditions of greater humidity than had existed during the episode of erosion.

The formations which succeeded the lacustrine deposits where the latter occur, or which rest on the lower brown earth where the lacustrines are wanting, are of two kinds. There is a fine whitish or light-gray stratum which exhibits the vertical structure characteristic of eolian loess and which also possesses the fineness and uniformity of wind-blown dust. The light color is peculiar and is not explained by any field observation. This white or gray loess is locally conformable to the brown sandy earth and again is separated from it by pockets of pink pebbly loess described below.

The formation which may be called pink pebbly loess, according to its color and constitution, is a fine-grained, light reddish-brown deposit, which includes small pebbles of the same material. The texture, homogeneity, and structure are eolian. The pebbles also could have been formed only by wind action, since the loess of which they consist would readily melt down in water and lose its form. The formation thus suggests arid conditions. It occurs characteristically in wind-eroded hollows which are more or less undercut, and thus it indicates the activity of the wind as it erodes and fills. Were it not for the intervening lacustrine formation there would be no reason for separating the episode of erosion during which the basal stratum was sculptured from the episode of erosion and filling which is marked by the pebbly loess, and the climatic variation would be simply from more humid to more arid. But the occurrence of the lacustrine deposits in the hollows cut in the basal stratum and the fact that they are themselves sometimes cut out by the hollows filled by the pebbly loess indicate that between two episodes when wind erosion was favored, presumably by aridity, there was an interval of precipitation adequate to produce ponds.

The horizon of the whitish-gray loess and of the pink pebbly loess is characterized by great irregularity of deposits, and is thus distinguished from the higher horizon immediately overlying them, which is occupied by a fawn-colored eolian earth most examples of which are a structureless loess, but some of which exhibit columnar structure. The fawn-colored loess is the highest of the formations in the Barrancas del Norte and forms the upper third to half of the bluff. It is continuous with the pink pebbly loess, which changes gradually in color and loses the pebbly inclusions from below upward. It is strongly contrasted in color with the whitish-gray and the plane between them is clearly marked, but is flat and not eroded. Thus the fawn-colored loess may be regarded as the upward continuation of these two dissimilar deposits with which it corresponds in being of wind origin. It merges upward into the black soil, which is derived from it.

In the foregoing descriptions of the *original* characters of the formation in the Barrancas del Norte, the secondary feature, the occurrence of limestone masses, or *tosca*, has purposely been omitted, it being regarded as a deposit from ground waters subsequent to the deposition of the earth in which it occurs.

There are two horizons in the Barrancas del Norte at which limestone is strongly developed. One is near the base of the cliff, somewhat less than a meter below the upper surface of the dark-brown sandy earth that forms the base of the exposed section. There is a heavy horizontal plate of limey rock, in many places two-thirds of a meter thick, and fairly constant in occurrence. According to the writer's understanding of the process of tosca formation, it represents the zone or horizon within which the ground water rises and falls, while diffusing by capillary action and evaporating from the surface. The conditions which are most favorable are those of semiaridity. The density and continuity of the residual lime deposit constitute a measure of the time during which the action continued at the horizon, and as this formation is both dense and continuous it appears to correspond to a notable episode. Thus, the lower plate or stratum of tosca strengthens the evidence for an arid or semiarid epoch, following the deposition of the brown, sandy alluvium.

The upper horizon of strongly developed tosca is at the base of and in the fawn-colored loess that constitutes the upper third or half of the barrancas. The limey rock occurs in irregular branching masses that are longer vertically than horizontally and are more or less separated from one another. The forms and occurrence are adjusted to the structure of the loess, which is itself irregular and occasions their irregularity. This horizon seems to indicate an episode of climatic condition favorable to evaporation—semiaridity—

BARRANCAS DEL NORTE, MAR DEL PLATA
Showing unconformity, due to effects of erosion, between basal bed and deposit of loess.

than the upper, but exhibits similar evidences of erosion and eolian deposition. At Miramar and Necochea the formation, which is exposed in the low bluffs also, consists of loess-like alluvium, the surface of which has been eroded and filled in by wind. Similar characters may be seen at Monte Hermoso and, as shown in plates 2 and 3, at Mar del Plata. According to Ameghino, the exposure at Monte Hermoso shows at the base a member of the Pampean terrane which is even older than the lowest exposed in the Barrancas de los Lobos. There is nothing in the lithologic or physical characters of the deposit which would enable one to form an opinion on this point. Ameghino's view is based on the faunas of the respective localities.

Whatever the relative ages of the various deposits that are to be seen in the sea cliffs of the eastern coast may be, they all exhibit the evidence of identical physical conditions and point to alternations of humidity and aridity during the time of their distribution.

It is not necessary to pursue in detail the geologic and chronologic problems connected with these older formations of the Pampean, for the present investigation is concerned primarily only with those formations which are related to the problem of man's existence in the region, and the writers have not been able to find any evidence which would show that he lived during Pampean time. Human remains have been found, so far as the writers have been able to observe, only in recent deposits, some of which are classed by them as the Upper Pampean and others as post-Pampean formations. The later phases of the Pampean may now be considered.

UPPER PAMPEAN AND POST-PAMPEAN

To Dr. Santiago Roth the writer is indebted for having pointed out the distinction between the Upper Pampean and the Middle Pampean of Roth's classification, as exposed in sections near La Plata; near Anchorena, on the Rio de la Plata above Buenos Aires; in the Arroyo de Ramallo; and at San Lorenzo, near Rosario. Doctor Ameghino designated as Upper Pampean two deposits seen at and near Mar del Plata.

All of the deposits which were thus referred to the Upper Pampean are characterized by the features which distinguish eolian loess. The material is finely pulverent, not firmly consolidated, often columnar in structure; it is light-gray or fawn colored and contains secondary limestone only in relatively small amount as compared with the older Pampean formations. It is a formation which obviously is composed of material eroded by the wind from the older Pampean and redeposited in favorable localities in the form of eolian drifts. It does not appear probable, considering the conditions of development and the present irregular distribution, that the Upper Pampean ever formed a widespread mantle in the region of its occurrence. It is distinctly a drifted formation and occurs with the irregularity which characterizes drifts.

It is doubtful whether we may safely speak of an Upper Pampean epoch in the sense of a definite division of geologic time. We have seen that eolian loess occurs as a characteristic constituent of the older Pampean terranes. The material for the formation of eolian drifts has been available and winds to erode and redeposit it have been active in later epochs also. From the time when the earliest alluviums of the Pampean terrane were formed to the present, deposits possessing the physical characters of the Upper Pampean have been developed. Thus it seems impracticable to distinguish an Upper Pampean formation on physical characters alone. There is paleontologic evidence, but it rests primarily on the physical, for the biologic lines of descent can not be established except by observation of the stratigraphic sequence. Those fossils which have been found in the superficial eolian loess have been assigned to the Upper Pampean, because they occurred in a position above the older Pampean and in material having Upper Pampean characteristics. In these criteria, however, there is nothing by which to distinguish the oldest Upper Pampean loess from the most recent, and it is not impossible that the range of time represented by such loess deposits corresponds with a large part or all of the Quaternary period.

While the writer is thus in doubt as to the stratigraphic and chronologic value to be given the term Upper Pampean, there are certain relations which serve to set an earliest date before which the Upper Pampean did not develop in the superficial position in which it is now recognized. These limiting relations are physiographic and climatic. As will be seen by referring to the description of the Arroyo de Ramallo, to that of Mar del Plata, and to other occurrences of the Upper Pampean, the Upper Pampean deposits occupy peculiar positions in the eroded surface of the older formations. In so far as this may be generally true they could not have been deposited until after the surface had been eroded, and the erosion could not have taken place until the older formations had been elevated above base level. There is thus a recognizable effect of deformation which intervenes between the Upper Pampean and any older formation.

The Upper Pampean did not develop, however, immediately after the elevation of the region. The relations which may be seen between Buenos Aires and Rosario show that shallow valleys were formed by small confluent streams that grew out of the Parana and that they afforded the appropriate locus for deposition of the Upper Pampean. (Plate 4.) Valley erosion by these local streamlets does not seem consistent with simultaneous valley-filling by winds. The two seem to have been distinct in time, the latter succeeding the former. Thus we may probably recognize an episode during which the alluvial plain formed by the surface of the older Pampean was raised to its present altitude above base level, an episode of humid climate during which the drifts of eolian loess, the Upper Pampean, were deposited. As those drifts are now cut through by the streamlets, a later episode of erosion is distinguishable, which appears to coincide with the present time.

"Upper Pampean" thus gains a certain definiteness as a geologic term by virtue of the physical relations in which the characteristic deposits occur, and may have value in systematic classification if it be limited to deposits formed during that episode of aridity which preceded the present humidity. The writer has not seen enough of the field, however, to know whether such a distinction is valid or not, and it does not appear that the term has been thus critically applied.

Post-Pampean deposits fall into four classes, namely: Lacustrine, alluvial, dune, and marine formations, all of which are dependent on topographic features as they now exist. In order to develop the conditions of deposition, it is necessary to describe the topography and the Atlantic coast of the pampas with reference to their origin and stage of growth. We will take up first the topography of the pampas.

The word *pampa*, signifying "flat plain," describes the pampas correctly only in so far as it applies to the general aspect of the surface. One must look beyond the foreground in order to see the extraordinary flatness of the pampas. In detail they are not flat, and yet in the foreground itself there are rarely those inequalities of the surface which are common in plains traversed by running streams, even where they are least eroded. The absence of running water and of the landscape forms which it produces is one of the most striking though negative phenomena of the Argentine plains. The characteristic surface form of the pampas is a gentle hollow or an equally imperceptible swell, each of them entirely devoid of line or sharp accent and each melting without distinction into the other. A horseman galloping over the apparently dead level surface sinks partly out of sight like a ship beyond an ocean swell and remains perhaps below the plane of vision while he rides a mile or more. A rabbit startled from the grassy flat is lost in sameness of color until he suddenly appears in silhouette against the sky as he tops the swell and beyond it disappears. These broad hollows and swells have no systematic relation to any structure of the Pampean earths, nor to any system of drainage. They are probably related to the prevailing direction of the winds which produced them, whether such winds be those of the present climatic episode or were those of a preceding time; but if such a relation exists the forms which may betray it will be discovered only by careful

topographic mapping. Nevertheless, the wind origin of the surface
features of the pampas is obvious in the general form of the hollows
and swells. Anyone who has studied a loess-covered landscape knows
the long sweep from plain to mountain which is the characteristic
form of equilibrium that is produced where the wind is deflected
upward from the plain. Like the slope of equilibrium of the beach it
varies in declivity with the material and the force of the moving element, and like the drumloid curve produced by ice it is definitely
characteristic of the fashioning medium. The pampas everywhere
bear the impress of the wind which has scoured, hollowed, and molded
their vast flat expanses of fine brown earth.

The surface which is thus characterized as an effect of wind sculp-
ture is modified along the right bank of the Parana, in what is now
the most humid region of the Province of Buenos Aires, by stream
erosion. A number of small valleys have their rise in the pampa and
extend more or less directly to the river. Those which the writer has
particularly examined are at Alvear and Ramallo; another is crossed
by the railroad near Baradero. These are but examples of similar
valleys of erosion which occasion the frequent up and down grades on
the Ferrocarril Central between Buenos Aires and Rosario. The
Arroyo de Ramallo is characteristic. (Pl. 4.)

The Arroyo de Ramallo debouches into the Parana with a low flood
plain about a kilometer in width. Between 2 and 3 kilometers from
the Parana the little valley is much narrower and is bordered by
steep banks and low bluffs. A kilometer higher up the stream has
been dammed and affords a fall of about 3 meters. Its channel
extends a very considerable distance farther back into the plain, but
only as a shallow talweg.

The little valleys of which the Arroyo de Ramallo is a type are in
an early stage of development. They are due to little confluent
autogenous streams that have grown back from the Parana into the
pampas and as yet have reached no more than a youthful growth.
Their history embodies, it is true, the early episode of erosion, which
was followed by partial filling with eolian loess, and most recently by
reexcavation of the talweg, but when we consider the softness of the
Pampean earths as opposed to the eroding power of a stream, we are
obliged to recognize that these little streams have accomplished but
a small amount of erosion.

In the photograph shown in plate 5, we see the bank of the Parana
at San Lorenzo, above Rosario. The level Pampean plain extends at
an elevation of 12 to 15 meters above the river and ends in nearly
vertical bluffs, which are scarcely attacked by erosion. Talus is also
wanting and the scarp is very young. It overlooks the wide channel

ARROYO DE RAMALLO

Showing terrace of eolian Pampean (Superior Pampean) deposited in the older arroyo cut in the Middle Pampean.

BANKS OF THE PARANA AT SAN LORENZO

of the Parana and the alluvial islands on the farther side, and it is apparent that the great river is corrading—literally cutting away—the bank faster than talus or gullies can develop. But though the river is a powerful agent of erosion it has not accomplished a great deal in widening its flood plain at this favorable point. The work is only begun.

In describing the warped surface of the old continent it was stated that the Parana and the Rio de la Plata occupied a downwarp. Southwest of their depression the Pampean plain rises very gently in an upwarp to an altitude of between 30 and 40 meters above sea. The highest part of the plain lies in a line which trends from northwest to southeast, some 50 kilometers southwest of Buenos Aires. About 50 kilometers still farther southwest there is another depression whose axis is approximately parallel to that of the Rio de la Plata and which is occupied by one of the several salt rivers (Rio Salado) of the country. This depression constitutes the eastern portion of the Province of Buenos Aires, in latitude 36°, and is an area in which extensive drainage canals have been thought necessary. The general elevation of the plain rises from near sea level to 25 meters in the valley of the Salado, but there is no perceptible slope and the extraordinary flatness of the surface is such that during the rainy seasons of wet years rain water has stood over many square kilometers where during drier years there spread the grassy plain. The channel of the Salado, meandering through this flat, is shown in the photograph (pl. 25). It will be noticed that the river is in a peculiar state of equilibrium. It is not deeply corrading, neither is it aggrading the channel. It has sufficient fall to carry away the silt which it brings and therefore does not build up its banks above the neighboring plain, as is the habit of rivers in their deltas, nor does it appear to be obstructed. Yet its force is not sufficient to excavate its channel to a greater depth below the surface than is required to carry its waters. The river may be said to flow practically at base level. The writer observed these relations in the vicinity of the stations called Villanueva and General Belgrano, and noted them as an illustration of a surface which, although elevated considerably above sea level, and traversed by streams, does not exhibit any of the features sculptured by running water. This condition may be attributed to the fact that confluent streams have not yet developed on the gentle slopes that descend from the northeast and from the southwest toward the Rio Salado. Due allowance must be made for the effects of wind erosion, which has produced very broad and shallow hollows in the plain, in which the rain waters gather and evaporate instead of running off. Nevertheless, the period of time is short during which such a surface, when elevated, may retain its integrity. The drainage systems have not had time to develop since the Pampean was warped up to its present position.

Thus observations of the effects of erosion along the Parana and in the valley of the Salado show that streams have done very little work on the Pampean formation. Indeed, the features which they have sculptured are insignificant. Hence, the elevation of the pampas may be regarded as recent. If, however, it should appear on further study that stream erosion has been retarded by the peculiar character of the pampas to a greater degree than now seems probable, and that there have been one or more epochs of aridity during which stream erosion was reduced to practically nothing, there would be reason for extending the time that has elapsed since the uplifting of the surface, and it might be that this later history would cover the Quaternary period.

It has already been stated that those eolian deposits, which are characterized as Upper Pampean by both Roth and Ameghino, lie in hollows sculptured in the surface of the Pampean, and the same holds true for the still younger deposits of alluvium and dune sands. All of these, including the Upper Pampean, appear to the writer to fall in the Quaternary. It may or may not follow that the earlier Pampean formations were deposited during the later Tertiary (Pliocene and late Miocene), though this is probable; but they also may be in part of the Quaternary age.

ATLANTIC COAST OF THE PAMPAS

If now we turn from the consideration of the pampas to that of the eastern coast of Argentina, we must recognize at once that the coast line has reached its present position by virtue of wave erosion on the uplifted mass of the Pampean. In order to place this proposition in its appropriate relations, we may consider the development of the coast as the result of the attack of the ocean on the inert mass of the Pampean earths.

A shore is fashioned by waves and currents, driven chiefly by winds. In the course of their attack they destroy headlands, build bars, spits, and beaches across embayments, and eventually establish a coast which is adjusted to and in equilibrium with their activities. A young coast is distinguished by irregularity, an old coast by smoothness. On a young coast the wave-cut terraces and sea cliffs are conspicuous features; on an old coast the cliffs due to wave action are modified or obliterated by subaerial erosion. It may happen that sea cliffs cut in enduring rock stand for a relatively long time, but a cliff of earth, however compact, is a very transient feature.

BARRANCAS DE LOS LOBOS

View southwest of Mar del Plata, near the northeastern end of the sea cliffs; part of the recent and rapidly changing coast of the Province of Buenos Aires.

The eastern coast of Argentina is composed, to a great extent, of sea cliffs of the Pampean earths. Many of these are too steep to climb and are frequently undercut by the waves that beat against the base. Their height depends on the elevation of the plains and is usually not more than 10 to 15 meters, but in the Barrancas de los Lobos, south of Mar del Plata, the cliffs attain an altitude of 28 meters. (See pl. 6.) As one walks beneath these bluffs of clay and notes the fallen masses of earth disintegrating at the foot of the cliff, one can not but recognize that the present coast line is a transient thing. It evidently changes measureably from decade to decade and no feature of it can be many centuries old. Thus no bank or slope or eroded surface between the plain and the beach, nor any deposit built upon such a slope, can be considered to be older than very recent.

The coastal deposits which may be observed along the recent coast of Buenos Aires are of three kinds: Beach, dune, and coquina formations. The beaches are deposits of sand formed between the base of the cliffs and the sea and are usually so narrow that they are covered by the rising tide. Except as subordinate features at the foot of the bluffs, they are entirely wanting. Sometimes their shoreward limit is formed of dunes.

Dunes are conspicuous features. These occur wherever there is a source of sand and a surface upon which they can accumulate. They appear to be absent only where the sea cliffs are so steep and high that a dune can not find lodgment. Even then sand is blown into the hollows wrought by wind and waves in the face of the cliff, and lies in banks and festoons which sometimes simulate interbedded sandy strata. The universal activity of the wind and its efficiency in transporting sand constitute most striking facts in the present condition of the coast. The writer's observations cover particularly the stretch from Mar del Plata to Bahia Blanca, but the data regarding the direction and frequency of winds are available for the stretch from Buenos Aires to Bahia Blanca. In his work on the climate of the Republic of Argentina,[1] Davis gives two tables, one for Buenos Aires and the other for Bahia Blanca, which embody the results of observations taken three times daily and referred to a scale of 1,000 monthly observations. The original data are arranged with reference to the months and eight points of the compass, namely, north, northeast, east, and so forth. For our purpose we may group these observations into two classes, one representing winds which may be said to blow from the sea, and the other those which blow from the land. The first class comprises winds from northeast, east, southeast, and south, and the second those

---

[1] Davis, Gualterio G., Clima de la República Argentina, Buenos Aires, 1909, pp. 41–44.

from southwest, west, northwest, and north. The figures taken from
Davis's tables then yield the following:

Month	Buenos Aires		Bahia Blanca	
	NE. to S.	SW. to N.	NE. to S.	SW. to N.
January	685	315	389	611
February	593	393	376	624
March	677	323	308	692
April	555	445	235	765
May	446	554	151	849
June	422	578	136	864
July	486	514	207	793
August	587	413	225	775
September	663	337	280	720
October	703	297	353	647
November	668	332	376	624
December	646	364	334	666
	7,131	4,865	3,370	8,630

These figures show that at Buenos Aires the winds blow far more
frequently from the sea than from the land, whereas at Bahia Blanca
the reverse is the case. Davis comments on this fact and states that
if the data were to be given for a number of intermediate stations it
would be seen that the variation in frequency of the winds changes
from north to south in a regular manner in obedience to a physical
law. An examination of the isobaric and isothermal charts for different seasons, accompanying Davis's work, shows clearly the nature of
this law and its relation to the observed variation. According to the
same official source of information, the mean annual velocity of the
wind at Buenos Aires is 15.8 kilometers per hour and there is no
month in the year in which the mean monthly velocity falls below 13
kilometers per hour. At Bahia Blanca the annual mean is 14.9 and
the least monthly mean is 10.2.

The effect of the barometric and thermometric conditions is to
produce winds which, along the northeastern coast of the Province
of Buenos Aires, blow prevailingly on shore, and this condition
extends to a point south of Mar del Plata. The coast then trends
away southwest, while the prevailing direction of the wind veers in
the same direction, but through even a greater angle, so that as we
go from Mar del Plata southwestward toward Bahia Blanca the prevailing winds blow more and more nearly in a direction parallel to
the coast. The effect of these relations on the work of the wind is
seen in the distribution of sand dunes, which become high and
numerous and occupy a relatively broad belt along this shore where-
ever the sea cliffs do not prevent.

By reference to the local description of the coast northeast of
Necochea it will be seen that there are older and younger dunes, which

clearly belong to different episodes of development. The older ones lie inland in a zone behind the younger. They are grass-grown and sink away to low mounds till they merge into the plain. Where the drainage is ponded behind them there are little lakes. Beneath them is a layer of black earth representing the soil of the former plain over which the dunes advanced with the advance of the sea upon the coast. The younger dunes are composed of moving sand. They rise directly from the existing beach, to which they are obviously related, and form a zone a kilometer or more in width. They vary from less than 10 to more than 20 meters in height, rise in a long, wind-wrought curve from southeast to northwest, and on the northwest side are as steep as the sand will lie.

At the mouth of the Rio Quequen, near Necochea, the dunes are 12 to 15 meters high and advancing from the southwest have pushed the river northward so that it flows through a restricted channel beneath a cut bank in the loess 12 meters high. At Monte Hermoso the zone of large grass-grown dunes is 3 to 5 kilometers wide, and the dunes themselves attain a height of 25 meters or more above the sea. Monte Hermoso is a dune 27 meters in height, the upper 20 meters being sand and the base consisting of the Monte Hermoso formation. These brief descriptions will suffice to indicate the effective work which is being accomplished by the wind along this stretch of coast, and to make it clear that the dunes are a strictly coastal formation dependent on the proximity of the sea, formed from the beach sands, and moved by the winds whose prevailing direction depends on existing relations of land and sea. More detailed descriptions are given in the accounts of the specific points visited.

The *coquina* which forms on the eastern coast of Argentina is intimately related to the dunes in origin, since the wind is the chief agent in its production. But, whereas the sand dunes are developed by the more regular winds, the coquina is the product of the storms. It consists chiefly of broken shells mingled with sand and gravel, but includes also any pebbles or other large objects, such as bones, which may happen to occur with the sand. It is usually more or less indurated, and this character, together with the fact that it contains fragments of fossils identical with those which occur in the underlying Pampean, has led to its being considered a Tertiary formation. The writer regards it as strictly equivalent in character and origin with the coquina of the Florida coast, in regard to which we may quote the following description:[1]

"One of the most common of the marine Quaternary deposits is the coquina which occurs at various points along the coast. This consists of a mass of more or less water-worn shells cemented by calcium-carbonate. The amount of cement is seldom great enough to close

[1] Sellards, E. H., State Geologist, in *Second Annual Report of Florida State Geological Survey*, 1908–09, p. 153.

the openings between the individual shells, though in some localities the process of cementation has proceeded far enough to produce a rather compact fossiliferous limestone.   There is usually more or less sand present, which is commonly in the form of thin laminæ separating the shell beds, and various gradations from sand rock to shell rock may be noted along the Florida coast."

Sellards quotes from an account published by James Pierce in 1825, in the *American Journal of Science:*

"Extensive beds of shell rock of a peculiar character occupy the borders of the ocean in various places from the River St. Johns to Cape Florida.   They are composed of unmineralized marine shells of species common to our coast, mostly small bivalves, whole and in minute division, connected by calcareous cement.   I examined this rock on the Isle of Anastasia, opposite St. Augustine, where it extends for miles, rising 20 feet above the sea and of unknown depth. It has been penetrated about 30 feet.   In these quarries horizontal strata of shell rock of sufficient thickness and solidity for good building stone alternate with narrow parallel beds of larger and mostly unbroken shells, but slightly connected. · · ·   The large Spanish fort and most of the public and private buildings of St. Augustine are constructed of this stone.   The rock extends in places into the sea with superincumbent beds of new shells of the same character."

In the report from which these quotations are given the Quaternary is divided into Pleistocene and Recent and the coquina is placed in both Pleistocene and Recent, along with beach sands and eolian deposits.   The various deposits of coquina along the coast have repeatedly been observed and studied by both Dall and Vaughan, and their Quaternary age has been determined by these observers.

From the example of the coquina of the Florida coast we learn that indurated formations may be even as modern as the Recent epoch. They may also be Pleistocene, and the question of age determination depends in a large measure on their relation to other formations or to physiographic features.   Paleontologic evidence also has bearing, but there are two conditions which may qualify it.   The life range of species may cover the time of development of different masses of coquina which are physiographically distinguishable, for the movements and accidents of coastal development are constantly affording new and different conditions under which shells may be assembled and cemented.   Again, in case a coquina contains remains of both living and extinct species, the latter belonging to an older formation from which they may be derived, we can not accept with any confidence the evidence of these older fossils as to the age of the coquina.

The coquina of the Argentine coast may then be studied with reference to its constitution, hardness, and the capacity of existing agencies to cement it; in regard also to its relation to the existing coast line and the special features thereof; and finally as to the fossil content.

The Argentine coquina is composed, in the several places where the writer observed it, of materials derived directly from the adjoining strand. The sand, the pebbles, the larger stones, and the shells are all identical, so far as they possess similar characteristics, with those which make up the latest beach deposits. The sand is both white and black, being composed of grains of quartz and of various dark grains derived from volcanic rocks. The pebbles are in large part those which have been styled "Patagonian," because they are the same as those which form the widespread pebble deposit of the Patagonian plateaus. They are brought along the shore by the prevailing northerly drift of the inshore currents. The shells and shell fragments are those of thick-shelled bivalves which occur in limited quantities on the beach and live in adjacent waters. Thus, as regards constitution, the coquina is identical with the beach.

The physiographic relations of the coquina are definite. It occurs only in immediate relation to the present coast within reach of the waves or spray. It usually lies at the beach level. In one case, however, namely, at the mouth of the Arroyo del Barco, to the south of Mar del Plata, the coquina occurs up to a maximum altitude of 9 meters above the beach; and again at the Boca del Moro, north of Necochea, it was observed just above the modern beach, lying in a slope continuous with the beach, but eroded by gullies. At the Arroyo del Barco the coquina lies in an angle of the coast, at the head of the Playa de Peralta, where it is open to the storm waves of the Atlantic and at a point where the converging shores concentrate them and give them exceptional force. At the Boca del Moro the occurrence of the coquina may be within the reach of an unusual storm, but it is not unreasonable to postulate that the shore currents have built out the sandy beach and have thus widened the strand sufficiently to remove the zone of former wave action from that of the present breakers. Another occurrence of this formation is on the slope of Punta Porvenir, south of Mar del Plata. It there consists of a mingling of sand and loess and extends from the low bluff back of the beach to a distance of 110 meters from the shore, that is to say, to the limit which may be reached by spray from the storm waves breaking on the prominent point. It was in this deposit that the Ameghinos found the carapace of a glyptodon associated with hand-worked stones. Just north of Punta Piedras at Mar del Plata the coquina occurs on the beach in the lee of the quartzite point, where the waves have washed in the material which goes to make up the conglomeratic and pebbly deposit. It also consists largely of shells and is cemented by lime. A peculiar interest attaches to it because it appears to underlie a portion of the bluff, which is here composed of eolian loess. This loess is assigned to the Upper Pampean and still greater age is allotted to the coquina beneath it. The coquina is not to be seen in section beneath the loess, but is said to have been struck in numerous wells that were put down through the bluff. This lee, or sheltered place, behind which the coquina occurs, was produced when the waves cut out the little bay that is now protected by the quartzite of Punta Piedras, and the eolian deposit, like the coquina, is genetically related to the present strand line.

The fossil content of the coquina is well known to consist of shells of living species, but is said to include also shells and bones of extinct species. A number of specimens brought by the writer from the localities where he examined the coquina, between Mar del Plata and Necochea, contained shells of living species only. In one fragment a shell of an extinct species was found; the specimen came without a label and the locality from which it was derived could not be identified with certainty.

In the coquina at Arroyo del Barco, Doctor Hrdlička and the writer observed a bone which was too firmly imbedded in the rock to be secured, but which appeared to be a jaw or pelvis, possibly of an ungulate. Ameghino stated that the formation contains bones of extinct species peculiar to the Pampean formation (Ensenadean) upon which it rests. In view of the fact that the coast is eroded from this same formation and that any bones contained in it must be washed out and swept along with the beach sands and gravel, it is to be expected that the more massive ones or portions of them may have become imbedded in the coquina. It is said that delicate or articulated bones have been found in the formation. They could hardly survive in such a deposit as that at the Arroyo del Barco, as it is composed of very coarse material which could be moved only by use of considerable force, but the mingled loess and sand of Punta Porvenir might bury lighter objects, either weathered out upon the surface of the underlying Pampean or contemporaneous with the recent deposit. Thus the carapace of the glyptodon found on Punta Porvenir may be a fossil from the older Pampean (Ensenadean) or it may indicate the survival of that species down to the recent time when the coast developed in its present position and the eolian deposit was formed. In this case the paleontologic evidence must derive its significance from the more direct and unequivocal stratigraphic and physical relations.

SUMMARY OF GEOLOGIC RELATIONS

In the preceding pages the facts which the writer regards as most essential to an understanding of the geology of the region under review have been briefly sketched. They may be summarized as follows:

1. Beneath the Pampean is an ancient land surface which was formerly a plain or nearly so, it having been long subjected to erosion. The plain subsided and became covered with the alluvium of rivers which brought silt from the north and especially from the west. The rate of subsidence and the rate of sedimentation were related to one another somewhat as they now are in the Mississippi embayment, so that the surface of the river deposits remained above sea level although the mass was sinking. Marine deposits, therefore, do not enter the area.

2. The alluvial deposits constitute what is now called the Pampean terrane. They resemble the deposits which are made by the Hwang River in the delta plains of eastern China, and which consist of eolian loess redistributed by river action. The loess of China originates in the deserts of central Asia, and by inference the Pampean earths originated under similar arid conditions. The lands to the east of the Andes now have an arid climate because the high mountains dry out the western winds. If this hypothesis of the origin of the Pampean earths be valid there is a relation between the Pampean and the Cordillera, since the elevation of the Cordillera was required to establish the genetic conditions for the production of the loess that was subsequently deposited as the alluvium of the Pampean terrane. By this hypothesis it seems probable that most of the Pampean is of late Tertiary age, but there is nothing in the process of deposition which precludes Quaternary age for the later part of the formation.

3. During the deposition of the Pampean terrane eolian processes involving erosion and redeposition were certainly active. They appear to have been particularly active at certain epochs which alternated with others of dominant fluviatile action. This alternation may have been local and have occurred in different places at different times, but the phenomena as they are displayed in the sections on the eastern coast of Argentina suggest that there were one or more epochs when wind erosion prevailed over a wide area and was favored by some special climatic condition, such as aridity. The deposition of secondary limestone appears also to indicate climatic variation, and the two lines of evidence—wind erosion and limestone deposition—appear to coincide in their indications. Hence it is inferred that Pampean history has been varied by climatic change, and it is suggested that the ultimate subdivision of the Pampean terrane into distinct formations will be based on climatic variation. The writer has not formed any opinion as to the relations which might exist between such a classification and any of those which may have been published. It would seem probable, however, that no attempt to classify the Pampean terrane, a mass of lenticular alluvial deposits produced by several rivers, according

to the methods that apply to more uniform marine strata, could be successful.

4. The criteria by which the several more or less theoretic divisions of the Pampean have been distinguished are primarily lithologic—composition, texture, compactness, structure, and the proportion of secondary limestone or tosca. The differences in these characters are not marked. At first the writer did not easily recognize them. Eventually he saw them without difficulty, but he did not learn to rely on them as a means of classification. It seemed to him that local conditions affecting the source of the material and the character of the deposit might be more influential than the greater or less age of the formation. It was apparent in clearly exposed sections that deposits of distinct epochs might occur in the same plane in close proximity or in contact with one another. Sections are few and the distances between them are great. Under these conditions the subclassification of the Pampean is a problem of extreme difficulty, in which there is great liability to error.

5. If we turn from the physical to the paleontologic criteria as a means of classification, we are confronted with the fact that the sequence of faunas can be determined with certainty only when we know the sequence of formations. But, inasmuch as we do not surely know the succession of Pampean formations, we can not have confidence in any theoretic development of faunas. There is urgent need in this matter to withhold judgment and to preserve a conservative attitude of agnosticism in regard to the relative age of hypothetic divisions of the Pampean terrane and the supposedly distinct faunas.

6. Among the divisions of the Pampean which have been proposed the distinction between the Upper Pampean and all older formations of the terrane seems to be one of the safest. In many places there is a distinct unconformity beneath the deposits of the Upper Pampean, which is a result of uplift and erosion. Elsewhere there is entire conformity, as, for instance, at San Lorenzo on the Parana, and apparently continuous deposition from the older Pampean up into loess deposits of the Upper Pampean type. This is not surprising, for the surface of the pampas is now and has been in the past sufficiently warped to bring about conditions of erosion in one locality concurrently with those of continuous deposition in another. The Upper Pampean is identified lithologically as an eolian loess. It is eolian not only in texture and structure but also in distribution, and occurs generally in drifted deposits rather than as a widespread stratum. The conditions for its formation may have been peculiarly favorable during some recent epoch of aridity, and if so the formation would acquire a certain unity and individuality. But the writer is satisfied that not all of the irregularities of the surface which gave

rise to wind eddies, nor all of the loess drifts that accumulated in them, can be assigned to a single epoch. He believes that the deposition of various local deposits of the Upper Pampean type has been distributed over a considerable interval of time and is still going on. If so, fossil remains found in them may be similarly distributed.

7. Although the pampas may be described as elevated plains, they have suffered but very little erosion. The development of valleys is in an incipient stage. There are extensive areas which are not drained by streams, and the characteristic topographic form is a shallow wind-scooped hollow. The flatness of the surface and the meagerness of the rainfall undoubtedly retard the growth of erosion channels, but the Pampean loess is easily eroded and can not long have been exposed at the elevation and with the slopes which it now exhibits, without dissection. Hence it is inferred that the elevation is a result of recent warping. Some of the Upper Pampean deposits occur in the incipient valleys tributary to the Parana. The valleys are consequent on the slope due to elevation, and are therefore younger, and the Upper Pampean drifted into the valleys is younger still.

8. The coast of Argentina presents a line of sea cliffs and beaches which are being vigorously attacked and are in process of constant changes. The sea is constantly eroding the land, and the coast line is geologically a very transient feature. It must shift from century to century to a perceptible degree and can not have occupied its present position at most more than a few thousand years. Upon this shifting shore the winds and waves have built certain equally temporary formations, among which the dunes are the most conspicuous and the coquina is the most interesting, at least in the study of man's supposed antiquity. The physical evidence of the relation of the dunes and the coquina to the recent coast line is definite and positive. Those formations are as recent as the coast line is, and any organic remains found in them, whether human or otherwise, or any artifacts which they contain as contemporaneous deposits, must also be recent. The only exception to this conclusion is found in the possibility that fossils weathered out of older formations may become incorporated in the younger.

REPORT ON SHELLS COLLECTED BY BAILEY WILLIS AND A. HRDLIČKA IN ARGENTINA

By WM. H. DALL

Geologist and Paleontologist, U. S. Geological Survey

The following is my report on the shells brought [by Dr. Hrdlička and Mr. Willis] from Argentina and submitted to me for determination. The age of the various beds from which the specimens come is difficult to estimate, as the shells prove to be all of recent species, that is, species still having, so far as known, living representatives. There is one specimen without label, and it proves to be the only one carrying an extinct species.[1]

Detailed notes:

Current numbers	U. S. National Museum numbers	Locality	Observations
1	5352	Arroyo del Barco, south of Mar del Plata, Argentina, May 31, 1910.	The shells in this lot comprise *Glycymeris longior* Sowerby, *Eutivela perplexa* Stearns, and *Olivancillaria auricularia* Lamarck, all recent species.
2	5353	Mar del Plata, Pta Piedras, southeast side ("Inter-Ensenadean").	*Mactra patagonica* and Orbigny and *Glycymeris longior* Sby.
3	5354	Punta Porvenir, south of Mar del Plata (typical "Inter-Ensenadean").	*Glycymeris longior* Sby.
4	5355	Mar del Plata, 8 miles south of the city, on the plain back of the seabeach, southwest of Pta Mogote, May 25, 1910.	Indurated beach gravel containing fragments and worn valves of *Glycymeris longior* Sby., and *Mactra patagonica* Orb., later bored by *Lithophaga* and perhaps other boring bivalves.
6	5356	Los Falos, La Plata....................	Loose sand with valves of *Mulinia isabelleana* Orb., *Venus tehuelca* Orb., *Tagelus platensis* Orb.; *Petricula* sp., *Paludestrina* sp., *Columbella* sp., and *Buccinanops gradata* Desh.
8	5358	Arroyo del Barco, south of Mar del Plata ("Inter-Ensenadean"), May 31, 1910.	Similar to the last but indurated, the fragments somewhat larger and many of them derived from sessile barnacles.
9	5359	Mar del Plata, north side H. W. ("Inter-Ensenadean").	*Glycymeris longior* Sby.
10	5360	Mar del Plata, north of mouth of Arroyo de Peralta, May 25, 1910, H. W.	Venerid shell, decorticated but resembling *Venus tehuelca* Orbigny, now living.
11	5361	South of Mar del Plata, on the southern side of Pta Mogote, about one-half mile from the lighthouse, May 26, 1910.	Worn valves and fragments of *Glycymeris longior* Sby.
29	5371	Mar del Plata, Argentina, 8 miles south of city, at Punta Mogote.	Blackish sand and earth with a few minute apparently recent land shells *Succinea* and *Thysanophora* (?), some of them quite fresh.
30	5372	Miramar, sea level coast ½ mile south of the bathing houses; shell marl of fresh-water lake, supposed by Ámeghino to be Lujanean, June 1.	Myriads of a single species *Paludestrina*, which agrees with figures of description of *P. parchappii* Orb., which that author states inhabits nearly all the streams and lakes of Argentina.
12	5362	Lake deposit from mouth of Rio Quequen.	*Paludestrina* sp. and *Bulimulus* sp. both probably recent, but perhaps undescribed.
7	5357	Necochea, plain by the sea, 25 feet above high tide, June 5, 1910.	Loose sand containing minute worn fragments of shells, probably bivalves.
13	5363	"Inter-Ensenadean," Boca del Moro, northeast of Necochea.	*Tegula corrugata* Koch (*Tegula patagonica* Orb.).

[1] Label lost during transportation; specimen from the coast, but the exact locality can not be ascertained.—A. H.

Current numbers	U. S. National Museum numbers	Locality	Observations
14	5364	"Magdalena" (Necochea).............	Indurated shell fragments of *Venus tehuelca*, young *Mulinia* sp., *Paludestrina* sp., probably estuarine assembly.
15	5365	Terreno Guerrico, from black earth above tosca. (Necochea).	Valve *Glycymeris longior* Sby.
16	5366	Mouth of Rio Quequen, Necochea, from barranca said by Ameghino to be Ensenadean, more than 1 meter below considerable, irregular layer of tosca.	*Bulimulus sp.* (recent).
17	5367	No label	Indurated calcareous sediment containing valves of the extinct *Erodona* (or *Azara*) *prisca* von Martens; probably Pleistocene.
18	....	Coast 25 miles north of Necochea, near the beach; so-called Eolian phase of "Inter-Ensenadean" of Ameghino, from beneath heavy layers of tosca; at first identified by Ameghino as "Ensenadean," but distinguished by black sand grains.	No shells; loess well indurated, with scattered water-worn pebbles; many root holes.
19	5368	Mouth of Rio Quequen, Necochea, fresh-water deposit forming barranca on north side, June 9, 1910.	Looks like loess but shows no root holes; no shells.
20	....	Coast 25 miles north of Necochea, bluff 5 feet above beach; loess of the "Ensenadean" of Ameghino from just below that called "Inter-Ensenadean" (contact not seen).	No shells; indurated fine white sand with numerous root holes.
21	....	Necochea, Argentina; plain by the sea, 25 feet above high tide, 200 yards southwest of hotel; superficial harder layer of "Inter-Ensenadean" formation beneath which the human skeletons were said to have been found, selected by the man who dug up the skeletons.	No shells; material like the last.
22	/5369	Coast 25 miles north of Necochea near Laguna Malacara; sand with shell from digging near the hole where skeletons were found in same material, June 7, 1910.	Contains a fragment of *Glycymeris longior* Sby.
23	5370	Coast 25 miles north of Necochea, near Laguna Malacara near beach; so-called "marine Inter-Ensenadean" of Ameghino; hard coquina.	Considerably bored by marine worms or *Cliona;* contains *Tegula corrugata* Koch, and fragments of other shells.
24	....	Coast 25 miles north of Necochea, near the beach; tosca from "Inter-Ensenadean," June 8, 1910.	No shells.
25	....	Coast 25 miles north of Necochea, 15 feet above beach; so-called "marine Inter-Ensenadean;" coarse sand, calcareous cement holding larger tosca pebbles.	Do.

Current numbers	U. S. National Museum numbers	Locality	Observations
26	....	Necochea; plain by the sea 25 feet above high water, 200 yards west of hotel; tosca in recent sand, same as last material, June 5, 1910.	No shells.
31	....	Necochea, Argentina; plain by the sea 25 feet above high tide, 200 yards west of Necochea Hotel; selected by Ameghino as "typical Inter-Ensenadean," June 5, 1910.	No shells, except fragments of sessile barnacles, and unrecognizable shell sand.

As already noted, the only sample containing a species not now living (so far as known) in the region is No. 17.

IV. TIERRA COCIDA; SCORIÆ

By Bailey Willis

Tierra cocida, or burnt earth, occurs in the Pampean terrane at various horizons, as shown by the researches of Ameghino, Roth, and others. The material resembles brick, or in places scoria, and occurs commonly in the form of small pebbles. Occasionally larger masses have been found. Ameghino has described the tierra cocida with accuracy and in great detail. Through his courtesy the writer has been able to verify the descriptions by examination of the original specimens, which form part of the collections of the Museo Nacional at Buenos Aires.

The burnt earth varies in character and color from brown or fawn-colored loess, through various tints of pink or brick to dark iridescent or black scoria. Some specimens are of close texture, like a fine-grained brick, but the scoriaceous specimens are very porous. It occasionally contains impressions of strongly ribbed grasses, and in rare instances includes bits of carbonized grass stems, little bones, and other things of organic origin. There are also specimens which are distinguished by a dark color and slaggy appearance. These are heavy, though scoriaceous, resemble volcanic scoria, and have been described as such. They have been found mainly on the coast of the Province of Buenos Aires, where volcanic scoria may occur as wash brought along the coast from tuffs in the territory of Rio Negro. It is important in considering their character and origin to distinguish between those which are washed up on the beach and those which occur in the Pampean terrane, as will appear presently.

The writer collected specimens of the so-called tierra cocida in company with Doctor Ameghino and Doctor Hrdlička on the eastern coast, with Roth at Saladillo near Rosario, and alone in the delta of the Rio Colorado south of Bahia Blanca. The last-mentioned occurrence is modern, while the others pertain to the Pampean terrane. Brief descriptions of the observations made in the course of this work will be found in the following pages.

On visiting Saladillo with Doctor Roth, a section of the dark-brown loess loam, which Roth classed as Upper Pampean, was found

45

exposed by the little Rio Saladillo where it issues from a small reservoir. Thirty to forty meters from the reservoir and close to the stream is a layer 30 cm. thick, composed of the brown earth with many little pebbles the size of a pea, more or less. Most of these consist of secondary limestone or tosca, but pebbles of burnt earth are not uncommon. They are precisely like little water-worn fragments of brick. On following this horizon down the valley, other bits of burnt earth were found, including one 2 cm. to 3 cm. in diameter. All of these were imbedded in the Pampean earth. They exhibited no impressions and contained no inclusions which might give a clue to their origin.

On the eastern coast, near Miramar, the sea cliff affords a section of the Pampean terrane, in which Ameghino identifies two formations, the upper one of which he calls Ensenadean and the lower one Chapalmalean. The latter is a brown ferruginous loess-loam and forms the lower part of the bluffs. In it, at a height of 1 meter above the beach, 8 kilometers north of Miramar, occurs a mass of distinctly reddish, orange, and blackish earth, not bricklike, which contrasts with the surrounding brown loess-loam. Its horizontal length is about 1 meter; its thickness is 30 cm. The upper surface is irregular and there are small isolated masses of the red surrounded by the brown clay. The principal mass of red clay is 60 cm. long and 10 cm. thick. It is banded in various shades of red. At the bottom it is distinguished by a sharp contact, where it passes in the distance of approximately a millimeter from the red into a larger, dark-brown and black mass that fades away below into the brown loess.

The red earth is a portion of the loess loam, which has been dehydrated. The darker brown color is also due, in all probability, to a peculiar condition of the iron oxide. The black, which occurs chiefly, if not exclusively, on joint planes in the clay, is caused by a film of specular iron oxide.

This coloring might have been occasioned by a fire burning on the surface that is now red. Similar effects of dehydration occur, however, not infrequently as a result of a slow process of chemical change, without heat, producing more or less distinct ferruginous nodules. Fine ferruginous clays in which capillary moisture circulates are favorable to the reaction. This is undoubtedly the explanation of the particular occurrence observed in the Chapalmalean north of Miramar.

In contrast to the preceding *fogón*, which the writer does not class with the tierra cocida, there are certain specimens found somewhat nearer Miramar, but also in Pampean terrane—whether in that portion which Ameghino would class as Chapalmalean or as Ensenadean, the writer is not sure. The specimens are small pieces of red tierra cocida, and distinct masses of heavy black scoriæ ranging up to 8 or 10 cm. in diameter. The latter resemble an opaque slag, imperfectly fused, and cooled from a pasty state into irregular individual lumps. Each specimen of the four that were gathered was complete in itself, not a fragment of a larger mass. They occurred imbedded in homogeneous loess, in which they were in place, like pebbles in shale. Judging from their general appearance that they might be of volcanic origin, the writer carefully noted that they were not washed up on the beach and buried in a recent deposit of the loess. They occurred in the undisturbed Pampean, and if they were volcanic would demonstrate that scoria of appropriate character had existed in a place from which these masses could have reached their present position. According to Mr. Cross, whose opinion is quoted below, they are probably not volcanic. This inference therefore fails but it is still possible that scoriæ of volcanic origin should be found in this locality, as they occur along the same coast farther south, and tuffs and basalts cover a large area in the territory of Rio Negro near the Colonia Valcheta and elsewhere, as observed by Señor Moreno in 1873–74. Masses so derived and washed along the coast would occur only in modern formations, for the present coast is modern. During the Pampean epoch the shore was farther east and the coastal wash could not have reached this position. Hence the importance, above referred to, of distinguishing the precise relations in which any such supposed volcanic scoria occurs.

Mr. Whitman Cross, of the United States Geological Survey, reports as follows on the specimens collected from this locality near Miramar and submitted to him:

"Among the explanations of the occurrence of 'tierra cocida' in the Pampean is one advanced by early writers, as quoted by Ameghino, to the effect that burning grasses had calcined and fused the loess. To investigate this suggestion the writer burned several heads of the great Pampas grass or cortadera, both growing and dead. The growing tussocks consist in the winter season of a large, almost solid head, which is green, and of dried leaves. The latter burn readily down to the green head, but the fire does not reach the ground. When cortadera is dead the head also burns and the fire lasts a number of hours. A large plant, fired at 5 o'clock of an afternoon, was still a glowing mass at 7 the next morning. The effect on the underlying earth was, however, slight. The loess was reddened to a depth of 10 millimeters, more or less. It was not calcined to a bricklike or scoriaceous mass. The ground was dry at the time. The fire had been intense and had burned 14 hours. It had, however, been practically on the surface, and the writer infers that superficial heat does not notably calcine loess."

A different result follows when the grass and loess are intimately mingled. Esparto is a grass which sends up blades from root-stocks below the surface. The blades grow close together, catch more or less dust between the stems, and become partly buried to a depth depending on local conditions, perhaps 10 or 15 cm. or more. When esparto burns, the loess about the grass stems is calcined down to and around the roots below the surface of the plain. The writer observed an instance in the delta of the Rio Colorado. A bright-red spot in the greenish-brown plain attracted attention. On riding to it, it was found to be an area a hundred meters more or less in diameter, where the esparto, which grew in tufts all about, had recently been burnt. The stems and roots were burned out, leaving a spongy mass in which a horse sank to his fetlocks. It was composed of thoroughly calcined earth, varying in color from pink to brick-red, in part scoriaceous. Coherent masses 10 cm. or more in diameter could be picked up, but they were penetrated in every direction by hollows formerly filled by the stems and roots, and were very fragile. They carried impressions of grass stems, bits of carbonized grass, etc., and in these respects corresponded with specimens obtained from the Pampean by Doctor Ameghino and described by him.

These observations lead the writer to give weight to the views of those early observers, who attributed the tierra cocida of the Pampean terrane to the burning of grasses.

There is nothing, however, to connect the burnt earths of the Pampean with man, so far as the occurrences were observed by the writer. Any fire whatever, whether originating in spontaneous combustion, in lightning, or in other natural conditions, independent of man, would have the effect of burning the earth under favorable conditions. In order to prove that man maintained a fire which burned a particular mass of tierra cocida it would be necessary to bring independent evidence of his handiwork. Two classes of facts have been cited to demonstrate his agency: The presence of supposed artifacts and the arrangement of a mass of burnt clay; chief among the former are split, broken, or scratched fragments of bone, and it appears to the writer that these may be referred, with greater probability, to weathering, biting, gnawing, and accidents incident to the wanderings of bones, as strata were eroded and redeposited. Certainly the proofs of man's agency should be uncontrovertible and the possibility of explanation by other than human action should be positively excluded, before the conclusion that he intentionally or incidentally burned the earth can be accepted.

This critical test should be met equally by occurrences where the mass of burnt earth and its relations to the surrounding unburnt loess suggest that man built and maintained a fire over the spot.

Dehydration by slow chemical change produces a red mass, which may grade by color variation into the brown loess, simulating the effect of heat.   But the red earth thus produced is not hard like brick.   The occurrence observed 8 kilometers north of Miramar is a case in point.   If an unquestionably burnt earth should occur in place in the Pampean in a notable mass, it would be necessary to prove that man gathered the fuel and maintained the fire, for the accidental burning of matted vegetation buried in the earth would produce the same effect.   The hills of Dakota and Montana in the western United States are banded by red clays burnt to the consistency of tile by the combustion of lignite beds, without the agency of man, and what occurs in that region on an extensive scale may well have taken place on the pampas from the combustion of matted masses of grass.

The specimens of tierra cocida and scoria collected by the writer and Doctor Hrdlička have been submitted to the Geophysical Laboratory of the Carnegie Institution of Washington for an exhaustive investigation of their physical characters and conditions of origin, which Mr. F. E. Wright of that laboratory has kindly agreed to make. His report on the subject will doubtless form the basis for further discussion.

NOTES BY ALEŠ HRDLIČKA

The writer has recorded a number of personal observations on the subject of the tierra cocida which will serve to supplement the preceding.

The present coast of the Province of Buenos Aires, north of Bahia Blanca, is devoid of forests, and very poor in wood of any kind, nor are there any indications that it was more favored in this respect at any time during the formation of the Pampean deposits.   In consequence it is probable that there has been always a dearth of fuel. This doubtless led to the habit, common in the region to this day, of making fire, where it could be made at all, in small, usually quadrangular excavations in the ground, about 4 to 8 inches deep.   A number of these holes were examined by the writer.   The ground lining the hole was generally found blackened, and where the heat had been more intense, there was some reddening of the earth beyond the blackened surface; but both the blackened and the reddened soil (where the latter existed) crumbled readily in every instance, showing but little, if any, cohesion.   Nothing was found even remotely resembling Pampean tierra cocida specimens thought by some to demonstrate the presence of man.   In one instance, at the Laguna de los Padres, some miles inland from Mar del Plata, the remnants of two particularly large and intense fires were observed which had been fed, as seen from the unburned pieces, by large quantities of dried branches of the hard, thorny brush growing in that locality.   One of these fires was on the surface and represented merely the burning of a pile of brush; the other, probably remade a number of times, was in and about a hole in the ground, such as described above, and filled with ashes and bones.   Fires of this size are exceptional, and it is in the highest degree improbable that they would ever have been equaled among the aborigines; yet even here there was no approach to a production of tierra cocida, or scoria.   The surface fire acted on the black vegetal soil; that in the hole principally on the yellowish loess.   In both cases there was superficial blackening, and beyond this some obscure reddening of the soil to a maximum depth of approximately $1\frac{1}{2}$ inches, but no baking to cohesion.   All this indicates the improbability, if not the impossibility, of the production by the fires of primitive man of the tierra cocida, or of scoriæ, such as were seen in the Argentine museums or were collected on the expedition.

A variety of stout grass, growing in big bunches and known, from the sharp, cutting edges of its blades, as *paja brava* or *cortadera* (*Gynerium argenteum*) occurs in many localities in Argentina.   The burning of this grass has been reported by Descalzi, Romero, and Ameghino (see Bibliography) as resulting in the production of baked earth and scoria.   During the writer's trip to the Puerto San Blas, this grass was found in spots among the dunes south of San Blas, and instances were seen in which the dried bunches had been burned.   In every one of these cases, however, the heart of the bunch was still alive and there was no burned earth or scoria.   Men on the ground said that only rarely will one of these bunches die, in which case, if fired, it burns out; but no one has observed anything resembling the tierra cocida or scoriæ ascribed to them.   This shows that the ordinary burning of cortadera is not (at least not commonly) associated with products such as those under consideration.

Small particles, and occasionally larger masses of tierra cocida, were found by Mr. Willis or the writer in a number of localities along the coast from northeast of Miramar to Monte Hermoso, and were relatively abundant in the deposits exposed in the barrancas at the former locality.   They occur at different depths from the surface, to below the sea level at ordinary low tide.   The pieces collected are all compact, with the exception of two or three that show on one side a transition to scoria.   While there is a general resemblance, they all differ in aspect and weight from the very porous, light products of the burning of the esparto grass, collected by Mr. Willis on the Colorado.

Large masses of tierra cocida are called *fogónes* (fireplaces) by the local investigators.   One of these, about 3 paces long and proportionately broad, was reported by one of the natives employed by Professor Ameghino for watching the coast and collecting fossils, to exist off the barranca of Monte Hermoso, but it became exposed only at the lowest tide and could not be examined. None of the few observed cases in which the tierra cocida would be taken for a fogón, or remnants of the same, was accompanied by the slightest evidences of the presence of man; but burnt bones, carbon, and other substances that might possibly be due to man have been reported as found at or near fogónes in other localities.[1]

The scoriæ were very abundant on the gray *playas*, or denuded flats, near the seashore northeast of the Arroyo Moro, the region of Necochea. Farther inland, even on the playas, they were absent. Many hundreds, in fact thousands, of specimens could have been collected. They were fairly uniform in character, grayish-black, porous, without sharp points or angles. They ranged in size, as far as seen, from small bits to pieces as large as the two fists. Farther south they were scarce, and on the coast between Rio Negro and Puerto San Blas they were wholly absent, but the writer picked up on the shore near San Blas an oval, water-worn piece of a different, clearly volcanic red scoria more than 12 inches long.

On the whole, none of the evidence relating to tierra cocida and scoriæ seen in the Argentine Museums or in the field, has proven at all convincing that these products, even if not directly volcanic, are due to man's agency. Messrs. Wright and Fenner's report, which follows, bears out these impressions.

The principal bibliographical references in connection with this subject are as follows:[2]

DESCALZI, N. Diario del descubrimiento del Rio Negro de Patagones. Revista del Rio de la Plata, I, 1854, p. 97; and in Albarracín, S. J., Estudios generales sobre los rios Negro, etc., II, Buenos Aires, 1886, pp. 51, 63–64, 600–602.

HEUSSER, J. C., and G. CLARAZ. Essais pour servir à une description physique et géognostique de la Province Argentine de Buenos-Aires. Mém. Soc. Helvétique Sci. nat., XXI, Zurich, 1865, pp. 1–140.

AMEGHINO, F. Nouveaux débris de l'homme et de son industrie, etc. Journal de Zoologie, IV, Paris, 1875, pp. 527–528.

BURMEISTER, H. Description physique de la République Argentine, II, Buenos Aires, 1876, pp. 178, 387.

AMEGHINO, F. Catalogue spécial de la section anthropologique et paléontologique de la République Argentine, Paris, 1878.

---

[1] See Ameghino, F.,Énumération chronologique et critique des notices sur les terres cuites et les scories anthropiques, etc.; in *Anal. Mus. Nac. Buenos Aires*, XX (ser. iii, t. XIII), 1911, pp. 39–80 (separate, 1910).

[2] Principally after Ameghino. For additional minor references, see that author.

AMEGHINO, F.   L'homme préhistorique dans le bassin de La Plata. Congr. int. sci. anthr., Paris, 1878, p. 346.

———— L'homme préhistorique dans La Plata.   Rév. d'Anthr., 2me sér., II, Paris, 1879, pp. 242–245.

———— La plus haute antiquité de l'homme dans le Nouveau-Monde.   C. R. Congr. int. Amér.   3me sess., Bruxelles, 1879, II, pp. 216–217.

———— La antigüedad del hombre en El Plata, Paris-Buenos Aires, II, 1881, pp. 427–428, 451, 461, 476–478, 489–490, 535.

———— Escursiones geológicas y paleontológicas en la provincia de Buenos Aires.   Bol. Acad. Nac. Cienc. Córdoba, VI, Buenos Aires, 1884, p. 161 et seq.

———— Monte Hermoso, Buenos Aires, 1887, pp. 5–6, 10.

MORENO, F. P.   Informe preliminar de los progresos del Museo La Plata, etc., Buenos Aires, 1888, pp. 6–7.

———— Breve reseña de los progresos del Museo de La Plata, etc., Buenos Aires, 1889, p. 27.

AMEGHINO, F.   Contribución al conocimiento de los mamíferos fósiles de la República Argentina, 2 vols., Buenos Aires, 1889, pp. 50–69.

ROTH, S.   Ueber den Schädel von Pontimelo (richtiger Fontezuelas).   Mitth. anat. Inst. Vesalianum zu Basel, 1889, pp. 8–9.

LEHMANN-NITSCHE, R.   L'homme fossile de la formation pampéenne.   C. R. Congr. int. d'anthr. et d'arch. préhist., XII sess., Paris, 1900, pp. 145–146.

AMEGHINO, F.   Paleontología Argentina, Buenos Aires, 1904, p. 77.

STEINMANN, G.   Ueber Diluvium in Süd-Amerika.   Monatsb. deutschen geol. Ges., No. 7, 1906; also in Rév. gén. sci. pur. et appl., Paris, 1907, pp. 626–633.

STEINMANN, G.   Das Alter des Menschen in Argentinien.   Bericht über die prähistorischer Versammlung zur Eröffnung des Anthropologischen Museums in Cöln, 1907, p. 73.

LEHMANN-NITSCHE, R.   Nouvelles recherches sur la formation pampéenne, etc.   Rev. Mus. La Plata, XIV, Buenos Aires, 1907; including communications by C. Burckhardt, pp. 143–171; A. Doering, pp. 172–190; F. Zirkel, pp. 455–456; and G. Steinmann, pp. 461–462.

AMEGHINO, F.   Notas preliminares sobre el *Tetraprothomo argentinus*, etc.   Anal. Mus. Nac. Buenos Aires, XVI (ser. iii, t. ix), 1908, pp. 106–107.

OUTES, F. F., with E. H. DUCLOUX and H. BÜCKING.   Estudio de las supuestas "escorias" y "tierras cocidas," etc.   Rev. Mus. La Plata, XV, Buenos Aires, 1908, pp. 138–197.

AMEGHINO, F.   Las formaciones sedimentarias de la región litoral de Mar del Plata y Chapalmalán.   Anal. Mus. Nac. Buenos Aires, XVII (ser. iii, t. x), 1909, pp. 358, 372, 401, 421.

AMEGHINO, F.　Productos píricos de origen antrópico, etc.　Anal. Mus. Nac. Buenos Aires, XIX (ser. iii, t. XII), 1909, pp. 1–25.

OUTES, F. F.　Les scories volcaniques et les tufs éruptifs de la série pampéenne de la République Argentine.　Rev. Mus. La Plata, XVI, Buenos Aires, 1909, pp. 34–36.

AMEGHINO, F.　Le litige des scories et des terres cuites anthropiques, etc., Buenos Ayres, 1909, pp. 1–12.

——— Dos documentos testimoniales á propósito de las escorias producidas por la combustión de los cortaderales.　Anal. Mus. Nac. Buenos Aires, XIX (ser. iii, t. XII), 1909, pp. 71–80.

BOULE, M.　Produits pyriques d'origine anthropique dans les formations neogènes de la République Argentine.　L'Anthropologie, XX, Nos. 3–4, Paris, 1909, pp. 381–383.

ARLDT, TH.　Feuerproducte von menschlichem Ursprunge in den neogenen Formationen der Argentinischen Republik.　C. R. Naturwissenschaftliche Rundschau, XXIV, No. 31, Braunschweig, 1909, p. 397.

G. A. J. C.　The Antiquity of Man in South America.　Nature, LXXXI, London, 1909, p. 534.

BRUNET, L.　Étude des prétendues scories et terres cuites de la série pampéenne de la République Argentine.　Analyse du mémoire de MM. Outes, Herrero Ducloux et Bücking, en Révue Générale des Sciences pures et appliquées, 20e année, No. 21, Paris, 1909, p. 890.

AMEGHINO, F.　Examen critique du mémoire de M. Outes sur les scories et les terres cuites.　Anal. Mus. Nac. Buenos Aires, XIX (ser. iii, t. XII), 1909, p. 459.

OUTES, F. F., and H. BÜCKING.　Sur la structure des scories et "terres cuites" trouvées dans la série pampéenne.　Rev. Mus. La Plata, Buenos Aires, XVII, 1910–11, pp. 78–85.

AMEGHINO, F.　Énumération chronologique et critique des notices sur les terres cuites et les scories anthropiques des terrains sédimentaires néogènes de l'Argentine.　Anal. Mus. Nac. Buenos Aires, XX (ser. iii, t. XIII), 1911, pp. 39–80 (separate, 1910).

V. PETROGRAPHIC STUDY

OF THE SPECIMENS OF LOESS, TIERRA COCIDA, AND SCORIA COLLECTED BY THE HRDLIČKA-WILLIS EXPEDITION

By FRED. EUGENE WRIGHT AND CLARENCE N. FENNER

INTRODUCTION

The petrographic examination of the rock specimens collected by the Hrdlička-Willis expedition in Argentina was undertaken by the Geophysical Laboratory of the Carnegie Institution of Washington, at the request of the Secretary of the Smithsonian Institution. Although descriptive work of this kind is hardly germane to the purposes of the Geophysical Laboratory, it was apparent that, if the problem were to be solved at all, exact laboratory methods of attack would have to be used and that, even in case the material available was not sufficient or characteristic enough for a satisfactory solution, the precise data gathered by the laboratory would nevertheless be of value. The descriptions below apply only to the material examined.

The problem submitted to the laboratory was to determine the kinds and nature of the rocks in the collection. Ordinarily such problems are not difficult and can be solved by the usual petrographic methods, but in the present instance several of the rocks are so extraordinary in type that previous investigators have been unable to agree as to their nature, whether volcanic, or sedimentary, or both, and the matter has become one of controversy based more or less on opinion.

In approaching this problem, three lines of attack were followed: (1) the usual detailed petrographic-microscopic examination of the rocks; (2) chemical study of the different rock types; (3) thermal study of the rocks at different temperatures and comparison of the products thus obtained, with the natural products. From these three lines of independent evidence which will now be presented, it should be possible to obtain a fair idea of the nature of the rocks and possibly also of their genesis.

The tools and methods used in the examination of the different specimens.—Ordinarily it is not customary to cite the particular instruments and methods which have been adopted in the study of any particular problem, but in the present instance the methods applied were not the usual methods and merit, therefore, a brief word of description. In the petrographic-microscopic examinations the methods employed were those specially adapted to the study of fine-grained preparations. They have recently been described in a paper by one of the writers [1] and need not be considered in detail here. The specimens were examined both in the thin section and in powder form. In the thin section the texture of a specimen can be studied to best advantage, while in the powder the optical properties of its several mineral components can be ascertained most readily and accurately.

The chemical analyses cited below were made by Mr. J. G. Fairchild, of the United States Geological Survey, and the methods used in his determinations were the standard methods of the Geological Survey laboratory.

In the thermal work the standard thermo-electric apparatus and methods of the Geophysical Laboratory [2] were adopted. The material to be heated was placed in a platinum crucible and suspended therein in an electric resistance furnace where it could be brought to any desired temperature and held there for any length of time. The temperature of the furnace was determined by means of a platinum-rhodium thermoelement inserted into the furnace together with the charge. This method for ascertaining high temperatures has been thoroughly tested in the Geophysical Laboratory and furnishes temperature readings whose probable error is not more than 2° C. Throughout this paper the temperatures are expressed in degrees centigrade.

In the present series of experiments the conditions were varied considerably, but not to extremes which departed widely from natural conditions. One point of difference, however, should be noted. The amount of material used in an experiment was small, only a few grams at most, while in nature kilograms and usually tons are used and the resulting products are on a corresponding scale. The small charge in the platinum crucible oxidizes readily and the iron is converted almost entirely into ferric iron (hematite), while in the natural products a lower state of oxidation (magnetite) is present. The attempt was made to overcome this difficulty by mixing a reducing agent, generally graphite, with the charge before treatment, but this proved insufficient for the purpose. In another

[1] Fred. E. Wright, The Methods of Petrographic-microscopic Research. Their Relative Accuracy and Range of Application. *Publication No. 158*, Carnegie Inst. of Washington, 1911.

[2] A. L. Day, E. T. Allen, and J. P. Iddings, *Publication No. 31*, Carnegie Inst. of Washington; A. L. Day, E. S. Shepherd, and F. E. Wright, in *Amer. Jour. Sci.*, 4th ser., XXII, 265–302, 1906; W. P. White, in *Phys. Rev.*, XXV, 334–352, 1907, and in *Amer. Jour. Sci.*, 4th ser., XXVIII, 453–489, 1909.

series of experiments, however, larger charges (about 100 grams) of material were heated in a Fletcher gas furnace and with them the oxidation was found to be much less, the center of the charges containing magnetite and resembling the scoriæ more closely than did the smaller charges. The dependence of the product obtained on the mode of heat treatment to which it had been subjected, was thus clearly demonstrated, and is a factor which should be taken into account in all such work.

DESCRIPTIONS OF SPECIMENS

SPECIMENS FROM BUENOS AIRES

No. 263702. Specimen label. *"Samples of the Pampean formation (brown and green) from excavation on Veinte Cinco de Mayo, Buenos Aires."*

Under this number two distinctly different earths are included; the first, a light-brown, porous earth of fine, even grain, the second, a pale ashy-green earth, mottled in appearance and noticeably different from the first in composition. Under the microscope the powder of the brown earth was found to consist largely of fragments of plagioclase feldspars, glass, and fine earthy material, the last usually stained with iron oxide. The plagioclase feldspars range in composition from oligoclase to labradorite and often show zonal structure. The glass particles are usually colorless and angular or splintery in outline and are relatively fresh. Occasional grains of pyroxene, hornblende, biotite, quartz, sanidine, apatite, zircon, and magnetite were also observed and are all fairly fresh. Most of these minerals and the glass are of igneous origin and have evidently been assembled from various types of igneous rocks, the majority of which were probably andesitic or dioritic in character.

The second type of earth consists largely of fine calcite with occasional larger grains of plagioclase, quartz, and volcanic glass. Some argillaceous material is apparently also present. The plagioclase is usually fresh and often exhibits zonal structure. This earth differs from the first chiefly in its high calcium carbonate content.

On immersion in water the brown earth in this specimen softens and crumbles into brown mud, while the gray earth remains intact and hard. On testing the water solution above the earth with silver nitrate, only a trace of chlorine was detected.

No. 263747. Specimen label. *"Locality: Buenos Aires, on the old Moreno place, where an elevation that rises above the general level of the plain is being graded down. Material: White earth which occurred in lenticular layers 1 inch to 3 feet thick in the brown loess that looks like upper Pampean. Probably volcanic ash."*

A loose, white, incoherent earth of even grain consisting in large measure (about 90 per cent) of volcanic glass in angular and splintery fragments, which often show evidence of viscous flow. Gas inclusions are abundant in the glass. The remainder of the material is made up of scattered grains of plagioclase, quartz, hornblende, pyroxene, relatively abundant biotite, zircon, epidote, apatite, spinel (or garnet), and cryptocrystalline calcite. This material is essentially shattered volcanic glass (volcanic ash) with which are mingled mineral fragments, some of which are not of volcanic origin. This ash was tested with silver nitrate solution, and only a slight trace of chlorine obtained.

The powder of this specimen, heated between 720° and 727° C. for 45 minutes, became flesh-colored, but otherwise remained loose and noncoherent; heated to 1,100° for one-half hour, it became agglomerated and shrunk to a hard, compact mass, but was not fused. Held at 1,200° for 3 hours and then at 1,150° for 2 hours, it fused to a pale-gray glass, which contained microscopic fragments of plagioclase and particles of iron oxide. Gas bubbles were relatively common, but no secondary microlites were observed. The refractive index of the glass was fairly constant and averaged about 1.485.

SPECIMENS FROM ALVEAR

No. 263715. Specimen label. *"Locality: Alvear, on the Paraná. Material: Loess from the deposit in the ravine, selected by Santiago Roth for comparison with that from the Middle Pampean at a higher level. This material appears to be a secondary deposit derived from, and younger than, the Middle Pampean, but Roth regards it as underlying and older. B. W. 26 June, 1910."*

A pale-brown, porous aphanitic earth, which consists largely of plagioclase, quartz, and glass, with considerable argillaceous material. Minor components are pyroxene, hornblende, biotite, and magnetite. Most of the silicate fragments show some decomposition. The mineral grains average about 0.1 mm. in diameter and are usually sharp and angular.

This earth was mixed with bituminous coal and heated to 1,300° for 30 minutes. It was then reheated at 1,300° for 2 hours and held at 1,100° for 17 hours. The resulting gray glass contained fragments of the original minerals and flakes and needles of hematite and acicular microlites of a substance of medium birefringence and refractive index considerably higher than 1.52. The minute crystals showed parallel extinction, with the least elliptic axis parallel to the direction of elongation, but they proved too fine for satisfactory determination. The refractive index of the glass ranged from 1.505 to 1.525.

No. 263716. Specimen label. *"Locality: Alvear, on the Paraná. Material: Loess selected by Santiago Roth to represent the Middle Pampean, which he regards as younger than the deposit in the bottom of the ravine. B. W. 26 June, 1910."*

In general appearance this specimen is practically identical with the preceding. It is a light-gray, even-grained earth, coherent but not indurated, which consists microscopically of plagioclase, quartz, glass, and argillaceous material. Minor components are hornblende, pyroxene, magnetite, and spinel (or garnet (?)). As in the preceding specimens, igneous and volcanic materials constitute the major part of the specimen. Both this earth and the preceding disintegrate when immersed in water. Treated with silver nitrate, they give a slight chloride reaction.

This specimen of earth, which is practically identical with 263715, was moistened and heated to 510°. The material was caked but not reddened by this treatment. At 710° it was slightly reddened. Held at 1,000° for 4¾ hours, the color became a bright brick-red and the material was considerably indurated, but no sign of fusion was observed under the microscope. This material was noticeably like some of the tierras cocidas, but was not so hard.

No. 263717. Specimen label. *"Locality: Alvear, on the Paraná. Material: Loess from the Middle Pampean of Roth, taken from the bank 3 feet from, and on the level of, the burnt clay. B. W. 26 June, 1910."*

A light-gray, rather compact, earth of fine, even grain. Similar in texture and general appearance to the two specimens just described from the same locality. Microscopically, this specimen exhibits the characteristic minerals of many of the loess specimens of this region. Plagioclase, quartz, and glass, and argillaceous material constitute the bulk of the rock, while occasional grains of hornblende, pyroxene, biotite, and magnetite are scattered through the specimen.

This earth disintegrates partially to a lumpy aggregate when immersed in water. Its water solution gave only a slight trace of chloride when tested with silver nitrate.

Fragments of this specimen heated to 870° for 16 hours became bright brick-red and indurated and could not be distinguished from some of the fragments of 263729. Heated to 1,200° for 3 hours, the earth was fused to a dark-purple mass, in which fragments of the original minerals appeared under the microscope, embedded in a colorless to pale-brown glass. The colorless glass was filled with minute specks of iron ore, while the pale-brown glass was relatively free from such specks and had a slightly higher refractive index (n = about 1.530) than the former (n = about 1.510).

Chemical analysis.—Although this loess contains argillaceous material and can not be constant in its composition, it does contain much volcanic material and should express this fact in the chemical analysis. Since some of the tierra cocida specimens are evidently baked loess, it was of interest to have an analysis made of one of the typical loess specimens. This and the following analyses were made by Mr. J. G. Fairchild in the laboratory of the United States Geological Survey:

	I	Ia				
SiO_2	66.81	1.108	Q	42.26	42.26	
Al_2O_3	15.04	.147	Or	13.95		
Fe_2O_3	3.11	.019	Ab	15.25	37.00	85.89
FeO	Trace	----	An	7.80		
MgO	1.03	.025	C	6.63	6.63	
CaO	1.65	.029	Hy	2.74		
Na_2O	1.79	.029	Hm	3.11		
K_2O	2.31	.025	Ru	0.65		6.62
H_2O-	3.34	----	Ap	0.12		
H_2O+	4.07	----				
TiO_2	0.65	.008				
CO_2	None	----				
P_2O_5	0.06	.0004				
S	Trace	----				
MnO	0.12	.0017				
	99.98					

Ratios

$$\text{Class} \quad \frac{Sal}{Fem.} = \frac{85.89}{6.62} > \frac{7}{1} \text{------ I}$$

$$\text{Order} \quad \frac{Q}{F} = \frac{42.26}{37.00} < \frac{5}{3} > \frac{3}{5} \text{----- 3}$$

$$\text{Rang} \quad \frac{Na_2O' + K_2O'}{CaO'} = \frac{.054}{.028} < \frac{7}{1} > \frac{5}{3} \text{----- 2}$$

$$\text{Subrang} \quad \frac{K_2O'}{Na_2O'} = \frac{.025}{.029} < \frac{5}{3} > \frac{3}{5} \text{------ 3}$$

I. Loess, Alvear. J. G. Fairchild, United States Geological Survey, analyst.
Ia. Molecular proportions of I.

In the calculation of this analysis the method used in the quantitative system of Cross, Iddings, Pirsson, and Washington has been adopted. This system applies strictly only to fresh igneous rocks and was not intended for use with sedimentary or altered rocks of any description. It is used in the present instance only as a convenient method for expressing the analysis of a rock which contains an abundance of eruptive material. Characteristic for this rock are the large amount of salic components and the abundance of free corundum in the norm, which is probably due to the argillaceous material of the loess.   If the rock were an eruptive rock its analysis would be classified along with those of certain granites and rhyolites, which in the quantitative system are included in the subrang Tehamose of the persalane class.

No. 263718.   Specimen label.   *"Locality: Alvear on the Paraná. Material: Brick from the tower near the mass of burnt clay."*

A brick of ordinary red color and usual appearance.   Under the microscope angular fragments of quartz, plagioclase, and colorless glass are seen to be embedded in a microcrystalline, reddish matrix which is evidently argillaceous.   The deep-red color is probably due to the presence of hematite which has resulted from the dehydration and breaking down of the limonitic material in the yellowish and brownish matrix of the original earths.   The hematite is so fine, however, that the microscope is of little assistance in the direct determination, and the character of the microscopic red dust is inferred rather than definitely determined.   The thermal experiments on the earths of this collection prove that many of them are suitable for brickmaking.   In the present specimen there is no trace of fusion. When immersed in water this material remains intact.   No trace of chloride was obtained with silver nitrate solution.

No. 263729.   Specimen label.   *"Locality: Alvear on the Paraná. Material: Burnt clay from the remains of the lower part of the mass or fogón originally discovered by Roth.   B. W.   26 June, 1910."*

A brick-red, terra-cotta-like material considerably indurated and of fine, even grain.   Under the microscope small angular fragments of plagioclase, quartz, and glass were observed embedded in a fine reddish matrix, evidently argillaceous in character.   In comparison with the earth (specimen 263717) the present material is similar in composition and general texture except that the individual mineral grains are possibly slightly smaller in average size.   Both specimen 263717 and specimen 263729 exhibit cavities coated with chalcedony and are intersected by films and threads of manganese oxide.

This specimen remains intact when immersed in water and does not crumble.   When treated with silver nitrate only the slightest trace of chloride was obtained.   In this respect the present specimen resembles the two preceding specimens.

This specimen was heated first to 1,300° for 30 minutes and then held at 1,100° for 16 hours.   The resulting melt was dark-purple in color and consisted chiefly of glass in which occasional remnants of the original mineral fragments were embedded and also numerous microlites of hematite and rarely a minute, lath-shaped crystal, which was too fine for satisfactory determination.   The major part of the glass was colorless, with a refractive index about 1.510; occasionally brown-colored glass fragments with refractive index about 1.53 were observed.

Chemical analysis.—

	I	Ia					
SiO_2	65.67	1.089	Q	44.02	44.02		
Al_2O_3	16.25	.159	Or	13.39			
Fe_2O_3	4.89	.031	Ab	14.20	31.77	85.28	
FeO	Trace	----	An	4.18			
MgO	0.87	.021	C	9.49	9.49		
CaO	1.44	.026	Hy	2.33			
Na_2O	1.66	.027	Hm	4.96		8.79	
K_2O	2.29	.024	Tn	1.50			
H_2O-	1.98						
H_2O+	3.44						
TiO_2	0.90	.011					
CO_2	None						
P_2O_5	Trace						
S	Trace						
MnO	0.12	.0017					
	99.51						

Ratios

Class $\quad \dfrac{\text{Sal}}{\text{Fem}} = \dfrac{85.28}{8.79} > \dfrac{7}{1}$ - - - - - - - - I

Order $\quad \dfrac{Q}{F} = \dfrac{44.02}{31.77} < \dfrac{5}{3} > \dfrac{3}{5}$ - - - - - 3

Rang $\quad \dfrac{K_2O' + Na_2O'}{CaO'} = \dfrac{.051}{.015} > \dfrac{5}{3} < \dfrac{7}{1}$ - - - - - - 2

Subrang $\quad \dfrac{K_2O'}{Na_2O'} = \dfrac{.024}{.027} < \dfrac{5}{3} > \dfrac{3}{5}$ - - - - - 3

I. Tierra cocida, Alvear. J. G. Fairchild, United States
Geological Survey, analyst.
Ia. Molecular proportions of I.

This analysis is similar to that of the loess 263717 from the same locality. The relations of the several elements are not greatly different, and the calculation of the analysis on the assumption that it was made from a fresh eruptive rock leads to the same subrang Tehamose of class 1 of the quantitative classification.

The last three specimens, Nos. 263717, 263718, 263729, are evidently modifications of the same material. This is indicated by (1) their mineral composition, which was found to be practically identical under the microscope except for the reddening of the argillaceous material in 263718 and 263729; (2) the close similarity between the chemical analyses of 263717 and 263729; (3) the presence of chalcedony lining the cavities in 263717 and 263729; (4) the close resemblance in texture and color between fragments of 263717, baked at 870° over night, and fragments of 263718 and 263729. The fragments of 263718 were baked in general slightly harder than those of 263729. (5) the identity of the glassy products obtained by fusing 263717 and 263718. (6) The absence of sodium chloride from all three specimens. These facts prove with reasonable certainty that the earth, the tierra cocida, and the bricks, just described from Alvear, are of the same material, and that the last two have been heated under the same general conditions. The tierra cocida in this case is probably the fragmental baked material from the old brick kiln in which the bricks were made. •

No. 263738. Specimen label. *"Locality: Saladillo near Rosario. Material: Burnt clay, calcareous concretions, and animal bones from the conglomeratic layer in the 'Middle Pampean' of Roth. B. W. 25 June, 1910."*

As indicated in the specimen label, a number of different rock types have been included in this lot: (a) Soft-brown loess of the usual characteristics and composition (chiefly fragments of quartz, plagioclase, hornblende, magnetite, and argillaceous material); (b) pieces of baked loess ranging in color from brick-red to brown and often containing dark linings of probable manganese oxide; (c) nodules of finely crystalline calcite; (d) black nodules rich in phosphate and evidently associated with (e) bones which have been highly altered and contain fine, microcrystalline calcite and black phosphatic material and a pale-yellow to white, microcrystalline substance of weak to medium birefringence and refractive index about 1.60. This substance occurs in so intricately intergrown and overlapping aggregates that further optical properties could not be determined with certainty. (f) Rounded pebbles of a substance which agreed in its properties with the white substance just described were also observed and tested chemically. The pebble tested was examined under the microscope and found to be practically homogeneous. Heated in a closed tube a small amount of water was obtained. The substance is completely soluble in dilute hydrochloric and also nitric acid with strong effervescence of carbonic-acid gas. Phosphoric acid was found to be one of the principal constituents; also calcium. The mineral is evidently a hydrated calcium carbonate-phosphate. The only mineral listed in Dana's Mineralogy of this nature is dahllite, whose optical properties, so far as determined, agree approximately with those recorded above. The density of this substance, however, is about 2.53, which is quite different from that given for dahllite (3.053). Unfortunately not enough of this material is available for a chemical analysis or for detailed tests.   It appears to have resulted from the interaction of calcium carbonate- and calcium phosphate-bearing solutions, the calcium phosphate having been derived from the bones which appear in this stratigraphic horizon.

SPECIMENS FROM THE VICINITY OF MAR DEL PLATA

No. 263704.   Specimen label.   "*Locality: Four miles north of Mar del Plata in the Barrancas del Norte.   Material: Greenish loess forming a stratum near high tide.   Ameghino's Belgranean.*"

A pale greenish-gray, pulverulent material consisting in large part of plagioclase, glass, and argillaceous substance.   With this specimen a special concentration test was made to determine as completely as possible the minerals present, for the purpose of ascertaining whether any mineral of other than igneous origin occurred.   A considerable quantity of material was first washed with water and the clay and major part of the lighter minerals thus removed.   The remaining part was then separated in a heavy Thoulet solution and a heavy, dark-colored, residual sand obtained which consisted of a great variety of minerals.   Inclusive of the lighter constituents the following minerals were recognized: (1) Plagioclase (andesine, and labradorite, the grains often showing zonal structure); (2) quartz; (3) sanidine; (4) pyroxene (diopside, augite, and titaniferous augite); (5) hornblende; (6) glass, colorless and brown.   Many of the characteristics of volcanic glass are clearly shown in this specimen.   The particles often appear as elongated rods and frequently contain long-drawn-out gas inclusions. Splintery and pronglike forms are not uncommon and often show conchoidal fracture.   Birefringent spherulites occur in certain instances and practically replace the volcanic glass.   The glass does not appear to have suffered much attrition, but the individual grains are too small to be affected seriously by water transport.   That this volcanic glass does not have the same composition throughout is evident from the variation from grain to grain in the refractive index, which ranges from about 1.50 to 1.54.   Evidently material from different sources has been brought together by water action.   (7) Magnetite; (8) biotite; (9) and (10) epidote and zoisite in considerable quantity and of various types; (11) zircon; (12) tourmaline; (13) titanite; (14) apatite; (15) garnet; (16) spinel (probable); (17) brucite (probable); (18–22) five minerals which could not be positively identified.   One agreed well in its optical properties with monazite; another was suspected to be wulfenite.

Most of these minerals are typical of igneous rocks, but a few of them, as epidote and zoisite, which are abundant, are metamorphic rather than igneous minerals.   Tourmaline is a common contact mineral, but occurs also in certain kinds of igneous rocks.   Some of the doubtful minerals are also at home in metamorphic rocks or in veins rather than in igneous rocks.

On immersion in water this earth does not break down easily. The water solution above it was found to contain abundant chloride in the form probably of sodium chloride derived from salt water.

On heating this earth to 1,100° for 30 minutes, a hard, fused lump with glazed surface was obtained, purple in color and containing microscopic fragments of quartz, plagioclase, pyroxene, and magnetite embedded in a nearly colorless glass base, which was often clouded by innumerable specks of iron oxide. On heating another portion to 1,200° for 3 hours and then at 1,150° for $3\frac{1}{2}$ hours, the melt was found to have settled in the crucible to a dark purplish-brown glass, which still showed under the microscope fragments of the original minerals. The glass in this case, however, was noticeably brown in transmitted light and contained innumerable minute hematite scales which had evidently crystallized from the glass; no evidence of other secondary crystals was obtained. The colorless glass ($n=1.50$) has a lower refractive index than the brown-colored glass ($n=1.515$ to 1.525).

No. 263713. Specimen label. *"Locality: Barrancas del Norte, about 4 miles north of Mar del Plata. Material: Samples of pebbly loess, filling hollows in the green and brown loess beneath. Formation: Ameghino's 'Bonaerean.'"*

A light brownish-gray, fine-grained earth containing many rounded fragments which are of similar material, but slightly more indurated. Under the microscope the matrix was found to consist largely of argillaceous material usually stained with iron oxide. Plagioclase and glass are also abundant. Hornblende, pyroxene, epidote, and magnetite are present in subordinate quantity. The pebblelike fragments consist of practically the same substances. In them pyroxene seemed slightly more abundant, and spinel and apatite were observed in addition to the minerals noted in the matrix. This earth disintegrates in water to a lumpy mud. Its water solution contains abundant chloride (probably common salt from sea water).

No. 263706. Specimen label. *"Locality: Barrancas del Norte, north of Mar del Plata, 600 feet south of Arroyo Camé. Material: Loess from stratum in which wind-hollowed pocket was excavated, 4 feet above high tide."*

A fairly hard, grayish-brown earth, consisting in large part (60 per cent or more) of isotropic, colorless glass, which appears in angular splinters or in rodlike forms produced evidently by the drawing out of viscous glass. Gas inclusions in the shape of fine capillary tubes are characteristic of such glass rods. Besides the volcanic glass much argillaceous material is present; also fragments of plagioclase, quartz, hornblende, biotite, pyroxene (evidently several varieties in shades of brown, green, and purple), magnetite, apatite, zircon, tourmaline, epidote, and probably spinel. Except for the larger proportion of volcanic glass this specimen is similar to specimen 263704.

On immersion in water this earth does not break down easily. The water solution surrounding the earth gives a strong chloride reaction when treated with silver nitrate.

A portion of this earth was mixed with graphite and heated to 1,300° for a few minutes and then held at 1,100°±30° overnight (16 hours). A pale greenish glass resulted, which contained isolated remnants of the original quartz and plagioclase fragments. Hexagonal crystals or aggregates of hematite, which had been formed from the melt, occurred frequently and were the only evidence of crystallization from the magma. The refractive index of the glass was found to vary considerably (from 1.50 to 1.525).

No. 263708. Specimen label. "*Locality: Barrancas del Norte, north of Mar del Plata, 600 feet south of Arroyo Camé. Material: Filling of wind-hollowed cavity, taken 4 feet above high tide.*"

A pale-brown, fine earth containing microscopic fragments of plagioclase (andesine and labradorite, the individual crystals often showing zonal structure), volcanic glass, quartz, sanidine, hornblende, biotite, pyroxene, magnetite, and zircon. The plagioclase is fairly abundant and fresh. Argillaceous substance, often stained with iron oxide, is scattered through the specimen and coats the individual mineral grains. In this specimen, as in most of the preceding, the average diameter of the grains is about 0.1 mm. Compared with specimen 263706 this specimen contains noticeably less volcanic glass.

When immersed in water this earth crumbles somewhat, but not entirely, many large resistant lumps remaining intact. The water solution above it gives a strong chloride reaction when treated with silver nitrate.

No. 263711. Specimen label. "*Locality: Beach 1½ miles north of Mar del Plata. Material: Pebbly loess resembling in the bed a soft volcanic agglomerate. Formation: 'Ensenadean' of Ameghino.*"

The present hand specimen gives practically no hint of the pebbly character of this formation, but appears to be a uniform gray-brown earth, even grained, and fairly coherent. Under the microscope the principal components are plagioclase and glass, both much decomposed. Hornblende, biotite, pyroxene, magnetite, and epidote were also observed in scattered grains. In general aspect and composition this earth is not greatly different from those preceding. Argillaceous substance is abundant and is evidently due in part to weathering.

On immersion in water this specimen disintegrates readily into a lumpy mud. The water solution above was found to contain abundant chloride (probably common salt).

No. 263742. Specimen label. "*Locality: Mar del Plata, Barrancas del Norte. Material: 'Toscá,' from the 'Ensenadean' of Ameghino.*"

A light-gray-brown, stony material of fine, even grain. The microscopic examination of the specimen revealed the presence of very fine-grained calcite, in which are embedded many larger grains of plagioclase, quartz, colorless glass, and a little pyroxene. Both macroscopic and microscopic evidence indicates a concretionary limestone or nodule in the loess formation.

On immersion in water this specimen remains fairly intact. Tested with silver nitrate solution it gives a strong chloride reaction (probably common salt).

No. 263740. Specimen label. "*Laguna de los Padres, 10 miles west of Mar del Plata. Material: Baked loess from hole about 12 inches deep in which there had been a large hot fire.*"

A burnt-looking earth, light-brown to black in color, which crumbles to a fine, soft powder. Under the microscope the most abundant components were found to be plagioclase and glass, both partly decomposed and stained with iron oxide. Hornblende, pyroxene, zircon, apatite, epidote, and magnetite (often altered) were present in smaller quantities. Argillaceous material is widely disseminated through the rock. The color of the black portion appears to be due to carbonaceous material, and merely the blackening from the fire. There is no evidence of fusion.

Immersed in water this specimen remains fairly intact and only here and there crumbles down to mud. Its water solution contains abundant chloride (probably sodium chloride).

No. 263703. Specimen label. "*Locality: Bajada Martinez de Hoz-Barrancas de los Lobos. South of Mar del Plata. Material: 'Tosca' from lower part of the 'Chapadmalean'* [1] *formation of Ameghino.*"

This large specimen is not homogeneous throughout but includes two different types of material—a light-brown earth and a grayish-brown, stony substance which is evidently concretionary in character. The brown earth was found under the microscope to consist chiefly of earthy argillaceous substance, plagioclase, and volcanic glass. The argillaceous material was usually stained brown by iron oxide. The plagioclase fragments were quite fresh and ranged in composition from andesine to labradorite, the individual fragments often showing zonal growth. Orthoclase and quartz were also observed and occasionally grains of magnetite, pyroxene and hornblende. In general aspect this earthy specimen is not unlike No. 263702 from Buenos Aires.

[1 Written also Chapalmalean.]

The indurated part of the specimen consists largely of fine, almost aphanitic calcite. Occasionally coarser-grained patches of the calcite occur, especially near and in the druses which are not uncommon in the rock. Accessory components are plagioclase, quartz, magnetite, and some hornblende. This part of the material is evidently concretionary limestone and similar in formation to the Loess-kindel of Germany.

The earthy part of this specimen disintegrates to a fine mud in water; the calcareous part remains practically unchanged. A strong chlorine reaction was obtained with silver nitrate from the water solution which contained the earth.

The concretionary calcite and the earthy portions of this specimen were mixed together in about equal parts and heated to 1,050°; brick-red, indurated material resulted but no melting. On another charge, held at 1,200° for 30 minutes, incipient fusion was observed; heated to 1,300° for 2 hours the powder melted down to a vesicular glass, which was reheated for one-half hour at 1,300° and then cooled to 1,100° and held at about that temperature for 16 hours (over night). During this last period the temperature may have varied 30° or 40°. The product thus obtained was pale-brown, compact, and stony in appearance. Under the microscope, the original mineral fragments were found to have disappeared and the glass to have recrystallized in large part. In the crystalline aggregate sections of a colorless substance of medium birefringence, maximum refractive index about 1.655, parallel extinction on square sections, apparently uniaxial and optically negative, predominate and are probably gehlenite. Minute specks of a higher-refracting, weakly birefracting substance occur in the gehlenite sections but were too fine for satisfactory determination. Low-refracting isotropic glass particles were not uncommon. None of these crystallized substances were found in the scoriæ.

No. 263712. Specimen label. *"Locality: Bajada Martinez de Hoz-Barrancas de los Lobos. South of Mar del Plata. Material: Loess of the 'Chapadmalean' formation of Ameghino from the lowest part of the exposure near high-tide level."*

A fine-grained, gray-brown earth, similar in appearance to specimen 263711, from the north of Mar del Plata. The mineral components observed under the microscope are plagioclase, quartz, sanidine, hornblende, biotite, zircon and magnetite. Volcanic glass and argillaceous subtance are also present, the glass being relatively less abundant than in many of the preceding specimens. The plagioclase is relatively abundant and appears in broken, twinned grains averaging about 0.1 mm. in diameter; zonal growth is characteristic of many of its fragments. In general type and composition this earth is similar to the earths described above. Characteristic for the entire group is the abundance of siliceous volcanic glass and minerals derived from igneous rocks.   This earth disintegrates readily in water to a fine mud.   The water solution above it contains abundant chloride (probably sodium chloride).

Part of this specimen was powdered, mixed with bituminous coal and heated to 1,300° for 30 minutes; a fused product was obtained. After heating at 1,300° for 2 hours it was held at 1,100° over night (17 hours).   A dark, glassy mass resulted, which contained remnants of the original fragments of quartz and plagioclase set in a glass matrix out of which hematite crystals in separate individuals and stellate groups had formed in abundance; more rarely minute acicular crystals, either isolated or in radial clusters, occurred (probably pyroxene).   Their optical properties, so far as determined, were: Refractive index high; birefringence medium to fairly strong, extinction angle often large, with elliptical axis c nearest the axis of elongation.   The refractive index of the glass ranged from about 1.510 to 1.525.

SPECIMENS FROM MIRAMAR AND VICINITY

No. 263701.   Specimen label.   *"Locality: Miramar.   Coast for a mile north.   Material: Portion of 'Ensenadean' (Ameghino), representing the deposit above the intraformational unconformity."*

A grayish-brown, distinctly conglomeratic rock in which hardened nodules, ranging up to 3 cm. in diameter, but generally less than 1 cm., are included in a fine softer matrix.   Scattered through the matrix are, furthermore, hard, brown, cherty grains, round, and from a half to 1 cm. in diameter; microscopically these grains consist in large part of quartz and chalcedony more or less filled with fine particles of iron ore.   The pale-gray nodules on the other hand consist essentially of calcite in minute grains and clusters, associated with which are a few larger grains of plagioclase (mostly albite and oligoclase with occasional grains of labradorite), quartz, glass, pyroxene, hornblende, and magnetite.   The subangular appearance of these nodules indicates that they were not formed in place but were derived from rocks not far distant.   The rounded and polished chert grains, on the other hand, have evidently been transported long distances.   The matrix contains chiefly plagioclase, glass, and argillaceous material.   Minor components are quartz, pyroxene, hornblende, biotite, magnetite, and zircon.   This earth falls into pieces when immersed in water; the soft material crumbles into mud and the nodules remain intact.   When tested with silver nitrate this earth gave a strong chloride reaction.

No. 263710.   Specimen label.   *"Locality: Miramar.   Exposed 'Ensenadean,' ¾ mile north.   Material: Ferruginous segregation regarded by both Ameghinos as 'Tierra Cocida.'"*

This specimen is a rounded piece of brown ferruginous earth, which has evidently existed as a unit and been exposed to wind or water transportation. Its outer surface is coated with small, rounded particles and grains of quartz, plagioclase, pyroxene, magnetite, and limestone, which are embedded in the fine, earthy material of the specimen proper. The earth itself consists of argillaceous material and fragments of quartz, plagioclase, pyroxene, hornblende, magnetite, and zircon. The darker-brown, ferruginous areas, which are distributed irregularly through the specimen, are similar in composition except for the pronounced accumulation of limonitic material, which is evidently the cementing material. Here and there in the broken specimen long, canal-like cavities were observed, which evidently mark the course of grass roots that have now disappeared. On immersion in water this earth crumbles to a fine brown mud. Its water solution gives a strong chloride reaction when tested with silver nitrate.

No. 263709. Specimen label. *"Locality: About five miles north of Miramar. Bluff of Chapadmalean and Ensenadean. Material: Tierra Cocida from a fogón or fireplace 4 feet above beach in situ in the Chapadmalean. B. W. 2 June, 1910."*

A light-brown, fine, evenly grained earth which consists of microscopic grains, averaging 0.1 mm. in diameter, of quartz, plagioclase (albite, oligoclase), a little biotite and hornblende. Glass is also present but appears decomposed and no longer clear. Argillaceous material is abundant. Finely crystalline aggregates of a low-refracting substance, possibly opal, were observed in several parts of the specimen. A uniaxial negative substance of medium birefringence and refractive index about 1.55 was encountered in the powder section, but was not identified with certainty. This earth crumbles and breaks down into mud when immersed in water. Its water solution gives a strong chloride reaction when treated with silver nitrate.

The earth was heated with graphite to 1,300° for 30 minutes and then held at 1,100° over night. The product was a dark-green glass, in which microscopic fragments of the original minerals were still visible. An unusual amount of hematite had crystallized from the melt; also occasionally a minute silicate microlite which was too fine for satisfactory determination. In a second experiment a portion was heated to 1,300° with graphite. After fusion more material was added and the whole mass reheated to 1,300°. This was repeated several times. Finally the glass was crushed, mixed with graphite, heated to 1,300° for 40 minutes and then held at 1,000° over night. The resulting glass was dark-green in color and contained occasional traces of the original mineral fragments. In addition there were present numerous clusters of microlites of fairly strong birefringence

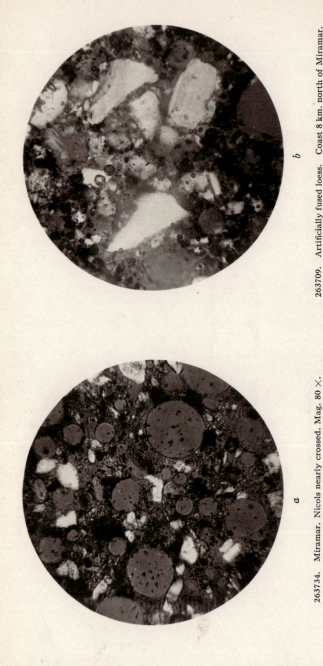

a

263734. Miramar. Nicols nearly crossed. Mag. 80 ×.

b

263709. Artificially fused loess. Coast 8 km. north of Miramar. Nicols nearly crossed. Mag. 150 ×.

SCORIÆ FROM THE ARGENTINE COAST

and refractive index noticeably greater than 1.53; the microlites extinguished parallel with their elongation but were too fine for identification. The refractive index of the glass ranged from 1.51 to 1.53. Neither hematite nor magnetite was present except in traces around the microlites. To vary the conditions of heating a larger quantity of the earth was taken (100 grams) and heated in a Fletcher gas furnace at 1,100°–1,200° for half an hour and then quickly withdrawn and allowed to cool in air. The product thus obtained was highly scoriaceous and resembled closely some of the natural scoriæ. The glass which had been formed was streaky, and varied in refractive index from about 1.515 to 1.540. Grains of the original quartz and plagioclase, pyroxene, and magnetite fragments were still visible. The cooling of the magma was rapid and no new crystals were formed as a result. A second charge consisting of lumps of the earth was heated in a similar way in the gas furnace but at slightly lower temperature. The lumps assumed a glassy surface and although entirely melted were evidently so viscous that little evidence of flow was noticeable. On both these samples red hematite was formed on the outer glassy surface but, in the interior of the lumps, the mass was gray-black in color and no new hematite was observed with certainty. The original magnetite fragments were still visible. New crystallization had evidently not taken place. In both cases the glass was full of small bubbles and streaky, and variable in composition and refractive index (1.515 to 1.54). (Pl. 7.) The evidence from the different methods of heating adopted above indicates that the character of the product is dependent somewhat on the heat treatment it has undergone.

No. 263725. Specimen label. *"Locality: Miramar. Material: Disseminated scoria."*

A pale-brown earth of uneven grain in which are imbedded pieces of a grayish-black, scoriaceous substance of variable size and ranging from large lumps to small pellets. The vesicles of the scoria have usually a glazed surface and are often filled with the earth which surrounds them. There is no evidence of a transition between the scoria and the earth. Clinging to the scoria and firmly wedged into some of the small cavities are rounded grains of quartz, calcite, plagioclase (oligoclase, andesine, and labradorite), pyroxene, garnet, magnetite, and volcanic glass. These grains are noticeably coarser than the earth which surrounds the scoria and have evidently been blown or washed into their present position. The larger pieces of scoria often appear freshly broken, but at the contact of undisturbed scoria and earth the surface of the scoria suggests an original smooth, rounded surface similar to the surface of a volcanic bomb or scoria rather than that of an originally angular fragment which has been subsequently rounded by attrition during water transportation.

Even the small scoria pellets in the earth frequently impress the observer as presenting in large measure the original glass surface. These relations indicate that the scoriæ were not derived from a large, compact lava mass. Microscopically the scoria is essentially a microlite-bearing glass crowded with fragments of plagioclase, quartz, pyroxene, and magnetite. The refractive index of the glass varies rapidly even in short distances and ranges from above 1.55 to below 1.52. Near the microlites which have crystallized from the glass, the color of the glass is often a pale-brown. The microlites appear in radial spherulites and irregularly grouped acicular crystals. They are colorless to pale-brown, of medium birefringence and of average refractive index, slightly greater than 1.65. The lath-shaped individuals often show high extinction angles; $c : \mathfrak{c} = 40°$ was measured in one instance. The optical character is positive. The optical properties agree, so far as determined, with those of pyroxene. This microlitic pyroxene does not agree in its properties with the larger green pyroxene crystal fragments noted above. The large, fragmental crystals never show normal crystal outlines but are always broken and irregular in outline. They are similar in shape, size, and composition to the crystals found in the earthy loess of the country. They often appear partially resorbed by the magma. Some of the crystals are even fractured. At certain points the thin section is crowded with angular fragments, each one of which represents a portion of a single crystal, and these are set in a paste of glass in which there has been very little crystallization. The occurrence of these fragments of plagioclase and also of quartz in a glass out of which they were not observed to recrystallize is good evidence of the melting-down of originally crystallized material. The variation in refractive index of the glass and also in adjacent plagioclase fragments (observed values ranged from 1.55 to 1.565) is evidence that the rock is not a volcanic rock of any normal type. In a cooling magma or lava the composition of the residual glass is fairly uniform, whereas in the present rock the refractive index (and consequently the composition) of the glass varies rapidly. Different explanations may be offered for the formation of such a rock type, all of which involve a partial melting-down or assimilation of originally crystallized material containing fragments of quartz, plagioclase, pyroxene, and magnetite. It is noteworthy in this connection that no fragments of original rock-types were observed, only isolated mineral fragments such as occur in the fine earths of this region. These fragments appear embedded in a glass base out of which radial pyroxene crystals are formed. The evidence at hand is not sufficient to determine definitely the mode of formation of these scoriæ.

The earth surrounding the scoria is of the usual fine, evenly grained type and consists of fragments of plagioclase (oligoclase, andesine, labradorite), quartz, hornblende, pyroxene, magnetite, colorless volcanic glass of low refractive index, and argillaceous material. On immersion in water this earth crumbles slightly. Its water solution contains abundant chloride (tested with silver nitrate).

Part of the earthy material which surrounds the scoriæ in this specimen was heated to 1,100° for 30 minutes; then it remained at 1,200° for $3\frac{1}{2}$ hours, and finally at 1,100° for $1\frac{1}{4}$ hours. The product was a vesicular, purple-colored glass, in which the original fragments of quartz and plagioclase were still visible under the microscope. In transmitted light the glass appeared colorless, but was filled with fine, dust-like particles of hematite. No new development of crystals was observed. The refractive index of the glass was about 1.51. The scoriaceous part of the specimen was heated at 1,240° for 1 hour and then held at 1,000° for $1\frac{1}{2}$ hours. The resulting glass was greenish-brown in color and had evidently settled quietly in the crucible. Under the microscope numerous grains of the original quartz and plagioclase fragments were observed. Clusters of acicular microlites of medium birefringence, parallel extinction, and refractive index greater than 1.53 are abundant, but are too fine for satisfactory determination. The refractive index of the glass, which appears pale-brown in transmitted light, varies from about 1.515 to 1.54.

No. 263727. Specimen label. *"Locality: Miramar. Material: Tierra cocida and scoriæ combined. Contact transition."*

The hand specimen shows a regular and uniform transition from a dark-gray scoria filled with small vesicles to a brick-red material, which bears a close resemblance to some of the specimens of baked earth. It is different from the latter, however, in this respect, that, while the baked earths have a close, compact texture, the portion of this specimen which resembles them most (observed with a binocular magnifying glass, magnification 65 diameters) is filled with minute holes and is distinctly glassy in character. A thin section which was cut across both the black scoria and the transition zone to the bright-red material bore out this observation. The black scoria is filled with fragments of quartz, plagioclase (acid oligoclase to basic labradorite), pyroxene, and magnetite, set in a glassy matrix in which a few microlitic crystals have developed, but which is essentially an undifferentiated glass except for a black dust, probably of magnetite. On passing toward the compact red portion the principal change observable is the replacement of the black dust by red dust, which is more prominent and tends to cover up the crystallized fragments and even the minute vesicles. In the more compact red portion the red iron oxide is so prominent that the mineral fragments are almost veiled to view. A careful determination of the mineral fragments in the black and the red portions of the specimen proved them to be of the same general size and kind, chiefly

quartz and different varieties of plagioclase, ranging from oligoclase
to basic labradorite, and occasional grains of pyroxene. Superficially
the red portion of this specimen resembles the baked earths, but
closer examination has shown it to be distinctly different. Its glassy,
vesicular texture throughout is indicative of melting; the red coloration may be the result of alteration or oxidation, whereby magnetite
has been changed to the red oxide of iron. It seems probable from
this evidence alone that the whole of the present specimen represents
an originally vesicular rock in the red part of which the iron is in
a more highly oxidized state than in the dark-gray part.

No. 263728. Specimen label. *"Locality: 3 miles north of Miramar. Bluff on the coast, 5 feet below the top in Ameghino's, 'Ensenadean.' Material: Scoria and adjacent loess."*

This specimen is an irregular, slaglike piece of scoria, consisting of
a dark, olive-green glass, almost pumiceous at certain points and
filled with vesicles which are often so large and numerous as to leave
only thin walls of the glass between them. The outer surface of this
scoria has plainly been in contact with the loess, some of which still
clings to it and is of a light-brown color. The division between the
scoria and the loess is sharp and there is no indication of a transition
between the two. In the cavities of the scoria there is an accumulation of rounded grains of magnetite, olivine, quartz, and plagioclase,
measuring up to 1 mm. in diameter. These have reached their present position either by wind or by water action. Microscopically this
scoria is similar to specimen 263725. Angular and rounded fragments of quartz, plagioclase, and pyroxene are set in a streaky,
brownish glass out of which lath-shaped microlites, showing high
extinction angles and medium birefringence, have crystallized; these
are probably pyroxene. The refractive index of the glass is not constant, but ranges from about 1.515 to 1.55, and occasionally shows
birefringence resulting evidently from strain.

The brown earth surrounding the scoria is of the usual type and
consists chiefly of argillaceous material, fragments of plagioclase,
quartz, pyroxene, and magnetite. Volcanic glass is less abundant
than usual.

Part of the scoria was heated to 1,240° for 1 hour and then held at
1,000° for 1½ hours. Under this treatment it melted down to a dark,
brownish-green glass, in which many of the original mineral fragments (quartz, plagioclase, and pyroxene) were still visible. Newly
formed microlites of high refractive index, medium to fairly strong
birefringence and parallel extinction, were also abundant, but were
too fine for satisfactory determination. Occasionally radial aggregates
of a lower-refracting, medium to weakly birefracting, substance were
observed, which may have been plagioclase feldspar. Particles of

iron ore were widely disseminated through the glass. The refractive
index of the glass ranged from 1.52 to 1.545.

Chemical analysis.—

	I	Ia				
SiO_2	61.30	1.016	Q	5.43	5.43	
Al_2O_3	14.15	.139	Or	21.20		76.52
Fe_2O3	0.91	.006	Ab	46.27	71.09	
FeO	2.86	.040	An	3.62		
MgO	2.46	.061	Di	12.79	16.23	
CaO	4.63	.083	Hy	3.44		
Na_2O	5.47	.088	Mt	1.39	2.45	20.29
K_2O	3.62	.038	Il	1.06		
H_2O-	0.24	----	Ap	1.55	1.61	
H_2O+	2.03	----	Pr	.06		
TiO_2	0.54	.007				
CO_2	None	----				
P_2O_5	0.71	.005				
S	0.03	.001				
MnO	0.08	.001				
	98.99					

Ratios

Class $\quad\dfrac{\text{Sal}}{\text{Fem}}=\dfrac{76.52}{20.29}>\dfrac{5}{3}<\dfrac{7}{1}$ ----------II

Order $\quad\dfrac{Q}{F}=\dfrac{5.43}{71.09}<\dfrac{1}{7}$ ------------- 5

Rang $\dfrac{K_2O'+Na_2O'}{CaO'}=\dfrac{.126}{.013}>\dfrac{7}{1}$ ------------- 1

Subrang $\quad\dfrac{K_2O'}{Na_2O'}=\dfrac{.038}{.088}<\dfrac{3}{5}>\dfrac{1}{7}$ ----------- 4

I. Scoria, Miramar. J. G. Fairchild, United States Geological
Survey, analyst.
Ia. Molecular proportions of I.

Compared with the analysis of the tierra cocida, No. 263722, this
analysis presents several noticeable differences. The alumina is
lower, also the ferric oxide and the water, while the ferrous oxide
and alkalies are notably higher. Lime and magnesia are also slightly
higher. Considering this analysis as that of a fresh eruptive rock,
the calculation places the rock in the subrang Umptekose of Class II
of the quantitative classification. On comparing this analysis with
the others of this class listed in Washington's Chemical Analysis
of Igneous Rocks, the relatively low alumina and alkali content is
noticeable; also the relatively large amount of magnesia and of lime.

There is nothing, however, in the analysis alone which precludes an igneous origin for this rock.

No. 263731. Specimen label. *"Locality: Miramar. Material: Scoria and Tierra Cocida."*

This specimen includes three distinct types of material: A grayish-black scoria, brick-red earthy material, and pale-brown loess. The scoria is vesicular and full of small bubbles. Parts of the outer surface of the scoria are often glassy and smooth and indicative of an original cooling surface. Where this surface is fractured, the small cavities are more or less filled with brown earth and with coarser rounded crystals of quartz, plagioclase, magnetite, and pyroxene. These grains have evidently been lodged in their present position either by wind or by water action. On one side of the specimen a brick-red, compact earth fills the small cavities and is evidently different from and older than the normal brown loess. In the cavities containing the brick-red earth, no rounded, coarser grains of the minerals, noted above, were observed. This red earth is more or less indurated and closely resembles the tierra cocida from Alvear described above and probably owes its color to a baking process at higher temperatures. There is, however, no transition between the glassy scoria and this red earth. The glassy walls of the vesicles are sharply marked and the red earth was evidently introduced into the cavities after their formation and is of later origin. Microscopically the composition of the scoria and the red earth is noticeably different. The red earth contains abundant red iron oxide and chalcedony, besides fragments of quartz, sodic plagioclase (oligoclase chiefly) and pyroxene and colorless glass. These same minerals are present in the scoriæ, but the plagioclase is noticeably more anorthic (andesine and labradorite) and pyroxene is less abundant. The glass is pale-brown and streaky, the colors appearing often along curved bands as though the molten glass had flowed. The microlites which have crystallized from the glass show medium birefringence, but are not sufficiently well-developed to be satisfactorily determined. At many points in the specimen a thin shell of the glass lining the cavities has devitrified and scales off in thin flakes.

The brown earth is of the usual type, a friable, pale-brown loess containing argillaceous material and fragments of quartz, plagioclase (labradorite), pyroxene, magnetite, and glass. This material is obviously later than both the scoria and the red earth.

Portions of the scoria and of the adjacent earth, each mixed with graphite, were heated simultaneously in separate crucibles to 1,200° for 2 hours and then cooled slowly for 2 hours from 1,200° to 1,000°. The scoria was found to have melted down to a dark olive-green glass which took the shape of the crucible. Microscopically it contained remnants of the original mineral fragments and also a few minute microlites. The magnetite of the original scoria appears to have been largely absorbed. The earthy material in the second crucible also melted down to a thick viscous glass which did not flow rapidly enough to take the shape of the crucible during the time of exposure. In it the original mineral fragments are still visible. The glass present was colorless, but was filled with fine, dust-like particles of iron ore. Its refractive index was about 1.51, while that of the brown-colored scoria glass ranged from about 1.515 to 1.54.

No. 263719. Specimen label. *"Locality: Miramar. Material: Washed-in bits of Tierra Cocida and Scoria."*

A pale-brown loess of the usual type containing fragments of scoria and red indurated material. The vesicular cavities of these scoriæ often contain rounded grains of quartz, chert, magnetite, plagioclase, and pyroxene; these grains are occasionally tightly wedged into the small bubble cavities. The loess contains much argillaceous material and minute fragments of quartz, microcline, plagioclase, magnetite, pyroxene, and colorless glass. Small worm-like cavities are common and are evidently due to former grass roots. The scoriæ pebbles are similar to specimen No. 263734 in appearance and composition. The red earth contains much brick-red, argillaceous material and also minute fragments of quartz, acid plagioclase (oligoclase), pyroxene, hornblende, and colorless volcanic glass. This red earth resembles in its properties that of specimen 263731. This specimen crumbles slightly and softens when immersed in water. Tested with silver nitrate it gives a strong chloride reaction (probably common salt derived from sea water.)

No. 263720. Specimen label. *"Locality: Barrancas 3 to 5 miles north of Miramar. 0 to 5 feet above the base, i. e., from the lowest formation above the beach. Ameghino's Chapadmalean. Material: Scoria and burnt earth."*

This specimen consists of a large fragment of scoria, similar in appearance and properties to No. 263728, embedded in pale-brown loess of the usual properties and closely allied to No.263719 in texture and composition.

Nos. 263724, 263726, 263733, 263734, 263737. Specimen labels. *"Locality: Miramar. Material: Scoriæ and Tierra Cocida."*

These specimens are similar to the specimens noted above from this locality. The scoriæ are of the same general appearance and composition and contain in a pale-brown, streaky glass irregular and rounded fragments of quartz, plagioclase (andesine, labradorite), pyroxene, and magnetite. (Pl 7, a.) The glass base is full of fine bubbles and is often streaky and variable in refractive index and composition. In No. 263737, the vesicles are large and elongated. In one part of this specimen elongated drops of the viscous scoria are visible and testify to the flowing of the molten scoria. In all of these specimens of scoria bright-yellow spots occur here and there and may possibly be due in part to admixture of iron chloride. On immersing in distilled water clean particles from such colored patches, a distinct precipitation of silver chloride was obtained on adding silver nitrate to the solution.

Specimen 263733 contains occasional vesicle fillings of red earth which are indurated and evidently different from the loose brown earth adhering to the specimen at other points.

On these specimens, as in the above, many of the cavities of the scoriæ are filled with rounded grains of various minerals, as quartz, plagioclase, garnet, magnetite, and pyroxene. These grains are apparently confined to the upper, exposed part of the scoria. In many cases the lower part of a scoria specimen is covered with loess which still adheres to it and in which evidently the fragment was originally embedded, with its surface protruding above the level of the loess. In this position wind or tide may have swept the rounded particles of foreign material over the scoria and lodged the observed grains in their present position. Such grains may also have been gathered by the scoria during water transport; the grains on its underside may be so intermixed with the present loess as to be covered up and not easy to separate from the finer earth. It seems probable, however, in the absence of field data, that the first supposition is the correct explanation of the presence of these grains.

No. 263737. This scoria after heating at 1,100° for 40 minutes was noticeably fritted. Another fragment heated to 1,400° for 1½ hours, and cooled slowly for 1 hour to 1,100° and then held at 1,100° for 1½ hours became a dark-green glass which contained a small quantity of magnetite and rarely a trace of the original mineral fragments. The refractive index of the glass varied greatly, from 1.505 to 1.56, the more deeply brown-colored fragments having the higher refractive index.

Nos. 263721, 263722, 263732. Specimen labels: *Locality: Miramar. Material: Tierra Cocida.*"

These specimens range in color from brick-red to dark-brown and are fine-grained, indurated earths which resemble in texture the brown loess of this region. Microscopically they consist of fragments of quartz, plagioclase (andesine, labradorite), microcline, pyroxene, hornblende, magnetite, colorless volcanic glass, and argillaceous material often deeply stained with iron oxide. The outer surface of these indurated fragments is often pitted; these pits are not deep but often contain rounded grains of magnetite, quartz, and plagioclase similar to the grains observed in the cavities of the scoriæ. They have probably been lodged in the pits by wind or wave action.

All of these specimens contain some sodium chloride. They are indurated and do not break down and disintegrate as does the loess when immersed in water.

Chemical analysis. No. 263722.—

	I	Ia						
SiO_2	62.49	1.036	Q	23.34	23.34			
Al_2O_3	16.45	.161	Or	13.39				
Fe_2O_3	4.30	.027	Ab	29.45	60.95	85.92		
FeO	0.65	.009	An	18.11				
MgO	1.56	.039	C	1.63	1.63			
CaO	3.62	.065	Hy	3.92				
Na_2O	3.45	.056	Mt	0.46				
K_2O	2.26	.024	Hm	4.00		9.44		
H_2O-	2.44	- - - -	Il	1.06				
H_2O+	2.44	- - - -						
TiO_2	0.57	.007		95.36				
CO_2	None							
P_2O_5	Trace							
S	Trace							
MnO	None							

100.23

Ratios

$$\text{Class} \quad \frac{\text{Sal}}{\text{Fem}} = \frac{85.92}{9.44} > \frac{7}{1} \quad \text{- - - - - - - - - - -} \quad \text{I}$$

$$\text{Order} \quad \frac{Q}{F} = \frac{23.34}{60.95} < \frac{3}{5} > \frac{1}{7} \quad \text{- - - - - - - -} \quad 4$$

$$\text{Rang} \quad \frac{K_2O' + Na_2O'}{CaO'} = \frac{.080}{.065} < \frac{5}{3} > \frac{3}{5} \quad \text{- - - - - - - -} \quad 3$$

$$\text{Subrang} \quad \frac{K_2O'}{Na_2O'} = \frac{.024}{.056} < \frac{3}{5} > \frac{1}{7} \quad \text{- - - - - - - -} \quad 4$$

I. Scoria, Miramar. J. G. Fairchild, United States Geological Survey, analyst.

Ia. Molecular proportions of I.

Except for the high percentage of water this analysis might easily be mistaken for that of a biotite-granite or granodiorite or quartz-mica-diorite. It differs from the analysis of the scoria from Alvear in its noticeably higher alkali content and consequent less amount of corundum and quartz in the norm. Both the lime and magnesia are higher, but their proportions do not suggest any abnormality in the composition, if the rock were considered an eruptive rock. The eruptive material predominates to so great an extent that it determines the general character of the analysis.

SPECIMENS FROM THE VICINITY OF NECOCHEA

No. 263745. Specimen label. *"Locality: Playas near the sea in the neighborhood of Laguna Malacara, north of Necochea. Material: Scoriæ."*

No. 263746. Specimen label. *"Locality: Coast north of Necochea, beyond the Boca del Moro, Laguna Malacara vicinity. Material: Scoria found on the surface of various playas where the Ensenadean is exposed."*

These two samples include a number of specimens which are practically identical in external appearance and in the thin section. In the hand specimen they bear a close resemblance to normal lava scoriæ and might easily be taken for such, but under the microscope they do not resemble any known type of lava. (Pl. 8, *a*.) Fragments of quartz, plagioclase, and pyroxene are set in a streaky-brown glassy matrix out of which radial and irregular groups of acicular pyroxene crystals and less frequently of plagioclase have been precipitated. The pyroxene was determined optically by its high extinction angles, high refractive index, fairly strong birefringence, square-end section, and positive optical character. It is usually colorless or pale-brown in color while the larger fragmental pyroxenes are pale-green in color, have higher refractive index, and are usually rounded in outline. It is evident that not only did they not crystallize out of the glass but they were unstable in it and were attacked and corroded by it. The plagioclase microlites are lath-shaped in section and apparently andesitic in composition. They proved too fine for more exact determination. The glass varies in composition from point to point, as is evident from its streakiness and the differences in color and refractive index (ranging from 1.515 to about 1.55). Fine dusty particles, possibly magnetite, are abundant in the glass and frequently become so abundant as to impair seriously the transparency of the glass. The cavities of these scoriæ are often filled with rounded grains and pellets of quartz, plagioclase, magnetite, chert, and limestone. Some of these grains are tightly wedged into the cavities and have evidently been lodged there either by water or wind action, possibly during the transport of the scoriæ.

Fragments of the scoriæ 263745 were heated at 1,000° for 30 minutes and showed but little change; after being held at 1,100° for 30 minutes the product was found to be tightly sintered and the glass base of the original material largely crystallized to brown acicular crystals of medium to fairly strong birefringence, refractive index slightly above 1.66, and high extinction angles. These optical properties agree with those of pyroxene. The crystals were too small for a more definite identification. Another portion of the scoria, heated to 1,200° for 2 hours and then cooled gradually to 1,050° for one-half hour, where it was held for 2 hours and then cooled to 1,000°

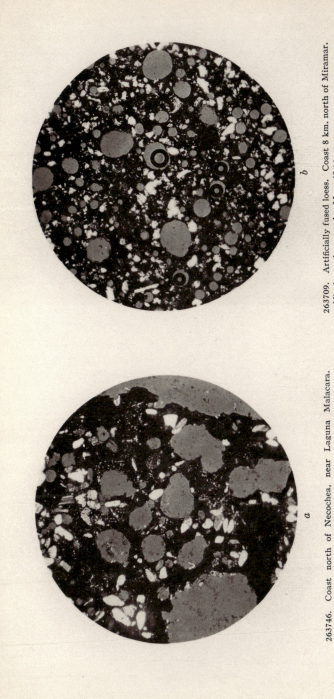

b

263709. Artificially fused loess. Coast 8 km. north of Miramar. Nicols nearly crossed. Mag. 40 ×.

a

263746. Coast north of Necochea, near Laguna Malacara. Nicols nearly crossed. Mag. 28 ×.

SCORIÆ FROM THE ARGENTINE COAST

for one-half hour, was found to have been melted to a dark greenish-brown mass in which remnants of the original plagioclase and quartz fragments were still visible under the microscope. Some glass was still present but it had largely crystallized to a substance which agreed with pyroxene in its optical properties, so far as these could be ascertained. Fine specks of iron oxide were noted frequently in the section.

Fragments of the scoriæ 263746 heated to 1,000° for 30 minutes exhibited a slight change in color but were not profoundly altered. Held at 1,100° for 30 minutes the mass had sintered together and the change was more noticeable. Heated at 1,150° for 3½ hours, the material was completely fused to a dark brownish-green, vesicular glass which still contained numerous fragments of the original minerals. Acicular microlites resembling pyroxene in optical properties were abundant; also iron oxide particles. The refractive index of the glass was unusually high, ranging from 1.55 to 1.59. It is of interest to note that in all these heating experiments the minerals which crystallize out of the melt are not those which appear in fragmental state in the glass and which were present in the original material that was subjected to the heat treatment. The same holds true of the fragmental mineral grains in the scoriæ from Miramar and Alvear.

Chemical analysis. No. 263746.—

	I	Ia				
SiO_2	56.27	.933	Q	5.49	5.49	
Al_2O_3	12.79	.125	Or	11.71		62.49
Fe_2O_3	2.55	.016	Ab	34.70	57.00	
FeO	7.24	.100	An	10.59		
MgO	3.14	.078	Di	26.76		
CaO	8.89	.159	Hy	1.22	27.98	
Na_2O	4.07	.066	Mt	3.71		37.33
K_2O	1.96	.021	Il	5.02	8.73	
H_2O-	0.36		Ap	0.62	0.62	
H_2O+	0.44					
TiO_2	2.62	.033				
CO_2	None					
P_2O_5	0.23	.0016				
S	Trace					
MnO	None					

100.65

Ratios

$$\text{Class} \quad \frac{\text{Sal}}{\text{Fem}} = \frac{62.49}{37.33} > \frac{5}{3} < \frac{7}{1} \cdots \quad \text{II–III}$$

$$\text{Order} \quad \frac{Q}{F} = \frac{5.49}{57.00} < \frac{1}{7} \cdots \quad 5$$

$$\text{Rang} \quad \frac{K_2O' + Na_2O'}{CaO'} = \frac{.097}{.038} < \frac{7}{1} > \frac{5}{3} \cdots \quad 2$$

$$\text{Subrang} \quad \frac{K_2O'}{Na_2O'} = \frac{.021}{.066} < \frac{3}{5} > \frac{1}{7} \cdots \quad 4$$

I. Scoria.   North of Necochea.   J. G. Fairchild, United States
   Geological Survey, analyst.
Ia. Molecular proportions of I.

This analysis places the rock on the border between Class II and Class III of the quantitative classification.   In the Tables of Chemical Analyses of Igneous Rocks, by Washington, rocks ranging from syenite and trachyte to diorite and andesite and even basalt are included in the subrang in which this analysis falls.   Characteristic of the analysis is the high percentage of ferrous oxide and of titanic oxide.

SPECIMENS FROM MONTE HERMOSO

No. 263705.   Specimen label.   *"Locality: Monte Hermoso near the old lighthouse.   Material: Red loess-sand of the Monte Hermoso formation from the lower bench just above high tide."*

A light-reddish, earthy material, in part indurated and stony, in part loose and friable.   Under the microscope the stony part is seen to be composed almost entirely of microscopic calcite grains and clusters usually stained with iron oxide.   The earthy, loose part consists largely of cryptocrystalline, argillaceous material.   Disseminated through the rock are quartz and plagioclase fragments, and some glass, pyroxene, hornblende, biotite, and magnetite.   The calcareous portion of this specimen is evidently concretionary in origin.   On immersion in water this earth crumbles to a lumpy mud.   It gives strong chloride reaction when tested with silver nitrate solution.

A small quantity of the earth was mixed with graphite and heated to 1,300° for a short time, after which the temperature was dropped to 1,100° and held there over night (16 hours).   The resulting mass was found to have been completely fused, no trace of the original material being visible, and to have largely recrystallized.   Pyroxene crystals predominated, in lath-shaped prisms, and exhibited the usual optical characteristics: refractive index about 1.66, birefringence, fairly strong, extinction angle *c: c* usually high; the square-end section of the prisms extinguished along the diagonals.   A colorless mineral of weaker birefringence and refractive index about 1.57 occurred in overlapping aggregates which were too fine for satisfactory determination but may have been plagioclase. Some glass with refractive index about 1.525 was also present.

No. 263707. Specimen label. *"Locality: Monte Hermoso near the old lighthouse on the coast east of Bahia Blanca. Material: Loess-sand of the Monte Hermoso formation from exposure above high tide."*

A light brownish-gray, firm, but distinctly sandy, material consisting of plagioclase, quartz, and colorless glass. The plagioclase is occasionally fairly fresh but more often slightly decomposed and stained with iron oxide. Minor components are hornblende, pyroxene, apatite, and magnetite. The grains are generally of fair size and rounded from transportation. Scattered through the rock are minute needles and cryptocrystalline material which is too fine to identify with certainty. It is in part evidently argillaceous in character. When immersed in water this earth crumbles into a lumpy, sandy mud. Tested with silver nitrate it gives a distinct chloride reaction.

No. 263714. Specimen label. *"Locality: Monte Hermoso near the old lighthouse. Material: Yellow-brown loess of the Monte Hermoso formation from the upper bench 5 feet above tide."*

A light-brown, porous earth, fine and even-grained and consisting in large measure of argillaceous material with some plagioclase, volcanic glass, and occasional grains of pyroxene and biotite. On making a concentration test with the powder of this specimen, plagioclase of different compositions, quartz, pyroxene, hornblende, biotite, apatite, zircon, magnetite, spinel (or garnet), and epidote were observed; also possibly olivine and monazite and two other minerals which were not identified. Most of these minerals are of igneous origin but several are of metamorphic origin. In water this earth disintegrates into a lumpy clay. Its water solution gives a strong chloride reaction when treated with silver nitrate solution.

This earth, heated to 1,200° for 1 hour, fused to a brown glass in which many of the original crystal fragments of quartz and plagioclase were still visible. Hematite in minute crystals was found to have crystallized from the melt and at certain points to be so abundant as to render the glass nearly opaque. The refractive index of the glass ranged from 1.525 to 1.54. On heating the earth to 700° for 45 minutes its color was found to have changed from brown to brown-red.

No. 263741. Specimen label. *"Locality: Monte Hermoso near the old lighthouse. Material: Basal layer of cross-stratified sands (the Puelchean) upon Monte Hermoso formation."*

An indurated, light-brown material composed apparently of a mixture of clay and quite coarse sand through which numerous pebbles of various colors (white, gray, red, brown, and black) are scattered. These pebbles range from 1 mm. to 1 cm. in diameter and are more or less rounded and distinctly water-worn. They appear to be in large measure quartzose and cherty in character. Under the microscope much argillaceous material was observed. The sand grains consist largely of plagioclase and quartz, both stained or coated with iron oxide. Isotropic glass, usually considerably altered, is present in noticeable quantities. Minor components are pyroxene, magnetite, and spinel (or garnet). Many of the pebbles consist of quartz which appears to be vein quartz. Other pebbles are composed of chalcedony of typical fibrous structure. The dark-red and brown pebbles contain so much fine iron oxide as to be practically opaque. They contain either quartz or chalcedony and resemble ferruginous chert in general appearance.

This specimen crumbles into a muddy sand when immersed in water. Its water solution gives a noticeable chloride reaction when tested with silver nitrate.

No. 263743. Specimen label. "*Locality: Monte Hermoso near the old lighthouse. Material: Volcanic ash from the Puelchean.*"

A light-gray, gritty material of fine even grain which microscopically consists largely of colorless volcanic glass, the refractive index of which is fairly constant and averages about 1.500. Some argillaceous material is present, as are occasional grains of plagioclase and quartz. After washing away the major part of the glass, grains of plagioclase, quartz, hornblende, pyroxene, biotite, magnetite, apatite, zircon, spinel (or garnet), and epidote were found in the concentrates.

This ash crumbles but little in water. Its water solution, when tested with silver nitrate, gives an abundant silver chloride precipitate. The chlorine is evidently present in sodium chloride.

SPECIMENS FROM RIO COLORADO

Nos. 263730, 263739. Specimen labels. "*Locality: Delta of the Rio Colorado, 100 miles south of Bahia Blanca. Material: 'Tierra Cocida,' or burnt earth, produced by burning the 'esparto,' a rank grass growing in swampy ground. Area burnt about ½ acre. Earth all burnt to tender crusts to a depth of 3 to 5 inches.*"

These specimens are brick-red in color, fine-grained and indurated. They are full of irregular holes and cavities and carry numerous impressions of grass leaves. Under the microscope numerous fragments of quartz, plagioclase, pyroxene, magnetite, colorless volcanic glass, and abundant argillaceous material deeply impregnated with iron oxide are visible. Except for the red oxide of iron, this composition is similar to that of the original loess from which these burnt earths were derived. Microscopically this burnt earth resembles closely the natural tierras cocidas 263721, 263729, 263731, 263732. Whether the latter were produced by the burning of grass can not be definitely ascertained. Their relatively compact texture and the absence of grass-leaf impressions are not in favor of this view.

These specimens do not disintegrate when immersed in water. The water solution does show, however, the presence of a fair amount of sodium chloride.

No. 263739. Fragments of this artificial tierra cocida were held at 1,100° for 2⅓ hours and were found to have melted to a viscous glass, in which many of the original mineral fragments are still visible under the microscope. The glass is so filled with fine particles of red iron oxide that it is opaque at many points.

It is of interest to note the lack of compactness of this earth baked by the burning of grass. The product is extremely porous and full of holes, many of which evidently mark the position of former grass roots. The specimens of tierra cocida from Miramar and Saladillo, on the other hand, are large, compact masses; for their formation a much greater quantity of uniform, confined heat was required than for the Rio Colorado material. The source of heat supply for the baking of the tierra cocida was probably volcanic contact action. This hypothesis is developed at greater length below in connection with the formation of the scoriæ, but it applies with almost equal force to the formation of the tierra cocida of this region. The assumption that the large specimens of tierra cocida were formed simply by the action of open fires is hardly possible in view of the quantity of heat involved, which must have acted through a period of time on large masses of material to have produced the effects observed.

SPECIMEN FROM SAN BLAS

No. 263744. Specimen label. *"Locality: Coast near San Blas, north of Rio Negro. Material: Scoria or pumice."*

A dark, reddish-brown, pumiceous scoria containing here and there a minute feldspar phenocryst, but otherwise aphanitic and stony in appearance. Under the microscope occasional phenocrysts of plagioclase (labradorite, Ab_1An_1) and pyroxene were observed. The groundmass is filled with fine specks of opaque, ferruginous substance which renders it for the most part nontransparent. Fine laths of plagioclase were noted in the clearer parts of the groundmass, but so far as could be determined it is largely isotropic and glassy. Both megascopically and microscopically this specimen does not differ in any essential feature from many andesites, and there is no reason to doubt its volcanic origin.

Chemical analysis.—

	I	Ia				
SiO_2	56.09	.930	Q	12.54	12.54	
Al_2O_3	16.04	.157	Or	10.60		76.17
Fe_2O_3	8.81	.055	Ab	31.02	63.63	
FeO	0.90	.013	An	22.01		
MgO	3.21	.080	Di	3.72		
CaO	6.09	.109	Hy	6.19	9.91	
Na_2O	3.68	.059	Hm	8.80		
K_2O	1.79	.019	Il	1.98	11.87	22.40
H_2O-	0.43	....	Tn	1.09		
H_2O+	0.49	....	Ap	0.62	0.62	
TiO_2	1.67	.021				
CO_2	None	....				
P_2O_5	0.29	.002				
S	None	....				
MnO	None	....				
	99.49					

Ratios

Class $\frac{Sal}{Fem}=\frac{76.17}{22.40}<\frac{7}{1}>\frac{5}{3}$ - - - - - - II

Order $\frac{Q}{F}=\frac{12.54}{63.63}<\frac{3}{5}>\frac{1}{7}$ - - - - - - 4

Rang $\frac{Na_2O'+K_2O'}{CaO}=\frac{.078}{.079}<\frac{5}{3}>\frac{3}{5}$ - - - - - - 3

Subrang $\frac{K_2O'}{Na_2O'}=\frac{.019}{.059}<\frac{3}{5}>\frac{1}{7}$ - - - - - - 4

I. Scoria, near San Blas. J. G. Fairchild, United States Geological Survey, analyst.
Ia. Molecular proportions of I.

This analysis places the rock in the subrang Tonalose of the new quantitative classification, a division in which many andesites and diorites occur. Characteristic for the rock is the high percentage of ferric oxide and low amount of FeO. This finds expression in the red color of the rock. Except for this unusually high Fe_2O_3, the analysis is that of a normal andesite.

RECAPITULATION

THE LOESS SPECIMENS

*Petrographic microscopic features.—*Characteristic of all the specimens of loess in this collection is the relatively large amount of distinctly igneous material present. Fragments of quartz, plagioclase, pyroxene, magnetite, and acid volcanic glass predominate and are, as a rule, remarkably fresh and unaltered. The amount of volcanic glass present varies within wide limits. Specimens 263743 and 263747 consist almost entirely of colorless volcanic glass which has many of the characteristics of tuffaceous material. The glass fragments are splintery and irregular and often contain streaks of elongated bubbles. The refractive index of the glass and its chemical composition are fairly constant in each specimen; in 263743 the refractive index averages about 1.500, in 263747 about 1.485. These refractive indices are both low and indicate a high silica content, specimen 263747 being slightly more siliceous than 263743. In other loess specimens the glass is less abundant and may even become rare. In all cases it is colorless or nearly so and of very low refractive index. In contrast to this the glass in the scoriæ is usually colored and of higher but variable refractive index, which ranges from about 1.51 to 1.56 and above in some of the specimens.

The mineral fragments in the loess are usually angular and average about 0.1 mm. in length. They occur almost invariably in single isolated grains and not in crystalline aggregates nor embedded in a groundmass. No fragments of an eruptive rock were observed with certainty.

The quartz grains are irregular in shape, and rarely, if ever, show crystal outlines. They are of normal quartz which has suffered little deformation and may be in part eruptive quartz and in part vein quartz. The plagioclase occurs in angular, broken individuals twinned after the albite law and rarely after the Karlsbad and pericline laws. The composition of the plagioclase is not the same in the different specimens and often varies within wide limits in the same specimen. In the one its composition may range from albite-oligoclase to andesine; in another, from andesine to basic labradorite. Zonal structure is not uncommon, but is by no means the rule. The pyroxene crystals are prismatic in form, generally pale-green in color and unusually fresh and free from alteration. They are ordinarily of the diopside-augite varieties and are more abundant than the green hornblende grains which occur in many but not all of the loess specimens. The magnetite is relatively abundant and occurs in irregular, more or less equant, grains and octahedra. The other minerals noted in the descriptions above are less common and less constant in their occurrence. The relatively fresh, unaltered state of practically all the grains is noteworthy. They are often covered with fine, cryptocrystalline, argillaceous material, but do not appear to have altered into it to any appreciable degree in most cases.

Chemical evidence.—The predominance of eruptive minerals in the loess is clearly expressed in the chemical analyses, which might easily be mistaken for those of eruptive rocks, were the water content a little lower.

Thermal evidence.—On heating these loess specimens to temperatures between 850° and 1,050° distinct sintering occurs. The brown, earthy material assumes a brick-red color and shrinks to a compact, indurated mass, resembling brick in all its properties. Between 1,050° and 1,150° it melts to a thick, viscous glass, in which the mineral fragments appear to be set as in a thick paste. On continued heating the mineral fragments are slowly dissolved by the molten glass. By lowering the temperature 100° or more microlites crystallize out, whose optical properties agree with those of pyroxene, but of a variety different from that of the pyroxene fragments in the original loess. Occasionally minute laths of plagioclase were also precipitated, together with the pyroxene microlites. The glass thus formed is streaky and evidently variable in its composition. Its refractive index varies rapidly from about 1.51 to above 1.56 in some of the specimens. On heating the loess to the temperature at which melting first occurs the glass formed is practically colorless and contains many opaque particles of iron oxide. On raising the temperature the magma dissolves these particles and the resulting brown-colored glass has a notably higher refractive index; the more pronounced the color of the glass, the higher its refractive index.

In the thermal experiments with the loess specimens it was found that the mode of treatment and size of the charge had great effect on the resulting product. Small, loose charges of powdered material were necessarily exposed during heating to the oxiziding effect of the air and the iron present was converted largely into the ferric state, with the result that the product was colored dark-red. With heavy charges of large lumps of the loess, the air found less ready access to all parts of the material and the outer portions only of the lumps were thoroughly oxidized, the centers of the lumps being dark-gray in color and resembling the scoria in appearance. (Pl. 7.) In conducting thermal experiments of this kind in imitation of natural processes, it is highly essential that the physical conditions of experiments be as nearly like those which obtain in nature as it is possible to make them, otherwise totally different products may result and the conclusions deduced therefrom be in error to that extent.

TIERRA COCIDA

Petrographic microscopic features.—Under this title three distinct types of rock are included:

(1) Indurated, brick-red earths, which, under the microscope, resemble the ordinary loess specimens except for the red particles which have evidently resulted from the heating of the argillaceous material. The mineral composition of the tierras cocidas both with respect to kind and size is practically identical with that of the

loess. Chemically also they are practically identical, as analyses 263717 and 263729 show. The percentage of H_2O in 263729 is lower than that in 263717 as was to be expected. In both the amount of FeO present is very slight. This is also true of analysis 263722 of the tierra cocida from Miramar and is in accord with the conditions under which the tierras cocidas have probably been formed. Many of the specimens of tierra cocida are so large and compact that one is forced, in explaining their mode of formation, to assume long-continued and confined heating at a fairly high temperature, such as would be encountered near the contact of an intrusive igneous or volcanic mass, but not beneath an open fire made of grass or small timber.

(2) Some of the scoriæ contain bright-red patches, which resemble the tierras cocidas superficially, but which on closer examination are seen to be glassy and to have been melted, just as the gray parts of the scoriæ have been melted, the chief difference between the two parts being the state of oxidation of the iron. These will be considered below, together with the scoriæ to which they belong.

(3) Brown ferruginous earths (specimen 263710) have also been considered tierra cocida by some investigators. A careful microscopic examination of these specimens has shown that they are simply loess in which ferruginous material abounds (ferruginous concretion) and acts as a weak cementing material, causing the specimens to appear more indurated than the surrounding loess. On immersing such specimens in water they are seen to crumble and break down readily. The red tierras cocidas or baked earths do not crumble in the least under these conditions.

THE SCORIÆ

Microscopic petrographic features.—Under the microscope the scoriæ from both Miramar and Necochea exhibit abnormal features. Irregular fragments of quartz, plagioclase, pyroxene, and magnetite occur embedded in a colorless-to-pale-brown glass, out of which aggregates of acicular crystals, probably pyroxene, crystallize. The mineral fragments have been considered phenocrysts by some observers. On this assumption the rock would be classed with the andesites and has been described as such. The chemical analyses of the present paper might be considered confirmatory evidence in favor of this view. A careful microscopic examination of the mineral fragments, however, precludes this hypothesis. The mineral fragments are broken and irregular in outline. (Pl. 7, *a* and pl. 8, *a*.) They were evidently not stable in the molten glass and were attacked and dissolved in part by the same. The plagioclase feldspars are not uniform in composition. In the same microscope-field fragments of oligoclase and labradorite can often be seen, the fragments of both being homogenous throughout and without zonal texture. Such rapid variation in composition in the nonzoned phenocrysts of effusive rocks is unknown to the writers and would be abnormal in view of the mode of formation of phenocrysts. Zonal structure does occur in some of the grains and the composition follows then the usual succession, with the more anorthic plagioclase in the center of the grains. The zoned individuals are often broken across so that the whole series of compositions was exposed to the action of the melted glass. Taken as a whole the mineral fragments in the scoriæ resemble in kind, in size, and in general character and outline the mineral fragments in the loess. In the specimens of scoriæ from Miramar, however, there is a decided difference in quantitative mineral composition between the scoriæ and the loess adjacent to them. This difference also found expression in the thermal behavior of the two materials as noted above under specimen 263731.

The character of the glass base is another feature which is difficult to reconcile with the view that the scoriæ are normal andesites. The glass base is streaky and varies rapidly in composition, its refractive index ranging from about 1.51 to 1.56. In the glass resulting from the cooling of a normal lava such great differences have not been described and are not to be expected. The presence of fine particles of iron oxide embedded in a colorless glass base in some parts of the scoriæ and their absence in other parts, whereby the glass is colored brown and has a higher refractive index, is strikingly like the features observed in the loess specimens which had been heated at different temperatures.

It is interesting to note that the glass obtained by heating the loess and burnt earth specimens has about the same refractive indices and variation in refractive indices as the glass of the scoria from Miramar. In the glass of the Necochea scoria the refractive indices are slightly higher than those of the Miramar glass and the Necochea scoria is correspondingly less siliceous in composition. The mineral fragments in the melted loess specimens are practically identical in size and kind with the mineral fragments in the scoriæ. In both cases the fragments are unstable in the melted glass and have been partly dissolved by it. The new microlites which crystallize from the melt agree with pyroxene and have the same general aspect in both cases. The products differ chiefly in the state of oxidation of the iron, but this difference is evidently due, as noted above, to the different conditions under which the products were formed, the conditions of experiment not agreeing in all details with those of nature under which the scoriæ were formed.

Chemical evidence.—The chemical evidence given in the analyses 263728 and 263746 does not of itself preclude a volcanic origin for the scoriæ. In both analyses the ferrous iron predominates over the ferric iron; in this respect the analyses differ notably from those of the tierras cocidas.

Two analyses by Dr. E. Herrero Ducloux cited by Col. Antonio A. Romero,[1] of a "tierra cocida" and an "escoria" from Chapadmalal do not show this relation between the iron oxides. For the sake of comparison these analyses have been expressed in the quantitative system and both found to belong to the same subrang; but in this subrang no analysis of an igneous rock has yet been found to occur. This in itself is indicative of the abnormal character of the rocks.

Chemical analysis, of Dr. E. Herrero Ducloux.—

	OO	a				
SiO_2	66.600	1.104	Q	45.59	45.59	
Al_2O_3	16.350	.160	Or	1.95		
Fe_2O_3	5.030	.031	Ab	14.25	34.11	86.33
FeO	0.350	.005	An	17.91		
MgO	1.422	.035	C	6.63	6.63	
CaO	3.880	.069	Hy	3.52		
Na_2O	1.947	.0314	Mt	.70		
K_2O	0.325	.0035	Hm	4.48		9.50
H_2O-	0.651	------	Il	.30		
H_2O+	2.715	------	Ap	.50		
TiO_2	0.180	.002	NaCl	.50		
P_2O_5	0.211	.0014				
Cl	0.340	.001				
MnO	0.019	------				
	100.02					

Ratios

Class $\dfrac{\text{Sal}}{\text{Fem}} = \dfrac{86.33}{9.50} > \dfrac{7}{1}$ -------- 1

Order $\dfrac{Q}{F} = \dfrac{45.59}{34.11} < \dfrac{5}{3} > \dfrac{3}{5}$ ----- 3

Rang $\dfrac{K_2O' + Na_2O'}{CaO'} = \dfrac{.0306}{.0643} < \dfrac{3}{5} > \dfrac{1}{7}$ ----- 4

Subrang $\dfrac{K_2O'}{Na_2O'} = \dfrac{.0035}{.0271} < \dfrac{1}{7}$ -------- 5

OO. Tierra cocida. Chapadmalal, E. H. Ducloux, analyst.
a. Molecular proportions of OO.

In calculating this analysis, the rules prescribed by the authors of the quantitative classification for the calculation of the Cl were not followed by the writers. This procedure would have indicated

---

[1] In *Anales del Museo Nacional de Buenos Aires*, XXII (ser. iii, t. xv), pp. 11–31 (separate, 1911).

the presence of a relatively large amount of sodalite together with a large excess of quartz, which is obviously contrary to experience. The tests with silver nitrate cited above indicate that the chlorine is contained in NaCl, which has probably been derived from sea water, and this assumption was made in calculating the analysis in order to obtain the most favorable conditions for proving the eruptive nature of the rock. But even with this assumption, the analysis does not resemble that of any known lava.

Chemical analysis, of Dr. E. Herrero Ducloux.—

	OI	a			
SiO_2	65.950	1.094	Q	43.84	43.84
Al_2O_3	15.010	.147	Or	2.90	
Fe_2O_3	4.750	.0297	Ab	10.36	37.22 84.73
FeO	.410	.0057	An	23.96	
MgO	1.872	.046	C	3.67	3.67
CaO	4.872	.087	Hy	4.63	
Na_2O	1.224	.0197	Mt	.86	
K_2O	.488	.0052	Hm	4.16	9.95
H_2O-	0.789	------	Il	.30	
H_2O+	3.370	------			
TiO_2	.160	.002			
P_2O_5	0.062	.0004			
Cl	0.034	.001			
MnO	0.021	.0002			
	99.012				

Ratios

Class $\dfrac{Sal}{Fem} = \dfrac{84.73}{9.95} > \dfrac{7}{1}$ ---------- I

Order $\dfrac{Q}{F} = \dfrac{43.84}{37.22} < \dfrac{5}{3} > \dfrac{3}{5}$ ------ 3

Rang $\dfrac{K_2O' + Na_2O'}{CaO'} = \dfrac{.0249}{.086} < \dfrac{3}{5} > \dfrac{1}{7}$ ------ 4

Subrang $\dfrac{K_2O'}{Na_2O'} = \dfrac{.0052}{.0197} < \dfrac{3}{5} > \dfrac{1}{7}$ ------ 4

OI. Escoria. Chapadmalal, E. H. Ducloux, analyst.
a. Molecular proportions of OI.

The calculation of this analysis indicates its close similarity with the first. Both analyses belong to subrangs for which no representative has yet been found in normal lavas. These rocks are abnormal and the conclusion of Dr. H. Bücking and Colonel Romero that the rocks are normal andesites can not be considered justifiable.

Scoria from San Blas.—Both the microscopic and chemical evidence prove that this rock is a normal andesitic lava. It is unusually vesicular and even pumiceous but no evidence was obtained to suggest even a relation between this rock and the scoriæ from Miramar and Necochea.

General Conclusions and Summary

In the foregoing pages the attempt has been made to present the data of observation and experiment on the collection of rocks submitted to the writers for determination. Throughout the investigation but little attention has been given to the works of others on the same general problem. The present writers have not personally studied the rocks in the field and are not in a position, therefore, to discuss the more general problem of which the rock problem is only a part. In the descriptions attention has accordingly been directed to the facts of observation rather than to the possible theories of genesis which, without a definite basis of fact, become simply matters of opinion.

The most important facts noted during the present investigation are:

(1) The loess consists in large measure of volcanic and eruptive material. Siliceous volcanic glass is present in practically every specimen and may become so abundant that it constitutes 90 per cent of the whole. The minerals present are remarkably fresh and unaltered. The amount of argillaceous material present is relatively small in most of the specimens. These facts may be considered indicative of tremendous and widespread volcanic activity of the explosive type during or just preceding the formation of the loess. The variation in composition of the loess may be due in part to the effect of wind action on original tuffaceous deposits, the wind blowing the lighter matter farther away from the source, and thus producing a rough separation of the components in some instances. That volcanic action was widespread and not confined to one vent is evident from the enormous quantity of volcanic material in the loess.

(2) The specimens of tierra cocida are, for the most part, composed simply of loess fragments which have been indurated and reddened by heat action between 850° and 1,050°. Except for the red particles which have resulted from the oxidation of the iron in the argillaceous material of the loess, the loess and most of the tierra cocida are identical in general character and composition. Analyses of both are closely similar and, except for the high water content, might be mistaken for analyses of igneous rocks. This is well shown by specimens 263717, 263718, 263729 from Alvear, whose microscopic features, behavior on heating, sodium chloride content, and the chemical analyses of 263717 and 263729 are as nearly alike as can possibly be expected from such material and prove their original

identity conclusively. Under the title "tierra cocida" specimen 263710 has been included. It is, however, simply a loess rich in limonite, which forms the cementing material and renders the fragments slightly harder and more resistant than the adjacent loess.

Specimen 263731 has also been labelled "tierra cocida," but it belongs strictly to the melted scoriæ.

THE SCORIÆ

These rocks are the most interesting specimens in the collection and have been the subject of much discussion in the literature. They are abnormal in type and do not agree with any known eruptive rock or lava in their microscopic features. They contain fragments of various minerals (quartz, plagioclase, pyroxene, magnetite) embedded in a streaky glass base, out of which pyroxene microlites, different in composition from the large pyroxene fragments, have crystallized at certain points. The composition of the plagioclase fragments is not constant and in extreme cases may pass in the same thin section from oligoclase in one grain to labradorite in an adjacent grain. Zonal structure is present in some of the grains and these may then be broken across so that the different zones are in contact with the glass. The feldspars show indications, moreover, of resorption by the molten glass base and were evidently not crystallized from it as they are in a normal lava. (Pl. 7, *a* and pl. 8, *a*.) Practically the only microlites which have crystallized from the glass have the optical properties of a pyroxene which is of a different color, refractive index, and composition from the larger fragmental pyroxenes. The glass base itself is streaky and variable in composition, as is shown by the variation in its refractive index from point to point. ($n = 1.51$ to 1.56 and above.) Variations of this magnitude in the glass base of a normal lava have not been recorded. The minerals occurring as fragments in the scoriæ are practically identical with those observed in the loess, both as to kind, size, and composition. The melted loess products obtained by heating charges in the electric furnace resemble the scoriæ in all details except for the degree of oxidation of the iron; with large masses products were obtained in which the iron was less oxidized and at the center of large lumps were practically identical with the scoriæ. The scoriæ are not, in general, of the same composition as the loess immediately adjoining them and behave differently on being heated to high temperatures. (Specimen 263721.) This proves that part of the scoriæ at least were not formed in situ from the adjacent loess but have been transported to their present position. No zone of transition between the scoriæ and the loess was observed; in view of the high temperature to which the scoriæ must have been heated (1,050° or above) and the ease with which the loess is reddened (at 800° and above), this unaltered condition of the loess is another proof that these particular scoriæ were not formed in situ. The scoriæ of specimen 263731 do contain, however, in some of the vesicles red baked loess, which, in turn, is of a different composition from the friable brown loess adhering to other parts of the same specimen. This indicates again transportation of the scoriæ; also that at some period in their formation these scoriæ came in contact with the loess and that the temperature at that time was between 850° and 1,050°. No evidence was found in this specimen that the scoria had melted down the loess.

Taken as a whole the evidence recorded above proves that the scoriæ are not nórmal volcanic scoriæ. They are not lava in the ordinary sense of the word. But they have been melted down under conditions which protected them from oxidation; they were not melted down, in short, in the open air, otherwise the iron oxide would have passed largely into red hematite as in all the experiments cited above. The temperatures and quantity of heat required for melting the large masses of Necochea scoriæ postulate long-continued heating at a very high temperature, much higher, in fact, than is possible in the open air under ordinary conditions. This fact, together with the observed lack of oxidation of the scoriæ, precludes the possibility that they have been formed by the melting down of loess by bonfires or any type of fire in the open air.

The microscopic and thermal evidence practically proves, however, that the scoriæ have been produced by the melting down of an original clastic material which resembled in all its details the loess of this region. The observed facts indicate, in brief, that the scoriæ are simply fused loess, melted under conditions which protected the molten mass from oxidation.

In this connection the relatively local distribution of the scoriæ near the coast is significant. Had the scoriæ been transported from the far West their size and number would naturally increase in that direction, but the field observations show that the opposite is the case.

In seeking for a possible explanation of these phenomena and, in particular, of the genesis of the scoriæ, the writers have been forced to adopt the following hypothesis as the only reasonable one in view of the evidence at hand. This is presented, not as an established theory, but only as a tentative hypothesis which needs further verification but which accounts satisfactorily for the observed facts. According to this hypothesis the loess formation was intruded by igneous masses which melted down the adjacent loess and formed the present black scoriæ. These intrusions may have been submarine or beneath the land area. In either case oxidation would not have been serious, although a submarine extrusion might favor less oxidation and more pronounced vesicular character of the

scoriæ than a subaerial extrusion. In view of the exceedingly large
amount of volcanic glass and minerals of igneous origin in the loess
of this region, the assumption that volcanic action has been directly
responsible for the formation of these scoriæ and also of the tierra
cocida, in the manner suggested above, is not unreasonable. It
is surprising, however, that the present collection does not contain
any specimens of normal lava from either Necochea or Miramar.
This may possibly be due to the fact that the collection is a small
one and probably does not include all the rock types which occur in
these localities; or it may be that the volcanic extrusion was of the
explosive type, whereby the lava (possibly siliceous in character and
largely glassy) was shattered and reduced to dust, which fell to the
surface as volcanic ash and now constitutes an integral part of the
loess formation. Under these conditions the cooler, viscous, melted
loess fragments would remain intact and be ejected as scoriæ and
resist attrition and breaking down more effectively than the shattered volcanic lava.

Similar contact phenomena between lava intrusions and adjacent
rhyolite pumice breccia have been observed in Nevada by Professor
Iddings.[1] There basaltic lava was plainly visible and the mode of
formation of the contact scoriæ was obvious. The broken mineral
fragments occurred embedded in the glassy base which, in some of
the sections, still showed the brecciated character of the original
material. These relations are clearly stated in the following paragraph from the general description of the rocks from this region by
Professor Iddings in the monograph cited above (p. 183):

"Thin section 200 is the most interesting of all the alteration
products, on account of its undoubted relations to the basalt and its
higher degree of metamorphism; it is traceable directly to the same
deposit of pumice as 199, and lies in apparently undisturbed layers
directly over basalt, which did not in this instance reach the surface,
but thoroughly altered the overlying pumice, breaking through it
lower down the slope. In thin section it is a whitish gray, fine-
grained breccia of about the same grain as 199. Under the microscope the porphyritical crystals are seen to be angular fragments of
quartz, sanidine, and plagioclase of the same size and abundance as
those in the last-named section; pyroxene, however, is wanting and
only a little biotite is present, besides a single grain of garnet. The
groundmass has retained its brecciated character, though the pumice
fragments have lost their original form and appear to merge into one
another; but the degree of crystallization is far more advanced,
hardly any portion of it being without influence on polarized light.

[1] See Arnold Hague, Geology of the Eureka District, Nevada. *U. S. Geological Survey Monographs*, No. 20, 381–385, 1892.

As a natural result of its brecciated character the structure is most varied, which is the more pronounced between crossed nicols. It is partly spherulitic and axiolitic and partly cryptocrystalline and in places it is microcrystalline in irregular grains."

In many respects this description might serve for the thin sections of the Miramar and Necochea scoriæ. Similar irregular broken fragments of quartz, plagioclase, and other minerals are present and the groundmass is variable both in composition and in degree of crystallization. The hypothesis suggested above for the genesis of the scoriæ of Necochea and Miramar is therefore not new to geology and is without question a probable working hypothesis for rocks of a similar nature in any other part of the world.

Petrographic-Microscopic Examination of Bones Collected by Doctor Hrdlička

The writers received in addition to the above collection of rocks a small collection of bones with the request that their mineral composition be determined so far as possible. The specimens were examined accordingly in powder form and no attention was given to the structural features of the bones. In many of the bones fine mineral particles from the adjacent loess, in which they probably occurred, were observed but, as these minerals bear no relation to the alteration of the bones, their presence is not recorded in the descriptions below.

Practically only one type of alteration was observed. The cryptocrystalline bone substance is replaced by a mixture of micro-crystalline calcite and of a weakly-to-medium birefracting substance of refractive index about 1.61 and resembling in appearance the mineral described under specimen 263738 above. In some of the specimens the calcite is not present and the weakly birefracting substance is proportionately more abundant. In all of the specimens a considerable amount of fine, low-refracting, often isotropic or cryptocrystalline, material occurs but is too fine for satisfactory determination. In the following paragraphs the results of the examinations of the powdered specimens of bone are recorded briefly.

The conclusions which may be indicated by these observations have probably been given in the foregoing Hrdlička-Willis report, which the present writers have not seen.

No. 263748. Specimen label. " 'Fossil' man. Human bones from the Necochea skeleton."

In the powder of this bone fine, microcrystalline calcite is abundant. The calcite is coarser-grained in this specimen than in any of the other bones in the collection. Grains of a weakly-to-medium birefracting substance, usually pale-yellow in transmitted light and of average refractive index about 1.61, are common and have evidently resulted from the alteration of the original bone substance. In optical properties this substance resembles that described under specimen 263738. Fine grains of an isotropic, low-refracting substance also occur but are too fine for identification.

No. 263749. Specimen label. "*Weathered modern bone from playa of 'fossil man,' near Laguna Malacara, north of Necochea.*"

This bone contains abundant cryptocrystalline calcite which has evidently replaced much of the original bone substance. The weakly birefracting substance, noted above and probably phosphatic in composition, is also present in considerable quantities.

No. 263753. Specimen label. "*Cow, very recent; exposed to elements; lower jaw. Playa Peralta, near Mar del Plata.*"

In this specimen no calcite was observed. The material consists chiefly of a cryptocrystalline, weakly birefracting, low-refracting substance which is probably slightly altered bone substance. Evidently this bone has suffered but slight alteration.

No. 263754. Specimen label. "*Rib. Necochea 'fossil' man.*"

Contains both cryptocrystalline calcite and the weakly birefracting substance noted above. Has evidently been altered considerably.

No. 263755. Specimen label. "*La Tigra skull.*"

In powder form this bone closely resembles the foregoing. In both specimens the calcite is evidently a replacement product.

No. 263756. Specimen label. "*Ovejero. Skull No. 1.*"

Practically no calcite was observed in this specimen. The powder consists largely of a fine cryptocrystalline, weakly birefracting, low-refracting substance which is probably bone substance. The material is evidently not highly altered.

No. 263757. Specimen label. "*Fontezuelas skull.*"

Contains both cryptocrystalline calcite and the weakly birefracting phosphatic material, besides a lower-refracting isotropic substance. This bone has obviously suffered considerable change.

No. 263758. Specimen label. "*Homo pampæus. Necochea.*"

Resembles 263755 closely and has evidently suffered the same kind of change.

No. 263761. Specimen label. "*Sea lion; very recent. Punta Mogote.*"

But very little calcite was observed in this specimen and was then associated with yellow, iron-stained argillaceous material. A weakly birefracting substance not unlike that described in many of the specimens above constitutes the major part of the powder.

CARNEGIE INSTITUTION OF WASHINGTON,
    Geophysical Laboratory, Washington, D. C.

VI. PECULIAR STONE INDUSTRIES OF THE ARGENTINE COAST

By Aleš Hrdlička

HISTORICAL ACCOUNT

THE "SPLIT-STONE" INDUSTRY

During 1908, while studying the sedimentary formations of the coast of the Province of Buenos Aires, Professor Ameghino discovered certain peculiar stone implements, which he regarded as of a hitherto unknown type; their seemingly primitive form and especially their apparent association with earlier geologic deposits led him to the conclusion that they are the work of a geologically ancient man of this region, assigned by him to the Pliocene.

The first report of this discovery made by Ameghino appeared in 1909.[1] Referring to Punta Porvenir, a point on the coast a few miles south of Mar del Plata, he says:

"This locality, the mammal fauna of which indicates the upper part of the Ensenadean or the lowest portion of the Bonaerean formation, is of special importance, on account of the quantity of fossil bones contained in the less compact superficial sand, and because of the proof that this accumulation of bones is due to the man of those times. . . .

"This tongue of land was at that epoch a seashore site (*paradero*) of man. I collected there the carapace of a *Sclerocalyptus pseudornatus*, which was found standing vertical, resting on the caudal end, with the dorsal aspect toward the sea and the ventral concavity toward the west, looking as if it had been made to serve as a shelter against the sea winds. The interior of this carapace contained no skeletal parts of the animal, but there were bones of small ruminants, parted longitudinally, and other extraneous remains, while the border of the posterior aperture of the carapace, on which it rested, shows artificial cuts. About the carapace, to a rather considerable distance, were found artificially split bones of mammals, burned bones, marine shells which appeared to have been subjected to the action of fire, and very crude stone implements of an unknown type."

---

[1] Ameghino, F., Las formaciones sedimentarias de la región litoral de Mar del Plata y Chapalmalán; in *Anales del Museo Nacional de Buenos Aires*, XVII (ser. iii, t. x), 1909, pp. 343–428.

On page 398 of the same report Professor Ameghino returns to the subject of these worked stones and expresses the view that "The larger pebbles were utilized by the man of that epoch [Inter-Ensenadean], giving origin to a stone industry entirely distinct from any of those known up to date. This industry is in certain respects more primitive than that of the eoliths of Europe."

In April, 1910, the same author published an article devoted entirely to the "New Stone Industry." [1] The principal parts of this report are here quoted.

In 1908, at Mar del Plata, "I had the good fortune to find an ancient stone industry different from all those hitherto known. . . .

"This industry comes from the inferior Pampean and from the middle part of the Ensenadean, i. e., the eolo-marine strata corresponding to the Inter-Ensenadean marine transgression . . .

"It is in these eolo-marine strata that is found the débris of *Homo pampæus*, and it is also from these same strata that the stone objects here dealt with are derived. It is therefore the stone industry of the *Homo pampæus*, who at this epoch inhabited the seashore. These stone objects are nearly always isolated, and lay almost invariably on the surface of the eolo-marine bed from which they have become exposed by the denuding action of water during a period of thousands of years."

However, not quite all the implements gathered by Ameghino lay on the surface of the eolo-marine Inter-Ensenadean strata; "there were also found such as were still inclosed in the original deposit, and among those that were already loose there are some which still retain a strongly adhering, fine and often very hard grit, characteristic of these deposits."

As to the material from which these stone objects were made, it "consists [p. 190] of rolled and elongated pebbles of quartz, porphyry, basalt, phonolith, and other eruptive rocks, which man gathered from the seashore at low tide. These are absolutely foreign to the country and to-day are not found except in the Inter-Ensenadean layer. The material is entirely similar to that which constitutes the great formation of rolled pebbles that covers the surface of Patagonia, and without doubt a strong marine current which ran along the coast at that time transported these pebbles from Patagonia up to Mar del Plata."

As to the characteristics of this stone industry, Ameghino still considers it (p. 192) "different from all those that are known."

In the way of further information about the locality of the finds, Ameghino states (p. 192) that—

"Mar del Plata is a point or peninsula formed by a heavy stratum of Paleozoic quartzite which projects into the sea. This mass is

---

[1] Ameghino, F., Une nouvelle industrie lithique: L'industrie de la pierre fendue dans le Tertiare de la région littorale au sud de Mar del Plata; in *Anales del Museo Nacional de Buenos Aires*, xx (ser. iii, t. xiii), 1911, pp. 189–204 (separate, 1910).

covered by sedimentary deposits consisting of red Pampean and pre-Pampean (Araucanean) clays, and is exposed only at a number of points of limited extent. This coarse-grained quartzite is the result of the transformation of sedimentary deposits of coarse sand and gravel and presents a texture and density which make dressing it impossible. Man who in former times inhabited this locality was not able, therefore, to employ this material for the manufacture of his implements.

"But at the epoch of the Inter-Ensenadean transgression the sea threw on the beach water-worn pebbles which the marine currents brought from the coast of Patagonia. These pebbles fractured with greater facility.

"The *Homo pampæus* probably commenced to gather these stones and to break them between two blocks of quartzite, in order to utilize the pointed and edged chips which resulted. Later, and with experience, there came to him the idea that these pebbles could be fashioned in a more uniform manner by making a cutting edge at one of their extremities. Not knowing true flaking by percussion, but only breaking by means of strokes with a stone hammer and with the help of a block of quartzite employed as an anvil, he tried, probably, to split the pebbles, supporting them on the anvil-stone. He attempted this splitting not as in simple breaking, but by strokes at one end of the long axis of the pebble."

The technique of making the implements Ameghino explains as follows (p. 193):

"I shall call the two ends of the long axis of the pebbles its two poles. That placed on the anvil-stone was the inferior pole, while the other, destined to receive the blows of the hammer, was the superior one. To obtain the desired instruments, the man made a selection from among the pebbles, etc., always utilizing the more elongated and flattened ones, one extremity of which was to be held by the hand, while the other was to be fashioned to a cutting edge. The larger end, the one easier to hold in the hand, was the inferior pole, by which the pebble was placed upright on the block of quartzite. The other end, which pointed upward, was the superior pole, on which the operator directed blows until he obtained the form he desired."

At this point Ameghino explains the mode of production of the anvil-stones (pp. 193–194):

"Naturally, during the first trials at shaping the stone, the rounded butt of the pebble, which was placed on the block of quartzite, must have tended to slip thereon. Possibly in some blocks a natural depression insured a vertical position of the pebble in such a way that the stone could not slide, notwithstanding the blows of the hammer.

"From that moment man chose pieces of quartzite which appeared to him most suitable and cut into their surfaces small elliptic cavities

of different sizes, destined to receive the inferior pole of the pebbles
to be chipped, in order to keep them in position.   Holding the pebble
in place and upright with one band, he grasped the hammer with the
other and directed a sharp blow on the superior pole.   As a result of
this first blow there were detached from the superior pole or end two
flakes, smaller or larger, according to the force of the blow, one on
each of the opposite large faces of the pebble.   Almost invariably
one of these flakes was much larger than the other.   The two facets
or planes produced by the separation of the two flakes converged
upward, terminating in a small cutting edge.   Repeating the blows,
there was finally obtained at the superior pole of the pebble a transverse cutting edge."

As to the occurrence of similar types in other parts of the world,
the author says (p. 195):

"It is true that there have been found elsewhere some more or less
similar objects, but they are very rare, isolated, their manufacture
not constituting a veritable industry.   The form is accidental, and
the pieces were not obtained by the procedure that I have described,
which consists in cleaving the stone on an anvil with the aid of a
percussor.   This procedure is not, to my knowledge, as yet known
from any other region, and it is for this reason that I designated the
industry as the *split-stone industry* (*l'industrie de la pierre fendue.*)"

The newly discovered stone industry involves, in the opinion of
Ameghino (p. 195), "three characteristic pieces: The chisel or hatchet-
chisel with a transverse cutting edge, which is the instrument desired;
and the two agents employed for its fabrication, namely, the anvil-
stone and the hammer."

Further details as to the characteristics of these three varieties of
stones are given as follows (p. 196):

"The hatchet-wedge or chisel is the simplest instrument that one
can imagine; very often a single blow on the superior pole of the
pebble sufficed to make it.   Notwithstanding this simplicity, however, the instrument presents a very large variety of forms, due
probably to the differences in shape, size, length, or thickness of the
pebbles employed, as well as to their dissimilarity of nature and
texture, from which it often resulted that they fractured in a different
manner or direction from that which the operator desired.   Often the
blow of the hammer not only detached one or two flakes from the
superior pole intended for the cutting edge, but the counter-shock of
the anvil also detached flakes from the inferior pole, destined for the
handle of the piece, and in consequence the implement occasionally
remained unutilized.   At other times the blow of the hammer split
the pebble from one end to the other, or crushed it, reducing it to useless fragments.

"The hatchet-chisel [p. 197] was an instrument for all uses; it served as a knife for cutting, as a wedge or hatchet for breaking the bones, as chisel, scraper, rasp, etc. When the edge became dull by usage it was revived by retouching, and when the wear became so great that the edge could no more be repaired the stone was utilized as a hammer. The size of this implement is variable; the smallest are no longer than 2 or 3 cm.; those of medium size, more abundant, measure from 4 to 6 cm.; the larger ones are from 6 to 8 cm., and some examples attain 10 cm. in length."

As to the anvil-stones, they (p. 198) "present so great a variety of forms that it can be said there are no two alike. Some are flat, almost like slabs; others are flat but very thick; others are circular in contour and flattened; others are rounded, and still others elongated, quadrate, ovoid, cylindrical, conical, etc. Some are nothing but angular blocks resulting from the natural breakage of the stone, while others show wear or even rolling by water. Some, especially among the smallest, have no more than a single cavity, but others have several, their number extending to more than a score. Sometimes one of the faces of the anvil-stone is slightly concave and much worn, as if some very hard substance had been triturated upon it. Their size is also variable, the smallest measuring not more than 6 to 7 cm. in diameter, while the larger ones reach considerable dimensions. One of the largest and most notable was found by Carlos Ameghino at Punta Mogote; I consider it a monument of its epoch. It is a nearly rectangular block measuring 25 cm. in length, 15 cm. in breadth by the same in height, and carrying some two score of cavities distributed over nearly all its surfaces. At Punta Porvenir I saw still interred in the Pampean earth, a large block of quartzite in the form of a slab, of which the part that protruded above the earth had more than half a square meter of surface and showed its flat upper part covered with similar cavities.   .   .   .

"The hammers are rolled pebbles of very hard stone whose elongated form permitted easy grasping by one extremity, and striking with the other the pebbles to be shaped, which were steadied with one hand in the hollows made in the anvils."

Besides the presence of the three above-described classes of stone utensils, the hatchet-wedge or chisel, the anvil-stone, and the hammer, there are according to the author, two other incontestable proofs of the special technique which he outlines (p. 201):

"The first is, that nearly all the hatchet-chisels present on the end opposite that of the edge a small surface showing characteristic traces of bruising, indirect results of blows of the hammer; there is the clearest evidence that these contusions were produced by the counter-shocks of the anvils on the surface of these inferior ends of the pebbles

placed in the cavities of the anvil-stones. The second proof consists
of the presence on stones, split from end to end, of two conchoid
facets, one at each end, without a transverse interruption between
their fields of irradiation."

In conclusion, Professor Ameghino declares (p. 203):

"The facts shown seem to me to be more than sufficient to justify
my first affirmation that we are in the presence of a new stone
industry."

Some attention is given to minor worked stone objects, flakes,
etc. (pp. 203–204):

"From the fabrication of this hatchet-chisel implement there
resulted, as was natural, a very large number of flakes of all forms,
which were utilized for cutting, scraping, or perforating, and on which
use has produced characteristic wear and defects which often give
these flakes interesting forms."

No mention is made of the numerous quartzite implements, etc.,
which occur in the same localities.

In a still more recent publication, Ameghino[1] makes further remarks
on the stone industry under consideration. He speaks of (p. 23) "the
fireplaces and crude worked stones which our faraway ancestors left
buried in the Miocene and Pliocene layers of Monte Hermoso, Chapadmalal, Mar del Plata, and Necochea." And again (p. 24) he reiterates:
"The stone industry of the *Homo pampæus* consists of oblong pebbles chipped at one extremity and of an aspect still more primitive
than that of the eoliths of Europe."

THE "BROKEN-STONE" INDUSTRY

In an article published on the occasion of the meeting of the
American International Scientific Congress in Buenos Aires, in July,
1910,[2] Ameghino reasserts his beliefs as to the stone industry previously described by him, and in addition reports still more primitive
and ancient worked stones from Monte Hermoso. The principal parts
of this last report are given below:

"It is only a couple of months ago that, in announcing the primitive split-stone industry, characteristic of the Middle Pliocene of the
Atlantic coast south of Mar del Plata, I said that this rudimentary
industry should have been preceded by another, showing the part-
ing of pebbles by knocking one against another, for the purpose of
utilizing the pointed and sharp fragments resulting from the separation.

[1] Ameghino, F., Geología, paleogeografía, paleontología, antropología de la República Argentina.
Estudio publicado en el Número Extraordinario de La Nación (Buenos Aires), del 25 de Mayo de 1910.
Separate, pp. 1–26.

[2] Ameghino, F., La industria de la piedra quebrada en el mioceno superior de Monte Hermoso. Congréso
Científico Internacional Americano, Buenos Aires, 1910, pp. 1–5.

"I have just succeeded in encountering this more ancient and more primitive industry which I will call *The Broken-stone Industry* (*industria de la piedra quebrada*).

"In 1889 I described and photographed a fragment of stone which I had found two years before at Monte Hermoso and recognized its primitive form, but without forming an exact notion as to the character of the industry of which it formed a part.

"Toward the end of the last of May and during the first half of June, I visited the Atlantic coast of Mar del Plata and farther south, accompanying the North American delegates, Messrs. Hrdlička and Bailey Willis, with the object of showing them the distinct deposits which yielded remains of fossil man or vestiges of his primitive industry.

"On the 11th of June, in the afternoon, we visited Monte Hermoso, where with difficulty we were able to stay a couple of hours.

"I found the barrancas of the locality modified into a form very distinct from that which I have known.

"The deposits of sands and sandy ground which rest above the Hermosean and constitute the Puelchean stratum, formerly visible over a small space of only about 40 meters, now appear exposed along the barranca for several hundred meters and also to a greater extent vertically.

"In the superior part of this formation of stratified sands I discovered a considerable number of fragments of quartzite of the most varied and irregular forms, all or nearly all angular and with cutting edges, from among which, the time being so short, I was able to collect only a small series.

"On examination these fragments proved to be those of water-worn pebbles of quartzite, derived from the nearby Sierra de la Ventana, which were broken by knocking strongly one against the other or with one on top of the other, without any determined direction.   This is the most primitive stone industry of which I have any knowledge, and I can not imagine anything more simple.

"The larger number of these fragments preserve still on one or two of their faces the natural surface of the rolled pebble, and on this surface are always observed scratches, bruises, abrasions, dints, etc., produced by strong and repeated blows given with other stones.   These signs of percussion are so fresh and so plain that they appear as of yesterday.

"The borders of these broken stones terminate in slender and sharp edges, but sometimes present irregularities, denticulation, and other effects produced by use.

"This industry is without doubt still more primitive than that of the eoliths, for the latter show retouching, either for sharpening the edges or to facilitate the accommodation of the instrument to the hand, but in the broken quartzite from Monte Hermoso there is absolutely nothing similar.

"On the other hand, these broken quartzites, however rustic they may appear, are surely the work of man or his precursor, for there can not be opposed to them the objections which are being made to the eoliths. In this case there can be no question of pressure by the rocks, of shocks produced by stones driven by water or due to falling stones, because, I repeat, they are loose in the sand, and are all separated one from the other.

"It is my duty to say that I have seen Doctor Hrdlička gather similar objects, but I do not know how he interprets them nor have I asked him. I declare myself, therefore, solely responsible for the significance which I give to the material in question."

Criticisms by F. F. Outes.—Shortly after the first announcement by Ameghino of his discovery of the new "split-stone industry,"[1] F. F. Outes published an article [2] in which he announced numerous finds of similar specimens in the same and also in other localities along the coast. He reported in at least one instance the association of such stone objects as are described by Professor Ameghino, with implements, rejects, etc., of quartzite, and he opposed both the geologic antiquity which has been attributed to the worked stones as well as the supposed great primitiveness of the workmanship. The principal features of the communication are cited below.

Visiting the localities of the highly interesting new stone industry, says Outes: "I was easily able to gather 187 different specimens belonging to that industry, not only in the locality indicated to me with notable exactness by the distinguished geologist and traveler, Don Carlos Ameghino, but in four others similarly situated along the coast.

"The barranca which constitutes the left boundary of the mouth of the Arroyo Corrientes is formed in the larger part of Pampean loess and of eolic deposit of the present era, on both of which denudation has acted extensively.

"On the surface, distributed irregularly, isolated, or in small gullies, but never covered by either earth or sand, I have found 91 objects belonging to the primitive industry referred to by Professor Ameghino.

"I gathered 56 other pieces at Punta Porvenir, a little spur of quartzite rounded by the beach and nearly submerged when the waters are very high. Over a large part of this point, in its folds, is found a veneer of eolic deposit, identical in composition with that of the mouth of the Arroyo Corrientes and equally as much denuded.

---

[1] The terms "split" and "broken" as applied to these industries should not be confused.

[2] Outes F. F., Sobre una facies local de los instrumentos neolíticos Bonaerenses; in *Revista del Museo de La Plata*, XVI, Buenos Aires, 1909, pp. 319–339.

Furthermore, I have observed that in the upper level the Pampean surface corresponds, even more than at Arroyo Corrientes, to the type of detritic accumulation, for among its component elements are fine sand, triturated fragments of shells, and rolled pieces of loess of dark-gray color. Surrounded by precisely these materials was found the carapace [1] of *Sclerocalyptus pseudornatus* Ameghino.[2]

"All the specimens attributable to the supposed new industry were found, as at Arroyo Corrientes, distributed superficially.

"The third locality in the department of Pueyrredon is situated at the distance of approximately a kilometer from the left bank of the Arroyo Chapadmalal. On the sand which covers the surface of the elevated platform, formed by oceanic erosion, which constitutes there the Bonaerean Atlantic coast, or distributed superficially over smaller areas where the vegetal soil is wanting and the sand is being reduced (in place of which there appears a calcareous deposit, called *tosca*, which covers as it seems a large part of the region), I obtained 29 very characteristic examples of the worked stones. In this case the special circumstances of the find are of great importance. The objects referred to were not isolated, as in the two previously mentioned localities, but associated and moreover mixed with a multitude of examples of flakes, knives, scrapers, etc., made of quartzite, or flint, and belonging to the well-known lithic industry, which is so little primitive in its characteristics that it occurs with considerable frequency in nearly all the Bonaerean culture-sites, even in those on the very surface of the land, as well as in those enveloped by the vegetal soil, especially along the borders of streams and on lake shores.[3]

"Finally, there are two other localities where these specimens occur in the department of General Alvarado, both on the right bank of the Arroyos Brusquitas and Durazno, respectively.

"In the former of these localities I found four isolated specimens on the sand which covered the surface of a small torrential gully or

---

[1 The Punta Porvenir specimen mentioned above by Ameghino.]

2 "The small excavation made [by Ameghino] in extracting the carapace of this *Sclerocalyptus pseudornatus* was still visible when I made my last visit to the locality in March of the present year and I was able to obtain samples of the soil which inclosed numerous isolated remaining plates from the carapace."

3 "Notwithstanding the bad weather and the misty and persistent rain, which formed an obstacle to my stay, I was able to gather on the great culture-site of which I speak, about 822 diverse objects: Flakes, knives, scrapers, and arrow points; but I did not find any fragment of pottery. Nevertheless, Don Carlos Ameghino told me that in other *paraderos* also near to the mouth of the Arroyo Chapadmalal, fragments of plain earthen vessels are sometimes found.

"The specimens which I gathered, nearly all worked on only one surface, belong, as I said above, to one of the most diffused neolithic industries in the Province of Buenos Aires and of which Dr. Florentino Ameghino made known many types and varieties (if a multitude of unstable forms can so be termed) in one of the most classical of his works (La antigüedad del hombre en El Plata, I, 213–267, Paris-Buenos Aires, 1880–1881). There is also an identity between the examples which form my large series and those that were described many years ago by Dr. Francisco P. Moreno (Noticias sobre antigüedas de los Indios del tiempo anterior á la conquista, etc., in *Boletin de la Academia Nacional de Ciencias de Córdoba*, I, Buenos Aires, 1874, pp. 130–149); and they are also identical with some mentioned by myself in a memoir published in 1897 (F. F. Outes, Los Querandíes, breve contribución al estudio de la etnografía argentina, 87–91 figuras 1–4, Buenos Aires, 1897)."

depression, that exists in the not very high barranca forming the coast, about 200 meters from the mouth of the Arroyo.

"From the other locality I obtained seven examples, which were also distributed superficially over the sand that covers in great quantities the right bank of the Arroyo at its mouth. With these pieces I found an interesting scraper of rude form of the type called "duckbill" by English archeologists, and further, two broken arrow points belonging to the same industry to which I referred in previous paragraphs.

"I believe that the objects described in this note [the chipped pebbles] belonged without doubt to the primitive stock of tools of the indigenous native of the Bonaerean time. The products in no way can be attributed to either natural or accidental causes . . . neither are the traces of workmanship, use, or retouching on these stones comparable with the apparent traces of such nature observed on the pseudo-eoliths; . . . nor, finally, can the specimens be attributed to the activities of those who actually live in these regions.

"I entertain no doubts on the subject of the antiquity of the material described and photographed in this note: It must be referred without exception to the neolithic period of these regions of South America.[1]

"All the specimens on the left bank of the Arroyo Corrientes were encountered superficially, and the same was true at Punta Porvenir.[2] In both localities I have removed the underlying deposits and have not found similar remains. On the other hand, at Chapadmalal and at the Arroyos Brusquitas and Durazno, all the objects came not only from the surface of the ground, but were also found mixed with implements and weapons of the pre-Spanish natives, representing the industry reported hitherto from nearly all the Bonaerean culture-sites covered by the vegetal earth, or exposed on the surface.

"The numerous objects of this last-named industry, gathered by me at Chapadmalal and in other localities of the department of Alvarado, present without exception the same luster and the same blunting of the edges as those described specially in this note— peculiarities which do not corroborate in any manner whatever a great antiquity, but are well explained by the polishing action of the sand carried by the waters or driven by the wind . . .

[1] In relation to Professor Ameghino's statements regarding the paleoethnologic importance of Punta Porvenir, Outes says: "It suffices to know that at Punta Porvenir the erosive agents have acted extensively; that the waters have moved the ground at all levels, and the wind has accumulated the detritic deposit of which I have spoken in the text. Hence it is probable, and a repeated examination of the terrane confirms my belief, that the fossils and diverse objects recovered from the 'looser upper sand' were not in an original deposit and that the suggestive picture of the primitive shelter described by Professor Ameghino . . . can be explained, without doing violence to the facts, by diverse accidental circumstances."]

[2] "However, supposing even that some of the specimens have been encountered buried in the ground, it would still be requisite to proceed with reserve, because of the very special character of all the localities, exposed to erosive agencies, which remove, transpose, and accumulate continually the earthy or sandy materials."

"The exhaustive examination which I made of the ground and of the objects associated in certain cases with the worked pebbles induces me to believe that these utilized or worked pebbles, gathered in the Bonaerean Atlantic littoral, constitute only a local phase of a certain portion of the tools of some of the neolithic native groups. Moreover, I incline to consider them contemporary with the rude implements and weapons of quartzite, shaped nearly always on only one surface, which appear to characterize the larger part of the more primitive neolithic stations, permanent or temporary. In my excursions I have found them not only in the departments of Pueyrredon and General Alvarado, but also on the coast of Necochea [1] and in the proximity of Puerto Belgrano." [2]

Outes has taken no notice of the anvil-stones.

Response to Outes's statements, by Ameghino.—To Outes's notes, cited above, Ameghino in his succeeding publication [3] answered as follows:

"A young archeologist, well known for his malevolence as well as for his obstinacy in defending the most impossible and paradoxical things, published about this industry a memoir filled with all sorts of inexactitudes. This young man had gone every year to Mar del Plata, had walked over the same localities and trodden upon the stones, without comprehending their significance. As soon, however, as my memoir appeared and with information obtained surreptitiously from those who accompanied me on my excursions, he went to Mar del Plata, gathered in the places that were indicated to him a certain number of specimens and at once thereon, without any serious examination of the question, declared that the case was that of neolithic implements (!), representing a local phase.

"Not possessing any geologic criterion, he mistook the Inter-Ensenadean beds veneering the ancient cliff for a detritic deposit of the present epoch; the Inter-Ensenadean marine strata, which underlie all the Superior Pampean and contain shells of extinct species, he considered recent accumulations on the way toward lapidification, whereas, on the contrary, they constitute an ancient formation on the way to destruction. The mammalian débris that are found in the eolo-marine deposit he regarded as having been brought out from the cliff against which this deposit is lying; but, as among

---

[1] "The specimens obtained in this locality were found at Punta Negra, on the surface of the continental flat, and also in another spot situated approximately 500 m. from the mouth of the Rio Quequen, partly covered by the movable sands of the dunes which there exist. In both cases, the worked pebbles were mixed with implements and weapons of the well-known recent industry to which I have referred in different parts of this memoir."

[2] "I gathered many examples over the surface at the foot of the Colina Doble, distant a few hundred meters from the military post, and I also found some isolated pieces in a *salitral* which exists on the road that leads from the last-named locality to Bahia Blanca."

[3] Une nouvelle industrie lithique. L'Industrie de la pierre fendue dans le Tertiare de la région littorale au sud de Mar del Plata, par Florentino Ameghino; in *Anales del Museo Nacional de Buenos Aires*, XX (ser. iii, t. XIII), 1911, pp. 189-192.

this débris there are whole or nearly whole carapaces of *Glypto-dontidæ* and articulated skeletons, the affirmation of this author resolves itself into one of those errors for which there is no excuse. Besides this, in these localities, the beds of the ancient cliff are completely sterile. And, moreover, this débris of mammals from the eolo-marine deposits is formed by species characteristic of the Ensenadean, without any vestige of a recent species. His complete ignorance of all these geologic and paleontologic questions is thus displayed in a very decided manner. Briefly, his malevolence, which perforce leads him to criticize everything, has resulted in filling his memoir on this ancient industry with errors so gross that they do not serve to honor him. To dwell more in detail on these errors, which one would say are the product of an infantile brain, would be a waste of time.

"There is, however, one point which prompts the following brief note on my part:

"The author in question criticises severely my statement that this industry is distinct from those existing to this day, and that to a certain degree it is more primitive than that of the eoliths. To demonstrate that what I have said is inexact, he enters into long considerations, with a large number of quotations which have no relation to the subject. Finally, he describes and photographs several of the implements to show their relation with others found in different regions, which he believes to be similar to those of Mar del Plata.

"According to these descriptions and the photographs with which they are accompanied, I perceive that the author has not appreciated the true character of this industry nor the technique of the fabrication, which is precisely that which distinguishes it from all other stone industries heretofore known, and as I have not said in what the novelty of this industry consisted, the result is that he has repeated the immortal combat of Don Quixote against the windmills."

So much for the published data relating to the "ancient stone industries" of the Argentine coast. The following pages contain the observations and views of the present writers on this highly interesting subject. In their work they have not been influenced materially by the publications cited, reliance being placed especially on personal observations in the field and on their own collections brought to Washington.

FIELD OBSERVATIONS

WORKED STONES OF REPUTED GEOLOGIC ANTIQUITY

The exploration, the results of which will be given in the following pages, was undertaken with eager expectations. Ameghino's publications on the strange ancient "split-stone" industry and on other finds from this very little known coast region, his personal information and enthusiasm on the subject, and the unquestionably peculiar characteristics of the archeologic specimens seen in his collection, impressed the writer considerably. It was soon recognized that all that was written or said on the subject could not be accepted, but the bulk of the data seemed of such importance that the visit to the regions which yielded the highly interesting specimens, especially in company with a geologist of experience, and with the promised presence of Professor Ameghino himself, was entered on with keen anticipations.

So far as collecting evidence and numerous specimens are concerned, the work was fortunate from the start; and, as time progressed, fact after fact appeared which threw light on the problems investigated different from and much more simple than that in which they were seen before. This was by no means changed later by the presence of Srs. Florentino and Carlos Ameghino, and the final conclusions reached by the Smithsonian expedition are completely at variance with the opinions held by these gentlemen.

The coast of Argentina, especially that of the Province of Buenos Aires, presents certain characteristic physical features found only rarely in other localities.

It is readily seen that the present coast line is very recent, that it is continually being changed by the action of the sea, and that a thousand years ago (not to speak of any greater length of time) it must have been much farther out, beyond the shallows that remain. As to the location of the coast line in the Pleistocene, or even earlier, there is no indication.

The flat or undulating surface of the interior, covered with sward, extends in some parts close to the sea, there ending abruptly in a more or less vertical wall or *barranca*. These bluffs, which range in height from 2 or 3 to more than 70 feet, are the result of the combined action of the sea wash and the crumbling down of masses of earth from the land facing the ocean.

At other points, parts of the surface of the land near the sea have been deprived by wind and water of the black vegetal soil and present smaller or larger barren, grayish stretches, in some instances sloping toward the sea, covered in varying degrees with sand, débris of tosca,[1] stones, triturated shells, etc.   The denudation by the elements

---

[1] Calcareous concretionary formation occurring at various depths in the loess; caliche.

has often been so great that the older geologic sediments are exposed, and bones of extinct species of animals lying in these sediments become more or less visible or even loose; in other instances, however, the erosion has been relatively slight, amounting to but a few inches below recent surface.

A third and most characteristic feature of the coast consists of the sand dunes, or *médanos*, which line the shore for great distances. They form a range of sand hills which, as the sea advances steadily and, in general, with considerable rapidity at the expense of the land, must be quite recent in their present location. This line of dunes varies from less than a mile to several miles in breadth and continues, with a few interruptions, from a short distance south of Mar del Plata to Bahia Blanca. The prevailing height of the individual dunes ranges from about 30 to 80 feet, but occasionally they are lower or higher. They are of various shapes, the conical and "hog-back" types predominating, differ considerably in bulk, and extend in many cases close to the beach. In some parts, as at Monte Hermoso, the sea front presents a barranca face surmounted by the médanos.

The sand dunes are of two principal varieties and the difference between them is of consequence archeologically. The first class, preponderant north of Monte Hermoso, are the barren, moving dunes, while the second consist of such sand hills as have become covered and more or less fixed by vegetation. It is the region of the barren médanos that is especially interesting anthropologically. In the fixed dunes whatever implements and other remains of aboriginal population there may be, lie buried within or under the sand and with rare exceptions escape observation. Among the barren and moving dunes, on the other hand, the force of the winds results in uncovering the implements and other remains, and these remain for a longer or shorter time exposed to view, so that they may be easily collected.

The barren dunes are shifted by the sand being blown from the slope exposed to the wind and falling down the opposite slope. On the exposed side the wind tends to remove all the sand down to the more resistant surface of the ground. If there are any stones, implements, or heavier human or animal remains anywhere in the sand or on the ground underneath, such objects sink down to, or remain in place on, the exposed harder surface, to be reburied, reexposed, and shifted from time to time as the wind currents assume different directions.

All the dunes connect at the base and inclose more or less extensive hollows. Some of these hollows are relatively shallow, circumscribed, and sandy. Other depressions are, however, much larger and deeper and often more irregular in form. In many instances these larger depressions connect at one extremity with the seashore, and their bottom in parts, or even in a large stretch reach to, or even somewhat into, the ground beneath the sand. The basal areas in the various depressions here referred to are sometimes called *playas*, a convenient term for the purpose, though more strictly applied to the beach only.

There are two distinct varieties of the dune-range playas, which may be distinguished by the color as the black and the gray. Most of the black are shallower than the gray, though the difference may be slight. They present level patches of closely packed fine sand and earth colored nearly black by manganese and possibly other mineral ingredients; the surface is often rich in archeologic specimens. These black playas are generally situated more inland, and owe their principal characteristics of form and color to water action. They represent the denser ground of the lowest parts of the dunes, or the top of the underlying soil, with additional material brought and deposited during rains. In heavier rains water in small quantities evidently accumulates over the surface of these patches, particularly of those that offer no easy outlet, and the mineral particles, as well as fine sand from the surrounding dunes, settle and form the black even surface. The amount of material thus deposited is generally small; yet it was found sufficient nearly to bury, in one instance, the skull of a viscacha, and in other cases to cover, in a degree, several stone flakes and implements. Generally, however, the stone objects and bones lie free upon the surface.

The second class of playas consists of the larger, sometimes extensive, irregular, denuded surfaces, similar to eroded areas occurring independently of sand dunes, as mentioned in the first part of this section, and containing débris of tosca, stones, shells, bones, etc., and also, in some localities, numerous pieces of scoria. In some places such large denuded patches show remnants, a few inches to more than 2 feet in height, of a former, comparatively recent surface, the rest of which has been removed by the action of the elements. In some instances the higher of such remnants are capped with darker earth, which represents, in all probability, the vegetal layer that has become covered by the sands. The gray floor itself belongs to older sediments and shows traces, in some localities rare, in others rather common, of skeletal remains of fossil animals, particularly the glyptodon and the scelidotherium. Most of these gray open playas are poor in specimens pertaining to man, although there may be sheltered nooks farther inland in which more of such objects will be brought to light in the future.

The archeologic remains found associated with the several above-mentioned features of the coast are, first, numerous stones with a few objects of other materials, showing man's handiwork; and, second, skeletal remains of man himself.

The worked stones consist of utensils, such as mealing- or grinding-stones, mostly in fragments; hammer-stones; peculiar anvil-stones (stones which show the effects of having served as supports on which other hard objects, probably stones, were worked); highly interesting implement-like chipped pebbles, of the types described by Ameghino and Outes, derived from hard pebbles of fluvial origin, which are found in large numbers along the shore in these localities; arrow points, scrapers, and nuclei of yellowish-white quartzite, brought to these regions from the inland hills; and a great many flakes and other rejects of manufacture. The smaller objects, in general, fall into two main classes distinguished as "white" and "black," the former proceeding from fragments of massive whitish quartzite, the latter from pebbles of jasper, quartzite, etc., ranging from black to various tints of red, brown, and yellow. (Pls. 9–12.)

These two classes of specimens—the light and the dark—were always found in association. On the playas, both black and gray, the worked stones and flakes, wherever they occurred, were invariably commingled. No single spot was found, and many were examined, where either the "white" or the "black" chipped stones existed alone. In the district of Mar del Plata the heavier objects, as mortars, pestles, mullers, and the hammer- and anvil-stones, are made from the coarse local quartzite, ledges of which are exposed in a number of places along the shore. In the more southern parts, quartzite is wanting and one finds occasionally hammers and anvil- stones made from stout pieces of tosca, utilized for want of better material. Now and then a smaller stone showing man's handiwork, of the Mar del Plata quartzite, will be found as far south as Necochea. The material of such specimens has undoubtedly been derived from the more northern locality.

The flaked stones and chips (particularly the black ones) are generally strewn over the surface of the playas, as they would occur on sites utilized by the natives for their shops. The depressions among the médanos, particularly the more sheltered and protected ones farther inland, were especially adapted for such a purpose. It is inferred that most of the implements made in these shops were carried away to be utilized inland, but a few, with the stones from which flakes were secured and with the refuse of the shaping work, remained on the ground. Some of the mealing stones and anvil-stones were found apparently in the exact places where they were last used, and often the flakage was more plentiful in the immediate vicinity of the latter than elsewhere. Of course, as the depres-

CAMPO PERALTA, NEAR MAR DEL PLATA

In the foreground are shown a number of worked stones which were gathered here.

sions shifted, being filled on one side and extended on the other by the changing sands, the native implement-maker moved his work place with them, and it is readily seen that in the course of time much of the surface of the ground underneath the sands would be supplied in this way with chips, nuclei, and rejectage, and these in turn would continue to be reexposed as new areas were uncovered by the winds.

There is nothing to indicate that either the "black" or the "white" flaked stones were brought in the worked state, accidentally or otherwise, to the sites where found. The proximity of the principal materials used—the quartzite in the north, the tosca in the south, and the dark pebbles on the adjacent beach—makes it practically certain that all of these materials were worked in the protected depressions among the sand dunes on the very spots where the numerous relics are now found. Had the few finished implements only been encountered on one or more of these playa floors, their presence might be regarded as due to accidental loss by hunters or other rovers of the pampas, but the hundreds of the flaked pebbles, the thousands of chips, and quantities of other forms of rejectage, strewn over practically all of the black and some portions of the gray playas, could not have been brought in and left by wayfarers from a distance.

The white quartzite, however, was, without question, brought in convenient masses from the low Sierra in the more western part of the province, and worked up at leisure among the médanos. A large nucleus of this stone was found by the writer near the Arroyo Corrientes, south of Mar del Plata, and some of smaller size were seen in other localities. It is plain that these are nuclei from which large pieces have been flaked, and thus is furnished clear proof of the importation and local utilization of this material. (Fig. 27.)

Of course, it is not assumed that all of both the "black" and the "white" stones showing human manipulation have been deposited at the precise level and in the identical spots at which they are found to-day. Some may have sunk from higher levels, as the lighter soil ingredients were removed by the wind and perhaps also by water, and some of the lighter flakes may have been moved directly by these agencies.

In rare instances only was a worked stone found imbedded in the surface of a playa. A careful search directed particularly to this phase of the subject resulted in the discovery of only five chipped pieces, three "black" and two "white," partly buried. All of these were observed in the black playas, in one of which there was also partly interred (nothing exposed except the teeth) the skull of a modern viscacha. Yet it is readily conceivable that specimens may be even entirely covered, and that not merely in the surface of the black, but also in that of the gray, playas, for cattle, horses, ostriches (rheas) and other animals occasionally visit these depressions, and, especially after rains, may press small stones into the ground; or rain water and the wind may contribute, by means of the material which they carry, toward the same end.   On the playas south of Punta

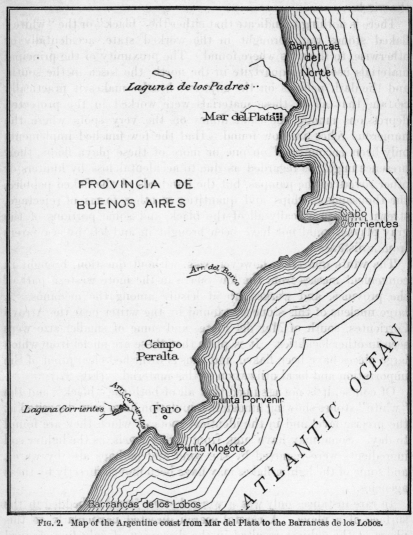

FIG. 2.   Map of the Argentine coast from Mar del Plata to the Barrancas de los Lobos.

Mogote, Mr. Willis and the writer observed several worked stones, as well as some recent bones, banked on the windward side with fine wind-blown material of the same color and apparently of the same geologic nature as the deposits underneath.   After a rain such accumulations might easily harden and thus appear as constituent parts of the older ground on which they are formed.

ANVIL-STONES

a, On grassy surface (apparently in situ) at Campo Peralta, south of Mar del Plata.
b, On denuded surface, near the sea, in vicinity of Arroyo Corrientes. Here is seen also refuse of
    pebble-stone flaking, with numerous unused pebbles, bones of seals, shells, and other objects.
c, A small collection from an area of less than an acre on an elevation just north of Arroyo Corrientes.

It is also highly probable that in exceptional instances a smaller chip or implement, moved by running water, wind, or gravity, is lodged in a hole or a depression where it eventually becomes covered by alluvial or eolic materials. Examples illustrating this were observed on the slopes of the Campo Peralta and will probably be reported from time to time from other localities. Similar agencies may explain the presence, mentioned by Professor Ameghino, of two black stones buried near the carapace of a glyptodon, on the small sloping denuded Punta Porvenir, which is about a mile distant from the Campo Peralta. (See map, fig. 2.)

In at least two localities worked stones were found on or in the black vegetal surface soil outside of the playas. One of these was the Campo Peralta, just south of Mar del Plata, and the other the north bank of the Rio Quequen, near the mouth of the stream, in the neighborhood of Necochea.

On the Campo Peralta the writer found several larger anvil-stones in the grass-covered, undenuded and hitherto undisturbed part of the surface. The stones lay more or less buried in the vegetal soil and, barring one or two exceptions, with the pitted surface upward. Some were near and some distant from the denuded part of the playa, on which were found numerous worked stones of all varieties. The difference in level between the sward-covered and more inland part of the playa and the uppermost portions of its denuded surface, rich in flaked stones, chips, etc., was only slight, not more apparently than a few inches.

Some of the stones observed in situ on the grass-covered black soil were photographed before removal (see pl. 10). When they were lifted, it was seen that the lighter ones were undergrown with grass roots and blanched grass, which made it appear at first sight as if the stones had been placed there recently; but on examination of other, unworked stones on the same surface, and also elsewhere, it was found that grass invariably forms such roots and etiolated stems under stones that are not very heavy or very large or deeply buried. On being shown these anvil-stones in the grass, Professor Ameghino surmised that they had been carried there by boys, ranch hands, or excursionists; but on careful consideration of the case this hypothesis, as applied to at least the majority of the specimens, seemed quite improbable. The locality is as yet without settlers. A single family lives in a depression half a mile away, but the children of this family knew nothing of the stones, which are not of a nature to attract ordinary curiosity. The place is distant from Mar del Plata and is not near the beach or other places where excursionists are likely to roam. Were it visited at all, it is reasonable to assume that the stone implements on the denuded part of the flat would have been taken or scattered. Furthermore, some of the anvil-stones were too heavy to be carried away easily by boys, and ranch hands would not be likely to take them from the barrens and scatter them over the pasture. It is much more probable that at least some of these stones remain to-day on the identical spots where they were left by the natives who used them.

An additional fact which may be mentioned in this connection is the find on the more inland portion of the denuded part of the Campo Peralta of two accumulations or arrangements of larger unworked stones, which showed man's agency. One of these was in the shape of a right angle and the other formed a small mound. The latter in appearance suggested a grave-covering, but on excavation no confirmation of this theory was discovered. A large and well-made metate and other stone utensils were placed there, in all probability by the original inhabitants, or those who worked the "black" as well as the "white" stones found in the vicinity. These artificial stone piles served to indicate even better than did the general level of the ground about them the small amount of denudation that has taken place on the spot since their construction. (Pl. 11.)

The second locality where worked stones were actually found by the writer in the black surface soil, was the top of the high north bank of the Rio Quequen, near Necochea. This locality yielded only small specimens, but a large quartz implement that might have been used as a hand ax was found deep in the ground in digging a well a few rods away. This specimen is in Professor Ameghino's hands. A very large quartzite object of the same type, but slightly cruder, was gathered by the writer from one of the black playas about 20 miles to the northward. Articles of stone were by no means rare in the surface soil in the locality under consideration, and were said by the writer's guide, the gardener employed by Professor Ameghino to collect antiquities in that neighborhood, to have been even more common formerly. Many have been exposed by wagons passing over and breaking the ground. In this locality there is no denuded playa or exposed old surface; yet the specimens here collected are identical in their characteristics with those from the playas among the sand dunes.

A special variety of flaked stones was discovered at Monte Hermoso. The writer found that the Monte Hermosean formation exposed in the now famous barranca was covered by more recent material. On the old formation rests a layer of volcanic ash, then some stratified sand, while the highest part is formed of a stratum of gravelly sand, continuous with the base of the sand dune situated above and a little farther inland from the edge of the barranca. The last-named surface material is unstratified and somewhat packed, but in no way consolidated, and bears every evidence of being very recent. It crumbles over the clearly marked, ancient Monte Hermosean deposit, and in

CAMPO PERALTA, NEAR MAR DEL PLATA

In the foreground are shown a number of stones, worked and unworked, many of them, including all in the right half of the illustration, in situ.

falling down becomes here and there lodged on the shelves or in the depressions of the old formation. In common with Professor Ameghino the writer found in such crumbled-down material some large irregular and entirely fresh-looking fragments or chips of quartzite, which indicate plainly the work of man. One of the heavier fragments had been employed as a hammer, portions of the periphery being distinctly worn by use. In addition, he found on one of the upper ledges a well-finished scraper of jasper. Subsequently he extracted a number of quartzite chips or fragments from the more gravelly part of the uppermost deposit itself, within 18 inches of the surface. No "black" or "white" material and no anvil-stones were seen in the neighborhood, but the visit was too short to determine their absence. It is probable, however, that such specimens are wanting entirely or are very rare, since in this part of the coast there is marked absence of the hard pebbles which were utilized so freely farther north and to some extent also farther south, near Bahia Blanca, by the Argentine natives.

From Monte Hermoso the writer proceeded to the southern limits of the Province of Buenos Aires and to northern Patagonia. Archeologic finds here also were quite numerous, and some discoveries were made which are of special importance in their bearing on the antiquity of the peculiar "black" stone "implements" of the more northern part of the Argentine coast.

These finds were made in and near the valley of the Rio Negro. In these regions, "black" pebbles comparable in size to those of the more northern parts of the coast are rare on the surface but not totally absent, and were utilized by the natives. In general, the stone work of this territory differs from that farther north in the profusion of chipped blades, arrow points, spear points, and drills. There are also stone mortars, pestles and mullers, and a peculiar type of ax. Yet, with all this, one finds occasionally a "black" flaked stone exactly resembling those of the neighborhood of Mar del Plata, Miramar, or Necochea. Several such specimens were collected at San Xavier (a locality well inland), in the neighborhood of Viedma (see fig. 39), and among the coast sand dunes near San Blas. A particularly important find, however, was that of two anvil-stones, absolutely identical in character with those of the coast of the Province of Buenos Aires, on the surface of the alluvium in the confines of a former settlement of the Rio Negro Valley natives, about 4 miles south of Viedma. Here all antiquity is out of the question, for the alluvial deposits of the Rio Negro, particularly those on the surface, are very recent. Furthermore, the neighborhood has yielded a collection of Indian skeletons and a large well-made stone mortar. Over the site were scattered numerous flakes and fragments of jasper of different colors, some of which at least were derived from pebbles.

It thus appears that the utilization of suitable pebbles, occasionally in the same way as at more northern points on the coast, and also of anvil-stones, can not be regarded as characteristic of any very ancient culture.   They must have been made and used by the Indians occupying some parts of the Argentine coast up to and probably even in historic times.

A word remains to be said as to pottery.   Potsherds are very rare along the coast from Mar del Plata to Bahia Blanca; nevertheless, a few specimens were found by the writer, these on the same black playas, among the sand dunes, with "white" and "black" chips, flakes, and implements.   The fragments are all of rather thin cooking vessels, without glaze or ornament.   Some potsherds of very much the same nature were found with worked "white" and "black" stones on the shore of the Laguna de los Padres, west of Mar del Plata.   At San Blas and in the eastern part of the valley of the Rio Negro, pottery is more common, although comparatively rare; this was occasionally well decorated by incised and impressed figures.   No pottery was found at the San Xavier settlement, which existed until historic times, nor at that south of Viedma.

Besides the many stone specimens and the pieces of earthenware collected on the journey, three objects were found which deserve special mention.   One, near the Laguna Malacara, was the piece of a shaft of the long bone of some animal, fashioned artificially on one side to a point, and having served very likely as a flaker; the second was a small turquoise bead, with central perforation, picked up by the writer with some of the "white" and "black" worked stones, on a playa southeast of Miramar; while the third is a large neatly finished arrow point, made of a flake of one of the black pebbles, found by the writer on one of the playas between Punta Mogote and Arroyo Corrientes, south of Mar del Plata.

The stone specimens, specially the "black ones," were found in numerous instances to present faint-to-marked signs of weathering. This feature was particularly noticeable in one limited region close to the seashore near the Arroyo del Moro, northeast of Necochea.   This weathering is due in the main to sand blast and is a phenomenon of but secondary importance.   Everything in these regions that is exposed to the wind, including recent bones of animals, fragments of glass bottles, pieces of driftwood, tosca, etc., shows before the lapse of many years the effects of weathering in greater or less degree.   A fragment of a stout wine bottle, collected by the writer among the dunes, had the exposed surface ground to complete dullness, while that buried in the sand preserves all its old luster.

No evidence was found that the natives ever actually dwelt, except temporarily, in the territory of the sand dunes.   They have had settlements in not very distant localities, traces of such being apparent at the Campo Peralta, at the Arroyo Corrientes, near the Laguna Malacara (north of Necochea), and near the mouth of the Rio Quequen, on the north side of the river, not far from Necochea. Farther south, especially in the neighborhood of the Rio Negro, settlements were located among the sand dunes, as at San Blas, but here the strip of sand dunes was narrow and inclosed several small fresh-water lakes.

Possessing their workshops among the sand dunes, with at least some of their settlements in the neighborhood, it is quite probable that the natives buried some of their dead in or among the dunes. This probability will be shown later to have a significant bearing on the question of the antiquity of some of the human remains obtained along the coast and claimed to be geologically ancient. Burials of precisely the same character have been made in numbers, both in the sand dunes and on the firmer ground among them, farther south, between the port of San Blas and Rio Negro.

CONCLUSIONS

Taking into consideration the extent of territory over which the various worked stones here dealt with are found; the relatively large numbers in which they occur, particularly in some localities; the relatively recent nature of the present sand-dune area, which is almost exclusively their home; and the additional facts, that they are as a rule on the surfaces of the playas, that they occur occasionally on or in the vegetal soil, that worked stones of corresponding types are found in some instances farther inland on recent alluvial deposits, and that many of the specimens are of fresh appearance—it appears that only one conclusion can be reached in regard to the age of these artifacts, namely, that they are not of great antiquity and certainly not of geologic antiquity.

The general and intimate association of the "white" and the "black" worked stones, with other considerations, leads to the further conclusions that these two classes of relics are the products of one culture and one period; that the "black" stone or pebble industry was the result of an ample local supply of such material coupled with scarcity of other material; and that the peculiarities of this industry were due to the nature of the material, connected possibly with some special local requirements.

Finally, as the "white" stone industry of the coast is identical with that of the Indians of the more inland parts of the same province, and as it is impossible to separate it from the "black" stone or pebble industry, the conclusion seems justifiable that they are both the work of the Indian.

It seems very probable that the natives, the remains of whose workshops exist among the médanos, were well acquainted with the "white" stone, or quartzite, industry before they began working the beach pebbles, which, or the flakes from which, were to serve as a substitute for the stone found farther inland. Finding, however, that they could not entirely replace the quartzite, they kept on bringing or importing a limited quantity of that stone and working it up among the dunes.

Whether the Indians used the "black" flaked pebbles to any extent as implements is not as yet certain. If used, they were utilized, in all probability, only locally and not by any of the inland tribes. The explanation of this appears simple. Inland the pebble material is absent, while the sources of the quartzite were frequently nearer. Furthermore, the pebbles were evidently of but secondary value as raw material, so that there was no incentive for carrying them to any distance, and they yielded nothing, so far as known, that would have been of special value for exportation.

We have found, then, on the coast of the Province of Buenos Aires archeologic remains of but a single culture, with a local phase in working pebbles; a culture that can be referred to only one period, though this may have been of some extent, and to only one people, namely, the Indian of the same province; and this culture can not possibly be of any great, especially of geologic, antiquity.

The archeologic report by Professor Holmes (p. 125), on the specimens collected, throws further light on this subject.

NOTES ON PLAYA AND CAMPO PERALTA

By BAILEY WILLIS

Immediately south of Mar del Plata is a little bay, between Cabo Corrientes and Punta Porvenir, the shore of which is known as the Playa Peralta (pls. 1, 21; also fig. 2). This shore is a slope rising at first slowly and then more sharply to the gently inclined plain, a part of which, east of the road that leads to the Punta Mogote lighthouse, is known as the Campo Peralta. The beach, though composed largely of sand, is strewn with pebbles of dense black or dark rock, and on the plain above are many worked stones of the same material. From this locality were collected a variety of artifacts, which are described by Doctor Hrdlička and Professor Holmes. The locality is of interest, because it was once the site of an industry in implements fashioned from the pebbles on the beach. Men lived on the gentle slope of the Campo Peralta. They collected stones from the beach. They carried them to their dwellings, possibly of a temporary nature, and worked them into shape—all within a distance of 200 or 300 meters. It is evident that the supply of stones attracted the workers and that they pitched their workshops where they could most conveniently reach the strand. The conditions are local. Northward and southward the coast is more precipitous and the beach is less accessible from the plain.

This relation between the local slope to the beach and the industry which was carried on in the immediate vicinity leaves no doubt in the mind of the writer that the industry is even more recent than the beach. It has already been stated that the coast is very young. It is developing, changing rapidly. Its actual features are forming now and endure but a short time. The industry is younger still. Several instances were observed of a precise relation between anvil-stones, and the immediate surface, which could hardly endure a century on this slope under the activities of wind erosion that now exist. There were also other evidences of a relatively recent occupancy of the place (see pls. 9–11). The writer does not think a century has passed since the stones referred to were used.

NOTES ON PUNTA PORVENIR

By BAILEY WILLIS

Punta Porvenir is a low point jutting into the Atlantic just south of Cabo Corrientes and forming part of the extreme eastern projection of the coast of Buenos Aires. The interest which attaches to the locality rests in the discovery of worked and unworked stones, which the writer has not seen, by Doctor Ameghino and his brother Carlos, in association with the carapace of a glyptodon on the point near the sea. Doctor Ameghino and his brother both accompanied Doctor Hrdlička and the writer to the place and pointed out the exact spot, where a hollow indicated the partly filled, not very large excavation. A piece of bone from the massive tail of a glyptodon lay on the surface near by. Ameghino stated that they had dug a hole to a depth of about a meter down through the superficial formation to the underlying Pampean terrane. The latter he styles "Ensenadean" and the former "Inter-Ensenadean." His view is that the superficial formation on the Inter-Ensenadean was deposited during a marine transgression which took place in the Ensenadean epoch. He places that epoch in the Pliocene, a reference which the writer regards as probably correct, and deduces thence the Pliocene age of the Inter-Ensenadean and its contained fossils. The writer is obliged to dissent from this deduction since the Inter-Ensenadean is marked as very modern by its intimate relation to the recent coast line at every point where Doctor Ameghino identified it. This relation has been discussed in connection with the coastal formations, but the occurrence on Punta Porvenir requires special description because of the delicate and temporary adjustment of conditions leading to its formation.

The Inter-Ensenadean of Punta Porvenir is a veneer of beach sand and loess spread over an irregular wind-eroded surface of the Ensenadean and slightly cemented by carbonates. It is thickest next the beach and thins to nothing at a distance of 100 to 110 meters from the beach. It does not extend beyond the reach of spray from storm waves breaking on the point. It lies on a gentle slope, from 4 to 6 meters above the sea, on top of the low bluff cut by the waves in the Ensenadean earth. The face of the bluff is concealed by sand blown from the adjacent beach, and this recent sand is continuous with and the same as the Inter-Ensenadean. Both sand and loess have accumulated, though from opposite directions, on the gentle slope to form the Inter-Ensenadean, the sand being blown from the beach, the loess from the bare surface of the Ensenadean that is exposed between the Inter-Ensenadean and the grass-grown plain still higher up. The sand gathers there because there is an eddy or lee on top of the bluff, when the wind blows from the sea. The wind sweeps up the steep face of the bluff, and being directed upward, does not blow directly across the gentle slope that tops the bluff. Sand is blown from the beach against the face of the bluff and accumulates there till a slope of equilibrium is reached, on which a wind can carry it up to the top. It then drops in the wind eddy on the slope. There is a certain sorting; black sand, being heavy, remains in larger proportion, whereas white sand, being lighter, is blown away in larger amount. Hence the black sand is more evident in the Inter-Ensenadean. Its presence is a characteristic by which Ameghino identified that formation in repeated instances on Punta Porvenir and elsewhere. It is a common constituent of the modern beach sands, which are partly derived from volcanic rocks of northern Patagonia and other districts to the south.

The loess which gathers to form part of the Inter-Ensenadean is caught in hollows or is held by moisture. It is blown off of the dry surface of the Ensenadean by land winds and lodges on any moist surface. This process was observed at Miramar on the plain close to the sea. The uneven surface had dried unequally and dust, blown into hollows where moisture lingered, was moistened and held. The moisture had evaporated from deposits made in a similar manner a few days or weeks previously, and they were slightly cemented. They contained specks of black sand and were identified by Doctor Ameghino as Inter-Ensenadean. On Punta Porvenir the Inter-Ensenadean is of the same character—a cemented mixture of loess and sand deposited in the zone reached by spray from the sea. It is thicker and more firmly cemented than the similar accumulations now forming at Miramar and the mass of it is doubtless older. Lying on one of the most exposed points on the coast, its seaward edge is liable to erosion by Atlantic waves, while its landward margin is extended inland as far as the sand and spray are blown together. Thus it is a transient formation that may last a few score years or so, but can not endure longer than the strand by which it is conditioned.

The glyptodon found in this Inter-Ensenadean is said to be characteristic of the underlying Ensenadean and to be of Pliocene age. If so, it is certainly older than the formation in which it was found, and may be regarded as weathered out and buried again. The writer questions, however, the extinction of this species in Pliocene time. The fact that it has been found in the eolian drift of the Arroyo Siasgo, which may be Pleistocene, but not older, and in this very recent coastal formation, suggests that the species may have ranged down into the Recent epoch.

Stone Implements of the Argentine Littoral [1]

By W. H. Holmes

The archeologic collections made by Doctor Hrdlička, with the aid of Mr. Willis, during their researches in Argentina, comprise numerous articles of stone, a limited number of fragments of pottery, some worked beads of shell, and a single bead of stone (turquoise). All of these specimens were derived from surface sites distributed along the coast between Mar del Plata on the northeast and the Rio Negro on the southwest, a distance of nearly 400 miles.

In previous sections Doctor Hrdlička and Mr. Willis have presented all necessary details with respect to distribution and manner of occurrence of the various classes of stone implements, and it remains for the writer to describe and illustrate the implements themselves and draw from their study such conclusions with regard to origin, manufacture, use, ethnologic significance, and chronology as may be suggested.

There are about 1,500 specimens in the collection, which in their general aspect suggest a primitive culture comparable with that of the tribes in possession of the region in the recent past, a culture corresponding somewhat closely in grade with that of the numerous tribes of the middle Atlantic coast of North America on the arrival of the English.

The implements, under which head are embraced all artificial objects that bear evidence of design, include the following varieties: Mortars, pestles, mullers, grooved hammers, discoidal hammers, pitted hammers, anvil-stones, bolas-stones, projectile points, knives, scrapers, axes, drills, and unspecialized blades. Associated with

---

[1] No attempt is made in these notes to consider or weigh the published data relating to the stone implements of Argentina. The collections at hand are classified and briefly described, and such conclusions are drawn as seem warranted by their character and manner of occurrence.

these, on the sites, were fragments, chips,[1] broken and imperfectly shaped forms, nuclei, and other refuse of manufacture, selections from which are included in the collections.

It is a noteworthy fact that, with the exception of a single turquoise bead from Miramar and a few shell beads from the Rio Negro, there are no ornaments; neither are there any articles that could safely be attributed to fiducial or ceremonial use. This would seem to indicate a people or peoples of simple manners and customs, little given to religious practices and poor in the arts that grow out of religious symbolism. It is probable, however, that the coastal districts were sparsely occupied, except by roving bands which hunted deer, ostrich, etc., on the land, and the seal along the shore, and gathered supplies of water-worn stones found along the beach, for the manufacture of implements.

It is convenient for purposes of description to arrange the objects in two geographic groups, those to the north obtained between Mar del Plata and Bahia Blanca, the principal localities being Mar del Plata, Miramar, Monte Hermoso, Arroyo del Moro, and Necochea, and those to the south of Bahia Blanca, gathered mainly from sites in the valley of the Rio Negro. This treatment has the advantage of making convenient a comparison of the art of the northern area with that of the southern, the differences being somewhat decidedly marked and possibly ethnologically significant.

NORTHERN GROUP

Use of Beach Pebbles

The seashore between Mar del Plata and Bahia Blanca furnishes in certain localities a liberal supply of beach pebbles of jasper, quartzite, and other fine-grained and generally black or dark-colored materials. These pebbles are mostly of small size, although occasional larger specimens weigh a pound or more. Since the surrounding region is poor in materials suitable for the shaping of small chipped implements, these pebbles were much sought after by the natives, the evidence of this fact occurring at a number of points. The principal shaping work consisted in fracturing the pebbles by blows with a hammer-stone, delivered generally at one end of the pebble, the other resting on a larger stone, conveniently called the anvil-stone. The anvil-stones are of various shapes and sizes, being merely suitable pieces of local rock—quartzite, sandstones, and limestone (tosca) utilized for the purpose. They are characterized by irregular, ragged surface pittings, the result, it is believed, of the impact of the pebbles

---

[1] Usage with regard to the terms chip, flake, spall, and teshoa is not well established, but, in order to avoid confusion in this paper, *flake* is employed as a generic term; *chip* applies to the smaller flakes; *teshoa* to large flakes, struck from bowlders or pebbles; and *spall* to large flakes derived from inchoate masses of stone.

under treatment (fig. 3). Some of the smaller of these scarred stones are flattened on one face by use as grinding stones or mullers, while others, as indicated by the scarred edges or peripheries, were employed on occasion as hammers, as illustrated in fig-ure 4.

Numerous hammer-stones were found on the sites examined and many of these doubtless pertain to the pebble-fracturing work. This is indi-cated not only by the shape and surface markings but by their close association with the anvils and the re-fuse of pebble-work-ing.

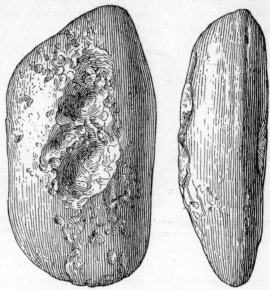

FIG. 3.   Anvil of limestone.   (⅛ actual size.)   Mar del Plata.

In form they are cylindrical, discoidal, globular, ovoid, and irregular. Nearly all are quartzite bowlders of suitable proportions

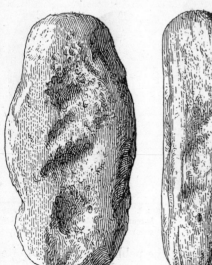

FIG. 4.   Anvil-stone of quartzite.   (⅛ actual size.)   Punta Mogote.

or are made of that mate-rial rudely chipped into desired shape. Some are battered at the ends merely (fig. 5) while others are pitted centrally on the broad faces and battered and scarred on the ends, lateral margin, or periphery (figs. 6–8). The scarring of the broad faces may be in cases the result of use as anvils. It is worthy of special note that some of the flatter hammers have been used as rubbing stones or mullers.

Certain discoidal exam-ples have beveled periph-eries and these and others (figs. 9–12,) are identical with the stone-working hammers of North America. All the above-described forms

were used unhafted. Certain others are grooved roughly or in neat
fashion and were probably not employed in the stone-shaping work.
They were hafted and, it may reasonably be assumed, served some
domestic purpose or on occasion for war and the chase. Examples
are presented in figs. 13, 14.

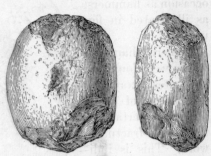

FIG. 5. Bowldei hammer of felsite, with
battered ends. (⅓ actual size.) Miramar.

FIG. 6. Hammer of felsite, with battered ends and
pitted sides. (⅓ actual size.) Necochea.

Associated with the hammers and anvils scattered liberally over
the surface of the sites near the beach, as described by Doctor
Hrdlička, are the fractured pebbles and the implements and flakage
made or derived from them.

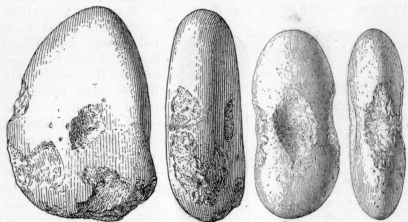

FIG. 7. Hammer of quartzite, with pitted faces and battered
end and sides. (⅓ actual size.) Campo Peralta.

FIG. 8. Hammer of quartzite, with deeply scarred and pitted faces. (⅓ actual
size.) Mar del Plata.

The processes employed in fracturing the pebbles have been quite
simple. It appears that although the free-hand stroke may have
been in common use for other kinds of stone-shaping work, as indicated by the occurrence of hammers of the type commonly employed
in free-hand flaking and pecking (figs. 10–12), the pebbles, held usually between the fingers and thumb of one hand, were set one end

upon the anvil-stone while the other end was struck sharp blows with the hammer.   As a result the ends of the pebbles were split or

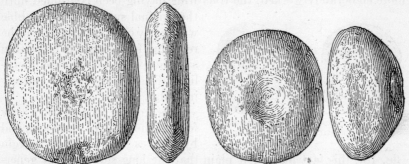

FIG. 9. Discoidal pitted hammer of quartzite,   FIG. 10.   Hammer made of a felsite bowlder, with
   with beveled periphery. (½ actual size.)   pitted sides. (½ actual size.)   Necochea.

splintered or flakes were driven off.   In some cases the blows were continued until the ends of the pebbles became quite battered and it

FIG. 11.   Chipped quartzite hammer, with battered   FIG. 12.   Small hammer of greenish fel-
   periphery. (½ actual size.)   Mar del Plata.   site. (½ actual size.)   Necochea.

is difficult to say always whether the strokes were repeated in the attempt to drive off other flakes or to reduce the ends of the pebble

to a desired shape.   It is seen that in numerous cases, as a result of the removal of flakes, one or both ends acquired a somewhat ragged edge which was squarish or slightly rounded in or notched, giving to the object, when both ends were so flaked, a shuttle - like outline

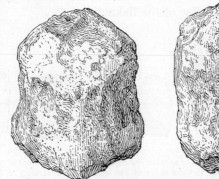

FIG. 13.   Roughly grooved hammer of quartzite. (½ actual size.)
   Campo Peralta.

(fig. 15).   In figure 16 two examples are shown, the first chipped at both ends and having the shuttle form and the second a very small

specimen chipped at one end only.   Nearly one-third of the worked
pebbles are chipped thus at one end only.   Occasionally examples are
more elaborately worked, the fracturing having been continued until

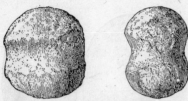

the original surface of the pebble
was nearly or wholly removed, the
resulting form being in cases thin
and somewhat rectangular in outlines (fig. 17) and again entirely
irregular.

It is worthy of note that very
few of the pebbles were chipped
by strokes on the long margin

FIG. 14.   Neatly shaped grooved hammer of sandstone. (½ actual size.)   Punta Mogote.

(fig. 18), this fact making it plain that the long side was not generally or even frequently intended to be elaborated as the edge of an
implement, as was usual in many sections; it is equally plain that

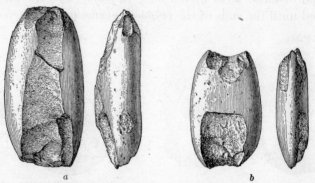

FIG. 15.   Quartzite pebbles chipped at both ends, having a shuttle-like
outline. (½ actual size.)   Campo Peralta.

flakes, if these were the object of the work, derived from the sides
were either difficult to make or on account of size, or shape, unsuited
for the purpose of the flaker.

FIG. 16.   Small jasper pebbles, one chipped
at both ends and the other at one end
only. (½ actual size.)   Campo Peralta.

FIG. 17.   Pebbles chipped into subrectangular forms.
(½ actual size.)   a, Jasper (Campo Peralta). b, Felsite
(Miramar).

It is observed that the pebbles selected for chipping were usually
oblong and flattish in form, these being chosen, undoubtedly, because

they yielded the requisite result more readily than any other.   Again, it is equally plain that the stroke on the end was expected to produce a particular kind of result and two results only could have been desired or anticipated: (1) the making of flattish, round, or oblong sharp-edged flakes of the teshoa[1] type (fig. 22, *b*) for use of the cutting edge or for elaboration by secondary chipping; (2) the shaping of one or both ends of the body of the pebble for use as an implement.   We are therefore called upon to determine whether one or .both of these results were actually utilized and in what way.

That there was a definite purpose in view for the flakes made seems practically certain.   Split pebbles and especially large

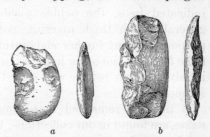

FIG. 18.   Jasper pebbles chipped irregularly from the side.   (¼ actual size.)   *a* (Campo Peralta).   *b* (Necochea).

teshoa flakes were almost universally employed by primitive peoples for cutting and scraping as well as for elaboration into projectile points and other implements.   Perhaps the most universally employed stone implement of Argentina is the plano-convex knife blade or scraper, the simplest and most readily made type of which is the teshoa flake.   An examination of the flaked pebbles—the nuclei—collected on the shore-land sites, shows that most of the flakes driven off were quite small, but that many were large enough for

FIG. 19.   Flakes from black jasper pebbles specialized for use as knives or scrapers.   (¼ actual size.)   Necochea.

use as knives and scrapers is shown by the presence in the collection of a dozen or more specimens which have been specialized by removing, probably with a pressure implement, a number of small chips from one margin of the convex face to make the cutting edge more stable and effective (fig. 19).   Others by more abrupt chipping were especially fitted for use as scrapers, while many others, both large and small, probably served for cutting and scraping without secondary

---

[1] This form of flake was found by Dr. Joseph Leidy, of the Hayden Geological Survey, in common use among the Shoshoni Indians of Wyoming for scraping skins and is thus conveniently referred to by its Shoshoni name.

chipping.   No one can estimate the number of these flakes that were
carried away for use elsewhere.   The flakes thus utilized were usually
substantial portions of the pebble, having a body of considerable
strength and one keenly incisive edge.   The relation of the half
pebble to the several varieties of flakes will be understood by an
examination of figure 20.   When split into approximate halves as
indicated in *a*, the pebble yields two potential implements, but
generally with thick margins, not particularly well suited to any
purpose without further elaboration.   The well-proportioned teshoa
flake *b* has on the other hand a rounded margin at the top and a thin
incisive margin below, well suited for immediate use for cutting or
scraping.

It may be remarked that comparatively few of the specialized
flakes are found in our collections, but if they were really the designed
product of the chipping work, they would not have been left, except

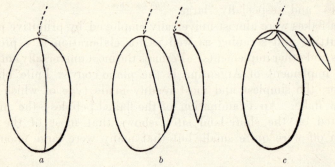

FIG. 20. The several forms of flakes. *a*, Split pebble. *b*, Large teshoa flake. *c*, Small flakes or chips.

incidentally, on these sites, but would have been carried away to the
permanent dwelling places for utilization in the practice of the primitive tribal arts.   No form of pebble other than the long flattish one
would yield suitable flakes so readily and no other process would be
more effective in producing these flakes than that employing the
hammer and anvil.

As a result of the above considerations, it is manifest that the
larger flakes made on these sites were much utilized, and it remains
to consider the possible utilization of the remaining portions of the
pebbles.

The pebbles from which the flakes were detached by strokes of the
hammer—the nuclei—took certain shapes already described and
fully illustrated in figures 15–17.   The questions of their purpose,
if they represent a purpose, and their use, if they were really intended
to be used, require particular attention.

There can be no doubt that these pebble nuclei occur on sites where
the pebbles were collected and worked by a Stone-age people.   The

presence of the hammers, anvils, and flakes make this entirely clear. That they were left on these sites in large numbers is attested by the many examples obtained by collectors. No one will claim that these sites along the arid seashore were very largely occupied for dwelling or for any industrial purpose other than that of making stone implements and it is safe to conclude that if the pebble nuclei were used at all, it was in the stone-shaping work, but we are entirely at a loss to imagine how these could have served in shaping any of the known implements of the Argentine coast.

That these flaked pebbles were not intended to be held in the hand as hatchets, chisels, or scrapers, is apparent from the fact that a majority of them are fractured at both ends and are so uneven as to injure the hand if thus used. The fact that all are not fractured at both ends signifies nothing more than that the fracturing blow or blows took effect at one end of the pebble only instead of at both as was more usual. Their shapes do not indicate in any way that they were intended for hafting, although hafting after the manner of hatchets, scrapers, or knives would not be difficult, either by setting them in a socket in a handle of wood or bone, or by fastening the haft about the middle by means of thongs; but there is no reason for assuming their utilization in any of these ways.

In advancing any theory of a possible purpose or use for these objects, we are met by the significant fact that they were left in large numbers on the sites of manufacture, whereas if intended for use they would not have been left but rather would have been distributed far and wide, especially to the sites of permanent dwellings in the vicinity of a fresh-water supply. That they have no particular adaptation for use is made apparent by an examination of the flaked ends, which are notched and bruised from the hammer blows and are rarely so even-edged as to fit them for cutting and scraping. The strongest claim they have to serious consideration is that in cases the flaked ends present an appearance of wear as if from use. This appearance is limited to a blunting or rounding of some of the fractured ends; but a close inspection shows that this result is such as might be produced and in all probability was produced by the repeated blows of the hammer in attempts to detach desirable flakes. That these chipped pebbles were occasionally devoted incidentally to some purpose to which they happened to be adapted is probable, but the claim that they were designed for any particular use can not be substantiated.

The facts that they were left on the sites of manufacture, that they show no clear adaptation to any particular use, that they present no certain evidence of having been used, that they show no trace of specialization beyond that produced by the direct blows of the hammer on the ends, and that the flakes made from them *were used* for most important and constant needs, tend to show in no uncertain manner that they were merely the rejectage of flake-making cast aside as of no particular value.

Feeling that the settlement of the questions here raised is of considerable interest and importance, the writer undertook certain experiments in pebble-working, the results of which are instructive. A large number of pebbles of the same general form as those used on the Argentine coast were gathered from gravel banks in the suburbs of Washington and subjected to tests which were, however, not altogether satisfactory for the reason that the pebbles were of quartz, most of them much flawed, or of quartzite, often tough, coarse-grained, and partially disintegrated. They were much more difficult to flake than the more homogeneous and fine-grained pebbles of the Argentine sites.

FIG. 21.   The principal percussive methods of stone flaking.   *a*, The anvil method.   *b*, The free hand method.

Proceeding on the theory, well supported by the facts just recited, that the principal object of the chipping work on the shore-land sites was the making of flakes suitable for knives, scrapers, and projectile points, and recognizing no other ideal toward which the aboriginal work could have been directed, effort was confined entirely to the production of such flakes. The pebble, held firmly between the thumb and fingers of the left hand, was set vertically on the anvil-stone and struck sharp blows with the hammer held in the right hand (fig. 21). This process was in occasional if not very common use among numerous North American tribes, the free-hand method (*b*) being more generally employed. These processes are almost equally effective in the making of simple flakes, but the former is effective in the work of crude primary fracture only, while the latter is capable of carrying forward a considerable degree of specialization of the implement forms. The result of the hammer stroke varied with the strength of the blow, the character of the pebble material, and the degree of hardness of the anvil-stone. The first stroke, if strong, shattered the pebble, split it into nearly equal parts, or removed flakes from one or both faces. When the anvil was of hard stone, the lower end of the pebble was also fractured, yielding flakes identical with those produced by the direct impact of the hammer. When the pebble was of tough or refractory material, several strokes were often delivered and with increasing vigor before even a single flake of moderate size was driven off. Continuation of the effort was encouraged by the fact that satisfactory flakes were often secured after the end of the pebble had become well battered. When it became apparent that further effort must be futile, the mutilated pebble was abandoned as mere waste. But whether good flakes were secured or not, the ends of the pebble under the hammer took forms entirely familiar to the student of the Argentine artifacts. In many

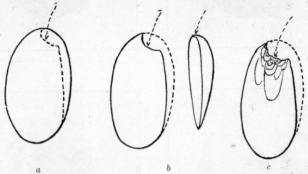

FIG. 22. Adventitious origin of the crescentic edge and the gouge shape of the pebble nucleus. *a*, The arrow point indicates the direction of the hammer blow. *b*, The flake removed and the slightly hollow bed left. *c*, The result of additional blows on the upper end of the pebble.

cases the fractured ends developed an incipient, yet purely adventitious, edge which was often bruised and dulled in such a way as to present the appearance of wear from use in some kind of manual operation.

Furthermore, it should not escape attention that the hollowed out, gougelike edge which appears in many cases and is interpreted by some to be the result of design, is purely adventitious. This is proved by the experiments made. The hammer stroke on the end of the pebble removes a flake from one face, leaving a slightly concave bed, which is deeper at the point of percussion (fig. 22, *a*), and a crescentic edge (fig. 22, *b*). A few additional strokes, designed to remove flakes from the other face of the pebble nucleus, bruises this edge and possibly removes small chips, giving the appearance of wear in use, and at the same time often deepens the notch, as shown at *c*. Proof that this nucleus is an implement showing design and traces of use is thus entirely wanting.   The fact that the pebble was nearly always an oblong one and flaked from the end has been used to support the view that the fractured end was intended to be used for cutting, scraping, or some like purpose.   The experiments, made, however, with a view to settling this point show that it is

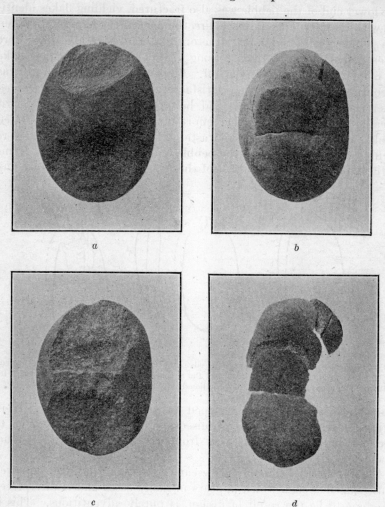

a   b

c   d

FIG. 23.   Examples of flaked pebbles from Argentina and District of Columbia. a, Pebble nucleus of fine-grained stone from the Argentine coast, from which two teshoa flakes were struck by the ancient workmen. b, Coarse-grained Potomac pebble nucleus from which flakes were struck by the author with two blows. c, The flakes restored to their place on the nucleus. d, The several flakes separated from the nucleus.

more difficult to strike off a well-proportioned flake from the side than from the end of a pebble.   Besides, a stroke having enough force to remove a large flake from the long margin of a pebble usually resulted in cross-fracture and failure.   In fact, all the features of

(Actual size)

PEBBLE NUCLEI

Forms resulting from attempts to produce flakes of a size suitable for use as implements: *b, c, d, i, j,* from the Hrdlička Argentine collection; *a, e, f, g, h, k,* made by W. H. Holmes from Washington pebbles.

the so-called pebble implements of the Argentine coastal sites—the chisel and shuttlelike shapes, the notched and curved edge and the appearance of wear from use—are exactly duplicated in the forms produced by these experiments.

As a result of his experiments, the writer is confirmed in the view that the hammer-anvil work was aimed at the production of the plano-convex flakes intended for use, unspecialized or specialized

FIG. 24. Chipped implements of black jasper (¼ actual size.) a, Leaf-shaped blade (Arroyo Corrientes). b, Rude blade, probably a reject from arrow-making (Necochea).

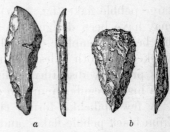

FIG. 25. Spikelike forms of black jasper pebble derivation, possibly rejects from arrow-making. (¼ actual size.) a, Miramar. b, Necochea.

as knives or scrapers, or for elaboration into other forms of implements, and that the body of the pebble, the nucleus, was not intended as an implement at all, and was never used as such, unless incidentally. Experiment can hardly fail to convince the most skeptical of the correctness of this view. Examples of the forms resulting from the experimental work are included in plate 12 in association with specimens of like genesis left by the ancient inhabitants of the Argentine coast.

Figure 23 is intended to illustrate further the pebble-fracturing work. In *a* we have a pebble nucleus from the Argentine coast from which two flakes have been removed by one, or at most, two strokes of the hammer. These flakes were of the teshoa type and doubtless served some useful purpose for the maker. Forms

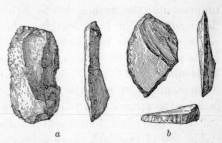

FIG. 26. Scrapers of jasper. (½ actual size.) a, Duck-bill scraper of brown jasper (Necochea). b, Flat scraper of olive jasper (Monte Hermoso).

b and *c* represent a Potomac pebble of similar shape which shows the result of two experimental blows with the hammer. In *b* the flakes have been removed. In *c* they are replaced, and in *d* they are separately shown. It may be added here that the hammer-stones and anvil-stones used in the experimental work described above display, as the result of the fracturing work, markings identical with those of the corresponding implements of the Argentine collection.

It is observed that the ancient pebble workers of the Argentine coast rarely aimed to make the ordinary leaf blade from the body of the pebble, as was the usual practice with primitive pebble workers elsewhere in roughing out projectile points and knives. Between Mar del Plata and Bahia Blanca only a single well-finished, pressure-chipped blade of ordinary leaf-shape type, made probably from a large pebble flake (fig. 24, a) was obtained by Doctor Hrdlička. It may have been designed as an arrowhead, the trimming and notching being incomplete. Another specimen, from Necochea, is slightly worked on both sides apparently by free-hand percussion, but it was probably discarded unfinished on account of the development of a high irregular hump on one face (fig. 24, b).

A few spikelike forms, closely related to the preceding, made from black pebble flakes, and specialized by rather irregular chipping on both margins of the convex face and remaining flat on the other, occur in the collection (fig. 25).

The collection of pebble-derived implements contains also an example of the duck-bill scraper made of a flake of brown jasper. It was picked up by Doctor Hrdlička, at Necochea (fig. 26, a). A second scraper of olive jasper, of related but less typical form, was found by the expedition, at Monte Hermoso (fig. 26, b).

It would appear from the foregoing examinations and experiments that the pebble workers employed anvil-stones and plain and pitted hammer-stones as well as pressure implements (probably of bone), in the shaping work and that the forms made include four varieties of implements; the teshoa blade either unmodified or sharpened by flaking on one or both margins; the spikelike form with flat under surface and high back; the duck-bill scraper; and the leaf-shaped blade worked on both faces. According to the evidence as interpreted by Hrdlička and Willis, the same people which shaped and used these implements used also the mortars, pestles, mullers, grooved hammers, bolas-stones, and pottery, as well as the quartzite implements yet to be described, found on the same sites.

The use of the dark shore pebbles and the implements made from them, as exemplified by the Hrdlička-Willis collection, extended from Mar del Plata to below Viedma, a distance along the coast, as already mentioned, of approximately 400 miles. It may be observed here that identical archeologic conditions continue along the Argentine coast to the north of Mar del Plata and along the coast of Uruguay. Explorations having been confined in the main to coast localities, the collection throws but little light on the distribution inland of these artifacts. However, one of the black worked pebbles was collected on the beach of the Laguna de los Padres, about ten miles inland.

CHIPPED WHITE QUARTZITES

The collection embraces many hundreds of chipped articles, flakes, and fragments made of a fine-grained, light-colored, somewhat glassy quartzite, a material not found along the coast, but obtained presumably from outcrops in the hills to the west. Occasionally small masses, apparently nuclei from which fragments and flakes have been broken off, are encountered along the coast, and one specimen of this kind

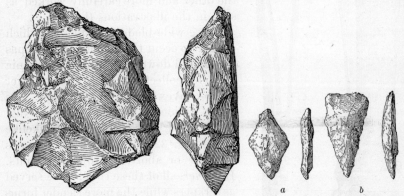

FIG. 27. Nucleus of quartzite from which flakes have been removed. (¼ actual size.) Campo Peralta.

FIG. 28. Arrow points of quartzite. (½ actual size.) Campo Peralta.

weighing several pounds was brought away by Doctor Hrdlička (fig. 27). These quartzite objects occur invariably in intimate association with the dark-pebble implements on the shore-land sites. They include arrowheads, duck-bill scrapers, flat-faced (plano-convex) blades, and spike- or drill-like forms, as well as numerous fragments and flakes—

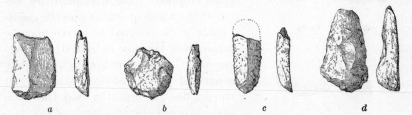

FIG. 29. Quartzite scrapers of duck-bill type. a, b, c, Campo Peralta. d, Necochea.

the refuse of local chipping. Examples are illustrated in the accompanying figures. The arrowheads are few in number and of ordinary types (fig. 28). The numerous scrapers, characterized by abruptly beveled edges, or more properly, ends (fig. 29), are identical with the scrapers used by the tribes south of Bahia Blanca as well as by many other tribes in both South and North America. They were probably hafted much as are the scrapers of the Tehuelche of to-day (fig. 30).

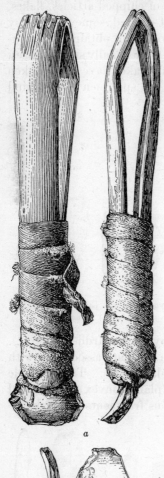

a

b

FIG. 30. *a*, Hafted Tehuelche scraper of duck-bill type, made of green bottle glass. (½ actual size.) Hatcher collection (southern Patagonia). *b*, The scraper removed from the handle for comparison with the ancient types. The strong curve was imposed by the curve of the glass fragment.

A number of blades, flat on one face and in cases handsomely chipped on the other, are especially noteworthy and may have servéd either as knives or as scrapers. As a rule, one of the edges is more decidedly curved outward than the other and more carefully worked, as seen in the illustrations (fig. 31).

These wide blades (see pl. 14), which appear to occur throughout the pampas region and down to southern Patagonia (Hatcher collection), grade into narrower plano-convex forms, the chipped face being decidedly arched or ridged (fig. 32, *a*), and these pass into spikelike forms (fig. 32, *b*), which may in cases be rude or abortive projectile points. However, all of these could have served as scrapers while the more slender forms could have been used as drills.

It is a noteworthy fact that the entire series of white quartzite artifacts, upward of 400 in number, contains only a dozen specimens chipped on both faces. Only two of the dark-pebble artifacts out of many hundreds of specimens are thus chipped. The dissimilarities between the white quartzite and the coast-pebble work referred to above may be interpreted by some as indicating differences in the people concerned, or widely separated periods of occupation, yet it should not be forgotten that the form and nature of the two kinds of raw material are so unlike as to account for somewhat marked dissimilarities, both in processes and in forms made, even if utilized by the same people at the same period.

DOMESTIC UTENSILS

Evidences of more or less sedentary occupancy of the coastal region are found in the presence on the various sites, of articles of domestic use, as mortars, pestles, mullers, and hammer-stones, in intimate association with the dark-colored and the light-colored stone implements described above, made of local materials, chiefly quartzite and sandstone. Their form in cases is so highly specialized and typical as to enable us to say with confidence that the makers were well advanced in the arts of barbarian life, and no good reason appears in the manner of ·their occurrence or in the specimens themselves for assuming that all do not pertain to the same or to kindred peoples and to the same or approximately the same time. Hammers or clubheads, which may have served in the domestic arts or in war and the chase are illustrated in figures 13 and 14. Two mortars, one a block of quartzite with a shallow depression in the upper

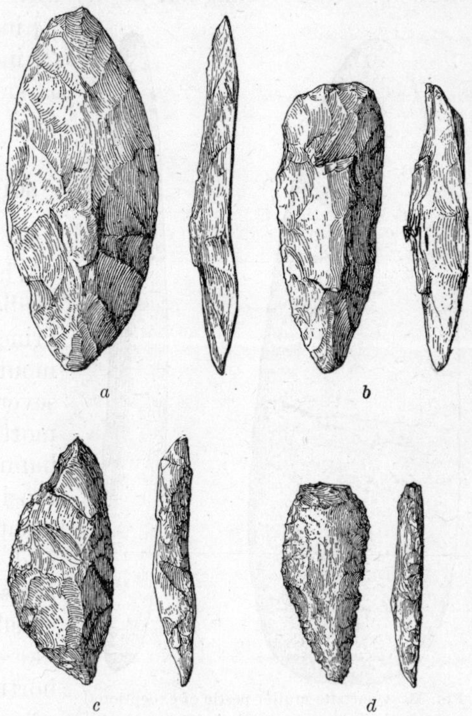

FIG. 31. Plano-convex blades of white quartzite, showing the carefully chipped convex faces and the profiles. (¼ actual size.) Campo Peralta. a, Neatly chipped and thin. b, High back and of reject type. c, Curved edge carefully chipped. d, Both edges carefully chipped.

surface and the other a large fragment of the same stone with a deeper depression, are included in the collection. A muller or muller-pestle of remarkable proportions is shown in figure 33; this is a symmetrical, well-finished slab of gritty sandstone 20¼ inches long, 7¼ inches wide at the widest part, and 1¾ inches thick. The flat faces, toward the middle, are somewhat smoothed by use. The feature that distinguishes this from kindred utensils is the narrowing to a point at one end. Another specimen of similar type, but smaller, is represented by a large fragment. A cylindrical pestle with a tapering top, made of the same stone as the above, is shown in figure 34; this is 7¼ inches long and 3 inches in diameter and is

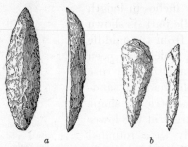

FIG. 32. a, Narrow high-backed blade of quartzite. (¼ actual size.) Laguna Malacara. b, Spikelike form of quartzite. (¼ actual size.) Playa Peralta.

smoothed at the larger end by use. Three other pestles somewhat pointed at both ends are slightly flattened on one side by use as mullers. One rectangular muller with rounded corners and margins, $5\frac{3}{4}$ inches long, $3\frac{1}{2}$ inches wide, and $2\frac{1}{4}$ inches thick, made of quartzite, is smoothed and flattened on one face by use.

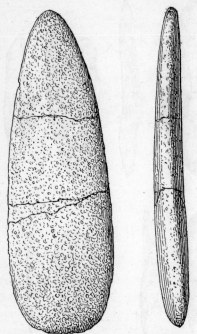

FIG. 33. Quartzite muller-pestle of exceptional size and shape. ($\frac{1}{5}$ actual size.) Campo Peralta.

SOUTHERN GROUP—RIO NEGRO DISTRICT

The collections made by Doctor Hrdlička in the southern area, principally on sites about the mouth of the Rio Negro, number several hundred objects, including mortars, pestles, mullers, anvils, hammers, bolas-stones, and an extensive series of chipped implements, unfinished chipped forms, and the refuse of chipping operations. The larger implements, chiefly domestic utensils, are much like corresponding varieties to the north of Bahia Blanca. The well-specialized mortars, pestles, and mullers were shaped by the pecking-abrading processes from masses of quartzite and sandstone. Excellent examples of mortars made of sandstone are shown in figure 35. The numerous mullers are well-shaped and finished and range in form from discoidal to subrectangular outlines. Two specimens are illustrated in figure 36, a, b. A cigar-shaped pestle made of quartzite, 15 inches in length and $2\frac{1}{2}$ inches in diameter at the middle part, is shown in figure 37, a. It tapers gradually from the middle to the rounded points. The surface, which has been finished by pecking, is somewhat smoothed by use toward the ends. A second specimen, made of sandstone, 16 inches in length, is unsymmetric in shape and appears to be unfinished. It is larger at the lower end and tapers somewhat irregularly to a rounded point at the top. The fragment of a third pestle is shown in figure 37, b.

FIG. 34. Pestle of gritty sandstone. ($\frac{1}{5}$ actual size.) Mar del Plata.

An exceptional specimen is the broad blade of an axlike implement, the upper portion or poll of which has been lost. It is made of sandstone, the surface being rather unevenly ground off. An engraved design appears on the lower part of the blade, as shown in figure 38. Axes of this general type prevail over a wide area in South America and extend even into the West Indies. The rather dull edge bears slight traces of use, but the presence of the ornamental figure suggests employment in some ceremonial office.

a   *b*

FIG. 35.   Mortars of sandstone.   (⅛ actual size.)   *a*, San Blas district.   *b*, Viedma.

There is a noteworthy scarcity of chipped pebbles of the type found in so great abundance up the coast, but this is probably due in large part to the fact that the district does not furnish the variety of pebbles so much sought and used in the north. Half a dozen anvil-fractured specimens were found near Viedma and 4 miles south of that place were collected on a site occupied in recent times by the natives, two pitted and scarred hammer-anvils, one of which has been used as a muller (fig. 39). The white quartzite of the north

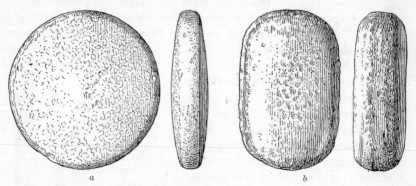

a   *b*

FIG. 36.   Mullers.   (⅓ actual size.)   *a*, Granite, well polished.   (Viedma.)   *b*, Sandstone.   (San Blas District.)

is absent. The chipped forms are distinct in a number of respects from both the pebble and the white quartzite implements of the northern area. They consist of projectile points, knives, drills, and scrapers, together with unspecialized leaf-shaped blades and the rejectage of blade-making. The material was obtained in the main from rather large water-worn pieces of jasper and other free-fracturing rocks and was rough-shaped by free-hand percussion with a hammer-stone and finished with a pressure implement. Practically all of the well-developed forms are of leaf-blade genesis, specialization having taken different directions according to the implement to be made. The few scrapers were made from flakes of proximate shape and correspond closely in type with the duck-bill scrapers of the white quartzite and pebble groups. The plano-convex knife-blades and the spikelike forms so common in the white quartzite and shore-pebble groups are of rare occurrence. Incipient blades unfinished or rejected because of imperfect fracture, of which there are numerous examples, are shown in figure 40, and a series of forms illustrating the relation of the first step in the shaping work to the more finished and specialized forms is given in figure 41. The ruder specimens are sometimes referred to as "paleolithic," but without other reason than that they are not well-finished. It is not assumed that the final form in this series is the only one that may have been employed as an implement, but the lack of specialization or careful finish of point or edge in the ruder forms supports the assumption that these were not finished implements.

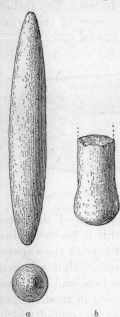

FIG. 37. Pestles. (⅓ actual size.) a, Quartzite pestle of cigar shape (San Blas District). b, Sandstone pestle, fragment (San Blas District).

A representative series of the arrowheads appears in plate 13 and a typical drill-point or awl is shown in figure 42.

To the North American student the most striking characteristic of these flaked forms is their remarkable analogy with North American types. The entire collection from the Rio Negro could be thrown together with corresponding collections from Arizona, Georgia, or New Jersey with the practical certainty that the student would be unable to separate more than a few of the specimens of the several regions.

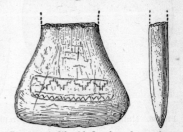

FIG. 38. Axlike blade of sandstone, bearing engraved design (⅓ actual size.) Puerto San Blas.

ETHNIC BEARING

A study of the lithic art of the region under consideration brings into prominence the fact that three groups of chipped artifacts, presenting certain noteworthy resemblances and differences, are represented. These groups are the hammer-anvil worked pebbles of the

(⅜ actual size)

ARROWHEADS OF JASPER AND AGATE

From the vicinity of San Blas.

coastwise sites and the several specialized varieties of implements of pebble origin belonging with them; the chipped white quartzites of the same localities; and the chipped artifacts of the southern or Rio Negro area. In addition there are the various pecked-abraded domestic utensils and weapons apparently common to the entire region examined. The question is necessarily raised as to whether

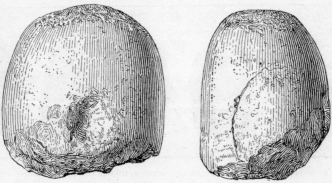

FIG. 39. Hammer-anvil of quartzite, used secondarily as a muller. (½ actual size.) Viedma.

more than one people is represented and the archeologist is called on to point out the bearing of the evidence.

It may be said that in any area occupied by primitive peoples having a range as great as 400 miles in length of coastal territory, it is to be expected that more than one tribe, possibly more than one linguistic stock, would be found, even at one and the same period. In California a dozen stocks occupy a like extent of coast at the present day. The culture of such contemporaneous tribes is not necessarily identical, but on the contrary is often decidedly unlike, and it does not seem unreasonable to suppose that separate tribes practicing forms of art in chipped stone as distinctive as

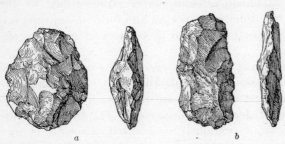

FIG. 40. Leaf-shaped blades of brown jasper, probably rejects of manufacture. (½ actual size.) San Blas.

those enumerated above should have occupied the middle coastal region of Argentina at one and the same time.

However, comparing the white quartzite work with the coast-pebble work, we find the artifacts of both groups distributed over exactly the same sites, never apart, and in like relations to the present surface of the country, which is a surface of to-day rather than of any early period. We find the plano-convex knife blade (pl. 14), the spikelike plano-convex point (figs. 25, 32), the symmetric doubly convex leaf-blade (figs. 24, 28), the duck-bill scraper (figs. 26, 29), and the chipping hammers in both groups. The use of the fracturing and the pressure implement in the shaping work was apparently common to both. The specialized arrowhead is found in the quartzite group

FIG. 41. Series of jasper leaf forms representing successive steps in the specialization of arrow points. (⅓ actual size.) San Blas.

only and in that but rarely. The anvil-stone can not be shown to be characteristic of either of the groups exclusively, although it certainly pertains in large measure to the pebble group, while the chipped pebbles are necessarily confined to the shore-pebble group. Fuller collections might show even still closer correspondence between the two groups. The differences do not seem so radical as to preclude the idea that a single people or closely related groups of people were responsible for all the chipped-stone work of these more northeastern coastal sites. This likelihood is considerably strengthened by the fact that differences in kind and form of material impose distinctions in the processes and in the things made.

FIG. 42. Drill-point of jasper. (⅓ actual size.) San Blas.

Comparing the whole work of the northern groups with that south of Bahia Blanca, it is seen that certain culture differences are quite marked. The prevalence of leaf-blade forms (fig. 41) and leaf-blade implements, variously specialized arrowheads and spearheads (pl. 13), and drill points (fig. 42), contrasts with the absence or decided rarity of these forms in the north. The rarity of the plano-convex knife blade (pl. 14) in the Rio Negro District (although it is common in southern Patagonia) is a noteworthy fact. The duck-bill scraper occurs much less frequently here than in the quartzite group of the north. The shaping processes are the same throughout, although the use of the anvil-stone was apparently exceptional in the south, being there devoted to the fracturing of pebbles and hence confined to the pebble-yielding areas.

(⅔ actual size)

PLANO-CONVEX KNIFE BLADES

From three widely separated groups: *a, b, c,* from the coast-pebble group; *d, e, f,* from the white quartzite group; *g, h, i,* from southern Patagonia (Hatcher collection). (See fig. 31.)

Bolas-stones of globular and ovoid forms are widely distributed over the area studied, but they are not made of local materials, and if Hatcher is right the bolas represents a very recent period, having superseded the bow and arrow as a weapon, after the acquisition of horses by the natives.

On the whole, in the writer's view the differences in general aspect between the northern and southern groups of chipped-stone artifacts are so pronounced as to favor the assumption that the two regions were occupied by peoples having somewhat distinct cultures—cultures, however, not differing very decidedly in grade, and presenting, as indicated above, numerous features in common.

That the aboriginal cultures of Argentina represented by the available collections are not separated by wide differences of culture grade and time is strongly suggested by the presence throughout Argentina of at least two flaked implements of highly specialized type, the plano-convex knife blade and the duck-bill scraper.   In plate 14 are shown photographic reproductions of three bevel-edge knives (a, b, c), belonging to the coast-pebble group and made of black-pebble teshoas; three of the same type of white quartzite from the white quartzite group (d, e, f); and three from Patagonia (Hatcher collection) (g, h, i).   The duck-bill scraper is of almost universal occurrence. The slight differences in general shape and specialization of the edge are only such as would readily arise in the utilization of different kinds and forms of material by the same people and for a common purpose.

The presence over the entire area north and south, of domestic utensils of ordinary types and weapons of well-specialized forms may be variously interpreted.   It may be thought to indicate a well-advanced people of general distribution quite distinct from the tribes responsible for the three groups of chipped-stone implements, or it may be regarded with more reason as indicating that the same or kindred peoples responsible for all the cultural phenomena extended over the whole area, the peculiar varieties of chipped-stone work being merely local developments due to peculiarities of local materials and activities.

The writer is well aware that other finds may have been made or may yet be made which will either entirely obliterate or, on the other hand, decidedly emphasize the differences here noted.   So diversified are the elements to be considered in this study and so limited relatively to the extent of territory the materials at hand, that the archeologist can not assume to reach definite and final results with respect to the peoples concerned, but it seems safe to conclude that although different tribes or racial groups may be represented, there is no satisfactory evidence that the cultures were widely separated from one another in grade or essentially distinct from the culture of the tribes occupying the region in historic times.

CHRONOLOGIC BEARING

The many hundreds of relics included in the collection were all obtained from the surface. None are known to have held any synchronous relation with the geologic formations, save with the surface soil, the shifting sands and sand dunes, and such other recently rearranged deposits as are constantly forming under the never-ceasing action of wind, water, and gravity along the outcropping edges of imperfectly consolidated strata. The chronologic order of these unstable deposits is of little consequence in these investigations since no sequence involving measurable periods of time can be established.

The facts that all varieties of the artifacts bear the same relation to habitable sites and to the seashore of to-day throughout nearly the entire region and that shapes and processes of manufacutre in all the groups, though differing in certain respects, have important features in common, as already pointed out, antagonize any theory of wide separation of periods.

The relation of the pebble-working sites to the coast line of to-day has a most important bearing on the theory of geologic antiquity for any of the relics of man's handiwork. It is seen that these sites which yield such large numbers of both the dark-pebble and the white-quartzite artifacts are ranged along the bluffs and slopes facing the sea. But the ocean front is not a stable line. It is not to-day where it was a century or a millenium ago. During the early stages of the Recent period (by which is meant the time since the land surface assumed approximately its present relative altitude) it probably lay farther out to the south and east. If this assumption be correct, it should be explained why the people of the auroral days of this period brought the pebbles from a distant shore to work them up and utilize them in the localities examined by Doctor Hrdlička. It would seem that if the pebble artifacts belong to the Recent period at all, they belong to its closing phases, during which the relations of the land and sea were practically the same as we find them to-day.

Again, if the pebble-using people occupied the region during either Quaternary or Pliocene time, how shall we arrange to have them occupy a series of sites along the line which just now happens to have become the shore of the sea between Mar del Plata and Bahia Blanca? Or are we to suppose that these people occupied the whole of the pampean region so fully during any one of these periods that the sea front at any and every stage of its recession toward the highland should yield to the archeologists of the time the rich harvest reaped by our representatives to-day? The number of specimens required to stock the whole of the pampas at this rate would be beyond the possibility of computation.

Besides we should also inquire as to where dwellers on the land surface exposed during either of the periods referred to could have obtained the pebbles which now occur only along the present beach. Can we explain the manner in which a people occupying a Pliocene horizon, for example (which, to accommodate these inhabitants, must have had for the time a suitable land surface), obtained a supply of pebbles belonging in underlying beds of an earlier period, since none occur, so far as Hrdlička and Willis have observed, in contemporaneous or superior formations. Is it to be assumed that the tribes of that time found the seashore with its bluffs and seaward slopes and supply of pebbles conveniently exposed as they are to-day and all along a line connecting Mar del Plata with Bahia Blanca?

Questions like these can readily be asked, but not so readily answered, and since the writer has great difficulty in answering them affirmatively, he finds it necessary to adopt the view that the tribes responsible for the several groups of relics collected by Hrdlička and Willis along the Argentine littoral occupied the various sites visited in recent centuries, under conditions corresponding in all essential respects with those of the present day. Nothing short of perfectly authenticated finds of objects of art in undisturbed formations of fully established geologic age will justify science in accepting the theory of Quaternary or Tertiary occupants for Argentine.

The writer has pleasure in observing that Dr. Félix F. Outes, of the National University, La Plata, Argentina, has given careful attention to the antiquities of the pampean coast and to the relation of these to the several geologic formations, and after visiting and thoroughly examining all the more important sites, has presented the whole group of phenomena in a way that in the end, with possibly slight exceptions, must meet with general approval.[1]

Subsequent to the completion of the foregoing pages Doctor Hrdlička drew attention to certain specimens collected by him along the barranca at Monte Hermoso, which had escaped particular notice on the writer's part. Attention was directed also to a brief pamphlet just received from Doctor Ameghino,[2] describing a series of similar specimens collected by him while examining this same barranca in company with Doctor Hrdlička. Considering the nature of the specimens and the manner of their occurrence, the observations and interpretation of Doctor Ameghino are so remarkable that the writer is constrained to refer to them in some detail.

The objects in question are about 20 freshly-fractured chips and fragments of coarse, partially fire-reddened quartzite, a larger frag-

[1] Outes, Félix F., Sobre una facies local de los instrumentos neolíticos Bonaerenses; in *Revista del Museo de La Plata*, XVI, Buenos Aires, 1909.

[2] Ameghino, Florentino, La industria de la piedra quebrada en el mioceno superior de Monte Hermoso, Buenos Aires, 1910.

ment of the same material used as a hammer, and a knife or scraper of jasper. All were found in a surface layer of gravelly sand capping the Monte Hermoso barranca, or on the broken face of the barranca itself. The latter were picked up on the ledges of the bluff face, where they had cascaded from above. The jasper knife or scraper is of a type familiar in the coast region as well as in Patagonia, as will be seen by reference to figures 26, *b*, and 30.

The quartzite pieces are from water-worn or weathered material, such as was used for mullers, anvils, and hammers all along the coast, and present the usual appearance of shop refuse so familiar to northern archeologists—just such objects as may be found on numerous sites in the Potomac Valley and of which countless numbers may be seen distributed along the bluff slopes within the suburbs of Washington. The fact that one of the larger fragments has been used as a chipping hammer is entirely in keeping with the writer's classification of these objects as the refuse of implement making carried on by recent tribes along the Monte Hermoso bluff. The inclusion of such objects in superficial deposits which are subject to rearrangement by the winds and by gravity is a perfectly normal and commonplace occurrence. That they present any unusually primitive features of form or workmanship or have had any significant association with ancient geologic formations seems to the writer altogether improbable.

Such differences as may arise between the writer's interpretations and those of Doctor Ameghino are probably due in large measure to the fact that the points of view assumed in approaching the problem of culture and antiquity are widely at variance. Doctor Ameghino takes for granted the presence in Argentine of peoples of great antiquity and of extremely primitive forms of culture and so does not hesitate to assign finds of objects displaying primitive characteristics to unidentified peoples and to great antiquity, or to assume their manufacture by methods supposed to characterize the dawn of the manual arts. To him all this is a simple and reasonable procedure.

The writer finds it more logical to begin with the known populations of the region whose culture is familiar to us and which furnishes lithic artifacts ranging in form from the simplest fractured stone to the well-made and polished implement, and prefers to interpret the finds made, unless sufficient evidence is offered to the contrary, in the illuminating light of known conditions and of well-ascertained facts rather than to refer them to hypothetic races haled up from the distant past.

EARTHENWARE

A small number of fragments of pottery were collected by Doctor Hrdlička on prehistoric sites along the margin of a lakelet near Puerto

(⅔ actual size)

POTTERY FRAGMENTS FROM VICINITY OF PUERTO SAN BLAS

San Blas. They represent bowls and cups of simple shape, not in any case exceeding 8 inches in diameter. The walls are thin, between one-fourth and three-eighths of an inch in thickness, and are of well-baked clay, gray and brown in color, and tempered with a large percentage of quartz sand. The surfaces inside and out have been well smoothed with a polishing implement. The rims are upright, or curved slightly inward or outward, and rounded or squared off on the margin.

Simple decorative designs have been added, in some cases encircling the rim, and again covering a large part of the body. These designs have been incised and indented with implements of varied shape, and display considerable taste on the part of the potter, as will be seen by referring to plate 15. Small fragments of similar, entirely plain ware were collected on the margin of Laguna de los Padres, near Mar del Plata, and also among the dunes and in the playas near the coast. In the grade of culture represented this ware corresponds closely with that of the stone implements and utensils of the same region. It differs but slightly in composition, color, and decoration from the simpler ware of the Atlantic slope in the United States.

VII. THE SKELETAL REMAINS OF EARLY MAN IN SOUTH AMERICA

By ALEŠ HRDLIČKA

THE QUATERNARY MAN [1]

In entering on the investigation of the skeletal remains relating to early man in South America the writer approaches a field of exceptional difficulties, where a clear and satisfactory report may not always be possible. The material for examination is widely scattered, it is for the most part in a very defective state, and further, much of it has suffered through imperfect restoration. The essential data concerning the most important circumstances of the finds will be seen in many instances to be extremely defective; the descriptions of the human remains run often into unnecessary minutiæ on one hand and fail in the essentials; and descriptions with measurements by different observers show a lack of agreement. Under these conditions the records to be given, and of necessity also the comparisons, are somewhat limited. Notwithstanding this, however, it will be found that there runs throughout, like an uninterrupted red line, evidence pointing in one direction only, which is that of a more simple explanation, with more moderate dating, of the numerous finds—thus harmonizing with the conclusions arrived at through the study of other material in the preceding sections of this work.

THE LAGOA SANTA DISCOVERIES (BRAZIL)

The Lagoa Santa remains are by far the earliest finds in South America that bear on the question of ancient man; these, which were discovered by P. W. Lund, a Danish explorer of note, between the years 1835 and 1844, in certain caves in the district of Lagoa Santa, Brazil, along with the bones of fossil as well as of recent animals, consist of a large series of more or less fully mineralized human bones.

---

[1] Exact chronologic classification of the subject dealt with in this report is not possible. Ameghino regards some of the specimens reported here as Tertiary. The only criterion that could be employed in arranging the separate reports was the seemingly prevalent opinion as to the geologic age of the various remains. The sections relating to "Quaternary" man will be given in the order of the dates of discovery, and those which relate to "Tertiary" remains will be arranged on the basis of the reputed antiquity of the specimens, beginning with the most recent.

HISTORY

The .first reference to these finds occurs in a letter dated August, 1840, written by Lund to C. C. Rafn, secretary of the Société Royale des Antiquaires du Nord.[1] Lund reports the discovery, in one of the Lagoa Santa caves, of human bones and of one stone utensil, in connection with the bones of certain animals of extinct species. The human remains were in part petrified and appeared to be in the same state of preservation as the ancient animal bones. The forehead in the human skulls was very sloping, as in the figures on some of the ancient Mexican monuments.

Shortly afterward, in a memoir dated at Lagoa Santa, January 30, 1841, and published one year later,[2] Lund speaks of the same subject somewhat more fully. He declares that, "as to the important question of the contemporaneity of man and extinct animal forms in this part of the world, I do not believe myself authorized as yet to modify the negative result at which I have hitherto arrived." This view was maintained by Lund notwithstanding the fact that he found in two caves skeletal remains of man which presented all the characteristics of really fossil bones. In neither of these caves, however, were the human skeletal remains in a condition to permit a safe conclusion as to their geologic age; in fact, they seemed to be of more recent origin than the animal bones in the•same caves. Lund did not feel himself warranted therefore in attributing to the human specimens special value as evidence of antiquity.

The circumstances of the discoveries in question are narrated as follows: [3]

"One of the two caves in question is situated on the border of a lake, the waters of which invade it in the rainy season, flowing afterward to the Rio das Velhas, half a league distant. In the galleries of the cave, dry at the time of the exploration, the ground was found covered by a thin layer of mellow black earth, freely mixed with the shells of snails of the species (*Planorbis, Ampullaria*) still existent in the lake and on its borders. In this soft earth lay bones of man, mammals, birds, reptiles, and fishes, distributed without order, and in very different states of preservation. Some could be distinguished from fresh bones only in that they were more fragile, lighter in weight, and of dark reddish-brown color; others were very heavy, hard, and of a brownish aspect on the surface as well as in fracture. Between the two extremes, however, there were many gradations." It is expressly noted by Lund that the human skeletal parts are included

---

[1] Lund, P. W., Letter of Aug. 20, 1840, to C. C. Rafn. Referred to in *Berlingske Tidende*, Feb. 12, 1841; in *Aarsberetning fra det Kgl. nord. Oldskriftselskab* for 1840, p. 5; in *Neues Jahrbuch für Mineralogie*, Stuttgart, 1841, pp. 502, 606; in *Nouvelles Annales des Voyages*, 1841, d., VI, p. 116; and published in full in Breve till C. C. Rafn, udg. af B. Grondahl, Kjöbenhavn, 1880, p. 247.

[2] Lund, P. W., Blik paa Brasiliens Dyreverden, etc.; in *Kgl. danske Videnskabernes Selskabs Skrifter*, 4de Raekke, Naturv.-mathem., Afhandl., IX, Kjöbenhavn, 1842, pp. 195–196.

[3] Lütken, Chr. Fr., Indledende Bemaerkninger om Menneskelevninger i Brasiliens Huler og i de Lundske Samlinger. En *Samling af Afhandlinger e Museo Lundii*, I, Kjöbenhavn, 1888, pp. 1–29 (with a good abstract in French). The quotations here given follow Lütken.

in the above statement, presenting all gradations in the conditions of their preservation and ranging from those that were light and fragile to those that were hard, heavy, and completely petrified.

The thoroughly petrified bones of animals belonged to extinct species (*Platyonyx, Scelidotherium, Chlamydotherium, Hydrochœrus sulcidens, Dasypus sulcatus, Antilope maquinensis*, etc.) [1]

As to the human skulls, it seemed to Lund that they indicated two different races, "some being smaller and relatively well-formed, and others larger, but of a most unfavorable (*d'une forme des plus désavantageuses*) form, with a forehead so sloping that it is lower than even that in many of the apes."

The second cave [1] is a great subterranean labyrinth, the lower chambers of which become inundated in the season of rains. In the lowest part of one of these chambers Lund encountered a large quantity of bones of different animals scattered throughout the earth which filled the space. The bones were in the main those of deer, peccaries, and pacas, doubtless of species that are still living, but with them were teeth and bones of the *Platyonyx, Chlamydotherium, Hoplophorus, Megatherium, Smilodon,* and other extinct forms. The human remains were not found associated with these bones, but far away in another part of the cave and in the immediate vicinity of one of its entrances; these, which belonged to only one individual, were broken, and lay at a slight depth in the ground in a narrow space only a few cubic feet in capacity; but they showed characteristics of fossil bones, being very fragile, even friable, pure white in fracture, and strongly adherent to the tongue. Their position, however, seemed to indicate a more recent origin [2] than that of the bones of the fossil animals.

Lund closes his communication with the statement "that he has said enough to show that the discoveries are not sufficient to decide the question of contemporaneity of man with the extinct animal forms, the remains of which are found in the youngest terranes of Brazil." [3]

In 1842 and again in 1844, Lund wrote other letters on his discoveries, to the secretary of the Instituto Historico Brasileiro. [4]

---

[1] Lütken remarks that this cave was, without doubt, the Lapa Vermelha.

[2] Lütken remarks, however, that of the above the antelope was shown to be the *Cervus simplicicornis*, a species still living, and that the *Hydrochœrus "sulcidens"* can not be separated as a variety from the *H. capybara*, although it might well be considered one of the ancient forms in which this species presented itself.

[3] "At han mener at have anført nok til at vise, at de ikke ere tilstraekkelige til at tjene som afgjørende Dokumenter i Spørgsmaalet, hvorvidt Mennesket var samtidigt eller ej med de undergaaede Dyreformer, hvis Levninger ere ophevarede i Brasiliens yngste Jordlag."

[4] Carta escripta da Lagôa Santa (Minas Geraes), ao Sr. 1°. Secretario do Instituto, pelo socio honorario, Sr. Dr. Lund, in *Revista trimensal de Historia e Geographia*, IV, 1842, Rio de Janeiro, 1843, pp. 80–87; and Carta do Dr. Lund, escripta da Lagoa Santa (Minas Geraes) a 21 de abril de 1844; ibid., VI, 1844, pp. 334–342.

These letters are also given in translation by Lacerda, in the *Mémoires de la Société d'Anthropologie de Paris*, 2me sér., II, Paris, 1875, pp. 522–535; and the earlier one is referred to in the following: *Köllner Zeitung*, Sept. 9, 1842; *Amer. Jour. Sci.*, XLIV, New Haven, 1843, p. 277; *Edinburgh New Philos. Jour.*, XXXVI, 1844, pp. 38–41; *L'Institut*, X, 1842, p. 356; *Neues Jahrb. für Min.*, Stuttgart, 1843, p. 118; *Proc. Acad. Nat. Sci. Phila.*, II, 1844–5, Phila., 1846, pp. 11–13.

All quotations here are translations from the originals in Portuguese.

These two communications repeat in the main what has already been cited, but there are also several additional statements.

In the earlier letter Lund states that notwithstanding the excellent opportunities he had to examine into the question of the contemporaneity of man in Brazil with the extinct species of mammals, he had not yet arrived at a definite conclusion, although he had made every effort to do so. He had explored up to that time nearly 200 caves and the number of mammal species alone which were found amounted to 115, of which only 88 are still living in the region.

The bad condition in which most of the cave bones of animals were found and the nature of the mutilations they showed convinced Lund that in the majority of cases their presence was due to savage beasts, which had the habit of bringing their victims or parts of them to their dens in the caves where the flesh was devoured.

"But," Lund continues, "among so large a quantity of bones, which indicate the existence of an order of things altogether different from that which exists to-day, I have never encountered the slightest traces of man. Yet, at an epoch when ferocious animals, among which some gigantic forms (e. g., *Smilodon populator*) abounded in this country, why should man, who is so feeble in contest with such formidable animals, have escaped the fate which overtook numerous victims many times stronger than himself?" This consideration, he was led to believe, settled negatively the question of man's contemporaneity with these animals, when, after six years of fruitless search, he discovered cave remains of human beings "which may possibly lead to a contrary solution of the question."

"I found these human remains," he says, "in a cave mixed with the bones of various animals of species entirely extinct (*Platyonyx Bucklandii, Chlamydotherium Humboldtii, C. majus, Dasypus sulcatus, Hydrochærus sulcidens*, etc.), a circumstance sufficient to call attention in the highest degree to the interesting relics. Moreover, they presented all the physical characteristics of fossil bones. They were in part petrified, in part impregnated with ferruginous particles, which gave to some of them a metallic luster, akin to that of bronze, as well as extraordinary weight. There could then be no doubt as to their great age. But in view of the fact that the cave that contained the bones lay at the border of a lake, the water of which entered it annually during the rainy season, no definite conclusion can be reached as to whether the individuals to whom they belonged were or were not contemporaneous with the extinct species of animals with which their bones occurred. In consequence of this circumstance, successive introductions of animal remains into the cavern could have taken place and the bones of later introduction could have become mixed with those already deposited. This, it was demonstrated, had actually taken place, for among the bones of the extinct species were encountered others of animals whose species are still living.   These latter showed unequal states of preservation, according to their age, some of them hardly differing from fresh bones, while others approximated the submetallic state previously referred to; the majority, however, showed alterations intermediate between these two extremes.   A similar difference, but less considerable, was also noted in the human bones, proving undeniably the inequalities in their ages; but all presented sufficient alteration in composition or texture to indicate a considerable antiquity, so that, should they lose the right to serve as evidence of the coexistence of man with the great extinct species of terrestrial mammals, they would still retain sufficient interest from the latter point of view. . . .

"The researches of the European naturalists have demonstrated that none of the great species of terrestrial mammals whose bones are found in true fossil state have lived in historic times and that consequently the date of their extinction is further back than 3,000 years. Applying these results to the extinct species of Brazil, the bones of which present the same state of preservation as those of the extinct forms in Europe, and attributing to those human bones, which are found in an analogous state of conservation, corresponding antiquity, we obtain for these human remains an age of 30 centuries and more. As, however, the process of petrifaction is one of those that has been least studied, principally in relation to the time required for its consummation, and as, on the other hand, that time varies according to more or less favorable circumstances, we can not risk on this basis any more than vague approximations.   Be it as it may, there will always remain for these human bones a very considerable antiquity, which places them far back of the epoch of discovery of this part of the world, as well as beyond all the direct documents which we possess on the existence of man, considering that thus far there have been found in no other part of the world human bones in a state of petrifaction.

"It is then proved by these evidences, in the first place, that the population of Brazil is derived from very remote times and undoubtedly anterior to the historic period.

"Naturally the question then presents itself, Who were these most ancient inhabitants of Brazil?   Of what race were they?   What was their mode of life and their intellectual status?

"Fortunately the answers to these questions are less difficult and less uncertain than those relating to the antiquity of the bones. Having found a number of more or less complete skulls, I can fix the place which the individuals to whom they belonged should occupy in anthropology.   The sloping forehead, the prominence of the zygomatic bones, the facial angle, the form of the jaws and orbits, all assign these skulls a place among the most characteristic of the

American race . . .   In regard to the low forehead, these ancient crania show not merely a conformity with those of the American race, but some of them exhibit this feature in an excessive degree, extending to a complete disappearance of the forehead.

"It is then proved, in the second place, that the people, who in that remote time inhabited this part of the new world, were of the same race as those who occupied this country at the time of the Conquest."

In the following paragraph Lund expresses the opinion that this lowness of the forehead is a natural feature, not due to artificial deformation, and that it offers an explanation of the figures with similar low foreheads sculptured on some ancient American monuments.   He then proceeds:

"The bones of the skeletons belonged to individuals of both sexes; they were of ordinary size; nevertheless two among those of the males presented dimensions above the ordinary."

In conclusion, Lund expresses a rather poor opinion of the probable mental characteristics of the people from whom the remains came; this conclusion, he says, is "corroborated by an instrument of the most imperfect construction found with the bones.   This instrument consists simply of a hemispheric stone of amphibole, 10 inches in circumference and smooth on the plane surface, which evidently served for crushing seeds or other hard substances."

Besides the bones spoken of above, Lund mentions the finds of some human osseous remains, "whose characteristics were also those of fossil bones," in two other of the Minas Geraes caves.   "The bones were deprived of nearly all the gelatinous parts, and in consequence were very friable and white in fracture.   Unfortunately, they were found isolated and without being accompanied by the bones of other animals, so that the principal question raised by these finds, that of man's antiquity, remains undecided; nevertheless, the specimens corroborate the conclusions relative to the prolonged existence of man in this part of the world."

The main parts of the above letter were published in Philadelphia in 1845 and were quoted more or less extensively during the early forties, in other publications.[1]

The subsequent letter of Lund to the Institute (1844) contains less information than the one cited above, but there are several points of some importance.   The first concerns the mineralization of the various bones.   Lund's words in regard to this point are:

"The advanced decomposition of the [animal] bones contained in this deposit [evidently referring to the cave of Sumidouro] showed

---

[1] Strain, Isaac. G., Extract of a letter giving the synopsis of the translation, by himself, of a letter from Doctor Lund, R. S. A., Copenhagen, to the Historical and Geographical Society of Brazil; in *Proc. Acad. Nat. Sci. Phila.*, II, 1844-5, Phila., 1846, pp. 11-13.

plainly that they were very ancient.   Laid on glowing coals, they exhale no empyreumatic odor; they adhere strongly to the tongue, treated with dilute nitric acid, they dissolve completely and rapidly with a violent effervescence.   They are therefore wholly calcareous, that is in part petrified, offering thus all the characteristics of true fossil bones."

Having expressed himself on this part of the question, Lund proceeds to the examination of the bones from the zoologic standpoint, with the result that some of them are found to belong to species still living, while others belonged to animals which have already ceased to exist in that locality.   Among the latter specimens were some bones of the llama, but great surprise was occasioned by the presence also of some bones of a horse.   These did not belong to either of the two species of fossil horses known in the country, but "indicated a different species, so nearly similar to the domestic horse that no characteristics could be found in the fragments to distinguish them therefrom, though their proportions were notably superior to those of the races of the horse introduced into South America by the conquerors.

"In view of the facts to which I have here referred, there can then remain no doubt as to the existence of man on this continent in an epoch anterior to that in which the last races of the gigantic animals whose remains abound in the caves of this country became extinct, or, in other terms, as to his existence here anterior to the historic period.[1]

"As to the ethnographic peculiarities of the skulls from this deposit, I had occasion to confirm my former conclusions, namely, that they offer all the characteristic features of the American race; and I have also firmly convinced myself that the extraordinary depression of the forehead which is observed in some of the individuals, is not artificial.

"We see thus that America was already peopled before the first rays of history appeared on the horizon of the Old World, and that the people who inhabited it in those remote times were of the same race as that found here at the time of discovery."

In the subsequent paragraphs of his letter, Lund indulges in some speculations and gives interpretations of certain features consequent on the wearing down in the human skulls of the front teeth; these views are, however, in the light of present knowledge on the subjects, plainly erroneous.

The final, and in some respects the most important, communication of Lund on the subject of the Lagoa Santa human remains is contained in a long letter addressed by him, in March, 1844, to C. C.

---

1 By this Lund doubtless means the historic period of mankind in general as then known.—A. H.

Rafn, secretary of the Société Royale des Antiquaires du Nord.[1] The principal parts of this communication, which because of the relative inaccessibility of the originals, need to be given somewhat in extenso, are as follows:

"The limestone caves of Brazil, which are so rich in bones of animals, yield only very limited traces of the skeletal remains of man. My efforts to find the latter were for a number of years fruitless, a fact which strengthened more and more my belief in the generally accepted view that man was late in appearing in this part of the world. The researches of the last few years, however, have brought other results. Of more than 800 caves which I have examined, six at last yielded human bones, the majority of which, judging by their aspect, belong to very remote times; but the circumstances under which they were found did not afford at first any adequate criteria for the exact determination of their age.

"Usually the human bones were not associated with bones of animals which could shed any light on this point, but a single cave presented at last an exception. In this were found besides the human remains the bones of divers animals belonging to species both existing and extinct. Notwithstanding this, geologic criteria necessary for the determination of the relative age of these vestiges are unfortunately wanting, because the remains discovered were not found in their original positions.

"The cave in question is situated on the border of a lake, the waters of which invade it during the rainy season, a circumstance which explains how bones of different ages could have become accumulated within it without order. However, of all the caves which I have examined up to the present time, this was the only one that encouraged me to anticipate the possibility of finding the solution of a question of such importance as that of the age of the human genus on this continent. In consequence, I did not fail to profit by the opportunity afforded by the dryness of the previous year and submitted the cave to new explorations. These researches, although they have not yielded results capable of solving the problem of man's antiquity in a definite manner, nevertheless throw important light on several other points relating to that subject. . . .

"The cave is situated in limestone rock, which rises vertically on the southern border of a lake known as the Lagoa do Sumidouro. The lake, large during the rains, becomes entirely empty during the dry season. It is drained by means of several small crevices, named

[1] An extract from this letter was published in the *Antikvarisk Tidsskrift*, Kjöbenhavn, 1843–45, and a French translation of the larger part of it appears in "Notice sur des ossements humains fossiles, trouvés dans une caverne du Brésil," in *Mémoires des Antiquaires du Nord*, 1845–49, Copenhague (n. d.), pp. 49–77. The substance of the letter is given also by Lütken, op. cit. (see footnote 3, p. 154, herein), pp. 21–23, and references to it are found in his résumé; in *C. R. de l'Acad. Sci.*, XX, Paris, 1845, p. 1368; in *L'Institut*, XIII, 1845, p. 166; and in Froriep's *Neue Notizen*, XXXV, 1845, p. 16.

sangradores, which exist in the base of the limestone rock and lead to subterranean canals, by which the lake communicates with the Rio das Velhas, about half a league distant. . . .

"The highest of the above crevices opens into the cave, but the principal opening by which one reaches the latter is situated farther to the west, in a small wooded area, at an elevation slightly above the highest level of the lake. Descent is possible by two low passages a short distance apart, over large fallen stones, which obstruct the way to the cave.

"The cavern is spacious and comprises several large chambers and passages communicating with one another. The floor, which is everywhere strewn with large fallen rocks, slopes toward the middle, where there is a pool of water. Over the floor is a thick covering of mellow blackish earth, which dried in the air assumes a lighter grayish color, and contains numerous fresh shells belonging to a species of small fresh water snail living in the lake outside. This carpet of soft earth is a deposit left by the latest inundations. . . .

"A quantity of recent bones of small animals derived from a more ancient layer were found on and also in this soft earth. The original bed of these bones appears in the upper part of the cave. It consists of clay, different in quality and color, which fills the space between the large blocks of stone and continues deeper down. Toward its lower limit this clay is grayish and partly soft, partly more or less hardened by calcareous particles or by the shells of snails, which are mixed with it in great numbers. In measure at which this layer of clay becomes more distant from the center of the cave and consequently from the influence of the inundations, the gray color of the deposit passes insensibly from yellowish to dark brownish red, varied with some dark patches; these disappear farther on, and at last there is only clay of the color of a dark tile, similar to the original deposit which fills the spaces among the stones in the majority of the Minas Geraes caves. The quantity of the snail shells diminishes as the gray clay assumes more and more the red color.

"Many bones were exhumed from the different masses of this clay; and nearly as large a quantity of them was also found in the bottom deposit of the pool in the center of the cave. . . .

"This pool was entirely emptied, and many precious remains of animals were recovered from the spot. The bones found there resembled altogether those contained in the layer of the black earth, with the differences only that the effects of water were here more distinct. They were of a brown, red, or black color on the surface as well as interstitially; the majority of them were petrified and through being continually washed, their surface had a metallic polish. On account of this quality and their metallic sound when struck, they could have been taken for copies of bones in metal rather than for veritable bones themselves.

"The different classes of animals to which the bones found in the cave belong, are as follows:

"*Man.*—The human bones belonged to at least 30 individuals of different ages, from the newborn to the decrepit aged. They were for the most part broken, but the quality of the fractured surfaces indicates, in the majority of cases, that the injury took place after the bone had become fragile through advanced state of decomposition. . . . The massive blocks of stone, among which a large part of these bones were scattered, are sufficient witnesses of the great changes which the cave has suffered since the bones were introduced.

"The human bones were found scattered pellmell, without any order; some of them, nevertheless, formed an exception to the rule, presenting still their natural relations with the adjacent bones, which seems to indicate that they were originally deposited in the cave with their adhering soft parts. However, the large accumulations of human bones which were found at some points proved that these were removed from their original position and that they had been carried by water to the spots where encountered. The majority of the skulls were also heaped separately, while another pile was formed of small bones, as those of the fingers, toes, and the constituents of the carpus and tarsus.

"A number of small human bones appeared also in the uppermost portions of the black earth; these were distinguished by a reddish-brown color, which penetrated the bone more or less and was sometimes communicated to the entire specimen. They were entirely calcareous and more or less petrified, the measure of their red color corresponding to these changes. There were only a few human bones in the sediment of the pool. The largest number was found in the gray or yellowish clay, in its softer as well as indurated parts. Some of them existed also in the yellowish clay with blackish patches. In the indurated clay, they formed part of a sort of bony breccia of great hardness similar to that in which appears here the oldest débris of mammals of extinct species.

"The human remains had all the characteristics of fossil bones: the interior was of pure white; the surface was stained black by ferruginous substances. In those that had been broken there was as much of this black stain in the interior as on the exterior. They adhered strongly to the tongue; exposed to fire or laid on hot coals, they did not turn black and gave no odor; in dilute nitric acid they dissolved completely in a few minutes, with strong ebullition. They were in part petrified."

Mammals.—Among these remains was a piece of the femur of a species of extinct monkey. There were also a great quantity of bones of bats of varieties which still inhabit the cave, and those of many existing species of rodents. The bones of a number of individuals of a species of large extinct rodent, *Hydrochærus sulcidens*, were mingled irregularly with the human bones in the yellowish earth with blackish discolorations. The earth covering of the floor of the cave and the bottom of the pool also contained a quantity of the same.

There were bones of some species of *Didelphis*, which were nearly always found in the cave deposits, and those of carnivores, including the great fossil jaguar (*Felis protopanther*), belonging to a species that is extinct, or at least does not now exist in Brazil. The remains of this jaguar were found beside the human bones in the yellowish clay with black discolorations, and also in the floor covering of the cave and at the bottom of the pool. The bones in the first-mentioned deposit were of similar aspect externally to the human bones. Among the petrified bones of the pool and of the mold covering the floor of the cave were also those of a puma and an ocelot, identical with those of animals of these species still in existence.

The most interesting of the canine bones belonged to *Canis jubatus*, the existing wolf of Brazil. While the bones of the puma and the ocelot have been found occasionally in ancient layers of soil and in bone breccia, this is not true of the osseous remains of this wolf. The bones of this animal "were found mixed pellmell with those of man in the yellowish earth with black discolorations, and the staining was the same in the two species. The earth covering the floor and that forming the bottom of the pool contained also some débris of the troglodyte wolf (extinct), side by side with the bones of a small chacal similar to the one which still exists in the country." The bones of a species of otter, similar to the living *Lutra brasiliensis*, end the list.

The pachyderms were represented by peccaries of two living species. "Their bones were everywhere mingled with the human skeletal remains, but especially so in the yellowish earth with black discolorations." There were also traces of an extinct larger species of peccary and of tapir.

Besides the above, Lund found in the same cave, as reported in his earlier letter, the bones of a horse, differing from those of the two fossil species of this animal which existed in Brazil, but exhibiting "great conformity with the existing domesticated horse." However, these bones came from a stronger, taller animal than the ordinary horse of Brazil. They lay in the yellow as well as in the more reddish clay with blackish discolorations, and their state of decomposition was similar to that of the bones which surrounded them. They were calcareous, and in part petrified. Lund says: "This last circumstance creates a new and unexpected difficulty, the solution of which may one day lead to important results. No one could pretend that the

exhumed bones of this animal belonged to individuals descended
from the horse introduced by the Portuguese scarcely 100 years ago.
The relations under which these bones were found, with their state
of decomposition, prove incontestably a more remote age."

Ruminants were represented by four species, of which three,
those of deer, conformed with the living species. The remains of
two of these were found in the red clay and also in its more recent
modifications. They were found also, apparently removed from
their original bed, in the pool and in the earth which carpeted the
cave. The third species, which does not appear at present in the
country, existed in the clay and also in the pool as well as in the floor
deposits. The fourth species was the llama, not now known in Brazil. Its bones lay in the two most ancient modifications of the clay.

In addition to the above there were bones of several species still
living and some already extinct, of armadillos and other edentates, and
of numerous birds, reptiles, and fishes. Some of these bones were
still in a relatively fresh state, while others, of both living and extinct
species, were more or less petrified. The bones of the edentates were
encountered in the modified clay, as well as in the earth at the bottom
of the pool and on the floor of the cave. The remains of the birds,
reptiles, and fishes existed only in the two deposits last-mentioned.

In subsequent parts of his letter Lund considers the agency of
water in producing the conditions found in the cave, and the various
possible modes of introducing the animal remains into the cavern.
He then returns again to the human bones, with the following notes:

"I have already remarked that the skeletal remains of man which
were found in the cave belonged to individuals ranging in age from
the unborn to those of decrepit old age. The proportion of the latter
was very considerable. There were a number of lower jaws which were
not only without the teeth, but which presented such an absorption
of the bone that they resembled a bone lamina of only a few lines in
thickness. It is therefore probable that these skeletons belonged to
decrepit individuals who had died of old age and were thrown into
this cave, which thus appears to have served as a place of sepulture.
A similar explanation is applicable to the young individuals, whose
mortality as well known is greatest during the early years. . . .
A peculiarity which I discovered in some of the skulls warrants me, it
seems, in believing that the death of several of the individuals buried
in this cave did not result from natural causes. In several of the skulls
I discovered a hole in one of the temples, of a regular oblong form, the
long axis of which was parallel with the long axis of the head. This
hole was found to be of the same size and same form in all the skulls.
. . . It seems to me most likely that this hole in the temple is the
result of external violence which caused the death of the individual.
It should still further be remarked that the outline and size of the

puncture correspond quite closely to those of the pointed end of the stone axes, specimens of which are so often found in the excavations of antiquities, a fact which leads to the belief that they were produced by such an instrument. . . .

"If we consider these remains of man from the standpoint of the ethnographic traits which they present, we shall see that all the skulls bear the distinctive features of the American race. . . .

"The examination to which I have submitted the contents of the cave has thus led me to the following conclusions:

"1. The occupation of South America by man extends not only beyond the epoch of the discovery of this part of the world, but far back into historic times [i. e. historic time in general], and probably even beyond these into geologic times. A number of species of animals seem to have disappeared from the ranks of the creation since the appearance of man in this hemisphere.

"2. The race which occupied this part of the world in remote antiquity was in its general type the same as that which inhabited the country at the time of the discovery by the Europeans."

The above completes the original data concerning the Lagoa Santa cave discoveries.

Reports on Lund's Collections

Most of Lund's collections passed to the Zoological Museum of the University of Copenhagen; one of the Sumidouro cave skulls, however, was donated by him to the Historical and Geographical Institute of Brazil, in whose possession it remains to this day;[1] and a series of specimens, including the number of more or less mineralized human bones, was acquired by the British Museum.

The last-named collection was briefly reported on in 1864 as follows by Blake:[2]

"In the British Museum there exist some human remains purchased with the Claussen collection, and forming part of the series of specimens which were discovered by Lund and Claussen in their investigations in Eastern Brazil.

"Mr. W. Davies having kindly drawn my attention to them, I will give a short list of the specimens, without wishing to draw any further conclusions than that they probably belong to a period of great historical antiquity, although probably not coeval with the fossil fauna which Lund has described in the *Transactions* of various northern academies.

"1. Skull of young child. This skull is brachycephalic and asymmetrical, the right side being shorter than the left. There are evi-

---

[1] It was seen by the writer; it could be examined, however, only through the glass doors of a closet, the key of which had been lost.

[2] Blake, C. C., On Human Remains from a Bone Cave in Brazil; in *Jour. Anthr. Soc. London*, II, 1864, pp. CCLXV–CCLXVII.

dent traces of 'parieto-occipital' flattening, which has extended above the lambdoid and for a well-defined space on either side of the sagittal suture. None of the sutures are complex. Flattening on the left side of the frontal bone is manifest, indicating the direction in which the compressing force has been exercised throughout life. No other abnormal development is visible. The molar and premolar teeth in place, show little signs of erosion. The basioccipito-sphenoid suture having been present, the basioccipital bone has been broken away, as well as the right border of the foramen magnum and the right squamosal bone. The maxilla is slightly prognathic. The skull presents the most similarity to the skulls from Cañete, in Peru, described by Castelnau, and to some which I have seen from the uplands of the Argentine provinces, near Rosario.

"2. Broken maxillary (adult?) left side. The first premolar, as well as the broken fragment of the second premolar, are the only teeth which remain. Slight erosion is visible on the crown of the first tooth.

"3. Lower mandible, left ramus. Thickly incrusted with limonite and sand, which has filled up the alveoli. Only the first and second molars are in place, the second being turned out of its proper insertion, as well as the first being much worn. Both the molar teeth in place are much worn on the outer side of the teeth. All the other teeth, with the exception of the first premolar, are absent. No marked outward or inward inflection of the angle is present.

"4. Lower mandible, left ramus. This specimen exhibits the same general characters as No. 3, with the exception that the incrustation of limonite is not present. On the inner sides of m. 3 and m. 2, the upper angles of the cusps have been broken away, the whole surface of the teeth being much worn. M. 1 is much worn, and a small fracture of the alveolar process outside it has permitted that [sic] the two outer fangs to be elevated and dislocated from their own proper insertions and to form by this dislocation a grinding surface. The first and second premolars, as well as the canine and first incisor, are also much worn. The mental process of the jaw is high; the genial tubercles distinct; and the mental foramen, not as in No. 3, filled up with limonite. The coronoid process is high; and, although the angle is broken away, enough remains to lead us to conjecture that it was strong and powerful.

"5. Portions of parietal bones of average thickness, incrusted with ochreous mud.

"6. Upper part of supraoccipital bone, and lower and posterior portions of two parietals, exhibiting the confluence of the sagittal and lambdoid sutures. The supraoccipital bone is slightly elevated above the level of the lambdoid suture, which, as well as the sagittal, is very complex. There are no traces of wormian ossifications and on the inner side of the bone the sutures are perfectly closed.

"7. Broken glabella and fragments of nasals, as well as a piece of the supraciliary arch of a young individual; frontal sinuses small.

"8. Distal portion and shaft of humerus, gnawn by mice and by some larger rodent; thickly permeated by limonite.

"9. Distal portion and shaft of humerus; young or small individual; no marks of teeth.

"10. Proximal end of tibia, very young individual, wanting epiphyses; slightly gnawn by rodents.

"11. Shaft of femur; much gnawn by rodents.

"12. Proximal end of femur, including head and neck, and part of shaft, of young individual; gnawn by mice (*Hesperomys*).

"13. Distal end of femur, exhibiting frequent marks of the teeth of some rodent, probably one of the small mice (*Hesperomys*) of the caves, slightly infiltrated with ocherous mud, and with much of the animal matter absent.

"14. Tibia, long fragment of shaft; few traces of rodent action.

"The following three specimens are in the same condition as the fragments of the lower jaw, No. 3, above alluded to.

"15. Long bone (small humerus?) imbedded in limonite, which contains many fragments of fossil shells, exceedingly difficult of identification. A specimen of *Planorbis* (of which fresh-water type four existing species in Brazil are recorded by Mr. S. P. Woodward in his Manual of Mollusca) is recognisable, as well as the broken fragments of an elongated land-snail, probably *Bulimus*.

"16. Sections of three long bones, covered with sandy deposit containing large quantities of oxide of iron (limonite); the medullary cavity of the bones being filled with crystals of carbonate of lime.

"17. Distal end of femur, thickly incrusted with limonite, the animal matter being absent.

"18. Head of humerus, covered with limonite."

The next mention of the Lund specimens, referring to the main part of the collection at Copenhagen, occurs in the memoir of Reinhardt,[1] who occupied himself for years with the study of the animal bones collected by Lund in the Brazilian caves. In this memoir are mentioned also the human remains from the cave of Sumidouro. Reinhardt recognized that the disturbance of the primitive deposits in the cave necessitated great care in the drawing of conclusions from the find, nevertheless he says that the human bones resembled so exactly in their state of preservation those of extinct animals, that one can not doubt that they were introduced into the cave at about the same epoch as the latter. Reinhardt believed also that he could characterize the tribe from which the human remains proceeded as one of "quite tall stature, but somewhat delicate, dolichocephalic,

[1] Reinhardt, J., De brasilianske Knoglehuler og de i dem forekommende Dyrelevninger. En *Samling af Afhandlinger e Museo Lundii*, I, Kjöbenhavn, 1888, pp. 1–56. [Memoir read in 1866.]

and prognathic; with the summit of the skull elevated, nearly pyramidal, cheek bones prominent; with the front narrow, but not exceptionally depressed; with the interorbital space very large and the walls of the skull very thick (up to 1 cm.). In none of the skulls is seen any trace of an artificial deformation produced by pressure."

In 1876 the Sumidouro skull deposited in Rio de Janeiro was described by Lacerda and Peixoto.[1] The brief report reads as follows:

"*Fossil skull of Lagoa Santa, No. 7.*—It is a relatively small skull encountered with others in one of the caves of Lagoa Santa, where existed also fossil bones of animals of species already extinct. Externally it presents a metallic, bronzelike aspect; on fracture, there is clearly visible a calcareous alteration of the bone. Its weight is notable, as compared with that of other skulls which we have described. The zygomatic arches are broken in their middle part and the styloids are destroyed. In the right temporal region is seen a perforation, nearly elliptical in form, involving the squama of the temporal bone and measuring 4.8 cm. in length by 2 cm. in greatest breadth. The superior border of this defect reaches the beveled edge of the parietal, which is intact. The aspect of the borders of the opening, which are similar in nature and polish to the other unfractured parts of the skull, leads to the conclusion that this defect is not posthumous, such as appears to be true of the fractures of the zygomatic arches, which present an entirely different aspect. The form of this lesion, its extension, and the characteristics of its borders, lead us to believe that it was produced during life, by a cutting instrument. Considering the relations existing between the affected region and the brain, the wound must have resulted in the death of the individual. The skull is without the lower jaw. . . . The front is low and inclined backward as in nearly all of the skulls of the American race; the glabella is salient, the superciliary arches very prominent, the occiput flattened to nearly vertical; the external occipital protuberance is broad, plain, and very protruding. The plane of the occipital foramen prolonged forward would pass through a horizontal line drawn from one orbit to the other. The malar bones are prominent . . . the orbits quadrangular, the parieties of the skull vertical, the mastoid processes of small size, the parietal eminences prominent. Nearly all the sutures are consolidated, and their serration is for the most part simple except in the posterior portion of the sagittal, where it is complicated. There are vestiges of two Wormian bones in the lambdoid suture. In the upper jaw exist 14 dental alveoli, more or less damaged; of the teeth, there remains only the second left molar. . . . The anterior nasal aper-

---

[1] Lacerda, Filho, e Rodrigues Peixoto, Contribuições para o estudo anthropologico das raças indigenas do Brazil; in *Archivos do Museu Nacional do Rio de Janeiro*, I, 1876, pp. 63–65, pl. IV.

ture is heart-shaped, very irregular.   The canine fossæ are but little excavated; the occipital foramen presents oval form. . . . The cephalic index of the skull is 69.72; its capacity 1,388 cc.; its facial angle (Cloquet's) 67°."

Principal measurements:

	cm.
Diameter antero-posterior	18.5
Diameter transverse maximum	12.9
Diameter vertical	14.5
Arc, nasion to bregma	13.0
Arc, bregma to lambda	14.0
Arc, lambda to opisthion	12.0
Arc, from one auditory opening to the other	31.0
Basion–nasion diameter	9.3
Diameter frontal maximum	10.7
Diameter frontal minimum	9.2
Circumference, horizontal	51.5
Diameter bizygomatic	13.0
Orbital interval	2.2
Transverse diameter of the orbit	4.1
Vertical diameter of the orbit	3.3
Depth of the orbit	5.0
Distance from nasal suture to nasal spine	4.5
Breadth of the nasal aperture	2.4

The principal conclusion concerning the specimen under consideration is (pp. 72–73) that "the fossil cranium of Lagoa Santa, one of the precious objects of our collection, approaches in its charactertics very much the crania of the Botocudos."[1]

In 1879 Quatrefages made the Lagoa Santa remains the occasion of an extended report before the anthropologic meeting at Moscow.[2]

From the letters of Lund and the descriptions of the Rio de Janeiro skull by Lacerda and Peixoto, Quatrefages arrives, after a prolonged discussion of the case, but altogether too prematurely, it seems, at the following far-fetched conclusions:

"1. In Brazil, as in Europe, man lived contemporaneously with divers species of mammals which are absent from the present geologic epoch.

"2. The fossil man of Brazil discovered by Lund in the caves of Lagoa Santa existed certainly at the epoch of the reindeer; but, according to the opinion of M. Gaudry, he may not have existed at the epoch of the mammoth.

---

[1] During his visit at Rio de Janeiro the writer was able to see the skull in question, which is still preserved at the Instituto de Historia y Geografía in that city. Unfortunately the key of the closet in which the specimen is kept had been lost, so that the specimen could be inspected only through the glass. It was found that Lacerda's illustrations of the specimen were quite accurate. The skull is that of an adult, sex somewhat doubtful—either a male with submedium supraorbital ridges and moderate mastoids, or a female with these parts above average. No primitive characteristics. Orbits small, not sharp, relatively rather high, but not abnormally so, mesorhiny, small prognathism; upper alveolar process low, not strong. Vault moderate in size, apparently not deformed, dolichocephalic. Supraorbital ridges moderate; do not form complete arch. Color dark-brownish; specimen looks as if it had been treated with some preservative.

[2] Quatrefages, A. de, L'homme fossile de Lagoa-Santa (Brésil) et ses descendants actuels; in *Izviestia imper. obshchestva ljubitelei estestvoznania*, etc., III, Moskva, 1880, pp. 321–338. Also in *C. R. l'Acad. Sci.*, XCIII, Paris, 1881, p. 882.

"3. The fossil man of Lagoa Santa is distinguished from the fossil man of Europe by a number of characters, the most important of which is the coexistence of dolichocephaly and hypsistenocephaly.

"4. In Brazil, as in Europe, fossil man left his descendants who have contributed to the formation of the present populations.

"5. Lacerda and Peixoto have with reason regarded the race of Botocudos as a result of a mixture of the fossil type of Lagoa Santa with other ethnologic elements.

"6. The number and the nature of these elements remain to be determined, but one at least was brachycephalic.

"7. The fossil type of Lagoa Santa enters also in part into the composition of the Ando-Peruvian populations and is found again more or less pronounced in the littoral of the Pacific.

"8. In Peru and in Bolivia the ethnic element of Lagoa Santa manifests its presence quite as clearly as in Brazil. Nevertheless, (9) "it appears to have exercised a less general influence in Peru than in Brazil.

"10. The same ethnic element is found, according to all indications, elsewhere [in America] than in Brazil and Peru."

At about this time or a little later, a new communication by Lacerda,[1] on the subject of the Lagoa Santa man, appeared.

No new facts concerning the finds are given, but the author speaks of skulls having forms related to those of the Lagoa Santa caves from different parts of Brazil, and especially from the shell-heaps: "There are in the Museum of Rio a dozen skulls found by Hartt and his assistants in the *sambaquis* of the Provinces Paraná and Santa Catharina. Nearly all these have a sloping forehead; there are even some in which the front is very sloping. The bones of the vault are of a very considerable thickness. They are all provided with large lower jaws and with prominent and voluminous cheek bones. They are all dolichocephalic and more or less prognathic."[2]

Wear of the teeth, such as seen by Lund in the Sumidouro cave crania and considered by him as of special significance, was found equally in the *sambaqui* and other modern skulls.

An interesting section of the paper deals with "metallization" of bones. Speaking of the metallic impregnation of the Lagoa Santa specimens, Lacerda asks: "What space of time is necessary that this metallic impregnation should become complete? And has it need of special conditions of the environment to bring it about?

"It is not easy," he follows, "to give to-day an answer to these questions. What remains beyond doubt is that such a metallization

---

[1] Lacerda, A. de, Documents pour servir a l'histoire de l'homme fossile du Brésil; in *Mém. Soc. d'Anthr. Paris*, 2me sér., II, 1875, pp. 517–542.

[2] Lacerda mentions also the skull (portion) of Ceara, described by Lacerda and Peixoto in the *Archivos do Museu Nacional do Rio de Janeiro*, I, 1876, p. 67. The original, a piece of the vault, was examined by the writer; it is quite an ordinary piece, with a somewhat sloping forehead, which was badly posed and pictured. It can have no claim to be considered in connection with antiquity.

of bones bears relation to the presence of metallic substances in the terrane or deposit in which the skulls are found.   However, whatever may be the time necessary for this metallic impregnation to become complete, it is impossible to attribute on this basis any very great antiquity to the bones.   In fact, it is scarcely two years ago that we received from Para a skull that was buried in the mud on the shore of the Marajo, at its confluence with the Amazon.   In this skull also one finds all the characteristics of metallization of the bone; the specimen is relatively heavy, of a maroon color and has a metallic sound. Chemical analysis made on a part of this skull showed the existence of a very large quantity of oxide of iron and also a large proportion of alumina, two substances which do not enter normally into the composition of bone.   Nevertheless everything leads us to believe that this skull is a relatively very recent one; its craniologic characteristics are not at all similar to those of the skulls of Lagoa Santa; it was found in a rapidly forming estuary the age of which is plainly less than that of the caves.   Hence metallization of bones is not at all a special characteristic of fossil crania."

Lacerda expresses no decided opinion either for or against the acceptance of antiquity for the Lagoa Santa human remains, but his remarks are evidence of hesitation in assuming any great age.

On the occasion of the meeting of the Congress of the Americanists at Copenhagen, in 1883, some of the skulls and bones from the cave of Sumidouro were exhibited by Lütken,[1] who, at the same time, gave the principal data concerning the history of the discoveries.   In the report of this communication, we read (pp. 43–44) the following sensible remarks:

Lund himself did not go beyond the formal statement that "the most important criterion for fixing the relative age of these remains is absolutely wanting, because they were not found in their original position.   Reinhardt, who had a profound knowledge of the subject, although he did not have an opportunity to explore anew the Brazil caves, has given the opinion, it is true, 'that there is no doubt that the human remains were deposited in the cave at nearly the same epoch as those of the extinct animals,' and that 'the latter have been the contemporaries of man, at least in the last part of their existence.'   Nevertheless, I have not been able to convince myself that we are authorized to adopt this hypothesis other than as likely or probable.   I know well that de Quatrefages, in his discourse on 'The fossil man of Lagoa Santa in Brazil and his actual descendants,' at the Anthropological Congress in Moscow in 1879, arrived at the same conclusions as Reinhardt . . . that is to say, that the contemporaneity of man with the extinct species of animals is evident

---

[1] Lütken, Chr. Fr., Exposition de quelques-uns des crânes et des autres ossements humains de Minas-geraés dans le Brésil central découverts et déterrés par le feu Professeur P. W. Lund; in C. R. *Congrès international des Américanistes*, Copenhagen, 1883, p. 40.

and incontestable. However, although I do not wish to express myself except with reserve on a question of geology, I must nevertheless acknowledge that I range myself more with the naturalists who do not feel authorized to reach positive conclusions on the relative age of bones, objects, utensils, etc., which are found *in caves*, and which belong to different anthropologic and geologic epochs. It is a fact fully acknowledged by the explorers of caves, that very often there are found in such localities most ancient remains occupying a more elevated position than those from more recent periods, and that the grade of petrifaction of the bones may differ even in the two extremities of the same specimen according to whether it had been exposed or covered, more or less subjected to the action of water, etc. This shows what could have taken place, especially in such a cave as that of Sumidouro, which derives its name from the periodic penetration into it of the waters of the neighboring lake . . . It will be easily perceived that bones from different formations and periods could, under such circumstances, have become intimately mixed and could have assumed in the course of time, after having been exposed to the same influence of water, a similar aspect and the same degree of petrifaction."

In the remaining part of his communication, Lütken speaks of the fact that teeth worn as are those in the Lagoa Santa skulls are found in different primitive races. And in conclusion he says: "The question of the contemporaneity of man and extinct animals in Brazil would probably not be very much cleared by new excavations in the caves of that country; it is necessary in advance, that the relations between the extinct and the living fauna of Brazil be well fixed, and a solution of this important question will probably be found much more in the layers of the pampas than in the caves of the limestone hills."

In 1884 there appeared a communication on the subject of the Lagoa Santa skulls, by Kollmann,[1] who was able to examine the collection at Copenhagen and measured four of the best-preserved crania. These belonged to strong men; they are dark-brown in color, and heavy, owing to petrifaction. They resemble one another completely. Another skull, that of a female, presents the same characteristics and the same is true of six additional calvaria.

The skulls do not show very strong muscular ridges, with the exception of the *crista infra-temporalis*, which in all four of the male specimens is of an extraordinary development. The brain part of the crania is very well developed. "The old Lagoans are in this respect equally as well developed as our old long-headed Germans." The outline of the norma verticalis is a long oval. The forehead is vertical (!). The region of the greater wings of the sphenoid is in toto more depressed than usual. All the five skulls (including the Rio de

---

[1] **Die** Schädeln von Lagoa-Santa; in *Zeitschrift für Ethnologie*, XVI, Berlin, 1884, pp. 194–199.

Janeiro specimen) are hypsi-dolichocephalic, with average length-breadth index of *72.2* and an average length-height index of *80.2*. The face, in consequence of the strong outstanding of the zygomatic arches and small height, is chamæprosopic, the upper facial index averaging *47*. The nasal aperture is in all mesorhinic, the average nasal index amounting to *50.2*. The palate is very broad and is brachystaphyline. All four skulls show prenasal fossæ. The orbits are low, average index *78.3*. There is a rather strong grade of prognathism.

His determinations in regard to the racial characteristics of the Lagoa Santa skulls agree, Kollmann states, with those of Reinhardt, Quatrefages, and of Lacerda and Peixoto; but, "howsoever valuable all these individual features established by means of craniology are, much more significant still is the fact, which must impress itself upon everyone, that the skulls from Lagoa Santa have the *character of American crania, the racial features of the still-living Indians.*"

Curiously, however, the above does not lead Kollmann to any doubt as to the antiquity of the specimens; it is for him a proof rather of absence of changes in these features in America since the period of the American diluvium (p. 206).

The measurements (Kollmann's) of the specimens are as follows:

Crania of Lagoa Santa	No. 1	No. 2	No. 3	No. 4	Lacerda and Peixoto specimen	Average of the indices
Length of skull	18.0	18.0	18.9	17.7	18.5	—
Breadth of skull	13.5	13.0	13.0	13.4	12.9	—
Breadth of forehead	10.0	9.8	9.5	8.8	9.2	—
Height of forehead	14.5	14.6	15.0	14.5	14.5	—
Circumference, horizontal	51.2	51.0	52.3	55.4	51.5	—
Face, height (estimated)	11.0	11.6	11.3	11.4	—	—
Face, upper, height	6.0	6.6	6.3	6.4	—	—
Face, breadth	13.8	13.3	13.2	13.5	13.0	—
Nose, height	4.7	4.6	4.6	4.9	4.5	—
Nose, breadth	2.3	2.3	2.2	2.5	2.4	—
Orbits, breadth	4.2	4.2	4.1	4.2	4.1	—
Orbits, height	3.2	3.5	3.0	3.3	3.3	—
Palate, length	4.7	5.2	4.3	—	—	—
Palate, breadth	4.7	4.7	4.5	—	—	—
Length-breadth index	*74.9*	*72.2*	*68.7*	*75.7*	*69.7*	*72.2*
Length-height index	*80.5*	*81.1*	*79.3*	*81.9*	*78.3*	*80.2*
Breadth-height index	*107.4*	*112.3*	*115.3*	*108.2*	—	*110.8*
Facial index, upper	*43.4*	*49.6*	*47.7*	*47.4*	—	*47.0*
Nasal index	*48.9*	*50.0*	*47.8*	*51.0*	*53.3*	*50.2*
Orbital index	*76.1*	*83.3*	*73.1*	*78.5*	*80.7*	*78.3*
Palate index	*100.0*	*90.3*	*104.6*	—	—	*98.3*

Kollmann's conclusions, based in the main on this Lagoa Santa series, are as follows:

"1. The varieties of the American man show already in the *diluvium* the same face and skull forms as to-day. They have already the characteristics of the Indian.

"2. Man is therefore not only an old guest in America, but he is also furnished, already in diluvial times, with the same unmistakable racial characteristics as he presents this day.

"3. These racial characteristics, it necessarily follows from this evidence, originated even earlier.

"4. These racial characteristics were not further modified by environment.

"5. On the basis of the above observations and from the zoologic standpoint, a future change of racial characteristics of mankind is in the highest degree improbable."

In the present state of knowledge of the Lagoa Santa caves material, of the Indian in general, of American geology, and of the imperfect morphologic stability of the human organism, these opinions can have of course but little more than historic value.

In 1885 a brief report on the whole collection of the Sumidouro Cave human remains was published by ten Kate,[1] who had personally examined all the crania preserved at Copenhagen; other bones than the skulls were apparently not considered.

The crania were recognized by ten Kate as having close analogy with the Indian skulls of Lower California. With the probable exception of two, all the specimens are masculine. Their principal measurements are as follows:

Measurements of the Lagoa Santa skulls by ten Kate[2]

Specimen Nos.	Vault			Orbits			Nose		
	Length	Breadth	Index	Breadth	Height	Index	Length	Breadth	Index
MALES	cm.	cm.		cm.	cm.		cm.	cm.	
1.................	18.4	13.0	70.6	3.9	3.6	92.3	4.1	2.45	59.8
2.................	18.6	13.4	72.0	3.7	3.4	91.9	—	—	—
3.................	19.3	—	—	3.5	3.3	94.3	—	—	—
5.................	18.4	12.9	70.1	3.9	3.3	84.6	—	2.4	—
6.................	19.2	13.4	69.8	4.1	3.0	73.2	4.6	2.3	50.0
7.................	18.2	13.2	72.5	3.9	3.4	87.2	4.9	2.5	51.0
8.................	17.8	13.2	74.2	3.7	3.2	86.5	4.9	2.3	46.9
9.................	17.8	12.9	72.5	—	—	—	—	—	—
10.................	19.6	14.2	72.5	—	—	—	—	—	—
11.................	18.2	13.2	72.5	—	—	—	—	—	—
12.................	17.4	12.8	73.6	—	—	—	—	—	—
13.................	18.6	13.3	71.5	—	—	—	—	—	—
14.................	18.2	13.5	74.2	—	—	—	—	—	—
Average.......	18.4	13.25	72.1	3.8	3.3	86.9	4.6	2.4	51.6
Minimum.......	17.4	12 8	69.8	3.5	3.0	73.2	4.1	2.3	46.9
Maximum.......	19.6	14.2	74.2	4.1	3.6	94.3	4.9	2.5	59.8
FEMALES									
4.................	17.9	12.5	69.8	3.6	3.3	91.7	—	—	—
15.................	16.8	13.6	80.95	—	—	—	—	—	—

[1] ten Kate, H., Sur les crânes de Lagoa-Santa; in *Bull. Soc. d'Anthr. Paris*, 3me sér., VIII, 1885, pp. 240–244.
[2] Table rearranged by A. H.

The skulls are dolichocephalic, but in one of the females the cephalic index rises to brachycephaly. This skull differs from the others also in some other respects. It is difficult to say whether it represents an individual variation only or whether it is an evidence that there has been a mixture of different racial elements.

However this may be, "it is plain that if Kollmann had examined 15 instead of only 11 of the skulls, he would not have said that all the crania belonged to individuals of one perfectly pure race, and he probably would not have reached, on the basis of such homogeneity, the conclusion of a great antiquity.

"Nothing is less proven than the opinion that at the epoch of the race of Lagoa Santa, mixture of this with other ethnic elements had not as yet taken place."

As to the statements of Lund, Reinhardt, and Kollmann, that the skulls of Lagoa Santa offer well-defined characteristics of American crania and of those of the actual Indians, ten Kate says: "I accept willingly the view that the skulls of Lagoa Santa offer great analogies with other American series, notably with the Botocudos and natives of Lower California;" but he is not willing to admit, on account of the great differences in the craniologic characteristics of the different Indians, that the form of the Lagoa Santa skulls represents the typical form of the American aborigines in general.

As to the antiquity of the Sumidouro cave remains, "I am," says ten Kate, "with Mr. Lütken, rather of the opinion of those who do not accept as yet the contemporaneity of the man of Lagoa Santa with the extinct mammals of the Quaternary period in Brazil."

In 1887 the Lagoa Santa skulls are mentioned once more by A. de Quatrefages in his "Histoire générale des races humaines."[1] The author proceeds as if the antiquity of the remains was established beyond any possible doubt.

"These ancient inhabitants of Brazil," he says, "were also the contemporaries of now extinct species of animals; they belonged to the geologic age which preceded ours. . . . The man who left his bones in the cave of Sumidouro lived at an epoch corresponding probably to our reindeer age."

The next communication on the subject of the Lagoa Santa human remains is another paper by Lütken, published in the first volume of memoirs from the Lund Museum.[2] It deals principally with the history of the finds and with considerations relative to their age. The conclusions concerning the latter point are simple and judicial. Lütken says:

"None of the bones found in the caves showed any effect of man's activity, nor did the human bones show any traces of attacks by the

[1] Paris, 1887, pp. 82–83.
[2] Lütken, Chr. Fr., Indledende Bemaerkninger om Menneskelevninger i Brasiliens Huler og i de Lundske Samlinger. En *Samling af Afhandlinger e Museo Lundii*, I, Kjöbenhavn, 1888, pp. 1–29.

carnivores with whose bones they coexisted." And, as to their antiquity, "I do not believe that, on the basis of the information relating to the circumstances under which the human bones were found in the Brazil caves, mingled with the remains of mammals of species partly extinct and partly still living, one can draw other conclusions than this, that it is *permitted* to regard the contemporaneity of the aborigines of Brazil and of a number of species of extinct animals (Pliocene or Post-Pliocene) as more or less likely, but that this contemporaneity should not pass in any way for *demonstrated*, so it could serve as a basis of more extended conclusions."

In 1888, finally, the entire human skeletal material from the Lagoa Santa caves in the collections at Copenhagen and also that in London was examined by Sören Hansen.[1] The principal attention is given again to the crania, yet some remarks are devoted also to other bones of the skeleton, which, unfortunately, are for the most part fragmentary. Measurements of 17 skulls are given. The numbers designating the specimens are not the same as those used by Kollmann nor those of ten Kate, and the measurements differ in some respects from those of both previous observers. A number of dimensions in addition to those formerly recorded are given, as the height of the skull, circumference, etc. The measurements are as follows:

Measurements of the Lagoa Santa skulls by Sören Hansen [2]

Number; Collection	Vault			Basion-bregma height	Height-length index	Height-breadth index	Circumference	Transverse arc	Antero-posterior arc
	Length	Breadth	Index						
1. Copenhagen	19.4	13.0	67.0	—	—	—	—	—	—
2. Copenhagen	18.6	12.8	68.8	—	—	—	51.0	29.5	—
3. Copenhagen	19.2	13.3	69.3	13.4	69.8	100.8	52.0	31.5	40.0
4. Copenhagen	18.4	12.8	69.6	13.8	75.0	107.8	51.0	31.0	37.5
5. Rio de Janeiro	18.5	12.9	69.7	14.5	78.4	112.4	51.5	31.0	39.0
6. Copenhagen	18.6	13.0	69.9	—	—	—	—	—	—
7. Copenhagen	17.7	12.4	70.1	12.6	71.2	101.6	48.5	28.5	—
8. London	18.8	13.2	70.2	13.8	73.4	104.6	52.0	31.5	38.6
9. Copenhagen	18.2	12.8	70.3	13.6	74.7	106.3	50.5	31.0	38.0
10. Copenhagen	18.0	12.8	71.1	—	—	—	50.0	—	—
11. Copenhagen	19.6	14.0	71.4	14.0	71.4	100.0	53.5	32.5	39.5
12. Copenhagen	18.2	13.0	71.4	—	—	—	50.5	30.5	37.0
13. Copenhagen	18.3	13.2	72.1	—	—	—	50.5	31.5	—
14. Copenhagen	17.6	12.7	72.2	—	—	—	49.0	29.0	—
15. Copenhagen	17.2	12.5	72.7	13.0	75.6	104.0	48.0	29.5	37.0
16. Copenhagen	18.0	13.1	72.8	14.0	77.8	106.9	50.0	31.5	37.0
17. Copenhagen	16.6	13.4	80.7	—	—	—	48.0	31.0	—
Averages of Nos. 1-16	18.4	13.0	70.5	13.6	74.1	104.9	50.6	30.6	38.2

[1] Hansen, Sören, Lagoa Santa Racen. En *Samling af Afhandlinger e Museo Lundii*, I, Kjöbenhavn, 1888, pp. 1–37.

[2] Table rearranged by A. H., but order of records, based on cephalic index, as in original.

Measurements of the Lagoa Santa skulls by Sören Hansen—Continued

Number; Collection	Orbits			Nose			Miscellaneous		
	Breadth	Height	Index	Height	Breadth	Index	Basion-nasion line	Diameter frontal minimum	Length of foramen magnum
1. Copenhagen..	4.0	3.4	85.0	—	—	—	—	—	—
2. Copenhagen..	—	—	—	—	—	—	—	9.4	—
3. Copenhagen..	3.8	3.0	78.9	4.6	2.2	47.8	9.8	9.4	3.7
4. Copenhagen..	3.7	3.3	89.2	4.9	2.3	46.9	10.3	10.0	3.6
5. Rio de Janeiro	4.1	3.3	80.5	4.5	2.4	53.3	9.3	9.2	—
6. Copenhagen..	—	—	—	—	—	—	—	9.2	—
7. Copenhagen..	—	—	—	—	—	—	9.8	8.4	—
8. London......	3.8	3.5	92.1	4.8	2.5	52.1	9.8	9.7	3.7
9. Copenhagen..	3.9	3.6	92.3	4.6	2.4	52.2	9.8	9.8	3.4
10. Copenhagen..	—	—	—	—	—	—	—	9.4	—
11. Copenhagen..	—	—	—	—	—	—	10.8	9.5	3.5
12. Copenhagen..	—	—	—	—	—	—	—	9.2	—
13. Copenhagen..	—	—	—	—	—	—	—	—	—
14. Copenhagen..	—	—	—	—	—	—	—	—	—
15. Copenhagen..	—	—	—	—	—	—	9.3	8.7	3.1
16. Copenhagen..	3.8	3.3	86.8	4.8	2.5	52.1	10.2	9.0	3.8
17. Copenhagen..	—	—	—	3.9	2.0	51.3	—	8.8	—
Averages of Nos. 1–16	3.9	3.35	86.4	4.7	2.4	50.7	9.9	9.3	3.55

At the end of his article, Hansen gives the following résumé, in French, of the conclusions at which he arrived:

"The collection of fossil bones conserved at the Zoological Museum of the University of Copenhagen comprises 15 more or less complete skulls and a very considerable quantity of large and small fragments of crania, besides nearly 30 lower jaws, almost all broken, which give us the approximate number of individuals; in addition, there are numerous long bones, entire or broken, vertebræ, bones of the pelvis, bones of the hands and feet, etc. All these bones are calcareous and more or less incrusted by ferruginous agglomerations. Their color is quite variable and presents all the shades from yellow to dark-brown and passing into red, altogether as in the animal bones from the same caves.

"All stages of life are represented with the exception of the youngest infants. The teeth are often much worn, but rarely diseased. The wear of the incisors is in some cases so considerable that the roots are involved, in which case their surface presents a form elongated in the sagittal direction. Beyond this, it appears that the population from which these skeletal remains proceed was strong and enjoyed very robust health, nearly all pathologic alteration being absent, in the same way as traces of wounds or any kind of mutilations. . . .

"The fossil skulls of Lagoa Santa present, with about one exception, a remarkable uniformity. The 14 skulls of Copenhagen, that of Rio de Janeiro, and that of London, all have the same aspect, all are very high, very long and have a roundish [should probably read oval—A. H.] vault. The face is of medium breadth, the same as the orbits and the nose. The front is not sloping, but rather somewhat pyramidal, the supraorbital ridges are well-developed, the interorbital part is broad and strong. The skulls are very prognathic, the subnasal part especially. The bizygomatic diameter is large and the temporal root of the zygomæ is very strong, producing a considerable relief above the mastoideal region. The skulls are of a medium size, but their state of preservation does not permit measurements of capacity, of which a notion can be obtained only from the various measurements.

"The lower jaws are strong, with a well-developed chin and generally with large genial apophyses.

"According to the anthropologic terminology, the skulls of Lagoa Santa are dolichocephalic, hypsistenocephalic, prognathic, mesofacial, megaseme, mesorhinic, and phenozygous. The type corresponds perfectly to that of the Papuans, a fact already pointed to for the skull of Rio de Janeiro by de Quatrefages, but still more pronounced when one regards the complete series instead of the sole specimen which he knew. The uniformity of these skulls supports the theory of that savant concerning the existence of a primitive race, spreading over the larger part of South America and mixed with other elements (brachycephalic).

"The only atypical skull from the Lagoa Santa caves is brachycephalic, but in the remainder of its characteristics, corresponds quite well with the rest of the collection.

"The divers bones of the trunk present only a mediocre interest and the only remarkable thing is the frequence of transitory lumbosacral vertebra (three times for six sacra).

"The bones of the members indicate small or medium stature, but considerable strength, a new point of resemblance to the Papuans. The oleocranon cavity of the humerus is in many instances perforated. The ulnæ are somewhat incurved. The femora show a well-developed linea aspera as well as the third trochanter. The tibiæ are very platycnemic."

As to the antiquity of the remains, Hansen adduces (Danish and French text) that—

"The human remains were in no case so associated with the bones of animals that one could reach a conclusion with absolute certainty as to their contemporaneity with either a Tertiary or a Quaternary fauna. In the absence of all antiquities one can also know nothing about the absolute age of the population, although it is quite likely that it is very ancient."

As to geologic details, "I shall simply add that the contents of the cave of Sumidouro, the most important of all, were so disturbed when Lund came to its exploration that all determination of geologic age of the skeletal remains is impossible. . . .

"The fossil bones of Lagoa Santa were not found under geologic conditions sufficiently clear to permit the drawing of paleoethnologic conclusions with the absolute certainty demanded by science. Nevertheless these remains are precious documents for the definite solution of the great and important question of the antiquity of man, a question which by its delicate nature demands patience and prudence."

An additional original study of several of the Lagoa Santa crania in Copenhagen was made by Virchow, and is reported in his Crania Americana.[1] Virchow accepts, in general, Hansen's conclusions. He speaks of the remains only as "prehistoric," without regarding the crania as very homogeneous, at least so far as height, orbits, and nose are concerned, and points out on the basis of the Sumidouro material that "We must take account of the fact that already in the oldest settlements of the aborigines there were represented different races. Not only did brachycephalic and dolichocephalic tribes exist but the regions of their distribution lay close together."

Additional references to the Lagoa Santa skulls occur in a number of other authors, but with one exception they are without special importance.[2] The exception is Rivet's recent and able paper on "The Lagoa Santa race among the precolumbian population of Ecuador." [3] After giving a résumé of what has hitherto been published on the Brazil cave finds, and after enumerating the characteristics of the Lagoa Santa "race," the author shows conclusively that crania of the same type occur in some of the prehistoric burials of Ecuador and also in many other parts of South America, from Ecuador and Brazil to Tierra del Fuego, down to practically the present time. The skulls of Fontezuelas and Arrecifes belong evidently, according to Rivet, to the same race, and he feels inclined to add that of Miramar. As to the age of these specimens and of the Lagoa Santa remains, the author expresses reserve.

CRITICAL REMARKS

The evidence relating to the Lagoa Santa material may be compared with a considerable quantity of ore, which must pass through the reduction process to determine its grade. So far as the records of the

[1] Virchow, R., Crania Ethnica Americana, Berlin, 1892, pp. 32–33.

[2] For example Gervais, P., Zoologie et paléontologie générales, 1re sér., Paris, 1867–1869, p. 252; Topinard P., Éléments d'anthropologie générale, Paris, 1885.

[3] Rivet, P., La race de Lagoa-Santa chez les populations, précolombiennes de l'Equateur; in *Bull. et Mém. Soc. d'Anthr. Paris*, 5me sér., IX, fasc. 2, 1908, pp. 209–274.

characteristics of the bones are concerned, the data evidently correspond to rather low-grade ore. In fact, owing to differences in results reached by the different observers (the average breadth of the skulls being given, for instance, as 13.25 cm. by one, and as but 13.0 cm. by another, author), with the paucity of records on skeletal parts other than the skulls, the data on the Lagoa Santa material suggest the need of a thorough restudy of the whole collection, by students employing well-tested, modern instruments and approved methods.

The presence of the remains in caves is not of particular significance. Wherever caves were convenient, the American aborigines, as other primitive peoples, utilized them for habitation, shelter, storage, ceremonies, and burial. The cliff-dwellers of the southwestern United States, for example, made use of the caves and shelters of that region for all these purposes, and the Tarahumare and other tribes of Mexico do likewise at the present day.

The presence in the cave of Sumidouro of parts of the skeletons of upwards of 30 individuals of all ages, with the bones of some still in their natural associations, is sufficient evidence of the fact that the cave served as a place of burial. Whether the bodies were interred in the accumulations in the cave or were simply deposited on the floor is not apparent. It is well known that both methods have been employed even by a single people.

The absence from the Sumidouro cave of objects of ornament and of implements and utensils, with the exception of one muller, is a fact of secondary importance only, having little bearing on the problems of race antiquity. Objects of wood, fabrics, feathers, and other perishable articles decay rapidly where water has free access to them, or they may be carried away by running water. Many burials in caves, as most of those of late prehistoric times in Chihuahua, a number of which were explored by the writer, are lacking in objects of art except remnants of costumes and wrappings of the body.

The association in a single cave of human remains with bones of extinct animals can not be regarded as establishing by itself contemporaneity of the race and the animal species to which the bones belong. The acceptance of the theory of such contemporaneity requires proofs that both the animal and the human bones were in the cave before the extinction of the species represented by the former. On this point there is no satisfactory evidence in the present case. No part of the cave showed ancient deposits only; the red clay, which seemed to be the oldest and least disturbed sediment, contained on the one hand no bones of man, and on the other held bones of deer belonging to species still living. The extinct forms were represented by a few bones only, and in some instances, as that of the monkey, only by a piece of a single bone; and the fossil animal bones were irregular in both position and distribution, being mingled indiscriminately with human and with recent animal bones. These facts show that the period of deposition of the fossil bones themselves in this cave, which is provided with both vertical and lateral entrances and is periodically inundated, is entirely problematic; and from such facts it follows that the assumption of equal antiquity for the human and the fossil animal remains of the Sumidouro cave, on the basis of their association, is unwarranted.

While the presence in this cave of great quantities of shells and of bones of animals of species still existing, which were not inhabitants of the cave, would not *ipso facto* disprove the age of any other remains therein, it indicates the possibility of a casual, though not necessarily very recent, introduction by the elements of the fossil animal bones. And the distribution of the modern bones over the floor of the cave and at all depths in the deposits affords ample proof of the extensive disturbances which have taken place in these deposits through the periodic invasion of floods.

The strong point in the claim to antiquity of the human bones in this cave, as in so many similar cases in South America, is their more or less advanced alteration in color and composition, their state of partial petrifaction, and, furthermore, their similarity in these respects to the associated bones of extinct animals. This question of fossilization has often proved embarrassing to anthropologists. It is so fraught with uncertainties that probably no responsible paleontologist would risk maintaining that two animal bones, because of their similar color, weight, and other evidences of mineralization, are therefore of the same age, or even that either, by reason of these conditions, is necessarily geologically ancient. But let a human bone take the place of one of the animal bones and the case seems to assume a totally different aspect. Its "fossilization" brands it at once with the majority of observers as of great age. However, in the present case the facts in respect to this point are so readily interpreted that a safe conclusion regarding the relative age of the human remains should not be difficult.

The human bones from the Sumidouro cave present various grades of discoloration and progress of petrifaction. This is stated clearly by Lund and also by Hansen, and indicated by Blake, but it is not true, so far as shown, of the bones of the extinct animals. This fact led Lund at one time (see p. 157) to regard the human bones as derived from several periods. In this connection we have to consider the important and oft-repeated statements of Lund that the skeletal remains of the recent animals also showed changes in varying degrees (see p. 157), ranging from relative freshness to a state of mineralization corresponding to that of the fossil bones of extinct species. Some of the relatively modern species were apparently as fully petrified as any in the cave. Thus the changes in the bones of animals of still-existing species were evidently similar in general to those in the human bones, and there is equal justification in both cases for considering the remains contemporary with the extinct species.

In view of these considerations, petrifaction as an index of age in this particular cave must necessarily be regarded as of little value. The potency of mineral substances of the soil in altering bones is very pronounced, and this potency is materially increased by the presence of water, especially when the latter carries in solution, as it often does, the organic and inorganic constituents favoring fossilization. Such agencies are sufficient to account for the changes, within a few centuries, observed in the human and recent animal bones found in the Sumidouro cave. On the western coast of Florida, as reported by Vaughan and the writer on another occasion,[1] similar agencies are causing the rapid petrification of human bones and other objects subject to their influence, and these have produced also in relatively recent times in other parts of America changes in bones very much like those observed in the Sumidouro cave. One such instance is the cranium reported from the mouth of the Amazon by Lacerda (see p. 171), and many striking examples are seen among the brown and blackish-brown mineralized human remains collected by Moreno and also by the writer from the superficial and relatively recent alluvial deposits in certain parts of the valley of the Rio Negro.[2]

That the fossil animal bones from the cave under consideration presented the same degree of petrifaction as the associated human bones, rests only on statements and superficial evidence, but it is quite obvious, as already mentioned (see p. 7), that petrifaction under given conditions may proceed only to a certain stage, where it necessarily stops or becomes exceedingly slow. Hence two bones of widely different ages could well present the same aspect of petrifaction, a condition which in all probability exists in the Sumidouro cave.

There remain to be reviewed the anthropologic characteristics of the bones, and the first query that presents itself in this connection is, What has become of the low sloping foreheads which Lund so accentuated in his letters? It is certain that none of the examples described present any such feature. (Pls. 16, 17.) It may also be asked, Where are the human bones from the five or six other caves mentioned as having contained such remains? Also, trace seems to be lost of the skulls from the Sumidouro cave (excepting the specimen in Rio de Janeiro) bearing the characteristic wounds which Lund mentioned. However, this last point is quite immaterial.

---

[1] See *Bulletin 33 of the Bureau of American Ethnology.*

[2] See chapter on The Ancient Patagonians and that on the *Homo pampæus.*

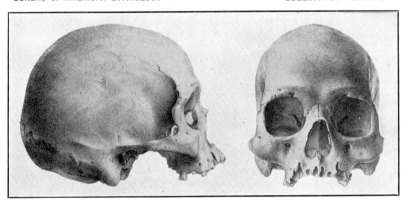

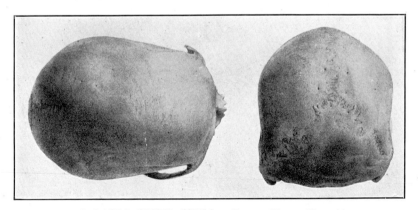

A LAGOA SANTA SKULL. (AFTER SÖREN HANSEN)

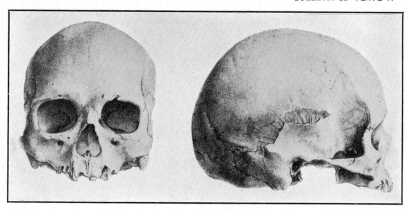

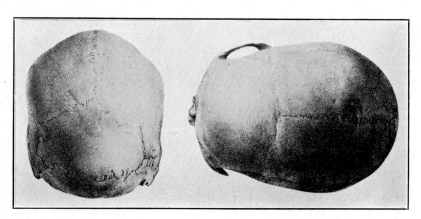

A LAGOA SANTA SKULL. (AFTER SÖREN HANSEN)

As to the actual anthropologic data on the remains, a summary of which has been given in preceding pages, it may be stated that notwithstanding the before-mentioned differences in the published records, the cranial type of the Lagoa Santa caves may be regarded as in general fairly well known; and this type agrees in every point of importance with what may be considered the fundamental traits of the American race, more particularly in the dolichocephalic strain of that race. The opinions to this effect of Lund, Kollmann, Hansen, as well as of ten Kate and Rivet, will doubtless stand without material alteration. The objection of ten Kate that there is no general American type, and his inclination toward regarding the American natives as racially heterogeneous, views entertained also by Rivet and many other authors, when the mass of present evidence is carefully considered can be admitted as true only to a certain rather limited extent. The fact is that the American stem or homotype is not homogeneous; it presents in different tribes and localities the extremes of head form and also numerous other pronounced differences. Yet, the living Indian, as well as his skeletal remains, are characterized throughout America, from Canada to the limits of Tierra del Fuego, by certain fundamental traits that indicate unity in a more general sense of the word. This is not the place, however, to go into detailed enumeration and discussion of these traits.[1] It may suffice to say that they apply especially to the facial features, the nasal aperture, the malar bones, the maxillæ, the base of the skull, the teeth; but they extend also to certain characteristics of the vault itself, and beyond that to the forms and relative dimensions of numerous parts of the skeleton. This general American type is more or less related to that of the yellow-brown peoples, wherever these are found without decided admixture with other strains. These yellow-brown people, including the American, represent one great stream of humanity. In this way it is explainable how the crania from Brazil, and again those of southern California, with still others, have been found to present resemblances to the Polynesians, or even to some of the less negroid Melanesians; it is a basal or *souche* relation, and the Americans may well be wholly free of any connection, except the ancient parental contact, with these branches.

Besides agreeing closely with the dolichocephalic American type, which had an extensive representation throughout Brazil, including the Province of Minas Geraes, and in many other parts of South America, it is the same type which is met with farther north, among the Aztec, Tarasco, Otomi, Tarahumare, Pima, Californians, ancient Utah cliff-dwellers, ancient northeastern Pueblos, Shoshoni, many of the Plains Tribes, Iroquois, Eastern Siouan, and Algonquian.

---

[1] See symposium on origin of American aborigines, in *Amer. Anthr.*, n. s., XIV, No. 1, 1912.

But it is apart from the Eskimo, who form a distinct subtype of the yellow-brown strain of humanity. Outside of the features assimilating them with the American dolichocephalic Indian type, the Lagoa Santa crania appear to present no characteristics whatever that could be regarded as more than individual variations.

Of the other parts of the skeletons there is unfortunately only the brief description of Hansen, but what he has said agrees with the prevalent holocene American type and suggests no geologic antiquity.

The assumption of racial kinship between the Lagoa Santa crania and the negroid Papuans is not justifiable. Resemblance of the vault is a character the value of which is as yet imperfectly understood, but within certain limits is not great; it alone, save in very exceptional circumstances, can not be regarded as decisive in racial differentiation.

In view of all the above facts and considerations, it seems quite evident that the human remains from the Lagoa Santa caves can not be accepted, without further and more conclusive proofs, as belonging to a race which lived contemporaneously with the extinct species of animals found in the same caves; and there is no reliable foundation in the remainder of the data relating to the specimens on which such geologic antiquity could be based.

THE CARCARAÑÁ BONES

HISTORICAL NOTES AND PREVIOUS OBSERVATIONS

In 1864 F. Seguin, a collector of and dealer in fossils, brought to Buenos Aires some fragments of human bones, which he said were found in the Pampean deposits of the banks of the Rio Carcarañá, about 25 leagues north of Rosario in the northern part of the Province of Buenos Aires, together with bones of the fossil bear and horse.

The find is mentioned for the first time in 1865 by Burmeister,[1] who, however, was not permitted by Seguin to see the specimens. A little later they were sent to France and were eventually bought, with the rest of the Seguin collection, by the Museum d'Histoire Naturelle in Paris. In 1869 they were mentioned, and 1873 briefly described, by Gervais;[2] in 1874 the find was discussed by Moreno;[3] in 1875 and again in 1879 by Burmeister;[4] in 1881 they were reported with further

---

[1] Burmeister, G., Lista de los mamíferos fósiles del terreno diluviano; in *Anales del Museo Público de Buenos Aires*, I, 1864–65, p. 298. See also, Ameghino, F., La antigüedad del hombre en El Plata, II, Paris-Buenos Aires, 1881, pp. 374–377; Lehmann-Nitsche, R., Nouvelles recherches sur la formation Pampéenne, etc., in *Revista del Museo de La Plata*, XIV, Buenos Aires, 1907, pp. 209–213.

[2] Gervais, P., Zoologie et paléontologie générales; Première série, Paris, 1867–69, p. 114; by same author, Débris humains recueillis dans la Confédération Argentine avec des ossements d'animaux appartenant à des espèces perdues, in *Journal de Zoologie*, II, Paris, 1873, pp. 231–234, figs. 1–4, pl. v.

[3] Moreno, F. P., Noticias sobre antigüedades de los Indios, del tiempo anterior á la Conquista, etc.; in *Boletín de la Academia Nacional de Ciencias de Córdoba*, I, Buenos Aires, 1874, pp. 130–149.

[4] Burmeister, G., Los caballos fósiles de la República Argentina; Buenos Aires, 1875, pp. 76–78; and, by same author, Description physique de la Republique Argentine, Buenos Aires, III, 1879, pp. 41–42.

details by Ameghino;[1] in 1907 they were touched on by Roth[2] and, finally, in 1907, an account of the find was given by Lehmann-Nitsche.[3]

In his first communication on the subject (1865), Burmeister merely mentions the alleged find and his unsuccessful efforts to examine the bones.

In his first note on the find (1869) Gervais also restricts himself to a simple mention of the bones and Seguin's information concerning them, but besides other remarks, makes this reference to the mingling of the human with fossil animal bones: "I leave it for others to decide whether there has not been some redistribution of earth sufficient to explain such a mingling." Nor is he less guarded in 1873, when the first description of the Carcarañá specimens appears from his pen.

"The human bones, which constitute part of the second Seguin collection, are quite numerous, but they are reduced for the most part to slivers. Among them are fragments of skulls, portions of the long bones, and some phalanges, the latter being mostly well-preserved. . . .

"These bones show two different varieties of coloration. Those of lighter color were scattered over the surface of the ground, having been removed from the deposit in which they lay and washed by water. The others, of brown color, were still in the ground. The piece of a femur, already partly exposed when found, is light in the half that was exposed and dark in the other.

"The teeth or parts of teeth found with this skeletal débris are not less characteristic and indicate at least two individuals. They consist of incisors and molars. The crown is in every case more or less worn off, and the incisors in particular show in this respect the transversal wear, such as is peculiar to primitive races. We possess about 30 of these teeth, several of which are shown in . . . this publication" (see fig. 43).

Seguin encountered also on the Carcarañá, "in common with the osseous débris mentioned above, stone implements comparable in certain aspects with those that characterize the paleolithic epoch in Europe. Specimens numbered 1, 2, and 4 are of quartzite; number 3 is of chalcedony. The last three pieces . . . are quite comparable with well-known forms; they also indicate a rather recent epoch, but they should be compared with implements of the same sort that are still used by some South American tribes, or with those which they employed before the Conquest."

---

[1] Ameghino, F., La antigüedad, etc., II, 1881, pp. 514–526.

[2] Roth, S., Ueber den Schädel von Pontimelo (richtiger Fontezuelas); in *Mitth. anat. Inst. Vesalianum zu Basel*, 1889, pp. 6–9; also in Lehmann-Nitsche, Nouvelles recherches, etc., 1907, pp. 470–477.

[3] Lehmann-Nitsche, ibid., pp. 212–213.

The illustrations given by Gervais show nine teeth, all of very ordinary form and size, and all somewhat worn (fig. 43), and four stone implements, more or less identical in form with quartzite implements from the Argentine coast (see section on Archeology).

F. P. Moreno, one of the most experienced of the Argentine men of science, referring in 1874 to the alleged finds of the remains of ancient man in Argentina before that time, voices his doubts much more freely:

"In the soil of the Province of Buenos Aires, above all in the banks of its numerous arroyos and lakes, there are discovered from time to time vestiges which indicate the existence of indigenous man anterior to the Conquest.

"These vestiges, which represent fragments of domestic objects and some weapons, belong undoubtedly to the epoch of modern alluvia.

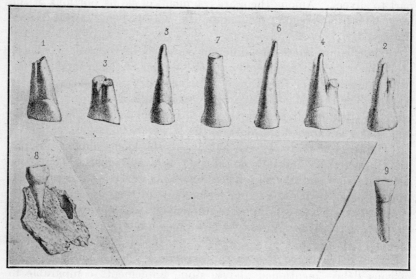

Fig. 43.—Teeth from the Carcaraña skull.   (After Gervais.)

Various authors have believed, nevertheless, that they should be assigned to an age contemporaneous with that of the great extinct American mammals; but the existence of Quaternary man in the Argentine territory is not yet certainly proven. . . .

"The discoveries which have been made in the Pampean strata during the last years are isolated and the human remains obtained have been brought to light by persons who are strangers to paleontology and little prepared for dealing with the problems of the pampas, and although these persons assure us that the remains were found mingled with the bones of the glyptodons and mylodons, we are not justified in attaching much importance to this circumstance.

"Many times the bones of these animals are encountered in what were originally Pampean deposits, but which have been moved and reaccumulated along the banks of the streams; or they are found interred in the vegetal soil mixed with sand from the channels of those streams. I myself have gathered bones of a mylodon, which, displaced from the great Pampean mass, have been brought into such accumulations in the way just named.

"The main reason of the announcements of such discoveries is, I am forced to say, the avidity with which certain persons, particularly those who in the Province of Buenos Aires occupy themselves with the collection of fossils for sale, desire to discover fossil man in the pampa. Relying on the great similarities of the works of the primitive man in Europe and those of the present natives in some parts of the South American continent, they believe themselves authorized in attributing the remains of the work of man distributed along the banks of the streams and lakes as well as among the sand dunes of the Atlantic coast, to an epoch contemporaneous with that of the cave man in Europe. I, myself, have had occasion to examine, although without much detail, the remains of the skull of an individual said to be fossil and alleged to have been found beneath the carapace of a glyptodon; but these remains had a great resemblance to some crania of the Tehuelche Indians of the period before the Conquest collected by myself along the southern bank of the Rio Negro. The wear of the teeth of the specimen, as well as that of the teeth pictured and described by Gervais (1873) is also characteristic of the Rio Negro skulls which I have mentioned and of those of the other primitive (but not fossil) races of our land. I believe that the remains and objects described by Professor Gervais and belonging to the collection of fossils which Seguin sold to the Museum of Paris, as well as the other human remains which, as I said above, I had the occasion to examine, belonged to some of the tribes which inhabited these regions before the Spanish occupation.

[p. 132] "Leaving aside, then, finds which prove only that man was here a witness of the formation of the last alluvial deposits, it is necessary that there be discovered in abundance and by competent persons, human remains, together with products of man's industry, in diverse parts of this Province, in undisturbed deposits. . . .

"The objects encountered up to this moment by the persons alluded to, and those which I myself have gathered in some of my excursions in search of fossil mammals, show the domestic and industrial status of those who first peopled our territory, namely, the bellicose Querandi, who inhabited the site where, in 1535, Buenos Aires was founded, and who were forcibly expelled from their lands by the first Spanish expedition."

And shortly afterward (1875) Burmeister expresses himself in much the same vein as Moreno:

"Some collectors have mentioned fossil remains of man extracted from the Pampean deposits, and they have even shown some of these to me, representing them as found in connection with fragments of *Megatherium, Glyptodon,* and other fossils of the antediluvian fauna of the pampa. I frankly confess that I do not find myself very much disposed to believe the affirmations of these collectors, because they know very well, through communicating with different persons, the scientific value of the discovery of fossil man, and, as they make their collections only with the intention of selling them, they believe with reason that there will be a large augmentation in the price if they can present among the objects they offer to the curious some rarity of the first order. Thus Seguin, who carried collections of fossil bones to Paris, had no other intention than to sell them; he was in the past a confectioner, and he followed the example of Bravard in making these collections when he comprehended the possibility of earning a fortune with the same. . . . The fame of the discoveries of fossil bones made by Boucher de Perthes in France has acquainted Seguin with the great value that they might acquire. He tried to augment, for this reason, the effect of his new collection, bringing his fossil bones to Paris and including with them the first examples of fossil man of the pampa."

In 1879, in the third volume of his Physical Description of the Argentine, Burmeister returns once more to the subject in the following words:

"The fossil bones described by Gervais [*Jour. de Zoologie,* II, 232] have been found in a deposit of gravel on the banks of the Rio Carcarañá, north of Rosario, at a place where excavations were made for a bridge of the Central Railroad. I have received from the same locality, through the kindness of the engineer charged with the construction of the bridge, a very numerous collection of bones from the same gravel, but without any human remains. The collection comprises a large quantity of bones of deer, all of a very fresh aspect and well conserved; and, as these animals belong to the superior level of the diluvial formation, . . . I can not concede to the human bones that came from the same layer any greater antiquity. It is true that there are also bones of more ancient species, but these are rare in comparison with the numerous fragments from more modern animals and their origin is problematic. I have received from excavations made in the same layer a fragment of a skull of *Typotherium* from a very young individual and as this species is evidently from the diluvial deposit and very rare in this gravel, I am disposed to believe that it had been transported from a more ancient stratum by running water, which deposited the entire layer of gravel. The same remark may be applied to the bones of the *Ursus bonæriensis*, which Seguin, the same who made the fortunate discovery of the human bones, found mingled with the latter; as there were found only very few fragments of the bones of the bear, I prefer to believe that they were not in their primitive position, but that they were detached from another more ancient stratum. . . . I prefer to believe that these bones [those of the fossil bear and the *Typotherium*] came from another deposit and were transported by the current which formed the gravel, and which mingled the bones of animals of more ancient formation with those of man which belonged to one more recent. My opinion is strengthened by the presence of objects worked by the hand of man found by Seguin in the same gravel. These objects are entirely similar to analogous objects worked by the Indians existing before the Conquest. The bones and the débris of examples of ancient Indian manufacture have probably been washed out from an ancient Indian tomb by modern currents of fresh water, and I do not see, after having ascertained their complete resemblance to similar objects found in the cemeteries and tombs from the period before the Conquest, any cause for attributing to them any greater antiquity."

An entirely different view of the subject, however, is taken two years later by Ameghino,[1] who saw the bones in Paris. He has nothing at all to say as to their anatomic features, nor was any chemical examination made to determine their "fossility," but he endeavors to sustain and to define their antiquity.

He states that, owing to Seguin's death, the exact location of the find was never ascertained; it was "on the borders of the Rio Carcarañá, a few leagues from its mouth." A manuscript catalogue of the collection, at the Paris Museum, contained the following data:

"Human bones collected near the Rio Carcarañá, in the same soil as the bones of various fossil animals (horse, bear, etc.), which appear contemporaneous with the latter; parts of the skeletons of four individuals; portions of upper and lower jaws, with teeth; various portions of skulls; 32 isolated teeth; various parts of the vertebræ, ribs, bones of the limbs (long bones and phalanges), etc.

"Also a large number of fragments of bones still enveloped in matrix (*gangue*), analogous in character to that which contains bones of various fossil animals.

"Knives and other cutting instruments, manufactured in ancient times by man, and discovered in the same deposits in which were found the above-mentioned bones, as well as those of various other animals."

---

[1] See La antigüedad, etc., II, 1881, p. 514 et seq.

The examination of the specimens showed Ameghino that the stone implements had "suffered absolutely no alteration of surface," and that they were "very well made, approaching, particularly in one case, recent forms." From this, and from the nature of the material of which three of the four implements are made (i. e., quartzite, the source of which is in the Sierra Tandil, 120 leagues distant), Ameghino deduced that "the stone implements brought by Seguin to Europe must have been encountered within the limits of the Province of Buenos Aires, and they proceed, without doubt, from the black earth of the surface. This, however, does not necessarily impugn Seguin's honesty; he was only mistaken. The worked stones may have tumbled from the superficial layer and have been transported onto Pampean deposits, where they were collected. . . . But the same thing did not happen with the bones. . . . Seguin, who collected fossils for 20 years, could hardly have committed such an error."

The bones, Ameghino continues, show different colors; many of them are in part or wholly bleached, indicating partial or complete exposure above ground. Some are still enveloped by the earth. On the banks of the Carcarañá there are distinguishable only two entirely different strata, the thin, black, superficial, vegetal (40–60 cm.), and the reddish Pampean argillaceous sediments underneath. The Seguin specimens show the yellowish color, which proves that they were derived from the Pampean deposits. Some of the bones are light, fragile—they lay in ground without carbonates or silicates; others are considerably heavier—they, though in the same terrane, became infiltrated with carbonate of lime; and others show in part one, in part the other, of these characteristics. The earth that still partly envelops some of the specimens is the Pampean sandy clay, and the same is found in their medullary as well as in their interstitial cavities. In some cases the adhering earth is hardened to tosca. "The presence of tosca, which adheres strongly to the bones, and which also fills all the cavities, constitutes itself an incontrovertible proof of the antiquity of these bones and of their contemporaneity with the great edentates of the Pampean formation." (P. 523.)

The bones of the fossil bear present, Ameghino says, the same characteristics as those of man. The surface of many of the human skeletal parts show a number of impressions which were recognized as due to gnawing by extinct animals (?) belonging to the genera *Hesperomys* and *Reithrodon;* and the bones of the bear show similar marks caused by gnawing. "It is evident that the *Hesperomys* and the *Reithrodon* have gnawed only fresh bones, a condition from which it is concluded that the man and the bear who left the osseous remains in this locality were not only geologically contemporaneous, but furthermore that they died within a very short interval of each other, if not at the same moment." (P. 524.)

"The human bones encountered by Seguin in the Province of Santa Fé are as fossil as the skeletons of the glyptodons, taxodons, and mylodons, which are to-day being exhibited in the principal museums of the world."   (Pp. 524–525.)

The author then proceeds to establish the horizon of the Pampean formation in which the bones lay.   His decision is that they came from the reddish Superior Pampean and belong to the same geologic horizon, slightly more or less, as the human bones found at the Arroyo Frias, near Mercedes.

In the same general neighborhood from which the Seguin collection came were found a number of other species of fossil animals, hence "the man whose remains Seguin encountered was contemporaneous with five genera and seven species of extinct mammals, namely, the *Arctotherium bonæriensis*, the *Hydrochœrus magnus*, the Mastodon, an equid, the *Megatherium americanum*, the *Lestodon trigonidens*, and the *Euryurus rudis*."   (P. 526.)   It would appear evident from the above that Seguin's death and his withholding the information as to the exact locality of the find, did not matter much after all.

Roth, who occupies himself briefly with the Seguin collection in his letter to Kollmann (1889), brings forth no facts touching directly on the human bones sold by Seguin, but questions the opinion of Burmeister that the bones came from a gravel deposit.   He says:[1]

"The opinion of Doctor Burmeister concerning the find of Seguin, given on page 42 in the third volume of the Physical Description of the Argentine Republic, is not justified.   Burmeister believes that the bones of the fossil bear may have been removed by water from a more ancient stratum and then deposited with human bones in a layer of gravel.   It is not likely that the water has torn from the hard loess a certain number of the bones of the bear (*Arctotherium*) to transport them into another place and there unite them; besides which, in the region cited, the borders of the Carcarañá, there does not exist any layer of gravel.   I know perfectly the place where the railroad from Rosario to Córdoba crosses the Carcarañá.   The banks consist of loess belonging to the Intermediary Pampean formation.   Above there exists a thin layer of humus and down below, in the bed of the stream itself, there are found from place to place deposits of an altogether insignificant extent of mud and of triturated calcareous concretions.   Had Seguin, instead of finding the human bones in the loess gathered them in these deposits, everyone who knows Pampean fossils would have seen at once that the débris did not come from the Pampean formation; but if these bones were really discovered in the loess traversed by the foundations of the bridge, they belong to the Intermediary Pampean strata.   .   .   .   Consequently,

---

[1] Ueber den Schädel von Pontimelo (richtiger Fontezuelas); in *Mitth. anat. inst. Vesalianum zu Basel*, 1889, p. 2.

without leaving place for any doubt, the human remains found on the borders of the Carcarañá are fossil and are derived at the least from the yellow loess, and it may also well be that they come from the Intermediary Pampean formation (brown loess)."

Finally Lehmann-Nitsche (1909), notwithstanding the facts that he has not seen the material and that he knew of the objection to the theory of antiquity of the Seguin specimens by Moreno and Burmeister, declares that "the fossil nature of the human débris from the banks of the Carcarañá can not be questioned."

And further on (p. 213) he says, following his quotation of Roth's above-given remarks: "Consequently, without leaving place for any doubt, the human remains from the border of Carcarañá are fossil and come at least from the yellow loess, and it may well be possible that they proceed from even the Intermediary Pampean (the brown loess.)"   In an even more recent publication [1] this author still considers the Carcarañá bones as belonging to the Superior Pampean.

CRITICAL REMARKS

The foregoing details are given because they relate to the first alleged discovery of ancient man in Argentina and also because this case is typical of practically the whole line of subsequent reports on the subject of early man in that country, as regards the defective nature of the basal facts, the frequently arbitrary treatment of the evidence that exists, and the strained reasoning indulged in on the basis of this evidence.

The actual facts of the Carcarañá evidence may be critically résuméd as follows:

1. The geographic data concerning the Carcarañá find are unsatisfactory, not precise enough for a case of any importance.

2. Direct geologic data are entirely wanting and the circumstantial evidence is inconclusive.

3. The bones were gathered by a nonscientific collector, whose discrimination regarding the essential details of the discovery at best would be open to doubt.   The further fact that the presence of fossil human remains, in the knowledge of the collector would heighten the value or facilitate the sale of the collection of animal bones can not be disregarded in the case of one who collected only to sell.

4. The quantity of human bones, with the statement in the catalogue of the collection that they were parts of four skeletons, points to the probability that the remains were derived from either several contiguous burials, or from a common secondary grave of a number of individuals; such graves were quite common in recent times farther south in Argentina.   The facts that the bones were in fragments or

---

[1] Lehmann-Nitsche, R., El hombre fósil pampeano; in *Bol. Ofic. Nac. Est.*, La Paz, Bolivia, VI, 1910, pp. 363–366.

slivers, that they represented nearly all the parts of the human frame, and yet comprised only small portions of the skeletons, indicate exposure of the bones, their fragmentation due to exposure, and perhaps other agencies, and either their removal from the original site, which could have been effected by running water, or the removal of the many missing parts, probably by the same agency. A possible alternative agency would be some great local disturbance, hard to be imagined, causing the fragmentation and the removal from *situ* of many of the broken parts of the skeletons.

5. Some of the bones were seen still embedded in, and others with the cavities filled by, Pampean loess, which in some instances was hardened to tosca. The presence of neither of these materials can be considered as proof of antiquity of the skeletal parts. Bones buried primarily or secondarily in loess (they could not well be buried elsewhere in the regions in question), on the disappearance of the marrow, especially if the bones be broken, become surrounded and filled with the material in which they lie, whatever may be its age. They may become thus filled and surrounded even if lying in, and especially at the edge of, a mixed deposit of loess and gravel. However, the relation of the bones in this case to gravel is entirely uncertain, and speculations on the point would be vain. Finally, if the loess carried moisture and lime salts, as it generally does in eastern Argentina, on drying some of it would turn to more or less compact cement, which would adhere to the bones. This would not be real tosca, such as exists already concreted within the loess, though this circumstance is not of great importance.

6. The bones of fossil animals found with the human bones are nowhere referred to as skeletons, or even as the larger undisturbed parts of the skeletons, of these animals. They were, it is plain, not such, or the fact would surely have been mentioned; and if only isolated parts, they could easily have been removed from their original resting place by torrential waters and deposited in contact with the human bones.

7. The "fossilization" of the human bones has been estimated without actual tests, leaving the subject in uncertainty. But even real mineralization, as mentioned in other parts of this report, is more a criterion of conditions than of age.

8. The implements stated explicitly by Seguin to have been found with the bones are such as were used by the Indians of other parts of the Province of Buenos Aires. No. 1 is not only identical in form with that found by Ameghino in the superficial layer at Lujan, but also with several brought by the writer from the coast of the Province.

9. The marks on the bones may well have been made by rodents, for markings of such origin are very common in Argentina, but it can

not be accepted as proven that they could have been made only by certain species of ancient rodents.

10. The contemporaneity of bones of fossil animals found in the same general region with the human bones under consideration lacks substantiation.

11. Finally, morphologically the Seguin human bones offer, so far as shown, nothing indicating primitiveness of form or great age.

On the basis of the above facts the inevitable conclusion is that the Carcarañá human remains should cease to be cited as representing a South American man of geologic antiquity.

THE ANCIENT PATAGONIANS

HISTORY AND OBSERVATIONS ON THE SPECIMENS

At the meeting of the Anthropological Society of Paris, July 1, 1880, Francisco Moreno read a communication on "Two prehistoric skulls brought from the Rio Negro."[1] This report marks the beginning of the written history of the so-called fossil Patagonian crania.

Sr. Moreno's communication was as follows:

"The two skulls come from the ancient cemeteries of the Rio Negro. They are representatives of races anterior to the Spanish conquest and already extinct before that time.

"The calva, which presents pathologic features, was exhumed by me from a layer of sandy, yellowish clay, which forms the ancient alluvia of the Rio Negro and appears altogether similar to the Quaternary loam of the pampas. This layer is not continuous, but occurs in knolls (mamelons) or ridges, which resemble old and but slightly elevated islands or banks of an ancient delta. Near this skull I found no bones of extinct animals, but, at the distance of some hundreds of meters, I came across a few fragments of the carapace of a glyptodon, which presented the same external appearances as the human skull. The color and the condition of the latter are quite the same as in the majority of Quaternary remains.

"The second skull is more modern but still very ancient; I extracted it from the ancient dunes, formerly mobile but now fixed, which in the past lined the islands of the old stream at its former mouth near Carmen. The first skull lay at a depth of nearly 4 meters, the second at 2 meters, [2] in the sand. The latter specimen is deformed in the Aymara fashion and shows some scraping below the parietal.

[1] Moreno, F. P., Sur deux crânes préhistoriques de Rio-Negro; in *Bull. rapportés Soc. d'Anthr.*, Paris, 3me sér., III, 1880, pp. 490-497.

[2] In answer to the question by Hamy as to the exact nature of the deposits in which this second skull was found, Moreno states in another part of the paper (p. 495) that the deposits are "ancient dunes, now solidified [this should be understood to mean settled, fixed, not solidified like stone.—A. H.], close to the ancient islands of the Rio Negro. The skull was found at a depth of 10 feet, in violet sand." There must be an error in one of these figures.]

"The two skulls are not the representatives of the two races which, in former times, inhabited the region of the Rio Negro near the ocean.

"In the ancient cemeteries [1] are found several cranial forms. The most ancient is that represented by the above-mentioned calva. This race lived, I believe, in the glacial time of Patagonia, which however, is more recent than the glacial epoch of Europe.

"Afterward (but not very long after, I believe), there comes a race, Neanderthaloid in type, very similar to the Botocudo. . . . The skulls of this race are interred in the ancient dunes.

"Still later there appears a cranial type with marked prognathism, and with the posterior or occipital part of the skull rounded instead of being very elongated. . . . There are normal as well as deformed (fronto-parietal compression) crania.

"The type known under the name of Aymara is seen afterward (of this I have found more than 100 skulls); the specimens belonging to this type are all blackish. It is difficult to say whether this is contemporaneous with or slightly subsequent to the just-mentioned flatheads, of which one can see about 50 representatives in the Archeological Museum of Buenos Aires.

"The most modern types in the valley and those which are perpetuated to this day, are those of the pampas, and the Patagonians or Tehuelches, with brachycephalic skulls that are generally deformed by flattening of the occiput. Some of the crania of these races are found painted red."

The foregoing report of Señor Moreno occasioned considerable discussion.

Mm. Bordier, Bertillon, and Broca considered the lesion of the first-mentioned skull evidently syphilitic.

Topinard remarked that the specimens "are the most authentically ancient skulls which we know from America. . . . Both come from the alluvia of glacial origin, of the Rio Negro; it is understood, however, that the term 'glacial' does not signify anything analogous in that country to the glacial epoch in Europe. We are still ignorant of even the rudiments of the chronology of the terranes and the faunæ of the Argentine Republic and Patagonia. Nevertheless, there is some reason to believe that the alluvia, the 'river beds' of the English, possess in these countries considerable antiquity and antedate by at least some thousands of years the Christian era." Both of the skulls "are artificially deformed, and one, especially, presents the classical, elongated, cylindric, low deformation, with its two characteristic, frontal and postbregmatic, depressions, known under the term *Aymara*. . . .

"The other skull, found by M. Moreno 15 feet beneath the surface, is also deformed but the type of the shaping is different. It is not the

---

[1] The author speaks only of those in the valley of the Rio Negro.

ordinary Aymara type, but a frontal deformation inclining gradually from the lowest part of the front to the vertex, similar to the Toulousian deformation recently presented before you by M. Broca. Some one remarked a while ago that this skull shows Neanderthaloid characters; this is an error, it is deformed."

Hamy said the black skull recalls, trait for trait, the crania of the Aymara.

Finally, Broca expressed the opinion that "it is necessary to be reserved in regard to the geologic chronology of America in general and especially that of South America. . . . Notwithstanding this, it would be of great interest to know to what epoch the deformed skull of which Hamy has just spoken and the form of which appears to me characteristic, belongs."

CRITICAL REMARKS

The foregoing citations include about all the information extant relating to the Rio Negro "fossil" crania. Nothing further concerning the specimens was published by Moreno.

Nearly 10 years later the finds under consideration were mentioned by Ameghino,[1] who, however, attached to them but little importance. In his work on the fossil mammals of Argentina he refers to them as follows:

"It seems that sites belonging to this epoch (Mesolithic) exist also at the southern extremity of the Province, in the valley of the Rio Negro, and the famous 'fossil' skull Moreno referred to in the Bulletin of the Anthropological Society of Paris came probably from one of these. Moreno said that he found the skull in a deposit of Pampean loam (*arcilla pampeana*) in the valley of that river, and that he also obtained from the same some scales of the carapace of a glyptodon. But, *there exist no vestiges of Pampean terrane in the entire lower course of the Rio Negro, nor has there ever been encountered, to my knowledge, the smallest fragment of a carapace of a glyptodon.* The skull in question shows by its fossilization that it belongs without doubt to a very remote epoch, but the general state of the bone and calcareous incrustation which it presents on its endocraneon surface, together with its texture and ashy color, locate it conclusively among objects derived from the Post-Pampean, and in all probability its antiquity, if greatest, may reach the Mesolithic epoch."

Lehmann-Nitsche, in his work on the Fossil Man of Argentina, makes no mention of the skulls under consideration and does not even refer to them in his bibliography, evidence that he does not consider the specimens as having any relation to the Pampean deposits.

The writer himself has not seen the skulls and can not speak of them at first hand, but Señor Moreno, now a member of the Chamber of

---

[1] Ameghino, F., Contribución al conocimiento de los mamíferos fósiles de la República Argentina; in *Actas de la Academia Nacional de Ciencias de Córdoba*, VI, Buenos Aires, 1889, p. 52.

Deputies and one of the most deserving men of Argentina, does not regard them, judging by expressions conveyed in conversations with him, as of great antiquity.   The writer's visit to the valley of the Rio Negro resulted in confirmed skepticism as to any considerable age of any of the remains from that region.   The present low, broad, flat, alluvial valley of the lower course of the river is evidently of recent formation; it is subject to occasional great inundations and in all probability its superficial deposits have been repeatedly disturbed or even wholly rearranged.

The incomplete condition of the two crania under consideration and their isolated position indicate a reinterment.   The depth at which they were found, in the unstable deposits of a powerful river, is a factor of but little chronologic value.   The artificial deformations of the crania are evidently only varieties of one form, the Aymara, and connect them with the native group which occupied the region and practiced similar deformations up to historic times.[1]   The alterations in color and other marks of mineralization of the specimens distinguish them but slightly from those of the shallow burials in mud at the Laguna de Juncal, south of Viedma.   Numerous skulls and bones from the latter place were collected by the writer and are mentioned in some detail in another part of this paper (see p. 298).

The unstable nature of the deposits of the Rio Negro and the great power of the river in periods of flood, were well illustrated during its last great inundation, somewhat more than 10 years ago.   The waters destroyed the town of Viedma, washed out and carried away bodies from cemeteries, and caused many changes in the surface of the valley.

In view of the facts presented above, it seems that the two "fossil" Patagonian skulls have no solid claims to geologic antiquity, the probability being strong that these crania belonged to relatively recent Indian occupants of the region.

THE ARROYO DE FRIAS FINDS

HISTORICAL NOTES AND PREVIOUS OBSERVATIONS

In 1875 F. Ameghino reports the second find of fossil human bones in Argentina.[2]   He says:

"In the small brook of Frias, on the outskirts of Mercedes, at the distance of 20 leagues from Buenos Aires, I found numerous fossil human bones, which lay at a depth of 4 meters in undisturbed Quaternary terrane.   I found some of these in the presence of Prof. G. Ramorino and of many other persons, mingled with a great quantity of charcoal, baked earth, burned and striated stones, arrow points, flint

---

[1] Compare chapter on *Homo pampæus*, p. 289.

[2] In his Notas sobre algunos fósiles nuevos encontrados en la formación pampeana, Mercedes, 1875, and in the *Journal de Zoologie*, Paris, 1875, pp. 527–528.

chisels and knives; and there were also a large quantity of bones belonging to about 15 species of mammals, in a large part extinct, such as *Hoplophorus ornatus* (Burm.), *Hoplophorus Burmeisteri* (Nob.), *Lagostomus angustidens* (Burm.), *Canis protalopex* (Lund), *Eutatus Seguini* (Gerv.), and *Triodon mercedensis* (Nob.)."

In 1881, in the second volume of his La Antigüedad del Hombre en El Plata (pp. 377–380), Ameghino speaks again of the discovery. He says, "In February, 1872, in the vicinity of Mercedes, I came across fragments of the carapace of a glyptodon, piled up by human hands, while at the same time I found on many fossil bones of animals signs of percussion, lines, grooves, and incisions, evidently produced by the hand of man.

"Toward the end of the same year I discovered on the banks of the Arroyo de Frias the first human fossil bones, accompanied with worked stones, bones of extinct animals, and other objects."

In 1874 Ameghino stated that he tried to interest Burmeister in his find of "fossil" human bones but without success. Somewhat later in the year, however, he was accompanied to the place of the discovery by Prof. Ramorino, "and, in his presence, continued the excavations at the Arroyo de Frias. We found some fragments of *tierra cocida* [baked earth], many pieces of charcoal, one vertebra, and one scaphoid bone of man, mixed with numerous fragments of the carapace of glyptodon, etc."

The discovery of the Argentine fossil man was soon afterward announced in a number of the Buenos Aires daily journals.

In 1875 the specimens in his possession relating to man's antiquity were exhibited by Ameghino at the Scientific Exposition of the Sociedad Científica Argentina, and the society honored the exhibitor with a diploma, one express object of which was to act as "a powerful stimulus for the continuation of these investigations."

In 1878 Ameghino presented to the same society a memoir bearing the title "El hombre cuarternario en la Pampa." This memoir was not accepted by the society for publication, some of the reasons for the refusal being as follows:[1]

"The problem which Señor Ameghino assumes to have solved is of considerable importance and can not be passed over lightly.

"Other analogous discoveries did not give the results which their authors anticipated.

"For this reason, and on account of the nature of the terrane in which the author of the memoir has made his investigations, and which was visited by one of our number, we are of the opinion that the problem can not be considered as solved until there shall be made a thorough prolonged study of the objects that were encountered."

[1] Ameghino, F., La antigüedad, etc., II, 1881, p. 397.

In a discussion concerning the memoir before the society [1] the secretary, Señor Zeballos, stated in reply to some objections, that the committee acted as it did in refusing the memoir because "its author had committed a fundamental error, attributing a very remote age to objects which were hardly three or four centuries old, and had declared fossil that which is contemporaneous with the modern alluvia."

In 1878, after much further discussion of the subject, and a second failure of the Argentine Scientific Society to publish the resubmitted

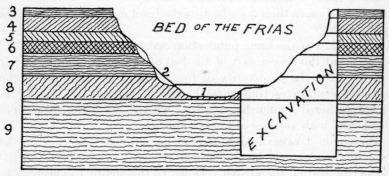

FIG. 44.   Transverse section of the stream Frias, demonstrating the geologic constitution of the strata at the point where the fossil man of Mercedes was found, together with a plan of the excavation made in exhuming the remains.

1. The water-level;

2. A thin layer of gravel found in excavating on the right side of the stream—material deposited by the stream which it had washed from more elevated portions of its bed;

3. A layer of vegetal mold 10 cm. in thickness, which contains numerous bones of domestic animals introduced into the country since its occupation by Europeans;

4. A stratum 40 cm. in thickness, containing the bones of animals indigenous to the country;

5. A very clayey stratum 20 cm. in thickness, containing the bones of extinct species of animals but in a poor state of preservation;

6. A marly layer 30 cm. in thickness, in which the bones of the great extinct mammals, *Mylodon, Glyptodon*, etc., are found;

7. A layer 60 cm. in thickness, not nearly so marly as the preceding; also contains remains of extinct animals;

8. A layer 55 cm. in thickness, of a reddish color, composed exclusively of fine sand and clay mixed together;

9. Stratum which contained the human bones.

Stratum No. 9, which is more than 1.5 m. in thickness, is distinguished from the preceding only in that it contains a larger proportion of clay.   In this layer of Pampean soil, at the base of the excavation indicated in the diagram and at a lower level than the bed of the stream human bones were discovered, together with rudely-shaped flints, apparently used in extracting the marrow from bones, a perforated femur of *Eutatus*, bones with incised, and some of radiate, markings and striæ, fragments of burnt bones, fragments of burnt or baked earth, and a great quantity of charred vegetal substances.   In the same deposit, mingled with the objects mentioned, were found also a great many bones of animals, which indicated the following species: [Here are named 12 genera and species of mammals and an ostrich.]

memoir,[2] Ameghino carried his collections to Europe and exhibited them at the Universal Exposition in Paris.   The same year he sent also a note regarding the find, accompanied with a sketch showing the strata at the Arroyo de Frias, to the *American Naturalist*.[3]

[1] In *Anales de la Sociedád Científica Argentina*, II, 1876; Ameghino, F., La antigüedad, etc., II, p. 399.

[2] See Ameghino, F., ibid., p. 400 et seq.

[3] Vol. XII, 1878, pp. 827-829.

The illustration is here reproduced (fig. 44) and the notes accompanying it are given in a slightly altered form.

The next notices concerning the Arroyo de Frias discovery are both from Ameghino and appeared in two publications in 1879.[1] The statements are again unsatisfactory as to essential details. In the first of the publications (*Compte-rendu*, etc., p. 219), the note reads as follows:

[Human bones from the epoch of the fossil edentates of Argentina], "although few in number, have been exhumed from the banks of the small Arroyo de Frias near Mercedes, where they were interred at a depth of more than 3 m. in disturbed soil mixed with the débris of glyptodon."[2]

On page 226 of the same publication occurs the following:

"Almost at the lowest part of the bed of the arroyo and in its left bank I found a large quantity of fragments of the carapace of the *Hoplophorus;* in extracting these I came to the stratum No. 7,[3] in which I gathered human bones mixed with those of several extinct animals and with vestiges of human industry.

"Thereupon I excavated a deep trench, which traversed all the strata in their natural lay and which I carried to 1.50 m. below the level of the bed of the arroyo. Down to this depth I continued to find the following objects: Human bones, worked stones, implements, fragments of burned bones, bones perforated, incised, grooved and striated, baked earth, and a great quantity of charcoal."

On page 227 Ameghino adds, after enumerating the bones of many fossil animals found during the same excavation:

"Some of these species were represented by entire skeletons with all their bones in undisturbed relation, a condition which demonstrates that the soil which inclosed them has not been moved and that they were enveloped by the earth at the same time as were the human bones and the worked objects. These last consisted of a small flint arrow point, another arrow point, more crude, and two flints showing beveling, with a perforated femur of the *Eutatus*, and an edged *lamina* from the tooth of a *Toxodon*."

In his article in the *Révue d'Anthropologie* (1879)[4] Ameghino adds nothing concerning the Arroyo de Frias find to what is said above, the two accounts being practically the same. In regard to the Arroyo de Frias bones he adds that they were in the same state of

[1] Ameghino, F., La plus haute antiquité de l'homme dans le Nouveau-Monde; in *Compte-rendu de la troisième session de Congrès International des Américanistes*, Bruxelles, 1879, pp. 198–250. Also L'homme préhistorique dans la Plata; in *Révue d'Anthropologie*, 2me sér., II, Paris, 1879, pp. 210–249.

[2] In the same paragraph Ameghino says, "other fossil human bones have been found mixed with the débris of *Megatherium* and of the *Great Ursid*, called *Arctotherium bonæriensis*, on the borders of the river Carcarañá." This can refer only to the Seguin find, in which, however, the bones were those of the great fossil bear and a horse, but not of the *Megatherium*.

[3] No. 9 of fig. 44.

[4] Vol. III, Paris, 1880, pp. 1–12.

preservation and of the same color as the bones of the fossil animals, and that their internal parts were filled with the same Pampean earth which forms the stratum in which they lay.

At the end of the later article (1880) are notes by P. Broca on the bones themselves, which read as follows:

"1. A portion of an iliac bone from the left side, belonging to an aged woman of very small stature; the border of the cotyloid cavity shows traces of dry arthritis.

"2. Four vertebræ more or less entire and three or four fragments without form. The former are the sixth and seventh cervical, with bifurcated spinous processes, and the first and second dorsals. They belong manifestly to the same subject of very small stature and present about their superior and inferior surfaces traces of pathological ossification referable to senile alteration, which in the articulation of the limbs one would qualify as dry arthritis or chronic rheumatism.

"3. Dozen ribs or fragments of ribs from one subject, again of small stature. One of the entire ribs presents on its inferior border an enlargement, which would make one believe that it belonged to another subject, if a similar condition in slighter degree did not exist on another rib; it is the result of senile hyperostosis of the same kind as that presented by the vertebræ.

"4. One scaphoid bone from the foot and one metatarsal. This is the smallest human scaphoid that one can imagine; the major dimension of its articular fossa does not measure more than 26 mm.

"5. Seven metacarpals, some of them deformed and showing at their extremities traces of dry arthritis. One, the metacarpal of the left thumb, is 38 mm. long.

"6. Eight phalanges of the hand.

"7. Head of a radius, very small.

"8. One tooth, probably a median upper incisor, of which the root is disfigured by an abundant deposit of cement, and the crown much beveled by use.

"From the above it is possible to conclude legitimately that *all these bones* belonged to a very old woman affected by senile alterations of the skeleton, one whose stature descended surely below 1.50 m."

In this publication (p. 11) Ameghino further states his belief that the strata which yielded the human bones are not Quaternary but Tertiary.

In his Antiquity of Man in Argentina[1] Ameghino occupies himself again with the finds of the Arroyo de Frias, more at length than in any preceding publication. But most of what is said[2] merely repeats

---

[1] La antigüedad, etc., II, pp. 483–511.

[2] Of this it will be possible to give here only a small part; for the rest the reader is referred to the original.

previously made assertions and supplements the arguments for the antiquity of the human bones.

The first interesting detail mentioned (pp. 486–489) is that relating to the presence of a large quantity of charcoal, found with and above the human bones. This charcoal extended from the top of stratum numbered 9 by Ameghino, slightly more than 6 feet (2.15 meters) from the surface, downward to the bottom of the excavation. The quantity increased with the depth of the excavation. And "on penetrating into the layer No. 9," Ameghino proceeds, "I encountered, mingled with the carbon and the bones of different animals, various human bones. Evidently I have come across the remains of the fossil man of Argentina; the man whose existence has already been revealed to me by striated bones and worked stones.

"The human bones in layer 9 were mingled with bones of different animals, worked flint, fragments of burnt bones, bones broken or perforated, others with incisions, etc., baked earth, and charcoal. . . . The vegetable carbon was so abundant that I calculated it to constitute at this point a fourth part of the total mass of stratum No. 9."

The carbon held, besides the human and broken animal bones, a quantity of fragments of ostrich eggs and some fragments of baked earth, also a piece of a burned scale of *Hoplophorus*. Ameghino especially advances this association as evidence of contemporaneity of man with that animal: "This fragment is of exceptional importance and offers irrefutable proof of the coexistence of man with the *Hoplophorus*."

The stone implements found in the same mass showed also traces of the action of fire. As to the nature of these worked stones, one is a quartzite implement of dark-yellow color, worked crudely on one surface only. The second specimen is a leaf or flake of "silex," prismatic in section; its inferior surface is smooth and concave. The third specimen is a small point of "silex," prismatic in section; its inferior surface is smooth and concave; it served probably as an arrow point. The fourth is equally of "silex;" judging by the illustration, this resembles a scraper; it is worked on one surface only.

The human bones (p. 496) "were found at the mean depth of 3 m.; of this only 50 cm., represented by layers Nos. 3 and 4, belong to the vegetal soil." . . .

"The soil could not have been moved [p. 498], because I did not obtain these bones on the surface of the ground, but interred at a considerable depth and at a lower level even than that of the bed of the Arroyo."

The fossil man of Mercedes, according to Ameghino, could not have been buried where he was found, because (p. 499), "If these were the remains of a skeleton buried in a recent epoch, the bones would not be found isolated, and scattered over a large surface."

The human bones are said to have lost completely all their organic material and are described as lustrous over a large part of their surfaces, as light, porous, and fragile, and adhering strongly to the tongue. All these characteristics "denote a most remote antiquity."

If the human bones had been from a modern inhumation, Ameghino argues, there would have been encountered with them bones of recent animals.

Returning once more to the stone implements (p. 501), we read that, "As these instruments themselves are more crude than those possessed by the Indians anterior to the Conquest, it must be admitted that they belong to an anterior epoch. This also proves that the human bones belong to a geologic epoch in which the physical conditions of the region (*comarca*) were distinct from those of the present day. The level at which the bones were encountered must then have been the surface of the ground; otherwise there would not remain any other explanation of the find except that of a modern burial, which, as already seen, would not accord with the facts; nor can it be admitted that savages armed with small fragments of "silex" could have done such work for the burial of their dead."

As to the animal bones found during the same excavation, Ameghino says (p. 503):

"Some animals were represented by nearly complete skeletons, but the larger part of the bones of the others were scattered without any order, those of the carnivora mingled with those of rodents or edentates. The human bones were found mingled and scattered in like manner without any order over the whole surface of the base of the excavation, more than 30 square meters in extent, which naturally suggests even a much larger area of dispersion. This is further proof that the human bones were interred at the same time as the bones of mammals which accompanied them."

On page 504 the statement is made, notwithstanding the former allusions to the great quantities of charcoal, that "the soil in which the bones occurred was the same in hardness, composition, and aspect as that found at the same level in following the barrancas of the arroyo;" from which again it is deduced that the man was contemporaneous with the animals found in these barrancas.

Later on (pp. 508–509) is mentioned a chemical analysis of the bones, but, with the exception of the statement that they are "fossil" and that they have "almost completely lost their organic matter" (compare with previous statement), no evidence is furnished that such analysis was actually made. In "fossilization," color, and other characteristics the human bones are said to be exactly the same as

those of a *Hoplophorus ornatus* from the same excavation; also the
cavities of both are filled with the same Pampean earth. "If the
bones had not remained from the beginning interred in this soil this
phenomenon could not have occurred."

In 1889 Ameghino published his large work on the fossil mammals
of Argentina in which also he treats of the "fossil" man, referring,
among other matters, to the finds at Arroyo de Frias.[1] This reference, while brief, contains one or two interesting new points. The
human bones are classed as belonging to the Superior Pliocene (pp.
65-66).

The first note in this work regarding the Arroyo de Frias (p. 50)
reads as follows:

"One human site from this epoch [the *mesolithic* epoch of the
Superior Quaternary], quite large in extent, is found near Mercedes
along the small Arroyo de Frias, approximately 1 league from its
mouth. The barranca, quite low here, shows:

"1. A layer of black vegetal earth 10-35 cm. thick;

"2. A layer of black earth, somewhat ashy, 25-30 cm. in thickness,
with vestiges of infusoria, small mixture of carbonate of lime, and
some *Ampullarias* and *Planorbis;*

"3. A layer of whitish soil, quite hard and compact, of some 40
cm. in thickness, with a strong proportion of lime; and

"4. The Pampean soil of yellowish-green color, corresponding to
the Lujanean stratum.

"From an exposure of the hard layer No. 3, there appear on the surface over a stretch of more than 200 meters slivers of long bones parted
longitudinally for the purpose of extracting the marrow, mingled with
ashes, carbon, small fragments of nearly unbaked pottery, pestles,
mortars, polishing stones and fragments of *bolas* made of diorite, as
well as crude flakes of quartzite. The bones which I was able to
determine belonged to three existing species, namely, *Auchenia
guanaco*, *Cervis campestris*, and *Rhea americana*, mingled with the
extinct species of *Paleolama mesolithica.*"

This note is very interesting in showing clearly the tendency of
Professor Ameghino to attribute too great age to his finds of human
remains, making them contemporaneous with the deposits in which
they occur. The antiquity of these deposits, compared with the age
ascribed to them by other observers, also appears very generally overestimated. Here we have, on the same Arroyo de Frias, near Mercedes, plainly an extensive site of occupancy of the modern Indian,
with his pottery, mortars, and even bolas; but because the remains
do not occur in what is regarded as the only Recent layer and
exposure, that is the present-day black vegetal layer, they are
referred to the Quaternary.

---

[1] Ameghino, F., Contribución al conocimiento de los mamíferos fósiles de la República Argentina,
Buenos Aires, 1889, pp. 50-65, 66, 83-84.

On page 65 of the above-mentioned work we read the following about the depth of the bed of the Arroyo de Frias:

"The Arroyo de Frias runs, as do nearly all the small streams in the Bonaerean flats, through a nearly horizontal plain of uniform geologic constitution, and its channel varies in depth from 2 m. to 2 m. 30 cm. . . .

"Vestiges of the activities of ancient man and human bones are encountered in the penultimate layer [1] at the level of the water of the Arroyo and lower in the last layer up to 1 m. below the bed of the stream.

"In 1870 I extracted at this point, on the left margin of the Arroyo, a human skull accompanied by a considerable part of the skeleton, and many bones of extinct animals. I attached but little importance to this find, and the skull was carried to Europe by a collector and given to the Museo Civico of Milan, where it is conserved without having as yet been described.

"Three years afterward, in September, 1873, I found at the same point additional human remains." Then follows a brief account, differing in a few particulars from those given above, of the find of the human bones under consideration in this chapter. Besides the bones of animals, Ameghino mentions again, as having been found with the human bones, "a considerable quantity of fragments of the shells of ostrich eggs."

On page 83 of the same work, finally, after giving some vague recollections concerning the skull found by him at the Arroyo de Frias in 1870, Ameghino adds: "Later on, as I have already mentioned, I gathered at the same place (en el mismo punto) other fragments, which I suppose belonged to the same individual." [2]

Lehmann-Nitsche, in his work on the human remains from the Pampean formation, deals with both of the Arroyo de Frias finds. [3]

As to the human remains collected by Ameghino in 1870 and taken to the Museo Civico of Milan, we learn that in 1890 Santiago Roth visited that institution in order to secure all the information possible on the subject, but no one was found who knew anything of the specimens, and an Italian, Morselli, who looked for them in the museum did not discover any trace of them.

The bones belonging to the second find, that of 1873, [4] were subjected anew to minute examination by Lehmann-Nitsche and Leboucq, of Gand. The results of these studies are that, while the

---

[1 Layer No. 8 of fig. 44.]

[2] No details are given as to the position of the skull, though such data would be, it seems, of much importance, and, curiously, no mention of this first find is made in the lengthy report on that of 1873 (La antigüedad, etc., II, 1881, p. 483 et seq.).

[3] Lehmann-Nitsche, R., Nouvelles recherches, etc., pp. 213–250.

[4] An erroneous statement is found on p. 215 and again on p. 244 of the Nouvelles recherches, etc. The text reads that the bones were found more than 2 meters below the level of the water in the arroyo; this does not correspond to any statement by Ameghino.

majority of the larger bones were found to belong to the skeleton of an old female, one of them, with some of the hand bones and foot bones, belonged probably to a second subject, of taller stature. The fragment of an iliac bone presents certain sexual and other peculiarities, but nothing on which any conclusions would be based. As to the vertebræ, Lehmann-Nitsche "was not able to discover any osteologic characteristic which might not be found in the vertebræ of contemporaneous man" (p. 241); and Leboucq makes almost the same statement in regard to the bones of the hand and the foot (p. 249): "The prehistoric bones of the hand and the foot collected at the Arroyo de Frias present no marked morphologic peculiarity which differentiates them from modern bones." The scaphoid, which Broca pronounced very small, presents really, according to Leboucq (p. 249), medium adult dimensions. The length of the second metatarsal surpasses the average length of the same bone in females and (slightly) even that in males. One of the metacarpals nearly equals the general masculine average in length.

The bones are described by Leboucq (pp. 245–246) as apparently thoroughly fossilized but no chemical tests are mentioned. They are dirty-gray in color, but the longer of the metacarpals, though also seemingly completely fossilized, is mahogany-brown.

Finally, in his latest publication on the subject of fossil man in Argentina,[1] Lehmann-Nitsche refers the Arroyo de Frias find to the Superior Pampean (Quaternary).

CRITICAL REMARKS

1. The antiquity of the human bones found at the Arroyo de Frias can not be accepted as established. It rests on the statements of one who at the time the discoveries were made could scarcely be regarded as a well-trained and experienced geologist, and is substantiated by no published record of any scientific witness, by no photograph or detailed drawings made on the spot.

2. The data and measurements given in the accounts of the find are not sufficiently precise; thus the human bones are said in one place [2] to have come from the depth of 4 meters, while the lowest limit of the excavation as given by Ameghino, in his figure and with his own measurements, was only 3.40 meters. In another place it is said [3] that the human remains were interred at a depth of more than 3 meters; still another statement[4] is to the effect that "The vestiges of the ancient existence of man and human bones were encountered in the layer before the last, at the level of the water of the arroyo

[1] Lehmann-Nitsche, R., El hombre fósil pampeano; in *Bol. Ofic. Nac. Est.*, La Paz, Bolivia, VI, 1910, pp. 363–366.

[2] *Journal de Zoologie*, IV, Paris, 1875, pp. 527–528.

[3] *Compte-rendu, 3me Congr. Int. Amér.*, Bruxelles, 1879, p. 219.

[4] Ameghino, F., Contribución al conocimiento de los mamíferos fósiles, etc., 1889, p. 65.

[which Ameghino's illustration shows to have been 1.75 meters from the surface.—A. H.] and lower, in the last layer, up to 1 meter below the base of the channel," this base corresponding exactly to 3 meters from the surface. The discrepancies in the statements are not limited to this important item only.

3. The find was made in the channel of a stream, a fact well calculated to weaken the evidence as to the bearing on antiquity. The geologist is well aware of the varied changes to which stream beds are liable. The waters, especially at periods of flood, remove, mingle, fill, cover, undermine, and cause subsidences or even the gouging out of great sections of the banks. The bed of earth in which the human bones lay had evidently been considerably disturbed and moved. This is indicated by the breaking, dissociation, and dispersion of the human remains, by the absence of many parts of the skeleton, and by the presence of the differently-colored bone from another body, pointed out by Leboucq. However, some degree of association still remained, as a score of separated parts of one skeleton and a considerable quantity of charcoal were found together. The conditions in general are suggestive of a burial or burials which had been disturbed by some such agency as the sinking or sliding of portions of the bank from pressure or undermining.[1]

4. The burial or burials, the remains of which were found by Doctor Ameghino, may have been made, however, in the incline of the bank or at its base, or even in the dry bed of the stream, and not in the flat surface of the pampa. In Argentina streams of the size of the Arroyo de Frias occasionally run dry, and at such time a burial might be made without hindrance at or even below the level of the bed of the stream, which would possibly offer less resistant ground.

5. A majority of the stone implements found with the human bones are of the same specialized worked-on-one-face-only type so characteristic of the work of the Indian tribes of Argentina, as shown in other sections of this report.

6. The state of fossilization of the bones, notwithstanding the numerous statements on this point by those who handled the specimens, has not been accurately determined, so far as can be found from the printed data on the subject. The statement that the human bones show the same color, consistency, and fossilization as those of extinct animals found in the same strata, lacks confirmation by a microphotographic and chemical demonstration. Mere appearances in instances of this nature are often deceptive, and can not be taken as

---

[1] Displacements of masses of earth by this agency are common along all streams running through unconsolidated formations. Instances of this kind in Argentina came more than once under the observation of Mr. Willis and the writer. Similar displacements were seen to occur in banks of reddish Pampean even far from running water. And the earth does not fall only in sections, but, in banks, also in circumscribed masses that leave large, irregular, deep gaps or holes, which offer good opportunities for introduction into lower levels of many objects from higher points in the surface.

definite facts. However, as already shown in other sections of this paper, and particularly in the report made by the writer on the human bones of reputed geologic age in North America,[1] the state of fossilization of bones, both as to mineralization and loss of organic constituents, is so dependent on local conditions as to be of little service in determining antiquity. Moreover, as also already discussed, the changes in bones are limited in character and extent by the physical and chemical agencies present, and are not cumulative beyond a certain stage. Hence, in a bone that has reached the limit of the alterations caused by the conditions of its surroundings, time would bring but little further alteration, and old as well as relatively recent bones may present quite similar "fossilization." This is observable in numerous instances with fossil bones of mammals from different epochs.

7. The value of the association of the bones of extinct animals with those of man, as a measure of antiquity is, it is necessary to repeat, frequently overestimated. The vital distinction between inhumation of the dead practiced by man since the earliest times and the natural inclusion of bodies of animals in various sediments is often overlooked by the paleontologist. Men dig graves for their dead regardless of the contents of the soil so long as these contents do not greatly impede their work. In ground rich in remains of extinct animals, it is quite probable that the gravedigger removed them and then left them in the earth above or near the body in the same manner as he would tosca, pebbles, or other objects found in the ground. It is also possible that some of the fossil bones incidentally became broken, cut, or otherwise marked and even burnt, either before the burial, or by those who attended to it. The significance of the association of fossil animal bones with human bones, even in the cases in which the former show effects of man's activity, is entirely problematic. The enumeration by the paleontologists in this and other cases, of long lists of names of extinct animals found with or near the the human bones, or in the vicinity, or in the same strata, is impressive, but alone counts for little as evidence of the age of the remains of man found in such relation. The scale of the *Hoplophorus* found with the Arroyo de Frias human remains proves only the action of fire, not the mode in which it was burned nor the time or cause of the occurrence.

8. As to perforated, grooved, and broken bones of animals, it should be shown in every case that their condition in these respects is not due to any agency other than man, and that the changes were made when the bones were fresh, in order that the evidence may be employed in determining man's contemporaneity with the animals which the bones represent. This also suggests the fact, which de-

---

[1] Skeletal Remains, etc., *Bulletin 33 of the Bureau of American Ethnology.*

serves careful consideration, that the date of the final extinction of some of these animals is still an unsolved problem.

9. Finally, it was seen that the anatomic features of the human bones are not incompatible with a recent date for the skeleton. The excessive wear of the teeth, the many signs of "dry arthritis," the size of the specimens, are all features well known among the Indians. As to the stature of less than 1.51 meters, the estimate was made in the absence of any of the long bones and may be too low, as the measurements of the metacarpal and metatarsal bones seem to indicate. However, individual females below 1.50 meters in height, especially among the aged, are really common among the Peruvian, Bolivian, and numerous Brazilian tribes. The feature has no weight as an indication of antiquity of the human remains under consideration.

The unavoidable conclusion regarding the antiquity of the Arroyo de Frias finds of human bones, reached after due consideration of all the above-outlined fragmentary and, in the main, inexpert evidence, is that they contribute practically nothing that can be relied on as decisive toward the solution of the vexed question of man's antiquity in Argentina.

THE SALADERO SKELETON

HISTORICAL NOTES AND PREVIOUS REPORTS

The remains known as the Saladero skeleton were found in 1876 by Santiago Roth, at that time a young collector of fossils.

According to his account, there are frequently seen in the pampas areas where the humus layer is wanting and the eolian loess appears upon the surface. These patches are called *desplayadas* or *comederos*. In course of time some of these areas become covered with vegetation while others remain barren.

It was in one of these desplayadas, less than 10 km. from Pergamino, and near the *saladero* of Señor R. Otero, that Roth found his first fossil man. He was collecting bones of fossil animals, being accompanied by José Mayorotti. Roth [1] says that after having searched for sometime this denuded locality he saw "in a gully about 3 meters deep, protruding from the loess, a portion of a skull. We dug this out and also the skeleton, which was exceedingly well preserved. Unfortunately it was afterward nearly all destroyed through bad handling; some small fragments only were sent by me much later to Señor Burmeister in Buenos Aires."

Further details regarding the find are given in Roth's letter to Professor Kollmann.[2] In this we read that Roth, after exploring the

---

[1] Roth, S., Beobachtungen über Entstehung und Alter der Pampasformation in Argentinien; in *Zeitschrift der deutschen geologischen Gesellschaft*, XL, Berlin, 1888, pp. 448–449.

[2] Ueber den Schädel von Pontimelo (richtiger Fontezuelas); in *Mitth. anat. Inst. Vesalianum zu Basel*, 1889, pp. 1–4; also in Lehmann-Nitsche, Nouvelles recherches, etc., pp. 470–487.

desplayada with his companion and locating some bones of fossil animals, "perceived, in the wall of a gully which was about 3 meters deep, a portion of a skull, which protruded slightly from the loess. Don José thought that the skull was that of an Indian, but I replied that more probably we were confronted with the results of some crime, because the Indians, not possessing utensils for digging, contented themselves with covering their dead with the little earth that they were able to scrape together, while this skeleton was interred at an unusual depth. The idea that these remains might belong to a man contemporary with the *Glyptodon* never even occurred to me. I did not examine the bones closely and had no intention of exhuming them. But as Mayorotti wanted to disinter the skeleton and take it home, I helped him in the work. The skeleton occupied a sitting posture, with the legs extended, the head slightly inclined forward. All the bones existed in their normal relations, as in life. We paid attention to this because I suspected a crime, and we also searched with care for any objects that might be present and that might decide whether the remains were those of a Christian or an Indian, but we found absolutely nothing. As to the form of the skull, which, besides, fell into a great number of pieces, I have no recollection. . . . About one year later I saw in the garden of Mayorotti some fragments of fossil bones and, on asking him where these bones were from, he responded that they belonged to the human skeleton which we dug out near Saladero; the bones were exposed to the sun and rain for the purpose of getting them bleached and they fell to pieces.

"In the interval I had made other excavations, which resulted in the discovery of a flint weapon (*silex-waffe*) on the site of the remains of a *Scelidotherium*. [1] This find puzzled me considerably. Señor Pedro Pico, to whom I communicated my finds, told me it was not the first time that such a case had presented itself, for another person had, in his knowledge, found a very similar implement in the midst of the remains of the *Machærodus*. [2] I left the implement with Señor Pico. At the same time I learned also that Seguin had found long before, on the borders of Rio Carcarañá, fossil human bones mingled with the bones of *Ursus bonaerensis*. These circumstances influenced me to gather the bones which still remained from the skeleton of Saladero, for the purpose of sending them to H. Burmeister at Buenos Aires. . . .

"I had completely forgotten my discovery of the fossil human remains of Saladero when, in 1881, I brought to Burmeister for examination the lower jaw of the skull of Fontezuelas. Burmeister

---

[1 On the banks of the Arroyo Zanjon not far from Pergamino; the object, apparently an arrow point, now no more to be found, is said by Roth to have lain under one of the thigh bones of the animal. (Lehmann-Nitsche, Nouvelles recherches, etc., p. 482, footnote.)]

[2 According to Lehmann-Nitsche, this was the arrow point found by the Breton brothers. Later the find was discredited.]

then produced from a case the still-existing fragments of the human remains from Saladero to compare them with those which I now submitted to him. He declared at once that the two were of equal age and belonged to the Pampean formation. The written statements of Burmeister, however, are not in accord with these remarks. In one passage he expresses himself as follows:[1] 'I saw myself the teeth said to be fossil, but could not distinguish the same by any characteristic from the teeth of ancient Indian skulls.' This observation could not have applied to anything except the human remains from Saladero which I brought him in 1877 and among which there were a large number of teeth. At this time Burmeister was evidently not convinced of the existence of man during the formation of the Pampean deposits; but why did he mention only the teeth, which are subject to the least change, and not also the fragments of other bones, which he himself declared later to be of the same age with the *Glyptodon*. [2] Every specialist who sees these bones must recognize that they proceed from the Pampean formation, because of the characteristic calcareous concretionary matter which adheres to them and even fills some of the medullary spaces."

Lehmann-Nitsche [3] examined such of these fragments as are still preserved in the Museo Nacional at Buenos Aires. He found two pieces of the left femur and a number of teeth. As to the femur, he reports that the cavities of the spongy part and the medullary canal are completely filled with solidified calcareous matter; the external layer, where it still exists, is of a light-yellow color and adheres strongly to the tongue; at the same time the bones are very friable. Anatomic observations were almost impossible owing to the fragmentary condition of the specimens. So far as could be seen, there were no remarkable features. "The teeth, nine in number, show all grades of wear; the enamel is perfectly preserved and presents in some places particles of tartar incrustation, easy to detach; the roots adhere to the tongue." The dimensions of these teeth are not unusual. As to age, the find is regarded by Lehmann-Nitsche as Quaternary, Superior Pampean. [4]

CRITICAL REMARKS

Judging from the position of the body and the natural relations of all the parts, the Saladero skeleton can be regarded only as representing an undisturbed, ordinary interment. The sitting position is found occasionally in Indian burials and is a modification of the contracted posture, which was general. It was due possibly to the effects of rigor mortis on the body before preparation for burial.

---

[1] Burmeister, H., Description physique de la République Argentine, III, Buenos Aires, 1879, p. 42.

[2] No such statement was found in the writings of Burmeister.—A. H.

[3] Nouvelles recherches, etc., p. 253.

[4] Lehmann-Nitsche, R., El hombre fósil pampeano; in *Bol. Ofic. Nac. Est.*, Las Paz, Bolivia, VI, 1910, pp. 363–366.

There are no data as to the exact depth at which the body lay, no photograph showing the remains; but granting that it was deeper than in an ordinary grave, who shall say that it was not buried in a depression or crevice, and that since the burial there were no additions to the general Pampean surface by wind or water or through the medium of the humus?

Roth's objection to burial, on the basis that the Indians had no means with which to dig a grave, is not tenable, for they always had bones of animals, and antlers, which are capable of making excellent digging tools, and they probably had also sticks, if no other implements. To scrape together enough earth for effectually covering a human body involves quite as much work, except in sandy places, as the digging of a not very deep grave, and necessitates the use of similar implements.

That the bones lay in the Pampean is natural. As everything beneath the vegetal stratum is regarded as Pampean, the body could not have been buried in anything else. That there was but little to direct special attention to the find at the time it was made appears plain enough from the words of Roth himself and from the subsequent neglect of the bones.

The state of fossilization of the specimens has not been chemically determined. As to incrustations, these are, even more than actual mineralization of a bone, an indication of environmental conditions; in this case it was the presence of lime in percolating or underground waters. There are in the United States National Museum several large Spanish olive jars, dredged from Atlantic coast waters, large portions of which are thickly incrusted with calcareous deposits. The teeth of the common horse from the beach of Laguna de los Padres, near Mar del Plata, and to a slight extent even the fresher ones from the lower jaw of a horse found at Ovejero (see p. 257), show similar deposits; and these are also occasionally found on the bones and pottery of the North American Indians. In the Argentine loess, the richness of which in lime and perhaps in other salts is attested by the very prevalent tosca formation, it would doubtless be a far greater rarity to find bones that have lain more than a few decades in the ground, and that were not cleaned at once after exhumation,[1] without than with more or less compact cement adhering thereto, and also more or less filling of the bone cavities by the same calcareous material. The "adherence of the bone to the tongue," which is often mentioned in these cases, especially by Lehmann-Nitsche, as a sign of "fossilization," is merely a sign of the presence on or in the bone of more or less mineral matter, particularly lime and will be equally manifest in a specimen that has suffered such change recently as in one in which the deposit or infiltration is of great age. The teeth of

---

[1] It was observed during the work in Argentina that sometimes loose earthy matter adhering to bones when taken from the ground becomes hard and adheres firmly after exposures.

the Saladero skeleton, it was seen from Roth's and Lehmann-Nitsche's statements, are but little altered, although showing advanced wear, as is generally met with in the more aged Indian. Their relative freshness would be wholly incompatible with any considerable age, especially geologic age, of the skeleton.

It is plain from the data extant on this find that there are many points relating to the Saladero skeleton which are not satisfactorily cleared up by the evidence, and that its antiquity is not substantiated. This is still another example of a case in regard to man's antiquity in South America which has been made to appear important but which will not stand critical tests. The bones were conceived of as ancient only because, long after their discovery, they were found to show some "fossilization."

THE FONTEZUELAS SKELETON

HISTORY AND REPORTS

The Fontezuelas skeleton represents another find by Santiago Roth. It was discovered by him in 1881, at the distance of slightly more than a mile (2–3 km.) from the Rio Arrecifes, in a locality called Pontimelo or, more properly, Fontezuelas.

The find took place under circumstances which were reported for the first time by Vogt in 1881.[1] Vogt was informed of the particulars by Roth himself through correspondence and later by oral communication. The data are as follows:

Roth was collecting the remains of extinct animals in the locality under consideration. The terrane of the region, according to him, is composed of (a) the surface layer of vegetal earth; (b) the upper layer of the Pampean formation, 5 to 24 m. in thickness, containing the remains of the glyptodon, hoplophorus, mylodon, and other fossil animals; and (c) a deeper Pampean layer, 1 to 3 m. in thickness, containing the remains of the mastodon, megatherium, panochthus, doëdicurus, and toxodon. Beneath layer c is a deep clayey stratum of unknown thickness.

Layers b and c were considered by Roth as Quaternary but with distinct faunas which were never found mingled. In 1888, however, that author published an account of the fossil animals which he had discovered,[2] and the details show that species found in stratum b were also not infrequently encountered in layer c, and vice versa.

The human bones were discovered in layer b. This layer had become exposed through denudation. Protruding from it were found the edges of the carapace of a glyptodon. The carapace lay slightly obliquely and with its convex part downward, hence in a position the reverse of the natural. Raising this carapace, there were gathered

---

[1] Vogt, C., Squelette humain associé aux glyptodontes; in *Bull. Soc. d'Anthr. Paris*, 3me sér., IV, 1881, pp. 693–699.

[2] In *Zeitschrift der deutschen geologischen Gesellschaft*, XL, Berlin, 1888, pp. 400–401.

also the pelvis and the femur of the animal.[1] A workman then observed to Roth that a "fossil gourd protruded from the ground. It was the top of a human skull.[2] This was excavated with great care. The lower jaw was in its proper place. The other bones of the skeleton fell to powder."[3]

Following the above, Vogt quotes Roth as follows:

"The ribs lay dispersed here and there; the cervical vertebræ were quite far from the skull; one of the femurs still held to the pelvis. The bones of the feet were scattered everywhere and a number of them were missing; the bones of one of the hands were still in place, those of the other being dispersed. I have not been able to find more than remnants of the vertebral column in a concretioned mass of earth, which I saved. All these bones were decomposed, the external parts being removed by decay, the cores alone being still recognizable. All the bones were at the same level, below the *Glyptodon*, in the steep bank of the stream.[4] Beneath the skull was found an oyster shell [5] 5 cm. long and 3 cm. broad, also an instrument of deer horn 18 cm. long and 1.5 cm. thick at its base."

Vogt's remarks are, in brief, that in the branch of the deer horn, a photograph of which he received, he was not able to recognize an intentionally made instrument; also, that after the receipt of the first letter from Roth he had answered him that the contemporaneity of the human skeleton with the glyptodons could not be admitted unless the probability of later interment was absolutely excluded. "It is possible, I told him, that the earth had been moved and that remains of very different ages were thus brought together." Roth responded that movements of the ground, except in cases where other proofs exist, can not be distinguished in the Pampean formation. The soil, he said, is so fine, yielding, and homogeneous that when excavated in making a pit and then returned to its place, it soon incorporates itself so well with the surrounding earth that it is impossible to find again the place of excavation. But as to an interment of the skeleton, that, he declared, he could not admit. "It would have been necessary to remove the whole carapace of the *Glyptodon* in order to place the cadaver in the position where I found the skeleton, and then to replace the carapace, bedding it well with earth so that it would keep the position in which I found it."

In 1882 and again in 1884 Roth speaks of the find under consideration, in his catalogue of the Pampean fossils.[6] This catalogue was not

---

[1] Erroneous; the bones were the pelvis and the femur of man; see further.

[2] Nothing is said in this place as to the level at which the skull was noticed.—A. H.

[3] This should probably read "some of the bones of the skeleton fell to pieces." See further.

[4 *"Sur la berge du fleuve"*; this point is confusing, for no other mention is made of a stream in close proximity. The Rio Arrecifes was given before as more than a mile distant.]

[5 Later, in other accounts, mentioned as a shell of a "bivalve."]

[6] Roth, S., Fossiles de la Pampa, Amérique du Sud; in Catalogue, San Nicolas, 1882, pp. 3–4 (2me éd.), Génova, 1884, pp. 5–7, pl. I.

obtainable, but the statement is quoted in full by Ameghino,[1] as follows: "The point where these fossil remains were discovered is situated on a slight incline which descends from a higher swell of land and unites the same with the border of the river, the place where the human remains were found being half a league, more or less, from the Rio de Arrecifes. The locality where the excavation was made has been denuded by rains, the vegetal earth being carried away. The human skull was found at the same level as the carapace, on the side toward the river. The bones of the human skeleton were found scattered slightly (*desparramados un poco*) in all directions; one femur and the pelvis (*cadera*) were beneath the carapace of the animal. The skull was by itself and in the vertical position, the lower jaw below, the instrument of deer horn under the lower jaw with which it was in contact; the ribs were scattered, the atlas and axis lying 1.50 m. from the skull. What I could gather of the spinal column lay by itself. The bones of the feet were scattered; those of one hand were together, those of the other separated. The shell of a bivalve was found in the pelvis [?] (*en la cadera*), and, on cleaning it at my house, I found in the earth that held it some little bones of a small edentate. The carapace of the *Glyptodon* was turned over on its back, its border projecting from the ground. The position of the human skeleton makes me suppose that it was covered by earth through atmospheric influences after having remained for some time exposed to the air and the rain, which explains why a certain part of the bones show destruction of their surfaces while others, covered more promptly, are well-preserved."

In 1883 the Fontezuelas find, and particularly the skull, are discussed by Virchow.[3] The account by Roth given in the preceding lines is repeated, with the additional remark that from the presence of the bones of the small edentate Roth concluded that the animal served the man as food.

Virchow does not enter into a critical consideration of the find. As to the antiquity of the human bones, he shows reserve. As to the skull, having only a photograph of its lateral aspect at hand, he misjudged its type, pointing out its apparent resemblances to the Sambaqui and the Pampean Indian crania.

A year later, at the end of a correction of some statements concerning the nature of the Pampean deposits,[4] Burmeister also refers in a few words to the Fontezuelas bones, saying that he has seen only the lower jaw, "which seemed to me to show nothing deviating from the type of the native race."

---

[1] Contribución al conocimiento de los mamíferos fósiles, etc., 1889, pp. 67, 84–85.

[2] In the letter to Vogt (see above) it is said that an oyster shell was found below the skull.—A. H.

[3] Ein mit Glyptodon-Resten gefundenes menschliches Skelet aus der Pampa de la Plata; in *Verh. Ber. Ges. für Anthr., Eth., und Urg.*, XV, 1883, pp. 465–467.

[4] Burmeister, H., Bemerkungen in Bezug auf die Pampas-Formation; ibid., XVI, 1884, p. 247.

The same year the skull from "Pontimelo" is considered by Kollmann.[1] There are no further data regarding the circumstances of the discovery. "The statements of Roth are admissible and there is no reason to doubt his reports, especially since Ameghino and Moreno [2] found traces of man in the same strata and with the same fauna." Kollman received a series of nine photographs of the skull and, using them as a basis, makes a number of determinations. Virchow's suppositions as to the form of the skull are equally erroneously confirmed. It belongs to the "chamæprosopic, brachycephalic, ancient race of the American diluvium." The forehead is not primitive in form but is broad, high, well-developed.

In 1887 the skull is referred to by Quatrefages, who also regards it as brachycephalic,[3] and in 1888 the principal points relating to the find are given by Roth in his good paper on the Pampean formations.[4]

Meanwhile the remains came into the possession of the Zoological Museum of the University of Copenhagen, and in 1888 a description of them was published by Hansen.[5] It was found that all the authors who based their opinions on the imperfect photographs of the skull reached erroneous conclusions. Its characteristics "are nearly the same as those of the race of Lagoa Santa. The skull is really dolichocephalic . . . and is even more hypsistenocephalic than the crania of the Sumidouro (Lagoa Santa) cave. . . . The facial parts had been broken and are not well restored," so that an exact description of the face is impossible. "For this reason it is necessary to restrict the remarks to the general statement that the face presents the same aspect as that of the race of Lagoa Santa. . . . If it is added to the above that the measurements of the long bones indicate a similar stature, it is seen that the individual should be regarded as a representative of the same ancient race, without any considerable divergence."

Concerning the find as a whole Hansen says: "A close examination of M. Roth's account gave the result that it is not possible to regard the contemporaneity of fossil man and *Glyptodon* as absolutely proven. This find does not suffice to solve the question of the antiquity of man in South America. . . .

[P. 30] "It is a circumstance of no small interest that the skeleton was found near a river, on a declivity on which the Pampean formation, consisting of a very fine clayey sand, was not covered by any

---

[1] Kollman, J., Schädeln von Pontimelo; in his Hohes Alter der Menschenrassen, in *Zeitschr. für Ethn.*, XVI, Berlin 1884, pp. 200–205.

[2] Reference can be only to Moreno's Rio Negro finds, which, however, were not made in the Pampean soil, nor were they accompanied by bones of fossil animals.]

[3] Quatrefages, A. de, Histoire générale des races humaines; in 2 pts., Paris, 1887–89, pp. 85–86, 105.

[4] Referred to in the earlier part of this section.

[5] Hansen, Sören, Det jordfundne Menneske fra Pontimelo (with abstract in French), in his Lagoa Santa Racen, in *Samling af Afhandlinger e Museo Lundii*, I, Kjöbenhavn, 1888, pp. 1–27, pl. IV.

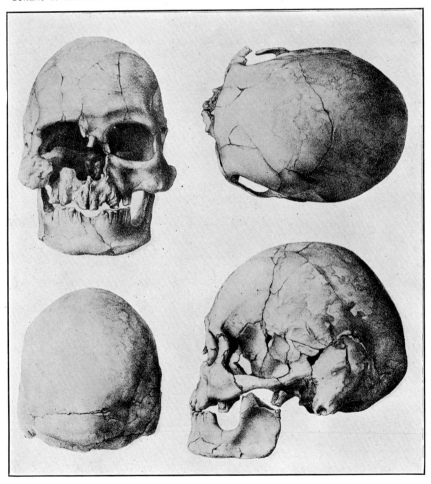

SKULL OF FONTEZUELAS. (AFTER SÖREN HANSEN)

layer of humus, because the individual bones did not occupy their natural relative positions, but were scattered over a rather large surface and seem to have been exposed to some change of location at a time when the water of the river stood higher.   The carapace of the *Glyptodon* mentioned was lying on the back, but somewhat obliquely, and projected from the surface above the pelvis and a femur of the same animal.[1]   However, no other bones of the animal were found, and the *Glyptodon* had remained undisturbed until Roth dug it up. Even if the human bones were in reality lying underneath the carapace, which is not quite certain, it is out of the question to regard the circumstances of the deposit as trustworthy proof that the Pontimelo man lived simultaneously with, or before, the *Glyptodon*. The Pampean layer consists of a mass so loose and mobile that the objects contained in it can not remain in all probability long in their original position. Roth himself in one of the letters to Vogt has given a very significant account of these conditions."

The principal measurements of the Fontezuelas skull are (Hansen):

	cm.
Length	18.5
Breadth	13.6
Cephalic index	*73.5*
Basion-bregma height, about	14.0
Circumference	52.0
Transverse arc	31.5
Nasion-opisthion arc	39.0
Diameter frontal minimum	9.7

The stature is estimated at 151.5 m.   The illustrations of the skull are here reproduced (pl. 18).

In 1889 Roth wrote to Kollmann on the subject of the "Pontimelo" skull.[2]   This letter was incited by the remarks of Hansen.   We learn from it that the statement in Vogt, which refers to the finding below the carapace of the glyptodon, of the pelvis and a femur of the same animal, is erroneous and should read "pelvis and a femur of man." Of the glyptodon there existed only a part of the carapace.   There are then references to the Carcarañá, Saladero, and Baradero finds of "fossil" human bones, with additional remarks on finds of ancient stone implements and baked earth, but there is nothing further concerning the details of the Fontezuelas discovery.

In answer to this letter, Kollmann (ibid.) says, "the decision [as to the antiquity of the skeleton] lies with the geologists. . . . We in Europe can contribute next to nothing to the solution of these pending questions; we can only bring forward, as Hansen did, doubts and reflections.   Fortunately the skull of Fontezuelas is not the

---

[1 Copies Vogt's error; should read "of man."]

2 Ueber den Schädel von Pontimelo (richtiger Fontezuelas): in *Mitth. anat. Inst. Vesalianum zu Basel*, 1889, pp. 1–4; and in Lehmann-Nitsche, Nouvelles recherches, etc., pp. 470–487.

only evidence which makes the existence of man in those regions in the time of the large South American mammals seem highly probable."

In 1889 also, as already mentioned, the Fontezuelas find is referred to, but with a bad error, in Ameghino's work on the fossil mammals of Argentina.[1] Ameghino concludes that, on the basis of the available data, "this skeleton belongs really to the Superior Pampean, to its most superficial layers, being much more modern than that of Mercedes [Arroyo de Frias] and that of the Rio Samborombón."

In 1891 Kobelt speaks of the find,[2] following Ameghino, and suggests indirectly the name *Homo pliocenicus* for the new species of man represented by the Fontezuelas skeleton.

In 1902 Virchow[3] returns in a few words to the "Pontimelo" skull. He says: "Of the oldest crania in America, such as could be ascribed to the diluvial if not to even the Tertiary period, there are known in general only peculiar cases, with which one can do but little;" and then deplores his error in having considered the skull of "Pontimelo," on the strength of a photograph, brachycephalic.

Some brief remarks concerning the Fontezuelas and other Tertiary skeletons are found in a later (1906) publication by Ameghino,[4] which read as follows:

"The remains of man from the Superior Pliocene (Fontezuelas) indicate a small race, reaching the height of approximately 1.50 m., with a frontal curve of medium elevation, without or with only slight supraorbital swellings, with a sternal perforation and 18 dorsolumbar vertebræ.[5] These last characteristics are very primitive and this race was made a distinct species, named by Kobelt *Homo pliocenicus.*"

Finally, in 1907, the Fontezuelas human bones are dealt with by Lehmann-Nitsche[6] who reexamined them and gave a detailed report on their physical characteristics. Nothing is added to the already-mentioned data concerning the circumstances of the find. Lehmann-Nitsche's own statement begins with the rather naive assertions that, "having studied personally the originals at Copenhagen, I can affirm without fear of being mistaken that all the débris of the skeleton came undoubtedly from the Pampean formation. All the peculiarities which they present are absolutely identical with those which one observes in the bones of the great mammals that are so well known, which fact has also been expressly remarked by Hansen

---

[1] Contribución al conocimiento de los mamíferos fósiles, etc., p. 67.
    The account speaks in one place of the skeleton as having been found in, instead of under, the carapace of a glyptodon, an error later copied by Kobelt.
[2] Ameghinos Forschungen in den Argentinischen Pampas; in *Globus*, Bd., LIX, Braunschweig, 1891, pp. 132–136.
[3] Crania ethnica americana, Berlin, 1892, p. 29.
[4] Les formations sédimentaires, etc.; in *Anal. Mus. Nac. Buenos Aires*, XV (ser. 3, t. VIII), 1906, p. 447.
[5] The last two features relate to the Samborombón skeleton (p. 233).]
[6] Nouvelles recherches, etc., pp. 253–296.

himself. They have the same dry, spongy constitution and they are very fragile, very friable. All are of a dark-yellowish color. Some of the bones, as for example the humerus, are covered with characteristic calcareous incrustations, which adhere strongly and can not be separated without taking with them the surface of the bone. Besides this, the detailed description which Roth published about his discovery and which he personally repeated to me, has convinced me fully of the contemporaneity of *Glyptodon* with the man of Fontezuelas."

The results of Lehmann-Nitsche's examination of the specimens are in the main as follows:

The description and measurements of Hansen, so far as they go, are correct. The basal parts and also the occiput show slight posthumous depressions. The facial parts also have been altered by pressure. Besides the posthumous compression, Lehmann-Nitsche believes there is a slight posterior artificial flattening.

The skull is dirty yellowish-gray in color and the bone adheres strongly to the tongue. The parietal region shows some calcareous incrustations. The cranium is very large and massive, its external form suggesting decidedly that of the modern Tehuelche skulls. The details concerning the external characteristics of the vault show no remarkable features.

As to sex, it is not unlikely that it is feminine.[1] The lower jaw, however, suggests a male rather than a female. It is very robust and massive and its body is voluminous; the ascending rami are nearly vertical but not particularly broad. The surface of the bone is covered with calcareous incrustations. The inferior outline of the jaw is angular, the chin part being square. The prominence of the chin is seen to be fairly developed.

The teeth in general are large; they are very much worn[2] and in the manner observed among the modern Indians of South America.

Measurements of the lower jaw of Fontezuelas

	cm.
Length from right condyle (middle of the posterior border) to the antero-superior border of the symphysis (the condyle is somewhat damaged), at least	11.0
Height of the ascending ramus, from the inferior border to the notch, in a direction parallel to the posterior border	5.2
Breadth of the ascending ramus, perpendicular to the preceding measurement[3]	3.7
Height at symphysis	3.3
Maximum thickness at symphysis (without internal spine)	1.7
Thickness of horizontal ramus between second and third molars	1.6
Angle (bigoniac)	*115°*

---

[1] A skull of such size, particularly if belonging to a short skeleton, with lower jaw, zygomæ, and mastoids as present in this specimen, can more safely be regarded as masculine. The strength of the humerus and the narrowness of the greater sciatic notch make the identification of the skeleton as that of a male quite definite.—A. H.

[2] The size of the teeth, ignoring extremes, can not be judged with any degree of certainty when the crowns are worn off in an advanced degree.—A. H.

[3] Breadth minimum?

The parts of the skeleton still in existence comprise: The atlas with portions of the axis, and the third cervical vertebra; remains of the rest of the vertebral column, conserved in the earth with which they are enveloped; a number of pieces of ribs; portions of the pelvis, including the two acetabula; some fragments of the scapulæ and clavicles; the two humeri, one nearly complete, the other very defective; the two radii, incomplete; one ulna, also incomplete; the bones of the right hand, nearly complete; the bones of the left hand, very incomplete; the two femora, nearly entire; the two patellæ, imperfect; the two tibiæ, nearly whole; the two fibulæ, very defective; some bones of the feet; and a large quantity of débris of bones from the same skeleton. It is plain that, notwithstanding the fact that the bones were somewhat scattered, as reported by Roth, there is very little, if anything, missing from the complete skeleton. Also, numerous bones appear to be in much better condition than the remarks in the earlier reports on the find would indicate.

The three cervical vertebræ are still in their natural position, enveloped in loess and forming one piece, but the bones are so defective that they offer but little for examination. The few measurements that could be taken present no special features.

The fragments of pelvic bones show a narrow greater sciatic notch, in marked contrast with that of the skeleton from the Arroyo de Frias, in which this notch was very wide.[1] A particular outline taken on one of the fragments "corresponds absolutely to modern types."

The right humerus is above medium in strength; it is not markedly platybrachic.

The principal measurements of the humeri	Right. cm.	Left. cm.
Maximum length, about	29. 0	.....
Maximum diameter at middle	2. 4	2. 1
Minimum diameter at middle	1. 7	1. 65
Index at middle	*70. 8*	*78. 6*
Circumference at middle	6. 9	6. 3

The measurements show that the right humerus is short and massive, while the left is weaker.

The radii are quite straight, but not very stout. The interosseous border shows the usual form. So far as can be determined, the ulna was quite strong.

As to the femora, the maximum length of the left bone was calculated by Hansen at 40 cm., the same by Lehmann-Nitsche at 39.7 cm., the bicondylar length at 39.6 cm. The bones are not very massive, the circumference at the middle measuring 8 cm. on the right, 7.9 cm. on the left. The platymeric index is *73.3*, which is not remarkable. The linea aspera is very broad in its whole extent but

---

[1] These are simply sexual characteristics, the wideness of the notch indicating a female; its narrowness, a male.—A. H.

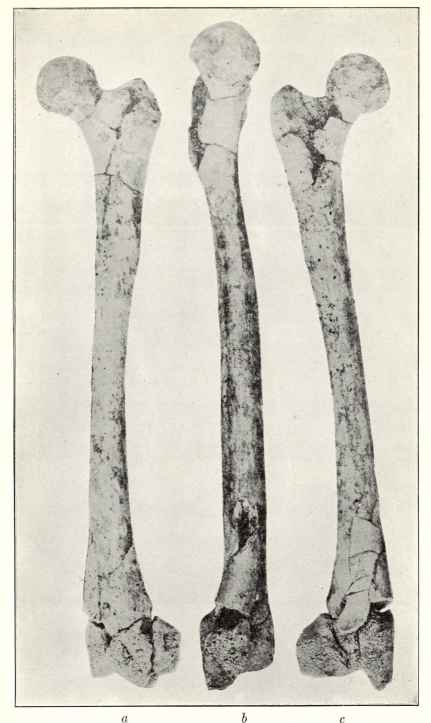

a   *b*   *c*

LEFT FEMUR OF FONTEZUELAS SKELETON. (AFTER LEHMANN-NITSCHE)

Anterior (*a*), medial (*b*), and posterior (*c*) views.

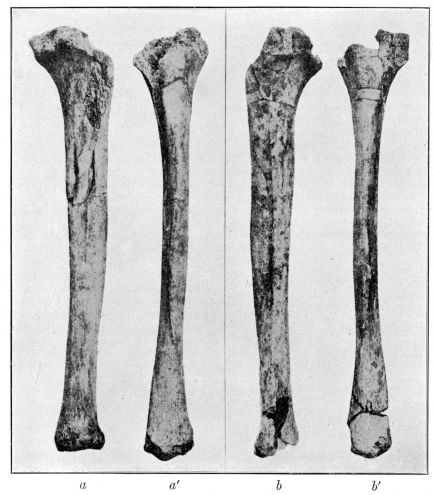

a   a'   b   b'

TIBIÆ OF FONTEZUELAS SKELETON. (AFTER LEHMANN-NITSCHE)

Right: a, lateral view; a', anterior view; Left: b, lateral view; b', anterior view.

there is no marked pilasterism. The pilasteric index of *112.4* on the right, and *112.5* on the left, corresponds very closely with that of the Saladero (Arizona), the Sioux, and other Indians. In general form the bones differ from those of the *Homo primigenius* and approximate to those of the present man. (Pls. 19, 20.)

The tibiæ "offer no special features." They are notably platycnemic. The retroversion of the head is marked.

Principal measurements of the Fontezuelas tibiæ

	Right. cm.	Left. cm.
Length between the articular surfaces	32. 5	32. 7
Diameter antero-posterior at middle	3. 3	3. 2
Diameter lateral at middle	2. 1	1. 9
Index at middle	*63. 6*	*59. 4*
Diameter antero-posterior at nutritive foramen	3. 6	3. 5
Diameter lateral at nutritive foramen	2. 1	1. 9
Index at nutritive foramen	*58. 3*	*54. 3*
Circumference at middle	8. 6	8. 3

"The fibulæ offer no particular features."

The humero-femoral index is about *73.2;* the tibio-femoral index about *82.6.* Both of these proportions are well within the range of variation of the modern man.

The stature is calculated at 151.2 cm., almost identical with the estimate of Hansen, this assuming that the skeleton is that of a female; if a male [and so it should be regarded], 153.6 cm.

The bones of the hands and the feet present no remarkable features.

As usual in this series of his reports, Lehmann-Nitsche avoids summarizing the results of his studies and conclusions; but his study has brought out no points about the skeleton that would suggest another species of man or even a type differing from that of the recent Indian.

As to its age, in a subsequent publication [1] Lehmann-Nitsche places the skeleton among those belonging to the Superior Pampean (Quaternary).

CRITICAL REMARKS

The pivotal question in regard to the Fontezuelas skeleton is, of course, that of its geologic age; and the criteria of age are stratigraphic position, association, alterations in, and the morphologic characteristics of, the bones. Let us test these several factors as applied to the case under consideration.

It should be stated to start with that the writer, who became personally acquainted with Santiago Roth, learned to appreciate highly the latter's integrity as well as his ability, and can not but regard his statements with entire confidence. However, his statements regarding the Fontezuelas find are not as detailed as desirable and are

---

[1] Lehmann-Nitsche, R., El hombre fósil pampeano; in *Bol. Ofic. Nac. Est.*, La Paz, Bolivia, VI, 1910 pp. 363–366.

not accompanied by exact measurements and photographic records, both of which in cases of this nature must be regarded as indispensable. We are told that there was only a part of the carapace, but are left in doubt as to how large that part was, how deep it lay, exactly how it was related to the human bones, and exactly how deep these were buried.

The barren surface in which the find was made is mentioned as "exposed through denudation," but it is not clear how deep this denudation was and whether it was recent or of ancient date. Most of the points here cited may not be of paramount importance, but in a case like this full and precise data relating to every particular are needed.

The carapace of the glyptodon, which lay inverted over the human bones, affords some means of estimating the depth of the latter beneath the surface at the time of the discovery. The complete carapace of a full grown glyptodon measures about 3 feet in height, but as in this case only part of the shield was present and as the border of this, moreover, protruded from the ground, the human bones must have been buried less than 3 feet deep. Even if it be granted that the locality had been denuded of its humus layer and perhaps even of the uppermost layers of the soil beneath, the depth at which the human bones lay must be regarded as having been moderate.

The different parts of the skeleton were somewhat scattered, yet larger or smaller fragments of practically all the bones remained. This does not seem to warrant the conclusion that the body lay until decomposed on the surface of the ground. If left thus, it would have fallen in all probability a prey to carnivorous animals and the body, or parts of it, would have been scattered, destroyed, or carried away. It appears much more probable that the body was buried and that most if not all the dissociation, fragmentation, and loss of parts of the bones, occurred subsequently beneath the surface, through the agency of inundations or other forces.

The theory of accidental burial, advanced by Roth, encounters, however, another serious objection. If the remains of the body were covered through natural means, as claimed, we must ask how the empty and overturned glytodon carapace came to lie directly over the human skeleton. Glyptodon skeletons occupying inverted positions may be common enough but here we have the carapace only, with no intimation or evidence that the spot was ever a bed or a gully into which a glyptodon could roll and die, lying on its back, directly over a human skeleton. Moreover, if the human remains had been covered with loess through natural means, it is reasonable to suppose that the same thing would have happened at least in part with the skeletal remains of the glyptodon other than the carapace, but no trace of any of the bones of the animal, or of the scales of the head or the tail was discovered. It is not probable therefore that the glyptodon rolled accidentally upon the human remains.

But if the above supposition is abandoned, then we must conclude that the carapace alone, or a part of it, as found by Roth, reached somehow the position over the human body or bones, or that it was placed there by man. It will be seen at once that in either case the relation of the carapace to the human skeleton ceases to be of value as evidence of antiquity.

An accidental presence above the human bones of the heavy upturned carapace would be difficult to explain, although it not infrequently happens that water, wind, and other agencies produce phenomena which are difficult or impossible to trace. Two interesting suggestions relating to overturned glyptodon carapaces, capable of throwing light on this problem, are found in Roth's own paper on the pampas formation. We read: "Burmeister believes that these carapaces [of glyptodons] were carried for some time by water, the rest of the bones [of the glyptodons] being lost. However, we often find isolated bones of the same animal lying next to the carapace and even under it." [1] If this is true, then it is conceivable that the carapace in question may have been deposited on higher ground during some flood of the not far distant stream. But its deposition directly over a human skeleton, though not impossible, would be a rare chance.

The most plausible solution appears to be the assumption that the carapace was placed over the human remains by man. This might have been done with or without the knowledge of the existence of the remains. In the latter instance the carapace might have been used on the same spot for a wind shield or for some other purpose, such use of these carapaces having often been referred to by the Argentine paleontologists.

It seems more rational to believe that the carapace was purposely laid over the human body as a covering and protection. In the absence of stone or heavier pieces of wood, if a carapace or a part of it was available, it is very likely that it would have been used by the natives who buried the body. As to the inverted position, it is not impossible a part of a carapace would be so placed originally. More probably, however, it was placed with the concavity downward and was disturbed subsequently by man, water, or some other agency; and the same agency may also have disturbed the bones beneath. Of course the carapace may already have been ancient when placed over the bones.

However, it is not here intended to build up any hypotheses. The fact is there is not the slightest proof that the animal, part of

---

[1] Roth, S., Beobachtungen über Entstehung und Alter der Pampasformation in Argentinien; in *Zeitschr. deutsch. geol. Ges.*, XL, 1888, p. 449.

whose carapace lay over the Fontezuelas human bones, was contemporaneous with the man to whom these bones belonged. This is true even though it is by no means yet established that the glyptodons passed away at a very remote date.

A petrographic examination of the bones with the view of determining their state of fossilization has not been made. Adhesions of indurated calcareous matter alone are not incompatible with the relatively modern character of the bones. This subject has been already discussed at length, however, in other sections.

In physical characteristics the bones are all closely related to those of the Indian skeleton; the femora and the tibiæ in particular are typically Indian. The shaft of the tibia, as can well be seen in the illustration (p. 261), presents a flat quadrilateral shape, due to the excessive development of a ridge between the tibialis posticus and the flexor digitorum longus muscles, which was frequent in the earlier Europeans, but occurs only very seldom in such a degree in the modern white, is not met with at all in the black, but is found again and again in the same form in the Indian.

The small stature of the individual, whether female, as claimed by Lehmann-Nitsche, or male, as believed by the writer, does not prove the existence of an early pigmy race, for such stature is not rare in the more central regions of South America, especially in Peru and Bolivia.

The correctness of the preceding statement will best be seen from the following figures: The bicondylar length of 200 Peruvian femora, taken without selection from the United States National Museum collection, ranges from 33.9 to 44.6 cm., the average being 40 cm. Of the 200 bones, 98 (49 per cent of the whole), show a length less than that of the Fontezuelas femur.

Again small stature is also met with frequently among the living Indians. It was shown by the writer on another occasion [1] that the minimum stature in normal males, even in tribes in which the average height is fair, often descends well below 160 cm. In six of the tribes it actually descends below that estimated for the Fontezuelas skeleton. If the skeleton were that of a female, the conditions would be still less exceptional, for among the 19 tribes in which the women were measured the minimum stature in all but one is below that estimated for the Fontezuelas individual and in two tribes, the Aztec and the Tarasco, neither of which has ever been considered a tribe of pigmies, even the average stature of the women falls below that of the subject under consideration.

On the whole, the study of the Fontezuelas find leads to the conclusion that, even if some circumstances of the find can not be

---

[1] Hrdlička, A., On the Stature of the Indians of the Southwest and of Northern Mexico; in Putnam Anniversary Volume, Cedar Rapids, Iowa, 1909, p. 42.

fully explained, they are not incompatible with the recent age of the human remains; and the skeletal parts, when considered in the light of our present knowledge, speak so strongly for their Indian and modern origin that, unless additional proofs tending to establish the contrary are supplied, they can not but be so regarded.

THE ARRECIFES SKULL

HISTORICAL REMARKS AND EARLIER REPORTS

The first notice of the Arrecifes skull is found in Ameghino's work on the fossil mammals of Argentina.[1]   After making certain remarks concerning the Fontezuelas skeleton, he says:

"This region of the Rio de Arrecifes appears to have been at that epoch more populous or more suitable for man's habitation than the rest of the province, for, while writing these lines, I have received notice of the discovery of a human skull, evidently fossil, more or less under the same conditions as the preceding [Fontezuelas], at the distance of about 4 leagues from the town of Arrecifes, near the small Arroyo de Merlo and at a short distance from the channel of the Rio Arrecifes, on a declivity of the Pampean terrane denuded by the waters.   I have not as yet seen the locality, but the aspect of the skull and its state of preservation show plainly that it proceeds from the red Pampean ground."

On page 85 of the same work we read the following additional remarks in regard to the specimen: "The skull, of which I have two photographs, was recently found in the same northern region of the province [as the skull of "Pontimelo"].   It is evidently of a distinct race, [2] dolichocephalic, with an index that should be in the proximity of 75, and also hipsistenocephalic, but of narrow and very low front, very pronounced supraorbital arches, and strong temporal crests."

And without further data or consideration the skull is accepted as representing a variety of ancient man, for the following lines read: "We hold, then, the proof that during the formation of the Inferior [probably should read "Superior"—A. H.] Pampean, the province of Buenos Aires was inhabited in the same regions, although we have no evidence that it was absolutely synchronically, by two distinct human races, one dolichocephalic and with marked characteristics of inferiority in the skull; the other brachycephalic. . . .

"The representatives of both races were hipsistenocephalic and of very small stature."

No other account of the discovery has ever been published by Ameghino.   But in 1906, in his work on the sedimentary formations,[3]

---

[1] Contribución al conocimiento de los mamíferos fósiles, etc., 1889, pp. 67, 85.

[2] From that represented by the Arroyo de Frias, Samborombón, and Fontezuelas skulls.—A. H.

[3] Les formations sédimentaires, etc.; in *Anal. Mus. Nac. Buenos Aires*, XV (ser. III, t. VIII), 1906, pp. 446–447.

this author gives another illustration of the Arrecifes skull, marking it as "Inferior Quaternary," and offers the following remarks (p. 447), which ill agree with those quoted in the preceding lines: "The man of the Quaternary epoch [fig. 344 = the skull] does not appear to differ from that of the present period, but his remains are very interesting because they seem to indicate that he is the result of an evolution effected on this continent."

A few details concerning the find, based on personal information obtained from Ameghino, were published in 1907, with a description of the skull, by Lehmann-Nitsche.[1] The skull was found by M. Monguillot, a preparator formerly attached to the Museo Nacional, in the locality mentioned above, "in terrane belonging to the Pampean formation, which was left exposed by water." Ameghino acknowledged he "did not know the locality; but the aspect of the skull, its state of preservation, and the information given by the preparator, proved to him conclusively that the specimen came from the upper layers of the Superior Pampean formation."

The above is absolutely all that has been reported of this discovery, and the case must be regarded as one of the most striking illustrations of the poor foundations on which the structure of the theory of ancient man in South America is built.

The skull is now the property of the Museo de la Facultad de Filosofía y Letras, Buenos Aires, where it was examined by Lehmann-Nitsche and also by the writer, thanks to the courtesy of Señor Juan Ambrosetti, director of the museum (fig. 45).

Lehmann-Nitsche's principal remarks and conclusions in regard to the specimens are as follows (p. 299 et seq.):

"As to the question whether the cranium really is derived from the Upper Pampean loess, it would be equally possible to sustain that opinion or oppose it.

"In favor of the antiquity of the specimen is the circumstance that the parts of the bone which have been freed from calcareous incrustation adhere strongly to the tongue; they have all the aspect of fossility, a yellowish-white color, fragile structure, etc. Besides that, the ventral surface of the skull is covered by a very irregular granular layer of strongly effervescent carbonate of lime. Similar calcareous covering over the external surface reaches in some spots a thickness of more than 1 millimeter, and is composed of at least three perfectly distinct layers. This differs from the known incrustations which cover animal bones from the Pampean formation and resembles the stalactite that forms on objects plunged into

[1] Nouvelles recherches, etc., pp. 298–320; also the somewhat earlier publication on the same subject in the *Revista de la Universidad de Buenos Aires*, VIII, 1907, reprint, pp. 1–46. The two accounts differ in a number of secondary particulars. All quotations and references that follow are from the Nouvelles recherches, etc.

mineral waters containing much lime in solution, as those of Carlsbad. . . .

"Against the opinion which attributes the skull to loess, may be advanced, as proof, the lack of data regarding the find, as well as the relatively satisfactory preservation of the osseous substance; but in reality the bone has been protected by the calcareous envelope which covered it.[1]   The chocolate-colored stains visible on some parts of the lamina interna suggest exactly the color of the ancient Patagonian

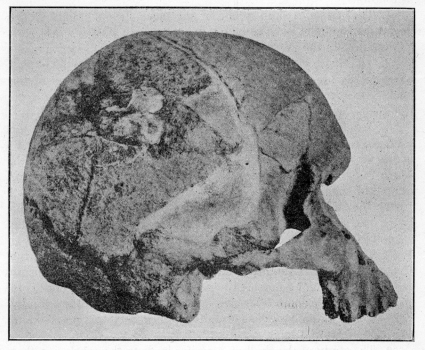

FIG. 45.   Skull of Arrecifes, *norma lateralis*.   (After Lehmann-Nitsche.)

skulls from the Rio Negro, of which an important series exists in the Museo de la Plata, the 'Quaternary' age of which is affirmed only by Ameghino.[2] . . .

"However this may be, I consider the skull, without hesitation, very ancient, without venturing to call it absolutely fossil, and I believe that the term subfossil would well express the idea of its great age."

[1 Experience with Indian skeletal material from limestone caves in California has been quite to the contrary, bones or parts of bones coated with or embedded in stalagmitic deposits showing advanced changes; there is marked loss in organic matter, the bones are yellowish-white to white in color, and where there is no interstitial infiltration of lime, they are fragile.]

[2 This statement is unjust to Ameghino who, at the place indicated, states with emphasis that Pampean deposits are absent from the entire lower part of the valley of the Rio Negro and that the skull in question (Moreno's collection) is unquestionably Post-Pampean (see also p. 196 of this report).   As to the stains, such disseminated black or brown spots are very common on bones and usually are devoid of all significance as to the age of the specimen.]

Of the various specimens described in this paper, Lehmann-Nitsche continues, "the subfossil skull of Arrecifes seems to be the most recent. I am firmly convinced that it may proceed from the Pampean formation.[1] All its characteristics indicate that it is very ancient and is comparable in this respect with all the other human remains which were studied in this work."

The preceding excerpt is from page 300. On page 320, at the end of the study of the specimen, Lehmann-Nitsche states his opinions as follows:

"1. The Arrecifes skull is one of the most ancient crania of the Argentine Republic, even though it is not possible to attribute it with all certainty to the Pampean formation.

"2. The length of the cerebral part of the skull surpasses the human average, the breadth equals exactly that average; the index of the vault is mesocephalic; the height, great absolutely, presents, in relation to the length, a figure that is relatively rather low (platycephaly).

"3. The breadth of the forehead corresponds absolutely with the average; relatively (in regard to the breadth of the skull) it corresponds to the American type. The frontal and bregmatic angles, which indicate inclination backward of the front, are such as occur in man of the present day.

"4. The facial part of the skull is more or less chamæprosopic; the index occupies an intermediary position among the human races in general [2] and among the various American tribes in particular.

"5. The supraorbital arches are well marked and prominent; the supramastoideal crests are well developed; the mastoid incisure presents the form of a notch (American type); the digastric crest is in the form of a rude comb (*d'un gros peigne*); the groove for the occipital artery is also notchlike. The occipital torus is very well marked and forms one long and large swelling.

"6. The study of the skull of Arrecifes leads to the conclusion that it belongs to the actual human type and especially to the American type."

In view of the last paragraph and of the almost entire absence of data concerning the find of the specimen under consideration, it is difficult to see on what the statements in paragraph 1 of the above conclusions and the statement on page 300 in Lehmann-Nitsche's work are based.

The more important of Lehmann-Nitsche's measurements of the skull are as follows:

---

1 "*Je suis fermement convaincu qu' il peut provenir de la formation pampéenne.*"

[2 The comparisons with mankind in general must be regarded as carried too far. The state of precise anthropologic knowledge concerning many important groups of humanity is as yet very imperfect, especially etiologically.]

cm.

Length, maximum	18. 6
Breadth, maximum	14. 1
Diameter frontal minimum	9. 6
Diameter bizygomatic maximum, about	14. 2
Nasion-alveolar point height, about	7. 5
Circumference, horizontal	53. 0
Circumference, transversal	33. 5
Circumference, antero-posterior, frontal	13. 2
Circumference, antero-posterior, parietal	14. 3
Diameter antero-posterior frontal, about	11. 5
Diameter antero-posterior parietal	12. 4
Auricular height	12. 3
Frontal height	8. 5

More recently [1] Lehmann-Nitsche classes the skull of Arrecifes with those of Frias, Saladero, Samborombón, Fontezuelas, Chocorí, Miramar, and Necochea, all of which, with the Carcarañá bones, are regarded as Superior Pampean and hence Quaternary. But these crania "represent no somatologic characteristic which is not found also in the existing natives of South America and especially in the same Pampean and Patagonian regions, and there is even noted a certain amount of variation in the different examples."

Finally, in 1910 the Arrecifes skull is also briefly reported on by Mochi.[2] This author shows that the norma verticalis of the specimen is ellipsoid; the vault is not chamæcephalic, as classified by Lehmann-Nitsche, who must have made an error in his figures, but, as already noted by Rivet, it is hipsicephalic; the face is pyramidal, chamæprosopic, the orbital index low. The "new characteristics" brought out "demonstrate that the skull belongs to the cranial group of the type known as that of Lagoa Santa, and thereby shows an affinity with the dolicho-acrocephalic oceanic type, with the *Ellipsoïdes pelasgicus* of Sergi, and with the Quaternary (or regarded as such) European skulls of Galley Hill, Engis, and Brno [Brün]. On the other hand, it has nothing in common with the types which, rightly or wrongly, are considered essentially American."[3]

These conclusions impress one, especially one who knows personally the sympathetic author, as very unfortunate. They involve in the comparison racial and ancient elements which are wholly irrelevant to the specimen under consideration, and largely so to the whole subject of man's age in South America in its present hazy stage. On what common basis, for instance, can the late diluvial skull of Brno be compared with the skull of Arrecifes, even if the latter

---

[1] El hombre fósil pampeano; in *Bol. Ofic. Nac. Est.*, La Paz, Bolivia, VI, 1910, pp. 363–366.

[2] Mochi, A., Appunti sulla paleoantropologia argentina; in *Arch. per l'Antr. e la Etn.*, XL, Firenze, 1910, pp. 214–218.

[3] "*Non ha invece niente di comune con i tipi che a torto o a ragione si considerano come essenzialmente-americani.*"

should belong to the Upper Pampean? The statements appear possible only from a worker well versed in the anthropology of Europe, but less so in that of America, a condition reflected also by the works cited. The last sentence quoted is wholly untenable. To make this clear, one needs only to point to the recent well-considered conclusions of Rivet on the same subject.[1] There are cranial types which may be justly considered essentially American, and, as recognized by Lehmann-Nitsche and as will be shown later on, the Arrecifes skull has everything in common with such of these types as it approximates in cephalic index.

The measurements given by Mochi are those of Lehmann-Nitsche. Two estimates, one of the basio-bregmatic height and the other that of the greatest bizygomatic breadth of the skull, are both too high, and others of the facial structures, in view of the defective state of those parts, can not be given much weight.

As to the geologic age of the find, Mochi is inclined to believe, on the basis of the alterations of the bone and the calcareous incrustation, that the skull "belongs to one of the final phases of the Quarternary."

EXAMINATION BY THE WRITER

What the writer observed in his examination of the Arrecifes skull may be briefly stated as follows:

The specimen is a normal, symmetric, and beyond any doubt masculine, skull. The subject was adult but not old. The sutures seem to be patent, but the teeth show rather advanced wear.

The skull has been fairly well reconstructed from about 24 pieces. The facial and basal parts are to a large extent defective. Parts of the temporals have been rebuilt in mastic, and the same is true of parts of the malars; furthermore, the mending substance is seen also between the parietals and the occipital, and between the mastoid portions and the parietals, slightly enlarging the vault.

The dorsal surface is covered with grayish, semigranular, calcareous incrustation, which measures from a fraction of a millimeter to about 1 mm. in thickness. Ventrally the bones are covered with similar coating but to a lesser degree. The skull is quite heavy, but the weight is evidently due largely to the incrustation. Nevertheless the bones and the teeth also seem somewhat mineralized interstitially.

What remains of the facial structures shows a medium prognathism, with a low upper alveolar process (about 1.3 cm.). The teeth, so far as can be determined, were of ordinary Indian size and form. The dental arch is regular. The palate was not unusually broad nor above moderate in height. The malar bones, badly damaged and defective, present no special features; marginal processes are of medium

---

[1] Rivet, P., La race de Lagoa-Santa chez les populations précolombiennes de l'equateur; in *Bull. et Mém. Soc. d'Anthr. Paris*, 5me sér., IX, 1908, p. 209 et seq.

dimensions. The zygomæ show masculine development. Orbital borders dull; interorbital breadth rather above, size of orbits rather below, medium. The naso-frontal suture is patent; the nasal articular surface on the frontal looks nearly down. Nasion depression moderate; nasion itself situated high, a frequent characteristic of Indian skulls in Argentina.

The supraorbital ridges are well developed, but not excessively so for a male, and extend over the medial two-thirds of the supraorbital border. The glabella is in a slight depression between the ridges. As is frequently the case, there is a shallow depression above the distal parts of the supraorbital ridges; none above the medial parts. The lateral angular processes are rather stout.

The forehead is well-arched and quite high, with a single diffuse median convexity; there are no lateral frontal eminences and no crest.

There exists no post-coronal depression. The sagittal elevation is very moderate and mainly perceptible about the summit, in the usual position. The parietal bones present no features worthy of special notice.

The temporal regions are not bulging. The temporal crests run at a good distance from the sagittal suture, their nearest approach to the same being about 6 cm. on each side, and are in no way unusual.

The occiput (including the posterior portion of the parietal region) is slightly uneven, the right side being the larger, but this is probably due in part to defects in repairing the specimen; its prominence is not above medium. The occipital torus is rather pronounced, broad, horizontal, and reaches nearly from side to side of the occipital. Depressions below the crest are ordinary.

The mastoids are good-sized, masculine; the mastoidal crests are well-marked.

Serration of sutures rather simple, as usual in Indians.

Outline of norma superior approximates elliptical; that of norma posterior is pentagonal.

The face was of medium height and moderate breadth, and in general of a type common among Indians of similar cephalic form.

The thickness of the skull is not excessive; the incrustations prevent direct measurement.

Ventrally, there are seen a short and moderately high metopic crest and some impressions of brain convolutions.

Measurements:[1]

Vault: cm.
Diameter antero-posterior... 19. 0
Diameter lateral maximum 14. 4
    (Owing to the imperfections in the repairing and to the thin crust, each of these measurements should be reduced slightly, perhaps as much as 3 mm.)

---

[1] The values obtained agree in general fairly closely with those of Lehmann-Nitsche, some differences being due doubtless to unlike allowances for the imperfections of the skull. Measurements that would have to be based principally on estimate are excluded.

cm.

Height, biauricular line–bregma, approximately........................... 12. 4
Circumference (above supraorbital ridges), approximately................. 52. 9
Transverse arc (from roots of zygomæ above meatus, across bregma)......... 31. 6
Breadth of base between points of mastoids............................... 11. 8
Breadth between the distal parts of the lateral angular processes of the frontal
 bones... 11. 0
Breadth between the points of intersection of orbital border and fronto-malar
 suture... 9. 8
Diameter frontal minimum.. 9. 7
Diameter frontal maximum, near.. 12. 0
Nasion-bregma arc... 12. 4
Bregma-lambda arc (before repair was probably slightly smaller).......... 14. 3

The skull shows no trace of disease.

There is absolutely nothing more primitive in form or size or in individual features of the specimen than is generally met in crania of the American Indians.

Conclusions.—As a result of the above examination, and after due consideration of the meager data relating to the specimen, it is the writer's opinion that, on account of defective information in regard to the circumstances of the find, and on the basis of the somatologic evidence, the Arrecifes skull should be excluded from all further consideration relative to early, i. e. geologically ancient, man in America.

The whole subject of antiquity in this case appears unfounded. Holding in view the known facts concerning the Arrecifes skull, it is impossible to settle on a single feature of importance which would point unequivocally to any great age of the specimen. Under these circumstances, the question forces itself: What could not be made, in a similar manner, out of such North American remains as the Osprey (Florida) skeletons, described in the writer's report on early man in North America. One of these specimens is inclosed in hard rock, another is more nearly petrified than the bones of a mastodon from another part of Florida, and the third is embedded in and converted into iron ore. There are, moreover, in our possession, cave skulls and skeletons embedded in solid breccia, or thickly covered with calcareous deposits, as well as more or less petrified human remains from shell mounds. But there is still another question that presses strongly, namely: What may be the results of further years of similar loose gathering and of so easily satisfied anthropologic work?

THE SAMBOROMBÓN SKELETON

HISTORY AND REPORTS

The first mention of the Samborombón skeleton is found, in 1884, in Burmeister's note on the Pampean formation.[1] This reads simply: "A second fossil human skeleton has been found here by Sr. de Carles."

The first details regarding the discovery are not met with until 1889 in Ameghino's Fossil Mammals of Argentina.[2] On page 47 of this publication we read: "In 1882 D. Enrique de Carles, traveling naturalist of the Museo Nacional of Buenos Aires, exhumed from the Superior Pampean of the Arroyo de Samborombón a nearly complete human skeleton, interred at a considerably lower level than some bones of a *Scelidotherium* and other extinct animals. The report on this specimen, which is most noteworthy in many respects, has not as yet been published."

On page 66 this is supplemented by the following: "The Arroyo Samborombón, in the vicinity of its confluence with the Arroyo Dulce, has a channel 3 to 3½ meters in depth. Its banks, now vertical, now sloping, are formed, with the exception of the uppermost humus layer, which does not reach 40 cm. in thickness, of reddish Pampean deposits, in which are intercallated here and there small deposits of yellowish-green lacustrine Pampean sediments. The latter are nearly always of slight thickness as well as extent.

"In one of these deposits of the lacustrine Pampean along the same Arroyo of Samborombón, at a very short distance from the mouth of the Arroyo Dulce, there was found by the traveling naturalist of the Museo Nacional of Buenos Aires, E. de Carles, a nearly complete human skeleton, with the exception of the skull, of which there remains only the basal part of the occiput and the lower jaw. The bones were found articulated, although the skeleton was divided into two parts, the trunk and the superior members with the skull being in one, and the pelvis with the sacrum and the bones of the lower limbs in the other, at a distance of 1 meter from the first. The only visible part exposed by the waters was the skull, of which, on account of the exposure, there remains only a relatively small portion.

"This lacustrine deposit or layer in which the skeleton reposed was 40 or 50 cm. in thickness; it rested on the red Pampean and was covered by the reddish deposits, 1 meter in thickness, belonging to the same Pampean formation.

[1] Burmeister, G., Bermerkungen in Bezug auf die Pampas Formation; in *Verh. Ber. Ges. für Anthr., Ethn., und Urg.*, Ber in, 1884, p. 247.
[2] Ameghino, F., Contribución al conocimiento de los mamíferos fósiles, etc., pp. 47, 66, 85.

"In the lacustrine deposit which contained the skeleton, there were no other vestiges; but in the reddish Upper Pampean layer and a short distance off, if not precisely above the skeleton, de Carles gathered the base of the antler of a large deer, now preserved in the Museum of Buenos Aires, and the mandible of a species of *Scelidotherium*."[1]

On page 85 of the same publication there are, finally, a few words concerning the skeleton itself, as follows: "The third skeleton of the fossil man from the Superior Pliocene, gathered in the Rio Samborombón, has hitherto been mentioned only by Burmeister, without a single word having been said about its features. It has remained undescribed in the possession of its discoverer.

"I have seen this specimen, though but casually, and observed in it some characteristics which attracted my attention. Among these were the small stature of the individual, who probably was of the female sex, and the possession of 18 dorso-lumbar vertebræ, an extremely rare anomaly in the existing races, but which should have been more frequent in the races of antiquity and without doubt was a constant characteristic of some of man's ancestors. In the sternum there also exists a vacuity or perforation, I do not now recollect at what height, an anomaly that is equally rare in the existing races. The lower jaw is in a perfect state of preservation, is strong and massive, and evidently belonged to a brachycephalic skull, without doubt of the race which Roth encountered."

These few and ill-estimated results of a casual examination of the skeleton serve as a basis for some important conclusions. Referring to the Samborombón skeleton and to that of Arrecifes, Ameghino says (ibid.): "We hold thus a proof that, during the formation of the Inferior [2] Pampean, the Province of Buenos Aires was inhabited over the same area, though it is not shown that it was absolutely synchronically, by two distinct human races; one dolichocephalic and with marked signs of inferiority in the skull, the other brachycephalic, of a skull apparently more elevated, and representing by the characteristics of the skeleton—if the existence of 18 dorso-lumbar vertebræ, in the only example with an entire vertebral column thus far known, is not an anomaly (which would be peculiarly rare)—a very inferior race. The representatives of both races were hipsistenocephalic, and of an exceedingly small stature."

---

[1] A written statement on the subject, made by Señor Carles to the writer while accompanying him on the way to the Ovejero finds, reads as follows: "At the confluence of the Rio Dulce and Samborombón, in a barranca of gentle declivity and in a small pocket of bluish-green lacustrine mud, probably deposited in an excavation in the loess (red Pampean), I found the human skeleton, without any vestige of any object of industry. It was divided nearly in the middle into two portions which were at a short distance one from the other, but in the same locality and at only a few meters distance (in the red Pampean) I found a piece of the lower jaw of *Scelidotherium leptocephalum* and a part of an antler of a large deer."

[2] Should probably read "Superior."—A. H.

In 1890 a brief report on the remains was presented to the Congress of Americanists at Paris by Vilanova.[1]   In it we read that "the lower jaw is very large; the condyles are slightly oblique to facilitate movement from before backward, which with the type of wear presented by the crowns of the teeth, indicates the frugivorous diet of the individual. The foramen magnum occupies a more backward position than in civilized man, which would give a somewhat inclined position to the body. The sternum presents a natural perforation, a very strange thing in our species. Finally, the dorsal part of the spine contains 13 instead of the usual 12 vertebræ. These remains were found by Señor Carles in the channel of the Rio Samborombón, an affluent of the Rio de La Plata, at a very slight distance from a nearly complete skeleton of a *Megatherium* in the Pampean formation."[2]

Shortly before this skeleton had come into the possession of the museum at Valencia, Spain. It had never been studied thoroughly. Notwithstanding this, however, it was later, and gradually with more and more definiteness, classified by Ameghino as a representative of a race characterized by sternal perforation and 18 lumbodorsal vertebræ. In 1906[3] the skeleton was attributed to the uppermost Tertiary strata. The remarks concerning this are as follows:

"The remains of man from the Superior Pliocene indicate a small race, reaching the height of approximately 1.50 m., with a frontal curve of medium elevation, without, or with only slight, supraorbital swellings, with a sternal perforation and 18 dorso-lumbar vertebræ. These last characteristics are very primitive and this race was made a distinct species, named by Kobelt *Homo pliocenicus.*"[4]

Finally, in Ameghino's "Geología, Paleogeografía," etc. (1910), the Samborombón find is apparently connected with that of the Arroyo Siasgo; the "race" becomes a definite new species characterized (p. 24) as follows:

"In the Superior Pampean, in the more recent strata of the Bonaerean horizon, we encounter the *Homo caputinclinatus*, of stature equally small (1.40 to 1.50 m.) and of 18 dorso-lumbar vertebræ, with a front scarcely a little less depressed than in the *Homo pampæus*, but without supraorbital arch; the skull is excessively long and narrow (cephalic index in the neighborhood of *66*), the parietal region is very high, glabella strongly inverted downward but not backward, the nasal bones very broad and without transver-

---

[1] Vilanova, J., L'homme fossile du Rio Samborombon, in *C. R., Congr. int. Amér*, 8me sess., 1890, Paris, 1892, pp. 351–352.

[2] De Carles: A piece of the lower jaw of *Scelidotherium*. Ameghino: The lower jaw of *Scelidotherium*. Vilanova: A nearly complete skeleton of *Megatherium*.

[3] Ameghino, F., Les formations sédimentaires, etc.; in *Anal. Mus. Nac. Buenos Aires*, XV (ser. III, t. VIII, 1906), pp. 447–448.

[4] In *Globus*, LIX, Braunschweig, 1891, pp. 132–136.

sal depression at the root; the orbits extraordinarily superficial, and consequently the rostrum very much prolonged forward; finally, the foramen magnum is situated in the posterior part of the skull, farther back than in many apes, giving the head a position strongly inclined downward."

In 1907 [1] Lehmann-Nitsche refers to the skeleton. He brings forth no additional information and assumes, it seems entirely too readily, that "there is no reason to doubt the geologic age of the skeleton." In his latest paper [2] he classes it as from the Superior Pampean.

CRITICAL REMARKS

To the writer it appears that there is much room indeed for doubt as to the antiquity of the Samborombón human bones, and as to the propriety in assigning them to a period preceding or contemporaneous with that of the scelidotherium, a portion of whose lower jaw was found at a few meters distance from the human remains and in different soil. The original data are, in fact, so inadequate and unsatisfactory that on their basis alone the specimen can never legitimately receive serious consideration as bearing on the problem of man's antiquity in South America, while the anatomic peculiarities which it shows are without significance in that connection.

The presence of 18 dorso-lumbar vertebræ [3] and of a perforated sternum [4] are both features not very rare in the American Indian or in other races, and there is no justification whatever for making one sole instance of this nature (even if fully substantiated) the distinguishing feature of any race or species.

The presence of the skeleton 3 feet or somewhat farther below the surface, and the close proximity of the spot to two streams, are circumstances quite compatible with the theory of a modern burial. The completeness of the skeleton and in general the natural relation of its parts speak strongly for burial. The separation of the skeleton into two nearly equal portions without disturbance of the various bones is explainable only by faulting or motion in the earth of the bank, having no bearing on the age of the human remains. The fact that the body

---

[1] Nouvelles recherches, etc., p. 298.

[2] El hombre fósil pampeano, etc., p. 364.

[3] There are three such specimens, two Indian and one Eskimo, in the special series of the U. S. National Museum and a large proportion of the material has not as yet been examined. See also Rosenberg, E., Über eine primitive Form der Wirbelsaüle der Menschen; in *Morph. Jahrb.*, XXVII, I, Leipzig, 1899; Dwight, Th., Description of the Human Spine showing Numerical Variation; in *Mem. Boston Soc. Nat. Hist.*, V, No. 7, Boston, 1901, pp. 237–312; and Bardeen and Embryo, in *Anat. Anzeiger*, XXV, Jena, 1904, pp. 497–519. See also Regalia, E., Casi di anomalie numeriche delle vertebre nell' Uomo; in *Arch. p. l'Antropol. & Etnol.*, X, 1880, p. 305 et seq.

[4] More common than preceding anomaly. See, ten Kate, H., Sur quelques points d'ostéologie ethnique imparfaitement connus; in *Revista del Museo de la Plata*, VII, Buenos Aires, 1896, pp. 271–272 (found perforation in 16 among 120 Indian sterna in the Museo de la Plata). Also Hrdlička, A., Description of an Ancient Anomalous Skeleton from the Valley of Mexico, with Special Reference to Supernumerary and Bicipital Ribs in Man; in *Bull. Amer. Mus. Nat. Hist.*, XII, New York, 1899, pp. 95–96.

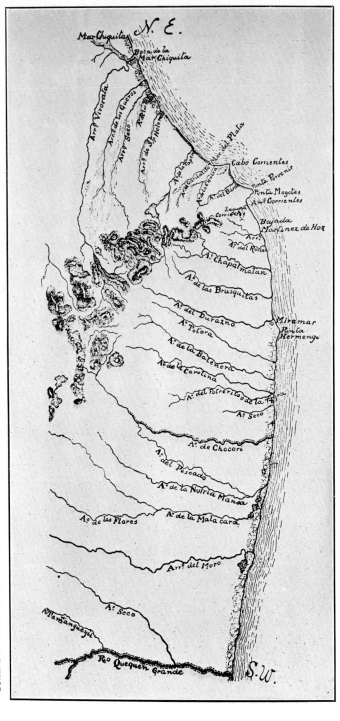

MAP OF THE LITTORAL OF MAR DEL PLATA AND CHAPALMALAN. (AFTER AMEGHINO)

lay in a pocket of lacustrine (?) mud has no significance if the body came there through burial; it is quite possible that soil there offered less resistance to digging than in other parts of the surface.

It is only too apparent that no antiquity for the Samborombón skeleton has been proved, and the specimen can not well serve further as indisputable evidence of the existence of early man in Argentina.

THE CHOCORÍ SKELETON

HISTORY AND EARLIER REPORTS

The skeleton of Chocorí was found in 1888, and is reported for the first time by Lehmann-Nitsche in 1907.[1]   It comes from near the coast not far south of Miramar, from the same region as the Miramar skull described in another place in this report.   (See pl. 35; also map, pl. 21.)   The details concerning the find are given by Lehmann-Nitsche as follows:

"About the year 1888 Francisco Larrumbe, an employee of the museum [de La Plata], discovered in the vicinity of the small village of Mar del Sud, situated on the seashore in the southern part of the Province of Buenos Aires, abandoned on the surface of the ground, in the midst of the lands between the Arroyo Chocorí and the Arroyo Seco, at a distance of about 100 meters from the beach, a human skull, with some remains of other bones of the same skeleton. . . . These remains had been almost completely covered by indurated sand, but the wind and water had partially removed the layer and left the skull exposed to the extent of some centimeters.   In this state it was discovered, with the rest of the osseous remains, by Larrumbe, who brought away all these specimens.   I have these details from himself.

"The fossilization of the bones can not be doubted; their character is identical with that of the bones of fossil animals from the Pampean formation.   The skull is of a color varying between whitish and yellowish; some parts are impregnated with a blackish substance. . . . The external compact layer has been destroyed in nearly its whole extent by weathering in such a way that the surface became rugose, and in parts where the destruction has penetrated farther, deeply eroded.   In the localities not attacked by the destroying agencies, that is to say, at small irregularly disseminated points and in more extended patches over the whole post-coronal region of the skull, the external lamina is covered by very hard calcareous concretions which can be removed only with difficulty without damaging at the same time the surface of the bone."

The lot of bones consists of a defective skull with a defective lower jaw, and of fragments of a humerus, radius, femur, tibia(?), and a rib.   Lehmann-Nitsche's examinations of these remains gave him in the main the following results:

---

[1] Nouvelles recherches, etc., pp. 321–334.

The vault of the skull is reconstructed in part, but Lehmann-Nitsche has full confidence that the reconstruction is accurate. The sex of the individual he judges to be feminine. The thickness of the bones is ordinary. On account of the defective condition of the specimen only a limited number of measurements is practicable. The norma frontalis "offers, so to speak, no noteworthy feature." The front appears narrow, the parietal eminences are pronounced. The skull is very long and relatively narrow; the cephalic index is calculated as *71.1*. Both dorsally and ventrally the occipital bone shows nothing in common, with the exception of a deep cerebral fossa, which is "extremely remarkable." "The norma basalaris offers nothing particular." The norma lateralis shows somewhat prominent supraorbital arches and a deep nasion depression. The frontal curve is not pronounced. The skull is very high. The capacity of the skull is calculated as 1,528 cc. The lower jaw shows "very pronounced human characteristics," the ascending ramus is narrow, the angle wide. It is notable by the prominence of the chin. Nothing out of the ordinary was discovered in the curve of the body. "It represents absolutely the recent European type. The teeth are small."

As to the fragments of the long bones, that of the right humerus is robust. The radius was very powerful and only slightly though regularly curved. The rib presents no special features; its "constitution indicates an individual of a stature above the medium and very vigorous."

Lehmann-Nitsche's measurements of the Chocorí bones [1]

	Humerus	Radius	Femur
	Cm.	*Cm.*	*Cm.*
Diameter maximum (near middle)	2.5	1.65	2.8
Diameter minimum (near middle)	1.8	1.25	2.4
Index (near middle)	*72.0*	*75.76*	*116.67*
Circumference (near middle)	6.9	4.2	8.0

In 1910 the Chocorí skull was briefly examined by Mochi and is reported on in his paper on Argentine paleo-anthropology.[2] It was found to be dolicho- and chamæcephalic. The norma superior is pentagonoid. As to sex, the author is inclined to consider it mas-

[1] Lehmann-Nitsche does not express directly his notion of the age of the Chocorí skeleton, but, as on p. 300 of his Nouvelles recherches, etc., he considers the Arrecifes skull "seemingly the most recent" of those dealt with in his work, it is evident that he regards the Chocorí specimen as more ancient. His statement on p. 321 that "the Chocorí bones are completely identical in character" with those of fossil animals from the Pampean formation—a statement somewhat at variance with certain views of Ameghino and Roth, as well as with the writer's observations—points in the same direction. Finally, in his most recent publication (El hombre fósil pampeano) he classes the skull with those of Arrecifes, Miramar, etc., as belonging to the Superior Pampean formation, which he regards, with the exception of its uppermost parts, as Quaternary.

[2] Mochi, A., Appunti sulla paleoantropologia argentina; in *Arch. per l Antr. e la Etn.*, XL, Firenze, 1910, pp. 218–220.

culine.   Looking again on the specimen from a European rather than an American standpoint, he considers it related to cranial forms prevalent in the Mediterranean littoral and especially among the north European dolichocephals; and probably likewise with the Quaternary and modern skulls of the Cro-Magnon type.   It corresponds to the platydolichocephalic Patagonian type of Verneau, which is found, though very rarely, among the existing South American natives. In the few measurements given, Mochi seems to follow Lehmann-Nitsche, still augmenting, however, the length (he gives 19.6 cm.). The basion-bregma height is estimated at 13.3 cm.

EXAMINATION BY THE WRITER

Through the courtesy of Doctor Lehmann-Nitsche the writer had the opportunity of studying the Chocorí bones.   The examination brought out a few additional points but none of great importance.

The bones apparently all belong to one skeleton, adult and much more probably male than female.   In color superficially all the parts are yellowish-white, with not very marked, scattered, blackish, probably manganese spots, such as are frequently seen on skulls of prehistoric and even more recent times.   None of the bones is decidedly heavier than normal, and there is no evidence of any considerable degree of mineralization.

The skull presents traces of a bilateral posthumous compression, especially of the temporal regions; on the left, this compression extends somewhat farther backward.   The foramen magnum and the basal parts anterior to it have been narrowed by the compression. There is no trace of any artificial deformation in life.   In general type the cranium approximates the skull of Arrecifes (see fig. 45).

The left side of the skull has been reconstructed of nearly 20 pieces, and the temporal region of that side has been largely rebuilt in mastic; a similar rebuilding with the same kind of material has been employed extensively along the coronal and forepart of the sagittal suture; the neighborhood of the foramen magnum also has been rebuilt.   All this work has evidently been as well done as possible, without, however, rendering the specimen safe as a subject for exact measurement.

The surface of the skull is nearly everywhere more or less abraded, in many places down to the diploë.   It is yellowish in color, but where scaled or worn off it is grayish-white.   Ventrally, it is still yellowish, of exactly the shade shown by many relatively modern skulls.   The facial parts, from slightly below the nasion, are wanting, and the same is true of most of the base.

The skull is that of an elderly person; the sutures appear to be for the most part obliterated, though their exact state is difficult to ascertain, and the teeth are worn.

As to the individual features, the nasion depression is marked. The situation of the nasion is ordinary, 1.1 cm. beneath the line connecting the highest parts of the borders of the orbits. The interorbital width is moderate. The orbits themselves were rather small.

The glabella prominence is well-marked, not excessive. The supraorbital ridges are of moderate dimensions, but the whole supraorbital region protrudes somewhat forward and there exists a shallow depression above it (2.8 cm. above the nasion). Yet this protrusion does not constitute a real supraorbital arch; it is due to a somewhat defective advance of the brain and consequently of the frontal squama forward. The forehead itself is fairly well arched, but quite

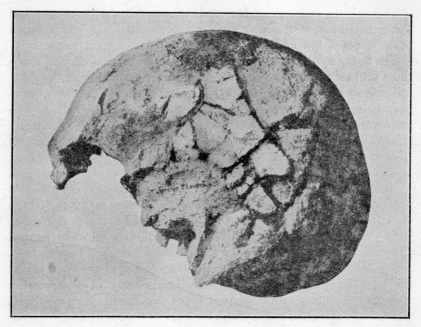

FIG. 46.   Skull of Chocorí, *norma lateralis.*   (After Lehmann-Nitsche.)

low, a type often seen in skulls of Indians. The frontal eminences are but slightly pronounced. There is no median crest.

The sagittal region is oval from side to side, the parietal eminences are well-marked, and the outline of the norma superior is accordingly pentagonal. The temporal ridges are indistinct but run at a good distance (between 5 and 6 cm. on each side) from the sagittal suture.

The occiput is slightly protruding but the muscular ridges and depressions thereon are only moderate. The mastoids are of about medium masculine size.

The thickness of the bones of the skull is moderate.

A portion of the upper jaw shows a nasal aperture of approximately 2.6 cm. in breadth; this is a very common dimension of the cavity among the Indians. The alveolar process was seemingly largely absorbed.

The lower jaw is defective but shows a square chin, of good prominence. The bone is of subaverage strength for a male. The teeth are moderate in size and were apparently normal in number; they show advanced degree of wear. Ventrally, there is but a slight reinforcement of the alveolar arch in the molar region, extending along the second and third molars. The genial tuberosities are moderate. In general the jaw shows no signs of great muscularity.

Measurements of the Chocorí skull and jaw:

Vault:	cm.
Diameter antero-posterior maximum	[1] 18.6
Diameter lateral maximum, approximately	[2] 13.9
Cephalic index, in the neighborhood of	75.0
Height, basion-bregma?, auditory meatus—line bregma, about	11.2
Circumference (above supraorbital ridges), approximately	53.0
Nasion-opisthion arc (probably shorter originally)	41.1
Lower jaw:	
Height at symphysis, approximately	3.3
Height between first and second molars	3.1
Thickness at second left molar	1.3
Angle, measurement unsafe.	

The observations as well as the measurements show, on the whole, features that could be duplicated without any difficulty in modern Indian crania.

Other bones of the skeleton:

Femur.—A portion of the left bone; surface much worn and apparently somewhat diseased, but defective character of specimen makes it difficult to be certain on the latter point. Is decidedly masculine. Shaft, in cross section approximates No. 1 (prismatic) in shape. The linea aspera is high and strong. Correct measurements impracticable on account of erosion.

Piece of a long bone.—Difficult of identification, possibly tibia; very irregular and apparently diseased surface, but no thickening of wall.

Humerus.—A portion of the right bone. Very stout and unquestionably masculine. The antero-posterior and lateral diameters at about the middle, measure, respectively, 2.85 [3] and 1.85 cm. The deltoid eminence is long and shows considerable development. There is also a well-marked tuberosity at the insertion of the lateral head of the triceps, and the ridge marking infero-posteriorly the

---

[1] Lehmann-Nitsche gives 19.4 cm.

[2] May have been originally slightly in excess of this. Lehmann-Nitsche gives 13.8 cm. for the breadth between the parietal eminences.

[3] Lehmann-Nitsche must have measured at a different level.

musculo-spiral groove is pronounced. The shaft shows characteristic Indian flatness; its shape at middle is intermediary: 1-cc. (prismatic—plano-convex); it presents a slight bend forward and inward about the middle, but this is nothing remarkable.

Radius.—Piece of one of the bones representing about the middle two-thirds of the shaft. Shows masculine strength. Curve exactly like that in modern bones, also shape of shaft and anterior concavity about the middle. Interosseous border moderate. Not diseased. Dimensions at about middle: diameter antero-posterior, 1.25 cm.; diameter lateral, 1.75 cm.

The bones, especially the lower jaw, indicate more conclusively than the skull that the individual under consideration was a male.

CRITICAL REMARKS

The Chocorí remains afford a still further example of the utilization of finds which have no satisfactory geologic and no anthropologic claims to antiquity, to swell the ranks of early man in America. They have been drawn on for that purpose simply because of the adhesion of calcareous matter to the surface of the lower bones and a possible slight mineralization of the same. Found by an unscientific museum employee near the surface of the ground, fragmentary and imperfect, restored approximately, presenting no features more primitive than the Indian and none to distinguish them from the Indian, and not even mentioned in the literature of the subject for 19 years after discovery, it seems that these remains should surely be omitted from further consideration as a factor in the discussion of the problems connected with early man on the South American continent.

HUMAN REMAINS FROM OVEJERO AND NEIGHBORHOOD

REPORTS AND HISTORY

The only information thus far published concerning the finds of human remains in the vicinity of Ovejero, is furnished by Ameghino. The first mention occurs in his paper on the *Tetraprothomo*,[1] in a footnote reading as follows:

"Ovejero is a locality in the Province of Santiago del Estero, on the Rio Dulce, at a distance of some 30 kilometers from the station Gramilla. The traveling naturalist of the Museo Nacional, Sr. Enrique de Carles, found in the uppermost strata of the Pampean formation at this locality a series of human remains (crania, long bones, etc.) belonging apparently to two distinct races, one of which was pigmy. I have entrusted the examination of these remains to the distinguished anthropologist, Dr. R. Lehmann-Nitsche, who

---

[1] Notas preliminares sobre el *Tetraprothomo argentinus*, un precursor del hombre del mioceno superior de Monte Hermoso; in *Anal. Mus. Nac. Buenos Aires*, XVI (ser. III, t. IX), 1907, pp. 115–116.

will publish in a short time, the result of his studies in these *Anales*. Meanwhile, however, having observed that the femur of the larger race preserves certain very notable primitive features, I have permitted myself to utilize it for certain comparative observations, which will not be without importance in the interpretation of the various morphologic peculiarities of the femur of the *Tetraprothomo*."

The femur in question is then repeatedly mentioned by Ameghino in comparison (pp. 118, 139, 141, 150–1, 153–4, 156–9, 167, 169–71; illustrations: 172–3, 238). In general, Professor Ameghino notes many and important similarities between the femur under consideration and that of the *Tetraprothomo*, besides other primitive forms, while other features of the bone are stated to be more like those of present man.

On page 238 of the memoir there is another reference to a "pigmy" race of Ovejero, which reads as follows:

"The man of the Pampean formation was really of a low stature, about 1.50 m., although superior in this respect to the races named above [*Homo pampæus*, etc.]. But there have been races, now extinct, of a considerably smaller size. In speaking of the fossil man of Ovejero, I said that he was accompanied by the remains of a dwarf race. I give here illustrations in natural size of the distal extremity of the humerus of a very old individual from the dwarf fossil race of Ovejero . . . and beside it the corresponding part of the humerus of a natural man of medium stature . . . in order that the great difference in size between the two may be appreciated; the stature of the dwarf races of Ovejero could not have been more than 1.30." [1]

The Ovejero remains are mentioned again by Ameghino in 1910, in his "Geología, Paleogeografía," etc. On page 24 of that work the author says:

"In the Quaternary of Santiago del Estero appear remains of a race (the race of Ovejero) which perhaps became isolated at an earlier epoch, for it is of very small stature, only 1.30 m., possesses a mandible with a strong chin, and has a skull that is short, broad, and smooth, presenting a distant likeness to the negrito type of Asia and Africa."

Still another notice concerning these finds, also by Ameghino, soon follows: [2]

"In Santiago del Estero (Rio Hondo) [3] were discovered fossil skulls and bones of two very distinct races of man; one strong and of

---

[1] "There exists an incomplete skull of the same individual of a size also very small, but I abstain from entering into the details in respect to this statement for the reason which I have expressed in the footnote on page 115." —AMEGHINO.

[2] Ameghino, F., Descubrimiento de un esqueleto humano fósil en el pampeano superior del Arroyo Siasgo; *Congreso Científico Internacional Americano;* separate publication, Buenos Aires, 1910, pp. 1–6.

[3] See Ovejero specimens.—A. H.

large stature, which does not seem greatly different from the normal form, and the other very small, which seems to show some relationship with the negritos (?)."

Before the last two of the above articles appeared in print, the writer's attention was called by Professor Ameghino to the Ovejero and other specimens, all of which are in the Museo Nacional. But the only information obtained was that "some of the specimens came recently from the Superior Pampean and are fossil; while others came possibly from superposed, more recent formations."

With one exception the specimens themselves were not catalogued or numbered and there was already confusion of the different lots and also confusion as to their particular localities.

The examination of the specimens yielded no results which would justify their acceptance as anything but relatively modern and in all probability as ordinary Indian, differing only as to age and sex of the subjects. In view of the recentness of the finds, however, the writer and Mr. Willis decided to visit the locality. In this endeavor we received very valuable assistance at the hands of Professor Ameghino, who sent Sr. de Carles, the collector of various remains, to accompany us. Thanks are due also to Sr. de Carles himself, who assisted the party in every way possible and who gave the writer as detailed an account of the various finds as he was able to furnish.

The data thus obtained are as follows: About 1906 de Carles made a visit to the valley of the Rio Dulce to see what objects of scientific interest could be found there, and during his search near a little settlement known as Ovejero discovered outside of a *viscachera* (lair of the viscachas) fragments of human bones. He dug into the viscachera and found other bones, including a humerus and two skulls. These remains were about 1 meter below the surface. The exact spot was slightly lower than the village and about one *cuadra* from the river. The bones were in soil washed by the river during periods of flood. There were found also in the same excavation bones of animals, including possibly those of the guanaco, with carbon, *Ampullaria* shells, broken unios, and fragments of plain pottery.

On the journey during which the first finds were made, Sr. de Carles found somewhat farther up the river, in a shallow barranca and at less depth than in the first case, portions of human bones and a skull; these were partly exposed in the face of the barranca.

On a subsequent journey Sr. de Carles discovered one "petrified" human skull and a small part of another, with some fragments of bones, in a deep barranca near a place called Sotelillo. These bones were near the base of the barranca, which might have been, as far as he remembers, about 9 m. below the surface. Nearby, at about the same level, he found bones of ordinary viscachas.   Nothing was found with the human bones.   The locality was on the opposite side from Ovejero and about 60 m. from the river.

At one point near Sotelillo, on a small elevation, de Carles found unbroken tosca covering 1 foot or more in thickness; on breaking this, several teeth of a common cow were found, segregated; these were for the most part entirely within the tosca, which was so hard that it had to be broken with a hammer.   The specimens are now in the Museo Nacional, Buenos Aires.

La Cañada bones: The place here mentioned is situated about midway between Sotelo and Las Thermas, on the Rio Hondo.   Here in a barranca facing the river, in a kind of alluvium which is deposited unconformably upon inferior araucanian sediments and is much inclined, Sr. de Carles found a piece of a human skull, one long bone, and fragments of other bones of a human skeleton.   These remains were "petrified" and when struck "sounded like a bell"; the walls of the long bone were stout, leaving but a small medullary canal.   The barranca was about 5 m. high, and the skull was about 2 m. from the surface.   The bones lay irregularly.

A femur of a megatherium was found somewhat farther on, in the alluvium at about the same level; there were no other objects.   At the base of the barranca, in what may have been fallen earth, were two small pieces of "petrified" human bones.

In front of Thermas and on the same side of the river as Ovejero, is a locality known as Las Tinajas.   No human remains were found here, but the skeleton of a modern dog was discovered by Sr. de Carles 2 m. below the surface of the ground in the face of a barranca. The bones of the skeleton, which were quite fresh, were scattered over about 5 sq. m.   In these deposits, which are of the same nature as those in the barranca at Sotelo, were several bones of *Eutatus*, some of these lying superficially.   There were also parts of *Dycotilio*, sp.; these were on the surface and were eroded.   When it rises, the river reaches these localities.   The *Dycotilio* consisted of only the skull with scattered teeth, without lower jaw or other bones.

Finally, a short distance below Sotelo and about 100 m. from the houses of this settlement, toward the river, Sr. de Carles found the skull of an infant.   A part of the face of this skull was exposed on the surface in a shallow depression.   There was no barranca in the neighborhood.   Besides the skull there were parts of bones (perhaps of the same skeleton) in bad condition.   No objects were discovered with these bones.   The locality is about 400 m. from the river.

Observations by the Writer

The localities from which the "fossil" human bones under consideration were collected, are from 20 to 35 miles southwest of the small railroad station Gramilla.   The road to this place passes through the primeval *bosque*, or forest. The surface is level nearly to the valley of the river; here two large swells in the ground, running apparently about parallel with the river, are crossed, beyond which is a gentle slope toward the river with here and there a sandy surface. Within about a mile or less of the stream the declivity becomes more apparent and in places is traversed by branching ravines or washes which descend toward the river. These have, for the most part, irregular, vertical walls, exposing pinkish homogeneous loess.

The small and scattered Indian settlement of Sotelo is located to one side of one of these branching washes. On the arrival of the party at the place the writer undertook at once an examination of the walls exposed in the different parts of the wash, and in less than half an hour discovered in one of these barrancas, 2 meters from the surface, the partially exposed and very imperfect remains of a human skeleton (pl. 22).

In the same and in other barrancas at similar as well as at considerably lower levels, down to perhaps 4 m. below the surface, were found *Ampullaria* and other shells, all of which, as will be seen from Doctor Dall's report (see p. 247) are of living species. Finally, near the base of one of the barrancas, on the side of the wash opposite the place where the human skeleton lay, was found firmly embedded in the loess, with only a small part protruding, half of the mandible of a common horse (pl. 23).

After the deposits and remains had been examined by Mr. Willis, the human bones were extracted from the ground. They proved to be without doubt the remains of one masculine skeleton and still showed to some extent their natural relations; but for the most part they had been moved by the settling of the ground, so that the original position in which the skeleton lay was no longer determinable; numerous parts of the skeleton, including fragments of the bones that remained, had been lost through exposure. Nothing was found with the bones or in the excavation of about 2 cubic yards of earth from below, on the sides, and above them.

The work of examining the barrancas and of removing the bones consumed a large part of one day and, owing to untoward circumstances, the stay of the party could not be prolonged, so that no other washes were examined.

The information was elicited from the Indians of the village that the settlement is a very old one and that before the present cemetery was established, about 100 years ago, the dead were buried in various places in the neighborhood.

The human bones recovered will be described later in this report; at this point it may be stated merely that they are partially mineralized, and agree well in physical characteristics with the Indian.

HUMAN SKELETON IN SITU, NEAR SOTELO

Found by Hrdlička in the loess of a barranca, 6 feet (2 meters) below the surface.

A number of shells, about forty in all, were collected from various levels of the Sotelo barrancas. Some of these lay very near the skeleton discovered by the writer; others were at lower levels, down to about 15 feet from the surface. The shells were of two kinds, with an occasional fragment of a third, and were seen in many parts of the deposits, so that ten times as large a number could have been collected without much difficulty. Those gathered were submitted for identification to Dr. Wm. H. Dall, who reports as follows:

"The shells from Sotelo, Argentina, which you left with me are *Epiphragmophora tucumanensis* Doring; *Odontostomus dædalus* Deschayes; and *Ampullaria cornucopia* Reeve, all recent species of the region."

THE OVEJERO SKELETAL MATERIAL [1]

Skull No. 1.—No. 4850, Museo Nacional (Buenos Aires) collections. The specimen is a portion of an adult, masculine, apparently nondeformed calvarium, rebuilt out of about 25 pieces and partially restored in mastic. A moderate frontal and parietal depression is the result of imperfect restoration. The parts present comprise portions of the frontal, parietals, and occipital. The right side is less incomplete than the left.

The bones are brownish-pink in color on both surfaces, with some blackish spots. On fracture they are white, though not chalky, and seem largely devoid of animal matter. They are not unduly heavy. Their thickness is somewhat above the medium for whites, parts of the frontal squama reaching 10 mm., but this would not be extraordinary for Indians.

In the median line, 2 cm. above what was the center of the supreme occipital line, is a round hole 6 mm. in diameter and about 7 mm. deep, apparently made by a drill. This does not pass through the bone; it seems to be artificial and not recent.

The cranium was of fair but not large size and apparently mesocephalic in form. There is no frontal or sagittal crest. The forehead was not low, though its exact build can not be seen. The parietal eminences are moderate. The ridges on the ventral surface of the occipital are stout. The ventral surface in general is poor in impressions of convolutions. Of sutures, nothing is visible except a part of the coronal, which seems to have been obliterated in a marked degree.

The foregoing is about all that can be said concerning the specimen, owing to its imperfect condition. No feature that can be clearly discerned is primitive or striking.

---

[1] The identification of most of these specimens with the particular localities from which they came could not be made with certainty.

Skull No. 2.—The cranium of a female, probably adult, exact age not determinable; base and jaws missing (fig. 47).

The dorsal surface of the specimen is covered with a thin pellicle of grayish-white calcareous matter and a less pronounced deposit of the same nature is seen all over the ventral surface. The bone on fracture is cream-white and probably largely devoid of organic matter, but it is not heavy or petrified.

There is no deformation or disease. Over the glabella and lower part of the frontal are seen a few clusters of superficial, small, straight or curving grooves, apparently made by the teeth of small rodents;

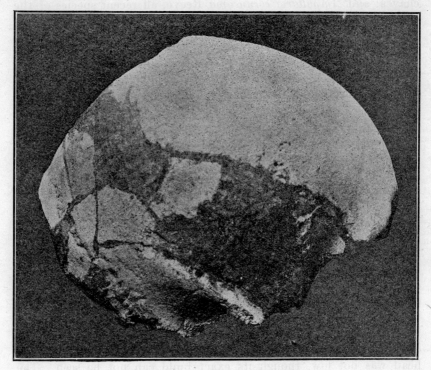

FIG. 47.   Ovejero skull No. 2 (side view).

the depth of the most pronounced of these grooves does not exceed 1 mm.

The parts present include the frontal (damaged), the larger part of the right and a small part of the left parietal, the right temporal (defective) and a part of the left temporal with the mastoid. The specimen is well reconstructed, so far as it goes, from 13 pieces; the right squama is restored in mastic.

The skull was of moderate feminine dimensions, and in form is either highly mesocephalic or somewhat brachycephalic, and of medium height.

There is a fairly well marked nasion or rather supranasion depression, but the whole region is decidedly female in character. The nasal process is quite well developed and reaches well down below the line connecting the uppermost points of the orbital border on each side. The glabella is slightly convex, not prominent, and there are small, feminine supraorbital ridges extending over the median half of each orbit. There is no approach to a supraorbital arch nor is there any depression above the supraorbital ridges.

The forehead is only moderately high, but fairly convex, with scarcely a trace of the lateral eminences, and there is no frontal or sagittal crest, only a barely visible median elevation.

The parietal eminences are large but not specially prominent. The outline of the norma superior was nearly ovoid. The temporal crests were not pronounced; the nearest approach of that on the right to the sagittal suture is 3.6 cm. The supramastoideal crests are well marked, the mastoid itself is slightly above medium feminine; the digastric groove is deep.

Of the sutures, the frontal and the sagittal are plainly traceable dorsally but seem to be in an advanced state of obliteration ventrally. Their serration was submedium.

Internally is seen a moderate metopic crest extending over less than one-half of the frontal squama. Impressions of brain convolutions are few and shallow.

What remains of the base on the right side shows a glenoid fossa of ordinary features and dimensions.

It will be seen from the above that no part of the specimen presents morphologic peculiarities, primitiveness, or anything that would be incompatible with the skull of an ordinary Indian. Thickness of the bones of the vault such as shown here is common enough in the latter race.

Measurements:

Nasion-bregma arc,[1] about .... 11.8 cm.
Right half of transverse arc, about .... 13.7 cm.
Antero-posterior arc over the middle of the right parietal, near .... 11.5 cm.
Thickness of frontal squama .... 7 to 8 mm.
Thickness of the right parietal bone .... 6 to 9 mm.

Skull No. 3.—A large, masculine, adult skull, with possibly a slight fronto-occipital deformation. Ably reconstructed from more than 30 fragments.

Surface of bones covered, as in skull No. 2, with a thin deposit of grayish calcareous matter, not enough perceptibly to affect the measurements.

The specimen is quite heavy, but the weight is mainly due to the calcareous coating. The bones are apparently largely devoid of

---

[1] Eliminating incrustation.

animal matter, being generally in the same condition as skulls Nos. 1 and 2 from this region.

The left mastoid and neighboring parts appear to have been cut out by a rodent with broad teeth; and there are also some cuts, most probably gnawings, over the occipital bone and on the fore part of the right temporal crest.

A small depression, evidently a scar, 3 mm. high by 4 mm. broad and 1.5 mm. at greatest depth, is seen on the frontal, a short distance above the most prominent part of the left supraorbital ridge. From the depression run three small radiating lines, not fractures.

The nasal process is ordinary and the nasal depression fairly well marked. The glabella is medium, somewhat less prominent than the ridges. The supraorbital ridges are of masculine proportions and occupy the median two-thirds of the supraorbital space; above them extends from side to side a shallow concavity.

The forehead is rather low, sloping backward from 4 cm. above the glabella. It presents one broad median convexity; no lateral eminences present. Above the convexity is a slight flattening, approximately 4 cm. long, possibly the result of intentional compression.

There is no medio-frontal and only a slight sagittal crest. The parietal eminences are well-marked but diffuse. The outline of the norma superior was a long ovoid.

The temporal crests are not specially pronounced; the nearest approach of that on the right to the sagittal suture is 5.7 cm. The mastoids were rather large masculine.

The occipital region is somewhat more prominent on the left and the frontal bone on the right, so that the skull is moderately plagiocephalic. The occipital crest is pronounced, double-semilunar in form.

The auditory canals show partial occlusion by posterior and also anterior exostoses, such as are quite characteristic, especially among aged individuals, of the Peruvian Indians.

The basilar process presents a small pharyngeal fossa; the rest of the base is defective. The foramen magnum was in the usual position.

The sutures of the vault seem to have been quite well serrated; the sagittal is still plainly traceable outside as well as inside.

Ventrally is seen a submedian metopic crest; there is a paucity, with shallowness, of convolutional impressions.

Measurements:

	cm.
Diameter antero-posterior maximum, approximately	19.4
Diameter lateral maximum, approximately	14.7
Diameter frontal minimum	9.4

	cm.
Nasion-opisthion arc [1]	37. 4
Nasion-bregma	12. 4
Bregma-lambda	12. 9
Lambda-opisthion, about	12. 1
Transverse arc, approximately	30. 8

The bones of the vault are rather above medium in thickness, the left parietal above and along the squama measuring from 6 to 8 mm., the frontal 8 to 9 mm., with the occipital in places less, in others slightly more massive.

All the above features are of ordinary nature, especially when the skull is compared with those of Indians, and there is nothing that indicates geologic antiquity.

Specimens marked "Post-pampean fossil man from Rio Dulce de Santiage, 2 leagues north of the baths of Rio Hondo. Carles 2d journey."

Skull A.—An adult male skull of an individual beyond middle age. Shows marked occipital flattening. The bones are yellowish and grayish on surface, nearly white on fracture. They are not mineralized and the skull is not, so far as can be judged by hand, of more than ordinary weight.

The skull is large and shows no primitive characteristics. The supraorbital ridges were not excessive; the forehead is well arched; and there is a rather heavy occipital torus. The face and base are wanting.

Measurements:

	cm.
Diameter antero-posterior from ophryon	18. 3
Diameter lateral maximum	15. 8
Height, biauricular line, bregma, approximately	12. 7
Diameter frontal minimum	9. 9

Skull B.—This is a masculine cranium of an adult near middle age. It is in general well-developed but presents a moderate occipital flattening. The bones are brownish on the surface and fragile but are not perceptibly mineralized. The specimen has been partially restored. The glabella and a part of the right supraorbital ridge have been gnawed away to some extent, although the loss of substance is not deep.

Principal measurements:

	cm.
Diameter antero-posterior maximum, about	17. 9
Diameter lateral maximum	14. 2
Basion-bregma height, approximately	13. 4

The supraorbital ridges are of moderate masculine dimensions. The forehead is well-arched. A slight sagittal elevation extends for some distance beyond the bregma. The mastoids are of good masculine size and ordinary form.

---

[1] This is probably slightly in excess of what it was originally, owing to imperfections in repair.

The face is wanting. The lower jaw is present though defective. It is quite large and strong, and presents throughout ordinary Indian-like features. The symphysis is approximately 3.8 cm. high; between the first and second molars the height of the bone is 3.4 cm., and the smallest breadth of the ascending ramus is 3.6 cm. The maximum thickness of the left horizontal ramus (the right being deficient) is 1.7 cm. The chin is somewhat square and of medium prominence. The whole ascending ramus is strong. The notch is deep.

Femur.—A portion of a right, adult masculine femur.

The surface of the specimen has been covered with a thin deposit of grayish calcareous matter, most of which, however, has been rubbed off.

The bone was about 41 cm. long and moderately strong, the principal diameters at middle being: lateral 2.45 cm., antero-posterior 3.15 cm., at subtrochanteric flattening, antero-posterior (minimum) 2.4 cm., lateral (maximum) 3.15 cm. They give a pilasteric index of *128.6* and a platymeric index of *76.2*.

The bone shows numerous markings, which Ameghino regards as the work of man, but all of which were evidently made by the teeth of rodents, especially by those of a rodent of large size, probably a viscacha. In this way the large trochanter has been entirely cut away, the marks of teeth all radiating from the cavity of the bone. Four parallel cuts, all exactly alike, are seen below the edge remaining after the cutting away of the great trochanter. Large gnawings are also visible on the linea aspera, while still other traces of teeth exist in two places on the shaft. These cuts are all transverse. Most of them are in the form of V-shaped grooves with one plane wider than the other, and were made by a rodent's incisor cutting sideways, a frequent practice with these animals. Other cuts are more nearly square, with flat bottoms. On the postero-external surface, just below the middle, there are two parallel cuts of the latter variety, which dispel all doubt as to the rodent origin of the incisors. On the linea aspera, 11.4 cm. from the upper edge of the bone, are six such flat-bottomed cuts; these are in pairs, each pair being separated from the neighboring marks by a slight vertical ridge; and the best marked among these are each slightly more than 1 mm. broad. It would be impossible to produce this effect with a knife. There is not a single feature about all these cuts that points to man's instrumentality; they were produced, plainly, by a sharp-edged chisel-like tooth. The region from which the bone came contains the viscacha; in fact some of the human bones collected here, as stated by de Carles, came from a viscachera. This rodent brings all sorts of bones about and into its lair, some of which it probably uses, as rodents in general use hard objects, for the benefit of its teeth, which otherwise would grow too long.

Descriptive notes: The shape of the shaft at the middle, with exception of the linea aspera, is nearly round; this type is more proper to youth, but is found now and then in adults, in Indians and also in whites. The thickness of the walls is moderate. There was a pronounced linea aspera, in part compensatory for a rather marked backward bend of the shaft. It also reached lower than in some bones, but not abnormally so. Its inferior termination presents the common form. Besides this backward curve, the bone presents also, above the middle, a trace of a bend outward. Both of these features are common enough in the femora of Indians as well as in those of other races.

The specimen shows further pronounced lateral torsion, so that the lateral axis of the shaft at the middle and that at the widest part of the subtrochanteric flattening form together an angle of about 55 degrees. Instances of similar torsion, however, are not rare in Indian femora.

There is no third trochanter, and the trochanter minor is in exactly the place in which it is found in a modern femur used by Professor Ameghino for comparisons.

The angle of the neck was very obtuse, indicating a male of no advanced age. The line of the insertion of the vastus internus and the cruralis is fairly well marked and runs obliquely down from below the head to the linea aspera, being in exactly the same place as on the modern laboratory femur, above referred to.

The rest of the bone is so ordinary that further description would be superfluous.

Other bones.—Besides the above, the material from Ovejero and vicinity seen at the Museo Nacional consists of a not entirely normal skull of a child (probably slightly hydrocephalic), and of numerous fragments of various bones. A separate description of each of these pieces would unnecessarily overburden this paper. They do not present one feature of any special morphologic significance, and, with all the separately mentioned specimens, may be confidently classed as ordinary Indian.

A number of the larger pieces of long bones show gnawings and possibly also claw scratches, some of which may resemble cuts with a knife; but, on close examination, especially with a magnifying glass, one can generally detect characteristics, particularly occasional doubling and parallelism of the cuts, peculiar to the teeth of rodents. The same phenomenon is frequently observed in Indian bones buried in the loess in North America. One piece of a femur shows pathologic thickening of the walls.

The Sotelo skeleton found by the writer.—This specimen (No. 263964, U.S.Nat.Mus.) is represented by more than a dozen fragments of the skull, four isolated molar teeth with parts of the jawbones adhering to the roots, the larger portions of a humerus, a femur and tibiæ, fragments of other long bones, some defective phalanges, pieces of ribs, clavicles and tarsal bones, and some slivers.

The bones are dirty-yellowish in color, and all are covered with traces, or well-marked pellicles, or small masses of firmly adhering, gray, rough, sandy cement, which covers also more or less the medullary surfaces and fills many of the cells of the spongy bones that were exposed through fracture. When the bones were taken from the earth, no such hard, firmly adhering coating existed, except on those that had been exposed. It was noted specifically that, had the proper facilities been at hand, as a brush or water, the bones could have been thoroughly cleaned on the spot with ease. The cement now on them is the result of consolidation, in drying, of the loess that was left adhering to the bones. In some of the medullary cavities filled with loess this can still be removed easily and completely, except at the ends, where it was exposed to the air, causing it to harden and adhere to the bone.[1]

Because of their thin cement covering, the bones, when they strike one another, sound like so many potsherds; but they are not visibly petrified interstitially and preserve considerable animal matter.[2] The enamel of the teeth preserves its natural luster, is not much altered in color, although slightly more yellowish, and shows no cracks. In a number of places the larger fragments show old surface defects and gnawings by rodents.

Morphologically the lot, owing to its defectiveness, is of but little importance. There is enough to show that the bones are those of a strong adult man, not below general medium in stature.

The skull was of moderate thickness. A fragment of the frontal shows that there have existed pronounced supraorbital ridges, with a tendency to extension into an arch, as occasionally seen in the American natives. Nothing can be said as to size or form of the skull. The teeth (molars) are of good size and two show considerable wear.

The right humerus measured approximately 33 cm.; the principal diameters of its shaft at middle are 2.35 by 1.8 cm.; the form of the shaft approaches prismatic. There are no specially noteworthy features.

The femora were strong, pilasteric, with very moderate upper flattening. The right measures at about the middle of the shaft 3.3 by 2.65 cm., giving the pilasteric index of *124.5*. Other measurements are impracticable. The shape of the shaft approximates the prismatic.

---

[1] A portion of a humerus of a bird, found with the human bones, looks quite fresh, but the surface is already covered with thin grayish-white calcareous pellicles.

[2] Detailed chemical analysis was not practicable, the bones not arriving until six months after being sent by express.

The tibiæ were platycnemic. The right shows above the middle a shaft of type 4 (nearly lozenge-shaped in section) and measures at about the height of the nutritive foramen 3.8 by 2.3 cm.; this gives the low index of *60.5*. The form, platycnemy, and other features agree well with those of Indian tibiæ.

Racial identification of the skeleton can not be arrived at definitely, of course, from material so defective, but what there is all suggests a common Indian.

CRITICAL REMARKS ON THE OVEJERO REGION FINDS

The examination of the bones reveals nothing that even distantly suggests the Negrito. It does not show the presence of two distinct races; there is not enough properly to show even one. What there is agrees with the Indian.

The formation in which the bones occur is plainly recent, partly the effect of the floods, to which the nearby river, according to local information, is particularly liable, but mainly accumulation by the winds, which are said to blow across the valley protractedly and occasionally with much force. However, this part of the problem will be dealt with by the geologist of the expedition.

NOTES ON THE LOCALITY OF SOTELO

By BAILEY WILLIS

The old Indian village of Sotelo is situated on the eastern or left bank of the Rio Dulce near the boundary between the Provinces of Tucuman and Santiago del Estero. There are a church and burying-ground said to be more than a century old, and the locality was inhabited long before these came into existence. Not far away is Ovejero, where human remains were found in a superficial loess and at Sotelo Doctor Hrdlička found a skeleton, which he describes. These notes deal with the aspects of the locality and of the formation in which the skeleton was discovered.

The Rio Dulce is formed by numerous streams, which flow from the Aconguija Range, that rises to a height of 3,000 meters in western Tucuman. There are no notable tributaries from the east. In that direction stretch the arid plains of northern Santiago del Estero, covered with thorny desert bush and cactus.

Near Sotelo the valley of the Rio Dulce is between 1 km. and 2 km. wide and is sunk perhaps 5 m. to 10 m. below the plain. The right bank of the river is a bluff which exposes a section of loess characterized by a distinct pink color. Low bluffs of the same material face the river plain locally on the left side near Sotelo, and the formation appears to underlie the entire valley.

East of the river the superficial formation is of different character. It is a light-gray to buff or pinkish sandy loess, composed of fine rounded sand grains, mica scales, and very fine clay. It is slightly cemented by lime but readily crushes in the hand to a fine dust. Sections 3 m. to 4 m. deep show great uniformity and an absence of horizontal structure. On the contrary there is the incomplete vertical structure, characteristic of loess. The formation is thus distinctly eolian in texture and structure. The sand and mica scales are derived from the river bed and the clay from the pink loess of the underlying formation.

The prevailing winds of the district blow from the north or northwest down and across the river valley, where these materials are deposited and exposed by the stream. The origin of the superficial formation is thus sufficiently obvious. It is an eolian loess, blown out of the river bed.

The original surface of this superficial loess was a slope or plain, very gently inclined toward the river. It is a surface which implies somewhat uniform and gradual accumulation of the deposit. Dunes are absent. At the present time the plain is cut by branching gullies, 2 m. to 5 m. deep, which have extended from the river bank back into the loess to a distance of one-half a kilometer. The gullies are of recent origin and are growing. Since the observation of the writer and his colleague was limited to the immediate vicinity of Sotelo, these may be of local character and occasioned by a special condition, which gave storm rains an opportunity to initiate and develop the single system of branching channels that were observed.

Restricting the inference to this particular locality, there may be distinguished the earlier episode of loess accumulation, which was general and may be still in action, and the immediate incident of erosion. The latter may have been in progress a score of years or half a century, scarcely more, for in this soft loess the growth of channels is very rapid, even where rains are occasional.

Any fossils indigenous to the loess must be older than the gullies. This would be true also of any human burials exposed in the side of a gully, such as were found, for no burial would intentionally be made where it would be liable to exposure. Accidental burials might occur, however, in holes in the loess near the temporary head of a growing gully, as is explained in a subsequent paragraph in connection with the finding of a horse's jawbone. The writer would thus distinguish three conditions of occurrence, any one of which might apply to any remains found in the loess: (1) Occurrence as a fossil indigenous to the loess and contemporaneous with the stratum in which the remains occur; (2) intentional burial, younger than the formation, but older than the gullies where the bones are exposed by erosion; (3) accidental burial, which may coincide with the growth of the gullies.

BARRANCAS AT SOTELO

These barrancas are west of Gramilla, in the valley of the Rio Dulce de Santiago.   Here is shown a jawbone of a common horse, buried in eolian loess 9 feet (3 meters) below the surface.   When found, the
front end of the bone extended into the bank 7 inches (18 cm.), the rear end 3 inches (8 cm.), so that
the angle only was exposed.

The relative ages of these possible occurrences would be somewhat as follows: The last-mentioned (accidental burial), taking place during the growth of the gullies would be the latest, and in the writer's estimate, would not be more than half a century old, as the gullies are probably not of greater age. The second (intentional burial) would probably antedate the cemetery of the church, which is said to have been established a hundred years. The first would date back to the formation of the deposit. The source of the material in the river bed, the winds to transport it, and the plain of deposit are favorably related at the present time. The formation is genetically related to them and may be ascribed with confidence to the present geologic epoch.

In the superficial loess were found the jawbone of a horse and the remains of a human skeleton, at points about 100 m. apart, in the nearly vertical sides of a gully which passes just south of and close by the village of Sotelo.

The jawbone of the horse lay in the gray loess at a depth of slightly less than 3 m. (about 9 feet) below the surface (pl. 23). The front of the jaw was buried 18 cm. in from the face and the articular process about 10 cm. Only about 1 cm. of the lower edge was exposed when found. The loess above the jaw appeared laterally continuous with that on each side and in firmness and structure exhibited closely similar if not identical characters. Close examination detected rounded loess pebbles or concretions of darker color than the mass, which did not occur in the adjacent loess and which might indicate a secondary deposit. The bone was that of a modern horse.

If we may regard this jawbone as a fossil indigenous to the loess, the latter is more modern than the writer would otherwise infer. If it represents a case of accidental burial, it is related merely to the growth of the gully and probably somewhat in the following manner.

When a pool of water gathers on a surface of loess, as it may in a shallow hollow during a rain, and sinks in, the water has a capacity for mixing with a considerable proportion of loess and rendering it fluid. This capacity depends on the fineness of grain of the loess particles which may be contained in the thickness of a capillary film and thus become part of the liquid. The mixture flows like a fluid. When such a mass finds an exit at a lower level, as in a gully, it flows out and leaves a vertical pit having a horizontal outlet at the bottom. The writer saw a number of such pits in the loess of China and thinks they might readily form in the loess at Sotelo, although he did not observe any in the small area inspected.[1]

It is easy to understand that a bone might fall into such a pit and become buried by loess blown from the immediate formation. There

---

[1] They were seen later by both the writer and Doctor Hrdlička in loess banks in Argentina.

is, however, little to support the suggestion except the somewhat doubtful pebbly appearance of the loess above the horse's jawbone. The evidence is not adequate to determine whether the jawbone is to be regarded as an indigenous fossil or as an accidental burial occurring after the deposition of the loess.

The human remains were found in the superficial loess at a depth of approximately 2 meters below the surface. The position and attitude are shown in plate 22, and are described by Doctor Hrdlička. According to the writer's observation the loess above them was identical with that on each side of and below them. If they were buried here the process of rearrangement of the disturbed loess has obliterated the evidence of disturbance by producing a structure identical with that of the undisturbed earth. The movement of rain water, sinking in and rising again by capillary attraction, is adequate to accomplish such a rearrangement in a moderate interval of time, and this may be the case. But considering the depth at which the skeleton lay, the homogeneity of the material above and around it, and the conditions favoring loess accumulation, the writer inclines to the view that the skeleton should be regarded as a fossil in the modern superficial loess formation. It may thus have an antiquity exceeding one or two centuries.

THE TERTIARY MAN [1]

THE BARADERO SKELETON

HISTORY AND REPORTS

In 1889, in his letter to Kollmann,[2] Santiago Roth announced the discovery by himself of still another geologically ancient skeleton, and the bones are represented as proceeding not from the Superior but from the Intermediary Pampean.

The find, made in 1887, is thus reported: "The place where I found this human skeleton is distant about 2 kilometers from the Baradero Railroad station and a short distance from the Bañado, which exists between Baradero and San Pedro.

"At this locality there was made, in constructing the railroad, a cut through the loess, and one of the feet of the skeleton was partially uncovered. The remaining parts of the skeleton were still in the loess bank, and the bones lay in normal relations, except that the head was bent forward so that not the face, but the vault of the skull, pointed upward. The lower jaw was wide open. The circumstance which impressed me most was that the bones of the

---

[1] The finds under this head are dealt with, as before stated, in the order of the antiquity attributed to them, proceeding from that regarded as the most recent to the most ancient.

[2] Ueber den Schädel von Pontimelo (richtiger Fontezuelas). (Briefliche Mittheilung von Santiago Roth an Herrn J. Kollmann); in *Mittheilungen aus dem anatomischen Institut im Vesalianum zu Basel*, 1889, p. 10–11; also in Lehmann-Nitsche's Nouvelles recherches, etc., p. 485.

upper limbs, which were stretched along the sides of the body, reached as far down as the knee joint. One hand was united with one of the knee joints by calcareous concretions. It is a matter of regret that, as is frequently the case in this class of sediments (eolian loess), the individual bones were not well-preserved. Although the bones lay in general in their true relations, I still do not believe that the body was buried but rather that it was gradually covered by the dust brought by the wind and storms. The bones showed splitting and other unmistakable signs of weathering, such as are seen only on bones which have been exposed for some length of time in free air. . . .

"That the skeleton belongs to the Intermediary Pampean will not be doubted. The case is still further strengthened by the fact that directly opposite this place is found a bank with the Tertiary oyster shells of the Entre Rios formation. Any one who will examine the case will satisfy himself of the contemporaneity of these two strata."

There are no further data by Roth. In 1889, however, the locality of the find was visited, under the guidance of Roth, by Carl Burckhardt and Lehmann-Nitsche, and the report on the observations made is given by the latter.[1] From this report it appears that the Baradero skeleton lay at no great depth, apparently only about 1 meter, below the surface. The oyster shells collected from the opposite bank were declared by von Ihering and Steinmann to be "relatively modern, probably Quaternary and intimately connected or even identical with the living forms." And the conclusions in Burckhardt's contribution to the subject are as follows (p. 162):

"Basing our opinions on these data [given in preceding lines], we can not accept the ideas of Roth that the marine bank corresponds to the formation of Entre Rios and that, consequently, a part of the loess and the fossil man of Baradero are Tertiary.

"We are obliged to hold, on the contrary, that the bank is relatively modern, very probably Quaternary, and in consequence that the fossil man of Baradero is himself probably also diluvial."

Again it is seen that, as in other cases already referred to in this report, the possibility of an ordinary burial from the surface is given no consideration.

Long before the foregoing excerpt appeared in print, the skeleton was sold to the École Polytechnique Fédéral of Zürich, and there in 1901 the bones were studied by Rudolf Martin. Martin's report is included in Lehmann-Nitsche's work just mentioned; its principal features are as follows (pp. 374–386):

"The state of conservation of the Baradero bones leaves so much to be desired that, notwithstanding my good will, I have arrived at the

---

[1] Nouvelles recherches, etc., pp. 144–165.

conviction that it is impossible to deduce from the study of this material any far-reaching conclusions. It would seem that previously the skeleton, and especially the skull, were in better state. . . .

"The petrifaction of all the skeletal parts is complete [?]; the loess which still adheres to them is so hard and so firmly attached to the bones that it can not be separated except by the action of heat or acids. . . .

"The larger part of the skeleton has been submitted to strong pressure, as the result of which one of the femurs, for example, presents to-day more than 60 fragments. These are solidly reunited [by the loess] but not exactly in their natural positions, from which has resulted an important modification in the original form of the bones. On the basis of this fact, I do not believe that I can follow Roth's opinion, which is that the present eroded and cracked condition of the bones is due to weathering. In my opinion it is more probable that the bones were thus broken within the ground.

"The remains of the skeleton consist of the following parts: Fragments of the skull, formed of small pieces of the vault in very irregular agglomeration. The majority of the fragments belong to the frontal and the parietals," others representing parts of the occipital and the right temporal bones. There are present also a portion of the upper jaw, two parts of the lower jaw, the shafts of the two femora, the tibiæ and fibulæ (broken and much compressed), and a fragment of the left *os calcis*.

All the better-preserved parts indicate, according to Martin, that the skeleton was that of an adult male, of stature well above the medium for whites.

The remnants of the skull are in such condition that no safe conclusions can be drawn from them as to the cranial form. The bones are not thick. The dental arches were evidently massive and strongly developed. The lower jaw is stout, short, and high. Below the oblique line and in front of the insertion of the masseter, there is a strong protuberance or *lateral* mandibular eminence. The surface of the insertion of the masseter is deeply grooved. The height of the horizontal ramus in the region of the second molars amounts to 3 cm., its thickness at the same point to 1.6 cm. The molar teeth, all of which are preserved, although showing extreme wear, are large but their characteristics are typically human.

"The dimensions of the teeth are without doubt superior to those which we encounter in European skulls, but they would not surprise us in the Indians of South America, who belong almost without exception to macrodont varieties."

The bicondylar length of the femur has been fixed by Martin at 47.2 cm., which corresponds to the stature of about 1.70 meters. The middle part of the shaft gave the diameters of 3.2 by 2.9 cm. on the right, and 3.3 by 3 cm. on the left; the circumference on the right was 9.5 cm., on the left 10 cm. The upper part of the diaphysis ol. the left measured transversely 3 cm., antero-posteriorly 2.7 cm., showing an eurymeric form.

The measurements of the shaft of the tibiæ at about the middle were as follows:

	Right cm.	Left cm.
Diameter antero-posterior	3. 95	4. 0
Diameter transversal	2. 35	2. 35
Cnemic index	*59. 4*	*56. 2*

The shaft, as shown in the illustration (fig. 48) presents in a typical form the quadrilateral shape.[1]

The conclusions reached by Martin on the basis of his examinations are as follows:

"It is really to be regretted that this skeleton has come to us in so defective a state, because it constitutes the most ancient specimen from Argentina, found under circumstances which are sufficiently well-known. As it is, the results of our examination do not afford a basis solid enough to enable us to conclude that the skeleton belonged to the race of Lagoa Santa.

FIG. 48. Tibia of Baradero: Transverse section of the shaft.

"It is possible to affirm, however, without fear of being in error, that in divers fragments of the skeleton which are in our possession to-day, there exists no character which is not equally encountered in modern man, especially that of South America. The man of Baradero does not represent, therefore, a human form specifically different from the man of the present day."

CRITICAL REMARKS

To the writer the only possible conclusion, from what has been learned about the Baradero find, is that the antiquity of the skeleton can not be regarded as satisfactorily demonstrated. Nothing has been advanced which could be accepted as proof that the case could not be one of merely a prehistoric holocene burial. The presence of all the parts of the skeleton in their normal relations, as reported by Roth, speaks for an intentional, or a speedy accidental, interment. Intentional Indian burials in an extended position are more rare than those in a more or less contracted one, but they occur in many parts of America and are explainable either by a modification of the usual custom, due to some special motives, or from inability to bend the body on account of *rigor mortis*. The notion that burials in fossæ were not practiced in northeastern Argentina, on account of the

---

[1] Type 4, A. H. This feature, while of rather widespread ancient as well as recent occurrence, is especially characteristic of the Indian.

absence of implements, is not correct; even if some burials were quite superficial or in shallow mounds, the fact does not, as seen again and again in North America, exclude other forms of inhumation in the same locality, at the same or other periods. No photographic study was made of the bones. That they are solidly covered with calcareous concretions indicates no great age. Finally, as seen from Martin's report, the bones so far as preserved show close morphologic relations with those of the ordinary American natives. Strong and high lower jaws are especially frequent in Argentina.

Cases of the nature · of the Baradero find have no prospect of ever being generally accepted as representative of geologically ancient man in America. They are full of uncertainties and are incapable of furnishing positive proof of the contentions as to antiquity, which are based on some of the unusual phenomena connected with the circumstances of the find or with the bones themselves. The subject of man's antiquity on this continent, as elsewhere, is of so great importance that it demands much more than an opinion or assumption by any observer. It calls in every case for a definite, unequivocal demonstration, which permits of no legitimate doubt, and any find that does not come up to this requirement can have no right to further consideration as an evidence of man's antiquity. Doubtful cases, as that of Baradero, marked by scanty geologic records, poor material, and the absence of all conclusive evidence of great age, are really, until definitely excluded from further consideration, obstructions to the progress of scientific research.

HOMO CAPUTINCLINATUS—THE ARROYO SIASGO SKELETON

HISTORY AND EARLIER REPORTS

The Arroyo Siasgo skeleton is one of the latest finds in Argentina of human remains attributed to antiquity   It was made by Carlos Ameghino and was reported before the International Scientific Congress in July, 1910, by Florentino Ameghino.

The report was published shortly afterward [1] and, as it is rather inaccessible, the contents are given here with more detail that is perhaps absolutely necessary. Professor Ameghino says:

"The year 1909 and that part of 1910 which has already passed have been particularly fruitful in finds relating to fossil man in the Argentine territory.

"It would seem that we have assisted at the awakening from *ultra tumba* of the ancient and now extinct species and races of man which inhabited our lands, in order that they might present themselves, even though only with their inanimate bones, at the celebration of the Centenary.

---

[1] Descubrimiento de un esqueleto humano fósil en el pampeano superior del Arroyo Siasgo; *Congreso Científico Internacional Americano;* Separate publication, Buenos Aires, 1910, pp. 1–6.

"In Santiago del Estero (Rio Hondo) fossil skulls and bones of two very distinct races of man were discovered; one strong and of large stature, apparently not widely different from the normal form, and the other very small and seeming to present some relations with the Negritos (?).[1]   At Necochea new examples of *Homo pampæus* were gathered.   To the north of the [Arroyo] Moro, fronting on the Laguna Malacara, some 60 km. north of Necochea, there were recently discovered in the ancient Pampean two skeletons with their skulls, belonging not to a race merely, but to a real (*verdadera*) extinct species, of reduced stature, with only four lower molars in place of five (the posterior being absent), and possessing a lower jaw without a chin, like that of Spy and Krapina.   And in the Superior Pampean of Arroyo Siasgo there was discovered a skeleton of human type, but exceedingly primitive and as simian, or perhaps even more simian, than the *Homo pampæus.*

"The last-mentioned species is named by me *Homo caputinclinatus.*"

The specimen representing the species "is a fossil human skeleton, found in January of the present year by the traveling naturalist of the Museo Nacional, Sr. Carlos Ameghino, in a barranca of the Arroyo Siasgo, some 300 meters from the house of the *estancia* 'La Georgina' belonging to Sr. J. M. Mendez, in the Department of Ranchos, near the station Villanueva of the Southern R. R.

"With the object of satisfying myself as to the position which the skeleton occupied, I visited the locality about the middle of last March.

"The Arroyo Siasgo is a small affluent of the Rio Salado.   .   .   .

"Before coming to the Salado, which it reaches through a very narrow channel, the valley of Siasgo broadens in an extraordinary manner, forming a deep depression 4 km. long and 2 km. broad. This hollow, now dry, was in a recent epoch a lake which dried up, its waters draining into the Salado.

"This depression is limited on the east by a barranca, about 8 meters high, against which broke the waters of the lake.   This barranca is a part of the remnant of an ancient and high table-land, which, in other times, separated the Siasgo from the Salado; the most elevated part of it has already disappeared.

"The terrane of this table-land (*meseta*) is formed by a layer of vegetal earth, some 50 cm. in thickness, which passes gradually into a light eolic loess of reddish-gray color, that somewhat lower becomes more compact.

"This loess deposit of the barranca of the Siasgo was described in a masterly manner in 1863 by Burmeister, who encountered in it many fossils, now preserved in the Museo Nacional of Buenos

---

[1 The Ovejero specimens (q. v.).]

Aires. One carapace of a *Glyptodon*, nearly complete, was found, Burmeister says, only 1 foot below the surface of the ground.

"The human skeleton was found buried in this unmoved deposit of loess, at a depth of 1.80 meters from the surface of the ground, deeper than many remains of *Glyptodon*, *Sclerocalypus*, *Eutatus*, etc., which we have collected in the same locality.

"The skeleton consists of a skull, of which the lower jaw and the facial parts are missing, and of various long bones, numerous vertebræ and ribs, the sacrum, the pelvis, and a number of the bones of the feet, among them a nearly intact astragalus.

"The long bones indicate that the individual was still young; compared with those of the actual man, they would correspond to one of 16 to 18 years of age. Moreover, it was an individual of very reduced stature, probably not greater than 1.40 meters.

"The bones of the skeleton present very notable peculiarities, of which for the present I shall mention only the superficial form of the 'ectal' articular facet of the astragalus, which is not deeply concave as in actual man, but much flatter; and the form of the femur, whose linea aspera is scarcely visible, and which presents toward the middle of its length a nearly circular transverse section, like the femur of many apes.

"The skull is excessively small and very dolichocephalic. . . . [1]

"It is very low anteriorly and excessively high posteriorly, so that the vertex falls far back of the bregma, more or less in the posterior two-thirds of the parietals, in which characteristic the skull coincides with the *Homo pampæus*.

"I have not measured the cranial capacity, but I calculate that it does not surpass 1,000 c. c.

"Posteriorly there is no torus occipitalis, the inion region is not prominent but rounded and all the muscular insertions are but little developed.

"The sutures, including the lambdoid, are exceedingly simple and nearly straight. The mastoids are very small. The frontal region, much depressed, rises gradually toward the back, and the vault continues to rise in this way up to the vertex. . . .

"The frontal bone is very prominent by reason of its elongated and narrow form, in which it presents a remarkable similarity to the formation proper to the *Diprothomo*. In a straight line, without paying regard to the curve, it measures 106 mm. in anteroposterior, and 98 mm. in its greatest transverse diameter. The post-orbital narrowing is very slight, the minimum transverse diameter at this point being 91 mm., only 7 mm. less than the maximum transverse diameter.

[1 The two measurements that follow are those of the writer.]

"From this it follows that the anterior part of the front is proportionately very broad, in which it differs absolutely from the *Homo pampæus* which on the contrary possesses a frontal region that is exceedingly narrow. The front of this skull appears thus not only very long and narrow in the back but also of a very characteristic rectangular contour.

"The whole frontal appears arched from before backward, forming a convex curve not very pronounced but very regular.

"This regularity extends also to the anterior supraorbital part, which has no vestiges of the supraorbital ridges nor of the transverse depression which accompanies the same, but the frontal eminences are plainly visible.

"Of the post-glabellar depression there remain also no visible vestiges nor is there any visor (*visera*). The glabella does not protrude but curves notably downward; the interorbital part of the frontals descends especially low below the superior border of the orbits, but its inferior border does not present a backward inversion, so that the nasion did not lie in a transverse depression as in modern man; by this characteristic this new type of man accords with the *Diprothomo* and the *Homo pampæus*. . . .

"The conformation of the orbits is peculiar; to judge by the superior part, which still exists, and by the arched border, they appear to have been notably more high than broad, as in the *Homo pampæus;* moreover, they are *excessively* superficial, their roof forming with the external surface of the frontal region an angle that is nearly obtuse; they are much more superficial than in the *Diprothomo*.

"The posterior part of the skull is not less singular. At the first view, the eye is struck with the fact that the occipital aperture is situated more posteriorly than in existing man. The occipital bone, instead of being continued by a long, more or less horizontal space back of the foramen magnum, as is the general rule, ascends rapidly, so that the opening appears as if located nearly in the posterior part of the skull, in a way more accentuated than in many apes."

In the following paragraphs Ameghino speculates as to the "orientation of the skull during life." The conclusion is that "a skull with a sloping front directed downward and an occipital opening located nearly in the posterior part of the specimen, indicates a head which in life must have presented a notable grade of inclination downward. It is for this reason that I designate the species, now completely extinct, by the name of *Homo caputinclinatus*."

In the latter part of 1910 a brief report on the Arroyo Siasgo remains is made by Mochi.[1] This author says he was able to exam-

---

[1] Mochi, A., Appunti sulla paleoantropologia argentina; in *Arch. per l'Antr. e la Etn.*, XL, Firenze, 1910, pp. 250–253.

ine the skull only cursorily, a fact which doubtless accounts for his failure to notice that the present color of the specimen is due to its having been treated with a preservative, that it presents a posthumous deformation, and, what is even more important, that it belongs to the skeleton of a child.[1] He further regards Ameghino's reference to 18 lumbo-dorsal vertebræ as applying to this skeleton, while it relates to that of Samborombón, which Ameghino includes, in the paragraph that Mochi quotes on page 250, with the Arroyo Siasgo skeleton in the new species of *Homo caputinclinatus*. Finally, the hasty examination is also probably accountable for the one or two errors that have entered into the figures of Mochi's measurements. These are given as follows:

	cm.
Length	16. 6
Breadth	11. 5
Height (basion-bregma)	13. 0(?)
Diameter frontal minimum	10. 2

Mochi recognizes that the skull is artificially deformed, in the circular or Aymara fashion. The "far back" situation of the foramen magnum and the rapidly descending roof of the orbits, insisted on by Ameghino, "are both caused by the orientation of the calvarium." With an approximation to the ordinary anthropologic posing of the specimen "the foramen magnum assumes a position which has nothing extraordinary in a skull with a slightly flattened occiput, and the roof of the orbits comes to lie in a much different way from that in Ameghino's orientation."

"On the whole," Mochi well concludes, "this species seems to me a very doubtful one."

EXAMINATION BY THE WRITER

Through the courtesy of Professor Ameghino, the writer was able to examine all that remains of the Siasgo skeleton. The results, as will appear, differ in some very essential points from those quoted above.

It is the skeleton of a child, probably not 12 years of age.

The portion of the *skull* remaining (pl. 24) consists of only the vault, without the facial parts and most of the base; the vault presents a perceptible degree of Aymara deformation.[2]

There is also a posthumous, unrestored depression, affecting the posterior two-thirds of the lateral part of the right parietal and diminishing the maximum breadth of the skull by 2 or 3 mm.

The skull would be small for an adult but is not so for a child.

---

[1] The latter error is possibly due to the thickness of the bones of the vault, which resemble those in an adolescent, to the absence of all the parts(teeth , face, base) that indicate the age of a skull, and to failure to see the remaining parts of the skeleton.

[2] The photograph does not afford a good view of this feature, which is plainly recognizable in the specimen.

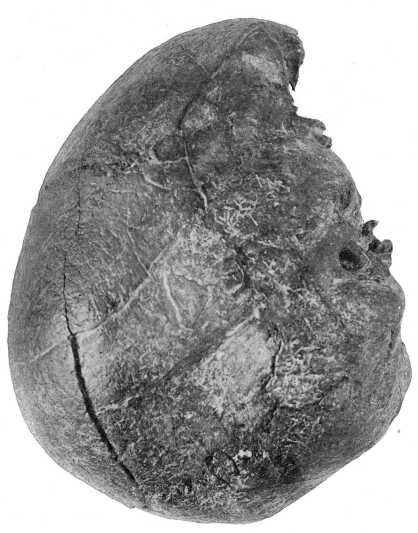

ARROYO SIASGO SKULL (LATERAL VIEW)

It is brownish and yellowish in color, but has been treated with a preservative. It does not seem to be devoid of animal matter to a great extent, though it may be somewhat mineralized. Morphologically, beyond the effects of the deformation and the lack of development due to youth, the specimen presents no peculiar features. This statement applies equally to every other part of the skeleton.

The thickness of the bones of the vault is medium, or slightly above, for a child. The sutures show only slight serration and all are patent. There are six unimportant small to medium-sized Wormian bones. The pterions are both of the H variety and of moderate width.

The mastoids (right) are fairly well developed for a young subject and of ordinary form. The floor of the auditory meatus presents on the left a large, on the right a small, dehiscence; these defects, rather common in all Indians, are of great frequency in those of Bolivia and Peru.

The frontal process and the upper parts of the orbits show childlike characteristics, otherwise no unusual features. The former is still divided inferiorly for some distance by a remnant of the metopic suture.

Owing to the deformation of the vault, the foramen magnum appears as if situated farther backward than usual; but this feature is commonly observed in skulls with Aymara deformation.

Principal measurements of the Siasgo cranium:

	cm.
Diameter anterior-posterior maximum	16. 9
Diameter lateral maximum	11. 5
(but was larger; is diminished somewhat by both artificial and posthumous deformation.)	
Height, auditory canals line to bregma, approximately	11. 7
Circumference (above supraorbital ridges)	46. 1
Nasion-opisthion arc	35. 4
Nasion-bregma	11. 9
Bregma-lambda	11. 8
Lambda-opisthion	11. 7
Transverse arc	27. 1
Diameter frontal minimum	9. 2

The remaining parts of the skeleton have been treated for the most part, as has the skull, with a solution of some preservative. Those treated thus are brownish-yellow; those not treated, light-gray.

Pelvis.—The three constituents of the ossa innominata are as yet entirely separate, and as the rami of the ischium and the pubis commonly unite about the tenth year, the youth of the subject is evident. The pubic, crest, ischial, and sacral articulation epiphyses are wanting as well as those of the acetabulum and of the border in front and above it. The bones are of fair strength and usual form.

Ribs.—These are light, dry, quite easily broken and apparently not mineralized in any degree. They indicate a child. They are all regularly formed. A few appear slightly thicker than usual,[1] owing largely, if not entirely, to the age of the subject.

Vertebræ; sacrum.—There are present 10 pieces, representing several dorsal, lumbar, and sacral vertebræ. All the epiphyses are wanting. The sacrum is represented only by separate, immature segments. The right lateral mass of the fifth lumbar is large, sacral-like, articulating with the uppermost segment of the sacrum; later in life it would doubtless have become part of the latter. The neural canal of this vertebra measures from above 2.5 cm. in breadth and 1.4 cm. in its antero-posterior diameter.

Femora.—None of the epiphyses are attached; the bones are light with no fossilization perceptible. The shape of the shaft approximates cylindrical, which is typical of childhood. Its antero-posterior bend is very moderate, the lateral slight. The external lip of the subtrochanteric flattening is well differentiated. The right bone shows on its posterior aspect four fresh cuts.

Measurements of the Siasgo femora:

	Right. cm.	Left. cm.
Length, minus epiphyses	(?) near	34. 0
Diameter antero-posterior at middle	2. 1	1. 95
Diameter lateral at middle	2. 0	2. 05
Pilasteric index	105. 0	92. 9
Diameter maximum, at upper flattening	2. 65	2. 60
Diameter minimum, at upper flattening	1. 95	1. 95
Platymeric index	73. 6	75. 0

Tibiæ.—Left bone only, without epiphyses. Shape of shaft prismatic. Anatomically without special features. Head deficient. Surface of bone eroded as if by roots.

Measurements of the Siasgo tibia:

	cm.
Diameter antero-posterior at middle	2. 5
Diameter lateral at middle	2. 0
Index at middle	80. 0
Diameter antero-posterior at the nutritive foramen	2. 8
Diameter lateral at the foramen	2. 2
Index	78. 6

Ulna.—Fragment, upper epiphysis wanting; lower? No special features.

Radius.—Part of the proximal extremity; epiphysis wanting; no special features.

Astragalus.—The bone measures 4.75 cm. in its greatest length, 3.85 cm. in its greatest breadth, and 2.60 cm. in its greatest height

---

[1] One of the longer ribs measures at middle of the shaft 0.65 x 0.9 cm.: another, from a slightly lower part of the thorax, 0.4 x 1.4 cm., and still another, from about the middle of the thorax, 0.6 x 1.0 cm.

(the last-named measurement taken with the specimen laid on the border of the table). The posterior facet for the calcaneus is probably less concave than usual in adults. The right astragalus is defective and quite useless for study but was apparently similar in size and form to that of the left side.

None of the above-mentioned bones present any intravital injury or disease.

CRITICAL REMARKS

The fundamental errors of the original description of the Siasgo skeleton are shown plainly enough in the preceding pages. The age of the subject was much overestimated, and through lack of comparative material, no doubt, features of the skull due to artificial shaping were mistaken for natural characteristics and made the basis of a new species of man.

The remains consist of a few very ordinary, immature, and defective bones, which show little if any fossilization and, it is safe to say, would not be recognized as exceptional if placed with a series of similar remains from, for instance, the graves of Bolivian Indians.

However, there is other good evidence that the skeleton in question has no claims whatever to antiquity. On his return from the Sierra Ventana Mr. Willis visited the locality of the find. He was shown by the owner of the hacienda the exact spot from which the bones came and which was still plainly in view. His observations are embodied in the pages that follow.

OBSERVATIONS ON THE ARROYO SIASGO FIND

By BAILEY WILLIS

The Arroyo Siasgo Valley is a peculiarly broad and shallow but winding hollow in the Pampa. It has been described by Ameghino as a lake basin and may have been partially filled at times of excessive rains, although the writer saw no shore features, as an established lake would make. The valley itself is an abandoned stream channel widened by wind. It lies in the east-central part of the Province of Buenos Aires in that broad lowland through which the Rio Salado winds. The region is one in which drainage channels are but slightly developed and which has exhibited extensive flooded areas during rainy years up to a recent time, when the construction of drainage canals provided channels in which the waters might flow away. The writer does not recall ever having seen a more perfect plain or one from which evidences of erosion were more completely wanting. From the vantage point of the railway train the plain could be scanned for many leagues and exhibits everywhere the same dead level. Even the long hollows, characteristic of much of the wind-sculptured surface of the pampas, are here developed in only an insignificant degree.

The Rio Salado flows in a meandering channel whose character is shown in the photograph (pl. 25). It is peculiar that the river is like a canal, flowing between steep banks, apparently in perfect equilibrium and of uniform regimen. The fall seems to be just sufficient to carry off the waters and the sediment which they bring, and there is no evidence of flood waters, sufficient at least to rise above the banks and spread out on the flood plain. Thus the level grassy surface of the pampas stretches straight to the river bank without elevation or depression, and one does not realize that the river is there until one is upon it.

Within sight of the station General Belgrano, but at a distance of an hour and a half's drive from it, there is a low ridge which is a conspicuous feature in the level plain. From near the surface of this ridge, on the *estancia* "La Georgina" belonging to Señor George M. Mendez, Doctor Ameghino found a human skeleton. Guided by his directions, the writer visited the spot on June 23, 1910, for the purpose of studying the topographic and geologic relations in which the skeleton had been found.

The central features of the locality are the ridge and the hollow known as that of the Arroyo Siasgo, which winds along its southern base. The writer approached the ridge from the east and followed its northern base for about 3 km. It is not continuous, but consists of three or more long low elevations. The northern slope is gentle, sinking imperceptibly into the perfectly level plain, which stretches away to the northward. At the estancia "La Georgina" the ridge was crossed at a point where it sinks away to the westward, and the southern slope and the Arroyo Siasgo came into view (pl. 26). The southern slope of the ridge is relatively steep. At the top it shows effects of wind erosion and portions of the grass-covered margin have slid down. Toward the bottom it is gentler and passes into the hollow by a curve similar to that of the lower part of an earthy talus. It is covered with vegetation. Near the top the sod is broken by sliding and undercut by the wind. The Arroyo Siasgo is a winding hollow. Water from a recent rain was standing in pools in the lowest parts of it, but it was all overgrown with herbage. The width of the hollow is somewhat indefinite, since it has no well-defined southern bank. From the lowest portions, which are below the general level of the plain, there is a very gentle rise southward for perhaps a kilometer before the uniform altitude of the plain all about is reached.

The hollow and the hill have a definite relation to each other. The hollow is a winding depression; the hill is a winding ridge which closely follows its northern side. According to an estimate based on observation in driving past and in walking over the hill and through the hollow, the volume of the one above the plain is about equal to that of the other below the plain. The position of the hill is to

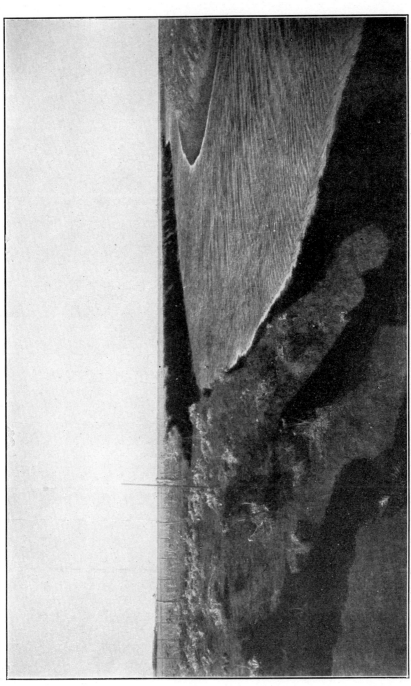

RIO SALADO

Near the stations of Villanueva and General Belgrano, Province of Buenos Aires.

ARROYO SIASGO

Looking southeast across the arroyo from the top of the ridge where the skeleton was found (cross indicates position of skeleton).

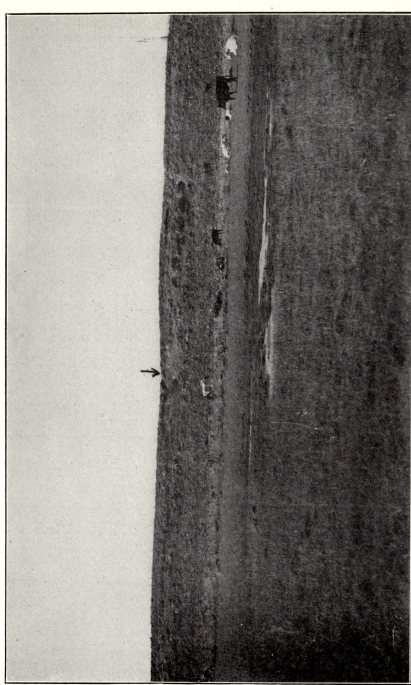

ARROYO SIASGO

View of barranca from which skeleton was excavated (at point marked by arrow)—looking northwest from arroyo toward loess-dune.

that he had noted at one side of the excavation a small quantity of black earth, like a pencil in an upright position, which was probably due to a root. Señor Pirez said that he was not present when the bones were disinterred but learned the facts when Doctor Ameghino made a second visit for the purpose of searching for some missing portions.

A reasonable interpretation of these facts, as it seems to the writer, is that the body was buried on the summit of the hill in the soft eolian loess and in the position which would naturally be chosen for such a purpose; that in course of time the earth in which it was buried slid somewhat, as it is evident that much of the face of the hill at this immediate point is, even now, sliding. Some portion of the earth which was originally above the body may have been removed by wind erosion, and possibly the discovery of the bones was facilitated by this fact. There is nothing in the topographic or geologic relations, nor in the situation in which the bones were found, to indicate that the skeleton is of any antiquity.

HOMO SINEMENTO—ARROYO DEL MORO; NECOCHEA

THE ARROYO DEL MORO FIND

The Arroyo del Moro, or more properly the Laguna Malacara, find was made sometime in the earlier half of 1909 by José Oliva, a sailor guarding a stranded *chata* [1] on the desolate beach about 7 miles northeast of the Arroyo del Moro, some 35 miles northeast of Necochea. As he told our party, he was out with his wife and boy hunting, and in crossing one of the flats among the sand dunes, situated about 15 minutes walk north of his temporary home and at a somewhat shorter distance from the Laguna Malacara, his wife and he saw on the ground from a distance a white rounded object, which they took at first for a large ostrich egg, but which on closer view was found to be the top of a human skull. The sailor dug out the skull with a knife, and when an opportunity presented itself he sent a notice of the find to the gardener, L. Parodi, at Necochea, who was known to be interested in bones in behalf of the Museo Nacional at Buenos Aires. The information reached also Dr. E. Cavazutti, an amateur local collector of Necochea.

The place was then dug over by the sailor, his boy, and the gardener, who found two skeletons; what was saved of these came through Doctor Cavazutti to the Museo Nacional, where the specimens, especially the skulls, were repaired and partially reconstructed.

Later on the locality was visited by Florentino and Carlos Ameghino, who collected over the same flat numerous fossils and also many worked stones of the dark variety. [2]

---

[1] A flat-bottom boat. The *chata* in question is a stranded steel barge.
[2] See section on Archeology.

The human remains under consideration were recently described by Professor Ameghino, and they have been made by him the representatives of still another South American species of man, namely, the *Homo sinemento*.

They are first mentioned in print in a commemorative number of "La Nacion." [1]   Following a statement concerning the *Homo pampæus*, we read the following (p. 24):

"From the same epoch as the *H. pampæus* or perhaps somewhat more recent is the *Homo sinemento*, which, retaining some very primitive characteristics, has in other respects surpassed in its evolution *Homo sapiens*. Its representatives were pigmies (1.40 m.), of a very prognathic rostrum, of lower jaw without chin, as in *Homo primigenius*, but with orthognathic and very regular denture, and without the last molar. It is a species which disappeared without leaving descendants."

Somewhat later, on the occasion of the meeting of the International Scientific Congress in Buenos Aires, the find was reported and published more in detail. The following principal statements were made by Professor Ameghino: [2]

When the human bones in question reached the Museo Nacional, where they were cleaned and reconstructed, "it was possible to establish the fact that they were fossil bones enveloped by the Pampean loess, in parts strongly hardened by calcareous concretions or tosca, which is so characteristic of the Pampean formation."

When subsequently Professor Ameghino, with his brother Carlos, visited the place where the remains were found, he saw that "the fossæ, from which the skeletons were extracted, were excavated in unmoved (*in situ*) terrane, traversed by lines of tosca absolutely identical with that which envelops and also fills many of the human bones. From the earth that was dug out I still gathered some fragments of the skeletons, various bones split longitudinally, and an instrument made from a fragment of long bone intended for retouching stone flakes.

"The whole surface of the ground was sown over with worked stones, some representing real instruments, others rejects and residuum. It is the industry of the split stone (*piedra hendida*).

"I gathered also many fragments of scoriæ and some of baked earth.

"Finally, over the whole locality there were numerous fossil bones, especially from young animals. . . .

---

[1] Ameghino, F., Geología, paleogeografía, paleontología, antropología de la República Argentina. Estudio publicado en el Número Extraordinario de La Nacion, Buenos Aires, May 25, 1910; separate, pp. 1–25.

[2] Ameghino, Florentino, Descubrimiento de dos esqueletos humanos fósiles en el pampeano inferior del Moro; special separate, *Congreso Científico Internacional Americano*, Buenos Aires, 10 á 25 de Julio, 1910, pp. 1–6.

[Fifteen genera and species are enumerated.]

"We collected also incomplete fossil human remains of various individuals. [1] . . .

"As to the skeletal remains, they represent a hitherto unknown race, with characteristics so profoundly distinct and peculiar that I consider it a true species, which I designate by the name of *Homo sinemento*.

"They were very small people, almost pigmies, whose approximate height I calculate at about 1.40 cm.

"All the bones of the skeleton indicate not only a race of very small stature but also slender people, not very robust, in consequence of which the muscular insertions on the bones are little marked. Some of the bones, as the femur, calcaneus, and astragalus, present very peculiar features, but their examination would require too much time. I shall occupy myself solely with the skulls.

"These, in agreement with the stature, are very small. . . . Both are clearly dolichocephalic. There is nothing extraordinary as to their general form. The mastoids are small and the muscular insertions in general but little developed. There is no *torus occipitalis* and the inion shows scarcely any prominence.

"The vault is rather low and the front is regularly convex and without a supraorbital arch. There are no supraorbital ridges, but there exists a well-marked transverse depression extending from one to the other of the orbital apophyses of the frontal.

"The frontal is short and broad, and the coronal suture is nearly transversal, i. e., but little inclined forward and but little arched backward.

"The glabella in its inferior part does not present an inversion backward, so that the nasion was not located in a depression; in this the specimens agree with the *Homo pampæus* and the *Diprothomo*.

"The orbits are deep, and to judge by the more complete skull they were of greater height than breadth, a primitive character which we already know in the *Homo pampæus*.

"The rostrum is quite prognathic, but this prognathism is due almost exclusively to the maxilla, which advances much forward.

"The most noteworthy peculiarities of these skulls are those which relate to the dental apparatus and the conformation of the mandible.

"The teeth are small in proportion to the size of the skull, but well-formed and worn horizontally all to the same level. The canines are more or less of the same size as the incisors and premolars, and their crowns do not reach higher than those of the contiguous teeth.

---

[1] It is puzzling that not a word is said of the numerous white quartzite flakes, rejects, and implements which strewed the same playa, some of these, as was seen later, being in close proximity to the grave. These stones were considered by F. Ameghino much more recent than those included in the above-mentioned industry of *piedra hendida*.]

The true molars diminish in size gradually from the first to the last, the first being notably larger than the second. This difference is especially marked in the lower molars. The last lower molar does not exist and there are no signs that it has ever existed. . . .

"The implantation of the superior incisors, canines, and premolars shows a small slant forward, producing slight dental and subnasal prognathism. In the inferior jaw the same teeth show reversely a slight inclination backward; that is to say, the mandible instead of being prognathic is orthognathic, or, more than that, ultra-orthognathic.

"This characteristic is so much more surprising, as the jaw lacks absolutely the chin prominence, reproducing in this respect the conformation of the mandibles of Naulette, Spy, and Krapina, which are classified as belonging to the *Homo primigenius*.

"In the *Homo primigenius*, however, the absence of the chin is accompanied by a strong prognathism of the anterior part of the alveolar region and also of the teeth which are inserted in this part, especially the incisors and the canines; moreover, these teeth are proportionally of larger size, and the canine is not only larger but its crown is also higher than that of the neighboring teeth.

"This conformation in the *Homo primigenius* has been interpreted as very primitive, as an ape character inherited from the anthropoids.

"It is known that I have combatted this view for many years. For me the Neanderthal or *Homo primigenius* type represents an extinct species, greatly specialized in the direction of bestialization. The pronounced dental prognathism which characterizes this type and the absence of chin are characteristics acquired secondarily. I maintain the opinion that the primitive humanoid (*hominideo*) type presented orthognathic denture without great canines and with the symphisis of the lower jaw vertical or nearly vertical.

"The discovery of this new fossil type overthrows in a definite manner the theory of the simian descendants of the Neanderthal type. If this theory were true, the absence of the chin should always be accompanied by a great dental prognathism. Here we have a case completely contrary to that. The absence of the chin is accomplished by a denture implanted vertically [1] and by an orthognathism as perfect as that in the most elevated existing human races. The theory that the type of Neanderthal is the phylogenetic intermediary between man and the anthropomorphs is overturned by this sole fact.

"The new type under consideration represents by these characteristics a form anterior to that of the Neanderthal man or of the *Homo primigenius*."

---

[1] Compare previous lines.—A. H.

The new species differs from *Homo primigenius* also "by the absence of prognathism,[1] by the more human conformation of the denture, and by an absolutely different conformation of the anterior region of the skull.[2] It is therefore a new species of man, which I have designated by the name *Homo sinemento*.

"With this, we have in the Pampean formation, without taking account of the *Homo sapiens* of the uppermost strata, four distinct species of *Hominidæ*, namely the *Diprothomo platensis*, the *Homo pampæus*, the *Homo caputinclinatus* and the *Homo sinemento*. These four species show among themselves differences much greater than those which we observe among the actual human races that are farthest apart. This not merely proves specific differences but also brings new evidence for the South American origin of man, because it is here where he acquired his greatest diversification and where he was represented by the greatest number of species."

A brief note only on the Arroyo de Moro specimens is found in the recent paper on the Argentine fossil man, by Mochi.[3] He did not have time to study the remains relating to *H. sinemento*, but what he saw made him doubt the validity of the new species.

OBSERVATIONS BY THE WRITER

In June, 1910, the locality of the find was visited by the party consisting of Srs. F. and C. Ameghino, Mr. Willis, the gardener Parodi, the sailor from the *chata*, and the writer.

The place was found to be in the inland terminal part of a long, irregularly outlined, denuded flat or *playa*,[4] lying within the belt of barren, moving sand dunes, near the small lake Malacara, far from any human settlement. One whole day and parts of two others were spent in the examination of the spot and the vicinity. The following is a transcription of the principal notes made there by the writer.

The "skeleton playa"[5] is a somewhat broadened end portion of a long denuded depression, which connects with a barren flat that reaches down to the beach. It is situated in the midst of the sand dunes, slightly nearer the open land than the sea.

The surface of the playa is grayish and blackish, with irregular remnants of a former level, 1 to 2½ feet (about 30 to 75 cm.) high. Below the discolored surface the earth is yellowish loess. Here and there within the loess are seen streaks of tosca.

The irregular earth banks, when cut, show color and composition which appear to be similar to those of present surface of the playa; but in one of the elevations, about 2½ feet high, not far from the spot

---

[1] Compare previous lines.—A. H.

[2] This probably refers to its narrowness antero-inferiorly.—A. H.

[3] Mochi, A., Appunti sulla paleoantropologia argentina; in *Arch. per l'Antr. e la Etn.*, XL, Firenze, 1910, p. 253–254.

[4] See p. 112.

[5] For convenience the depression in which the find was made will be referred to under this term.

EXCAVATION NEAR LAGUNA MALACARA

From this excavation, north of Necochea, parts of two skeletons were taken by the gardener Parodi and the sailor's boy, who are here shown in the positions, according to their recollection, which the skeletons had occupied. The illustration shows also the eroded surface of the "Ensenadean" formation, the hollows being partly filled with a deposit of younger and softer sandy loess, in which the bodies were buried. In the middle background is a grass-grown dune and on the left a large modern moving dune.

where the human bones were found, the earth for about 8 inches from the top was blackish, evidently a remnant of a former vegetal surface.

On closer inspection there were still found scattered over the surface of the terminal part of the playa and even close to the spot where the human skeletons were discovered, black as well as white chipped stones. As previously mentioned, the Ameghinos collected during their former visit many examples of the black variety.[1] Pieces of a quartzite grinding-stone and a few anvil-stones were also found by the writer on the "skeleton playa," and chipped stones of both the "black" and the "white" variety were numerous over some of the black playas in the neighborhood.

In a portion of the "skeleton playa" were seen in several localities protruding bones of the glyptodon and other fossil species; all these lay clearly in the undisturbed deposits.

A narrow part of the playa, connecting the inland portion of the flat with that extending toward the sea, where remnants of human bones were previously found on the surface by the Ameghinos, was examined. It differed in no way from the rest of the playa and was not more deeply denuded. It yielded some stone chips but no other specimens.

Careful attention was given to the site that contained the principal human remains. The cavity from which the two "fossil" skeletons came was found to be filled with loess and sand blown in since the bones were removed. As to its original contents, the gardener as well as the sailor and his son said that it held the remains of two bodies. These lay with the heads at the opposite sides of the hole, the feet nearly touching. Both were in a contracted, somewhat crouching position, which the two men later demonstrated most vividly (pl. 29). A narrow line of tosca, not very hard, ran through the soil that covered one of the skeletons, in a direction transverse to its axis; the earth itself was not hard. Some of the bones were fragmentary or in poor condition and some became broken at or after the excavation. With one of the skeletons was found a quantity of red and some white mineral pigment, in the form of small concretions. There were no animal bones with those from the human subjects, nor in close vicinity.

The second day of the stay of the party at the *chata*, the force that made the first excavation was engaged to help clear out the cavity they had previously made, and to extend the digging in several directions. This work, in which the writer took part, resulted in gaining some interesting information, which was recorded on the spot as follows.

---

[1] For meaning of the term "black" and "white" and further details, see the archeologic sections of this report.

The skeleton cavity exists in an irregular elevation upward of 3 yards in diameter and rising to about 18 inches above the surrounding surface. This elevation, due in a slight degree to the earth thrown out at the former digging, is one of the remnants of the earlier plain.

The cavity is plainly a double or joint grave. There seems to be some possibility of judging of the depth of this beneath the old surface. The blackish earth, which, as previously mentioned, was found to form the top of an elevation a few steps from the skeleton cavity, can be interpreted only as a remnant of the former vegetal earth of the plain. Extending toward the skeleton cavity the horizon of the old surface indicated by this black earth, and remembering that the uppermost part of the skull of one of the skeletons was somewhat above the surface of the low elevation in the floor of the playa which contained the grave, it is seen that the original vertical distance between the top of the head of one of the buried bodies and the old surface of the ground was only about $1\frac{1}{2}$ or at most 2 feet. It appears therefore that the interment might easily have been a fairly modern burial.

Ameghino says the Indians of these regions did not bury in graves but made stone piles and that they had nothing to dig with. But the sailor has now parts of two Indian skeletons dug out from graves, with the earth still in and about the bones. Nothing at all was seen or learned of cairns or stone piles in the region; in fact there are nowhere any stones except the tosca and the pebbles near the beach. Burials in the ground were found previously along the coast (Moreno) and constitute the rule in the valley of the Rio Negro and in the sand dunes farther north, toward San Blas. Besides, a large artificially-edged piece of white quartzite, that would serve well for digging in even hard ground, was found farther north by the writer,[1] and there were available at all times bones, antlers, and sticks suitable for digging in the friable deposits of the surface.

No trace of loose or broken tosca, as was said to have existed at one place in the earth covering the skeletons, can be found in the earth remaining from the former digging nor in the cavity itself. But its existence would be no standard of antiquity, for calcareous concretions form readily in the Argentine loess.

In cleaning out the hole in which the human skeletons lay, it is noticed, after the removal of all that had been blown in, that on digging deeper than the first excavation, the earth is still soft, in one place to the depth of about 8 inches. This is possibly earth that had been removed in preparing the grave. It is not a part of the undisturbed deposit which constitutes the flat and which offers wherever exposed in the cavity, much greater resistance.

---

[1] One quite similar in size, shape, and material but of still better make, from near the left bank of the Rio Neuqen, a short distance from Necochea, came shortly afterward into the possession of Professor Ameghino through the gardener, Parodi.

The burial cavity is of an irregular oblong form, approaching somewhat an hourglass in shape. Its longest diameter from east to west measures a little more than 9 feet (3 m.); its greatest breadth in its more western part is just 3 feet (1 m.), while the greatest breadth of the more eastern enlargement is slightly more than 2 feet (65 cm.). The greatest depth of the larger part of the fossa is 25½ inches (64 cm.), while that of the smaller portion is only 14 inches (36 cm.). The sides are slightly sloping, the cavity growing smaller toward the bottom. The greatest depth of the depression below the former surface of the soil, estimated on the before-explained basis, was not far from 4 feet (1.25 m., more or less), a very common depth for an ordinary burial; it could, in fact, hardly be less with bodies interred in the contracted position.

In the cavity and its immediate vicinity were found numerous little stones, some of which yielding red coloring matter were shown later to be impure ocher, while a few others were a white mineral pigment. According to the gardener and the sailor's boy, these lay with one of the skeletons; if so, they can represent only "paint" stones that were buried with one of the bodies.

These few crude pigment stones, to which no attention was paid when the skeletal parts were removed, are objects of paramount importance in considering the problem of antiquity of the remains. They afford strong evidence of the fact that these were burials, and are also a proof of the use of such pigments, whether for adornment or other purposes, and of a belief in a future existence, in which the paints would be of use as in the present life. All this signifies a certain grade of culture entirely incompatible with "the first *homo*, not to say even a *prothomo*," of Ameghino; moreover, it is in harmony with a widespread practice among the Indians, though more usually paint is buried with the man than with the woman.

Besides the pigment stones there are found on or in the earth formerly thrown out from the grave a tooth and the piece of a jaw containing several teeth, which are taken by Professor Ameghino; also a middle cuneiform, secured for the United States National Museum. All these pieces, especially the teeth, resemble in a remarkable degree fairly recent bones, and the specimen brought by the writer is as rich in animal matter as any Indian bone from the more modern, even post-Columbian burials.

The presence of undoubted Pleistocene, or possibly even older fossils in the floor of the "skeleton playa," at about the same level as the human bones, can afford no criterion whatever for determining the antiquity of the latter for, as repeatedly pointed out in other parts of this paper, a grave may penetrate any unconsolidated strata, whatsoever their geologic antiquity or paleontologic contents. It may even happen that fossil bones dug out in making the grave would be thrown in again with the rest of the earth, on or above the body. These facts would seem to be self-evident, yet they apparently received no consideration in this instance.

EXAMINATION OF THE SKELETAL REMAINS

The examination of the skeletal parts resulted as follows:

Malacara, or Moro, skeleton No. 1.—The remains representing this skeleton consist of a skull and a number of more or less eroded and defective bones. The skull is that of a middle-aged female, and the bones are probably from the same individual.

The skull (pls. 30–32) is not deformed. Cemented earth (not tosca) adheres to the surface along the sagittal and along parts of the lambdoid suture, forming a lump 0.3 mm. to about 3 mm. in thickness, on upper part of anterior half of right parietal. Ventrally, there are small scattered remnants of similar hardened loess-like earth.

The walls of the skull are rather thin and of nearly ordinary weight, though probably somewhat lacking in animal matter.

The left parietal presents slightly posterior to the coronal and along the anterior third of the sagittal suture, a noticeable bulging, approximately 3.5 mm. long by 2 mm. broad, with a small circular perforation in its anterior portion. This swelling corresponds to two depressions in the ventral surface of the parietal, produced apparently by moderate-sized tumors or abnormal growths of some nature. Two somewhat similar depressions are seen more posteriorly, one on each side, but these do not affect the outer wall.

The frontal bone presents a slender and long nasal process, the nasion lying 11.5 mm. below the line connecting the highest parts of the orbital borders. The minimum breadth of the process (i. e., interorbital distance) is 2.05 cm.

The nasion depression is shallow, the glabella of only moderate prominence. The supraorbital ridges are somewhat above the medium for a female, without reaching the average of males, and extend over the median half of the supraorbital space on each side. A shallow depression, such as frequently seen in modern Indian crania, extends from side to side above the supraorbital ridges. Over the outer part of the orbits the surface of the frontal slopes backward in the usual way. There is no approach to a supraorbital arch.

The forehead is well built; shows no separate frontal eminences, only one large median convexity. There is no frontal or sagittal crest.

The parietal eminences are large but dull. Outline of norma superior is ovoid, that of norma posterior pentagonal, with low summit.

The temporal crests are not pronounced; their nearest approach to the sagittal suture is to within 4.9 cm. on the right and 4.5 cm. on the left side.

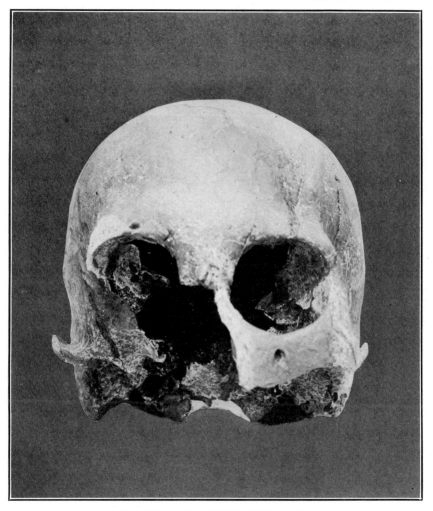

MALACARA (OR MORO) SKULL NO. 1

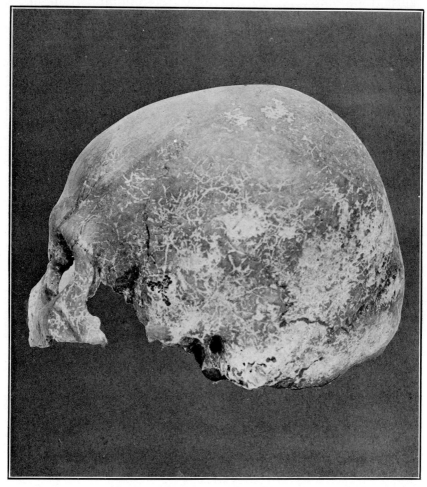

MALACARA (OR MORO) SKULL NO. 1

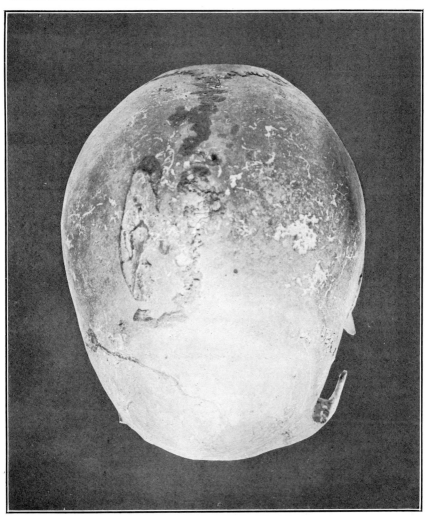

MALACARA (OR MORO) SKULL NO. 1

The mastoids are somewhat above medium feminine in size; the supramastoidal crests are but slightly developed.

The occiput is moderately protruding. Postero-inferiorly a portion of the bone is depressed, posthumously. Dorsally the surface is rather smooth, though a fairly marked transverse ridge exists under the insertions of the trapezii.

The sutures, particularly the lambdoid, show submedium serration, as general among Indians; they are all patent or nearly so externally, but ventrally the coronal sagittal and lambdoid are obliterated. There are no Wormian bones.

The basal parts show feminine development, otherwise no special features. The occipital condyles are small.

The facial structures are defective. The orbital borders are sharp. The nasal and orbital region indicates a feminine skull.

On the whole the examination shows plainly an average, moderate-sized Indian cranium, not one feature of which points to anything more primitive. The entire specimen shows nothing whatever "bestial" or that could not be found in a modern female Indian skull, particularly in that of a woman of small stature.

Measurements:

	cm.
Vault:	
Diameter: ant.-post. max., 17.4 cm.; lat. max	13. 2
Cephalic index	75. 9
Basion-bregma height, approximately	12. 6
Height between line connecting auditory canals and bregma	11. 6
Diameter frontal: min., 8.4 cm.; max	10. 5
Face:	
Diameter bizygomatic maximum	12. 7
Circumference, maximum (above supraorbital ridges)	48. 0
Nasion-opisthion arc	35. 8
Nasion-bregma, 11.7 cm.; Bregma-lambda, 12.1 cm.; Lambda-opisthion	12. 0
Transverse arc, approximately	28. 0
Maximum length of right temporal	8. 6
Foramen mag., max. length, 3.1 cm.; max. breadth, approx	3. 0
Thickness of left parietal above and along the squamous suture mm.	3 to 5
Thickness of frontal bone at points corresponding to eminences mm.	5

The module (mean diameter) is 14.4 cm., and the capacity of the skull may be estimated at or near 1,200 cc.

As every anthropologist who has occupied himself with American skeletal material will recognize, the above measurements are just about such as could be expected in a subdolichocephalic Indian female of small stature. The data relating to the female California skulls published by the writer in 1906[1] may be given for comparison.

The two sets of measurements are so similar that further comments on the Indian nature of the skull would be superfluous.

---

[1] Contribution to the Physical Anthropology of California; in *University of California Publications*, IV, No. 2, Berkeley, 1906, p. 51 et seq.

Comparison of the measurements of the Malacara or Moro skull No. 1, and of 14 female California Indian crania

Measurement	Malacara skull No. 1	Average of the California skulls	Measurement	Malacara skull No. 1	Average of the California skulls
	cm.	*cm.*		*cm.*	*cm.*
Length	17.4	17.24	Circumference	48.0	48.10
Breadth	13.2	13.37	Sagittal arc	55.8	34.42
Height	12.6	12.75	Thickness of parietal	.5	.54
Module	14.4	14.41	Breadth of face	12.7	12.88

Other parts of the skeleton.—The bones are rather frail, short, feminine. All are eroded and defective. No exact measurements of lengths are possible.

A remnant of the right humerus shows decidedly moderate proportions. The breadth and thickness of the shaft at the middle were about 1.9 cm. by 1.4 cm. The shape of the shaft closely approximates type 4 (prismatic with anterior border broadened into a fourth surface). A slight vertical ridge exists in the situation of the supracondyloid process. The specimen presents no unusual characteristics as to form.

The remnants of the radii and ulnæ present no features worthy of special mention.

The femora were between 39 cm. and 40 cm. long (estimated); they were slightly longer than modern female Guayaquil femora in the Museo Nacional collection and correspond to a stature of between 1.50 m. and 1.55 m. They present no special features as regards form except perhaps a greater than average stoutness of the external border of the subtrochanteric flattening. On the right side this border forms a surface 11 mm. broad. Each of the bones has a medium-size third trochanter. The whole shaft presents a moderate physiologic curvature backward and also a slight curve outward. The torsion is not unusual.

Measurements of the femora:

Diameter antero-posterior at middle: Right, about 2.3 cm.; left 2.2
Diameter lateral maximum: Right, about 2.2 cm.; left 2.3
Pilasteric index: Right, *104.6* cm.; left *95.7*
Diameter max., at subtrochanteric flattening: Right, 3.0 cm.; left 3.2
Diameter min., at subtrochanteric flattening: Right, 2.0 cm.; left............ 2.5
Index of platymery: Right, *66.7* cm.; left..................................... *78.1*

All these proportions are entirely compatible witl the assumption that the subject was an Indian.

What remains of the tibiæ shows that the shaft was prismatic with a slight concavity of the external surface and also a slight tendency toward the formation, by a vertical intermuscular ridge, of a double posterior surface. Both of these features approximate the bones to the Indian. At the middle, the antero-posterior diameter measures, on the right, approximately 2.6 cm., lateral 1.85 cm.; on the left, the antero-posterior 2.5 cm., the lateral 1.75 cm., giving the ordinary indices of *71.2* and *70.*

The pieces of the fibulæ indicate weak bones; they show no special features. A portion of a clavicle is of normal shape but almost child-like in size. The astragalus is small and of ordinary form. On comparison with other astragali no significant difference can be perceived.

The calcaneus presents a separation by a groove 5 mm. broad of the anterior and middle facets for the astragalus. The sustentaculum tali protrudes considerably. The cuboid facets are as usual concave from above downward and moderately convex from side to side. There are no primitive features.

Measurements of the calcaneus:

Maximum length: Right, 7.3 cm.; left, 7.1 cm. Minimum height of body: Right, 3.4 cm.; left, 3.5 cm. Breadth of body (5 mm. back of the most posterior part of the large astragalus facet): Right, 2.4 cm.; left, 2.4 cm.

All of these features agree well with the Indian provenience of the specimens.

There are ten vertebræ, probably nine dorsal and one lumbar. The bones are still in their natural position, cemented by sandy calcareous loess, consolidated on the surface but loose inside. The surface of this part of the skeleton has been treated with a solution of *gomma laca blanca* to prevent efflorescence; this hardens the bone (and it may be, to some extent, the loess also) without causing discoloration.

The pelvis, so far as preserved, shows ordinary features; it is of moderate size and badly damaged. A piece of the shaft of an ulna adheres to the right ilium, being cemented to it by the hard loess (which Ameghino includes under tosca), and a portion of the head of the femur is cemented to one of the acetabula.

A portion of the upper part of the sacrum is present, but unfortunately the specimen is so defective that it is not possible to take measurements. What remains of the bone shows no peculiar features.

Another piece consists of a cluster of five right ribs from near the middle of the thorax, cemented together like the vertebræ by hardened loess. The bones are of moderate size and anatomically present no special features.

In addition to the specimens which have just been mentioned, there are in the same lot some hardened slivers of bone the origin of which could not be determined. These may not be parts of the human skeleton.

The sum of the results of the study of the bones under consideration is that they present very ordinary human characteristics and that all their distinguishing features agree with those of the bones of the modern Indian. They show, as do the bones of any given skeleton, a few individual peculiarities, but these are without importance.

Malacara, or Moro, specimen No. 2. (pls. 33, 34).—This is the specimen on which the species *Homo sinemento* in the main is founded.

It is a small female adult skull, probably very slightly deformed in the Aymara fashion. It has been repaired from pieces and partially restored. This cranium is apparently somewhat "fossilized," especially the teeth, which have a brownish-pinkish glance.

The forehead shows above the faintly marked frontal eminences two slight lateral flattenings, which are probably artificial. There is also a shallow broad depression under each parietal eminence, such as might have resulted from the application without much force of a band about the head.

The glabella is moderately developed. There are traces only of supraorbital ridges and but a faint depression above them. The forehead is well-arched though not high, and there are slight indications of frontal eminences. A moderate sagittal elevation is noticed from the bregma to the summit.

The parietal eminences are well-marked; the outline of the norma superior is intermediary between ovoid and pentagonal, the outline of the norma posterior pentagonal. A slight asymmetry exists in the posterior part of the parietal region, due possibly to imperfect mending.

The occiput is moderately convex and rather smooth. The mastoids are of medium feminine size.

The walls of the skull are rather thin, the left parietal measuring, above and along the squamous suture, 3.5 mm. to 5 mm.

On the whole, the form of the vault can not be regarded as entirely natural, though nearly so.

The face was made too high in the reconstruction. It shows a shallow nasion depression, ordinary form of nasal articulation and ordinary nasal process, with quite sharp orbital borders. The nasal aperture was rather narrow, being about 1.8 cm. in greatest breadth. Its inferior border is not dull and there are no subnasal fossæ. The nasal spine is damaged.

The upper alveolar process is somewhat prognathic (it appears more so owing to defective condition of the nasal structures) and not high (approximately 1.7 cm.). The palate presents no unusual features. The suborbital (canine) fossæ are fairly hollowed out. The molars are submedium in size, rather prominent anteriorly.

The lower jaw presents almost (but not absolutely) vertical symphysis; there is, as can well be seen in the illustration (pl. 33), a distinct though very moderate median chin prominence.

BUREAU OF AMERICAN ETHNOLOGY

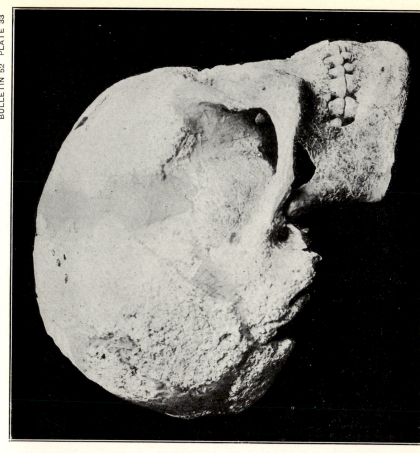

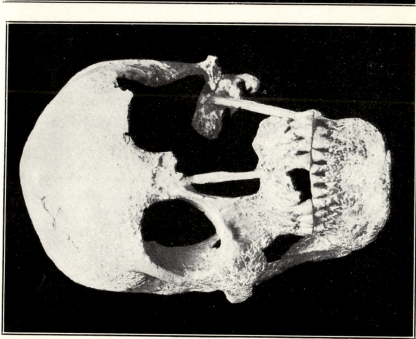

MALACARA (OR MORO) SKULL NO. 2 ("HOMO SINEMENTO," AMEGHINO)

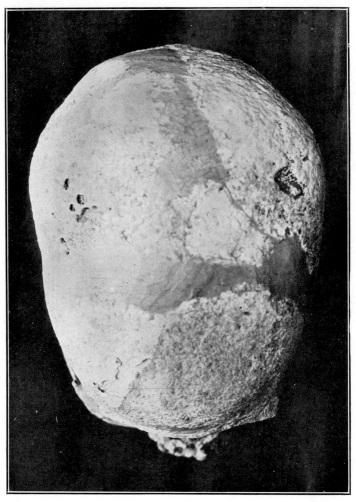

MALACARA (OR MORO) SKULL NO. 2 ("HOMO SINEMENTO," AMEGHINO)

This feature, which has been made much of, is in this case not a theroid or Neanderthaloid character, due to a strong preponderance of the dental portion of the bone over the basal part, but an infantile form, a lack of normal development restricted to that spot. It is on par with other localized infantile characteristics encountered now and then in the skull or other bones, particularly in those of females, though perhaps less frequently than some other such features. It occurs, however, now and then in the Indians and even in whites (see fig. 49).

The lower border of the chin is angular, approximating square. Ventrally the bones show a fairly strong submalar (or supra-mylohyoid) reenforcement.

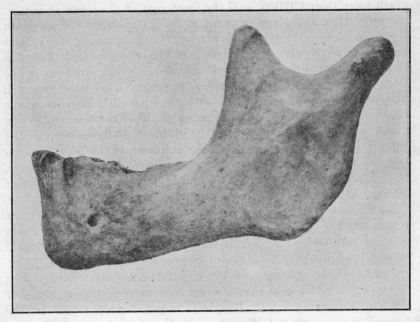

FIG. 49. Lower jaw of modern man showing only a slight chin prominence; unidentified, but either white or Indian.   (U. S. Nat. Mus. No. 227323.)

The teeth are feminine in size and moderately worn. The right lower third molar has never appeared; left (?) There is no unusual feature in the relative size of the molars. The canines are inconspicuous, no diastemæ.

Measurements:

Vault:	cm.
Diameter: Ant.-post. max., 16.8 cm.; lat. max	12. 8
Cephalic index	73. 2
Height auditory canals line to bregma, approximately	11. 7
Height basion-bregma (estimated)	12. 7
Circumference (above supraorbital ridges)	46. 2

Vault—Continued.

	cm.
Nasion-opisthion arc, about 33 cm.; transverse arc	27. 5
Diameter frontal: Min., 8.3 cm.; max	10. 7
Face:	
Height: Total, chin point to nasion, about 10.5 cm.; upper	6. 5
Breadth (?) (moderate).	
Interorbital breadth, minimum	2. 2
Lower jaw:	
Height: At symphysis, 2.9 cm.; between first and second molars	2. 5
Vert. ramus: Breadth, min., 3.5 cm.; height, about	4. 9
Thickness of horizontal ramus, between first and second molars (at right angles to the vertical axis)	1. 3

The specimen, it is seen, is quite small. The cranial capacity, though the walls of the skull are rather thin, could not have been much more than 1,150 cc. and the front part of the forehead is very narrow. However, these facts are striking only when the specimen is compared with the standards among whites, or among the Indians developed physically more highly, as the Patagonians. Let this skull with its mate be contrasted with crania of the same sex of the Bolivians (with whom the individual to whom it belonged may well have stood in blood relation) or with those of other dolichocephalic and small-statured American tribes, and the dimensions will seem quite ordinary; in fact they will be still, especially as regards the capacity, somewhat distant from the extremes of the normal variation in these crania. Moreover, the minimum frontal diameter, though often naturally small in the Indian, is invariably further diminished through the Aymara kind of deformation.

As examples of similar smallness of skull from other parts of the continent, the before-mentioned California series may be again referred to. Out of 11 female skulls in which the capacity could be measured, it was in 8 less than 1,200 cc. and in 5 less than 1,110 cc. In many of the Tarahumare (Mexican) females the capacity falls below 1,100 cc., and a similar condition prevails among some of the old Pueblos. As to Bolivia, 7 adult female crania in the United States National Museum collection have a mean diameter frontal minimum of 8.3 (8–8.5) cm., and in the large collection of such skulls in the American Museum of Natural History, New York, there are many not only with narrow forehead but also with small internal capacity. Finally the most modern-looking skull the writer brought from the Rio Negro Valley (No. 264117, U. S. N. M.), which is slightly deformed in the same Aymara fashion, has the diameter frontal minimum at the closest approach of the temporal crests of only 7.7 cm.

From Peru the writer recently brought a large number of crania, among which have been found thus far 21 adult female skulls, showing no abnormality or disease, but with capacities ranging from 1,050 cc. to 920 cc.

Outside the features just discussed, the skull is, so far as can be seen in its present state of preservation, entirely Indian-like, and there is not even a remote possibility that it is ancient.

GEOLOGIC NOTES ON THE LAGUNA MALACARA (ARROYO DEL MORO) REGION

By BAILEY WILLIS

The Malacara find.— At a point somewhat more than 30 miles north of Necochea, not far from a small lake known as Laguna Malacara, two skeletons were exhumed from a *playa* among the sand dunes. The geologic formations of the vicinity may be described as follows:

The basal formation is dull-brown loess-loam or waterlaid deposit composed of eolian loess. It is quite compact, contains much secondary limestone or tosca, which occurs in flat layers and in places has been uncovered by wind erosion so that it constitutes the floor of hollows among the sand dunes. In color, texture, firmness, and its tosca the formation is lithologically identical with that seen south of Mar del Plata; in both localities it is styled "Ensenadean" by Ameghino, who assigns it to a Tertiary age.

Overlying the Ensenadean is a discontinuous deposit that takes on several forms. One facies may be described as a brown loess containing films of tosca in suncracks. It is grayish on fracture, earthy rather than sandy, and hard to cut with a knife or to dig with a shovel. The fact that it contains specks of black sand serves in the opinion of Doctor Ameghino to identify it as Inter-Ensenadean. The writer interprets it as a playa deposit formed of dust from the Ensenadean which was blown on a moist surface, wetted by absorption, dried and cracked, and in which secondary lime was deposited from ground water. This process is entirely consistent with a Recent origin.

Another facies of the Inter-Ensenadean is a fine compact brown sand, mingled with loess, which may easily be cut with a knife or dug with a shovel. Its surface lies from a few inches above to 3 feet or more below that of the harder facies, and it appears to occur around masses of the other, occupying hollows eroded by the wind. The two are scarcely distinguishable in color, but the softer is easily recognized on digging. At the line of contact one may observe that the films of secondary limestone in the harder of the two do not extend into the softer and in the latter was observed no tosca deposit of any kind. A general examination of the ground showed that the harder facies of the two presents a very irregular surface, having a relief of

1 or 2 meters due to wind erosion,[1] and that the softer, as already stated, has been deposited in the hollows (see pl. 29).

It was in the softer of these two deposits that the skeletons were found, and it was in similar formation in another part of the playa that part of a carapace of a *Glyptodon munizi* was observed by Hrdlička and the writer. Neither the skeletons nor the remains of the glyptodon appear to have any relation to the formation as fossils indigenous to it.

A formation which is possibly younger than the sandy softer facies of the Inter-Ensenadean is a layer of sandy black earth, which in some places is probably the soil of the pampa where the vegetation has been destroyed by advancing sand dunes, and elsewhere is an eolian deposit blown out from the pampa and mingled with sand and broken shells. Ameghino assigned it to a Recent date. It constitutes the floor of smooth flat hollows among the sand dunes, to which the name "black playas" was applied. Quantities of chipped stones were scattered over these playas.[2] About a dozen large and small exposures of the formation in a range of 7 kilometers along the coast were examined, but no fossil bones of extinct animals were seen, although bones of ostriches and of modern domestic animals were not uncommon.

Capping the black-soil layer are dunes composed of brown-to-gray sand, which are overgrown with grass and fixed. They form an inner zone of low mounds on the margin of the pampa and sink away inland on the plain. Where they are eroded and exposed in sections, their relation to the underlying black soil is plainly to be seen.

The latest formation in the district is that of the great sand dunes which rise to a height of 20 to 25 meters. These consist of marine sands, shells, and some loess, blown up by the southerly winds. They are in constant motion. Their distribution with reference to one another is determined by the interaction of the winds from the south or southeast, that build them up and move them, with the winds from the northwest that blow across them. The latter tend to maintain open passes across the broad zone of moving sand hills, and thus prevent the constructive winds from building up continuous ridges. It was in one of these passes through the zone of sand dunes that the two skeletons were found together.

The writer regards the moving sand, the older dunes, the black soil, and the brown sandy faces of the Inter-Ensenadean, all as Recent formations, on the ground that they are all related to the phenomena of the coast and owe their genesis to the erosive or constructive activities of the winds. The harder facies of the Inter-

---

[1] See Doctor Hrdlička's account.

[2] Similar worked stones, chips, etc., " black " and "white," were found scattered over the flat in which were discovered the two skeletons.

Ensenadean may pertain to the Ensenadean and may be of Tertiary age. The skeletons were found in that facies of the Inter-Ensenadean which the writer regards as Recent. But the age of the formation has no bearing on the age of the skeletons, since it is evident from the shallowness of the hole and the attitude of the bodies, as illustrated in plate 29, that they were buried in the soft sand by human hands.

GENERAL CONCLUSIONS REGARDING HOMO SINEMENTO

By A. H.

After what has been said in previous pages, no further extended consideration of the subject on the writer's part seems necessary. The antiquity of the finds and the identification of a new species of man fail wholly to be substantiated by either geologic or anthropologic evidence. On the contrary, the evidence all points to a relatively modern age of the interments and to the ordinary Indian derivation of the bones.

HOMO PAMPÆUS

HISTORY AND REPORTS

Homo pampæus is, according to its sponsor, Professor Ameghino, "the most ancient representative of the genus *Homo* (possibly even a species of *Prothomo*), of which we now possess the skull, and it preserves many of the characteristics of the *Diprothomo*." [1]

The species is based on an imperfect cranium, known as the skull of Miramar, or La Tigra, found accidentally about 1888 by A. Canesa, a nonscientific employee of the Museo de la Plata, near the arroyo La Tigra, not far from Mar del Sud, south of Miramar.

Since the above date a number of other specimens have appeared, which are placed by Professor Ameghino in the same class. He enumerates them as follows:

"I designate examples of skulls of *Homo pampæus*, which are actually known, in this order:

"First example: The skull found by Canesa south of Miramar, preserved in the Museum of La Plata, which has served me as a type upon which to found the species. . . . It is the skull of a male.

"Second example: The incomplete cranium discovered by Dr. Rodolphe Faggioli at Necochea, with some other bones of the skeleton.

"Third example: This is the most complete skull which I have brought from my journey to Necochea . . . there are also numbers

---

[1] Ameghino, Florentino, Le *Diprothomo platensis;* in *Anales del Museo Nacional de Buenos Aires*, XIX (ser. iii, t. XII), Buenos Aires, 1909, p. 151; also p. 156, footnote.

of bones of the rest of the skeleton, but they are in a very bad state of preservation.   It is the skull of a female.

"Fourth example: Pieces of another cranium, which accompanied the preceding and presents the same features."

The principal characteristics of the crania of the *Homo pampæus* are outlined by Ameghino in footnote 3 on page 127 in his paper on the *Diprothomo*, where, speaking of the Necochea skulls, he says:

"These three skulls are of the same age as that of Miramar on which I have founded the *Homo pampæus*. They all present the same characteristics, including the excessively sloping forehead, which is natural and not the result of an artificial deformation, as has been alleged; all have the rostrum much prolonged forward and the alveolar border and the denture orthognathic; all present a glabella without backward inversion below, so that there is no fronto-nasal depression; all present the last molar placed forward of the most posterior part of the anterior border of the orbits; all show the inferior border of the orbit placed considerably more forward than the superior one; all are very dolichocephalic, with excessively narrow forehead, great orbits, and other characteristics."

In consequence, "Judging from the paleontologic standpoint, *Homo pampæus* is a species very different from *Homo sapiens;* it differs much more from the latter than the *Homo primigenius*.   It is even possible that when better known the *Homo pampæus* will result to be a veritable *Prothomo*."

The various specimens above named call for separate detailed consideration.

The Miramar (La Tigra) Skeleton

HISTORY AND REPORTS

The Miramar skull (pls. 35, 36) was first mentioned and pictured by Ameghino in 1898.[1]   In 1900 the announcement was commented on by Sievers[2] and by Lehmann-Nitsche.[3]   The skull is mentioned again prominently by Ameghino in 1906,[4] and was described with the rest of the bones of the skeleton by Lehmann-Nitsche in 1907.[5] Finally the cranium was noted extensively by Ameghino in 1909.

Strangely enough, with all the prominence and attention the specimen has been given, almost nothing of importance is known about its discovery.   Ameghino[6] gives merely the general locality, with the

[1] Ameghino, F., Sinopsis geológico-paleontológica; in *Segundo Censo Nacional de la República Argentina*, 1895, Buenos Aires, 1898, I, p. 148, fig. 15.

[2] Sievers, P., Review of Ameghino's Sinopsis, etc., in *Petermanns Mittheilungen*, XLVI, 1900, p. 72.

[3] Lehmann-Nitsche, R., Review of Ameghino's Sinopsis, etc.; in *Centr. für Anthr., Ethn., und Urg.*, V, Jena, 1900, pp. 112-113.

[4] Ameghino, F., Les formations sédimentaires du crétacé supérieur et du tertiaire de Patagonie; in *Anal. Mus. Nac. Buenos Aires*, XV (ser. iii, t. VIII), 1906, pp. 447-450.

[5] Lehmann-Nitsche, R., Nouvelles recherches, etc.

[6] Ameghino F., Le *Diprothomo platensis;* in *Anal. Mus. Nac. Buenos Aires*, XIX (ser. iii, t. XII), 1909, pp. 156-190.

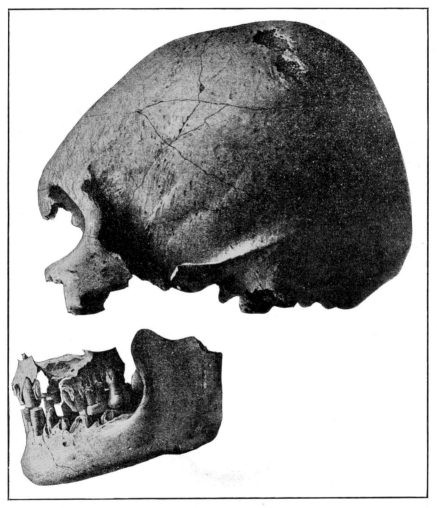

MIRAMAR (LA TIGRA) SKULL. (AFTER LEHMANN-NITSCHE)

Type of *Homo pampæus* (Ameghino).

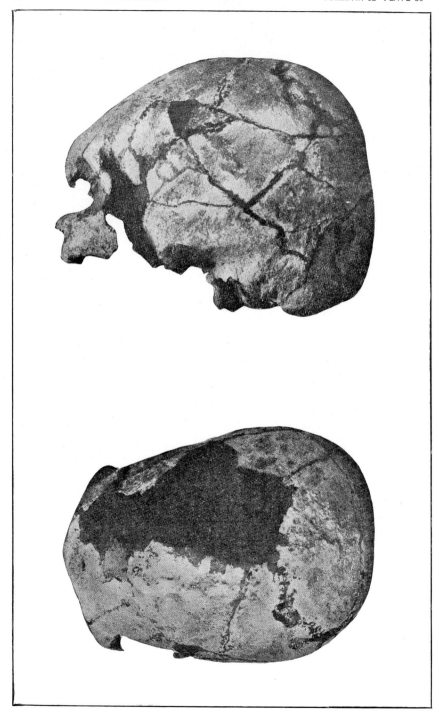

MIRAMAR (LA TIGRA) SKULL. (AFTER LEHMANN-NITSCHE)

Type of *Homo pampæus* (Ameghino).   The separate portion of the upper jaw is missing.

name of the finder, and states that it comes from the Lower Pliocene. Lehmann-Nitsche,[1] after having become a member of the staff of the Museo de la Plata, found that the discoverer of the specimen was no longer employed by the institution, but obtained the following details from Preparator E. Beaufils: "Beaufils, charged with collecting Pampean fossils, discovered [in about 1888], among other things, in a place near the cliffs which face the sea, not far from the little village Mar del Sud, between the arroyos La Tigra and Seco, mentioned already in connection with the Chocorí find and near the place where these human remains were discovered, the carapace of a *Glyptodon*. . . . One month later, Andreas Canesa, charged also with collecting fossils for the museum, thought that at the same point, which was still plainly recognizable by the eminences of earth that covered it, he could still find more fossils. He excavated in the neighborhood and discovered a human skull." This is all that was learned from Beaufils in regard to the find; from Canesa himself there is no information whatever.

About eight years after the find, in 1896, according to Lehmann-Nitsche,[2] Messrs. Moreno, Roth, Nordenskjöld, and Lahitte visited the locality from which the skull came and found there some bones of a scelidotherium and other fossil animals.[3] On this occasion Roth identified the deposits from which the specimen was believed to have come as Quaternary, Superior Pampean.

This wholly insufficient evidence regarding the most important data bearing on the antiquity of the specimen would seem to be alone more than sufficient to cause the discarding of the Miramar skull from serious consideration as a representative of early man in Argentina, or at least to relegate it to the uncertain. But the cranium shows fossilization as well as some peculiar morphologic features, and owing largely to these was given by Professor Ameghino the consequential position of the *Homo pampæus*, genetically the first representative of the human family. For Lehmann-Nitsche, who carefully studied every part of the skeleton but did not remain uninfluenced by the "fossility" of the skull, the bones are not so ancient nor so important as claimed by Ameghino, nevertheless they are accepted, in spite of the defective evidence, as belonging to the Superior Pampean deposits, believed to be of Quaternary age.[4]

---

[1] Nouvelles recherches, etc., pp. 335–336.

[2] Ibid., p. 335; a reference is here given as to where this information was first published (in *Globus*, Braunschweig, 1891, No. 9, p. 135), but the place indicated is occupied by an article on Korsika.

[3] There are no details.

[4] "Under no condition can the skull come from the Inferior Pampean and consequently it should not be attributed so great an antiquity; it is certain *that the skull is fossil in the true sense of the word and that it is derived from the Superior Pampean,* from which other human remains are already known."—Lehmann-Nitsche, Nouvelles recherches, p. 335, in the brief account of the visit to the locality with Moreno and others, mentioned above in the text.

The peculiar morphologic features of the Miramar skull, as seen by Professor Ameghino and in part already outlined (p. 290), are specified more in detail as follows:

Of all the specimens representing the *Homo pampæus*, the Miramar cranium "shows the ancestral characteristics most accentuated,[1] having no supraorbital ridges and presenting a front more sloping than any hitherto observed on a human skull that was not artificially deformed. In this respect it surpasses the Neanderthal skull, from which it differs by the absence of the gross supraorbital swellings; it seems to differ from the same also in its posterior portion, which is more developed vertically and less prolonged backward, but it is probable that this may be due to an occipital compression produced during infancy, although not intentional.

"This skull, which is distinguished from those of the *Homo primigenius* or Neanderthal by a glabella without prominence and the absence of the supraorbital ridges, and differs from that of *Homo sapiens* by a forehead more sloping than that in the *Homunculides* and in some of the living apes, can not belong to the same species as existing man; it represents an extinct species, which I named *Homo pampæus.*"

And in the paper on the *Diprothomo*,[2] we read (pp. 156–158): "The rostrum of the Miramar skull is prognathic, nearly as much so as in the *Arctopitheci* and only a little less than that shown by the reconstruction of the *Diprothomo;* . . . there is no subglabellar depression; . . . the inferior border of the orbits is placed considerably more forward than the superior; . . . there is a prolongation forward of the glabellar region, which assumes the form of a truncated cone, a conformation almost absolutely identical with that which I have described in the *Diprothomo.* . . .

"The cranial vault is not less extraordinary. It is ultra-dolichocephalic with a cephalic index of approximately *60* and with nearly parallel parieties. . . .

"A simian peculiarity of the skull of the *Homo pampæus* which merits serious attention is the great development of the zygomatic arches and their bulging outward in such a manner that their transverse diameter from the external border of one zygomatic arch to the other much surpasses the greatest transverse diameter of the skull. This is a conformation unknown in normal, that is to say, nonpathologic skulls of *Homo sapiens*, but it is frequent among the apes."

(Page 164) "In proportion to the rostrum the orbits of the *Homo pampæus* are very large and, placed below the very small forehead, they give the face an aspect which is truly bestial, which is further augmented by the circumstance that laterally one can not see the

---

[1] Les formations sédimentaires, etc., p. 449.

[2] The data relating to the *Homo pampæus* are given piecemeal on various pages of the *Diprothomo* memoir.

slightest vestige of the vault of the skull, owing to its narrow and elongated form. . . .

"The forehead of the *Homo pampæus* is so sloping that in this feature it surpasses numerous monkeys."

The posterior part of the skull is elevated; "the conformation of the frontal [in all the *Homo pampæus* skulls] is natural, without any vestige of artificial deformation" (p. 170); the last molar teeth are placed forward of a vertical line drawn from the most posterior point on the orbital border (p. 172). As to the lower jaw, "the chin is very prominent;" but "this conformation, which is believed to be recent, is, on the contrary, excessively ancient and reaches probably to the very origin of the *Hominiens*" (p. 173).

On the whole, the "characters of inferiority of the skull of the *Homo pampæus* are so apparent," according to Señor Ameghino, "that they can not pass unperceived by any anatomist" (footnote, p. 172).

On the other hand, Lehmann-Nitsche, who studied the Miramar skeleton in detail,[1] fails to find about it any very extraordinary features. The skull "presents no sign of inferiority" (p. 334–335); but its fossility is such that "the bone adheres to the tongue and has the same characteristic constitution as presented in general by the bones of vertebrates [fossil], which make the reputation of the Museo de la Plata" (p. 336). The view Ameghino takes of the specimen, in attributing it to a particular species of man, the *Homo pampæus*, "is absurd" (p. 336).

The skull (pls. 35, 36), which is probably masculine, shows, according to Lehmann-Nitsche, a posthumous and an artificial deformation, the latter consisting of a fronto-occipital flattening (pp. 337–338). It is extraordinarily narrow (p. 340), "supremely dolichocephalic"— cephalic index *68.59* (p. 341).

The glenoid fossa presents features which correspond exactly with those observed by Martin in ancient skulls from Patagonia (pp. 342–344).

The palate is very low, the front teeth are small, the crowns of the third molars rather large (p. 346). The left upper third molar is probably congenitally absent (p. 350).

"The reconstructed profile of the La Tigra skull shows a very strong prognathism," and "in the lower jaw we are equally surprised by the strong prominence of the chin" (p. 349).

"The capacity of the skull, calculated by Welcker's method, is 1,464 cc." (p. 349).

As to the lower jaw, the ascending ramus is broad, but this Lehmann-Nitsche considers "characteristic of Americans" (p. 351); "the features of the chin region, ventrally, belong to the common human type" (p. 356); the curve of the jaw approaches the more primitive U shape, and the bone is stout.

---

[1] Nouvelles recherches, etc., pp. 334–374.

As to the other bones of the Miramar skeleton, including the long bones, they are compared principally with those of Bavarians, hardly a satisfactory procedure; they present but little worthy of special notice.

The length and other dimensions of the femur approximate closely the average of the Bavarian bone (pp. 262–268). Both femora are very platymeric.

The tibiæ are platycnemic, the fibulæ relatively strong.

The stature of the individual is calculated to have been approximately 1.634 m. (p. 374).

The skull of Miramar was also considered, in 1908, with some of the other finds reported by Ameghino, by Giuffrida-Ruggeri,[1] who expresses himself (p. 24) as follows:

"Ameghino gives illustrations of these skulls, from which I perceive that the Quatenary one (Arrecifes), as well as the one from the Upper Pliocene (Fontezuelas), presents an entirely modern aspect; and so far as the skull from the Lower Pliocene (Miramar) is concerned, the specimen conveys a very distinct impression of being deformed. Ameghino was led himself to say that as to the appearance of the occiput, 'it is probable that that is due to an occipital compression produced during early infancy, although not intentional.' Unfortunately, however, for this 'nonintentional' characterization, it happens that, in my opinion, the forehead also is deformed, in the same manner as in pre-Columbian natives of America. It can not be accepted that the front slopes naturally as a result of a defective brain development, for the brain development in the posterior half of the specimen is even excessive, standing in marked contrast to the fore part. Such a feature would be opposed to all experience and would puzzle the observer, who would not comprehend why the brain pressed on the back part of the skull and not also on the frontal bone, arching it in such a manner that it would afford greater accommodation for the organ. If the brain failed to exert pressure on the frontal bone (and unintentional pressure exerted on the occiput would have forced the brain of the young man against the frontal bone), it was because there existed also over the forehead a band or some other appliance which pressed upon it. Under these conditions, however, it is to be feared that the period of the Lower Pliocene (to which the skull was attributed) becomes the age of the discovery of America."

In 1909 and again in 1910 Sergi[2] utilized the *Homo pampæus* without critical consideration of the specimen, in his theory of polygenism and in a new classification of man.

---

[1] In *Globus*, Bd. xcIV, Braunschweig, 1908, pp. 21–26.

[2] Sergi, G., L' apologia del mio poligenismo; in *Atti Soc. rom. antr.*, xv, fasc. 2, Roma, 1909, pp. 187–195; and Paléontologie sud-Américaine, in *Scientia*, vIII, Bologna, 1910, xvI–4.

In 1910 the Miramar skull is casually referred to by Schwalbe[1] in his critical study of the *Diprothomo*. Speaking of the faulty figures of the *Diprothomo*, Schwalbe says: "On this occasion let it also be stated at once that Ameghino's *Homo pampæus* skull, pictured in the same work (fig. 24, p. 157 of Ameghino's memoir on the *Diprothomo*), is falsely posed for the norma verticalis." If the position is corrected, the inferior orbital border, which in the illustration is advanced considerably more forward than the upper, assumes the same position as in recent man.

Finally, in the latter part of 1910, the *Homo pampæus* remains from Miramar and Necochea are considered by Mochi in his notes on the Argentine paleoanthropology.[2]

As to the Miramar skull, however, Mochi's observations are restricted. He recognizes that it is artificially deformed. Except for the deformation, it presents considerable resemblance to the skull of Fontezuelas. This is somewhat in accord with the opinion of Rivet, who inclines, in a brief note on the specimen,[3] to class it with those of Lagoa Santa.

OBSERVATIONS BY THE WRITER

The results of the writer's examination and measurements of the Miramar skeleton differ considerably from those of Ameghino, and somewhat also from those of Lehmann-Nitsche, though with the latter there are many points of agreement.[4]

The skeleton is that of an adult male, of advanced middle age. The sexual identification of the skull can be safely based on the lower jaw, which can not be other than masculine; the remaining parts of the cranium show the sexual features less pronounced than ordinary. The long bones indicate a male of moderate stature and musculature.

The poor development of the sexual characteristics of the vault, otherwise of little importance, is surely not a feature of any great primitiveness or one pointing toward antiquity.

The surfaces of all the bones are discolored to yellowish-white (very much as in the specimens from Chocorí, p. 239), and in general very defective, being worn or scaled off. In a number of places on the skull and bones there are incrustations of loess cemented by lime, and a few

---

[1] Schwalbe, G., Studien zur Morphologie der südamerikanischen Primatenformen; in *Zeitschr. für Morph. und Anthr.*, Bd. XIII, Heft 2, Stuttgart, 1910, pp. 242, 253.

[2] Mochi, A., Appunti sulla paleoantropologia argentina; in *Arch. per l'Antr. e la Etn.*, XL, Firenze, 1910, p. 253–254.

[3] Rivet, P., La race de Lagoa-Santa chez les populations précolombiennes de l'Équateur; in *Bull. et Mém. Soc. d'Anthr. Paris*, 5ᵐᵉ sér., IX, 1908, p. 209 et seq.

[4] To insure greater independence of procedure and view in this case, as in that of every other object reported on in this paper, with the exception of the *Diprothomo*, the details published by Ameghino, Lehmann-Nitsche, and others, concerning these specimens, were not read until after the writer's results were on paper.

parts of the skull, including its ventral surface, show more or less infiltration with calcareous matter. The cavities of the long bones are filled with dark-yellowish loess, which crumbles quite as readily as would that from an ordinary well-settled deposit; at the ends, however, where there has been more exposure, the loess is hardened.

The above description indicates approximately the extent of the visible "fossilization" of the skeleton. With exception of the parts that are incrusted or infiltrated with lime, the bones are not perceptibly heavier than the average, and are not chalky, retaining probably considerable animal matter.

To obtain a more precise view of the "fossilization" of the specimen, a small fragment of bone from the vault of the skull, with other specimens from *Homo pampæus* and some modern but weathered and more or less fossil-appearing bones from the coast,[1] were subjected to a limited chemical analysis. The work was done by Mr. J. G. Fairchild, under Prof. F. W. Clarke, at the United States Geological Survey, and the report is given below. In a letter accompanying the report Professor Clarke says:

"It is worth while to notice that the three specimens which purport to be fossil were not perceptibly lower in phosphoric acid than the others. They all give a strong odor of charring when burned, indicating the relative quantities of organic matter."

DEPARTMENT OF THE INTERIOR,
UNITED STATES GEOLOGICAL SURVEY,
Division of Chemistry.

Report of Analysis No. 2523. (*Material received from Charles D. Walcott for A. Hrdlička:* "*Fossil*" *bones from Argentina*)

Specimens	Effect of heat	Loss on ignition.	S_1O_2	P_2O_5	Indication of carbonates
263759. Scelidotherium from near Laguna Malacara, north of Necochea.	Slight odor of charring.	19.12%	4.00%	25.40%	Effervescence strong.
Homo pampæus (Miramar) skull.....	Strong odor of charring.	25.56%	1.66%	25.92%	Effervescence strong.
263754. "Fossil skeleton" from near the Laguna Malacara, north of Necochea.	Marked odor of charring.	16.12%	2.92%	30.48%	Effervescence strong.
"Fossil man" from near the beach of Necochea (remains of skeleton in U. S. N. M.).	Strong odor of charring.	20.67%	1.89%	25.44%	Effervescence not so strong.
Modern animal bone, weathered, from Necochea.	Marked odor of charring.	14.30%	8.06%	27.61%	Effervescence fairly strong.
Seal bone, weathered, from sands at Punta Mogote, south of Mar del Plata.	Strong odor of charring.	18.20%	0.64%	31.40%	Effervescence strong.

[1] Picked up on the beach or the sands and identified as belonging to recent species by Mr. J. W. Gidley, the United States National Museum paleontologist.

Report of Analysis No. 2523—Continued

Specimens	Effect of heat	Loss on ignition	S_1O_2	P_2O_5	Indication of carbonates
Sea lion bone, weathered, fossil-like, from a flat near the beach Punta Mogote, south of Mar del Plata.	Very strong odor of charring.	17.40%	7.42%	29.61%	Effervescence mild.
Guanaco bone, from Miramar (extinct in that region).	Slight odor of charring.	16.38%	2.74%	30.10%	Effervescence mild.
Horse tooth, looking much fossilized, but recent, from beach of Laguna de los Padres, west of Mar del Plata.	Strong odor of charring.	17.16%	3.32%	31.44%	Effervescence mild.
Deer bone, modern, much weathered, from sand dunes at Punta Mogote, south of Mar del Plata.	Strong odor of charring.	21.84%	1.32%	31.51%	Effervescence strong.

Examined by J. G. Fairchild and reported January 9, 1911.

F. W. CLARKE, *Chief Chemist.*

It is seen from the above data that the Miramar man gives evidence of the retention of at least as much animal matter as the weathered bones of the modern seal, horse, and deer, and of decidedly more than a relatively recent guanaco or the more ancient scelidotherium. Nor do the other tests indicate mineralization; but parts of the skull that are more covered or impregnated with lime would doubtless give somewhat different results.

The retention of animal matter is the most important point brought out. The mineralization of a bone, human or otherwise, is a matter the importance of which, as pointed out in other parts of this report, is very often overestimated. The process is far more a question of environment than of time and can serve only under exceptional conditions as an index of antiquity. As mentioned before, the United States National Museum possesses parts of human skeletons fossilized in almost every possible manner and degree, some of the specimens being entirely petrified and showing greater mineralization than do the bones of the mastodon and other long extinct animals, and yet it is well-determined that none of these remains are of even moderate geologic antiquity. This whole subject was treated more at length in the writer's report on the "Skeletal Remains Suggesting or Attributed to Early Man in North America."[1] Conditions favoring strongly the covering and infiltration of bones, especially with calcareous matter, are present along a large portion of the Argentine coast, and apparently elsewhere in the country where there are loess deposits. This is seen in the constant presence of the formation within the loess of these regions of the tosca or calcareous concretions,

[1] *Bulletin 33 of the Bureau of American Ethnology.*

which in many places assume the form of whole layers, and also in the effects observed on recent bones of animals as well as of man.

The writer brought an astragalus of a cow picked up among the refuse in front of an occupied hut on the coast near Mar del Plata, which shows marks of cutting with a sharp knife. This bone undoubtedly came from a limb the flesh of which was eaten some years ago by the family occupying the dwelling, but already it presents a metallic luster and a darkened surface as well as increased weight, being plainly on the road toward fossilization.

From slightly farther south, near the Arroyo Corrientes, the writer brought a large part of the pelvis of a cow which had been partially buried and partially exposed to the air; the part that was buried is of a dark color and has a smooth, hard, shining surface decidedly fossil in appearance, while the rest of the bone is quite white. Other bones were picked up from the sands and playas, which had been exposed for a long time to the sun and to the wind blast; these are weathered, some hardened and some crumbling, dry, fossil-like. One and the same bone occasionally presents these different features in different parts, which evidently were subjected to unlike conditions. Several specimens of the teeth of the common horse were picked up on the broad, flat beach of the Laguna de los Padres, all belonging to the modern horse, hundreds of living specimens of which are feeding about the lake; these teeth are yellowish-brown in color, with blackish somewhat lustrous discoloration in places, and with a surface resembling that of petrified wood.

Finally, the writer brought from the valley of the Rio Negro, from the mud-soil of a shallow depression in the alluvial surface of the valley, which is occasionally filled with water, the remains of 10 Indian skeletons, including several complete skulls, all parts of which, except those for a time exposed to the air where they lay and in consequence bleached, are brownish-black, old bronze-like, shiny, somewhat heavier than normal, and in every way "fossil" in appearance. The teeth even more than the bones look fossil-like and the changes undergone by them are markedly different in the several specimens. The "fossil" as well as the other Patagonian skulls of Moreno belong to this same category.

The foregoing does not imply that every bone of man or animal on the coast of Argentina will become fossil-like or mineralized in a short time; but such cases are relatively common, and the mere fossilization of a bone can not be taken by itself in any instance, without decisive proofs of geologic and morphologic nature, as a criterion of the antiquity of the specimen. This applies particularly to cases in which the bone is found covered or incrusted with calcareous matter or concretions, for lime salts are more easily soluble than many other minerals; they are carried not only by the surface, but especially by the underground waters, the latter often rising sufficiently high, as shown by the tosca formation, to reach the bones of even a shallow burial. The deposition of lime takes place rapidly,[1] and, as we know from numerous specimens from the California caves, the Cuba and Isle of Pines caves, and from the shell-mounds, it does not affect merely the surface, but infiltrates parts of the bones, giving them the appearance of great age.

Skull.—The Miramar skull was restored from a number of pieces and partially reconstructed in mastic. The filling in the frontal comprises about one-fourth of the squama on the right side and extends from the supraorbital ridges to the coronal suture and beyond into the parietal. The restoration is near to nature, yet the forehead may have been a trace less sloping than it now appears. Some of the pieces from which the skull was reconstructed show signs of artificial beveling of the borders, evidently done by those who restored the specimen and because the pieces did not fit exactly. A slightly similar superficial beveling, besides other defects, is seen also over the mid-region of the frontal squama.

The surface of the vault of the Miramar specimen is for the most part worn and peeled off (as in the Chocorí skull). The same statement is especially applicable to the ridges of the frontal bone; that on the right appears as if partially cut off. In consequence of these defects the minimum frontal diameter can not be accurately determined and the front appears narrower than it really was.

The skull has been artificially deformed, showing mild frontal with moderate occipital compression; it bears also, perhaps partially corrected, a post-mortem deformation, the whole right side below the parietal eminence being somewhat pressed in, more so in front, less so over the posterior part of the parietal. This latter deformation still exists to an extent sufficient to diminish the breadth of the skull by approximately 2 mm. to 4 mm.

Of this double deformation of the skull, which was equally recognized by Lehmann-Nitsche but not by Ameghino, the alteration produced in life proves to be a very weighty indication against any great antiquity of the Miramar specimen.

As described above, the life-deformation in the Miramar skull is mainly in evidence on the frontal bone and on the occiput. Notwithstanding this, careful inspection shows that it is not of the "flathead" type but represents a lighter grade of the Aymara variety of intentional deformation, produced not by pressure of a plank or pad on the forehead but by the application of a bandage about the head.

In the "flathead" type of deformation, the skull in compensation invariably grows wider, and there is no such effect in this case; in

---

[1] "The rapidity with which *caliche* [Mexican term equivalent to *tosca*.—A. H.] may be formed under experimental conditions out-of-doors may be remarkable—2 inches in two years."—TOLMAN, C. F., in *Carnegie Institution Publication* No. 113, Washington, 1909; also reference in *Science*, June, 1910, p. 865.

the Aymara type, on the other hand, it never widens and often becomes even narrower than would be natural in the normal adult stage, a condition which agrees with what is observed in the Miramar specimen.

It may be adduced that in the Aymara form the impression of the compressing bandage can be plainly traced about the vault, and that there are marked secondary effects of the compression, particularly a coronal elevation and precoronal as well as postcoronal depression, besides a bulging, a protrusion, backward and upward, of the posterior portion of the parietal and the upper part of the occipital region. However, these effects are present in only a very moderate degree and are sometimes very nearly absent in cases of slight Aymara deformation, very much as in the skull of Miramar. Nevertheless, even the Miramar specimen (pls. 35, 36) is not entirely devoid of such marks, for the lower half of the parietals presents a faint concavity from above downward, extending over a larger part of the bones antero-posteriorly than usual; there is also a slight postcoronal depression and there is the heightening of the norma posterior, which does not take place without a simultaneous widening of the same in the fronto-occipital or simple occipital types of deformation.

Now, intentional deformation of the head, even among savages, is a ritual operation, denoting contact of peoples, an approach to a sedentary life of the family, and at least a moderate stage of native culture, all of which ill agrees with Professor Ameghino's "first representative of the human beings"—if not even "man's forerunner," the *Homo pampæus.*

Furthermore, similarly deformed Indian skulls have been found before and since in Argentina. Burmeister mentions[1] two deformed crania from the Rio Negro, but gives no details as to the type. Moreno reports several[2] and states in addition, referring to the Valley of the Rio Negro, that he found more than 100 skulls deformed in this manner. And Verneau[3] mentions four crania of the Aymara type of deformation from Viedma, also in the Valley of the Rio Negro.

Shortly after the arrival of Professor Ameghino, his brother, Mr. Willis, and the writer at the so-called *chata,* a stranded barge on the coast north of Necochea, the sailor occupying the boat, the man who discovered the principal representative of the Necochea *Homo pampæus,* brought in a box filled with black sandy vegetal earth, containing human bones. On examination it was found that the remains were parts of two, in no way "fossilized," but badly

[1] Burmeister, G., Sur les crânes, les mœurs et l'industrie des anciens Indiens de la Plata; in *Compte-rendu du Congrès international d'anthropologie et d'archéologie préhistoriques,* 1872, Bruxelles, 1873, pp. 342–351.

[2] Moreno, F. P., Sur deux crânes préhistoriques rapportés du Rio-Negro; in *Bull. Soc. d'Anthr. Paris,* 3me sér., III, 1880, pp. 490–497; also Description des cimetières et paraderos préhistoriques de Patagonie; in *Révue d'Anthropologie,* 1ere sér., III, Paris, 1874; Viaje á la Patagonia austral, emprendido bajo los auspicios del Gobierno nacional, t. I, 1876–77, Buenos Aires, 1879 (for review of this work, see last-mentioned Journal, 2me sér., III, Paris, 1880, pp. 303–309.)

[3] Verneau, R., Crânes préhistoriques de Patagonie; in *L'Anthropologie,* v, Paris, 1894, pp. 420–450. Also by same author, Les anciens Patagons, Monaco, 1903, pp. 126–129.

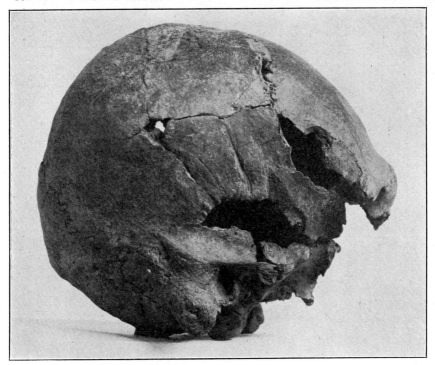

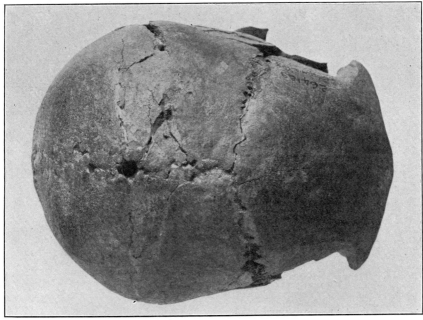

FOSSILIZED PATAGONIAN SKULL FROM VICINITY OF VIEDMA, ON
RIO NEGRO

This skull (No. 264129, U. S. Nat. Mus.), lateral and top views of which are here shown, is marked by
a slight Aymara-like deformation.

a

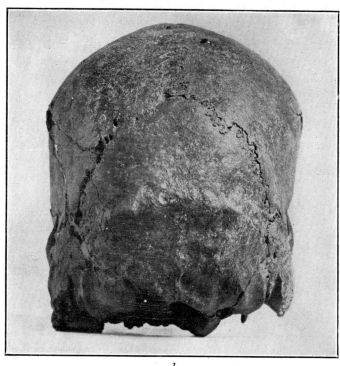

b

SKULL OF HOMO PAMPÆUS (*a*) AND PATAGONIAN SKULL (*b*)

Rear views. *a*, From Miramar (after Lehmann-Nitsche); *b*, No. 264129, U. S. Nat.
Mus., marked by slight Aymara-like deformation.

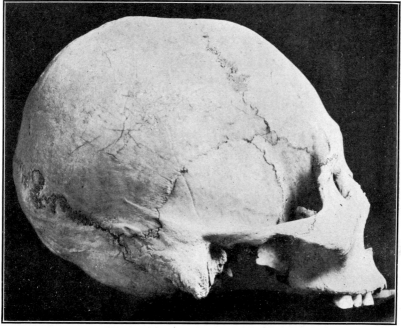

a

b

TWO PATAGONIAN SKULLS

a, recent, and *b*, fossilized, but of no great antiquity (though probably pre-Columbian), marked
by Aymara-like deformation in minor degree.

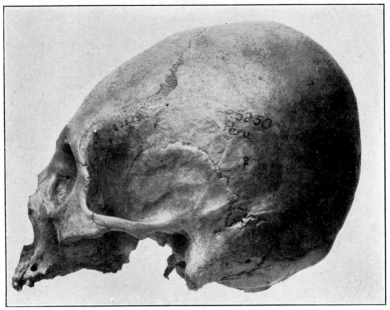

a

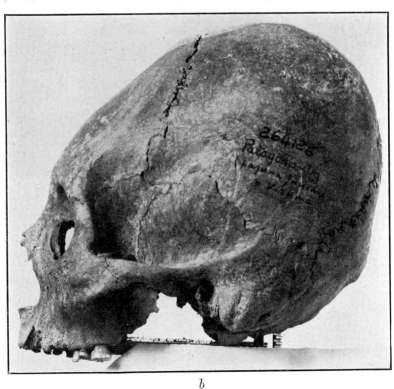

b

PERUVIAN (*a*) AND PATAGONIAN (*b*) SKULLS

Both skulls are in alveolo-condylian plane.
a, Showing Aymara-like deformation in a slight degree.
b, Probably pre-Columbian, from near Viedma, showing Aymara-like deformation in a marked
degree. (From same series as specimen on pl. 37 and skull *b* on pl. 39.)

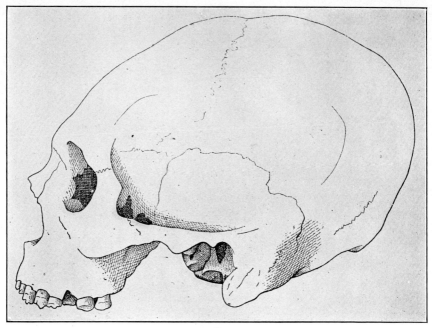

a

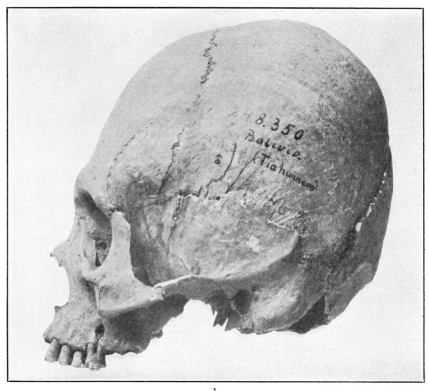

b

PATAGONIAN (*a*) AND AYMARA (*b*) SKULLS

a, From Viedma; shows marked Aymara-like deformation. (After Verneau.)
b, From Tiahuanaco; shows slight and aberrant Aymara-like deformation.

broken and decomposed skulls. One of these, an adult male, showed a plain case of moderate Aymara deformation, which fact, as well as the very evident recent character of the skull, after being pointed out by the writer, was freely acknowledged by Professor Ameghino. The remains were found, according to the sailor, in shallow graves somewhere north of the Laguna Malacara, which lies about a mile inland from the *chata*, but owing to an exaggerated notion of the money value of such objects the man would not reveal the exact location. He said, however, there were other similar burials. The fragments were, the writer understood, to be sent to the Museo Nacional, Buenos Aires, but a month later they had not been received.

Meanwhile the writer proceeded down to the Rio Negro, and there succeeded, through the help of Srs. D. Gallindez, the acting governor, and F. R. Cuestas, the inspector of police, in obtaining from the dry mud of the Paso de la Laguna de Juncal, about 4 miles south of Viedma, parts of 11 nearly black (except bleached parts protruding from the ground) skeletons; and 10 of the skulls (the eleventh being a part of that of a fetus) show more or less perceptible Aymara deformation. In only 1 case is the deformation of a greater degree than that in the specimen from Miramar (see pls. 35–41). Just before leaving the region the writer obtained a similarly deformed skull, but not stained or presenting any ancient characteristics or fossilization, from a superficial Indian burial-ground discovered accidentally in the southwestern limits of the town of Viedma itself (pl. 39).

It is evident from the above summary that a center of population practicing Aymara-like deformation of the head, existed at no very distant time in the lower part of the Valley of the Rio Negro, in the district of Viedma. The exact period of this occupation remains to be determined. As seen before, Moreno found a skull with Aymara deformation 10 feet deep in the sands. The crania found by the writer, similar in appearance to some of the Rio Negro skulls collected by Sr. Moreno, which were seen in the La Plata Museum, were all superficial, and that from Viedma itself, is plainly recent. The surface alluvium of the Rio Negro, a river which not infrequently overflows the flats, is of no geologic antiquity. The brownish-black discoloration of the bones is probably due to an abundance, in at least some localities, of manganese and iron salts, and may be also due in part to results of decomposition of organic matter; it is not a sign of antiquity. As mentioned before (p. 298) a similar discoloration is seen in a partially buried cow's pelvis collected by this expedition, and in other recent bones.

Both Necochea and Miramar are at no great distance from the Rio Negro center and the road offered no obstacles.

Thus, the artificial deformation, which suggests a limited former Aymara influence on a part of the Argentine population, offers nothing in support of and much against any great antiquity of the Miramar specimen. Such deformation connects it, as do also its main morphologic features (see p. 300), with an imperfectly-known native group of the Argentine coast, some living remnants of which have apparently persisted at Viedma and north of Necochea to relatively modern if not to historic times.

The original form of the Miramar skull, which is plainly determinable, was dolichocephalic. The principal measurements are: Diameter antero-posterior maximum, 19.2 cm. and diameter lateral maximum, 13.1 cm.; but the latter, as mentioned above, is surely somewhat diminished by the posthumous compression. The height of the vault, from the line connecting the auditory canals, to bregma, can not be accurately determined, but was slightly in excess of 12 cm.[1] These measurements, either singly or collectively, are in no way extraordinary compared with those of some modern dolichocephalic Indian crania, especially with some that have suffered a similar kind and grade of deformation. And as will be seen from the table below they approximate quite closely to those presented by the brownish-black crania brought by the writer from near Viedma and showing (with one exception) the same kind of deformity.

Fossil-like skulls from near Viedma

Cat. No. (U.S.N.M.)	Sex	Deformation	Length, maximum	Breadth, maximum	Floor of auditory canals line–bregma, height	Basion-bregma, height
			cm.	cm.	cm.	cm.
264128.............................	Male....	Imperceptible.	18.5	[2]13.6	(?)	(?)
264122.............................	...do....	Slight "Aymara."	18.5	14.2	(?)	(?)
264125.............................	...do....	Well-marked "Aymara."	18.6	[2]13.0	(?)	(?)
264130.............................	...do....	Moderate "Aymara."	20.4	[2]14.0	[2]12.7	(?)
264129.............................	...do....	Slight "Aymara."	19.0	[2]13.5	[2]12.9	[2]14.5
264127	Male?...	...do......	17.8	13.3	(?)	(?)
264126.............................	Female .	Typical "Aymara."	17.3	13.2	13.1	14.6
264117 more recent Viedma........	...do....	Slight "Aymara."	17.7	13.4	12.2	13.4

[1] Lehmann-Nitsche gives 12.3 cm. The basion-bregma height in undeformed dolichocephalic Indian crania is from 7 to 12 mm. greater than that between the floor of the meatus line and bregma; in deformed skulls the range of variation is still more extensive.

[2] Approximate.

The forehead is narrow but not more so than in many more or less recent Indian skulls. Lehmann-Nitsche, who may have measured the specimen while it was still in better condition, gives for the minimum frontal diameter 9.1 cm. Twenty-four southern Utah dolichocephalic masculine crania, measured by the writer, show for the same diameter a variation from 8.3 to 9.6 cm., with the average 9 cm.; 16 Tarahumare, from Mexico, the variation of 8 to 9.5 and the average 8.9 cm.; 4 Massachusetts Indian skulls the variation of 8.7 to 9 and the average 8.9 cm.; and 6 of the deformed skulls from Viedma in which the forehead is not damaged range from 7.7 (No. 264117, female, quite recent) to 9.4 cm., with the average 8.7 (average of the five fossil-like specimens alone, 8.9 cm.) It is evident from these figures that the narrowness of the forehead of the Miramar skull is very ordinary for America and can not be used in support of the antiquity of the specimen.

The nasion depression is submedium but it is not absent. However, a diminishing of the naso-frontal bent or angle is the rule in crania having the Aymara deformation and occasionally amounts to the entire loss of this feature. It is apparently the effect of traction upward and backward, induced by the band that deforms the skull. It is seen in all the deformed skulls brought by the writer from Viedma and to some extent also in the specimen from the same locality described by Verneau (see pls. 37–41).

The nasal process itself in the Miramar skull is of usual length and breadth. The orbits were of medium size, distantly approximating the quadrilateral in form, with borders of moderate dullness. There is no certain evidence that they were above the average in height, though if they were so it would merely agree with another common effect of the Aymara-like formation.

The forehead is artificially lowered but as usual in this type of misshaped skulls there is no marked flattening. There are no well-defined band or pad impressions now perceptible but such may have existed to a slight degree, becoming obliterated by the loss of substance on the surface of the frontal bone. There are no distinct frontal eminences, nor is there any median crest, conditions which agree with what is generally observed in skulls deformed in this manner.

The supraorbital ridges are of submedium dimensions for a male. This may be natural, for there are rare specimens of masculine skulls of American natives in which these protrusions are slight, but more likely it is, at least partially, the result of the artificial shaping, for it is still another feature that often attends the Aymara deformation. Were this not the case, then in face of what is well established as to the really early human remains, the small ridges would have

to be looked on as either an infantile feature or as an example of
recession, as is observed in these structures in the most highly civilized peoples of the actual time. Under no condition could they be
viewed as marks of primitiveness or antiquity. The ridges also extend
over only the median half of the supraorbital space, as in the great
majority of Indian crania. There is the usual slant of the outer part
of the supraorbital region, perhaps in this case slightly augmented
by the compression of the forehead, but there is no tendency toward
an arch such as characterizes the skulls representing well-known
earlier forms of humanity.

The parietal region is oval from side to side, there being no sagittal
crest. The parietal eminences are moderate. The outline of the
norma superior approximates to long ovoid, with the narrower end
forward. The temporal crests are not well traceable, but evidently
ran at a good distance from the sagittal suture.

The occipital flattening is only moderate yet plainly perceptible.
It extends quite high and there is no subinionic depression as in
highly misshapen Aymara skulls, but these features are common to
the less deformed crania of this type. They are shown by all the
fossil-like specimens, as well as by the more recent deformed skull
from Viedma and can be seen also on true Aymara skulls (pls. 37–41).
It is possible that in these cases there exists a combination of the
effects of the compress and the cradle-board. The occipital ridges
and impressions also are not very pronounced in the Miramar skull.

The sutures of the vault, with the exception of the temporo-parietal,
are apparently all synostosed, but the condition of the specimen permits no exact determination of this nor of the characteristics of the
sutures. The naso-frontal articulation is patent, at least to a large
extent. The pterions are both of the H form and of medium breadth.

The facial parts are very defective. The left malar shows no
features worthy of special remark. The nasal aperture was apparently of medium breadth, as in most Indians. The nasal spine is
broken. There are no subnasal gutters or fossæ. The upper alveolar process was rather low and but moderately prognathic.

The temporal region (left) is moderately and uniformly convex.
The mastoids are broken, the right, which is better preserved, showing moderate masculine size. The roots of the zygomæ are quite
stout. Nowhere in these parts is there any feature that would give
the impression of characteristics other than the ordinary in the
Indian.

The lateral angular processes are rather broad, though not abnormally so. The diameter between their most distal parts measures
10.4 cm. In a male Patagonian (No. 264109, United States National
Museum) the measurement is likewise 10.4 cm., while two other skulls

of the same sex and derivation (Nos. 264105, 264114) give each 10.5 cm.; in the most recent female Aymara-like skull from Viedma (No. 264117), the dimension is only 9.9 cm. and in two of the fossil-like skulls from the same locality (male, 264125 and female, 264126), where it is possible to make the measurement, they are respectively 10.5 and 10.7 cm.

The palate was quite spacious, regular, of moderate depth, and there is no torus. The upper teeth were 16 in number, of medium masculine dimensions; these are moderately worn, with the exception of the last molar on the left side, which shows no wear at all; the crown of this tooth is also slightly higher than that of the adjoining tooth, all these conditions indicating an absence of the corresponding molar in the lower jaw. The teeth are of dirty grayish-cream color, some looking as if covered with a thin, old pellicle of white paint. There are no anomalies in form and no features at all primitive.

Lower jaw: This bone is on the whole rather massive but of the usual modern Indian form. The chin is square, of medium prominence, inferiorly stout. A ventral reenforcement of the alveolar process, above and along the mylo-hyoid line, is quite marked and extends from the first molar backward; this feature is frequently met with in the American native.

The teeth in the lower jaw were not well restored. It can be ascertained, however, that there were congenitally only three incisors, and only two molars on the left side. The last molar on the right side is anomalous, having a crown 13 mm. long by 12.5 mm. broad. As to measurements, the thickness of the horizontal ramus (at right angles to its vertical axis),[1] opposite the second molar, is 1.8 cm.; height at symphysis, approximately 3.3 cm.; the bigonial diameter was about 10.9 cm. and the minimum breadth of the ascending ramus approximately 3.9 cm. At the chin, below the mental spines (which themselves are very moderate), the thickness of the bone is 1.6 cm.

In eight male lower jaws of Patagonians from San Xavier, Rio Negro, collected by the writer, the thickness at the second molar averages 1.7 cm., ranging from 1.5 to 1.9 cm.; while the height at symphysis varies from 3.5 to 4.2 cm., the bigonial diameter from 10 to 11.6 cm., the minimum breadth of the vertical ramus from 3.5 to 4.1 cm., and the thickness of the chin, below the mental spines, 1.4 to 1.65 cm.

The only measurement of the Miramar jaw that is slightly outside the range of the variation of this little series of specimens is the moderate height at symphysis. It has been noted that the upper

---

[1] Measured in the more ordinary way=1.6 cm.

alveolar process was also somewhat low. Both of these features may be due in part to reduction through age, for the teeth show some extrusion; but even if not so, they are signs of slight significance and point rather away from than to the primitive nature of the specimen. Yet relative lowness of the horizontal ramus, especially at the symphysis, often accompanies massiveness (as also exists in this specimen), and both of these features are not infrequently seen together with a broad ascending ramus, all standing evidently in relation with a functional use of the jaw greater than average.[1]

But the weightiest point against any great primitiveness of the jaw is the presence of the chin. None of the mammals, none of the apes, none of the truly primitive forms of man so far known, possess this feature. The chin prominence of the present human lower jaw is to a large extent merely a remnant, the result of a great reduction in the ancestral size of the teeth and the length of the alveolar processes, the lower and less functional portion of the jaw lagging behind. The lower jaw, with a very much reduced chin, may occur even in present man and not carry any great significance (see under *Homo sinemento*), but one with a well-marked chin can not possibly be very ancient and can not, so far as we are now able to judge, come from any very early representative of the human family.

Other bones of the Miramar skeleton.—Femora: These bones are of medium masculine dimensions. The right is somewhat pilasteric, with prismatic shaft; the shape of the shaft of the left bone is intermediate between prismatic and elliptic. Both bones show marked lateral torsion, as is frequently met with in the femora of the Indians. The usual bend backward is present to a moderate degree and extends over the whole shaft. Both bones are markedly platymeric, a feature which, while not exclusively Indian, is a characteristic of many of the Indian femora.

The surface of the bones is more or less defective, eroded. The left femur possesses a moderate third trochanter; on the right the parts are damaged.

The principal measurements of the two femora, with some comparative data, are given below.

The length of the bones indicates a man of medium stature, not far from 1.64 meters; and the other dimensions, but especially the pilasteric as well as the platymeric indices, agree closely enough with those of the ordinary natives of northeastern Patagonia. There is not a feature about the bones that points to any early species of man or to any man other than the ordinary Indian.

---

[1] See writer's "Contribution to the Anthropology of Central and Smith Sound Eskimo;" in *Anthr. Papers Amer. Mus. Nat. Hist.*, v, pt. 2, New York, 1910, pp. 170-280.

Comparison of the measurements[1] *of the* Miramar *and* Patagonian *femora*[2]

Locality	Number of male femora	Average length (bicondylar)	Middle			Upper flattening		
			Diameter antero-posterior maximum (a)	Diameter lateral (b)	Index at middle (a x 100) (b)	Greatest breadth (c)	Smallest thickness (d)	Index of platymery (d x 100) (c)
		cm.	*cm.*	*cm.*		*cm.*	*cm.*	
Miramar.................. {Right.		(?)	[3] 3.2	[3] 2.6	[3] *123.0*	3.6	2.65	*73.6*
{Left...		44.0	[3] 3.0	[3] 2.4	[3] *125.4*	3.6	2.4	*66.7*
Fossil-like bones from Viedma, Patagonia........... }7...... {		45.3	3.3	2.65	*124.1*	3.4	2.5	*73.1*
		(43.5–	(2.6–	(2.5–	(*98.2*–	(3.2–	(2.25–	(*67.6*–
		49.5)	3.8)	2.7)	*145.3*)	3.6)	2.75)	*78.3*)
Tehuelche,San Xavier,near Viedma, Patagonia....... }15..... {		45.7	3.1	2.6	*117.7*	3.45	2.5	*73.0*
		(43.6–	(2.6–	(2.4–	(*106.9*–	(3.1–	(2.3–	(*67.1*–
		46.8)	3.3)	2.9)	*130*)	3.6)	2.75)	*76.8*)

[1] For details as to the significance of these measurements and indices and for data on primate, early human, Indian, and various racial femora, the reader is referred especially to—

MANOUVRIER, L., La platymèrie; in *C.-R. du Congr. int. d'Anthrop. prèhist.*, Paris, 1889.

—— Étude sur les variations morphologiques du corps du fémur dans l'espèce humaine; in *Bull. Soc. d'Anthr. Paris,* 4e sér., IV, 1893.

LEHMANN-NITSCHE, R., Über die langen Knochen der südbayerischen Reihengräberbevölkerung; in *Beiträge zur Anthropologie und Urgeschichte Bayerns*, XI, 1894. Separate, München, 1895, pp. 50-51.

MARTIN, R., Zur physischen Anthropologie der Feuerländer; in *Arch. für. Anthr.*, XXII, Braunschweig, 1894, p. 155 et seq.

HULTKRANTZ, J. V., Några bidrag till Sydamerikas fysiska antropologi; in *Ymer Tidskrift utgifven af Svenska Sällskapet för Antropologi och Geografi*, XVIII, Stockholm, 1898.

KLAATSCH, H., Die wichtigsten Variationen am Skelet der freien unteren Extremität des Menschen und ihre Bedeutung für das Abstammungsproblem; in *Ergebnisse der Anatomie und Entwickelungsgeschichte*, X, Wiesbaden, 1900, p. 599 et seq.

VERNEAU, R., Les anciens Patagons, Monaco, 1903.

BELLO Y RODRIGUEZ, S., Le fémur et le tibia chez l'homme et les anthropoïdes; Thése p. l., Doctora Médecine, Paris, 1909, p. 109.

[2] Specimens in the United States National Museum.

[3] Approximate.

Tibiæ: Like the femora, the tibiæ are of medium masculine dimensions. Their ends are badly damaged, their surfaces eroded. They present the usual slight sigmoid physiologic curvature of the shaft and a moderate inclination backward of the head. The shaft at middle is in shape of type No. 3 (external surface markedly concave),[1] with the addition of a fairly well marked vertical ridge running down the posterior surface (approximating type No. 4), characteristics often seen in the Indian.

As to measurements, the length of the bones can not be determined. The principal diameters at the height of the nutritive foramen are, on each side, respectively, 3.9 and 2.6 cm., giving the moderately platycnemic index of *66.7.* Seventeen male Tehuelche tibiæ from San Xavier, near Viedma, Patagonia, give for the same dimensions the averages of 3.95 and 2.45 cm., with the platycnemic

[1] See Hrdlička, A., Typical Forms of Shaft of Long Bones; *Proc. Assoc. Amer. Anatomists*, 14th Ann. Session, Baltimore, 1900, pp. 55-60.

index of *61.6* (*51.2–71.6*),[1] and Bell, on 79 Patagonian tibiæ, obtained the index of *63.8*. A number of the individual San Xavier tibiæ show measurements and indices that are very close to those of the Miramar tibiæ. Thus, No. 264157–[9] = 3.95 by 2.65, ind. *67.1*; $'r$ = 3.8 by 2.6, ind. *68.4*; $'g$ = 4.0 by 2.7, ind. *67.5*; and $'n$ = 3.7 by 2.65, ind. *71.6*. These resemblances, as those in the measurements of the femora and other bones, do not indicate that the Miramar skeleton is that of a Patagonian, but they show forcibly that it is the skeleton of an individual related in many ways to the principal modern native type of eastern Argentina.

The fibulæ, of medium masculine development, are very defective. The shaft shows shape of type No. 4 (quadrilateral).

The humeri are of moderate masculine strength. The upper and lower extremities are wanting and the length of the bones can not be determined. The deltoid tuberosities are well-developed. Shape of shaft, nearly plano-convex.

Measurements at middle:

Diameter maximum (antero-posterior):   cm.
    Right 2. 45
    Left, about 2. 3
Diameter minimum (lateral):
    Right 1. 75
    Left 1. 7

A portion of an ulna shows a fracture below the middle of the shaft. Fragments of the radii present no special features.

On the whole, the bones of the skeleton other than the skull are in poor condition, worn and defective, and not very satisfactory for detailed examination. They all indicate, however, an individual of male sex and present no features which would make it possible to reach any other conclusion than that they represent the relatively modern aborigines of the region. It seems safe to say that had the Miramar skull and other bones been compared originally with sufficient skeletal material from eastern Argentina, they would occupy a much more modest place in anthropologic literature than, in absence of such comparison, has been assigned them.

SKELETAL REMAINS RELATING TO HOMO PAMPÆUS, FROM NEIGHBORHOOD OF NECOCHEA

HISTORY AND REPORTS

These remains come from a place in the barren soil of the irregular stretch of country a short distance to the right of the new road leading from Necochea to the coast, and about as far inland from the large hotel built on the shore. The human bones lay on or near the surface, some of them exposed by the wheels of the wagons which passed

---

[1] Bello y Rodriguez, S., Le fémur et le tibia, etc., Paris, 1909, pp. 107–109.

over the spot. They were first seen by the gardener, Parodi, who lives in the neighborhood, but were not taken out immediately; later on part of them were secured by a local physician, Doctor Faggioli, who donated them to the Buenos Aires museum, and the remainder were obtained later by the Ameghino brothers and Doctor Cavazzuti. They are partially reported on by Professor Ameghino in his memoir on the *Diprothomo*,[1] where (p. 127, footnote 3) we read as follows:

"It is several months ago that my friend, Dr. Rodolphe Faggioli, of Necochea, donated to the Museo Nacional, at my request, a fossil human skull, which he found in the ancient Pampean formation of that place. Last April I myself made an excursion to the locality to study its geology. I was accompanied by the naturalist-traveler of the museum, Carlos Ameghino, and by Dr. E. Cavazzuti. We explored the coast over a stretch of 80 km. with the greatest profit, for I brought away a multitude of objects. Among these there are two fossil human skulls from the same stratum as the one mentioned above; of these skulls, one is in fragments, but the other is very complete, with the rostrum, the lower jaw, and the teeth in nearly perfect condition."

As to the antiquity and principal characteristics of these specimens, it will be best to give once more Ameghino's own words. He says:

"These three skulls are of the same age as that of Miramar, on which I have founded the *Homo pampæus*. They all present the same characteristics, including the excessively sloping forehead, which is natural and not the result of an artificial deformation, as has been alleged; all have the rostrum much prolonged forward and the alveolar border and the denture orthognathic; all present a glabella without backward inversion below, so that there is no frontonasal depression; all present the last molar placed forward of the most posterior part of the anterior border of the orbits; all show the inferior border of the orbit placed considerably more forward than the superior one; all are very dolichocephalic, with excessively narrow foreheads, great orbits, and other characteristics."

And further on (p. 170) in the same memoir we read about the second Necochea cranium (third example of *Homo pampæus*):

"As in the case of the first example (Miramar), the conformation of the frontal region is natural without any vestige of artificial deformation; on this point there can not remain absolutely the slightest doubt."

Notwithstanding the fact that the front is excessively low and very sloping, "the superior outline of the skull lifts itself gradually

---

[1] Ameghino, F., Le *Diprothomo platensis;* in *Anal. Mus. Nac. Buenos Aires*, XIX (ser. iii, t. XII), 1909, pp. 127, foot-note 3, 170 et seq.; illustrations especially on pp. 171, 179, 185.

toward the posterior part and, in prolonging the same to complete the segment which is wanting, one obtains an almost identical contour of the vault as that of the first-known example [Miramar], which is raising so much unjustified criticism. . . .

"The prolongation forward of the rostrum gives rise to facial prognathism so considerable that the anterior alveolar border of the intermaxillary is 3 cm. more forward than the most prominent part of the glabella."

One of the characteristics which according to Professor Ameghino distinguish *Homo pampæus* is the position of the teeth; these are said to be placed considerably farther forward than in *Homo sapiens*, a "condition which stands in relation with the primitive prognathism of the rostrum." To obtain an idea of this forward position of the denture, one needs, according to Ameghino, only to trace a vertical line tangent to the most posterior point of the orbital arch—this line passes back of the last superior molar and the same is the case in the first example [Miramar]. "It is then plainly a distinctive characteristic of this species. . .

"This same vertical line if prolonged upward separates an anterior segment of the frontal bone the surface of which is flattened and faces upward in the *Diprothomo*, is feebly arched and facing upward and forward in the *Homo pampæus*, and is strongly convex in *Homo sapiens* of elevated race, forming an arch the convexity of which faces forward.

[P. 173] "As to the lower jaw, the chin is very prominent. In the third example [1] here figured the chin is as protruding as in the first [Miramar]. . . . This conformation, which is believed to be very recent, is to the contrary excessively ancient and reaches probably to the very origin of the *Hominiens*."

The foregoing information was evidently considered sufficient, for it is all that we have from Ameghino on the Necochea specimens of the *Homo pampæus*.

The Necochea finds here dealt with are merely touched on in 1910 by Lehmann-Nitsche [2] but are considered later in that year more in detail by Mochi.[3]

Lehmann-Nitsche sees nothing, morphologically, in these remains that would separate them from the Indians; in age he regards them as Quaternary, Superior Pampean.

Mochi devotes considerable attention to the Necochea skull No. 2 (*Homo pampæus*, example No. 3), the specimen described and pictured

[1] Third example of *Homo pampæus*, illustrated in Ameghino's "Le *Diprothomo*" memoir, in figs. 7–11 of Mochi's paper and in pls. 43–45 of the present work. It is No. 5008 of the Museo Nacional. The reference to these skulls as first, second, etc., is confusing.]

[2] Lehmann-Nitsche, R., El hombre fósil pampeano; in *Bol. Ofic. Nac. Est.*, La Paz, Bolivia, VI, 1910, p. 364.

[3] Mochi, A., Appunti sulla paleoantropologia argentina; in *Arch. per l'Antr. e la Etn.*, XL, Firenze, 1910, p. 224 et seq.

by Ameghino in his "Le *Diprothomo platensis*." He notes that Ameghino's orientation of the specimen is incorrect; moreover, his illustration has suffered from the specimen having been placed too near the camera; also there are faults in the restoration. But Mochi fails to recognize that the skull is deformed and that the face is so ill-repaired that the whole part, including the nose and the orbits, is much higher than naturally. The writer feels confident that, with a little more leisure at his disposal in the examination of the specimens, Doctor Mochi would have easily recognized the existence of these several important features.

Mochi does not agree with Ameghino in regard to the latter's characterizations of the glabellar and subglabellar region and especially as to the forward position of the denture. Both, especially the latter, are properly referred to the false orientation of the skull; in a similar pose quite the same features appear in nearly all human crania.

Finally, Ameghino's estimate of the stature of the individual to whom the skull belonged appears to Mochi too small.

OBSERVATIONS BY THE WRITER

The skulls in question, with all the other specimens from the neighborhood of Necochea, were freely placed by Professor Ameghino before the writer for examination. Further, the locality of the find was visited.[1] The results of these investigations sustain neither the claim for any special morphologic peculiarity nor that of considerable antiquity for these remains. They are, in brief, as follows:

Owing to some changes in the surface, produced by the winds and the blown sand, the exact spot from which the bones were taken could not be located, though the party was accompanied by the gardener who discovered them. It was, however, part of the general irregular wind-denuded surface which stretches inland from the coast. The wind erosion is not on the whole of great depth, for there are in the near neighborhood various piles of earth which still show the presence of vegetal soil and which yield numerous recent skulls and bones of the viscacha; these are the remnants of *viscacheras* which existed not very long ago, before the looser earth about them was blown away.[2] Over this denuded, uneven surface were found by the party more than thirty "white" and "black" chips or implements, and others had been picked up before by the gardener's children. As mentioned, the bones were so near the surface that they were exposed by the wheels of a wagon. So far as the gardener could recollect they represented at least one complete, or nearly complete, skeleton. Here was evidently a grave, which could not have been very deep beneath the surface of the plain

---

[1] Compare geologic notes on a part of the same locality, by Bailey Willis, under *Homo sinemento*.

[2] The viscacha burrows as a rule are found in low hillocks covered with bushes, the roots of which naturally retard wind erosion.

before its erosion by the winds.   No bones of fossil animals were found
with the human bones nor have any been discovered in the immediate
neighborhood, though from another part of these denuded coast-flats
the gardener had extracted a number of parts of a scelidotherium.

Homo pampæus skull No. 2 (Necochea No. 1).—The first specimen
in the lot under consideration or, according to Ameghino's enumeration, the second example of *Homo pampæus*, bears the number 5004
in the Museo Nacional at Buenos Aires.   It is a piece of the vault of
a female skull, consisting of a portion of the forehead and portions of
the two parietals (pl. 42).

The specimen is in the same general condition as the other Necochea
skull (No. 5008), the surface being deeply and irregularly eroded.
The bones appear somewhat fossilized.   On the right side, the parietals show dorsally spots of dark-gray calcareous incrustation.

Obviously this was not a large cranium but the exact size can not
be determined with certainty.   The thickness of the bones is rather
submedium.

The bones show externally in two or three places signs of disease.
These alterations are somewhat masked by the effects of erosion, but
an examination under a magnifying glass shows plainly proliferation
and other changes due to some inflammatory process, probably
syphilis.

Morphologically, the specimen presents a rather low, moderately
convex forehead, but the latter character would be less pronounced
were the surface of the frontal squama preserved.   Just posterior to
the coronal suture and parallel with it is a perceptible, though shallow,
broad depression, which, with the lowness of the squama, may indicate a slight Aymara deformation.

The nasal process is of ordinary feminine form.   The glabella is
moderate; the supraorbital ridges are small.   There is no frontal or
sagittal crest.

The sutures are obliterated.

Ventrally, the bones show no special features; the metopic ridge is
of moderate dimensions.

Homo pampæus skull No. 3 (Necochea No. 2).—This is the better
preserved of the Necochea skulls.   It was found with some long
bones and other bones, but these, being damaged and in bad condition, were not collected.   The specimen bears the number 5008 in
the Museo Nacional and is in Ameghino's enumeration the third
example of the *Homo pampæus*.   It is a skull of an adult of advancing age.   The sex is somewhat doubtful; the lower jaw is quite masculine in character, but other parts indicate the female rather than
the male.

The specimen (pls. 43–45) is very defective and has been reconstructed to a considerable extent in mastic.   The rebuilding is

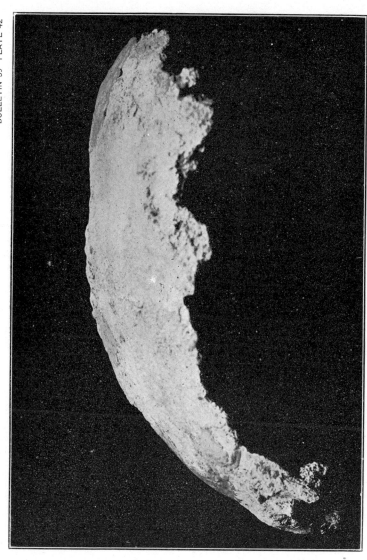

FRAGMENT OF SKULL FROM VICINITY OF NECOCHEA

Ameghino's "second example of *Homo pampæus*." (Collected by Dr. R. Faggioli.)

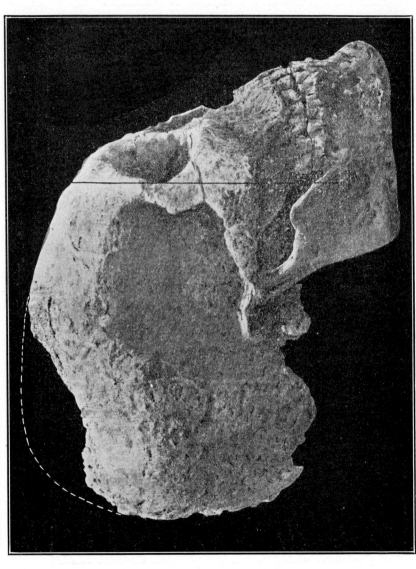

NECOCHEA SKULL NO. 5008

Third example of *Homo pampæus* of Ameghino. (As posed by Ameghino in his "Le *Diprothomo platensis*.") (In Museo Nacional, Buenos Aires.)

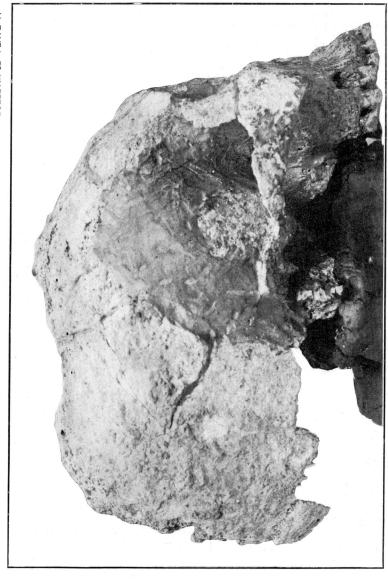

NECOCHEA SKULL NO. 5008

Third example of *Homo pampæus* of Ameghino. (Posed approximately in the alveolo-condylar plane.) (In Museo Nacional, Buenos Aires.)

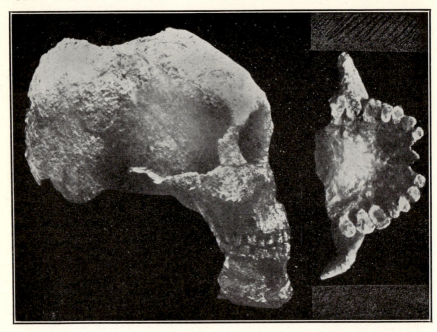

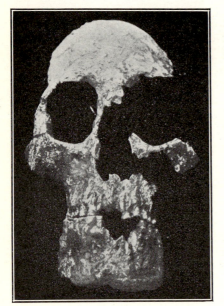
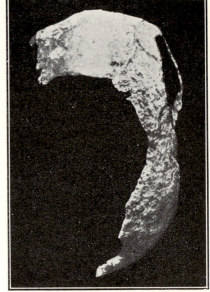

NECOCHEA SKULL NO. 5008. (AFTER MOCHI)

In Museo Nacional, Buenos Aires.

imperfect, especially as regards the face. The parts present include both jaws, the right malar and zygoma, the frontal bone, part of the right parietal, and the right temporal.

The surface of the bones of the vault is very defective and eroded, some of the losses of substance reaching nearly to the compact ventral layer.

The bones are not heavy, yet they appear somewhat fossilized; at least they are largely devoid of animal matter. Some dark mineral substance adheres to parts of what remains of the base.

The skull is without doubt artificially deformed, the type of the deformation approaching that of the Aymara.

There is nothing to indicate the age of the individual except the teeth, which show advanced wear. The condition of the sutures can not be determined; no trace is seen of the coronal.

In form the skull was doubtless dolichocephalic. The face also was originally, in all probability, rather long and narrow, but it has been made very perceptibly longer by faulty reconstruction. This applies particularly to the orbits and the nose.

The skull was of submedium size, though not microcephalic.

As to detailed features, there is a fairly prominent glabella. The supraorbital ridges are small and there is no tendency to supraorbital arch. The orbital borders are only slightly dull.

The forehead is very sloping, especially from a point about 3 cm. above the glabella. This slope is not natural, however, but is due to the above-mentioned artificial deformation. The posterior part of the parietals and the occipital bone are wanting, so that their exact character and the extent of the deformation in the rear can not be determined.

The forehead is also narrow but the diameter frontal minimum can not be measured or even closely estimated, owing to the destruction of the bone on the left side and its imperfect state on the right. There is no medio-frontal crest.

The parietals show but few features of interest. The eminences are large and quite prominent, though not pointed.

The base presents on the right side a deep glenoid fossa; the left side is deficient.

The walls of the skull were not thick. Ventrally there are seen a few shallow brain impressions.

As to the facial parts, the nasal bones and the nasal process show no unusual features. The nasal aperture was 2.6 cm. broad and was probably mesorhinic, in measurement and form typical of Indians. The nasal spine is of submedium dimensions as compared with that of the whites but very ordinary when compared with the average form among the American natives.

There are no subnasal grooves or fossæ. The prognathism is medium, again as in Indians. The suborbital (canine) fossæ were apparently shallow. The malars and zygomæ are of ordinary form and female dimensions.

The palate is fairly but not excessively deep, and the alveolar arch measures (by Turner's method) about 5.2 cm. in length and 6.4 cm. in breadth.

Dentition as well as the teeth was normal. The latter are of feminine size; their other characteristics are obliterated by wear. The crown of the third lower molar on the right side appears to be slightly longer than that of the second but the breadth is the same; above, the third molars were smaller than both the second and the first.

The lower jaw is entirely Indian in form. The prominence of the chin is well-marked. Height at symphysis, about 3.7 cm., anterior to the second right molar, 3.4 cm.; thickness opposite second right molar (at right angles to the vertical axis of the ramus), 1.25 cm. The height is unusual if the skull is that of a female, but lower jaws with high symphysis are particularly common in modern cranial material in eastern Argentina from the Parana to Tierra del Fuego.

Additional Homo pampæus specimens from Nechochea.—Besides the defective skulls noted in the preceding pages, there were found in Professor Ameghino's collection at the Museo Nacional in Buenos Aires, under the number of one of the skulls (5004), various fragments of a skull (the fourth example of *Homo pampæus?*) and bones, all in poor condition for examination, broken and eroded. They are all whitish-gray or yellowish-brownish white in color and possibly somewhat altered in their mineral composition.

The pieces include part of the left clavicle of a child. There are also several remnants of long bones which show disease, the lesions resembling very closely syphilitic alterations and scars; a portion of a femur presents also a thickening of the shaft. The pathologic changes are in the main of the same character as those seen in skull No. 5004, and the bones are in all probability part of the same skeleton.

The fragments indicate an individual of moderate stature and muscular development; anatomically none of them shows any characteristic at all which could be considered out of the ordinary.

This is all worthy of mention that the writer found in these earlier Necochea specimens, and it surely fails to substantiate the existence of anything so important as a separate species of man, a *Homo pampæus.*

Necochea skeleton (No. 263966 U. S. National Museum).—This skeleton is represented by about 150 fragments, the largest of which are (after repair) a portion of a humerus, 16.5 cm., and a piece of a femur, 8 cm. long. Most of the pieces are only slivers, and of the skull there are only a few remnants of little significance.

This specimen was found by one of the gardener Parodi's children, some of the bones having become visible after a wind storm which carried away most of the material about them. They lay on a gentle declivity in the barren lands near the sand dunes to the southeast of the lowest part of the Rio Quequen, and only a few rods from the Necochea–sea boulevard. They were not far from the Necochea specimens Nos. 1 and 2, found about the same distance from the sea to the southwest side of the same road, and were regarded by Professor Ameghino as of similar antiquity.

The bones were gathered together by the boy, but were left for some time on the ground near the place where they were found and finally became reduced to the state and quantity in which they are at present. Certain features of the environment of the bones as described by the gardener, as well as the fragments which represent almost all the larger parts of the skeleton, indicate that the remains represent one complete skeleton whose parts lay in fairly natural relation. No objects were found with the bones, but there were (even at the time of the writer's visit) numerous "white" and "black" chipped stones scattered over the elevation itself as well as in the denuded parts of the land in the neighborhood.

When the writer's party visited the locality, it was found that the sand had already re-covered the place where the bones were found. However, the spot was located and, in order to understand the conditions clearly, the writer made a large circle about it and removed all the recently accumulated sand down to the more solid ground. When this was done, there was seen near the center of the clearing a shallow cavity (pl. 46) 9½ inches (24 cm.) deep at maximum, slightly more than 3 feet (1.1 meters) long, and 33½ inches (85 cm.) at its greatest breadth, representing what remained of the fossa which held the skeleton. No additional material was discovered in digging about this cavity, which was evidently a remnant of a grave made in the former surface of the land or in the sand which covered it.

Through the kindness of Professor Ameghino the writer obtained for the United States National Museum the fragments of bones gathered by the gardener. These are whitish to yellowish-white in color, in many instances worn on the surface, and in the case of some of the slivers worn also on the edges. The pieces of shafts of the long bones appear hardened, but all retain animal matter. A number of the fragments show adhesions of earth cemented by lime. In the medullary cavities the earth or fine sand is hardened where exposed but flows out freely from the interior. These are the same conditions as presented by numerous others of the "fossil" specimens dealt with in this report.

Judging by the strength of the bones, they belonged probably to a male skeleton. Anatomically they offer but little requiring description.

The part of the left humerus is without either extremity. As with all the other pieces, it has an entirely ordinary modern human aspect. It was of moderate length as well as strength; the maximum and minimum diameters near the middle are 2.0 by 1.75 cm., but both have been diminished through erosion of the surface. The deltoid tuberosity and spiral groove are well marked. The shape of the shaft at the middle was nearly prismatic.

The upper portion of the left femur shows marked platymery (3.3 by 2.15 mm., index *65.1*), which brings it in close relation with the east Argentine Indian femora. It does not have a third trochanter.

Portions of an ulna, fibula, pelvis, and the skull present no features worthy of special mention.

All that can be said in conclusion about this skeleton is that neither the position of the bones nor any of their features justify an assumption of antiquity, nor will a new species of man be formed on their basis.

GEOLOGIC NOTES ON THE NECOCHEA REGION

BY BAILEY WILLIS

THE NECOCHEA FIND

At Necochea the plain approaches the sea with but slight altitude, and abreast of the town the shore is a beach surmounted by very low bluffs, behind which is a broad belt of drifting sand that locally rises into dunes as much as 10 m. high. An excavation in the town, a kilometer more or less from the sea, exhibits a section of black soil 70 cm. thick resting in sharply-defined contact upon laminated secondary limestone or tosca 2 m. thick. The upper layers of the limestone, although distinct from the black earth, enclose lenticular layers of it. On approaching the coast, one recognizes at once the drifting sands which the southerly wind blows along the shore from the beach. Beneath the layer of moving sand there is a somewhat firmer deposit of mingled sand and fine black earth and a more indurated formation, neither of which appears to contain any secondary limestone, and also a more indurated formation which does contain secondary limestone in very thin layers and in sheets filling sun-cracks. The last-named deposit varies in constitution from a sandy coquina to fine black loess, being thus composed of materials blown from the beach mingled with those blown from the plain. The surface is hard enough to retain the forms sculptured by wind and drifting sand and the material includes specks of black sand. These two characteristics, together with the occurrence of the secondary limestone or tosca, are regarded by

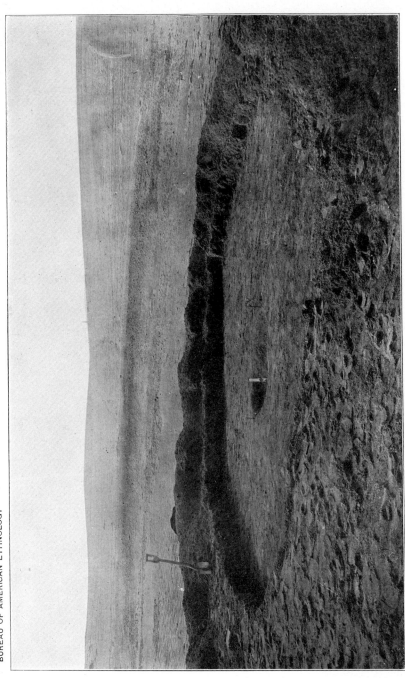

GRAVE OF "FOSSIL" SKELETON NEAR THE SEA AT NECOCHEA

Excavation by Hrdlička; the remains of this skeleton are now in the U. S. National Museum.

Ameghino as sufficient to distinguish the formation from the Recent deposits and to justify placing it in the late Tertiary under the name of "Inter-Ensenadean."

A careful examination of the so-called Inter-Ensenadean at this point showed that, as stated above, it consists of materials derived from the recent beach, as shell fragments, and also of black earth blown from the plain, where it forms the existing accumulation of soil. The presence of these modern materials in the formation appears to preclude any ancient date of deposition. Since lime is present in abundance in the ground waters, in the soil, and as shells in the material itself, it is naturally taken in solution and deposited on evaporation by the waters that rise and fall in the coastal plain. Little friable concretions of lime occur even in the deposits whose modern age is not questioned, and the difference between them and the thin sheets which occur in the so-called Inter-Ensenadean is rather one of conditions of deposition than of age. Still it is not questioned that the Inter-Ensenadean is slightly older than the drifting sand, though undoubtedly Recent.

The skeleton of a man was dug up in this superficial formation about 1 km. northeast of the Necochea Hotel, about 300 m. from the sea and between two large sand dunes. The material in which the bones were found was an incoherent brown sand, part of the formation over which the dunes are moving. Its surface was covered with loose pebbles of tosca and many chipped stones. The exact point from which the skeleton had been taken was indicated by Señor Parodi, and the hole, which had filled up with sand, was carefully reexcavated by Hrdlička down to the depth and far beyond the limits of the original excavation. The undisturbed material was distinguished from that which had blown into the hole, by decidedly greater compactness. The opening was 1.1 m. long and 85 cm. wide and had a maximum depth of 24 cm. As reexcavated the hole is shown in plate 46.

The more compact sand in which the skeleton occurred appears to belong to that formation which Ameghino styles Inter-Ensenadean and regards as Tertiary, whereas the writer looks on it as a modern shore formation slightly older than the dune sands that are drifting across it. Precisely similar deposits were seen in process of formation at Miramar, as may be noted by referring to the description of that locality. But the age of the formation is of no importance in connection with the age of the bones, for the shallowness of the hole and the lay of the bones, as described by Señor Parodi to Hrdlička and the writer, clearly showed that the body had been buried. In consequence, it was even younger than the sand formation.

FINAL REMARKS ON HOMO PAMPÆUS

By A. H.

If any *Homo pampæus* ever existed, it is safe to say that his remains have not as yet been produced. The case fails utterly thus far from the standpoint of geology, as well as that of anthropology. If the facts are carefully reviewed, it will be seen that geologically no substantial evidence has been brought forward favoring any great antiquity of the several lots of human bones assumed to represent this human species. And as to archeology and somatology, they both demonstrate that the specimens ascribed to *Homo pampæus*, the "earliest human representative—if not even a predecessor of man"—are fraught with no such possibilities, but that they point in no uncertain manner to the common American Indian. In view of all the facts, *Homo pampæus* must be regarded as merely a theory, without, so far as shown, any substantiation.

DIPROTHOMO PLATENSIS

HISTORY AND REPORTS

In 1896 the laborers employed by a firm of contractors in excavating a dry dock, now known as No. 1, at Buenos Aires, discovered a human skull. The specimen came to light at the commencement of the work on the rudder-pit, an additional small cavity in the bottom of the nearly finished dry-dock excavation.

An account of the circumstances of the discovery was published in July, 1909, by Professor Ameghino.[1] According to this: "The fragment of skull in question was found during the last stages of the work of deepening the port of Buenos Aires, in the excavations for the dry docks, in the north basin in dock No. 1, or that of the west. It was found in the deepest part of the excavation, even deeper than the floor of the dry dock itself, in a hollow made in the base of this for the manipulations of the rudder. There were some more osseous débris, but Mr. Junor,[2] having arrived somewhat late at the place of the discovery, was not able to save more than the specimen under consideration [p. 107]. . . .

"At the point where excavation for the dry-dock has been made the bed of the stream is 1.86 m. below the surface of the water at the ordinary low tide and the base of the dry dock is 10.50 m. below the bed of the stream; in other words, the latter is 12.36 m. below the level of the water. The additional hollow made in the bottom of the dry dock for the accommodation of the rudder is 50 cm. deep, and it

---

[1] Ameghino, F., Le *Diprothomo platensis*, un précurseur de l'homme du pliocène inférieur de Buenos Aires; in *Anal. Mus. Nac. Buenos Aires*, XIX (ser. iii, t. XII), 1909, pp. 107–209.

[2] A senior member of the Corps of Superior Employees of the works in the Port of Buenos Aires, and supervisor of the work.

was in digging out this additional basin that the skull was encountered. Accordingly, the latter lay at the depth of 11 m. below the bed of the stream, 12.86 m. below the ordinary level of the water at low tide, or 32 m. below the star on the portico of the Buenos Aires Cathedral. . . . All the information concerning the position of the skull has been furnished me by Mr. Edward Marsh Simpson, engineer and representative in Buenos Aires of the house of Charles H. Walker & Co., of London, the constructors of the port" (p. 108).

Professor Ameghino concludes from the information obtained from Mr. Simpson alone that the fragments of the skull came from the lower portion of the rudder-pit in Dry Dock No. 1 and from beneath *tosca*.[1] He states further, however (p. 121), that beneath the tosca was found a layer of quartzy sand followed by a stratum of gray clay, and that it was in this layer of gray clay, 50 cm. below the floor of the dry dock, that the skull-cap of the *Diprothomo* was discovered.

The foregoing are rather meager details concerning a specimen of so great importance. In consequence, the first endeavors of the writer and his associate, Mr. Willis, after reaching Buenos Aires, were to locate Messrs. Simpson and Junor as well as any others who might be able to give firsthand information, and to learn if possible additional particulars.

As good fortune would have it, both Mr. Simpson and Mr. Junor were found in Buenos Aires and both consented, very kindly, to tell what they knew in regard to the skull; and through these gentlemen it became possible to locate another person concerned in the find, namely, Mr. J. E. Clark, now of Bahia Blanca, the foreman of the laborers who discovered the specimen.

The results of the inquiry, however, proved in a large degree disappointing. The evidence is very largely indirect and, as 16 years have elapsed since the date of the find, during 15 of which no inquiries about it were made, the details, possibly even some important points, have been forgotten or have become obscured. This statement applies especially to the exact conditions at the rudder-pit and to facilities that might have existed for the transportation thither, accidentally or voluntarily, of the skull fragment.

Mr. Simpson stated that the find of the bones was made by the workmen; he was told there were more than one skull but neither he nor any other official of the firm was at the dock at the time of the find, nor was any investigation of the matter made. Mr. Simpson had nothing to do with the piece of skull or any other parts, made no examination of the spot, saw nothing of the specimen until after it was placed in the museum, and can not vouch for any statement made in connection with the discovery. He told Professor Ameghino

---

[1] Term applied, as explained before in this work, to calcareous sedimentary strata or concretions, in various stages of development, within the loess.

what he remembered having heard and furnished him with a sketch of the geologic formation as seen in the excavations for the docks, without locating the specimen. The excavations in Dry Dock No. 1 were never carried beneath the tosca except in the rudder-pit.

Mr. Junor states that he did not see the find, but was told of it the next day, or perhaps the second day after, by the foreman, Mr. Clark. No effort was made by Mr. Junor to examine the hole from which the bones came or to find or collect other pieces, for this might have resulted in delaying the work. He had an impression that there were five or six skulls discovered and that the workmen played *bochas*[1] with them, thus breaking them into fragments, but this seems to have been an error, as will appear later. The foreman brought Mr. Junor two pieces of the skull, and the latter saved them because they were said to have come from beneath the tosca, giving them later to the Museo Nacional. He had not been asked before by any one for details concerning the finds and is not responsible for any illustrations that may have appeared in print. No notice was taken for many years of the pieces he donated until they were taken up recently by Professor Ameghino. He has seen the specimen since—now only one piece, probably made by joining the two fragments; there is no doubt that the specimen is the same he donated.

As to the place from which the bones came, he remembers having been informed that the workmen had gotten through the floor of the dock into a sort of quicksand when the bones were encountered. Owing to this quicksand, the rudder-pit had to be concreted afterward to prevent entrance into the dock of water and sand. The bones must have been just beneath the tosca, for a small quantity of tosca was adhering to them. No animal bones were found in the pit or in this dock, and Mr. Junor has no recollection that any other human bones came to sight. He did not examine the site from which the skull fragments given him were supposed to have come. No inquiries were made of the laborers.

Mr. Clark states in his letter that the skull "was found at the commencement of the Rudder Pit at dock bottom"; he "is quite sure the skull was found at the Rudder Pit and under tosca"; and "it was the only one found in that locality, but there was another skull found in the sand at the entrance to Dock No. 4," which disappeared without his knowing what became of it. Further, he does not remember whether or not there were any loose bones.

Mr. Junor adds the following note:

"Clark told me the men had been playing 'bochas' with the skull; evidently they had only been tossing the one skull backward and

---

[1] A game played extensively in Argentina with wooden balls, which are rolled or thrown to strike and group with others.

Here are shown the exposed walls of the Pampean terrane and alluvium, the drain leading to the sump, or well, and the pumping machinery close to the side walls of the gate.

Here are shown the walls of the Pampean formation and alluvium still exposed after the concrete floor had been laid, with the sump and pumping machinery as in the view above.

EXCAVATION FOR DRY DOCK

(From original photographs in office of C. H. Walker & Co., Buenos Aires.)

FINISHED DRY DOCK

The rudder-pit is here seen in the place occupied by the sump during construction.   (From original photograph in office of C. H. Walker & Co., Buenos Aires.)

forward.   I supposed they had actually played at 'bochas,' which would require half a dozen skulls, hence my belief that five or six skulls had been found, whereas only one was found in the Rudder Pit."

The foregoing meager information concerning the circumstances of the find was all that could be gathered.   This differs from that published by Professor Ameghino mainly in that the specimen is represented to have been found not in the lowest but in the upper part of the rudder-pit, and in sand instead of clay; also, that another human skull was found in sand at Dock No. 4, but nothing more definite is known as to its exact position.   Finally, the excavations for Dock No. 1 yielded no bones of animals.   In Dock No. 3 a glyptodon skeleton was found in the tosca, and there was also a mastodon tusk at about the same level (Simpson).

Mr. Willis and the writer visited the dry dock, saw the rudder-cavity, and later on, through the courtesy of Mr. Simpson, they were able to obtain the photographs reproduced in the accompanying illustrations (pls. 47, 48), which show the condition of the dry dock at the time the rudder-pit was being excavated.

The specimen donated to the Museo Nacional by Mr. Junor was discovered in recent years in the collections of that institution by Professor Ameghino, studied minutely by him, and described[1] as a remnant of the skull of *Diprothomo platensis*, from the standpoint of evolution a second or premediate forerunner of man, who lived in the Lower Pliocene.

This far-reaching determination Professor Ameghino supports by an exhaustive geologic and comparative anatomic dissertation, the principal items of which are given in the following paragraphs.

As mentioned before, Professor Ameghino states that the fragments of the skull came from the lowest portion of the rudder-pit and that they lay in a stratum of gray clay below the tosca, which constitutes in part the floor of the dry dock, and below a subjacent layer of quartzy sand.   The gray clay he identifies as belonging to the uppermost portion of the Pre-Ensenadean stratum, which is the most inferior part of the Pampean formation (p. 120), and belongs to the base of the Pliocene.[2]

---

[1] Ameghino, F., Le *Diprothomo platensis*, un précurseur de l'homme du pliocène inférieur de Buénos Aires; in *Anal. Mus. Nac. Buenos Aires*, XIX (ser. iii, t. XII), 1909, pp. 107-209.   Pages cited below follow the work here cited.

[2] On page 116 the lower part of the Pliocene is represented as occupied by the Post-Puelchean hiatus, while in the table on page 124 the lowest part of the Pliocene is given to the Pre-Ensenadean, and the Post-Puelchean hiatus occupies the first part of the Miocene.

In a table on page 124 Professor Ameghino gives the stratigraphic position of the *Diprothomo* and also of other ancient remains relating to early man or his predecessors in Argentina.   It is as follows:

Quaternary.		Recent.	
		Platean. Querandine transgression.	
		Post-Lujanean hiatus.	*Homo sapiens.*
		Lujanean, and corresponding marine transgression.	Arrecifes and Ovejero skulls.
		Post-Bonaerean hiatus.	
PLIOCENE.	**Pampean formation.**	Bonaerean { superior.	Fontezuelas, Arroyo de Frias, Samborombón.
		Bonaerean { inferior.	Baradero, Chocorí.
		Belgranean transgression.	Industrial vestiges only.
		Post-Ensenadean hiatus.	
		Cuspidal Ensenadean.	*Homo pampæus,* Miramar (La Tigra), Necochea.
		Inter-Ensenadean transgression.	
		Basal Ensenadean.	Industrial vestiges only.
		Pre-Ensenadean.	*Diprothomo platensis* (vault of a skull).
Upper Miocene.	**Araucanian formation.**	Post-Puelchean hiatus.	
		Puelchean, and corresponding transgression.	Industrial vestiges only.
		Post-Chapalmalean hiatus.	
		Chapalmalean.	Industrial vestiges only.
		Post-Hermosean hiatus.	
		Hermosean.	*Tetraprothomo argentinus* (atlas, femur).

As to the name adopted for the new being, Professor Ameghino says (pp. 126–127): "The piece of skull found in the port of Buenos Aires is of a different genus from *Homo,* but one which by all its characteristics should, equally with the *Tetraprothomo,* be considered a real precursor of man, though nearer to man than the fourth forerunner. . . . I adopt for this new genus the name of *Diprothomo,* which I created in 1884[1] for the designation of the second precursor of man, the characteristics of which I have equally [with those of the *Tetraprothomo*] constructed by calculation.   The species I qualify as *platensis,* to recall the provenience of the specimen from below the bed of the great stream, the Rio de la Plata."

The line of evolution leading to man, and the position therein of the *Diprothomo, Tetraprothomo,* and the various other remains of South America attributed to early man, are, according to Professor Ameghino—it may be repeated—as follows:

---

[1] Filogenia, 1884, p. 380.

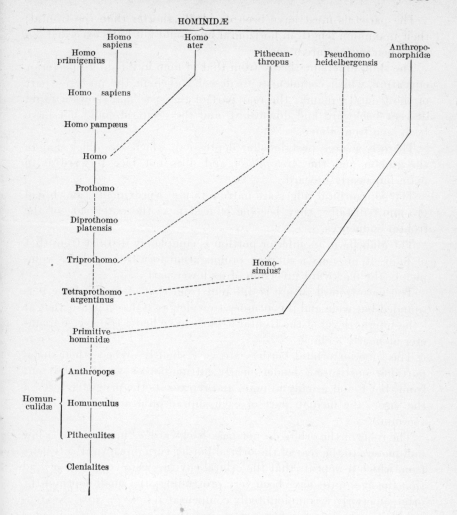

As to the anatomic features of the *Diprothomo* skull, Professor Ameghino advances in substance the following:

The skull was of small size, below the mean of human crania. Its capacity could not have exceeded 1,100 c.c., its greatest length 17 cm., and its greatest breadth 11.8 cm.

The skull possesses a very low vault; its front is so low that it surpasses in this feature the Neanderthal cranium.

The skull was narrow, with the parieties almost parallel and with a contour like that in the *Arctopitheci;* its greatest lateral diameter did not fall in the region of the parietals as usual but on the frontal; it was highly dolichocephalic, its breadth-length index being about *69.*

The frontal is very long and narrow, as in some of the lower Primates.

The parietals must have been decidedly shorter than the frontal; their maximum length in horizontal line could not have exceeded 5.5 cm., their surface arc 9 cm.

The skull differs markedly from that of man in its antero-posterior curvature, which commences to descend even in the posterior part of the frontal squama; the rear part of the specimen shows a rapid descent backward and downward, and the occipital could not have been seen from above.

There is a large postglabellar depression, which resembles that in the gibbon and the *Arctopitheci* and does not face forward as in man, but nearly upward.

The supraorbital ridges are narrow (5 mm.) proximally, and broad (15 mm.) distally; they become effaced near the outer side of the frontal eminences.

The glabella in its inferior portion is completely distinct from that of man; it presents a marked prolongation forward and lacks completely the backward inversion of its lower part.

The naso-frontal suture is different from that of man; above it is rounded but wide and it continues to widen as it descends, so that at "the inferior level of the frontal it must have had a transverse diameter of nearly 3 cm.".

The superior orbital borders are very slightly arched; their distal portions constitute a slender, nearly cutting border, which is different from that found usually in man, and represents the primitive form of the visor; the median part of each supraorbital arch is very stout (15 mm.).

The roofs of the orbits do not pass backward, as in man, but a few millimeters to the rear of the orbital border turn downward, a feature from which it appears that the orbital cavities were very shallow and that the eyes must have been very protruding; the small depth of the orbit superiorly was undoubtedly compensated for by a greater extension forward of each inferior part and there was pronounced facial prognathism; the orbital cavities were large, placed far forward. and visible to a great extent when looking at the skull from above.

The fronto-nasal suture is situated very nearly at the level of the superior border of the orbits; a horizontal line crossing it passes through the superior orbital borders.

The surface of insertion of the nasal bones looks forward; the nasal bones extended straight from the frontal and were very strong as well as very wide; also, they were directed forward with only feeble inclination downward.[1]

---

[1] For numerous additional details of less importance the reader must be referred to the original.

The writer reached Buenos Aires with the foregoing data before him and in consequence thereof with very eager expectations. But when the specimen itself was placed before him by Professor Ameghino there followed a rapid disenchantment, for it proved at every point antagonistic to the notion that had been formed of it on the basis of the published data. The first impression, in fact, amounted to incredulity as to its being the relic in question.

However, the specimen was subjected to a prolonged study and comparison, which resulted as follows:

The bone is a portion of the skull of an adult male, who, judging from the state of the coronal suture, was approaching middle age.

It is free from all deformation, effected either during life or posthumously.

It presents no pathologic features with the exception of an old shallow moderate-sized scar, situated just above the left frontal eminence. The injury left a trace also on the ventral surface of the bone, but is of no importance in the considerations that follow.

The surface of the fragment seems to show a slight calcareous covering and is discolored (wax to limonite-brown), particularly on the inside. The stained parts possess some luster, especially ventrally. The surfaces of the frontal sinuses are covered by a calcareous deposit resembling a thin pellicle of brown wax. The thin walls of bone between the frontal sinuses and the cranial cavity appear to be wholly infiltrated with calcareous and ferruginous matter, and the color of the interstitial parts of the bone where broken is blackish. There are similar black deposits in some of the cavities of the diplöe in the postero-external part of the free edge of the left parietal and there may be some interstitial infiltrations. Finally, in several of the exposed diplöe cells of the broken edge of the left parietal are seen remains of light earth with minute white crystals, possibly fine sand. Notwithstanding these conditions, the bone when struck does not sound as one highly mineralized and is not much heavier than normal. Furthermore, in ground as rich in lime salts as the pampean loess neither the above-mentioned discoloration nor these deposits can afford any index of antiquity.

Discolorations similar to those presented by the skull were found on numerous pieces of tosca recovered from the not very old strata exposed in an excavation for a new house in Buenos Aires (in Calle 25 de Mayo). They result from the deposition on such articles as calcareous concretions, bones, stone, etc., of ferruginous and perhaps other salts dissolved from the ground and carried by water, and in common with calcareous sediments in the cavities or on the surface of objects need under favorable circumstances no great duration of time for their formation.

ANTHROPOLOGIC CHARACTERISTICS

In a detailed study of the specimen it soon became plain that almost the entire original description by Ameghino had miscarried by reason of the fragment having been placed and considered in a wrong position. It had been viewed not in the indispensable approximation to either of the standard skull positions recognized in anthropology, but just as it lay on some pedestal or on the table. This accidental and faulty position of the fragment had changed the inclination of the plane of the articular surface for the nasal bones, had made the glabella and especially the roofs of the orbits look more forward, had changed a supraglabellar to a postglabellar space and made the same look nearly upward, had caused the forehead to appear much lower than it is and had given the sagittal line a slope backward different from that which it possesses. All these results of faulty orientation combined have helped to make the specimen look extraordinary and primitive, even unhuman.

The first step in the writer's examination of the fragment consisted in placing it in the position it would occupy in the alveolo-condylian plane of the skull. But as this could not be accomplished directly, owing to the defective nature of the specimen, an entire skull was looked for having a nearly related form and the same nasion-bregma diameter, which could therefore be utilized with propriety as a model. Such a specimen was found in No. 52, a modern male Indian cranium of unknown provenience, in the Museo Nacional, Buenos Aires, which not merely presents a frontal of the same length as the *Diprothomo* fragment, but resembles the latter also in other particulars. This specimen was brought into the alveolo-condylian plane, the inclination of the nasion-bregma axis was ascertained and then the *Diprothomo* specimen was placed so that its nasion-bregma axis formed the same angle as the model, with the horizontal (pls. 49, 50).

The results of the observations made were as follows:

The nasion was found to be 6 mm. beneath the horizontal line connecting the uppermost parts of the borders of the orbits.

The location of the point is undoubtedly high, but among 78 more or less modern Indian crania of the Museo Nacional collection, which were examined and measured for comparison, there were 9 in which its situation was equally high or even higher. The list below shows the distance of the nasion in these skulls from the line connecting the highest points on the superior border of the orbits (outside of the orbital foramina or canals):

	mm.
Diprothomo	6. 0
No. 3. Patagonian, male	4. 0
No. 25. Calchaqui, male	4. 5
No. 52. Indian, tribe not stated, male	4. 5

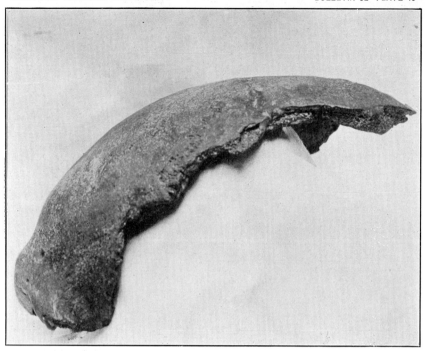

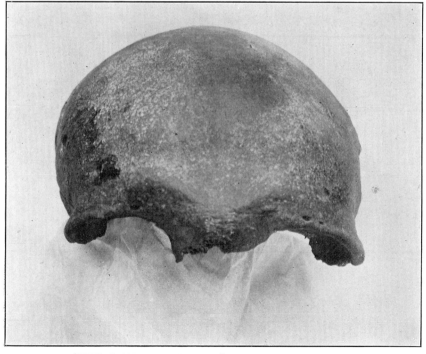

THE ORIGINAL OF THE "DIPROTHOMO" SKULL

Posed with the nasion-bregma plane approximated to that of another Indian skull, in which the nasion-bregma diameter is of the same value, and which shows form-relation to this specimen.

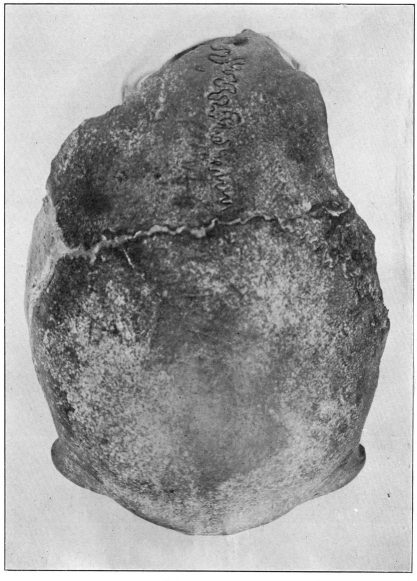

THE ORIGINAL OF THE "DIPROTHOMO" SKULL

Top view; fragment posed as in plate 49.

mm.

No. 13. Patagonian, male 5. 0
No. 42. Indian, tribe not stated, male 5. 0
No. 23. Patagonian, male 5. 5
No. 33. Araucanian, male 5. 5
No. 79. Calchaqui, male 5. 5
No. 49. Indian, tribe not certain, probably male 6. 0

These measurements show clearly that the situation of the nasion in the *Diprothomo* skull is very much like that in at least 15 per cent of the ordinary South American Indian crania.

The backward inversion of the lower part of the nasal process below the glabella, with the consequent nasion depression, exists, and the latter, while not deep, was quite as pronounced as in the average Indian or even white male. Of course, when the fragment is inclined backward more than it should be, both of these features become less appreciable. However, no great biologic importance could be attached under any conditions to these characteristics as found in a single case, for they are subject to considerable individual variation. The nasal process is convex from side to side, as usual in man. It measures 38 mm. in breadth between the supraorbital foramina and was about 26 mm. broad at its lower end, both of which dimensions are often met with in the modern Indian. In three masculine skulls belonging to the United States National Museum collection, a Piegan from Montana, an ancient Peruvian, and a Patagonian, they are respectively, 41 and 26, 44 and 27, and 42 and 27 mm.; while in 11 other male Patagonian skulls in the institution the lower measurements range from 23 to 27 mm.

The fronto-nasal suture presents a nearly semicircular form, as in the majority of modern Indian skulls.

The separation of the branches of the fronto-nasal suture at points 10 mm. distant from the nasion and corresponding closely, if not exactly, with the limits of the naso-frontal articulation, is 14.5 mm. A measurement of the diameter between corresponding landmarks, i. e., between the points at which the fronto-nasal changes to the fronto-maxillary suture, in 50 Peruvian and Patagonian skulls taken at random, showed an average of 12.5 mm., and 8 of the specimens (16 per cent) gave from 14.5 to 17 mm. This demonstrates the fact that the breadth, equally with the shape, of the fronto-nasal articular surface (with the intercallated nasal spine) in the dry-dock specimen can not be regarded as exceptional.

The depth of the nasal notch is somewhat exaggerated by the loss of the nasal spine. The maximum breadth of the articular surface on each side of the spine did not exceed 7 mm., a feature which points to a fairly, but not excessively, strong frontal border of the nasal bones. This border is always the stoutest part of the nasalia, particularly in adult males, though, like other dimensions of the nasal bones, it presents a considerable range of individual variation.

Finally, as to the inclination of the fronto-nasal articular surface, it was found that a line drawn on the left, or better-preserved, side from the nasion to the inferior end of the surface, forms with the nasion-bregma axis an angle of 71°, almost exactly the same as in a Piegan skull used for comparison (see pl. 51) and very much like that found in the average Indian. Naturally, the more the fragment is tilted backward, the more nearly vertical this surface becomes, as would be the case in any other frontal.

Resuming the subject, it is seen that the various characteristics of the nasal notch, particularly when the fragment is placed in approximately the position it would occupy in a naturally-posed head, are not merely entirely human but such that they may easily be taken for those of a modern Indian and in fact they could be even those of a modern white. On the other hand, they present important and in many instances radical differences from similar structures in the anthropoid apes as well as in the lower Primates, including the *Arctopitheci*.

The glabella presents a considerable, though by no means unique or especially unhuman, prominence. It is not massive. The region is brought forward, as can be seen from the broken parts below, by extraordinary development of the frontal sinuses, particularly their median chambers (pls. 49, 50, 52).

The following measurements relating to the protrusion of the glabella in the *Diprothomo* skull will make possible comparison with other specimens: An antero-posterior line from the center of the glabella to the ventral wall of the frontal bone, slightly to one side of the metopic ridge, on the right 22 mm., on the left 20 mm.; same, directly in the middle line (to a point 5 mm. above the foramen cæcum), 23 mm.

The prominence and form of the whole supranasal part of the frontal, though rare, can both be duplicated among Indian crania (see pls. 52, 53). They would not appear as they do in the *Diprothomo* fragment were the distal halves of the supraorbital ridges of that fragment well-developed; as it is, they are prominent over the median half and practically absent from the distal half of the supraorbital space on each side, a condition which accentuates the impression of protrusion of the middle region. And, what is more important, they are not inferior, zoomorphic characteristics. They diverge from, rather than approximate to, the specimen from Primates lower than man, for in these the glabella attains no prominence and no similar shape.

The unhuman appearance of the glabella in the drawings published with the first description of the specimen is due to the position the bone was given, and to the artist's interpretation of what he saw.

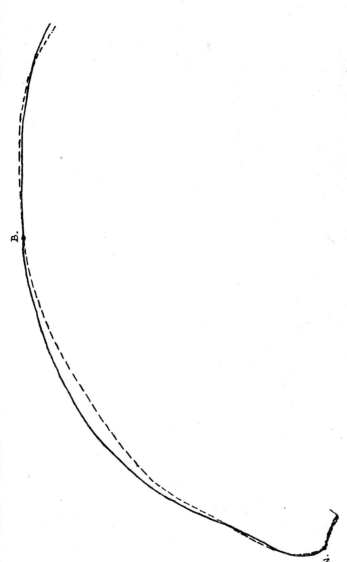

SAGITTAL CURVE OF "DIPROTHOMO" AND OF MALE PIEGAN SKULL

Piegan skull, No. 243673, U. S. National Museum.
—————— *Diprothomo*
··········· Piegan.

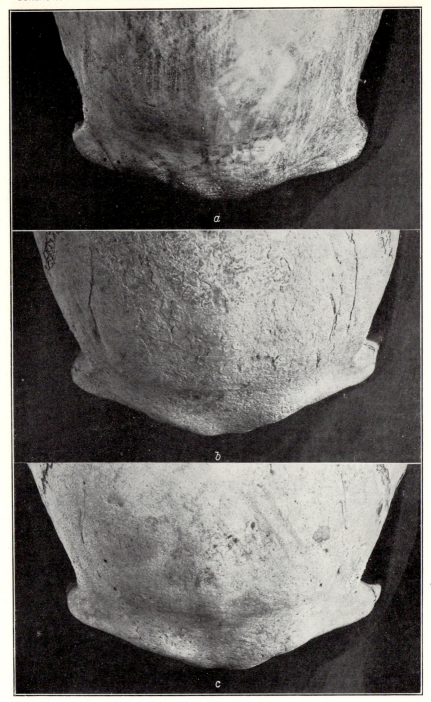

MODERN INDIAN SKULLS—GLABELLAR REGION

a, Piegan (No. 243672); *b*, Patagonian (No. 262149); *c*, Peruvian (No. 266141), all in U. S. National Museum. Comparable, with respect to glabellar region, to the *Diprothomo* specimen. All are posed in the alveolo-condylar plane; the maxillæ and malars are occluded.

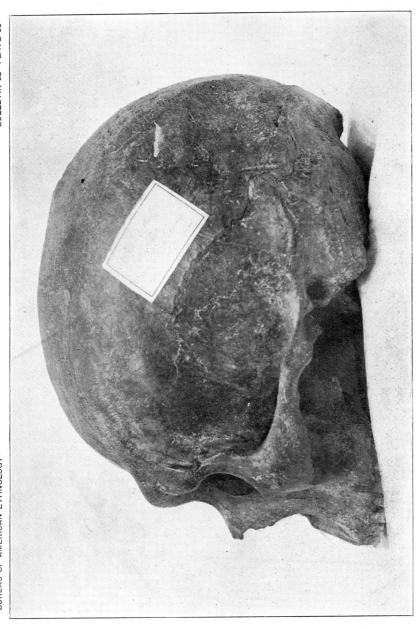

MODERN MASCULINE PATAGONIAN SKULL

From the Rio Chubut. Glabella very prominent and heavy. (No. 262149, U. S. National Museum.)

The frontal sinuses themselves differ somewhat on the two sides. On the right there is only one large cavity with a slight indication of a dividing septum; on the left there are a more median, antero-superior, partial septum, and another more complete wall about 3 cm. from the median line, in all three imperfectly separated spaces. The more median chamber on the left measures approximately 3 + cubic centimeters (15 by 15 by 20 mm.) in capacity and that on the right was even more spacious.

The supraorbital ridges arch, as already mentioned, over the median half of the supraorbital space on each side, following quite closely the curve of the orbital borders, exactly as in many modern Indian skulls. The ridges are prominent but not at all comparable with the heavy supraorbital welts of the Neanderthal and Spy skulls or even with those of some of the Australians. Their prominence is due not to size or massiveness but to the protrusion of the median parts of the outer wall of the frontal, caused by the large frontal sinuses. They would be regarded as quite ordinary in a masculine skull with fuller forehead. They are equaled and exceeded in some masculine crania of the modern Indian and occasionally even in those of whites.

The supraglabellar plane offers no extraordinary feature except that it is somewhat better marked than usual, owing to the prominence of the subjacent glabellar region. It is entirely human and modern in character, and the same is true of the moderate depression above the supraorbital ridges.

The distal halves of the supraorbital borders are normally formed; they are not massive or sharp, just ordinary. There is only a vestige of the supraorbital arch of the lower Primates, as usual in well-developed modern human crania. The *planum supraorbitale* is well-defined, smooth and slanting, precisely as in many modern masculine Indian skulls. In the lower Primates, especially in the adult males, this region is contracted, more or less deficient, and radically unlike that in man.

The lower portion of the cerebral part of the frontal is wide, wider than the average in the Indian, the diameter frontal minimum measuring 9.8 cm. This is surely no sign of primitiveness or inferiority.

The forehead is somewhat low and sloping as compared with well-developed skulls of the whites but is not exceptional if compared with the average masculine crania of Indians, particularly those of the dolichocephalic type. A number of modern Indian skulls were shown by the writer in his report relating to man's antiquity in North America [1] with lower and more sloping foreheads than in the *Dipro-*

---

[1] Skeletal Remains Suggesting or Attributed to Early Man in North America (*Bulletin 33 of the Bureau of American Ethnology*, p. 99 et seq. and pls. XII–XXI).

thomo. The curve of one of these, a modern and otherwise normal Piegan, is shown here in contrast to that of the *Diprothomo* (pl. 51). [1]

The frontal eminences are distinct. In the median line there is scarcely a trace of an antero-posterior ridge and in consequence the superior outline of the norma anterior was quite oval. There is no asymmetry and the whole formation of the frontal squama speaks for its ordinary recent human character.

The frontal bone does not give the impression of exceptional length, nor of exceptional narrowness; in fact, the conditions in regard to the latter particular are quite the reverse, as already partially shown by the dimension of the smallest frontal diameter. The arc or surface measurement from nasion to bregma is 12.6 cm., exactly the same as in No. 52 of the Museo Nacional, and a number of crania were found in the same collection in which it was very similar. In No. 33, the skull of the Araucanian Cacique Panchito, the nasion-bregma arc measures only 11.3 cm., while in Nos. 3 and 13, both male Patagonians, it reaches 13.9 cm. A frontal arc of 12.6 cm. is a very common feature of modern Indian crania, as well as of those of other races. The maximum breadth of the frontal amounts to about 11.4 cm., a very fair average for a dolichocephalic or mesocephalic Indian.

The temporal ridges are rather submedium in development for a male and run at a good distance (slightly less than 6 cm. on each side) from the sagittal suture. This is unequivocal proof that the temporal muscles were developed far less than in any adult male Primate below man, less even than in many a human savage. They were developed only about as much as they are in the modern, even in the civilized, man, a fact which leads inevitably to the conclusion that the jaws of this individual were of only moderate dimensions and that therefore the face could not have been massive or protruding.

In harmony with the distant and moderate temporal crests, the anterior part of the sagittal region shows only traces of elevation or ridge, which terminate at the summit. The latter is fairly distinct, 3.5 cm. posterior to the bregma.

The inclination of the fore part of the sagittal line when the fragment is placed in proper position is very slightly downward, but it is precisely so in the skull used as a model. (See pl. 51; also pl. xv in Bull. 33, B. A. E.) When the specimen is laid farther backward, the inclination of the line of the sagittal suture changes of course and points more nearly downward in direct ratio to the tilting. The posterior portion of the suture shows a descent, such as can be seen in many not unusually long modern crania.

---

[1] To insure accuracy, in the case of the *Diprothomo* the curve was drawn with a fine-pointed pencil along the cast of the fragment, cut in the median line, while in the Piegan skull it was drawn similarly along the nasion-bregma line of a cast of the frontal part of the specimen.

There is every indication that the parietals were of normal modern-human shape and size. The horizontal length of what remains of them is actually 6.3 cm. There is absolutely no evidence that the parieties of the skull were parallel or that the maximum biparietal did not exceed the greatest frontal diameter.

The orbits were of ordinary dimensions. The breadth of that on the right, from the lower extremity of the fronto-nasal suture to the point of meeting of the orbital border and the fronto-malar suture, is 39 or at most 40 mm., which is about the Indian average.

So far as can be judged from their upper portions, the orbits also were of no unusual form. The arching of the superior border is moderate but not subnormal, especially for a male. If a line is drawn from the nasion to the point of intersection of the fronto-malar suture and the limiting line of the orbit, the maximum elevation of the upper border of the orbit above this horizontal is 9 mm.; in a Peruvian male (No. 266023, U.S.Nat.Mus.) and in a Patagonian (No. 262149), neither selected for lowness of orbits, it is equally 9 mm., in the before-mentioned Piegan it is 9.5 mm., and in a Patagonian from San Xavier it is 8 mm. From a line connecting the orbital extremities of the two fronto-malar sutures, the highest point of the border is distant 16 mm.

The roof of the orbits, which received prominent attention in the original report on the *Diprothomo*, presents, when the skull is properly posed, no unusual feature. What appeared to be a peculiar inclination was due to the same cause as the apparent slope downward of the sagittal region, namely, the tilted position of the specimen. If a piece of an ordinary Indian skull corresponding in size to that of the *Diprothomo* be laid by the side of the latter in a similar position, or if the casts of the orbits from this and other skulls be compared, we find that the roof is similarly inclined in both, and also that in most masculine Indian crania which do not show more massive or protruding supraorbital arches the concavity of the outer part of the roof is somewhat shallow. Such shallowness was found in a number of the crania in the Museo Nacional, especially in No. 25, as well as in Nos. 3, 13, 23, and 42, and in numerous specimens in the United States National Museum. There is therefore no ground for an assumption that the eyes were bulging.

Finally, there is no indication, nor any probability, that the lower orbital borders protruded forward, so that they would have been visible from above with the skull in a standard position.

As to the vault sutures, the coronal is ventrally all obliterated but dorsally well traceable so far as the bone is preserved. The sagittal suture is patent both ventrally and dorsally. The serration of both the coronal and the sagittal is well-developed and actually more complex than usual in the Indian. The breadth of the serration of the sagittal increases in width as usual from before backward, reaching 11 mm. at the break.

Ventrally, the *Diprothomo* fragment shows some rather large depressions for Pacchionian bodies and shallow impressions of brain convolutions. The cavity for the frontal lobes is fairly spacious and the frontal portion of the brain was broadly rounded from side to side, as general in modern man. The metopic ridge is very moderate.

Finally, the thickness of the *Diprothomo* bone, ranging from 3.5 to 7.5 mm. for the frontal squama and from 4.5 to 9 mm. for the parietals, is quite ordinary as compared with the same measurement in the Indian and even in the white.

As to the size of the *Diprothomo* skull when entire, the evidence available indicates that it was between 18.5 and 19 cm. long, and between 13.6 to 13.9 cm. broad. It was fairly but not very high; its capacity was surely not below 1,350, more probably between 1,400 and 1,500 cc.

CONCLUSIONS

The sum of the results of the writer's study of the Buenos Aires skull fragment, regardless of its uncertain history, is that the specimen fails utterly to reveal any evidence which would justify its classification as a representative of a species of ancient Primates, pre-mediate forerunners of the human being, the *Diprothomo*. Every feature shows it to be a portion of the skull of man himself; it bears no evidence even of having belonged to an early or physically primitive man, but to a well-developed and physically modern-like human individual. While this individual was in all probability an Indian, a decisive racial identification in the absence of so many important parts of the specimen is impossible. The few peculiarities which the skull possesses are, even if taken all together, of only secondary biologic importance, such as are found in many Indians. The faulty anthropologic status given the specimen in the first report thereon was in the main the result of the before-mentioned fundamental error of placing and considering the fragment in a wrong plane, an incident which only accentuates the need of placing all similar specimens having an apparent or real bearing on man's antiquity, in the hands of an experienced anthropologist.

The ordinary nature of the fragment will be further appreciated from the measurements given in the table that follows:

Diprothomo—Comparative measurements

Skulls (Museo Nacional, Buenos Aires)	Nasion-bregma diameter	Uppermost point on upper orbital border, to bregma.		Point of contact of outer orbital border and fronto-malar suture, to bregma		Diameter between most external points on lateral angular processes	Diameter between points of contact of orbital borders and fronto-malar suture	Diameter frontal minimum	Diameter frontal maximum
		Right	Left	Right	Left				
	cm.	*cm:*	*cm.*	*cm.*	*cm.*	*cm.*	*cm.*	*cm.*	*cm.*
Diproth.	11.6	10.9	11.0	11.8	11.7	10.7	9.9	9.8	about [1] 11.5
3 [2]	12.3	12.0	11.9	12.9	12.5	11.0	10.0	8.7	11.6
7	11.2	10.7	10.6	11.6	11.4	11.2	9.8	8.7	11.2
13	12.3	11.8	11.7	12.8	12.6	11.1	10.0	9.5	12.5
23	10.2	9.8	9.9	10.8	11.2	10.8	11.1	9.2	11.3
25	11.4	11.1	11.0	12.3	12.4	11.3	10.2	9.85	12.9
33	10.4	10.0	10.3	10.9	11.5	11.2	10.3	9.0	11.1
42	10.7	10.3	10.4	11.4	11.6	10.3	9.3	9.8	11.3
43	10.2	9.8	10.2	10.6	11.2	10.4	9.8	9.0	10.3
49	10.7	10.2	10.3	11.1	11.3	10.3	9.3	9.1	near 11.3
52	10.9	10.7	10.7	11.8	11.9	10.8	9.85	10.0	11.9
79	11.2	10.7	10.8	11.6	11.7	11.2	10.5	9.6	11.6

[1] Between intersection of temporal ridges and coronal suture, 11.2 cm.
[2] The principal dimensions of the vault of these skulls are as follows:

	Length	Breadth	Basion-bregma height
	cm.	*cm.*	*cm.*
No. 3, male, Patagonian, not deformed, principal diameters	19.9 x	14.3	x 14.3
No. 7, male, Patagonian, not deformed	19.0 x	about 14.7	x 14.0
No. 13, male, Patagonian, not deformed	19.1 x	14.6	x 14.5
No. 23, male, Patagonian, not deformed	17.7 x	14.0	x 13.8
No. 25, male, Calchaqui, occiput flattened	15.9 x	15.3	x 14.9
No. 33, male, Araucanian, not deformed	about 17.5 x	14.0	x 12.9
No. 42, male, tribe? not deformed	17.2 x	near 13.7	x 13.5
No. 43, male, tribe? not deformed	about 17.1 x	about 13.0	x 13.6
No. 49, male, tribe? not deformed	17.2 x	13.2	x 13.3
No. 52, male, tribe? not deformed	18.0 x	14.0	x 13.3
No. 79, male, (probably) Calchaqui, occiput flattened	16.9 x	14.1	x 13.3

ADDITIONAL REPORTS ON DIPROTHOMO

Between the date of the original publication on the *Diprothomo*, by Ameghino, and the completion of the writer's study of the specimen embodied in this report, a number of publications on the subject, some of considerable importance, have appeared. Regrettably, notwithstanding the weight of the problems involved and the unsatisfactory condition of the data, in some quarters the new "precursor" is being accepted with scarcely any critical reflection, as demonstrated, but, as will be seen, there are also other opinions.

A good abstract of Ameghino's memoir on the *Diprothomo* is given by Rivet in *L'Anthropologie*.[1] There is no discussion of the subject, the reviewer ending his note with the expression that he "limits himself, without regret, to the rôle of a strict analyst."

[1] Vol. xx, Paris, 1909, pp. 573-576.

Sergi accepts Ameghino's main contentions without question and utilizes the Argentine finds, altogether too readily, in support of his theory of polygenism,[1] formulating on their basis a new classification of the human family.

Buschan enumerates the principal finds of Ameghino,[2] and reviews the "Le *Diprothomo platensis*" in his periodical.[3] He accepts apparently the Ameghino reports as for the most part satisfactory, hesitating only in regard to the American origin of man in general and to the continuation in America of the human line from the "precursors" to the Indian.

Senet publishes a résumé of the Ameghino finds relating to early man,[4] without critical consideration.

In the early part of 1910 the specimen is again spoken of by Sergi,[5] who as before accepts in the main Ameghino's conclusions and bases on the existence of the *Diprothomo* and other ancient remains of South America a special classification. The *Tetraprothomo* and *Diprothomo* constitute together parts of the genus *Proanthropidæ*, family *Homunculidæ*.

At about the same time the principal Argentine finds, including the *Diprothomo*, are given, as if they were established cases, by L. Wilser.[6]

On the occasion of the Seventeenth Congress of Americanists, held in Buenos Aires in May, 1910, while the subject was being studied by the present writer, the *Diprothomo* skull was examined also by A. Mochi, and his conclusions have since appeared in a brief publication.[7] Mochi declares that "from the commencement of my study of the specimen I became convinced that the major part of the characteristics attributed to this new genus depend strictly on the orientation given the fragment by Ameghino and were based solely on a complex of subjective views." The specimen was brought, by the help of the remaining orbital parts, into a more natural position, and as a result it "acquired a thoroughly human physiognomy." Nevertheless the skull presents a number of characteristics, "such as the extreme lowness of the vault, the form of the orbital arches and the glabella, perhaps the direction of the coronal suture, the small inclination backward of the nasal apophysis of the frontal bone, etc., on account of which we can consider it as representing a quite particular human type, and one so much more interesting in proportion (subject to contrary proof), as it is considered to have come from a geologic

[1] Sergi, G., L'apologia del mio poligenismo; in *Atti Soc. rom. antr.*, XV, fasc. 2, Roma, 1909, pp. 187–195.

[2] Buschan, G., Das Alter des Menschen in Amerika; in *Die Umschau*, XIII, 1909, pp. 949–956.

[3] Buschan, G., in *Zentralblatt für Anthropologie*, XIV, Braunschweig, 1909, pp. 368–371.

[4] Senet, R., Los ascendientes del hombre según Ameghino; in *Boletin de la Instrucción Pública*, II, No. 6, Buenos Aires, pp. 1–52.

[5] Sergi, G., Paléontologie sud-Américaine; in *Scientia*, VIII, Bologna, 1910, pp. XVI–4.

[6] Leben und Heimat des Urmenschen, Leipzig, 1910, pp. 17–22.

[7] Mochi, A., Nota preventiva sul *Diprothomo platensis* Ameghino; in *Revista del Museo de la Plata*, XVII, Buenos Aires, 1910, pp. 69–70.

horizon much more ancient than those to which belong all the other human remains known to date."

In September, 1910, there was published an answer to the above by Ameghino,[1] some parts of which deserve to be reproduced here in full.

Speaking of the anthropologists who during the earlier months of that year came to see or study the *Diprothomo*, Ameghino states: "I was able to note that the first impression produced by the sight of the specimen was one of surprise; then came reaction and they searched by one procedure or another, to pose the fragment so as to give it or make it assume a form resembling more or less that of the corresponding part of man. To obtain these results I have seen employed procedures which I do not believe to be scientific, for operating thus I could give a human aspect to the callotte of a chimpanzee and an aspect of a chimpanzee to the skull-cap of a human being." Doctor Ameghino does not understand why anthropologists are led to believe that he erred in the orientation of the specimen and, in respect to Mochi's contentions, makes the following double-edged admission: "What is most curious about all this is, that it is precisely those characteristics which Mochi makes disappear by a new posing of the skull which, according to my view, characterize clearly the *Diprothomo*, and which lead me to say that the *Diprothomo* is zoologically, in the broadest sense and without the possibility of a doubt, a genus distinct from '*Homo*.' . . .

"I still think," Ameghino says, "in the same way. I am convinced, or I shall say more—I am almost certain,[2] that the orientation which I gave the specimen in question is, if not absolutely the same at least very close to that which it must have had in life. I have figured it in the highest possible degree of elevation, so that I believe it could be placed still somewhat lower. It will be comprehended consequently that it is not possible to arrive at contrary results except by false posing and I believe that the one adopted by Doctor Mochi is of that nature."

In the remaining part of the paper Ameghino proceeds to prove by further minute examination, with the help of a fine steel wire, that his former conclusion, particularly in regard to the glabellar and subglabellar region of the fragment, are correct, and that "the characteristics which he has given are real and incompatible with a different orientation of the specimen." Particular stress is laid on the defect of the subglabellar part of the frontal process. In his words, "The *inferior glabellar projection* is formed by that part of the glabella or the interorbital prolongation of the frontal which descends

[1] Ameghino, F., Sur l'orientation de la calotte du *Diprothomo;* in *Anales del Museo Nacional de Buenos Aires,* XX (ser. iii, t. XIII), 1910, pp. 319–327.

[2] *"Je suis convaincu, je dirai plus, j'ai la presque certitude."*

below the superior orbital borders. This descending part is developed more or less in man, but it is *never missing*. *It is completely absent in the Diprothomo*."

The conclusion is that "notwithstanding the characteristics which approximate the *Diprothomo* to man, he departs from the same more than the *Anthropomorphs* and the larger part of other apes by the features which I have examined." And the last sentence is especially noteworthy: "The anthropologists can class it in the genus *Homo*, but from the point of view of the zoologists and the paleontologists it constitutes a distinct genus. one which is considerably removed from that of man."

Toward the end of 1910[1] Mochi published his second paper on the "fossil" human remains of Argentina but the *Diprothomo* receives no further consideration. Soon afterward, however, Ameghino published two more papers on the subject of the *Diprothomo* and some of the other "fossil" human remains of Argentina previously described by him. The first of these notes will be referred to later. In the second Ameghino[2] deals further with Mochi's statements: He points out that the Italian writer made his observations (in regard to the *Diprothomo* as well as on the other specimens he examined) too hastily and that he "falls very frequently into errors more considerable than those he pretends to correct." As to the geologic questions, Mochi "treated them superficially and without even a mediocre knowledge either of the facts or of the corresponding literature." As to the more recent strata, especially, his presentation "is a veritable pêle-mêle of ideas, facts, and of almost inextricable quotations, where the facts are tortured under all possible forms to make them accord with the prejudices which here burst from all sides" (p. 62). And there is more of this, for which, however, the reader must be referred to the original. It will suffice to say that the paper is devoted principally to the refutation of Mochi's statements of a geologic and paleontologic nature, Ameghino defending and retaining without any modification his position concerning the *Diprothomo* as well as the other finds he described. To Mochi's statement about the lack of proofs for the great age (Pliocene) of some of the human remains Ameghino answers that, "in closing one's eyes in presence of proofs, one forms for himself the illusion that they do not exist—which has happened to M. Mochi. The Pliocene age of the Pampean formation remains unshaken and consequently the human remains which it incloses are clearly of Pliocene age" (p. 72). As skeletal remains of man of Tertiary age have not been found elsewhere and "abound" in

---

[1] Mochi, A., Appunti sulla paleoantropologia argentina; in *Arch. per l'Antr. e la Etn.*, XL, Firenze, 1910, pp. 203–254.

[2] Ameghino, F., L'âge des formations sédimentaires tertiaires de l'Argentine en relation avec l'antiquité de l'homme; in *Anales del Museo Nacional de Buenos Aires*, XXII (ser. iii, t. XV), 1911, pp. 45–75.

Argentina, it follows that "the place of origin and the center of dispersion of man was the southern half of South America. . . . This conclusion is in perfect accordance with all the other facts that relate to man and in line with his physical characteristics. . . . The very abundance of those human remains indicates that one is at their point of origin and in the region of their greatest differentiation." [1]

In the lines quoted below, Ameghino mentions the discovery of another ancient species of man. In a recent letter to the writer he stated that there has just come to light, in the central pampa, another "*Diprothomo*" and the reference in the publication at hand applies in all probability to the same specimen, but it is now placed as "another intermediary type between *Diprothomo* and *Homo*." This makes already the sixth type of "*hominiens*," profoundly distinct from one another and from *Homo sapiens*, from the province of Buenos Aires, and "these six species of *hominiens*, cantoned in the same country, prove with all the eloquence of facts without appeal that here exists the center of origin, diversification, and dispersion of the human genus."

The remainder of the paper is given to reassertions concerning the antiquity of the various objects other than skeletal remains which have been reported from Argentina as signaling the presence of early man and which Mochi regards in general as of doubtful character. "The material of this kind which has been accumulated at the Museo Nacional of Buenos Aires is so considerable and contains pieces that are so characteristic, that only the blind could fail to recognize therein the hand of man—and the blind are to be pitied, nothing more." And there are announced new objects of this nature, from the Enterrian and Superior Eocene formations; also "eoliths," found from the Eocene onward. These vestiges, as well as incised, cut, scraped, and split animal bones, and objects showing the effects of fire, of similar antiquity, occur in the same strata with osseous débris of the most ancient precursors of the *hominiens* (= *Anthropos*, etc.), "to whom their first industrial vestiges can also be attributed."

"It is seen," Professor Ameghino continues, "that it does not matter from which point of view the case is considered; be it from that of the antiquity and abundance of fossil human bones; be it from that of the variety and great differentiation of fossil *hominiens*, or from that of the presence of skeletal vestiges of man's forerunners and of the precursors of the *hominiens*, which are totally absent from Europe; or be it finally from that of ancient industrial traces— South America possesses more ancient, more numerous, and more convincing documents than those that have been furnished up to this time by the old continent."

---

[1] " *L'abondance même de ces débris, indique qu'on est sur leur point d'origine et dans la région de leur plus grand développement.*"

The anthropologic discussion of Mochi's opinions is reserved by Ameghino for still another occasion and the paper ends without having brought forth what could be regarded as the slightest additional evidence on the *Diprothomo*, or on any of the other Argentine discoveries.

In a short paper, published toward the end of 1910,[1] referring to a lecture given in June of that year, Lehmann-Nitsche gives in regard to the *Diprothomo* skull the following: "It is probable that a human frontal bone discovered years ago in a dry-dock of the Puerto Madero (Buenos Aires) proceeds also [like the remains of the Baradero skeleton, p. 258] from the intermediary Pampean formation; by its characteristics it is distinguished in nothing from the corresponding bone of skulls that are derived from the Superior Pampean and consequently from the actual ones. There is, therefore, no justification for attributing this fragment to a new species or even a new genus of the *Hominidæ* and for calling it *Diprothomo platensis*, as has been done by Señor Ameghino."

At about the same time as the last-mentioned article there appeared an important contribution to the *Diprothomo* question, by Schwalbe.[2] No one is more competent to deal with questions relating to the morphology of man, particularly early man, than this author and his statements claim careful attention. In addition the paper contains an interesting contribution by Steinmann on the age of the formation in which presumably the specimen was discovered.

Steinmann regards the pampa formation as Quaternary. If the skull lay under a layer of tosca, it might be of a young diluvial age, or about as ancient as the Mousterian remains in Europe; but if it was not under the tosca, then it might be of even a very late alluvial origin.

In subsequent lines Schwalbe cites two other opinions concerning the *Diprothomo*. The first (p. 222) is from a letter by Lehmann-Nitsche, in which the correspondent states that "the skull-cap in question has long been known to him but that he was not able to see anything about it which would differentiate it from human." The other quotation is from a manuscript reference to the Paleontology of Vertebrates, by Deninger, to the effect that Ameghino's data concerning the *Diprothomo* are based simply on false orientation of the specimen.

Schwalbe himself finds that first of all the outline figures in Ameghino's memoir on the *Diprothomo* do not harmonize with the photographic ones, exaggerating some of the features. In the second place, Ameghino's reconstructions of the skull are wrong, worthless, and

---

[1] Lehmann-Nitsche, R., El hombre fósil pampeano; in *Bol. Ofic. Nac. Estad*, La Paz, Bolivia, VI, 1910, pp. 363–366.

[2] Schwalbe, G., Studien zur Morphologie der südamerikanischen Primatenformen; in *Zeitschr. für Morph. und Anthr.*, Band XIII, Heft 2, Stuttgart, 1910, pp. 209–258.

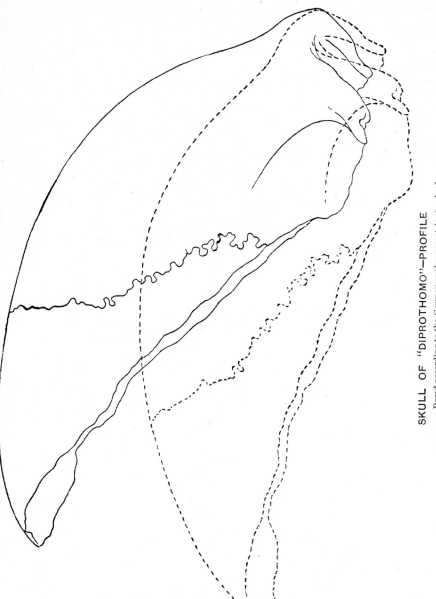

SKULL OF "DIPROTHOMO"—PROFILE

———— Posed according to the German anthropometric standard.
.... As posed by Ameghino.   (After Schwalbe.)

can not possibly correspond to conditions that actually existed. But, what is most important, the posing of the fragment was wholly incorrect and is responsible for the apparent resemblances to lower forms on which was based the genus *Diprothomo*. A number of Alsatian skulls were found to show characteristics of the frontal bone closely approximating those of the Buenos Aires fragment (fig. 50). "The skull-fragment of *Diprothomo* is that of a true man" and the size of the skull was very respectable. The frontal bone is not excessively narrow nor too long, "its breadth falls within the range of variation of the Alsatian crania," and its length, as well as the

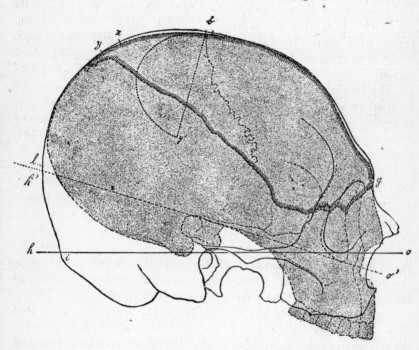

FIG. 50. *Norma lateralis* of *Diprothomo* fragment (shaded, and bounded by hatch-line) and Ameghino's "completion" of such fragment (shaded and bounded by broken line), compared with *norma lateralis* of Alsatian skull (unshaded and bounded by solid line). (After Schwalbe; slightly reduced.)

length-breadth index of the bone, is not seldom exceeded in modern man's skulls. Nor is there any indication that the parietals were relatively or absolutely too short. "All the rest of the features dwelt upon by Ameghino are referable to a *wholly false orientation* of the specimen."

On page 235 Schwalbe gives an illustration showing the differences in Ameghino's posing of the fragment and its consequent appearance, with an approximation of the same to the horizontal plane used by the German anthropologists. This drawing is here reproduced (pl. 54).

In regard to the position of the nasion with relation to a horizontal line connecting the uppermost parts of the superior orbital border, Schwalbe finds that, first of all, its high situation is encountered occasionally in man; second, the point is located at various distances below the line mentioned and on the whole lower than in man, in the American apes; and third, it is also, notwithstanding Ameghino's statements to the contrary, situated below that line (4 mm. as measured on the cast) in the *Diprothomo*. In consequence, the feature can not be regarded as a distinctive generic characteristic, separating the *Diprothomo* from man. There has existed also a nasion depression. The thickness of the interorbital part of the fragment compared with the biorbital breadth, shows itself to be well within the human variation and the inferior frontal construction is thoroughly human in type; finally, the greatest breadth of the skull was as usual in the parietal region.

"The fragment belongs to an entirely ordinary *Homo sapiens* and is equal in all parts to the most recent skulls of man. Ameghino's *Diprothomo* is to be stricken from the evolution-line leading to man." Subsequent examination by Schwalbe on the cast of the skull-cap only confirmed all the above observations.

The only comment the present writer can make on the above by Professor Schwalbe is that he agrees with every word written.

Another critical reference to the *Diprothomo* is made by Friedemann, which appeared toward the end of 1910, in the *Zeitschrift für Ethnologie*.[1] After giving the principal points from Ameghino's report on the *Diprothomo* and after pointing out the discord that exists between Ameghino and other observers in regard to the age of the formations in which the fragments were discovered, Friedemann says: "When Ameghino's data are tested critically there arises at once the question as to the orientation of the specimen. . . . Ameghino regards the callotte as it lies on the table, as 'naturally posed,'" the specimen assuming in this way the characteristics which Ameghino describes. When the fragment is properly elevated, "a considerable part of the given pithecoid features disappear;" . . . the nasofrontal articulation "is then directed forward no more than backward." The nasion is situated (on the cast) 3 mm. beneath the horizontal line connecting the uppermost planes of the border of the orbits.

On the basis of the foregoing and other considerations Friedemann reaches the result that for the present "we are not justified to see in the *Diprothomo* a proof for the correctness of the opinions expressed by Ameghino; it is much more possible to accept the probability that the skull-cap of the *Diprothomo* does not differ much from that of recent man."

---

[1] Friedemann, M., Vorlage eines Gipsabgusses des Schädeldaches von *Diprothomo platensis* Ameghino; in *Zeitschr. für Ethn.*, Berlin, 1910, Heft 6, pp. 929–935.

In discussion of the preceding communication [1] v. Luschan remarked that when he first learned of Ameghino's publication on the *Diprothomo*, he hoped that it would pass without notice, in which, regrettably, he was mistaken. "I want to say without reservation that I regard Ameghino's description as completely erroneous (*vollständige Entgleisung*). In another South American periodical there was once described with much emphasis a newly discovered intermediary form between the Amphibia and fishes, which afterward developed to be a tadpole. Ameghino's *Diprothomo* is scarcely a less sad error (*Entgleisung*) and must positively be refused to be accepted for what it is given. When the fragment is properly posed it becomes at once clear that it can proceed only from man who did not differ in the least from the normal average present-time European. Every large cranial collection contains dozens of modern skulls from Europe, Asia, America, and Oceania, from which could be cut out a piece entirely equal to that representing the *Diprothomo*. I place here side by side illustrations of one such piece and that of the *Diprothomo* fragment, and I also beg you to compare the skull from which the piece is derived with Ameghino's attempt at a reconstruction [of the skull of the *Diprothomo*]. . . . I believe that no more words are necessary to demonstrate the absolutely untenable nature of Ameghino's conception."

In the middle of February, 1911, Ameghino published his before-mentioned third paper which deals with the *Diprothomo*. In this he devoted himself particularly to the subject of the orientation of the specimen.[2] In the first paragraph we read: "The anthropologists, in their researches on the orientation which should be given to the *Diprothomo* callotte, continue to employ the method of direct comparison with man, seeking to give the fragment a position similar to that which a corresponding part occupies in man. The particular conformation of this specimen appears to their eyes only in a human form and, naturally, proceeding in this manner they obtain very different results from those which I have reached." And on the second page: "My morphologic conception is independent of measurements and of all mechanical procedure or of that of precision. In this case, having always in mind a perfect idea of simian morphology in general, my eyes judge on the basis of this conception, and I have more confidence in what my eyes see, in accord with my knowledge, than in all the mechanical procedures and measurements that can be imagined. I can turn the callotte of the *Diprothomo* in all the possible positions, turn it even upside down, and my eyes will always see it of the same form. I accept mechanical procedures, or those of

[1] See Friedemann, Vorlage eines Gipsabgusses des Schädeldaches von *Diprothomo platensis* Ameghino; in *Zeitschr. für Ethn.*, Berlin, 1910, Heft 6, pp. 935–938.

[2] Ameghino, F., La callotte du *Diprothomo* d'après l'orientation frontoglabellaire; in *Anales del Museo Nacional de Buenos Aires*, XXII (ser. iii, t. xv), 1911, pp. 1–9, pls. 1–4.

precision, simply as a means of confirmation of what is expressed to me by morphology."

And then, not moved in the slightest in his notions of the case by the various criticisms, Ameghino proceeds to develop an "absolutely exact" mode of cranial orientation or posing of his own. He invents an instrument ("craniorientor"), consisting of a vertical stand with a long horizontal branch and a shorter terminal descending part. The latter is applied to "the central glabellar point," which for Ameghino is the point of intersection of the antero-posterior median line with a horizontal passing between the highest points of the superior border of the two orbits. The second landmark is "the most elevated point of the skull, that is to say, the central point of the vertex." . . . "These two points, united by two lines that form a right angle, give the natural orientation of the skull." The two branches of the "craniorientor" supply these two lines. "To use this instrument, one places the skull, skull-cap, or frontal, on a wooden base in such a manner that the glabella comes in contact with the perpendicular descending branch of the instrument. Then, with the help of two superposed wooden wedges, the specimen is elevated or lowered until the perpendicular branch touches tangentially the central glabellar point. This obtained, the fronto-glabellar orientation of the skull has been reached, and on making the horizontal branch descend, this will come against the culminating point of the skull; that is, against the center of the vertex." The result reached by this procedure is shown in the accompanying illustration. The author states that he "does not pretend that the methods of orientation now in use should be abandoned for this one"; it is only to supplement them, as one more applicable to isolated frontal portions of skulls and one which will give more exact and less variable results. (Pl. 55.)

Oriented with the help of this instrument, the *Diprothomo* fragment "takes an absolutely different pose" from that of the skull of the present man or of the Neanderthal man, and also from that of a chimpanzee. "The vertex falls fully on the frontal, toward its posterior two-thirds.[1] The bregma remains much farther back. Immediately behind the vertex which, as seen, is placed extraordinarily forward, the rear curve of the skull descends rapidly, indicating an extremely low skull, a characteristic of inferior apes. Finally, one sees the enormous length of the frontal bone and the direction of the coronal suture which, instead of being transverse, descends obliquely forward in a form which is seen only in the monkeys and especially among American monkeys, as in the *Eriodes*, *Ateles*, and a number of others."

[1 "*Vers ses deux tiers postérieurs*"; the exact sense of this, as of some other of Doctor Ameghino's expressions, is difficult to determine.]

CALOTTE OF "DIPROTHOMO"

Posed in fronto-glabellar orientation.   (Ameghino.)

The concluding remark of the paper is: "The capital point to which I call attention is that the orientation which the callotte of *Diprothomo* assumes in the *craniorientor* is absolutely the same as that which I have given it on the basis of its morphologic characteristics. This orientation confirms therefore all the distinctive features which I attribute, in my preceding publications, to the *Diprothomo*."

Finally, in a terminal footnote of the paper just considered is found Ameghino's preliminary response to Schwalbe's study of the specimen under consideration. It reads: "At the moment of correcting the last proofs of this paper I learn of a recent publication by Professor Schwalbe—where, by means of comparisons that are simply empirical and with an arrogance that is almost aggressive, he affirms that my description of the *Diprothomo* rests on a false orientation of the callotte; besides which the work is a general criticism of my researches and my theories. My present memoir and former paper on the subject suffice to demonstrate that so far as the posing of the specimen is concerned he is in error. Nevertheless, I intend to counter-criticize the unfounded or badly founded criticism of Professor Schwalbe, in a forthcoming communication."

NOTES ON THE DIPROTHOMO FIND

By BAILEY WILLIS

The supposed antiquity of the fragment of skull which represents the *Diprothomo* of Ameghino is deduced geologically from the statement that it was dug out of the undisturbed Pampean formation beneath the Rio de la Plata in making the hole which was to serve as a rudder-pit in the floor of a dry dock. As there is no witness to the fact that it was actually found in place in the Pampean, it is peculiarly important to ascertain all attendant circumstances. To this end, Doctor Hrdlička and the writer called on Mr. Junor, who was immediately in charge of the dock construction at the time the fragment was found, and who had furnished the data published regarding its original position.

Mr. Junor was found at his home in Flores, a suburb of Buenos Aires, on the evening of May 7, 1910, and we were most courteously received. He appeared to be about 70 years of age, of sanguine temperament, still enthusiastic as in youth, and an ardent believer in the antiquity of man in Argentina. He recited freely his recollection of the finding of the skull, stating in substance: The piece of skull was brought to him by the foreman of a gang of workmen who were digging out the rudder-pit. He (Mr. Junor) was very much occupied at the time by duties of supervision of construction and did not see the skull taken out, nor did he examine the place afterward to see where it came from; but he had no doubt that it came out of the well, "probably" from between a layer of tosca and the underlying sand. The skull was said to have been found by a workman, who passed it to the foreman, who in turn gave it to Mr. Junor. The workman can not now be identified. It does not appear that he ever was questioned as to how the bone was found. Mr. Junor remembered that several skulls were found and that the workmen played *bochas* with them. In this game balls are tossed or rolled along the ground, and the skulls were thus broken up until only the fragment that is known as *Diprothomo* remained. But this recollection was afterward corrected by Mr. Junor to the original statement that the fragment alone was found.

On one point Mr. Junor was positive: The fragment of skull was taken out of the well. And although this statement rests on the say-so of the foreman who was told so by a workman, it appears to be the one item in the early history of the find that is not open to serious doubt. How, then, did the hard smooth skull-cap get into the well? Was it originally embedded in the Pampean terrane or did it happen to fall into the hole from some previous resting place?

The writer had understood that the dry dock was built out in the Rio de la Plata and had assumed that the space was inclosed by a caisson, an engineering device for excluding the water, which would necessarily keep out also any bones that might be buried in the river mud. When questioned on this point, Mr. Junor agreed that a caisson must have been necessary, but he could not clearly remember the structure. Subsequent inquiry at the office of C. H. Walker & Co., the contractors who built the dry dock, developed the fact that there was no caisson. The dry dock was excavated in the flat, which was awash with the water surface. The river was easily excluded by an embankment and the great excavation was kept dry by pumping from a sump or well at the lowest point. When the dock had been dug out a concrete floor was laid, then concrete walls were built, and when they were completed, the well for the rudder-pit was finally cleaned out and walled up. It was in digging the well that the *Diprothomo* was found. How it got there can not be positively ascertained, but two possibilities present themselves, namely, that it came there accidentally either before or after the dock excavation was made. During all the work up to the finishing of the walls the Pampean earth and river mud had stood exposed. Any objects contained in the material excavated or in the standing earth exposed at the side might have found their way into the close vicinity of the rudder-pit, if not into the pit itself. Three photographs which show the conditions were chosen from a number courteously shown us by Mr. E. M. Simpson, manager for the contractors; these are reproduced in plates 47 and 48. The first shows the finished excavation with walls of earth all about, a floor of earth and down the center a

"MIDDLE PAMPEAN" FORMATION. (ACCORDING TO ROTH.)

Exposure on Parana at Anchorena, near Buenos Aires, showing eroded surface favorable to accidental burials.

drain leading to a sump or well (later the rudder-pit), above which is the pumping machinery. Plate 48 represents the finished dock and shows the rudder-pit in the position where the well had been. During the progress of the work the river deposits, which no doubt contain remains of natives drowned in the Rio de la Plata, were completely exposed.

The second possibility is that the skulls, skull, or fragment came to the spot where found years before the building of the dock began. The character of the river bank was favorable to accidental burial to a considerable depth. We were told by Dr. Francisco P. Moreno that he, when a boy, used to go swimming where the dry dock now is, in deep pools, whose general character is indicated in plate 56. The photograph represents the bank at Anchorena, a suburb of Buenos Aires, but a few kilometers from the dry dock, where the Pampean terrane is of the same nature. The river has worked out deep irregular holes into which anything like the skull-cap called *Diprothomo* would readily sink and where it would become buried lower than the surface of the Pampean, but beneath recent river mud.

In view of the facts established by the photographs and of the probabilities suggested by the character of the river bank, the writer can not give weight to Mr. Junor's belief that the unknown workman who found the skull and gave it to the foreman who in turn gave it to Mr. Junor really dug it out of undisturbed ancient Pampean.

CONCLUDING REMARKS ON THE DIPROTHOMO

By ALEŠ HRDLIČKA

The new publications on the subject referred to in preceding pages are found to necessitate no change in the remarks and conclusions already presented by the writer. Schwalbe has considered the specimen from some additional standpoints, but the results are always the same: they show the fragment to be simply human and much like the corresponding part of a modern human skull. As to Ameghino's additional papers, they only tend to make the case against his farfetched notions the stronger by accentuating the defects of these notions. Accurate measurements and the relations of such measurements have in anthropology, as elsewhere, a fixed, solid value, which can not be lightly passed over. And as to the orientation of the fragment, if, as Ameghino objects, posing it like the corresponding part in man makes it look human, where then is the difference? Could the same part of any extinct or fossil primate or even that of the really ancient European man be made, no matter how posed, in shape and size so much like that of the modern man that it could not be readily distinguished by anthropologists of experience? The new method of orientation is radically wrong because it utilizes as a determinative a point (the glabella) which is capable of acting as a fulcrum on which the axis of the skull may be turned at will, or according to individual view, so long as the point of the true summit of the skull is not defined (as is often the case) with unmistakable precision. The position given to the fragment by Ameghino, particularly with the help of the "craniorientor," makes of it really a monstrosity, impossible both paleontologically and anthropologically. The only service the new appliance has indirectly rendered is that it has led to the publication of the most natural illustration of the Buenos Aires specimen presented (pl. 55) up to the time this illustration appeared.

TETRAPROTHOMO ARGENTINUS

HISTORY AND REPORTS

In 1887 F. Ameghino announced the discovery,[1] in the barranca of Monte Hermoso, a low cliff facing the sea in the central part of the coast of the Province of Buenos Aires, of vestiges of "a being, more or less closely related to actual man, who was a direct forerunner of the existing humanity." These vestiges consisted of fragments of "tierra cocida, fogónes [fire places]—some of the latter vitrified and having the appearance of scoria—split and burnt bones [of animals], and worked stones." In 1889 Professor Ameghino reached definitely the conclusion that such remains can not be the work of a being of the same species or of the same genus as the present man, but belong to "a precursor of man."[2]

Independently of the above, some time in the eighties (the exact date is not known), an employee of the Museo de La Plata made for that institution at Monte Hermoso a collection of fossils. Among these bones was found at the museum a humanlike atlas of subaverage size. When this átlas was seen by Señor Moreno, at that time the director of the La Plata Museum, it was still partially enveloped in yellowish or yellowish-brown earth.[3] Soon after its discovery the specimen was forgotten and lay unnoticed in the collections of the museum for many years, until finally it was observed accidentally by Santiago Roth, who freed it from the "loess," and seeing that the specimen appeared to be a human atlas of small size transferred it to the anthropologic collections of the institution. There again it lay for several years longer without receiving any special consideration,

---

[1] Monte Hermoso, Buenos Aires, 1887, 10 pp.

[2] Contribución al conocimiento de los mamíferos fósiles de la República Argentina; in *Act. Acad. Nac. Córdoba*, VI, Buenos Aires, 1889, p. 87.

[3] Ameghino (Tetraprothomo, etc., p. 174) says that the specimen was "still in a portion of the rock" but Señor Moreno expressly stated to the writer that it was in "earth" which held together but was not solidified. Whether or not this earth was sandy can not now be definitely determined. The fact that later the bone was cleanly disengaged from the mass shows further that it could not have been in "rock." Roth speaks of the bone as having been enveloped in "loess" (in Lehmann-Nitsche, Nouvelles recherches, etc., p. 386).

until a new discovery at Monte Hermoso attracted to it the attention of Ameghino. Through Lehmann-Nitsche Ameghino borrowed the specimen, studied it in detail, and published a description of it in his memoir on the *Tetraprothomo*, identifying the bone with that particular hypothetic genus of man's precursors.

At the same time a study of the atlas was undertaken and published by Lehmann-Nitsche,[1] who in turn attributed it to "a Tertiary primate of Monte Hermoso, the *Homo neogæus*."

Sometime during the early years of the present century Carlos Ameghino discovered in the same barranca of Monte Hermoso a peculiar bone, which eventually was referred to a supposed ancient parental form of man. It was a portion of the fossil femur of a being which F. Ameghino identified as a very ancient forerunner of man, the *Tetraprothomo argentinus*.

It was this specimen which excited interest in the Monte Hermoso atlas and which is responsible for the establishment of the new genus of Tertiary (Miocene) Primates or "precursors."

THE REPORTED FEATURES OF THE ATLAS

"This bone," according to Ameghino,[2] "does not belong to the genus *Homo*, but on the other hand it approximates so closely to the atlas of man that it doubtless comes from a form which was man's precursor, and this could have been no other than the *Tetraprothomo*."

As to the relatively considerable size of the bone, "comparisons have shown that other nonarboreal mammals which present a femur of approximately the same dimensions as the *Tetraprothomo*, have an atlas as large or even larger than the latter. It is also to be borne in mind that the femur of the *Tetraprothomo* indicates a body proportionately stouter than that of man, so that such a being had also a proportionately larger atlas. To this it should be added that some results of an examination of the bone demonstrate independently of the preceding consideration that it must have supported a skull proportionately larger than that of man, from which it is inferred that the atlas also must have been of proportionately greater size. Furthermore, if a correspondence in size is established between the atlas of a young chimpanzee of only 56 cm. in height, the atlas which I suppose to be that of *Tetraprothomo*—a being that according to the femur should have reached the stature of 1.05 to 1.10 m., and the atlas of a man of medium stature, it will readily be seen that the fossil atlas of Monte Hermoso corresponds perfectly with the height and corpulency of the *Tetraprothomo argentinus*. . . .

"Of course, the possibility that the two pieces, the femur and the atlas, may pertain to two animals specifically and even generically

---

[1] Nouvelles recherches, etc., p. 386 et seq.
[2] Tetraprothomo, etc., p. 174 et seq.

distinct, can not be absolutely excluded, but this would imply the existence at Monte Hermoso of *two precursors of man*, which appears to me for the present, I shall not say impossible, but highly improbable; and until further proofs appear to the contrary it seems to me more logical and prudent to refer the two specimens to but one form."

As to the morphologic peculiarities of the atlas, Ameghino expresses, to start with, the opinion that the atlas is beyond doubt "not only one of a primate, but it belongs to the same group which includes man and the anthropomorphs." It is further seen that the bone belongs to the "family of *Hominidæ* and not to that of the *Antropomorphidæ*." The features which demonstrate that the specimen does not belong to *Homo* but to a distinct and extinct genus are: The contour of the vertebral canal, determined by the ventral curves of the anterior and posterior arches of the atlas, approximates in man an ovoid figure with its longer axis in the antero-posterior direction, while in the *Tetraprothomo* the figure is elliptical and its greater axis is transverse. "This character is fundamental and separates neatly the *Tetraprothomo* from the genus *Homo*. . . . Certain other detailed features in the shape of the aperture approximate this bone to that of man."

The plane for the odontoid facet is vertical, indicating a "perfectly erect position of the body." The anterior tubercle of the bone presents the same form and development as in man.

As to the posterior arch, a feature which is particularly accentuated is the absence from the *Tetraprothomo* bone of the bridge covering the groove for the vertebral artery. "In the larger part of the mammals and in all the living Primates of the Old World, with the exception of the anthropomorphs and man, this vertebral groove presents itself covered by a bony arch; in *Tetraprothomo* this bridge does not exist, in which it agrees with man and the anthropomorphs. It is clear that the absence of a bridge over the vertebral artery groove is a primitive character and, although there are examples of human atlases in which the groove is totally or partially covered by an arch, these examples do not prove the existence of this bridge in man's precursors but indicate the commencement in man of a tendency toward the formation of the bridge. . . .

"This characteristic is of capital importance in a question of the relations of the distinct families of the Primates. It proves that man and the anthropomorphs constitute a great group or order (*Anthropoidæ*), which has no immediate relation either with the *Lemuridæ* or with the catarhine or platyrhine apes, and which has remained isolated, evolving independently, probably since the Upper Eocene."

Other very detailed features regarding the canals and grooves of the vertebral artery are discussed but the text is so involved that it is necessary to refer the reader to the original.

As to other parts of the bone, "the medium portion of the posterior arch of the *Tetraprothomo* [p. 191] is much more massive than in man, more broad or extended from above downward, with its posterior surface very convex and rough, but with a distinctly formed tubercle. The superior border forms in the median part a curve which is convex upward and the inferior border shows another curve, convex downward, in a manner even more accentuated. In the human atlas the inferior border forms usually a curve concave upward, although there are cases in which the border is straight or plane, but the characteristic convex form of the *Tetraprothomo* is so rare that among the numerous human atlases that have passed through my hands I have not seen it up to the present, except in a single example, and even there not to a similar degree. It is clear, therefore, that it is a case of atavic reappearance of a characteristic which reaches back to the ancient *Microbiotheriidæ* and which has been retained in the diminutive living *didelfids* which constitute the genus *Peramys*.

"In the *Tetraprothomo* the massive form of the median part of the posterior arch, the great breadth of the same in this region, and the great consequent extension of the rough surface which gives insertion to the cervical muscles, indicate that the latter were considerably stronger than they are in man, and that, therefore, the skull with relation to the stature was of notably larger size. In fact, this region of the posterior arch of the atlas of the *Tetraprothomo* is so different from that of *Homo* that it is permissible to suppose it subserved functions which have since become unnecessary."

This lower portion of the posterior arch leads Ameghino to the conclusion that the *Tetraprothomo* possessed a special cervical ligament of which no traces are encountered in the human atlas, except through atavistic reappearance. This ligament does not indicate that the skull of this being was inclined farther forward than in man; the ligament was necessary to insure the erect position of the skull and it could not disappear immediately after this was accomplished. "The great development of the cervical ligament in the *Tetraprothomo* proves that this is really the true forerunner of man; it demonstrates also that the erect position was in the *Tetraprothomo* an acquisition so recent that the cervical ligament referred to has not as yet, or has only recently, entered on the road to retrogressive evolution" (p. 194).

The lateral masses of the atlas with the articulation are, considered as a whole, "essentially human, but with notable deviations which bring the generic difference of the bone considerably into evidence."

The transverse processes, now defective, were very small. The superior articular facets are very different from those of the atlas of man; they are but slightly concave antero-posteriorly and the articular surface is shorter, broader, flatter, and less oblique. Their outline is not reniform but more regularly elliptical and considerably broader at the middle than in man, both relatively and absolutely. The declivity downward and inward of the facets is much less accentuated than in man—"which indicates a perfectly erect position."

The inferior articular facets show fewer differences from the human atlas than the superior ones. They are relatively much less oblique and flatter than in man; "these are features correlated among themselves and with the size and position of the skull, proving that the latter must have been of a proportionately larger size than in man and perfectly vertical on the vertical column."

Other features of the atlas to which considerable importance is attached by Ameghino are the large size of the ventral parts of the lateral masses; greater development of these masses in size and weight; greater breadth of the superior articular facets, and their advance on the canal of the bone. All these features "indicate a conformation destined to support in a vertical direction and in a perfectly natural equilibrium, on the vertical column in erect position, a skull heavier and consequently proportionately more voluminous than that of a man."

Reiteration of most of the above-mentioned points is found on page 205 of the Ameghino memoir.

In a postscript to his paper on the *Tetraprothomo*, Ameghino informs the reader that "this work was already completely finished and the paper was ready for printing, when to-day, the 23d of September, I received from my esteemed colleague, Dr. Lehmann-Nitsche, a leaflet from the *Rev. Mus. La Plata*, xiv, 286–299, without cover, without date, which bears the title of 'L'Atlas de Monte Hermoso.' Under the circumstances scientists will find it incomprehensible that the specimen is described at the same moment and under two distinct names by two authors. In order to obviate incorrect interpretation I am obliged to explain my position.

"I have stated before[1] that I have asked Lehmann-Nitsche for the specimen, which was not believed to be distinct from the corresponding bone in present man. As soon as I saw it I recognized that we were in the presence of man's precursor from Monte Hermoso, of which, as long as 20 years ago, I predicted the discovery. And I have even had long verbal discussion with Messrs. Lehmann-Nitsche and S. Roth to show them that the atlas in question was not identical with that of man. Seeing the little that was made of it, I requested permission to speak of it in my work on the femur, to which M. Lehmann-Nitsche at once acceded."

Subsequently Ameghino concludes: "But all that is of only secondary importance. That which is truly exceedingly important,

---

[1] Tetraprothomo, etc., p. 174.

and in which I am very happy to find myself in accord with Dr. Lehmann-Nitsche, is that he recognizes the *existence of the precursor of man at Monte Hermoso, and the age of the deposit as at least Pliocene.* The Tertiary age of the strata of Monte Hermoso having lately been admitted even by M. Steinmann, the existence of Tertiary man in Argentina becomes a definitely established fact."

The paper to which Ameghino refers above appeared later as a part of Lehmann-Nitsche's "Nouvelles recherches sur la formation pampéenne, etc."[1]

Lehmann-Nitsche goes also into considerable detail in studying the bone and compares it with 16 atlases of Indians of South America. The principal results of his examination are brought together on page 397. The "notable characteristics of the atlas of Monte Hermoso, which are *never* found in the same bone of the South American natives with which it was compared, follow:

"The entire form is remarkably *small* and *heavy;* the posterior arch is extraordinarily *broad* and its external surface elevates itself in the form of a *rectangular ridge* up to the median longitudinal line; the form of the superior articular facets is that of an *irregular ovoid* and rather *short* and *broad;* its longitudinal axis *diverges very slightly* backward; the inferior articular facets are large, proportionately to the whole vertebra."

Characteristics of the bone which were only rarely met with by Lehmann-Nitsche in the material used for comparison were:

"The internal border of the superior articular facets is *very slightly* outside the vertical line of the corresponding border of the inferior facets; and the posterior root of the transverse apophysis is *notably more developed* than the anterior."

The author then enumerates the differences and similarities between the Monte Hermoso atlas and those of the orang and gorilla; it is to be regretted that these comparisons apply, however, to only a single atlas of each of the anthropoids.

Among additional points of difference between the Monte Hermoso atlas and that of the South American Indian, there are, according to Lehmann-Nitsche, characteristics of inferiority in the former which denote a being with a brain but slightly developed. Nevertheless, the specimen is found "to approximate more closely the atlas of modern man than that of the anthropoids."

On the basis of the morphologic and geologic considerations, Lehmann-Nitsche proposes to regard the "Tertiary primate of Monte Hermoso" as a particular species of man "which certainly was very primitive and must have approached very closely the *Pithecanthropus,* and names it the *Homo neogæus.*

---

[1] In *Rev. Mus. La Plata,* XIV, Buenos Aires, 1907, pp. 386–410. Some copies of the part on the atlas were distributed preliminarily in leaflet form, as mentioned by Ameghino.

On pages 403–407 are given a number of very detailed supplementary notes on the bone, for which the reader is referred to the original, and on page 408 is given a table of measurements of the bone with comparative data on the 16 Indian atlases and the one atlas each of an orang and a gorilla, with which it was contrasted.

THE REPORTED FEATURES OF THE MONTE HERMOSO FEMUR

The first and so far the only report on this specimen is by F. Ameghino.[1]

As mentioned before, the history of the find is restricted to the statement that "this bone was encountered by Carlos Ameghino in his last voyage to Monte Hermoso."

The bone is that of the left side and its upper end is missing. The existing part, according to Ameghino, "measures 16 cm. in length but the entire bone must have measured about 19 cm. . . .

"The agreement in conformation between this bone and the corresponding one of man, is nearly perfect, although this great similarity does not become at once perceptible because of the enormous differences in size.

"The similarity of the specimen to the human femur appears evident in the different curves of the bone, in the femoral torsion, in the development of the linea aspera and its inferior bifurcation, in the subtriangular outline in section of the median part of the body of the bone, in the broadening and the anterio-posterior flattening of its inferior extremity, in the inversion inward of the internal condyle and the larger size of the same, etc."

It would be difficult to give a correct abstract of all the morphologic and comparative details given by Ameghino in his description of the bone and therefore for the less essential data the reader must be referred to the original. The principal items accentuated are as follows:

It is assumed that the head and neck of the bone were disposed as in man, and that the latter formed a similarly obtuse angle with the body of the bone.

The great trochanter was not of the quadrate form, as in *Homo*, but more like that of *Homunculus*.

The trochanteric fossa (which receives relatively little attention) "presents the same vascular perforations as in the human femur, and as in this is prolonged backward in the form of a canal or groove, which is quite extended and has a concave base in the transverse direction."

The minor trochanter is of large size, as in man, but shows a different form and is located on the internal border of the bone. "In

---

[1] Notas preliminares sobre el *Tetraprothomo argentinus* un precursor del hombre del mioceno superior de Monte Hermoso; in *Anal. Mus. Nac. Buenos Aires*, XVI (ser. iii, t. IX), 1908, pp. 108 et seq.

this position of the minor trochanter and of the lateral depression that accompanies the same, the *Tetraprothomo* constitutes a perfect transition between the *Homunculus* and *Homo.* . . . A conformation in some cases absolutely equal and in others very similar is met with in many other mammals, particularly in carnivores and rodents. As these are animals which have no parental relation with man and apes, and which besides are perfect quadrupeds, it is clear that the above-mentioned characteristic has no relation with the erect position and that man, as well as the anthropoid and catarhine apes and the other mammals in which it is present, have acquired it independently. . . ."

The posterior inter-trochanteric crest shows also an intermediary form between man and the *Homunculus.*[1]

The lower portion of the bone is intact. "The condyles are disposed very similarly to those in the human femur." The internal condyle shows the same characteristics as that of man, "from which it is deduced that in the *Tetraprothomo* both femurs were converged upward and inward, as in man, and that consequently the being had an entirely erect position."

The ligamentary depressions and roughnesses again are more or less intermediary between those of man on one hand and the *Homunculus* on the other. The internal muscles and ligaments of the joint were very strongly developed.

The external condyle is intermediary in form between that of man and that of the apes. "What is notable is an absolutely identical disposition of the ligament and tendon impressions on the dorsal surface of the external condyle in the *Tetraprothomo, Homunculus,* and *Homo.* . . .

"One of the greatest peculiarities of this region of the femur of the *Tetraprothomo* is the great semilunar depression, which is deep and excessively rough, located forward of the superior part of the external condyle, in the angle which the latter forms with the posterior border of the external surface of the bone. This ligamentary cavity is not encountered as a constant feature in any of the primates known to me, but I have observed it in different mammals of other orders, particularly in rodents and carnivora, and it is a constant feature of all the representatives of the family *Felidæ,* in which it generally acquires considerable size. This cavity is produced by the formation of the large sesamoid bone (the lateral sesamoid of the knee), which develops in the tendon of the popliteal muscle, serving on its postero-external surface for the insertion of fleshy fibers of the popliteal muscle, while on the other side it gives attachment to the strong sesamo-femoral ligament, which is inserted into the rough base of the cavity in question.

---

[1] This relates to the curved and totally unhuman rough line shown on pl. 65.—A. H.

"Notwithstanding all the other human characteristics which the
femur of *Tetraprothomo* shows, the presence of this large lateral sesamoid would have furnished sufficient cause to doubt that the bone
belonged to a primate, if it were not for the circumstance that the
same feature is at times observable in the anthropomorphs, especially
the orang, and above all for the fact that it occurs also, though very
rarely, in man. With the discovery of the *Tetraprothomo* there is now
explained the appearance of the bone in man and the anthropomorphs. It is a case in man of atavic reappearance of a character
which was proper to his more immediate ancestors. . . .

"In the *Tetraprothomo* the anterior border of the cavity for the
sesamo-femoral ligament is prolonged upward in the form of a rough
crest, which terminates in a supracondylar tubercle of an extraordinary development. In man this tubercle is very small or is replaced
by a simple rugosity, but there are cases in which it acquires a development as considerable as in the *Tetraprothomo*. It is therefore a
case, as in the preceding instance, of atavic regression. This tubercle
serves for the insertion of the medio-superior tendon of the external
gemellus. Now, the great development of the tubercle and the rugosi-
ties which accompany it up to the corresponding ligamentary impression of the external tuberosity indicate great development of this
muscle. It has already been seen above that the gemellus internus
was also much developed.

"This great development of the gemelli or gastrocnemii muscles is
exceedingly important, because the latter exercise the principal rôle
in biped progression. It is for this reason that they present greater
development in man than in any other mammal, without excluding
the anthropomorphs. It is the great development of the gemelli and
of the soleus which produces the enlargement of the limb known as
'pantorillas,' which under this form and at the present time are features exclusively of man. It being demonstrated that the *Tetraprothomo* possessed gemelli muscles as well developed as they are in
man, it must therefore have possessed also real 'pantorillas' and in
consequence a biped walk and erect position."

The inter-condyloid fossa "does not seem to present any differences
from that of the human femur, either in relative size or in disposition,
or they are, in view of the differences which the features show in man
according to races and individual varieties, insignificant and without
importance. . . .

"The patellar and condylar surfaces form a figure which narrows
from the back forward in a considerably more accentuated degree than
in the human femur. This difference is due to the fact that in the
Tetraprothomo the patellar surface is more narrow and that the condyles extend considerably farther backward, from which it results that
the patello-condylar field is of greater antero-posterior than trans-

verse diameter, while in the human femur it is of greater transverse than antero-posterior dimension.

"In the human femur the patellar surface is found separated from the condylar surface by two transverse depressions, sufficiently broad but of little depth; they are the 'transverse fossæ,' which, however, do not interrupt the continuation of the ridges which laterally limit the patellar trochlea. . . . These transverse depressions I have not observed in any of the mammals that I have had the opportunity to examine, not even among the primates, with the exception of the anthropomorphs, and it is indubitable that they are related with the biped and more or less erect position. . . . These depressions not only separate in the *Tetraprothomo* the patellar field from the condylar planes, but they also interrupt the ridges which limit laterally the patellar surface . . . further proof that the *Tetraprothomo* was a biped. . . .

"There are, however, between man and the *Tetraprothomo* some notable differences. In the femur of the latter the planes of the condyles are quite convex and they narrow notably backward, while in man they are nearly flat and in breadth nearly equal in front and behind, which gives to the inferior surface of the bone apparently a very distinct aspect.

"It is clear that the greater flattening of the inferior plane of the condyles and its posterior broadening in the femur of man are the result of the erect position; it is, however, also evident that man did not acquire these characteristics suddenly but very gradually, as a result of a cause which acted in the same direction during a long space of time, and it is natural to suppose that this flattening and broadening of the condylar surfaces continue still in augmentation at the actual time. In *Tetraprothomo* it can be said these characteristics are in the beginning of their formation. . . . The femur of Spy and that of Ovejero occupy an intermediary position between the actual man and that of the *Tetraprothomo* in these respects, but are still nearer the latter.

"The patellar trochlea is the part in which perhaps the femur of the *Tetraprothomo* is more distant from the same bone in man. It differs in the fact that it is farther extended from above downward, that it is more arched in the same direction, and is of a more symmetric form. The lateral ridges which limit the trochlea are more prominent and acute, characteristics which distinguish them from the same crests in the femur of man. . . . With this, the patellar trochlea of the femur of the *Tetraprothomo* extends farther from above downward than transversely, that is, it is of greater height than breadth, inversely to what succeeds in man, in whom it is notably more broad than high, while at the same time the external crest is stronger and more prominent than the internal and the superior border of the trochlea describes an oblique line descending gradually in an inward direction. As a consequence of this formation, the patellar trochlea of the human femur is at its internal side considerably lower than at its external, from which results that the patellar field appears as if located obliquely with reference to the longitudinal axis of the body of the bone. This is perhaps the greatest apparent difference between the femur of *Homo* and that of *Tetraprothomo*.

"However, to this difference must not be attributed more than a relative value. This obliquity of the patellar trochlea is due to the obliquity of the femurs of man, which incline, converging, from above downward, and the tendon of the extensor muscle moves in the same direction; as the patella is enveloped in the tendon mentioned, it is obliged to move somewhat obliquely instead of in a perfectly vertical direction, and it is the continuation of this oblique movement which has produced in man the transverse broadening of the patellar trochlea and its obliquity inward. This is a characteristic exclusively human, which has resulted from the biped progression in erect position. . . .

"But in the *Tetraprothomo* the biped and erect position was a characteristic of quite recent acquisition, which as yet had not acted during a sufficiently long time to be able to modify the form of this femoral region; notwithstanding which, it can be stated that such a transformation has already commenced. . . .

"The femur of *Tetraprothomo* presents 1 cm. above the trochlea quite a large suprapatellar fossa. . . . An equal fossa is seen in the femur of the *Homunculus*, but it is located proportionately a little farther above, besides which it is of smaller size and deeper. On another femur from the superior Eocene from Patagonia, which I attribute to the genus *Anthropops*, there exists an equal fossa but of a larger size and located somewhat lower. It constitutes a species of transition between that of *Homunculus* and that of *Tetraprothomo*, so that it is seen that the latter has inherited this conformation from its ancient predecessors of the superior Eocene.

"The suprapatellar fossa is present also in many apes of the old continent; it is, however, located not only lower than in the apes of the superior Eocene but also lower than in the *Tetraprothomo*. In the femur of man the suprapatellar fossa has descended still lower, until it has become located immediately above the superior border of the trochlea, but it has augmented in extension and diminished in depth. Furthermore, it has lost the subcircular or elliptic outline which it had in the ancient forms, to assume a triangular contour. Still, in the femur of the Man of Spy it is deeper [than in the present man] and its triangular contour is less well defined. . . .

"In the conformation of this region the *Tetraprothomo* occupies evidently an intermediary position between man and the apes.

Moreover, it is easy to perceive that in the *Tetraprothomo* this region was on the way of transformation in the direction toward the form characteristic of man."

The shaft of the *Tetraprothomo* femur presents "all the distinct curves of the human femur" and "a femur which presents reunited the conjunction of these curves can be regarded with certainty as proceeding from a primate of erect position. What is above all surprising and worthy of reflection is that in this case also the human characteristics mentioned are considerably more accentuated in the femur of the *Tetraprothomo* than in that of man. . . .

"The region of the greatest importance is the posterior surface of the shaft, because it carries the linea aspera, which is one of the characteristics which separate the femur of man from that of all the rest of the mammals, including the anthropomorphs, and which stands in correlation with the erect position. . . .

"In the femur of the *Tetraprothomo* the linea aspera in its general form is identical with that of the human femur, differing only by its scarcely smaller development and some other secondary details. . . .

"That being so, as the same organs must correspond to the same functions, the linea aspera of the femur of the *Tetraprothomo* must have subserved the same functions as the linea aspera of the human femur. In consequence, the *Tetraprothomo* was a biped of a perfectly erect position." . . .

The nutritive foramen is situated (with a slight difference in height) and directed as in man.

The popliteal space is convex in the transverse direction, instead of being slightly depressed or concave as in man. "This latter conformation, although very rare, is also observed in the femur of man. . . . There appears, however, in the middle of the convexity a small depression from above downward, with a rough surface and some small vascular perforations. This depression represents the commencement of a process of formation of a depression much more considerable than that characterizing the human femur."

The shape of the shaft at the middle is subtriangular, showing the relation of the bone to that of man. "In commencing the examination of the linea aspera, I said already that this is the feature which gave the body of the bone in the median part of its length a transverse section, with its larger axis in the antero-posterior direction while in all other mammals the section in the same region shows always a greater axis in the transverse direction (I have already mentioned the exception to this presented by some ungulates and also the fact that these have no value whatever in this question)."

On the succeeding pages (152–158) Professor Ameghino gives a number of sections of the shaft of the *Tetraprothomo* and other femora. It seems that some of the figures are not printed strictly antero-posteriorly; however, the bones show but little morphologic relation.

The torsion of the femur "is encountered, more or less accentuated, in all mammals, but reaches the highest grade in the femur of man and especially in that of the negro races.[1] Following man in this feature, come the anthropomorphs, especially the gorilla, which confirm the supposition that the higher grade of torsion results from the passage of the quadruped to biped locomotion. In this respect it would then be interesting to be able to determine the grade of torsion in *Tetraprothomo*. Unfortunately the head and neck of the bone are missing, but there exists the base of the specimen, which gives a sufficient sustaining point for the possibility of assuming that the femoral torsion has been still greater than that in the actual man. . . . This deduction finds complete confirmation in the lateral torsion of the shaft of the bone, to which it appears the anatomists have given as yet no attention, but which nevertheless, under this point of view, is of still greater importance than the femoral torsion determined by the change of orientation, in the inverse sense, of the extremities.[2] . . .

"The lateral torsion of the body of the bone and the remaining characteristics which accompany the same, are encountered only in the femur of man, although not in as accentuated a form as in that of the *Tetraprothomo*, owing to modifications which have been produced in relatively recent time."

Besides the foregoing, numerous other minor features of the bone are described, all of which according to Ameghino point in the same direction—that is, to the relation of the femur to that of man—while at the same time the specimen preserves generic differences. The femora of Spy and Ovejero show a still closer morphologic relation with the Monte Hermoso specimen than with the femur of the present *Homo*.

On the basis of the length of the bone the stature of the *Tetraprothomo* is estimated, as has already been seen, to have been not more than 1.05 to 1.10 m. The carriage of the body was perfectly erect and the body was in relation to the stature proportionately stouter than it is in the present man. The skull was, proportionately to the height of the being, of considerable size, in accord with and in relation to the stoutness of the body; the skull was also proportionately larger than in man.

As to the biologic classification of the *Tetraprothomo*, the being "can not be considered as an anthropomorph." In respect to both the femur and the atlas "it resembles man much more than it does any of the known anthropomorphs. . . . Therefore *Tetraprothomo*

---

[1] The fact is, on the contrary, that it is considerably less in the African and the Americanized negro than in either the whites or the Indians.—A. H.

[2] Expression not very clear.]

is decided to be a representative of the third genus of the family of the *Hominidæ.*" Nevertheless, "the distance between *Tetraprothomo* and *Homo* is from the morphologic and evolutionary point of view so considerable that it causes the presupposition of the possible existence of the three intermediary genera: *Prothomo, Diprothomo,* and *Triprothomo,* whose characteristics I determined many years ago theoretically" (p. 210).

In the last pages of Doctor Ameghino's memoir the preceding considerations form the basis of a new, complex, zoo-anthropologic classification, and also of a far-reaching theory of the evolution of mankind in and its spread from South America.

ADDITIONAL LITERATURE

Additional literature on the Monte Hermoso atlas and femur is as yet scarce. In 1909 Lehmann-Nitsche published a brief communication on *Homo sapiens* and *Homo neogæus,*[1] in which he repeats some of the principal characteristics of the Monte Hermoso atlas as found by his examination. Those features of the bone which in his earlier report on the specimen (Nouvelles recherches, etc., 1907) were specified as not having occurred in any of the other sixteen Indian atlases used for comparison, are now stated unqualifiedly as *never* occurring in any recent atlases, and some of these features are again said to bear relation to small brain development in the species. However, the atlas is "humanoid" and not "anthropoid."

In the same year the *Tetraprothomo* femur and atlas are dealt with at some length by Giuffrida-Ruggeri,[2] but the author restricts himself to a report of the cases and some secondary considerations, without giving any independent critical opinion.

The same year the two finds, with others of Ameghino, are already unreservedly utilized by Sergi[3] in support of his theory of polygenism and serve as a base of a new classification of mankind.

In 1910 Sergi reports[4] again on the latest finds relating to ancient man and his precursors in Argentina, accepts them apparently without any serious doubt, and advances again on their basis his new classification of the human family. The being or beings represented by the *Tetraprothomo* atlas and femur are placed among the *Proanthropidæ.* Lehmann-Nitsche's classification of the atlas as belonging to *Homo neogæus* is declared inadmissible, "because the atlas does not belong to man."

[1] *Homo sapiens* und *Homo neogæus* aus der argentinischen Pampasformation; in *Verhandlungen* XVI, *Internationalen Amerikanisten-Kongresses,* Wien, 1909, pp. 93-98; also in *Naturwissenschaftliche Wochenschrift,* N. F., Band VIII, Jena, 1909.

[2] Giuffrida-Ruggeri, V., Un nuovo precursore dell' uomo. Il "*Tetraprothomo argentinus*"; in *Rivista d'Italia, fascicolo di gennaio,* Roma, 1909, pp. 137-147.

[3] Sergi, G., L'apologia del mio poligenismo; in *Attt Soc. romana di antr.,* XV, fasc. 2, Roma, 1909, pp. 187-195.

[4] Sergi, G., Paléontologie sud-Américaine; in *Scientia,* VIII, Bologna, 1910, pp. XVI-4.

In 1910 also Lehmann-Nitsche says a few additional words on the Monte Hermoso atlas,[1] without, however, adding any new facts. His text reads as follows:

"From the inferior Pampean formation we know but a single small bone related with the human being. It is the first cervical vertebra or atlas, which has been discovered at Monte Hermoso. . . . It does not present likeness with the corresponding bone of the gorilla and orang-outang but is similar to the atlas of the actual man, so that at first view it can be taken as belonging to the latter. Nevertheless, it offers particular characteristics which are encountered only occasionally in the actual human genus and which always occur in an isolated manner, never jointly as in this case. This atlas is, before all, small and stout; its superior articular surfaces run in almost parallel directions, which proves that the bone was not obliged to carry a voluminous brain. The atlas of the present South American natives offers greater likeness to that of Monte Hermoso than any other atlas of other living races; however, superior articulate facets of the present-day atlas always diverge notably, being the supports of a larger and heavier brain. It results from this that the specimen must be considered as proceeding from a human or humanoid being, with tendency toward development into one of the actual human forms, especially that of some of the South American aborigines.

"The difficulty which existed in the classification of the carrier of this atlas whom I named *Homo neogæus* [man of the new world], with the remainder of fossil human remains and with the *Pithecanthropus* of Java, diminishes through the discovery by Prof. v. Ihering, of São Paulo, of which he gave an account before the Seventeenth International Congress of Americanists recently held at Buenos Aires. According to him there existed during the first half of the Tertiary a continent which disappeared long since, connecting eastern Asia with Central America. Moreover, mammals of the northern hemisphere which came to South America did not emigrate all at one time but in two distinct epochs. With this Miocene fauna emigrated perhaps also, towards Central America, the precursors of man, and in this manner the history of man may be most ancient in Argentina while it is most modern in North America. This removes, it is seen, the difficulty which existed in connecting the *Homo neogæus* with the cradle of the *Pithecanthropus*, but I shall not enter into conclusions which, for the moment, would be too anticipatory."

The same year the Monte Hermoso atlas and femur are also briefly dealt with by Friedemann.[2] This observer had seen the originals and

---

[1] Lehmann-Nitsche, R., El hombre fósil pampeano; in *Boletín de la Oficina Nacional de Estadística*, La Paz, Bolivia, VI, 1910, pp. 363–366.

[2] Friedemann, M., Vorlage eines Gipsabgusses des Schädeldaches von *Diprothomo platensis* Ameghino; in *Zeitschr. für. Ethn.*, Heft 6, Berlin, 1910, pp. 934–935.

possessed the casts of the specimens, but had evidently not subjected the case to a detailed study and has nothing to say on the atlas.   He remarks, however, that certain features in the conformation of the lower extremity of the Monte Hermoso femur are not such as are presented by the primate thigh bone.   "This region of the specimen reminds one more of the forms found among the *Felidæ* and *Canidæ*." And, "when Ameghino says that he must keep to his opinion until such a combination of characteristics is shown in another than a primate femur, the case may be reversed and the proof may be demanded before Ameghino's conclusions are accepted, that such a joint surface as that in the *Tetraprothomo* femur can occur among the primates."

In the discussion of Friedemann's paper v. Luschan makes only the following remark in relation to the femur:[1] "To speak here of the *Tetraprothomo* thigh bone appears to me, in view alone of its articular surface for the patella, wholly superfluous."

Toward the end of the same year an important remark concerning the *Tetraprothomo* femur occurs also in Schwalbe.[2]   In finishing his report on the *Diprothomo*, Schwalbe says: "In a following work I shall bring forth evidence that the intermediary member designated *Tetraprothomo* is also not retainable as a forerunner of man."   Regarding the atlas, he makes only the remark (p. 216) that, among the remains of "fossil" Primates in South America, there is "one, the atlas of Monte Hermoso,[3] in the highest degree humanlike."   In a recent letter to the writer, finally,[4] Schwalbe says that in regard to the Monte Hermoso atlas, he can not partake of the views of Lehmann-Nitsche and considers the bone purely human.

Subsequent pages will give the results of the writer's examination of the two bones, atlas and femur, attributed to the *Tetraprothomo* but it will be well to precede that part of the text by a brief report on the barranca of Monte Hermoso by the geologist of the expedition.

MONTE HERMOSO: GEOLOGIC NOTES

By BAILEY WILLIS

Monte Hermoso is a dune on the southern coast of Buenos Aires. It surmounts a short section of the Pampean terrane, which is exposed by wave erosion in a low bluff along the shore.   First described by Darwin, it has since been visited by many geologists who have studied the Pampean.   Its position, remote from other sections of similar geologic constitution, gives it peculiar interest, while at the same time its isolation makes direct stratigraphic cor-

---

[1] Friedemann, M., Vorlage eines Gipsabgusses des Schädeldaches von *Diprothomo platensis* Ameghino; in *Zeitschr. für Ethn.*, Heft 6, Berlin, 1910, p. 938.

[2] Schwalbe, G., Studien zur Morphologie der südamerikanischen Primatenformen; in *Zeitschr. für Morph. und Anthr.*, Band XIII, Heft 2, Stuttgart, 1910, p. 225.

[3] "*Ein dem menschlichen äussserst ähnlicher Atlas von Monte Hermoso,*" etc.

[4] Dated May 15, 1911.

relation impossible. The Pampean terrane, which forms the base of the section, contains a notable fauna and the geologic age of the formation has been much discussed. General opinion places it among the lowest or as the lowest of the divisions of the Pampean, and Ameghino regards it as Miocene. The writer does not consider the age of the so-called Monte Hermoso formation definitely established.

About half a kilometer southwest of the old lighthouse on Monte Hermoso the writer observed the following section (see pls. 57, 58):

RECENT { DUNE SAND, forming a steep grass-grown slope, part of the recent dune formation that constitutes a belt (3 kilometers or more in width along this part of the coast); at the base is a layer 15 to 40 cm. thick composed of gray sand, angular pieces of gray sandstone and pebbles, some fractured by man; marking an unconformity with the underlying formation.

Unconformity by erosion.

"PUELCHEAN" { GRAY SANDS, finely stratified, up to 1 meter exposed, forming a vertical face.

VOLCANIC ASH, in the form of hard white rock, forming a projecting ledge; thickness 20 to 40 cm.

GRAY SANDS, strongly cross stratified, slightly indurated, like those above the volcanic ash; forming an undercut slope; thickness 1½ meters.

GRAY SAND, with small white quartz pebbles and very small black pebbles, constituting a basal conglomerate at the bottom of the gray sands.

Unconformity by erosion.

"MONTE HERMOSEAN" { LOESS-LOAM, a yellow-brown compact earth, which is fine-grained like loess but lacks the columnar structure of typical eolian loess and is distinguished by firmness like soft pipe-stone; lies upon a wind-eroded surface of the underlying formation and has a pebbly structure, i. e. contains pebbles of loess where it fills hollows. These wind-eroded hollows and the filling by loess that contains wind-rolled pebbles of loess mark an uncomformity by erosion like those observed in the Barrancas del Norte, near Mar del Plata; 2½ to 3 meters.

Unconformity by erosion.

SECONDARY LIMESTONE OR TOSCA; locally developed in a thin irregular plate.

LOESS-LOAM OR LOESS-SANDSTONE, a red-brown sandy earth, very fine-grained, very compact and without lines of stratification or vertical structure; 1 to 1½ meters.

BEACH.

The features of this section are shown in plates 57 and 58 (from photographs). It comprises three recognized formations, which

MONTE HERMOSO

General section, showing the Monte Hermosean loess-loam at the base and the "Puelchean" sands and volcanic ash above, surmounted by recent dune sands.

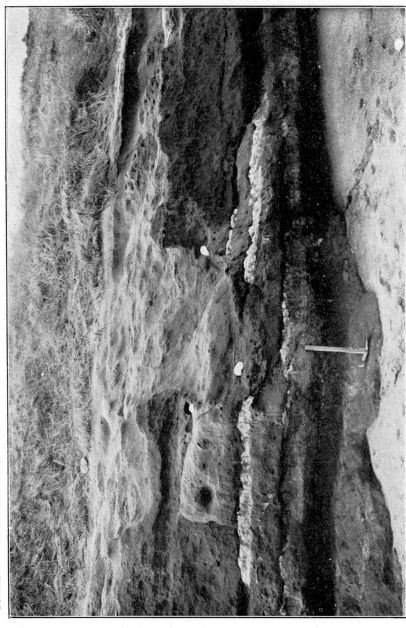

MONTE HERMOSO

Here are shown the "Monte Hermosean" formation, and the unconformity, due to the effects of wind erosion, between the upper and lower deposits of loess-loam. The upper part of the section consists of dune sands, which conceal the "Puelchean" formation.

Ameghino has named Monte Hermosean, Puelchean, and Recent, and which are separated by distinct unconformities.

The Monte Hermosean formation comprises the two deposits of brown earth or loess-loam, which are themselves separated by a plane of wind erosion. The formation is regarded as Miocene by Ameghino and as older than any other exposure of the Pampean.

The Puelchean consists of the stratified, slightly indurated, gray sands or sandstone, both above and below the volcanic ash, between two unconformities by erosion. It is a peculiar sandstone, marked by very striking cross-stratification and uniformity of gray color and grain. The writer regards it as an eolian formation. Later in the season, when studying the section exposed along the Rio Colorado from the delta to Pichi-Mahuida, he observed a very similar sandstone, which might be correlated with the Puelchean on grounds of lithologic identity. It is a thick widespread formation which is regarded as a Tertiary sandstone. The Pulechean, if the same, represents only a thin edge of it.

The Recent formation, as exposed in this section, is but a part of the extensive deposit of dune sands, which has become grass-grown and so fixed, but which does not yet show any signs of erosion. In driving some 10 kilometers diagonally across the belt the writer noted a general similarity to the grass-grown dunes observed north of Necochea, but near Monte Hermoso the supply of sand appears to have been much greater. The belt is very wide and the sand hills are high.

The distinction between the Recent dune sands and the Tertiary(?) Puelchean is not obvious. The two are identical in constitution; they are both eolian and may exhibit similar structures; the Recent formation may be consolidated almost or quite to the firmness of the older one. The unconformity between them suffices to establish the difference in age and is unmistakable when clearly shown in section (pls. 57, 58). Arrowheads or hand-chipped stones associated with the sands would mark them as recent, such objects being common in the belt of sand dunes which the Indians were in the habit of using as a line of march and cover in attacking Argentine settlements. At Monte Hermoso the dune sands and associated chipped stones had fallen from the upper slope onto various projecting ledges and chips were collected from the surfaces of the Monte Hermoso terrane.

Through the courtesy of Doctor Ameghino the writer saw at Buenos Aires 10 pieces of burnt clay which would appear to have formed a layer about 10 by 15 cm. in area and 5 to 10 mm. thick, collected by Ameghino from the Monte Hermosean formation below high-tide level. As stated in describing certain observations on the burnt earth of the Pampean, the writer finds that clays of that formation may be burnt without the agency of man, and he does not attach any significance to the occurrence of burnt earth as an evidence of man's existence in the Miocene (?) "Monte Hermosean."

EXAMINATION OF THE SKELETAL PARTS ATTRIBUTED TO THE TETRAPROTHOMO

By ALEŠ HRDLIČKA

THE MONTE HERMOSO ATLAS

The bone comes apparently from an adult subject.

In color it is now shiny brownish-black, but this is due to it having been treated with melted wax and resin. According to the museum preparator and others who saw the bone before it was thus treated, its color was yellowish or yellowish-brown, "like that of an ordinary earth."

Owing to the wax and resin it can not now be seen whether or not the bone was mineralized, or, if mineralized, to what extent. However, it is not heavy, and in knocking it against the teeth it gives much the same sound as would an atlas from a moderately old grave.

The bone is submedium in size and rather massive, but is in every respect human. An extensive comparison with human and other mammalian atlases settles its human provenience beyond question. It is more or less distant morphologically from the atlases of all the anthropoid apes and still more so from those of the monkeys, while the atlases of the Carnivora and other mammals present such differences that a comparison becomes entirely superfluous.

The specimen looks really smaller than it is, owing to the defective state of the lateral processes. It measures 3.85 cm. in greatest antero-posterior diameter[1] and was near 7 cm. in greatest breadth, exceeding in both dimensions five and equalling one of the Indian atlases from the series of 100 selected at random and used by the writer for comparison (pl. 59). The smallest normal adult atlas in this series measures 3.5 by 6.4 cm. Macalister[2] determined that the female atlas averages 4.2 by 7 cm., while the smallest adult specimen in his collection was only 3.6 by 6.1 cm.

The central aperture even more than the whole specimen gives the impression of being undersized. This is due partly to the optical effect of the rather stout arches and lateral masses which surround it, and partly to an encroachment on its lumen of the lateral masses. The actual measurements of the aperture, however, show that while submedium, it is by no means outside of the range of size variation of

---

[1] A cast of the atlas, donated by Professor Ameghino to the United States National Museum, while seemingly accurate as to form, presents in general slightly greater dimensions than the original. This is doubtless the fault of the artist or of the material, but the fact should be borne in mind by those who may desire to utilize any measurements on similar casts. All the measurements of the atlas given in this report were made on the original.

[2] Macalister, A., Notes on the Development and Variations of the Atlas; in *Jour. Anat. and Physiol.*, XXVII, London, 1893, pp. 519–542.

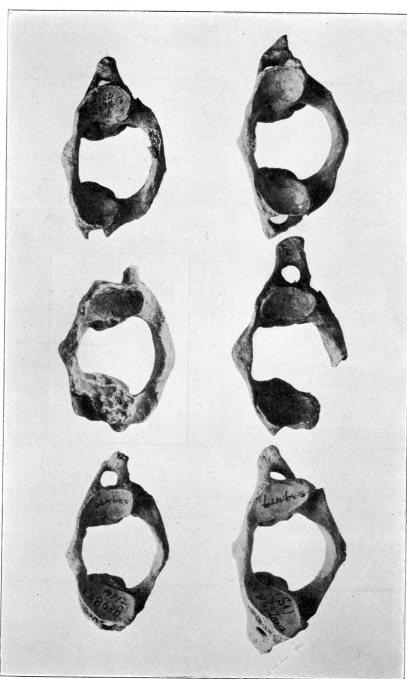

ATLASES OF "TETRAPROTHOMO" AND ADULT INDIANS

The *Tetraprothomo* atlas (photograph from cast) occupies middle of upper row. The other specimens, it will be noted, are of approximately the same size as, or even smaller than, the *Tetraprothomo*.

ATLASES OF "TETRAPROTHOMO," INDIANS, AND APES

Showing comparison of canal in atlas of Monte Hermoso with canals in atlases of four apes and eight Indians. Upper row (left to right): chimpanzee, gorilla, orang, baboon; in middle of next row: *Tetraprothomo*; the rest, Indians, principally Pueblos from Arizona.

the atlases of relatively modern Indians, for in the series of 100 of the latter used for comparison there were found 17 in which the greatest antero-posterior and also the greatest lateral diameter of the opening were either equal to those of the Monte Hermoso atlas or had one diameter equal and the other smaller, and there were two in which both the dimensions were smaller. (See pl. 60.)   A female Calchaqui atlas (No. 7–C in the La Plata Museum) approximates also very closely the Monte Hermoso specimen in this respect.

In shape the central aperture approximates a metal ax and is entirely humanlike, differing considerably from that of any other primate. (See pls. 60, 63.)   The anterior portion is somewhat narrow, owing to marked development of the lateral masses, and the posterior arch is rather shallow, but both of these characters only distinguish the bone still more fully from that of the anthropoid and other apes, in which the anterior part of the central aperture is as a rule broad, while the arch of the posterior portion in most cases is deeper than the average in the human species, and especially deeper than that in the Monte Hermoso specimen.   On the other hand a considerable number of the Indian atlases compared show precisely the same type of aperture.   Absolutely exact duplication can scarcely be expected, of course, in a feature liable to so much individual variation, but the same is true of the aperture of any other human atlas, or of any of the more important parts of the bone.

The anterior arch is entirely human in form.   The tubercle extends vertically over nearly the whole extent of the arch in the median line, as in modern man; in most of the apes it is confined to the lower part of the arch.   From the anterior tubercle to each lateral mass the anterior surface of the arch is flat and more distally it is perceptibly concave, as in most human atlases; a similar condition was found in a baboon (*C. porcarius*), but in the anthropoid and most other apes the anterior surface of the lateral parts of the arch near the tubercle is decidedly convex and only seldom is there a sign of the more distal depression.

The maximum height of the anterior arch, which corresponds to its middle portion, is 11 mm. and its thickness in the median line is 6 mm., both dimensions met with in many modern human atlases.

The facet for the odontoid is large and slightly higher than broad (13 by 11.5 mm.), as in many human atlases with higher anterior arches, but is radically different from what obtains in all other Primates that could be compared, for in these the facet is of greater breadth than height, besides differing more or less in shape from that in man and also from that in the Monte Hermoso specimen.   The axis of the facet in the Monte Hermoso atlas is vertical, as it is in most cases in man, while in the apes it is generally more or less inclined in such manner that its lowest portion is more anterior than the highest part. Finally, underneath the facet, the inferior border of the arch in the lower Primates projects downward as a well-marked point, of which in the Monte Hermoso atlas there is only a trace; in the Indian atlases there is either a similar trace or a total absence of this point.

The tubercle for the transverse ligament is fairly well represented, being, as in a large proportion of modern human atlases, more developed on the right, less so on the left side; and the same is true of the vertical groove on each side between the odontoid facet and this tubercle. The groove here referred to is less differentiated in or absent from the Primates lower than man.

The pit just back of each transverse ligament tubercle (the entoglenoid fossa of Macalister) is of submedium development, especially on the right, but similar conditions are often observed in man. In the anthropoid and other apes there is no pit at all, or it is small and shallow.

The oblique ridge ascending from below the fossa just mentioned to the hinder part of the median border of each upper articular facet, which is present as a rule in modern human atlases but is wanting or only feebly represented in lower Primates, is well-defined on both sides in the Monte Hermoso specimen.

The posterior arch is stout but this feature to the same or even greater degree is quite common in modern man; in most of the anthropoids and monkeys, on the other hand, this arch is more slender than the average in man.

The posterior arch is also high in its middle third, its maximum expanse measuring 12 mm. This is a less common, though not strictly a very rare, feature among human atlases, being equaled or exceeded by 8 of the 100 atlases used for comparison in the United States National Museum and by 7 out of 30 South American Indian atlases examined at the La Plata Museum. Among the anthropoid and other apes, however, the posterior arch is usually of only moderate height and where it is relatively more expanded in the vertical direction, as in some of the monkeys and rarely in an exceptionally powerful anthropoid ape, its height is quite uniform from side to side and is not concentrated, so to say, in the middle portion, as in the Monte Hermoso and other human atlases (pl. 61).

The proximal parts of the posterior arch in the Monte Hermoso atlas are flattened above and below, this feature being characteristic of all human atlases. An approximation to this is occasionally seen in the gorilla, but in all the lower anthropoids and apes the superior and inferior flattening is absent and the oblique sagittal diameter of the arch at these points is smaller than the vertical.

The curve of the posterior arch is slightly less than the average in human atlases, but equals or approximates that of a fair proportion

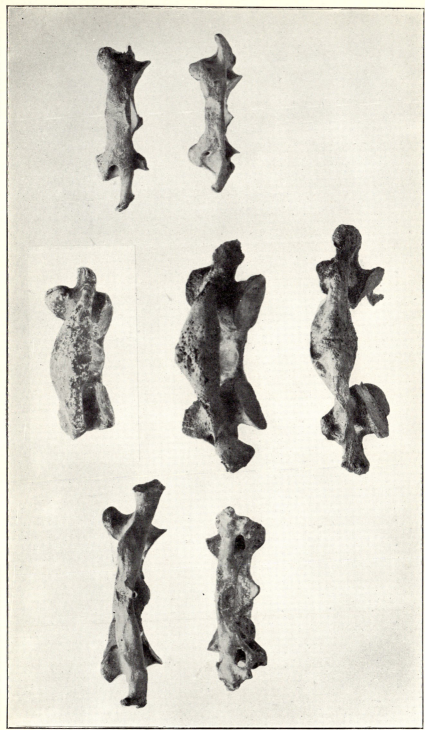

ATLASES OF "TETRAPROTHOMO," INDIANS, AND APES

Showing posterior arch, also inclination of inferior articular facets.

First vertical group: Gorilla (upper), orang (lower); Second group: *Tetraprothomo* (upper), from cast, two modern Indians; Third group: chimpanzee (upper), baboon (lower).

MONTE HERMOSO FEMUR
From photographs of the original.

The results of a critical examination and comparison of the bone failed, as seen in the preceding paragraphs, to sustain the former strained interpretations. There can not be even a shade of question as to the human provenience of the atlas, while the possibility of its belonging to an earlier species of man is opposed by the facts that such species is otherwise still a mere hypothesis, that there is nothing on hand on which to base the new species except a single imperfect bone of secondary anthropologic importance and of wide individual variation, that all of the peculiarities of this bone fall well within the range of such variation in modern human atlases, and that none of its features are more primitive than those of the atlases of Indians of comparatively recent times.

The normal range of variation in the more important characteristics of any part of the human skeleton extends, according to extensive observations of the writer, to from 50 to 250 individuals, adult and of one sex. If it can ever be shown that not one out of at least 100 adult male atlases of the Indians who occupied the region of which Monte Hermoso is a part, is the same as or closely similar to the "fossil" specimen, and if other atlases the same as or closely similar to this, but of thoroughly established geologic antiquity, are found in the same region, then another variety of man might perhaps be established on this basis. It would still remain to be shown, however, by skulls and other parts of the skeleton, that the peculiarities of the atlas are not those of a mere local group but those of a distinct species of humanity.

The writer's opinion, based alone on the structural characteristics of the Monte Hermoso atlas, is that it is a bone from a short, but by no means dwarf, and probably thickset, relatively modern, man. It is probable that the bone was accompanied by a rather massive skull, which is not a rare occurrence even in females among the Indians.

THE TETRAPROTHOMO FEMUR, FROM MONTE HERMOSO

The specimen is a left adult femur, complete in the lower extremity and the shaft, but with the upper end missing to a point just below the greater trochanter (pl. 64 and fig. 51).

The bone is nearly black in color, owing in this instance to fossilization, with a shiny surface. It appears fully petrified. It has the same appearance as the fossil teeth and bones of animals found by the writer in the Monte Hermoso barranca or seen by him in collections from that locality.

Morphologically, the specimen at first sight impresses one as bearing but little generic resemblance to the human thigh bone, but as approximating much more closely the femora of lower mam-

21535°—Bull. 52—12——24

mals. Yet, on closer view it is seen to present several rather singular features, which seem to bring it into some relation with the human thigh bone. The principal of these features are a relatively long median condyle; a supratrochlear fossa; a torsion of the shaft; a trace of backward bend of the shaft; and a very perceptible bend of the same, above its middle, outward. These few features are mainly responsible for the identification of the bone as that of a precursor of man and they demand therefore careful consideration.

Detailed study and comparison.—The shaft of the Monte Hermoso femur is rather planoconvex in shape, its posteromedial surface being flat. The lateral edge is sharper than the medial, owing to its correspondence with the downward extension of the gluteal ridge and lower down with the linea aspera.

The shaft is very slightly curved from before backward, but the curve is diffused over the lower

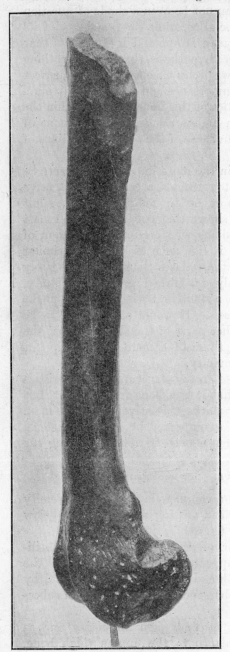
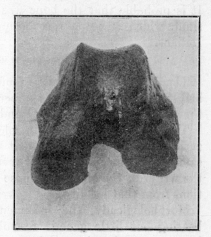

FIG. 51. The Monte Hermoso femur. (Photographs from original.)

half of the bone, while a bend backward above the middle, characteristic in general of human and to a less degree of other primate femora, is entirely wanting. On comparison a similar presence of the lower and defect of the upper curvature is seen to be common to the femora of many mammals, among which are a number of the Carnivora.

Besides the slight curve backward, the shaft presents above its middle a rather well-marked bend outward. This feature occurs in man but not regularly or exclusively so. It was also present and that to very much the same degree as in the *Tetraprothomo*, in the femur of an adolescent Bolivian bear in the Museo Nacional, Buenos Aires, and is found well marked in other bears, in the American Canidæ, and in fossil Felidæ.

The Monte Hermoso femur presents in its upper half a fairly well defined torsion outward. In this feature it may be said to approximate the femur of man more than that of the other Primates or of the modern cats, but it comes quite as near also to the modern Canidæ and to some of the fossil Carnivora, in which torsion is decidedly greater than in the apes or the modern Felidæ.

The stout median edge of the shaft shows a prominent secondary ridge running parallel with but more posterior to the border, and extending over slightly more than the middle third of the bone. A trace of such a ridge was found in a few of the Carnivora and in a baboon, possibly in an alouata, but none in other Primates or man.

From the great trochanter to the plantaris tuberosity below, the *Tetraprothomo* femur presents an antero-lateral surface, which is met with only occasionally and in a moderate degree in the upper fourth to two-fifths of the shaft in man and in some of the apes.[1] More closely related forms are seen in the hyena, jaguar, ocelot, jaguarondi, and gray wolf.

Postero-laterally the upper part of the bone presents remnants of a sharp but stout-based high ridge, which occupies the place of and is analogous to the occasional third trochanter in man but shows different form. This elevation is in direct continuation with the gluteal crest and the latter forms an inseparable constituent of the linea aspera. The upper portion of the anterior border of the third trochanter is somewhat overhanging, much as in the jaguar femur used for comparisons (25097, U. S. National Museum).

Laterally, below the third trochanter, there is in the *Tetraprothomo* no trace of the belly which forms, particularly in Indian femora, a prominent feature of the usual flattening of the bone at this point; the shaft is slightly flattened in this region as in some recent and fossil Carnivora and other mammals, but bears little resemblance to the human type.

---

[1] In one of the alouatas examined (*A. sen.*, No. 4785, U. S. National Museum), a narrow and almost wholly lateral surface extends from below the great trochanter over about five-sixths of the shaft.

The linea aspera descends straight from the third trochanter and the gluteal ridge as a marked postero-external border to the middle (in length) of the shaft, where it bifurcates, one well-developed ridge extending downward and slightly forward along the lateral aspect of the shaft to the pronounced plantaris tuberosity, while the other descends near the median line of the posterior surface, and at about the junction of the lower with the middle third of the bone divides into the medial and lateral epicondylic lines, of which the former is the more noticeable. The situation of the upper two-thirds of the linea aspera is much more lateral than in man or in any of the apes but is practically identical with that in many of the carnivores.

The nutritive foramen in the *Tetraprothomo* is situated 8.9 cm. above the lowest part of the external condyle, apparently near the middle of the bone. It is located close to the median lip of the linea aspera. In the femur of the Bolivian bear at the Museo Nacional the foramen is 8.5 cm. above the external condyle, the total "bicondylar" length of the bone being 17.4 cm., hence in very much the same position as in *Tetraprothomo*, but is placed more toward the middle of the posterior surface of the bone. The latter is also true of the jaguar and ocelot; in a jaguarondi and a coyote the canal was found placed both in height and laterally much as in the femur from Monte Hermoso. In man there are in most cases two canals for the nutrient arteries, one situated near the middle and the other, more constant, near the junction of the middle and superior thirds of the shaft, the upper one often in the linea aspera, the lower one in or near its medial lip. In most of the anthropoid apes and monkeys the canal appears to be situated near the upper third of the bone, in or near the median lip of the linea aspera and about the middle of the posterior aspect of the bone.

Below, a short distance (14 mm.) above the upper termination of the trochlea, the shaft presents a distinct shallow patellar fossa. This fossa measures about 9 mm. in length, 8 mm. in breadth, and 1.5 mm. in maximum depth. A very similar fossa was found by the writer in a chimpanzee, a baboon (*C. porcarius*), and a cinnamon bear. In a striped hyena a marked depression exists immediately above the trochlea. In a *Canis mexicanus* (No. 1384, U. S. National Museum) a shallow fossa exists 12 mm. above the trochlea, hence in about the same position as in the *Tetraprothomo*, and there is an additional large depression just above the trochlea. No fossa exists in the gorilla, orang, or gibbon. In a few American monkeys a slight hollow is found just above the trochlea. In man there is immediately above or very near the trochlea a more or less marked depressed surface, with some larger vascular foramina, but this surface is never clearly defined and never constitutes a distinct fossa as seen in the *Tetraprothomo*.

The uppermost portion of the bone shows features very much at variance with corresponding features of the human species. The anterior surface is less flat than in man. Nothing remains of the great trochanter except the base. This basal part is entirely unlike the same part in man and apes and is directly continuous with the base of the large and adjacent prominence corresponding to the third trochanter. Allied conditions are encountered in the jaguar, wolf, and other Carnivora. The greater trochanter must have been different in form from that in man and most Primates. Its base was weakest antero-laterally, where in man and the anthropoid apes, particularly the gorilla and orang, it is of pronounced strength. This weakness exists in connection with an extension far forward of the trochanteric fossa, which is a zoomorphic characteristic found in the monkeys, but more especially in the carnivores. On the other hand, the part of the great trochanter lying postero-laterally to the digital fossa and the groove leading from it to the posterior surface of the bone, is relatively stouter in the *Tetraprothomo* femur than in man or the Primates, owing to its strengthening by the third trochanter.

Beginning in the median line at the base of the great trochanter, about where in man we find the upper end of the anterior intertrochanteric line, and thence proceeding downward and outward to the lateral .border, just below that part of this border which is contributory to the third trochanter, there is a low but distinctive crest, a result of ligamentous or muscular attachment. This ridge is not to be confounded with a vertical muscular impression found on some mammal femora and rarely even on those of man. It is wholly distinctive and runs in an opposite direction from the anterior oblique or spiral line in man (which seems to be lost with the missing upper part of the bone), and corresponds probably to the interval between the crural and the vastus externus muscles. It was not found by the writer in any of the Primates, but was faintly indicated in the Bolivian bear, partially represented in the cinnamon bear and the jaguar, well marked in the striped hyena and the gray wolf, and is fairly distinct in the Indian dog from California.

Posteriorly the upper extremity of the Monte Hermoso femur shows features so unlike both human and primate that no close approximation of the forms is even suggested.

The minor trochanter lies much more mediad than in man and the gorilla, though slightly or no more so than in other apes; the closest analogies are found, however, in the Carnivora. (Pl. 65.)

The minor trochanter in the *Tetraprothomo* is also situated very high; with the bone in the bicondylar position the superior part of it is only 2 mm. lower than the base of the trochanteric fossa. This position is paralleled in a hyena and a coyote and approximated in other Carnivora, as well as in a cebus, but in none of the other Primates compared.

The form of the minor trochanter is that of a stout, dull, slightly intercepted ridge and not that of an isolated tuberosity, as in man and in all the Primates that were examined. In this respect it differs, even though to a less extent, from the modern and most of the ancient Carnivora whose femora were used for comparison. The lower part of the minor trochanter ridge extends downward and outward to the middle of the posterior surface of the bone, where it fades out. There is no trace of the posterior part of the spiral line, which is usually well-marked in the primates as well as in modern and in most fossil Carnivora, but it may be represented by the prolongation downward of the minor trochanter ridge just described.

The most striking peculiarity of this upper part of the posterior surface of the bone, however, consists in the presence of a well-defined, elevated semicircular crest (pl. 65), curving from the lower part of the minor trochanter downward, outward, and then upward to the upper portion of the rear part of the great trochanter, connecting with the lateral boundary of the groove which leads to the trochanteric fossa. This line forms the lower boundary of a surface which approximates circular form, is moderately concave from side to side and occupies fully the space between the trochanters. All these are features which find absolutely no analogy in and can have no generic relation to man or any of the Primates. They imply differing or at least much more developed muscle (quadratus femoris?) and differing function. But they occur in the Carnivora. The semicircular crest is represented typically in the ocelot and in less regular forms in the cinnamon bear, striped hyena, jaguar, gray wolf, *Canis mexicanus*, and the old California dog. It is also found, as will be shown later, in some of the fossil Carnivora. This character alone suffices to take the Monte Hermoso femur definitely out of the primate range.

The lower extremity of the *Tetraprothomo* bone is morphologically even farther removed than the upper, if possible, from the corresponding part of human and even ape femora. It is that of an ancient cat or a related carnivore and not that of a primate. (Pls. 66–68.)

It presents a high and narrow trochlea, narrow, high and deep condyles, and narrow, deep intercondylic notch. The separation inferiorly of the trochlea and the condyles is much more distinct than in man or any of the apes. The axis of the trochlea is more nearly vertical than in man or other Primates. The lateral ridges binding the trochlea are much more elevated and better defined than in any human femora or those of anthropoid apes, and they are much more nearly parallel than the lateral trochlear boundaries in man and most apes. The lateral ridge is higher, a trace less sharp, and extends farther up

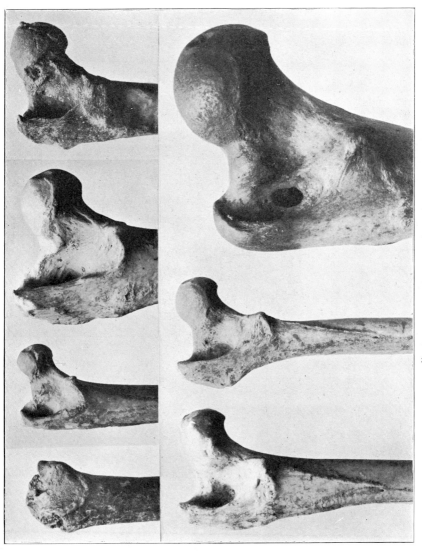

FEMORA OF "TETRAPROTHOMO" AND LOWER ANIMALS

Order: From left to right and from above downward—*Tetraprothomo*, ocelot, *Felis onca*, *Hyæna striata*, *Canis mex.*, gray wolf, and cinnamon bear. Specimens arranged to show especially the posterior intertrochanteric semilunar crest.

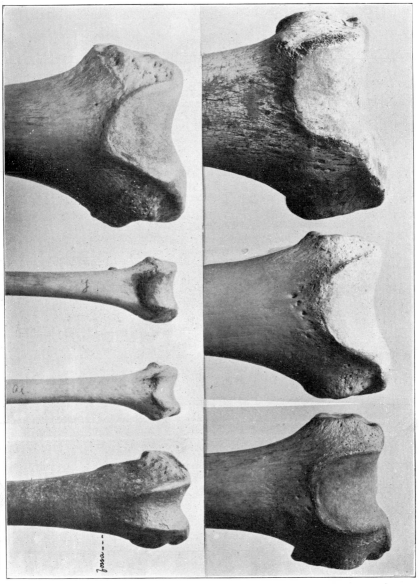

FEMORA OF "TETRAPROTHOMO," APES, AND MAN

Order: From left to right and from above downward—*Tetraprothomo* (from east), *Alouata sen.*, gibbon, orang, chimpanzee, gorilla, man. Lower extremity of each specimen is shown.   Specimens arranged on a horizontal platform and photographed from above.

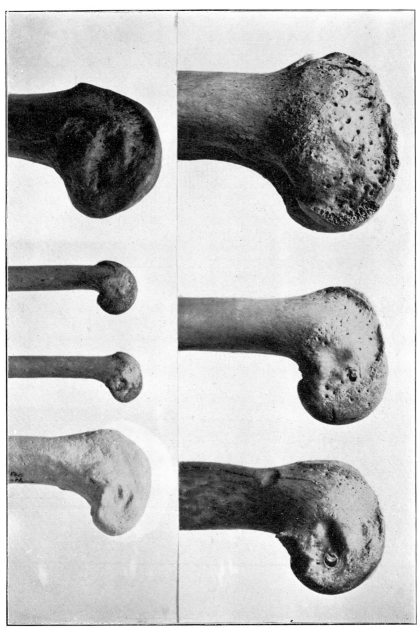

FEMORA OF "TETRAPROTHOMO," APES, AND MAN

Order: From left to right and from above downward—*Tetraprothomo* (from east), *Alouata sen.*, gibbon, orang, chimpanzee, gorilla, man. Here is shown median surface of internal condyle and shaft.

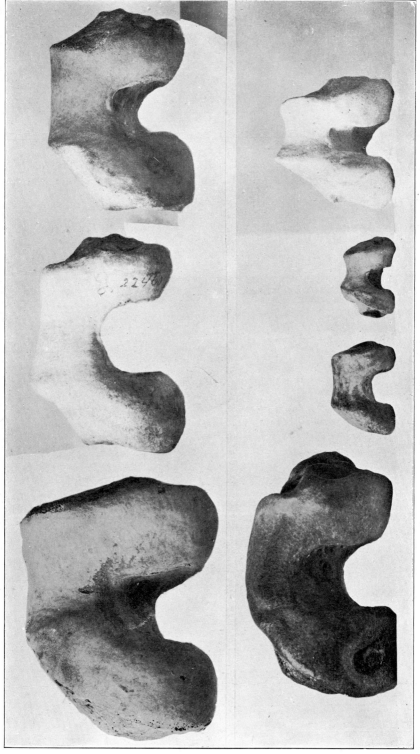

FEMORA OF "TETRAPROTHOMO," APES, AND MAN

Order: From left to right and from above downward—man, gorilla, chimpanzee, orang, gibbon, *Alouata sen.*, *Tetraprothomo* (from cast).   Here is shown inferior extremity of each specimen.   Specimens arranged in natural position and photographed in plane of shafts.

than the median one; and the upper boundary of the trochlear surface is less clearly marked than its other borders. All this points steadily away from the Primates and equally as steadily toward the carnivores, especially the cats.

The trochlea in the *Tetraprothomo* ranges in width from 15 mm. to 18 mm., and when the femur stands about vertical it reaches in height 19 mm. from the horizontal plane. Owing to the height, shallowness, and prolongation inferiorly of the border of the trochlea, it is impossible that the mammal from which this femur came walked with the hind limbs erect or even approximately so. The hind limbs were necessarily kept partially flexed, as general in cats, dogs, and other carnivores.

Finally the ligamental and muscular facets and elevations differ greatly, particularly along the lateral border of the bone, from those in the human and also in the ape species.

The plantaris tuberosity is very pronounced, much more so than in any primate, but very much as in the hyena and some of the feline species. Its outer boundary forms a part of the lateral border of the femur (of the lateral epicondylic line).

There is in the lateral epicondyle a very pronounced gastrocnemic notch (for the lateral head of the gastrocnemius), and almost vertically below this notch are two adjacent depressions, the lower for the external lateral ligament, the upper possibly for a slip of the biceps. Finally, below them is a well-marked popliteal groove.

On the median condyle is seen a marked depression for the adductor and another even larger for the medial head of the gastrocnemius. All these muscles were apparently strongly developed, in adaptation to jumping or running. As to the two facets on the lateral condyle besides those of the gastrocnemius and popliteus, they are met with in many of the carnivores but in none of the Primates examined. The remaining impressions agree in general with those in the Carnivora, particularly the Felidæ.

When the *Tetraprothomo* femur stands on a horizontal surface in the bicondylar position, the lower part of the shaft is seen to ascend less inclined outward than in man or in any of the anthropoid or other apes, except the baboon. This important difference is due to the relatively longer internal condyle in man and the Primates. ‘On the other hand, the axis of the shaft of the Monte Hermoso specimen is exactly the same in regard to lateral inclination as in the hyena, puma, jaguar, ocelot, wolf, and coyote, and much like that in other Canidæ.

Viewing the Monte Hermoso bone from below, the specimen is seen to resemble the femora of many of the Carnivora much more than those of any of the Primates, except in the relative antero-posterior dimension of the median condyle, which, in comparison with that of the lateral one, is somewhat greater than in any of the specimens with which it is contrasted except in the bear; the exact curves of the trochlear ridges, particularly of the external one, also approximate most closely to those of the bear.

The thickness of the shaft at the lowest portion of the diaphysis is relatively to its breadth much greater in the *Tetraprothomo* than in either man or any other primate, being precisely like that observed in many feline species.

Finally, the popliteal surface in the Monte Hermoso femur is perceptibly convex from side to side. In man and the majority of apes, it is slightly concave or flat, in the gibbon and some monkeys slightly convex, in the dogs slightly concave to slightly convex, in the cats flat to convex (ocelot, *Hoplophoneus*), as in the *Tetraprothomo*.

Conclusions.—The femur of the *Tetraprothomo* bears only a slight resemblance to that of man or the anthropoid apes, and but little greater to that of the lower monkeys. It presents no feature which would make obligatory or even possible its inclusion in the Primate class, but on the other hand it shows many features which approximate it to a distant family of mammals.

The class of mammals with which the characteristics of the femur connect it most closely are the carnivores, and among these especially the cats. All the evidence leads to the deduction that the Monte Hermoso femur is a femur of some extinct moderate-sized felid, though possibly a member of a subfamily other than that of the felines. It is probably useless to look for an exactly analogous form among the present South American or other modern cats, and this statement may apply even to the North American fossil Felidæ, but that does not affect its claim as a member of the same stem.

That Carnivora have not been found hitherto among the Monte Hermoso fauna does not prove their absence from the formation, for as yet this is known but very imperfectly; moreover, while looking over the Monte Hermoso fossils in the Museo de la Plata with Professor Roth, the writer came across the metatarsal of a large-sized carnivore, so that even the claim of the absence of this class of mammals from the Monte Hermosean deposit is no longer tenable.

Comparison with fossil Carnivora.—In order to make the identification of the Monte Hermoso femur still more definite, the writer examined, with the kind assistance of Mr. J. W. Gidley and Dr. W. D. Matthew, the femora of fossil dogs and cats present in the paleontologic collections of the United States National Museum and the American Museum of Natural History. The comparison was carried out especially with the Felidæ *Hoplophoneus* (Oligocene), *Nimraous* (Oligocene), *Dinictis* (Oligocene), and *Pogonodon* (Miocene); with the Canidæ *Daphænus* (Oligocene), *Ælurodon* (Miocene), *Enhydrocyon* (Miocene), and *Mesocyon* (Oligocene); and with the procyonid *Phlaocyon* (Miocene). All of these are North American forms, no South American fossils being available in the two institutions.

The substance of the results of the comparison can be stated in a few words: There follows in general a strengthening of the deductions resulting from the comparison of the *Tetraprothomo* specimen with recent forms. The Monte Hermoso femur is that of a carnivore. As might be expected, it presents complete identity with none of the fossil forms examined, but it possesses strong group relations with them all. As to family, it affiliates most closely with the Felidæ.

Entering more fully into detail, the comparisons showed that as to shape the shaft in all the fossil Felidæ that were examined and also in the *Phlaocyon* resembles very closely that of the *Tetraprothomo* femur, while in the Canidæ it presents perceptible differences.

The backward bend of the shaft, in general slight and diffuse, is quite marked in the *Pogonodon*, where it extends from the lower two-thirds of the shaft.

The outward curvature of the shaft is practically absent from the dogs, is present to a slight degree in the *Phlaocyon*, and is general in the cats; in the *Pogonodon* it is of very much the same grade as in the femur from Monte Hermoso.

Torsion of the shaft was found to be much like that in the *Tetraprothomo* femur or only slightly less in all the Felidæ, but it was decidedly less in the Canidæ and also in the Procyonidæ.

The linea aspera is of the same or closely related type as that in the *Tetraprothomo*, in the cats, and also in the *Daphænus*, while in the rest of the dogs and in the *Phlaocyon* it is distinct, running more mediad and being in general nearer the type shown by the Primates.

The gluteal ridge forms in all cases, as in the *Tetraprothomo*, a constituent and indistinguishable part of the linea aspera.

The third trochanter is present in all the fossil cats. It is usually an oblong and well-marked tuberosity forming a constituent part of the lateral ridge which, lower down, becomes the linea aspera, very much as in the *Tetraprothomo*. In the dogs, except the *Daphænus*, in which these features are much as in the cats, the third trochanter approximates more a distinct tuberosity, tending toward isolation from below. In the *Phlaocyon* the features are again much as in the Monte Hermoso femur. In nearly all these bones the superior part of the anterior border of the third trochanter is somewhat overhanging, as in the *Tetraprothomo* specimen.

As to height, the minor trochanter is situated in all the fossil Carnivora except the *Phlaocyon* (in which it is somewhat lower) much as in the Monte Hermoso femur, and most of the specimens bear also a similarity to the *Tetraprothomo* bone in the very median situation of the tuberosity, the only exceptions being the *Nimraous* and *Ælurodon*, in both of which the trochanter is somewhat less nearly medial, and the *Hoplophoneus*, in which it is even more nearly medial than in the *Tetraprothomo*. As to the form of the minor trochanter, in none of the specimens compared is this quite as ridgelike as in the bone from Monte Hermoso; yet in all the Felidæ and also in the *Enhydrocyon* and *Phlaocyon* it exists as a tuberosity arising from a ridge. In the rest of the dogs it is merely a pronounced tuberosity.

The anterior oblique line passing from the middle of the uppermost portion of the shaft to beneath the third trochanter, was not found in any of the fossil femora with the exception of the *Enhydrocyon*, in which there are traces of the same.

In all the dogs the posterior portion of the spiral line is entirely distinct and runs separate from the minor trochanter, proceeding downward to form the linea aspera. In the *Phlaocyon* it extends to the side of the minor trochanter and from this downward, as in the dogs. In the cats the upper portion of the spiral line is less distinct than in the dogs and tapers out without reaching the linea aspera; besides this there exists in the Felidæ a more or less marked ridge proceeding downward and outward from the inferior part of the minor trochanter itself, as in the *Tetraprothomo*.

The semicircular crest extending from the minor to the major trochanter and forming one of the most characteristic features of the Monte Hermoso femur, is present but situated high in the *Nimraous;* in the *Dinictis* it is well-marked but slightly less deep than in the Monte Hermoso femur; in the *Hoplophoneus* well-marked and nearly as in the *Tetraprothomo;* in the *Pogonodon* very much as in the *Tetraprothomo*. In the *Daphænus* and in the *Mesocyon* it is well represented but runs more nearly transversely, and there are only traces of it in the other dogs and the *Phlaocyon*.

The antero-lateral surface, so well defined in the Monte Hermoso specimen, is seen in very much the same form in all the Felidæ, and also in the *Enhydrocyon* and *Phlaocyon,* but in the remaining dogs it is not well or not at all differentiated.

As to the secondary ridge which runs along the median border of the *Tetraprothomo* femur, traces only of this are seen in the *Nimraous* and *Hoplophoneus,* the *Dinictis* being doubtful.

In the cats and the *Phlaocyon* the flatness of the anterior surface of the upper portion of the femur is slightly to moderately greater than in the *Tetraprothomo* and moderately to decidedly greater in the dogs.

The more or less marked flattening of the shaft below the third trochanter exists in all the fossils examined. (See measurements, p. 382.)

In the shape of the base of the great trochanter, and in the situation as well as the shape of the digital fossa, the femora of *Nimraous, Ælurodon,* and *Daphænus* approximate closely to the *Tetraprothomo,* the others being more distant.

The patellar fossa is absent from all the fossil Carnivora examined, except in the *Ælurodon,* in which it is low in position and shallow, and in the *Enhydrocyon*, in which it is both in situation and form exactly as in the *Tetraprothomo*. A femur of *Arctotherium* possesses also a very much similar patellar fossa.

In the principal features of its lower extremity the Monte Hermoso femur shows itself again typical of the carnivore and is again approximated most closely by the fossil cats, as it is by the modern Felidæ. The resemblance to the fossil femora, however, is even greater than to the modern, because several of the ancestral species present a decidedly longer (antero-posteriorly) median condyle. However, the morphologic relations of the bones extend to every important feature of the lower extremity. The fossil forms nearest in these particulars to the *Tetraprothomo* are the *Nimraous, Pogonodon,* and *Hoplophoneus,* then the *Dinictis* and *Mesocyon, Phlaocyon,* and the other dogs. The lateral ridge of the trochlea is higher, slightly less sharp, and reaches farther up than the median one, in the *Nimraous, Dinictis,* and *Pogonodon,* than in the Monte Hermoso specimen. The plantaris tuberosity is well marked in the fossil cats, particularly the *Hoplophoneus,* but in the *Daphænus* and the *Enhydrocyon* it especially resembles that in the *Tetraprothomo*. The lateral gastrocnemic notch in all the fossil cats is exactly like that in the *Tetraprothomo,* and in the other species is more or less closely related to that in the Argentine bone. In none of the fossils is the facet for the lateral ligament situated quite as high as in the Monte Hermoso specimen, but it approximates that location in the *Hoplophoneus, Pogonodon,* and *Daphænus.*

The axis of the *Tetraprothomo* femur, standing on the two condyles, is paralleled exactly by that of the *Pogonodon* femur and very nearly so by the femora of the other cats as well as by that of the *Daphænus.* In the *Pogonodon* the likeness extends to all the modifications of the axis.

In its inferior aspect the *Tetraprothomo* femur approximates more closely the fossil than the modern species and specially so the cats, owing to the greater length in the cats of the median condyle, but it also resembles closely the *Enhydrocyon, Mesocyon,* and *Phlaocyon.*

The thickness of the shaft at the lower portion of the diaphysis in all the fossil cats is very much like that in the *Tetraprothomo;* in the other fossils the thickness is somewhat less. (See measurements.)

The posterior surface of the lowest portion of the diaphysis (popliteal space) is moderately convex from side to side, as in the Monte Hermoso femur, in that of the *Nimraous, Pogonodon,* and *Hoplophoneus,* but in none of the other fossils.

Conclusions.—All the above details, combined with those derived from living forms, demonstrate that the Monte Hermoso bone can not possibly be other than that of a carnivore and that, on the whole, it approximates more closely the femur of the fossil as well as of the modern Felidæ than it does any other bone. These considerations justify the classification of the Monte Hermoso femur, at least provisionally, with this family.

In order to complete the study and comparisons of the Monte Hermoso specimen, the writer took a series of measurements, which are presented in the tables that follow. The figures only confirm and accentuate the visually noted differences between the *Tetraprothomo* femur and the femora of the Primates and its affiliations with the Carnivora, more especially the cats. The table of indexes is particularly worth perusal, for it shows in concentrated form the enormous differences between the bone under consideration and the corresponding bone of the Primate, and its close approximation to the corresponding bone in cats, in such important features as the relative proportions of the lower part of the diaphysis and those of the entire lower extremity.

Measurements of the Monte Hermoso femur and of femora of man and apes

	Tetra-prothomo	Man, white	Go-rilla	Chim-pan-zee	Orang	Gib-bon	Cyno-cepha-lus por-carius	Alo-uata seni-culus (a)	Alo-uata seni-culus (b)	Cebus hypol.
Diameters of subtrochanteric flattening:										
Maximum	2.1	2.7	2.9	2.85	2.9	1.2	1.9	1.25	1.1	0.9
Minimum	1.55	3.2	2.4	2.45	1.95	.95	1.45	.95	.9	.75
Platymeric index	73.8	83.7	82.8	86.0	67.2	79.2	76.3	76.0	81.8	83.3
Diameter of lower end of shaft just above gastrocnemius attachments:										
Breadth, maximum	3.1	6.2	5.7	4.8	5.5	2.0	3.2	2.15	1.85	1.6
Thickness, minimum	2.25	3.9	2.4	2.55	2.7	.9	1.55	1.0	.9	.95
Index	72.6	62.9	42.1	53.1	49.1	45.0	48.4	46.5	48.6	59.4
Diameter lateral of lower extremity (1), maximum	3.80	7.8	6.3	6.1	7.0	2.7	3.75	2.7	2.35	2.0
Diameter anteroposterior of lower extremity, maximum	3.80	5.9	4.9	4.55	4.9	2.0	3.2	1.8	1.8	1.65
Breadth-depth index of lower extremity	100.00	75.6	77.8	74.6	70.0	74.1	85.3	66.7	76.6	82.5
Diameter anteroposterior of inner condyle, maximum	3.8	6.2	5.1	4.8	5.7	2.2	3.3	2.0	1.85	1.8
Diameter anteroposterior of outer condyle, maximum	3.4	5.95	4.2	4.3	4.5	2.05	3.1	1.9	1.65	1.65
Percental relation of length of inner to that of outer condyle	111.8	104.2	121.4	111.6	126.7	107.4	106.5	105.3	112.1	109.1

Measurements of the Monte Hermoso femur and of the femora of some modern Carnivora

	Tetra-pro-thomo	Young Bolivian bear,[3] left femur	Jaguars (2), adult, left femur		Pumas (2), adult, left femur		Ocelot	Hyena striata
	cm.	*cm.*	*cm.*	*cm.*	*cm.*	*cm.*	*cm.*	*cm.*
Length, bicondylar, about...........	17.7	....	....	23.9	....	24.7	16.8	20.9
Length, bicondylar, to tip of minor trochanter, about..................	14.7	17.4	24.5	19.8	27.0	21.3	14.5	17.4
Diameters of shaft at middle:								
Maximum.........................	1.85	1.45	2.25	2.45	2.3	1.8	1.45	1.9
Minimum.........................	1.45	1.3	1.85	1.9	2.0	1.75	1.15	1.5
Circumference at middle.............	5.35	....	....	6.9	....	4.55	4.2	5.5
Diameters of subtrochanteric flattening:								
Maximum.........................	2.1	1.85	2.85	2.9	2.75	2.2	1.75	2.3
Minimum.........................	1.55	1.3	2.05	2.05	2.0	1.85	1.2	1.6
Platymeric index....................	*73.8*	*70.3*	*71.9*	*70.7*	*72.7*	*84.1*	*68.6*	*69.6*
Diameter of lower end of shaft just above gastrocnemius attachments:								
Breadth, maximum..............	3.1	....	....	4.1	....	3.1	2.2	3.3
Thickness, minimum.............	2.25	....	....	3.0	....	2.2	1.8	2.35
Index................................	*72.6*	....	....	*73.2*	....	*71.0*	*81.8*	*71.2*
Diameter lateral of lower extremity,[1] maximum...........................	3.80	....	4.9	5.0	5.4	4.3	3.15	4.05
Diameter antero-posterior of lower extremity,[2] maximum..............	3.80	....	4.75	4.80	5.6	4.2	3.0	4.1
Breadth-depth index of lower extremity..........................	*100.0*	....	*96.9*	*96.0*	*103.7*	*97.7*	*95.2*	*101.2*
Diameter antero-posterior of inner condyle, maximum.................	3.8	2.1	4.85	4.8	5.2	4.3	3.0	4.15
Diameter antero-posterior of outer condyle, maximum.................	3.4	1.8	4.7	4.9	5.15	4.25	3.0	4.05
Percental relation of length of inner to that of outer condyle............	*111.8*	*116.7*	*103.2*	*97.9*	*101.0*	*101.2*	*100.0*	*102.5*
Distance of nutritive foramen from lowest position on outer condyle....	8.9	8.5	....	....	....	....	8.3	....

[1] Rod of compass lying on both borders of trochlea.
[2] Anterior branch of compass lying on both borders of trochlea.
[3] Epiphyses detached, adolescent.

Measurements of the Monte Hermoso femur and of some fossil femora of Carnivora

	Tetra-pro-thomo	Nim-raous (Fel.)	Di-nic-tis (Fel.)	Hoplo-pho-neus (U.S. N.M.) (Fel.)	Hoplo-pho-neus (A.M.) (Fel.)	Pogo-no-don (Fel.)	Ælu-rodon (Can.)	Da-phæ-nus (Can.)	Enhy-dro-cyon (Can.)	Meso-cyon (Can.)	Phlao-cyon (Proc.)
Diameters of subtrochanteric flattening:											
Maximum..........	2.1	2.9	2.55	(?)	2.75	3.1	2.3	(?)	1.85	(?)	0.9
Minimum..........	1.55	1.75	1.7	(?)	1.8	2.2	1.55	(?)	1.35	(?)	0.65
Platymeric index.......	73.8	60.3	66.7	....	64.5	71.0	67.4	71.0	73.0	....	72.2
Diameter of lower end of shaft just above gastrocnemius attachments:											
Breadth, maximum	3.1	3.6	3.7	3.4	3.8	4.9	3.0	2.7	2.3	2.2	1.3
Thickness, minimum..............	2.25	2.8	2.4	2.45	2.8	3.6	1.9	2.2	1.4	1.65	0.9
Index...................	72.6	77.8	64.9	72.1	73.7	73.5	63.3	81.5	60.9	75.0	69.2
Diameter lateral of lower extremity, maximum.................	3.8	5.0	4.6	4.25	5.0	6.2	4.4	3.75	(?)	3.15	1.75
Diameter antero-posterior of lower extremity, maximum........	3.8	4.9	4.1	3.9	4.6	5.7	4.05	3.85	(?)	2.85	1.85
Length-breadth index of lower extremity....	100.0	98.0	89.1	91.8	92.0	91.9	92.0	97.4	....	90.5	94.6
Diameter antero-posterior of inner condyle, maximum..............	3.8	4.75	4.0	3.9	4.7	5.5	4.1	3.95	(?)	3.0	1.85
Diameter antero-posterior of outer condyle, maximum..............	3.4	4.9	4.2	3.7	4.4	5.75	4.0	3.7	(?)	2.85	1.7
Percental relation of length of inner to that of outer condyle......	111.8	96.9	95.2	105.4	106.8	95.6	102.5	106.8	....	105.3	108.8

Comparison of the principal indices of the Tetraprothomo specimen and other femora

	Platy-meric index [1]	Breadth-thickness index of lower end of diaphysis [2]	Length-breadth index of lower extremity [3]	Relation in length of medial to lateral condyle (lateral condyle=100)
Man	[4] *83.7*	*62.9*	*75.6*	*104.2*
Anthropoid apes	*78.8*	*47.3*	*74.1*	*116.8*
Monkeys	*79.3*	*50.7*	*77.8*	*108.2*
Tetraprothomo	*73.8*	*72.6*	*100.0*	*111.8*
Ancient North American Felidæ	*65.6*	*72.4*	*92.6*	*100.0*
Modern South American Felidæ	*73.6*	*75.3*	*97.9*	*100.7*
Ancient North American Canidæ	*70.5*	*70.2*	*93.3*	*104.9*
Modern North American Canidæ	*83.8*	*79.4*	*114.2*	*104.9*
Ursus Americanus	*60.5*	*60.3*	*97.3*	*125.7*
Hyena striata	*72.7*	*63.2*	*101.2*	*106.2*

[1] Diameter antero-posterior minimum of subtrochanteric flattening x 100 and ÷ by the diameter lateral maximum taken at the same height.

[2] Diameter antero-posterior of lower end of the diaphysis, just above the gastrocnemices insertions x 100 and ÷ by the diameter lateral taken at the same level.

[3] Diameter antero-posterior maximum of the condyles x 100 and ÷ by the diameter lateral maximum; measurements taken as indicated in footnote of table on p. 381.

[4] Average of 25 femora of whites, of both sexes.

Notes on identification of Monte Hermoso femur, by J. W. Gidley.— The cast of the *Tetraprothomo* femur was also submitted for comparison to Mr. J. W. Gidley, custodian of fossil mammals, U. S. National Museum, who kindly furnished the following report: "A careful comparison of the cast with numerous examples of both living and fossil mammals seems to show no characters in common with any of the Primates that are not also common to some or all of the carnivores. The proximal end, although broken, shows some especially characteristic features unlike those of any Primates. The trochanteric fossa is depressed to near the level of the lesser trochanter, the lesser trochanter is shifted to the extreme inner border of the posterior face, and the posterior area in this region is broadened and flattened. These features suggest a decided resemblance to many of the dogs, especially *Urocyon* and *Vulpes*. The distal end, however, in its more broadened patellar groove and general aspect is more cat-like in character, suggesting *Felis onca*, although the inner condyle is relatively longer [antero-posteriorly] than in any of the living species. In this respect the South American femur more nearly resembles the more primitive cats of the *Hoplophoneus* type. Thus, while it does not seem possible with the material at hand to determine definitely the particular group to which it may belong, the characters presented in this femur point undoubtedly to a carnivore rather than to a primate relationship."

FINAL REMARKS ON THE MONTE HERMOSO SPECIMENS

The preceding pages show that the identification of the Monte Hermoso atlas and femur as representing a human precursor, of whatsoever age, is in no way sustained.

In the first place the two specimens present a family difference and can not be considered together, the atlas being human, the femur carnivore.

As to the atlas, the geologic evidence of the find is entirely unsatisfactory, while the bone is not only thoroughly human but its characteristics are in no instance beyond the range of individual variation of the Indian atlas. Its identification as belonging to another species of man rests on the unwarranted assumptions of its antiquity and of the existence of such a species of man. It falls among the class of ill-starred specimens which have been dragged into the service of otherwise unsupported notions relating to the dawn of human history, only to be subsequently dropped of necessity into obscurity as having no bearing on the subject. Its extraction is problematical, but even if found in quite intimate relation with the real Monte Hermosean loess, it is not necessarily old. It may well have been derived from the dune above the Monte Hermoso barranca, which, as shown before, contains numerous traces of the modern native of the coast, and which fall from the crumbling edge above the ledges into pockets of the lower ancient formation.

As to the femur, it must be relegated to some ancient branch of the cat family or other related carnivore not as yet represented in collections elsewhere, for the discovery of which due credit should be given the most indefatigable and successful of South American collectors, Carlos Ameghino.

VIII. GENERAL CONCLUSIONS

The final conclusions reached as the result of the researches recorded in the preceding pages regarding early man in South America, may be thus briefly summarized:

A conscientious, unbiased study of all the available facts has shown that the whole structure erected in support of the theory of geologically ancient man on that continent rests on very imperfect and incorrectly interpreted data and in many instances on false premises, and as a consequence of these weaknesses must completely collapse when subjected to searching criticism.

The main defects of the testimony thought to establish the presence of various representatives of early man and his precursors in South America are: (1) Imperfect geologic determinations, especially with regard to the immediate conditions under which the finds were made; (2) imperfect consideration of the circumstances relating to the human remains, particularly as to possibilities of their artificial or accidental introduction into older terranes, and as to the value of their association from the standpoint of zoopaleontology; (3) the attributing of undue weight to the organic and inorganic alterations exhibited by the human bones; and (4) morphologic consideration of the human bones by those who were not expert anthropologists, who at times were misled in the important matter of placing and orienting the specimens and who accepted mere individual variations or features due to artificial deformation as normal and specifically distinctive characters.

As to the antiquity of the various archeologic remains from Argentina attributed to early man, all those to which particular importance has been attached have been found without tenable claim to great age, while others, mostly single objects, without exception fall into the category of the doubtful.

As to the many broken, striated, grooved, and perforated animal bones, the writers have not been convinced that these are in any case necessarily the work of geologically ancient man. In those instances in which the originals were examined, the markings observed were either clearly recognized as due to gnawing rodents or to other non-human agencies or as of doubtful origin.

The conclusions of the writers with regard to the evidence thus far furnished are that it fails to establish the claim that in South

America there have been brought forth thus far tangible traces of either geologically ancient man himself or of any precursors of the human race.

This should not be taken as a categorical denial of the existence of early man in South America, however improbable such a presence may now appear; but the position is maintained, and should be maintained, it seems, by all students, that the final acceptance of the evidence on this subject can not be justified until there shall have accumulated a mass of strictly scientific observations requisite in kind and volume to establish a proposition of so great importance.

IX. LIST OF PUBLICATIONS

RELATING TO THE SKELETAL REMAINS OF EARLY MAN AND HIS PRECURSORS IN SOUTH AMERICA [1]

(See also pages 51–53)

AMEGHINO, F. Ensayos para servir de base á un estudio de la formación pampeana. (Série d'articles publiée dans le journal La Aspiración, de Mercedes, d'août 1875 jusqu'à janvier 1876.)
——— Notas sobre algunos fósiles nuevos de la formación pampeana, Mercedes, 1875.
——— Étude sur l'âge géologique des ossements humains rapportés par François Seguin, de la République Argentine, et conservés au Muséum d'Histoire naturelle de Paris. (Not published. Quoted in his La antigüedad, etc., II, p. 421.)
——— Noticias sobre antigüedades indias de la Banda Oriental, Mercedes, 1877, p. 6.
——— El hombre fósil argentino, La Prensa, 28 de marzo 1877.
   (Also in Catalogue spécial de la section anthropologique et paléontologique de la République Argentine à l'Exposition de Paris, 1878.)
——— L'homme préhistorique dans le bassin de la Plata. (Compte-rendu Congrès international des sciences anthropologique, Paris, 1878, pp. 341–350.)
——— La plus haute antiquité de l'homme dans le Nouveau-Monde. (Compte-rendu Congrès international des Américanistes, 3me session, II, Bruxelles, 1879, pp. 198–250.)
——— L'homme préhistorique dans la Plata. (Revue d'Anthropologie, 2me sér., II, Paris, 1879, pp. 210–249.)
——— La antigüedad del hombre en El Plata, 2 vols., Paris-Buenos Aires, 1880–81.
——— Escursiones geológicas y paleontológicas en la provincia de Buenos Aires. (Boletín de la Academia Nacional de Ciencias en Córdoba, VI, Buenos Aires, 1884, pp. 168–195.)
——— Informe sobre el Museo Antropológico y Paleontológico de la Universidad Nacional de Córdoba durante el año 1885. (Ibid., VIII, 1885, pp. 347–360.)
——— Monte Hermoso. Article published originally in La Nación of March 10, 1887. (Boletín de la Academia Nacional de Ciencias, Buenos Aires, 1887, pp. 5–6, 10.)
——— Lista de las especies de mamíferos fósiles del mioceno superior de Monte Hermoso, hasta ahora conocidas, Buenos Aires, 1888, p. 4.
——— Contribución al conocimiento de los mamíferos fósiles de la República Argentina. (Actas de la Academia Nacional, Córdoba, VI, Buenos Aires, 1889, pp. 45–99.)
——— Sinopsis geológico-paleontológica. (In Segundo Censo de la República Argentina, mayo 10 de 1895, t. I, pp. 146–149.)
——— Paleontología argentina. (Pub. de la Universidad de la Plata, No. 2, Oct., 1904, La Plata, 1904, pp. 76–79.)
——— Les formations sédimentaires du crétacé supérieur et du tertiaire de Patagonie (Anales del Museo Nacional de Buenos Aires, XV (ser. iii, t. VIII), 1906, pp. 416–450.)

---

[1] Arranged alphabetically by authors, with the publications of each in chronologic order.

AMEGHINO, F. Notas preliminares sobre el *Tetraprothomo argentinus*, un precursor del hombre del Mioceno superior de Monte Hermoso. (Ibid., XVI (ser. iii, t. IX), 1908, pp. 107–242.)

—— Le *Diprothomo platensis*. (Ibid., XIX (ser. iii, t. XII), 1909, pp. 107–209.)

—— Geología, paleogeografía, paleontología, antropología de República Argentina. (Estudio publicado en el Número Extraordinario de La Nación, del 25 de Mayo de 1910, Buenos Aires; separate pp. 1–25.)

—— Descubrimiento de dos esqueletos humanos fósiles en el pampeano inferior del Moro. (Separate, Congreso científico internacional americano, Buenos Aires, 10 á 25 de julio de 1910, pp. 1–6.)

—— Descubrimiento de un esqueleto humano fósil en el pampeano superior del Arroyo Siasgo. (Ibid., 1910, pp. 1–6.)

—— Sur l'orientation de la calotte du *Diprothomo*. (Anales del Museo Nacional de Buenos Aires, XX (ser. iii, t. XIII), 1910, pp. 319–327.)

—— La industria de la piedra quebrada en el mioceno superior de Monte Hermoso. (Congreso científico internacional americano, Buenos Aires, 1910, pp. 1–5.)

—— Une nouvelle industrie lithique: L'industrie de la pierre fendue dans le Tertiare de la region littorale du sud de Mar del Plata. (Anales del Museo Nacional de Buenos Aires, XX (ser. iii, t. XIII), 1911, pp. 189–204.)

—— L'âge des formations sédimentaires tertiaires de l'Argentine en relation avec l'antiquité de l'homme. (Ibid., XXII (ser. iii, t. XV), 1911, pp. 45–75.)

—— La calotte du *Diprothomo* d'après l'orientation frontoglabellaire. (Ibid., pp. 1–9.)

—— L'âge des formations sédimentaires tertiaires de l'Argentine. (Ibid., pp. 169–179.)

(*See* GERVAIS, H.)

BABOR, J. Paleontologie člověka. (Věstník Klubu Přírodovědeckého, v Prostějově (Moravia), XIV, 1911.)

BLAKE, C. C. On Human Remains from a Bone Cave in Brazil. (Journal of the Anthropological Society of London, II, 1864, pp. cclxv–cclxvii.)

BOULE, M. Discussion and Reviews. (Compte-rendu Congr. int. d'anthr. et d'arch. préhist., XII sess., Paris, 1900, p. 148; and l'Anthropologie, XXII, No. 1, Paris, 1911, pp. 68–71.)

BURMEISTER, GERMAN.[1] Lista de los mamíferos fósiles del terreno diluviano (en Argentina). (Anales del Museo Público de Buenos Aires, I, Buenos Aires, 1864–1869: pp. 121–122 (brief reference to Lund's finds in Brazil; no fossil human bones as yet from Argentina); p. 298: El hombre fósil argentino (refers to Seguin's find; reproduced in Ameghino, La antigüedad, etc., II, 374–375.)

—— Sur les crânes, les mœurs et l'industrie des anciens Indiens de la Plata. (Compte-rendu Congr. int. d'anthr. et d'arch. préhist., 1872, Bruxelles, 1873, pp. 342–351.)

—— Die Ureinwohner der La Plata Staaten. (Verhandlungen der Berliner Gesellschaft für Anthropologie, Ethnologie und Urgeschichte, XVII, April, 1875, pp. 2–4.)

—— Los caballos fósiles de la Pampa argentina; also under German title, Die fossilen Pferde der Pampasformation—Buenos Aires, 1875.

—— Description physique de la République Argentine, tome II, Buenos Aires, 1876, p. 216; tome III, Buenos Aires, 1879, pp. 41–42.

—— Descripción física de la República Argentina. (Anales del Museo Público de Buenos Aires, III, 1879, p. 41.)

---

[1] Spanish form; in a number of publications the name appears in the German form, HERMANN.

BURMEISTER, GERMAN. Bemerkungen in Bezug auf die Pampas-formation. (Verhandlungen der Berliner Gesellschaft für Anthropologie, Ethnologie und Urgeschichte, XVI, Berlin, 1884, pp. 246–247.)

—— Lista de los mamíferos fósiles del terreno diluviano. (Anales del Museo Público de Buenos Aires, I, 1864–69, p. 298.) See also, Ameghino, F., La antigüedad, etc., pp. 374–377; and Lehmann-Nitsche, R., Nouvelles recherches, etc. (Revista del Museo de La Plata, XIV, Buenos Aires, 1907, pp. 209–213.)

BUSCHAN, G. Die tertiären Primaten und der fosile Mensch von Südamerika. (Das Ausland, LXV, 1892, pp. 398–700; also, Naturwissenschaftliche Wochenschrift, VIII, 1893, pp. 1–4.)

—— Das Alter des Menschen in Amerika. (Die Umschau, XIII, 1909, pp. 949–956; also, Zentralblatt für Anthropologie, XIV, Braunschweig, 1909, pp. 368–71.)

COMBES, P., Fils. Le Diprothomme. (Cosmos, Paris, 25th Sept., 1909 (N. s., No. 1287), pp. 344–46.)

DESOR, E. Homme des alluvions anciennes de l'Amérique du Sud. (In Mortillet's Matériaux pour l'histoire de l'homme, etc., 2e Année, Paris, 1866, p. 262.)

FRIEDEMANN, M. Vorlage eines Gipsabgusses des Schädeldaches von *Diprothomo platensis* Ameghino. (Zeitschrift für Ethnologie, 1910, Heft 6, pp. 934–35.)

GERVAIS, H., ET F. AMEGHINO. Les mammifères fossiles de l'Amérique du Sud, Paris and Buenos Aires, 1880.

GERVAIS, P. Zoologie et paléontologie générales. Première série. Paris, 1867–69.

—— Débris humains recueillis dans la Confédération Argentine avec des ossements d'animaux appartenant à des espèces perdues. (Journal de Zoologie, II, Paris, 1873, pp. 231–34.)

GIUFFRIDA-RUGGERI, V. Die Entdeckungen Florentino Ameghinos und der Ursprung des Menschen. (Globus, Bd. XCIV, Braunschweig, 1908, pp. 21–26.)

—— Un nuovo precursore dell' uomo. Il "*Tetraprothomo argentinus.*" (Rivista d'Italia, fascicolo di gennaio, Roma, 1909, pp. 137–47.)

HANSEN, SÖREN. Lagoa Santa Raceń. En anthropologisk Undersögelse af Jordfundne Menneskelevninger fra brasilianske Huler. Med et Tillaeg om det jordfundne Menneske fra Pontimelo, Rio de Arrecifes, La Plata. (En Samling af Afhandlinger, e Museo Lundii, I, 5, Kjöbenhavn, 1888, pp. 1–37.)

IHERING, H. von. El hombre prehistórico del Brasil. (Historia, I, Buenos Aires, 1903, pp. 161–172.)

KOBELT, W. Ameghinos Forschungen in den argentinischen Pampas. (Globus, Bd. LIX, no. 9, Braunschweig, 1891, pp. 132–136.)

KOLKEN, A. Die Vorwelt und ihre Entwickelungsgeschichte, Leipzig, 1893. (Discusses Roth's discoveries.)

KOLLMANN, J. Schädeln von Lagoa Santa. (Zeitschrift für Ethnologie, XVI, Berlin, 1884, pp. 194–99.)

—— Hohes Alter der Menschenrassen. (Ibid., pp. 200–05.)

LACERDA, A. de. Documents pour servir à l'histoire de l'homme fossile du Brésil. (Mémoirés de la Société d'Anthropologie de Paris, 2me sér., II, Paris, 1875, pp. 517–42.)

LACERDA, FILHO, AND RODRIGUEZ PEIXOTO. Contribuições para o estudo anthropologico das raças indigenas do Brazil. (Archivos do Museu Nacional, Rio de Janeiro, I, 1876, pp. 47–76.)

LACERDA, J. B. de. O homem dos Sambaquis. (Ibid., VI, 1885, pp. 175–203.)

LEHMANN-NITSCHE, R. Ueber den fossilen Menschen der Pampaformation. (Correspondenz-Blatt der deutschen Gesellschaft für Anthropologie, Ethnologie und Urgeschichte, XXXI, München, 1900, pp. 107–08. See also Virchow, pp. 108–09.)

—— Centralblatt für Anthropologie, Ethnologie und Urgeschichte, V, Jena, 1900, pp. 112–13, 138–41 (Reviews).

LEHMANN-NITSCHE, R. L'homme fossile de la formation pampéenne. (Compte-rendu Congr. int. d'anthr. et d'arch. préhist., XII session, Paris, 1900, pp. 143–48.)

—— In collaboration with C. Burckhardt, A. Doering, J. Fruh, H. v. Ihering, H. Leboucq, R. Martin, S. Roth, W. B. Scott, G. Steinmann, and F. Zirkel— Nouvelles recherches sur la formation pampéenne et l'homme fossile de la République Argentine. (Revista del Museo de la La Plata, XIV, Buenos Aires, 1907, pp. 143–488.)

—— *Homo sapiens* und *Homo neogæus* aus der Argentinischen Pampasformation. (Verh. XVI, Int. Amerikanisten-Kongresses, Wien, 1909, pp. 93–98; also in Naturwissenschaftliche Wochenschrift, N. F., Bd. VIII, Jena, 1909.)

—— El hombre fósil pampeano. (Boletín Oficina Nacional Estadística, La Paz, Bolivia, VI, 1910, pp. 363–366.)

LISTA, R. Sur les débris humains fossiles signalés dans la République Argentine. (Journal de Zoologie, VI, Paris, 1877, pp. 153–57.)

LOVISATO, D. Di alcune armi e utensili dei Fueghini, e degli antichi Patagoni. (Atti della r. Accademia dei Lincei, Classe di scienze morali, etc., memorie XI, Roma, 1883, pp. 194–202.)

LUND, P. W. Letter of Aug. 20, 1840, to C. C. Rafn. (Referred to in Berlingske Tidende, Feb. 12, 1841; in Aarsberetning fra det Kgl. nord. Oldskriftselskab for 1840, p. 5; in Neues Jahrbuch für Mineralogie, Stuttgart, 1841, pp. 502, 606; in Nouvelles Annales des Voyages, 1841, D., VI, p. 116; in Breve till C. C. Rafn, udg. af B. Grondahl, Kjöbenhavn, 1880, p. 247; and in Lütken, Chr. Fr., Indledende Bemaerkninger, etc. En Samling af Afhandlinger e Museo Lundii, I, Kjöbenhaven, 1888.)

—— Blik paa Brasiliens Dyreverden, etc. (Kgl. danske Videnskabernes Selskabs Skrifter, 4 Raekke, IX, Kjöbenhavn, 1842, pp. 195–96.)

—— Carta escripta da Lagôa Santa (Minas Geraes) ao Sr. 1° Secretario do Instituto. (Revista trimensal de Historia e Geographia, Rio de Janeiro, IV, 1842, pp. 80–87.)

—— Letter of Jan. 12, 1842, to Secretary of Instituto de Historia e Geographia, Rio de Janeiro. (Referred to in Köllner Zeitung, Sept. 9, 1842; American Journal of Science, XLIV, New Haven, 1843, p. 277; Edinburgh New Philosophical Journal, XXXVI, 1844, pp. 38–41; Froriep's Neue Notizen, XXIX, 1844, p. 247; L'Institut, X, 1842, p. 356; Neues Jahrbuch für Mineralogie, Stuttgart, 1843, p. 118; Proceedings of the Academy of Natural Sciences of Philadelphia, II, 1844–45, Phila., 1846, pp. 11–13.)

—— Carta do Dr. Lund, escripta da Lagoa Santa (Minas Geraes a 21 de Abril de 1844. (Revista trimensal de Historia e Geographia, Rio de Janeiro, VI, 1844, pp. 326–34.)

—— Letter of Mar. 28, 1844, to C. C. Rafn. (Referred to in Antiquarisk Tidsskrift, 1843–45, Kjöbenhaven, 1845, p. 154; in Mém. Soc. Roy. Antiquaires du Nord, 1845–49, Copenhague (n. d.), p. 49; in Compte-rendus Acad. Sci. Paris, XX, 1845, p. 1368; in L'Institut, XIII, 1845, p. 166; in Froriep's Neue Notizen, XXXV, 1845, p. 161; and in Lütken, Chr. Fr., Indledende Bemaerkninger, etc. En Samling af Afhandlinger e Museo Lundii, I, 1888, Kjöbenhaven, 1845, p. 5.)

LÜTKEN, CHR. FR. l'Exposition de quelques-uns des crânes et des autres ossements humains de Minas-geraés dans le Brésil central découverts et déterrés par le feu Professeur P. W. Lund. (Compte-rendu Congr. int. des Américanistes, Copenhagen, 1883, p. 40.)

—— Indledende Bemaerkninger om Menneskelevninger i Brasiliens Huler og i de Lundske Samlinger. (En Samling af Afhandlinger e Museo Lundii, I, 4, Kjöbenhavn, 1888, pp. 1–29, with a good abstract in French.)

MARTIN, R. Ossements humains, trouvés en 1887 par M. Santiago Roth à Baradero, etc. (In Lehmann-Nitsche's Nouvelles recherches, etc., 1907, pp. 374–86.)

MOCHI, A. Nota preventiva sul *Diprothomo platensis* Ameghino. (Revista del Museo de La Plata, XVII, Buenos Aires, 1910–11, pp. 69–70.)

—— Appunti sulla paleoantropologia argentina. (Archivio per l'Antropologia e la Etnologia, XL, Firenze, 1910, pp. 203–54.)

MORENO, F. P. Noticias sobre antigüedades de los Indios, del tiempo anterior á la conquista descubiertas en la provincia de Buenos Aires. (Boletín de la Academia Nacional de Ciencias de Córdoba, I, 1874, pp. 130–49.)

—— Description des cimetières et paraderos préhistoriques de Patagonie. (Revue d'Anthropologie, 1re sér., III, Paris, 1874.)

—— Viaje á la Patagonia austral, emprendido bajo los auspicios del Gobierno nacional, 1876–77, tomo I, Buenos Aires, 1879. (Reviewed in Revue d'Anthropologie, 2me sér., III, 1880, pp. 303–09.)

—— Sur deux crânes préhistoriques rapportés du Rio-Negro. (Bulletins de la Société d'Anthropologie de Paris, 3me sér., III, 1880, pp. 490–97.)

MORSELLI, E. Osservazioni critiche sulla parte antropologico-preistorica del recente "Trattato di paleontologia" di Carlo Zittel. (Archivio per l' Antropologia e la Etnologia, XXVI, Firenze, 1896, p. 140.)

NEHRING, A. Menschenreste aus einem Sambaqui von Santos in Brasilien. (Verhandl. Berl. Ges. für Anthr., Eth. und Urg., Sitzung vom 16 Nov. 1895, pp. 710–21.)

OUTES, F. F. Los Querandíes, breve contribución al estudio de la etnografía argentina, Buenos Aires, 1897, pp. 87–91.

—— AND C. BRUCH. Los Aborígenes de la República Argentina, Buenos Aires, 1910.

PAMPEAN FORMATION. The Man of the Pampean formation. (American Naturalist, XII, 1897, pp. 827–29. Based on Ameghino's work.)

QUATREFAGES, A. DE. L'homme fossile de Lagoa Santa en Brésil et ses descendants actuels. (Compte-rendu Acad. Sci. Paris, t. 93, no. 22, pp. 882–884.)

—— Histoire générale des races humaines. Introduction a l'étude des races humaines: [in 2 pts.] Paris, 1887–89, pp. 85–86, 105.

REINHARDT, J. De brasilianske Knoglehuler og de i dem forekommende Dyrelevninger. (En Samling af Afhandlinger e Museo Lundii, I, 4, Kjöbenhavn, 1888, pp. 1–56; Memoir read in 1866.)

RIVET, P. La race de Lagoa-Santa chez les populations précolombiennes de l'equateur. (Bull. et Mém. Soc. d'Anthr. Paris, 5me sér., IX, f. 2, 1908, p. 209 et seq.).

ROTH, S. Fossiles de la Pampa, Amérique du Sud, 2me catalogue, San Nicolas, 1882, pp. 3–4 (1re éd.); Genova, 1884 (2me éd.).

—— Beobachtungen über Entstehung und Alter der Pampasformation in Argentinien. (Zeitschrift der deutschen geologischen Gesellschaft, XL, Berlin, 1888, p. 400 et seq.)

—— Ueber den Schaedel von Pontimelo (richtiger Fontezuelas). (Briefliche Mittheilung von Santiago Roth an Herrn J. Kollmann). (Mittheilungen aus dem anatomischen Institut im Vesalianum zu Basel (1889), pp. 1–11. Reproduced in Lehmann-Nitsche's Nouvelles recherches, etc.)

SCHWALBE, G. Studien zur Morphologie der südamerikanischen Primatenformen. (Zeitschrift für Morphologie und Anthropologie, Band XIII, Heft 2, Stuttgart, 1910, pp. 209–58.)

SENET, R. Los ascendientes del hombre según Ameghino. (Boletín de la Instrucción Pública, Buenos Aires, II, no. 6, pp. 1–52.)

SERA, G. L. Sull' uomo fossile sud-americano. (Monitore Zoologico Italiano, XXII, Firenze, 1911, pp. 10–24.)

SERGI, G. L'apologia del mio poligenismo. (Atti della Società romana di antropologia, XV, fasc. 2, Roma, 1909, pp. 187–195.)

—— Paléontologie sud-Américaine. (Scientia, VIII, Bologna, 1910, pp. xvi–4.)

SIEVERS, P.   Review of Ameghino's Sinopsis geológico-paleontológica.   (Segundo
    Censo de la República Argentina, I, 1898, 148.   Petermanns Mittheilungen,
    XLVI, 1900, p. 72.)

STRAIN, ISAAC G.   Extract of a letter giving the synopsis of the translation, by him-
    self, of a letter from Dr. Lund, R. S. A., Copenhagen, to the Historical and Geo-
    graphical Society of Brazil.   (Proceedings of the Academy of Natural Sciences,
    Philadelphia, II, 1844–45, Phila., 1846, pp. 11–13.)

STROBEL, P.   Materiali di paletnologia comparata raccolti in Sudamerica, Parma,
    1885, 3 fasc., p. 34, pl. VI, fig. 47.

TEN KATE, H.   Sur les crânes de Lagoa-Santa.   (Bulletins de la Société d'Anthro-
    pologie de Paris, 3ᵐᵉ sér., VIII, 1885, pp. 240–44.)

TOPINARD, P.   Éléments d'anthropologie générale, Paris, 1885.

TROUESSART, E.   Les primates tertiaires et l'homme fossile sud-américain.   (L'An-
    thropologie, III, 1892, pp. 257–74.)

VALENTIN, J.   Bosquejo geológico de la Argentina.   (Article "Gea" in the third
    edition of the Diccionario geográfico argentino, of F. Latzina, Buenos Aires, 1897,
    p. 37.)   (Concerns Roth's discoveries.)

VARELA, F.   L'homme quaternaire en Amérique.   (Congrès international des
    sciences anthropologiques tenu à Paris du 16 au 21 août 1878, p. 288.)

VERNEAU, R.   Crânes préhistoriques de Patagonie.   (L'Anthropologie, V, Paris,
    1894, pp. 420–50.)

——— Les anciens Patagons, Monaco, 1903, pp. 126–29.

VILANOVA, J.   L'homme fossile du Rio Samborombon.   (Compte-rendu Congrès
    international des Américanistes, 8ᵉᵐᵉ sess., Paris, 1890, Paris, 1892, pp. 351–52).

VIRCHOW, R.   Ein mit Glyptodon-Resten gefundenes menschliches Skelet aus der
    Pampa de la Plata.   (Verhandlungen der Berliner Gesellschaft für Anthropologie,
    Ethnologie und Urgeschichte, XV, 1883, pp. 465–67.)

——— Crania ethnica americana, Berlin, 1892, p. 29 et seq.

VOGT, C.   Squelette humain associé aux glyptodontes.   Avec discussion (Mortillet,
    Zaborowski, Vogt).   (Bulletins de la Société d'Anthropologie de Paris, 3ᵐᵉ série,
    IV, 1881, pp. 693–99.)

WILSER, L.   Das Alter des Menschen in Südamerika.   (Globus, Bd. XCIV, Braun-
    schweig, 1908, pp. 333–35.)

——— Leben und Heimat des Urmenschen, Leipzig, 1910.

ZEBALLOS, E. S.   Estudio geológico sobre la Provincia de Buenos Aires.   (Anales
    de la Sociedad Científica Argentina, II, Buenos Aires, 1876, pp. 258–68, 309–21;
    III, 1877, pp. 17–35, 71–80.)

ZITTEL, K. A.   Handbuch der Paläontologie, München und Leipzig, 1888–94, p. 724.

ADDENDA

Since the preceding report was completed, four additional publications on some of the remains attributed to ancient man in South America have reached the writer, and he has learned that the subject is also dealt with in a more general way in three recent works which thus far he has not seen, namely:

BRANCA, W., Der Stand unserer Kenntnisse von fossilen Menschen, Liepzig, 1910; SERGI, G., L'Uomo secondo le origini, l'antichità, le variazioni e la distribuzione geografica, Torino, 1911; and FRASSETTO, F., Lezioni di Antropologia, 2 vols., Bologna, 1911.

Of the four special papers above mentioned the first to reach the writer was that "On ancient man and his predecessors in Argentina," by K. Stołyhwo,[1] one of the European delegates to the International American Congress of Sciences, held at Buenos Aires in July, 1911.

Stołyhwo examined the more important of the skeletal remains and his conclusions are as follows:

The skull of Arrecifes (p. 28): "On the basis of personal examination of the specimen I am of the opinion that its form is that of the contemporary man."

The skull of Miramar (pp. 33–34): "Shows an artificial deformation."

The Necochea specimens: "Skull No. I is not artificially deformed and its form corresponds completely to that of *H. sapiens.*" No. II shows traces of post-mortem deformation. No. III is deformed artificially besides showing poor reconstruction, including that of the orbits. Further, these specimens show no peculiar features in comparison with the skull of *H. sapiens* and should not be regarded as distinct therefrom. They differ in no essential features from skulls of the American natives.

As to the *Diprothomo* (pp. 34–38), the special features of the fragment as described by Ameghino became apparent only through faulty orientation of the specimen. The fragment "shows no important difference from a similar part in the present man." The length of the frontal, on which stress has been laid, is duplicated and even

---

[1] Stołyhwo, K., W sprawie człowieka kopalnego i jego poprzedników w Argentynie; in *Sprawozdania z posiedzeń Towarzystwa Naukowego Warszawskiego*, IV, No. 1, Warsaw, 1911, pp. 21–41.

exceeded in some of the modern skulls of whites in the Warsaw collections and in general the bone is entirely like that of *H. sapiens.* "The position of *Diprothomo* as a precursor of man is untenable;" though, should the geologic position claimed for the fragment become firmly established, the specimen would have much weight as evidence of the existence of man in the Lower Pliocene.

The atlas of Monte Hermoso (pp. 31–32) "is entirely like a human atlas." A comparison showed that in one of the recent atlases of the collection the main features that characterize the Monte Hermoso specimen are even more accentuated. The dimensions of the Monte Hermoso atlas are moderate, such as are found in *Homo sapiens.* The formation, on the basis of this specimen, of a new species of man, as attempted by Lehmann-Nitsche, is not justified.

The femur of Monte Hermoso (p. 30) "does not appear to me possibly to proceed from the same individual as the atlas. The specimen is of small size and belonged to a much smaller animal form."

Stołyhwo mentions two other communications by Polish men of science on the Argentine finds,[1] neither of which, however, appears to contain original observations or to be of special importance.

The next publications received relating to early man in Argentina were Schwalbe's postscript [2] and Sergi's paper [3] on the subject of the *Diprothomo.*

Schwalbe's paper is a discussion of several of the more recent publications dealing with or touching on the *Diprothomo* (Mochi, Ameghino, Sergi, Branca, Wilser, Friedemann, and v. Luschan). He finds that his views concerning the fragment as expressed in his former publication thereon need no modification; and the observations of Friedemann and v. Luschan coincide so closely with his own, that he "regards the *Diprothomo* question as definitely settled and considers it wholly superfluous and unnecessary to enter again into consideration of this phantasy-image, which proved to be purely human."

According to Schwalbe, Branca pronounces himself against the notions of Ameghino in regard to the *Diprothomo* as well as the *Tetraprothomo* specimens. The *Diprothomo* fragment is considered by Branca, as by v. Luschan, to be clearly of human origin.

On the other hand, Sergi opposes the opinions of Schwalbe, Friedemann, and v. Luschan, on the *Diprothomo.* He accepts as correct neither the orientation of the fragment as practiced by Ameghino nor that of Schwalbe, and essays to pose the same on a modern meso-

---

[1] Poniatowski, St., O klasyfikacyach wskaźników antropologicznych; in *Sprawozdania z posiedzeń Towarzystwa Naukowego Warszawskiego*, III, No. 7, 1910; and Majewski, E., O czaszce praczłowieka plioceńskiego, *Diprothomo platensis*, with discussion by K. Stołyhwo; ibid., II, No. 12, 1909.

[2] Schwalbe, G., Nachtrag zu meiner Arbeit: Über Ameghino's *Diprothomo platensis;* in *Zeitschr. für Morph. und Anthr.*, Band XIII, Heft 3, Stuttgart, 1911, pp. 533–540.

[3] Sergi, G., Sul *Diprothomo platensis* Ameghino; in *Rivista di Antropologia*, XVI, f. 1, pp. 1–12.

cephalic skull, the top of which has been cut off, on the basis of an approximation to a natural human position of the roof of the orbits.[1] The features exhibited by the fragment in this position show that the specimen "does not possess characteristics identical with those of recent human crania; its distinctive features are not even within the limits of the variation of recent man."

As a result of his observations, it seems to Sergi "that the *Diprothomo* may belong to the human family, to the Hominidæ, but it separates itself absolutely by many above-described characters from the living type of man. These characters do not constitute a type that would ordinarily be denominated as inferior; it is a type of its own, a type which is related with the hitherto known fossil human forms in Europe. . . . For my part," Sergi concludes, "I shall continue to denominate the *Diprothomo* as I have done in dealing with the descent of man, namely, *Proanthropus*."

Sergi entertains "no doubt regarding the antiquity of the fragment" and its age, in his opinion, is confirmed by its morphology.

Finally, still another reply to the criticisms of Mochi is published by Ameghino.[2] It is not possible to enter into the details of this extended paper. It relates almost exclusively to the various specimens representing the *Homo pampæus*, *H. caputinclinatus*, and *H. sinemento*. No new data concerning the circumstances of the several finds are brought forth, the discussion dealing with the morphologic characters of the skulls. Professor Ameghino acknowledges some errors in his former statements in regard to certain particulars, but retains and reasserts all his main views and beliefs. There are evident some incipient modifications or rather developments in these, but they do not lead in the direction of Mochi's opinions.

The above-mentioned publications contain nothing that necessitates any alteration of or addition to the writer's statements and conclusions recorded in the several sections of this report.

---

[1] A feature which presents considerable individual variations in all races, and hence can easily lead to error in such procedure as that adopted by Sergi. Only the *mean* inclination of these parts in different groups of man may be alike.—A. H.

[2] Ameghino, F., Observations au sujet des notes du Dr. Mochi sur la paléoanthropologie Argentine; in *Anal. Mus. Nac. Buenos Aires*, XXII (ser. iii, t. XV), 1911, pp. 181–230.

INDEX